THE UNITY OF HEGEL'S
PHENOMENOLOGY OF SPIRIT

SPEP Studies

in Historical Philosophy

General Editors David Kolb
John McCumber

THE
UNITY
OF HEGEL'S
PHENOMENOLOGY
OF SPIRIT

A Systematic Interpretation

Jon Stewart

Northwestern University Press
Evanston, Illinois

Northwestern University Press
Evanston, Illinois 60208-4210

Copyright © 2000 by Northwestern University Press.
Published 2000. All rights reserved.

Printed in the United States of America

ISBN 0-8101-1693-6

Library of Congress Cataloging-in-Publication Data

Stewart, Jon (Jon Bartley)
    The unity of Hegel's Phenomenology of spirit : a systematic interpretation /
Jon Stewart.
      p. cm. — (SPEP studies in historical philosophy)
    Includes bibliographical references and index.
    ISBN 0-8101-1693-6 (cloth : alk. paper)
    1. Hegel, Georg Wilhelm Friedrich, 1770–1831. Phènomenologie des
Geistes. 2. Spirit. 3. Consciousness. 4. Truth. I. Title. II. Series.
B2929 .S67 2000
   193—dc21   00-030563

The paper used in this publication meets the minimum requirements of the American National Standard for Information Sciences—Permanence of Paper for Printed Library Materials, ANSI Z39.48-1984.

Contents

CONTENTS

Preface

The structure of my text and a few of my editorial decisions may require a brief explanation. In particular, a word about the treatment of the Preface of the *Phenomenology* is in order, since it is the only part of the text which this commentary does not treat systematically. Hegel wrote the Preface to the *Phenomenology* last and intended it as a preface not just to the *Phenomenology* itself but to his entire philosophical system. I make reference to the Preface primarily in chapter 2 when it is helpful for understanding Hegel's methodology and his conception of philosophy in general; however, my own systematic analysis of the *Phenomenology* begins with an account of the Introduction in my chapter 3. Thus, the Preface, despite its importance, is treated in a more thematic fashion than the rest of the text.

In an attempt to remain faithful to Hegel's meaning as well as to be helpful to students struggling to understand his dense language, I have tried to keep close to the primary text and have relied heavily on quotations. Although this may at times make for cumbersome reading, nevertheless I have judged that the benefits gained from a close textual analysis far outweigh this inconvenience.

The key to reading and understanding the *Phenomenology* is to be able to identify correctly the beginning and the end of the individual analyses and arguments in the otherwise inchoate mass of text. Most students simply feel overwhelmed by the obscurity of Hegel's language and are unable to make out even the vaguest outlines of an argument, since they are not in a position to recognize its structure and component parts. But once the individual steps of the argument are made clear, the analysis as a whole emerges and becomes coherent. To aid the reader in this regard, I have divided my analyses up into individual sections corresponding to the sections in Hegel's argument which follow the same general pattern. In addition, I have inserted the extremely helpful paragraph numbers (following the Miller translation of the *Phenomenology*) at the head of my subtitles for the individual chapters and sections to help the reader identify the individual arguments more easily.

Acknowledgments

The composition of this work took place over a period of several years and with the invaluable help and support of numerous institutions and individuals. I am deeply grateful to the Deutscher Akademischer Austausch-dienst, the Heinrich Hertz-Stiftung, and the Alexander von Humboldt-Stiftung for extremely generous research grants (during the academic years 1989–90, 1992–93, and 1994–95, respectively), which allowed me sufficient time away from the usual rigors of teaching to pursue this project. I would also like to thank the Philosophy Department at the Westfälische Wilhelms-Universität, Münster for a Research Assistantship during the 1990–91 academic year which allowed me continued access to the library facilities there as well as the leisure time to make use of them. In addition, I would like to express my gratitude to the Philosophy Department at the University of California, San Diego for affording me the opportunity to try out my Hegel interpretation in the classroom during the 1991–92 academic year. I am grateful to the editorial staffs of the *Deutsche Zeitschrift für Philosophie, Idealistic Studies, Jahrbuch der Nietzsche-Forschung, The Owl of Minerva,* and *Philosophy and Phenomenological Research* for their generosity in allowing me to reprint here revised versions of some of the material which originally appeared as articles in these distinguished journals. Moreover, I am deeply indebted to a number of individuals without whose help this work could not possibly have been completed. Above all, the support and supervision of this project by Professors Robert Pippin, Frederick Olafson, and Ludwig Siep have been of inestimable value. A special note of thanks is due to Louie Matz for countless discussions and written exchanges about the *Phenomenology* and various aspects of Hegel's philosophy. I am profoundly in the debt of Dr. Jürgen-Gerhard Blühdorn for his unwavering support and enthusiastic encouragement as well as for innumerable instances of cooperative work, of which I was always the chief beneficiary. I would also like to acknowledge the help of several friends and colleagues for their proofreadings, criticisms, insights, and general feedback during the arduous composition of this work: Professor Steffen Dietzsch, Dr.

ACKNOWLEDGMENTS

Jim Dwyer, Chris Gilbertson, Robert Gillis, Bryan Harris, Professor S. Nicholas Jolley, Professor Michael Mendelson, Professor Alejandro Rosas, Loy Stewart, and Gale Vigliotti.

Abbreviations of Primary Texts

The English translations are all from the editions cited below unless otherwise noted. The only liberty I have taken is to have occasionally changed the translator's British punctuation and spelling to accord with standard American usage. For a number of the German secondary sources I have given my own translations unless otherwise noted.

Aesthetics I–II	*Hegel's Aesthetics: Lectures on Fine Art.* Translated by T. M. Knox. Oxford: Clarendon Press, 1975. Cited by volume and page number.
Aesthetik I–III	*Vorlesungen über die Aesthetik. SW,* vols. 12–14. Cited by volume and page number.
Briefe I–IV	*Briefe von und an Hegel.* Edited by Johannes Hoffmeister. Hamburg: Meiner, 1961. Cited by volume and page number.
Difference	*Difference between the Systems of Fichte and Schelling.* Translated by H. S. Harris and W. Cerf. Albany: SUNY Press, 1977. Cited by page number.
Differenz	*Differenz des Fichte'schen und Schelling'schen Systems der Philosophie. GW,* vol. 4, 1–92. Cited by page number.
Dissertatio	*Dissertatio Philosophica de Orbitis Planetarum/Philosophische Erörterung über die Planetbahnen.* Edited by Wolfgang Neuser. Weinhem: Acta Humaniora, 1986. Cited by page number.
EL	*Hegel's Logic: Part One of the Encyclopaedia of the Philosophical Sciences.* Translated by William Wallace. Oxford: Clarendon Press, 1975. Cited by paragraph number (§).
Enz.	*Enzyklopädie der philosophischen Wissenschaften. GW,* vol. 19. Cited by page number.
ETW	*Early Theological Writings.* Translated by T. M. Knox. Fragments translated by Richard Kroner. Chicago: University of Chicago Press, 1948; Philadelphia: University of Pennsylvania Press, 1975. Cited by page number.

First Phil. of Spirit	*First Philosophy of Spirit* in *G.W. F. Hegel, System of Ethical Life and First Philosophy of Spirit.* Edited and translated by H. S. Harris and T. M. Knox. Albany: SUNY Press, 1979. Cited by page number.
GW	*Gesammelte Werke.* Edited by the Rheinisch-Westfälische Akademie der Wissenschaften. Hamburg: Felix Meiner, 1968–.
Hist. of Phil. I–III	*Lectures on the History of Philosophy.* 3 vols. Translated by E. S. Haldane. London: K. Paul, Trench, Trübner, 1892–96; reprint, Lincoln: University of Nebraska Press, 1955. Cited by volume and page number.
Jena System, 1804–5	*G.W. F. Hegel, The Jena System, 1804–5: Logic and Metaphysics.* Translation edited by John W. Burbidge and George di Giovanni. Montreal: McGill-Queen's University Press, 1986. Cited by page number.
JSE I–III	*Jenaer Systementwürfe. GW*, vols. 6–8. Cited by volume and page number.
Letters	*Hegel: The Letters.* Translated by Clark Butler and Christian Seiler. Bloomington: Indiana University Press, 1984. Cited by letter number enclosed in brackets and by page number.
PhG	*Phänomenologie des Geistes. GW*, vol. 9. Cited by page number.
Phil. Diss.	Hegel, G. W. F. *"Philosophical Dissertation on the Orbits of the Planets* (1801). Preceded by the 12 Theses defended on August 27, 1801." Translated by Pierre Adler. *Graduate Faculty Philosophy Journal* 12 (1987), 269–309. (A translation of *Dissertatio,* above.) Cited by page number.
Phil. of Hist	*The Philosophy of History.* Translated by J. Sibree. New York: Willey Book Co., 1944. Cited by page number.
Phil. of Mind	*Hegel's Philosophy of Mind.* Translated by William Wallace and A. V. Miller. Oxford: Clarendon Press, 1971. Cited by paragraph number (§).
Phil. of Nature	*Hegel's Philosophy of Nature.* Translated by A. V. Miller. Oxford: Clarendon Press, 1970. Cited by paragraph number (§).
Phil. of Religion I–III	*Lectures on the Philosophy of Religion.* Translated by E. B. Speirs and J. Burdon Sanderson. London: Routledge and Kegan Paul; New York: The Humanities Press, 1962, 1968, 1972. Cited by volume and page number.

Phil. of Spirit, 1805–6	*The Jena Lectures on the Philosophy of Spirit (1805–6).* In *Hegel and the Human Spirit.* Translated by Leo Rauch. Detroit: Wayne State University Press, 1983. Cited by page number.
PhS	*Phenomenology of Spirit.* Translated by A. V. Miller. Oxford: Clarendon Press, 1977. Cited by paragraph number (§).
PR	*Hegel's Philosophy of Right.* Translated by T. M. Knox. Oxford: Clarendon Press, 1952. Cited by paragraph number (§) with the exception of the Preface, which is so noted and cited by page number.
Propaedeutic	*The Philosophical Propaedeutic.* Translated by A. V. Miller, edited by Michael George and Andrew Vincent. Oxford: Basil Blackwell, 1986. Cited by paragraph number.
RP	*Grundlinien der Philosophie des Rechts oder Naturrecht und Staatswissenschaft im Grundrisse. SW,* vol. 7. Cited by page number.
SL	*Hegel's Science of Logic.* Translated by A. V. Miller. London: George Allen and Unwin, 1989. Cited by page number.
SW	*Sämtliche Werke.* Jubiläumsausgabe in 20 vols. Edited by Hermann Glockner. Stuttgart: Friedrich Frommann Verlag, 1927–40. Cited by volume number and page number. Cited primarily for quotations from *PR* and from the various Berlin lectures.
TJ	*Hegels theologische Jugendschriften.* Edited by Herman Nohl. Tübingen: J. C. B. Mohr, 1907. Cited by page number.
VGP I–III	*Vorlesungen über die Geschichte der Philosophie. SW,* vols. 17–19. Cited by volume and page number.
VPG	*Vorlesungen über die Philosophie der Geschichte. SW,* vol. 11. Cited by page number.
VPR I–II	*Vorlesungen über die Philosophie der Religion. SW,* vols. 15–16. Cited by volume and page number.
Werke	*Georg Wilhelm Friedrich Hegel: Werke in zwanzig Bänden.* Frankfurt: Suhrkamp, 1970. Cited by volume number and page number. Cited primarily for the *Zusätze* in the *Encyclopaedia,* which are not included in the *GW* edition.
WL	*Wissenschaft der Logik. GW,* vol. 21. Cited by page number.
WL I–II	*Wissenschaft der Logik. SW,* vols. 4–5. Cited by volume and page number.

THE UNITY OF HEGEL'S
PHENOMENOLOGY OF SPIRIT

Introduction

A quick glance at the abundance of secondary literature on Hegel's philosophy and on the *Phenomenology of Spirit* in particular would quickly convince most people that there could not possibly be anything new or interesting that yet another book could unearth which has not been thoroughly exhausted by the existing body of material. Not only are there a number of full-length commentaries on all of Hegel's published works, but also there is a vast and growing body of literature dedicated to his unpublished manuscripts, letters, and other sundry *Nachlaß*. The profusion of secondary literature in Hegel studies has driven many scholars to great lengths to seize on an original thesis or an overlooked issue that could still be fruitfully explored. If the present study is not to fall into the usual academic traps resulting from this problem, what then could be the justification of a new book on Hegel or, more precisely, a new book on the *Phenomenology?* My objective in the present study is twofold: (1) to provide a detailed analysis of the *Phenomenology* that would be accessible to most intermediate students and nonspecialists; and (2) to make plausible Hegel's own conception of the *Phenomenology* as a part of a systematic philosophy.

With respect to the first goal, it seems to me that despite the overabundance of secondary literature on the *Phenomenology*, there is to date no single text in English which recommends itself as a simple yet thorough and accurate introduction to the work for the average undergraduate. A great deal of the secondary literature on Hegel fails in its task by not being in the first line concerned with explaining the primary text (which, with a thinker as difficult as Hegel, is a serious shortcoming).

My second major goal in undertaking this study has been to make a case for Hegel's own conception of philosophy as a system. Herein lies the academic or scholarly justification of the present work. The long-term trend in Hegel studies has been to regard as simply hopeless and indefensible Hegel's remarks about the systematic nature of his philosophy, the necessity of the dialectic, and the conception of speculative philosophy as a science. One commentator, referring to Hegel's

metaphorical discussion of the role of the *Phenomenology* as a ladder to
the philosophical sciences,[1] writes, "The idea of arranging all significant
points of view in such a single sequence, on a ladder that reaches from
the crudest to the most mature, is as dazzling to contemplate as it is
mad to try seriously to implement."[2] Given this premise that Hegel's
systematic pretensions are simply "mad," most interpretations of Hegel,
ignoring his own clear statements about the systematicity and unity of
his work, analyze his philosophy in a piecemeal fashion or, as is said in
Kant studies, as a "patchwork." This tends to obscure a good deal with
respect to the individual analyses in question, since it takes them out of
their larger systematic context from which they ultimately derive their
meaning and in which they were intended to be understood. I wish at
this point only to indicate the general interpretive strategy of the present
study. I have endeavored to understand the *Phenomenology* as a part of a
larger philosophical system and as a coherent and unified philosophical
work in its own right. Thus, the attempt has been made to indicate the
meaning and significance of the transitions as well as to point out the
parallelisms between the respective analyses. An effort has also been
made to trace some of Hegel's main themes—e.g., universal-particular,
mediacy-immediacy, etc.—through the text in order to demonstrate the
formal continuity. The analysis operates generally with two different perspectives: the first involves examining at the microlevel the particulars of
each dialectical movement, and the second perspective involves stepping
back periodically and analyzing at the macrolevel the role of the argument
in question in the context of the work as a whole.

I have also attempted to establish the continuity of the text by
understanding Hegel's argument in the *Phenomenology of Spirit* as a transcendental argument and by reading Hegel in this regard as the heir
of Kant. There have been two major schools of interpretation on this
matter. One group prefers to read Hegel as a metaphysician either of the
precritical or of the romantic sort.[3] As a precritical metaphysician, he is
conceived as the last rationalist who believed that everything was mind
or reason and who never really fully understood the import of Kant's
critique of metaphysics. As a romantic metaphysician he is thought of
as someone who believed, like Schelling, in some quasimystic world-soul
which he called "the Absolute." The other camp, with which I prefer to
affiliate myself, tries to read Hegel as developing Kant's transcendental
philosophy and as someone who was just as critical of metaphysics as
Kant.[4] This interpretive strategy tries to understand Hegel as reconstructing, in a Kantian spirit, the necessary presuppositions of human
cognition. For Kant, before we can talk about the objects of metaphysics,
we must first come to terms with the faculty of cognition by which we

know objects. Thus, what is needed is a transcendental philosophy, i.e., a philosophy which provides an account of the necessary conditions for the possibility of objective thought, and before we have such an account, we cannot have metaphysics. Hegel, according to this interpretation, tries in the *Phenomenology of Spirit* to reconstruct the necessary conditions of human cognition as well, but he goes well beyond the Kantian account by introducing social, quasihistorical elements into the account.[5] Hegel, like Kant, begins with an attempt merely to give an account of objectivity, that is, to explain what an object is, but in the course of this it is discovered that any such account necessarily presupposes an account of the subject. Thus, Hegel next tries to give an account of the subject, but in the course of this it is discovered that any such account of the subject presupposes an account of other subjects or, put differently, of the subject in the social sphere. Hegel's argument proceeds in this fashion, continually enriching itself by the addition of new, ever more sophisticated and complex elements. At each stage when the presuppositions of the specific claims are exposed, we see that a new account is needed and that the argument cannot go on without such an account.

On this reading of Hegel's texts, the *Phenomenology of Spirit* at least can be seen as offering a transcendental argument and thus as giving an account of the necessary conditions for the possibility of objectivity, whereas in the *Logic* and at the level of science proper, the distinction between transcendental philosophy and metaphysics collapses in Hegel's idealism, and there is no distinction between thought, or what is presupposed for objectivity, and reality, i.e., objectivity itself.[6] This account of Hegel as a transcendental philosopher, i.e., as one who tries to uncover the necessary conditions of knowing, will be used in the present study to help reconstruct the systematic unity of the *Phenomenology*. By following up on Hegel's transcendental account, we can come to see the necessity of the various analyses in the places in which they appear, and the understanding gained therefrom will then in turn allow us to avoid approaching the text in an episodic fashion. In this way, I have attempted to provide a picture of the *Phenomenology* as a unified and organically organized text which will be of practical use to Hegel students.

1

Preliminaries on Hegel's Life and Legacy

Hegel's Life

Hegel was born in 1770 and died in 1831, and his lifetime spanned one of the most interesting and dynamic periods of European history. He was a contemporary of (among other things) the French Revolution, the Napoleonic Era, the Congress of Vienna, and the July Revolution of 1830, and he died during the period of debate on the English Reform Bill, the so-called Great Reform, ultimately passed in 1832. He was deeply engaged in the social and political events of his day, and his philosophy can be seen largely as an outgrowth and response to these events. Moreover, he lived during the period which is usually regarded as the zenith of German culture and was personally acquainted with most all of the important intellectual figures of his day. These great figures, such as Goethe, Schelling, Hölderlin, and the brothers Humboldt and Schlegel formed the academic climate in which Hegel's philosophy grew and matured. Hence, his biography is not without interest to those attempting to come to terms with his thought.

Georg Wilhelm Friedrich Hegel was born on 27 August 1770 in Stuttgart in the Duchy of Württemburg and was one of three children. He attended the secondary school or *Gymnasium* there and distinguished himself early as a promising student. During this period he learned Latin, Greek, and Hebrew, and read the classical authors extensively. In addition to the ancient authors he also busied himself with the writers of the Enlightenment, of whom Rousseau was his favorite. He wrote down and summarized noteworthy passages from whatever he happened to be reading, hoping that by this method he could better internalize the thoughts of the writers he was working on. He kept a diary written in Latin during this period which exhibits the extremely self-reflective and inquisitive

4

nature of its young author. In 1788, at the age of eighteen, Hegel held the valedictory address upon graduating from the *Gymnasium*.[1]

He then went to Tübingen in the same year to attend a distinguished theological seminary or *Stift* at the university there. It was here that he made the acquaintance of and became close friends with fellow philosopher Schelling and the poet Hölderlin. During this period Hegel began his first serious study of Kant, whose work by this time had come to dominate German intellectual life. According to all accounts, life at the *Stift* was extremely oppressive,[2] including compulsory prayer, constant supervision, and a tightly controlled and invariable daily schedule. In this overbearing atmosphere, news of the outbreak of the French Revolution in 1789 caused great excitement among both students and faculty.[3] The students, who kept abreast of the events in Paris via French newspapers, founded a clandestine political club, which had among its activities the singing of revolutionary songs, planting a "Tree of Liberty," and giving political speeches. Although subject to the oppressive climate of the seminary and the backwards political institutions of the German states, the students found solace in contemplating the events taking place in Paris, which they were certain would prepare the way for a future which was brighter than the present that they knew.

After graduation from the *Stift* in 1793, Hegel went to Bern to work as house tutor for a noble family. Due to the extreme scarcity of academic positions at the time, work of this sort was quite common for scholars; indeed, we must bear in mind that Kant was the first genuine professional philosopher in Germany, the earlier generation of scholars in Europe (Descartes, Spinoza, et al.) being employed outside the academy. In Bern, Hegel was responsible for the education of two young girls and one small boy—a task which he did not cherish. He sorely missed being in close contact with the literary and academic affairs in Germany. Through the mediation of Hölderlin in 1796, he obtained a similar post in Frankfurt, where, to his great satisfaction, he moved at the beginning of the following year. During these early years in Bern and Frankfurt, Hegel produced a number of essays, which survive in handwritten manuscript form, primarily on the nature of religion.[4] Toward the end of this period, he also began work on an essay entitled "The German Constitution,"[5] which he completed a few years later in Jena.

At the turn of the century, the court at Weimar under the influence of Goethe had made the University of Jena one of the leading intellectual centers in Germany. Fichte, Tieck, A. W. von Schlegel, and Novalis had been at Jena, and Schiller, Schelling, and Friedrich von Schlegel were still in residence in 1801 when Hegel decided to go there as *Privatdozent*, or unsalaried lecturer, to begin his academic career. The inheritance he had received upon the death of his father in 1799 provided him with the financial stability to undertake such a venture. During his first year in Jena, he published a short book entitled *The Difference between the Systems of Fichte and Schelling.*[6] It is sometimes thought that this early work shows him to be still very much under the sway of his former school comrade Schelling, although some would find here the beginning of Hegel's own philosophical identity. Although Schelling was five years Hegel's junior, he had already become famous with, among other things, his *System of Transcendental Idealism* in 1800 and had already received a full professorship in Jena in 1798 at the remarkably young age of twenty-three. During this period, Hegel was relatively unknown and generally regarded as one of Schelling's followers. On 27 August 1801, Hegel defended his *Habilitationsschrift*, a work in Latin on natural philosophy entitled *On the Orbits of the Planets.*[7] This public defense was (and still is) a part of the formal requirements for becoming a professor and lecturing at the German university. From 1802 to 1803, Hegel and Schelling jointly edited a philosophical journal called the *Critical Journal of Philosophy*, to which both contributed a number of articles.

When Schelling abandoned Jena in 1803, Hegel was left alone to develop his own philosophy and was, indeed, under great pressure to do so. Since the beginning of the Jena Period in his lecture announcements he had been proclaiming that a book was forthcoming in which his own philosophical system would be expounded. From the surviving manuscripts from this period, the so-called *Realphilosophie*,[8] we can see that Hegel in fact had been diligently at work on a major project, much of which was to foreshadow his mature philosophy. Ultimately, in 1806, his efforts culminated in his most famous work, the *Phenomenology of Spirit*. His course announcement for Winter Semester 1806–7 reads, "[Professor Hegel lecturing on] Logic and Metaphysics, that is, speculative philosophy with the *Phenomenology of Spirit*, the soon to appear first part of his book *System of Science*, being treated first."[9] Although Hegel had offered his course on logic and metaphysics several times previously in Jena, this is the first occurrence of the word "phenomenology" that we find. This, along with other surviving fragments, shows that Hegel was continually reworking and rethinking the material which received its final form in the book we know as the *Phenomenology of Spirit*.

It is thought that Hegel, due to pressure from his publisher, composed the final sections of the *Phenomenology* in a short period of time in mid-October of the year 1806.[10] At this time Napoleon and the French army reached Jena and, at the Battle of Jena on 12 October 1806, defeated the Prussian forces and occupied the town. In a letter to Schelling,[11] Hegel reports that he finished writing the *Phenomenology* on the eve of the battle, and this is usually taken as evidence that he was under some strain to complete the manuscript. Despite the personal inconvenience caused by the battle, Hegel generally seemed to welcome the French conquest which he saw as a means of destroying the medieval institutions that were still firmly in place in Germany.[12] He was moved by the historical importance of Napoleon's campaigns which were effectively spreading the French Revolution to the rest of Europe. In another famous letter, he reports that he saw Napoleon, whom he so greatly admired, riding through the streets of Jena: "I saw the Emperor—this world soul—riding out of the city on reconnaissance. It is indeed a wonderful sensation to see such an individual, who, concentrated here at a single point, astride a horse, reaches out over the world and masters it."[13] The Battle of Jena closed the university and left Hegel unemployed. The *Phenomenology* was, however, at the publishers in Bamberg, and in January 1807 Hegel read the proofs and added the Preface. In April of that year the book appeared.

Hegel's academic career was for the moment at an end. He was, however, able through his friend Niethammer to obtain a post as a newspaper editor in Bamberg, where he was employed from 1807 to 1808. His task there was primarily to summarize the important daily events, usually making use of reports taken from French newspapers, Bamberg being at the time under French occupation. He began his return to the academic world as a headmaster or *Rector* at the *Gymnasium* in Nüremberg in 1808. This position was obtained once again through Niethammer, and it was Hegel's task to implement his friend's neo-humanist educational reforms at the *Gymnasium*. During this period, he published his second major work, the *Science of Logic*, in installments in 1812, 1813, and 1816.[14] At the *Gymnasium* he drew outlines from this most difficult and obscure of all Hegelian texts and lectured from them. It was also during this period that Hegel in 1811 married Marie von Tucher, the daughter of a noble family, who gave birth to two sons in 1813 and 1814, respectively. Hegel was in Nüremberg when the Prussians liberated it from French occupation—an event which he viewed with some skepticism.[15]

Hegel finally received an academic position again as professor at the University of Heidelberg, where he remained from 1816 until 1818. There he published the *Encyclopaedia of the Philosophical Sciences* in 1817, which many consider the most straightforward account of his philosophical system.[16] The *Encyclopaedia* consisted of three parts or three philosophical sciences, "Logic," "Philosophy of Nature," and "Philosophy of Mind," and was written in the form of a compendium for use in his lectures.

In 1818 Hegel accepted a prestigious professorship at the University of Berlin, which had just been founded in the year 1810 by figures such as Alexander von Humboldt, Fichte, and Schleiermacher. When Hegel arrived in Berlin, he found the Prussian capital in a tense state. After Napoleon's defeat by the allies in 1815, the Congress of Vienna, in its attempt to come to terms with the post-Napoleonic world, resolved to return to the age prior to the French Revolution and to restore the legitimate monarchs to the thrones of Europe. As a result of these measures, Germany consisted of a hodgepodge of some thirty-seven principalities and four republics, with no semblance of national unity. The powers in Prussia were particularly reactionary and oppressive in their attempts to eliminate anything that had the look of democracy or liberalism. In 1819 Prussia ratified the Karlsbad Decrees which called for, among other things, harsh censorship and the dismissal of agitating university professors or so-called "demagogues," who were critical of the state and who rallied student protest. In this atmosphere Hegel lectured on political philosophy, and in 1821[17] he published his final book, *Natural Law and Political Science in Outline: Elements of the Philosophy of Right*, known among scholars simply as the *Philosophy of Right*. During his years in Berlin, Hegel gave lectures on the philosophy of world history,[18] aesthetics,[19] the philosophy of religion,[20] and the history of philosophy,[21] which were extremely popular and which today count as useful supplements to his published works. In 1826 he founded a journal entitled the *Jahrbücher für wissenschäftliche Kritik*, which would serve as the ideological arm of Hegelian philosophy long after his death. At the peak of his career, he died suddenly during a cholera epidemic in Berlin on 14 November 1831.

Hegel, during his Berlin period, had come to be the leading philosopher in Germany. His lectures were popular, and through his books he enjoyed success in his own lifetime that few philosophers in Germany besides Kant had known. Berlin was the proper climate for this success, since by this time it had eclipsed Jena as the leading intellectual center in Germany, and because of this it provided Hegel with a wealth of extremely talented students. His colleagues at Berlin included Alexander von Humboldt, Arthur Schopenhauer, and Friedrich Schleiermacher, and among his students were Heinrich Heine, Bruno Bauer, David Friedrich Strauss, and Ludwig Feuerbach. Karl Marx arrived in Berlin in 1836, five years after Hegel's death, at a time when Hegelian philosophy was still very much in the air.

Due largely to the difficulty of his language, Hegel's *corpus*, and not least of all the *Phenomenology*,[22] was controversial and misunderstood in his own time. Immediately after Hegel's death his students divided into two antagonistic factions: the so called "right" and "left Hegelians." The central point of debate concerned originally Hegel's philosophy of religion. The right Hegelians, in whose number Bauer and Gabler are counted, read Hegel as maintaining orthodox religious beliefs concerning the existence and nature of God, the immortality of the soul, and the person of Christ. On the other hand, the left Hegelians, Feuerbach, Strauss, et al., contended that Hegel held a pantheistic conception of God. The theological debate developed into a political one in the context of which the terms "right" and "left" are more familiar. The right-wing Hegelians interpreted Hegel's famous dictum that the rational is the actual and the actual the rational[23] as the conservative claim that individual, real, existing conditions and institutions are rational and thus justified. Left-wing Hegelians, on the other hand, used the Hegelian dialectic as a critical tool by means of which they could criticize existing conditions as unjust and corrupt. These differences became ever more hardened in the years after Hegel's death, since most of the left Hegelians or "young Hegelians" were banned from the academic world by the conservative political forces then ruling in Europe and thus were compelled to pursue careers as political agitators and pamphleteers, while the right Hegelians enjoyed academic respectability and occupied the most important professorships in Germany.

Hegel's Influence

Hegel's influence has been extremely problematic. Rarely has the value of the work of any philosopher been so bitterly disputed. On the one hand, he has been raised upon the highest pedestal and hailed as the German Aristotle,[24] and, on the other hand, he has been reviled as a simple charlatan,[25] a reactionary ideologist for the Prussian state,[26] a protonazi,[27] and worse. Moreover, the matter is further complicated by the fact that Hegel has, like no other philosopher, been the victim of a number of myths or legends[28] that have badly distorted his philosophy and have provided a host of misunderstandings in the reception of his work during the years since his death. This wild diversity of views makes it all the more important to examine carefully Hegel's works themselves as the ultimate bar of judgment before we engage in the usual polemics about his philosophy. Here we can do no better than to heed the *hortatio* of the Hegelian Benedetto Croce:

> But the first condition for resolving whether to accept or to reject the doctrine which Hegel propounds . . . is to *read his books*, and to put an end to the spectacle, half comical and half disgusting, of the accusation and

the abuse of a philosopher by critics who do not know him, and who wage
a foolish war with a ridiculous puppet created by their own imagination,
under the ignoble sway of traditional prejudice and intellectual laziness.[29]

Whether hero or villain, the figure of Hegel indisputably marks
a major fork in the road in the history of Western philosophy. He is
most obviously seen as a major figure in the German idealist tradition
after Kant, Fichte, and Schelling. This, like the schools of rationalism
and empiricism which preceded it, forms a roughly continuous tradition
with many points of agreement about the nature and method of philosophical inquiry, but after Hegel all of this changes. With Hegel, modern
European philosophy splinters into a number of different and competing
camps. From Hegel's philosophy arise most all of the major schools of
modern thought. One can fairly say that the history of modern European
philosophy is in a sense the history of the influence and development of
Hegelianism.[30]

First, the tradition of phenomenology and existentialism that includes Nietzsche, Kierkegaard, Husserl, Heidegger, Sartre, and Merleau-
Ponty clearly owes a great deal to Hegel, despite the various criticisms of
him by precisely these figures.[31] This tradition inherited and developed
not only much of Hegel's terse vocabulary but also Hegel's methodology and philosophical problematic. For instance, Hegel's criticism of
the Kantian thing-in-itself or transcendent object was largely accepted
and developed by the earlier phenomenologists, Husserl and Heidegger, although their notion of "phenomenology" differed considerably
from Hegel's.[32] Borrowing from Hegel's criticism of formal accounts of
knowledge and from Hegel's theory of the relationship of a truth-claim
to the culture and time period within which it arises, the existentialists
concentrated on the situatedness of human knowledge and on the lived
experience. Hegel's celebrated account of self-consciousness and above
all the lordship and bondage dialectic can be seen as the forerunner of a
fair bit of existential psychology in the work of Sartre and others. Hegel's
philosophy of religion has also been influential in this tradition: his
contention that religion captures metaphysical truths in a metaphorical
fashion or with what has been translated as "picture thinking" has found
resonance in Schopenhauer's philosophy of religion.[33] Hegel's statement,
"*God Himself is dead*,"[34] foreshadows Nietzsche's famous dictum by more
than half a century.

Second, Marxism and the neo-Marxist Frankfurt School trace their
origins directly and fairly unproblematically back to Hegel. An important
point of intersection here, besides Marx himself, is Kojève's influential,
albeit idiosyncratic, lectures on Hegel at the Collège de France from

1933 to 1939.[35] The conception of the office of philosophy as an organ of social criticism can be traced back to Hegel's conception of the dialectic, which tests specific truth-claims for validity and rejects those which are self-contradictory, ideological, or in bad faith. His philosophy of history profoundly shaped Marx's account of history as a series of class struggles between workers and the owners of the means of production, as well as Marx's idea that certain social and economic conditions could be self-contradictory or, in his terms, ideological. Moreover, the teleology in Hegel, according to which philosophy is conceived as a process that progresses to ever higher levels of knowing until it reaches the ultimate level—absolute knowing—is found again in Marx's teleological conception of the history of class struggles leading ultimately to a classless society. In addition, Hegel's generally positive assessment of reason and his pro-Enlightenment belief in the efficacy of rationality[36] and of the dialectic finds its analogue in Habermas's conception of communicative action and theory of rationality.[37]

Third, the intellectual movement in the social sciences known as structuralism, with figures such as Piaget, Saussure, Lévi-Strauss, and Foucault, owes to Hegel its basic premise that underlying the apparent chaos of the manifold of individual cultures and peoples there is some fundamental structure that is accessible to human reason. Piaget's theory of childhood development, which proceeds in specific identifiable stages, strongly resembles Hegel's notion of the dialectical progress of knowledge.[38] Saussure's claims about universal linguistic structures and Lévi-Strauss's account of the universal structures of myths both reflect Hegel's methodology of trying to discover the rational behind the apparently inchoate phenomena of the world.[39]

Fourth, the classical American pragmatism of Dewey and James owes a great deal to the philosophy of Hegel.[40] Indeed, pragmatism would not have been possible without the surprisingly long intellectual tradition of Hegelianism in American thought. Toward the second half of the nineteenth century, St. Louis and Cincinnati became the main centers for the neo-Hegelian movement in the United States.[41] There, through the work of William Torrey Harris, Henry Conrad Brokmeyer, and John Bernard Stallo, Hegel was introduced into the world of American letters quite early. At the turn of the century, Hegel's philosophy became even better known and more respected through the lectures of Josiah Royce at Harvard.[42] It was from him that many of the pragmatists learned about Hegel. Although the pragmatist program developed in ways quite antithetical to Hegel, it nevertheless owes much to him.[43] The pragmatists' attempt to see philosophical problems of the tradition as contingent and as nested in a cultural and historical context which later is no longer relevant is derived directly from Hegel. Hegel's incorporation of a wide variety of seemingly nonepistemological or "pragmatic" factors in his account of truth and objectivity was, for the pragmatists, important in distinguishing him from the other philosophers of the tradition.[44] Likewise, their understanding of truth as something dependent on and functional only within concrete social-historical moments can also be traced back to Hegel.

Fifth, Dilthey and the brand of historicism and hermeneutics that runs through Gadamer was also strongly influenced by Hegel.[45] The attempt to understand truth as something arising out of the dynamic movement of historical epochs was taken up by Dilthey and developed in his theory of the comprehensive worldview or *Weltanschauung.* Hegel's attempt to formulate a philosophical system that integrated the various social and cultural forms such as literature, art, and religion was also adopted by Dilthey in his attempt to give a systematic account of the *Geisteswissenschaften* taken as a whole. This tradition has in turn had a profound influence on the social sciences of the twentieth century with what concerns methodology and subject matter. Modern disciplines such as the sociology of knowledge or social history can be traced back to Hegel via this tradition.

The other major strain of modern philosophy—the Anglo-American tradition of Wittgenstein, Russell, Moore, et al.—has defined itself largely in opposition to Hegel. This conflict can perhaps best be understood in terms of a generation gap among philosophers at the British university. At the end of the nineteenth century, T. H. Green and Edward Caird formed the first generation of Hegel commentators in Great Britain. Through their influence a thriving neo-Hegelian movement came about, whose leaders included scholars such as F. H. Bradley, Bernard Bosanquet, and J. M. E. McTaggart. It was against this movement that the incipient tradition of analytic philosophy reacted and later defined itself.[46] We could ask for no better example of a conflict between two entirely disparate conceptions of philosophy. For the neo-Hegelians, the analytic philosophers' concern with linguistic analysis and formal logic seemed obtuse, whereas the analytic philosophers saw the neo-Hegelians as sloppy, inexact thinkers concerned only with intellectual abstractions. They came to see the post-Hegelian tradition in European philosophy simply as a wrong turn in the history of philosophy which steered away from the correct conception of philosophy as a part of the project of the natural sciences.[47]

Today it can be said that one's academic identity in contemporary philosophical circles is defined largely by one's assessment of Hegel. Accepting Hegel commits one to endorsing the tradition of modern

European philosophy, and the particular aspects of his doctrine which one chooses to highlight determine specifically the school of European philosophy to which one belongs. On the other hand, a wholehearted rejection and dismissal of Hegel places one squarely in the Anglo-American tradition of contemporary philosophy. But no school of modern European thought can claim to be wholly devoid of the influence of Hegel. Thus, it is imperative to have some understanding of the philosophy of Hegel in order not only to understand the history and development of modern European philosophy but also to begin to evaluate and develop an informed opinion about the plethora of schools, camps, and research programs that make up the contemporary philosophical scene.[48]

The Kantian Background and Hegel's Methodology

Perhaps the best way to begin to understand Hegel's project in the *Phenomenology* is by means of a brief comparison with Kant's transcendental idealism, which played a crucial role in Hegel's philosophical development and to which Hegel in the *Phenomenology* was reacting. I do not pretend to be able to recount the entirety of Kant's theoretical philosophy here in order to give an exhaustive overview of Hegel's criticism or development of it, since this theme has been the topic of entire books. I wish rather simply to touch on a few points in Kant's philosophy and Hegel's reconstrual of them which will help us to understand better the interpretation at hand. Moreover, I cannot claim here to give a nonpartisan account of Kant's philosophy that avoids the much debated criticisms of his position or the many interpretive puzzles of Kant exegesis and criticism. My procedure has been simply to present Kant's philosophy as Hegel understood it. The larger questions about whether or not Hegel understood Kant correctly or whether or not he was fair to Kant I leave to other commentators.

The Determination of Objectivity and the Categories

Kant assumed an ambivalent posture with respect to the rationalist metaphysicians who preceded him. On the one hand, he was critical of the metaphysical systems of the rationalists who in his view unreflectively or "uncritically" accepted the existence of specific metaphysical objects or the validity of metaphysical principles or concepts—e.g., substance, causality, God, etc.—without first demonstrating how or that they were possible. This approach he called "dogmatism," since the fundamental metaphysical claims were dogmatically asserted and not philosophically examined or grounded. According to Kant, we must first analyze the faculties of the human mind in order to see to what extent we can meaningfully talk of metaphysical objects or principles. Only after we determine the powers and limitations of our cognitive faculties can we come to an understanding about the proper employment and status of metaphysical concepts. A precritical or dogmatic philosophy is one that begins straightaway with metaphysical objects themselves without previously examining the human cognitive capacity. "Dogmatism," Kant writes, "is thus the dogmatic procedure of pure reason, *without previous criticism of its own powers.*"[1] This dogmatism Kant contrasts with his own "critical philosophy," which undertakes an examination of the powers of the intellect and a "critique" of human reason.

However, Kant was not merely critical of his rationalist predecessors. He shared with the rationalists the idea that the perceiving subject played an active role in shaping and ordering the data of perception. He was likewise in agreement that rational human subjects were in possession of a priori knowledge or what the rationalists called "innate ideas," that is, knowledge that is inborn or derived solely from reason and thus not obtained empirically from experience or the senses; however, one of Kant's great innovations, which separated him from his rationalist predecessors, was his emphasis on form. For Kant, a priori knowledge was not something with content, i.e., Descartes's God or the *cogito*, but rather formal cognitive faculties which make perceiving and understanding possible in the first place. The *Critique of Pure Reason* can be seen as an attempt to demonstrate exhaustively the necessary forms of human cognition.

In the *Critique of Pure Reason*, Kant distinguishes (aside from reason itself) two fundamental sorts of cognitive faculties: that of sensibility and that of understanding. First, in the "Transcendental Aesthetic" he argues that space and time are what he calls the "forms of sensible intuition" (*sinnliche Anschauung*). All objects of sense or, put more exactly, all representations (*Vorstellungen*), must appear in space and time in order for them to be representations for us as perceiving subjects. Something outside of space and time is unrepresentable and thus meaningless for the human conceptual capacity. Space and time are subjective in the sense that they belong only to our faculty of sensibility, i.e., of perceiving and representing objects, and are not qualities of the things as they are in themselves apart from our understanding and perception. Space and time are thus not external, objective facts about the world but rather subjective facts about our faculties of representation.

Second, Kant introduces the "categories of the understanding," which are necessary for all judgments about objects that take place not in sensibility but in the understanding. The categories, twelve in number, are broken down into the following four groups:[2] (1) Quantity: unity, plurality, totality. (2) Quality: reality, negation, limitation. (3) Relation: inherence and subsistence (i.e., substance and accident), causality and dependence (i.e., cause and effect), community (i.e., reciprocity of agent and patient). (4) Modality: possibility/impossibility, existence/nonexistence, necessity/contingency. These categories carry with them a necessity which is not to be found in the mere perceptions themselves; thus, Kant argues, they must come from our own faculty of representing objects and not from the external world of things as they are in themselves. Causality, substance-accident, and so forth, are thus, for Kant, not qualities of things-in-themselves or facts about the world per se, but rather they are a part of the human faculty of understanding without which we would be unable to experience or conceptualize objects at all.

These faculties are then employed roughly as follows: raw empirical data is given to perceiving subjects in the chaotic manifold of experience, and the cognitive faculties, i.e., space, time, and the categories, spontaneously organize and render coherent the otherwise confused perceptions. In this way, disorganized perceptions are rendered into distinct representations or objects, or, put differently, the cognitive faculties *determine* (*bestimmen*) the objects of representation. One might use the analogy of focusing a camera in order to get a clear image. At first, the images are blurred and indistinct, and one cannot tell the one from the other. One sees only a manifold of colors and indistinct shapes. Then, as the camera is focused, the individual objects gradually become discrete and recognizable; by focusing we *determine* the individual objects. So also with Kant, the categories and the forms are our focusing devices, so to speak. However, there is, of course, no possibility of perceiving without these devices in the way that we can perceive without a camera. Without the application of the categories and the forms of intuition, we would not be able to perceive or conceptualize discrete objects at all. The objects of perception are then nothing more than just these organized representations. Thus, the cognitive faculties not only determine individual objects, but rather they determine objectivity in general, since objective experience would be impossible without them. The categories and the forms are thus necessary conditions for the determination of objectivity. Hence, the forms of sensible intuition and the categories of understanding are necessary presuppositions for human knowledge and objectivity.

According to what can be seen as Kant's "official view," truth concerns *our* knowledge, i.e., the objects represented through *our* representations. In other words, our representations are true objects and are thus objective not in the sense that there are external objects or things as they are in themselves which correspond to them, but rather in the sense that the representations are universally determined by the categories and the forms in the same way by all perceiving subjects.[3] Hence, truth or objectivity, for Kant, amounts to universal validity. Our representations are not simply subjective or solipsistic perceptions unique to each individual. The key to Kant's idealism lies in the fact that he believes that the human cognitive faculties not just reshape an already given manifold and thus distort it, but rather that these cognitive faculties make objectivity possible in the first place by their formative or constitutive function; without the categories and the forms of intuition, we would have no determinate objects at all. For Kant, objectivity issues from the side of the subject, and in this crucial point lies the heart of his idealism.

The tensions involved in Kant's "official view" and particularly in his doctrine of the thing-in-itself lead to what might be seen as his "unofficial view," which can be thought of as the natural result of his theory carried out to its logical conclusion. Kant's epistemology invariably generates the skeptical question of how our representations match up to the thing-in-itself, i.e., the object as it truly is in itself, understood apart from our subjective modes of representation. According to the "official view" the question is nonsensical: technically speaking, there is nothing for our representations to match up to, since things-in-themselves are not objects in the first place. Objects are by definition representations, and the thing-in-itself is not a representation and can never be one. However, the very idea of a thing-in-itself nonetheless tends to posit a second standard for truth in the external world independent of our representations. Moreover, this seems to be *the* standard for truth, since our representations, although universal among all rational subjects, are nonetheless subjective. They are subjective in the sense that they are only the result of the action of our cognitive faculties on the manifold of experience. Hegel describes this tension in the following way:

> This conclusion stems from the fact that the Absolute alone is true, or the truth alone is absolute. One may set this aside on the grounds that there is a type of cognition which, though it does not cognize the Absolute as science aims to, is still true, and that cognition in general, though it be incapable of grasping the Absolute, is still capable of grasping other kinds of truth.[4]

Kant tries to assert that even though we, limited as we are by our cognitive faculties (i.e., the categories and the forms), are unable to grasp the thing-in-itself or what Hegel here calls "the Absolute," nonetheless we still have another kind of truth, i.e., the truth bound up with the universality of our representations. Thus, our representations are true in some sense, albeit not in the sense that we know them to correspond to things-in-themselves. But this, on Hegel's view, leads to a confusing and ultimately unsatisfying division between two kinds of truth, one for us and one for God: "But we gradually come to see that this kind of talk which goes back and forth only leads to a hazy distinction between an absolute truth and some other kind of truth, and that words like 'absolute,' 'cognition,' etc. presuppose a meaning which has yet to be ascertained."[5] There are then two standards for truth which are posited, one in the universality of our representations—the official view—and one in the external world or in the nonsubjective dimension of the thing-in-itself. Yet we cannot help but believe that the external world, i.e., the thing-in-itself, is the higher standard. This seems to be confirmed by Kant's claim that God, not being limited by the forms and the categories, can directly intuit the thing-in-itself without mediation. This divine intuition then clearly appears to be higher than our human intuition and perception. Our human cognition and criteria for truth thus appear impoverished by contrast. Hegel expresses this in the *Science of Logic* when he explains how on the Kantian view the very idea of truth itself becomes weakened and even indiscernible: "In this self-renunciation on the part of reason, the notion of truth is lost; it is limited to knowing only subjective truth, only phenomena, appearances, only something to which the nature of the object itself does not correspond: knowing has lapsed into opinion."[6] Since our representations are only subjective and since we can never know the thing-in-itself, it appears that the very notion of truth itself is lost. As we shall see, Hegel's phenomenological method tries to provide us with an account that preserves truth in the deep sense and that is more satisfying than the Kantian view with its two-world split between representations and things-in-themselves.

To begin with, Hegel criticizes Kant's static account of the determination of objectivity. An important part of Kant's epistemology, which stems from his rationalist heritage, is the claim that the categories of the understanding and the forms of sensible intuition are a priori. In other words, the human cognitive faculty is, so to speak, hard-wired and static and thus has no relation to contingent or external elements such as history or familial or social institutions. Human cognition is, for Kant, unchanging and universal. It is precisely this point that Hegel wants to criticize. For Hegel, human representations are not ultimately determined by fixed categories and forms of intuition, but rather are continually molded and reshaped in something that resembles a historical process. Kant's epistemology can be seen metaphorically as a one-dimensional or horizontal account of human knowing, since, for him, the form of human representations is eternally and ahistorically fixed and cannot change. Objective truth, on this view, amounts simply to the universality of representations determined for all time in the same way among all perceiving subjects. Hegel's *Phenomenology*, on the other hand, is a multidimensional, vertical account of human knowing, which examines not just one set of categories or one conception of objectivity but rather several. In each chapter of the *Phenomenology*, we are presented with a different account of the determination of objectivity and a corresponding set of categories or what I will call "criteria for objectivity and subjectivity." By this I mean simply the very conceptions of objects and of ourselves as subjects that we form. To return to our camera analogy, for Hegel, just as there are many different sorts of cameras, infra-red, x-ray, etc., by which we can determine discrete objects, so also there are many different ways to determine objectivity and not just the one with the Kantian categories and forms.

Another important difference between Kant and Hegel that we need to keep in mind if we are not to be misled by this language of "the determination of objectivity" is that, for Kant, it is the subject which unilaterally determines the possible objects of representation. In other words, according to the Kantian picture, the categories and the forms of intuition, in short, all the formal elements which determine an object as such, are domiciled on the side of the subject.[7] Thus, it is the subject alone with his cognitive faculties who is responsible for the determination of objectivity. For Hegel, on the other hand, the categories or what I have called the "criteria" above have their own, so to speak, "inner logic" and are not considered to be the sole property of the subject. On Hegel's view, an object is nothing more than the result of a certain conception of objectivity or a certain conceptual scheme, e.g., as a thing with properties or as an unseen force behind the phenomena. Such conceptions, of course, need a subject to think them through for consistency, but they do not belong to the subject in the way the cognitive faculties for Kant are, so to speak, hard-wired in the subject. For Hegel, the various conceptions of subjects and objects work themselves out naturally or according to their own inner logic in the thought of each person in the way that, for instance, the various elements of a scientific theory arrange themselves in accordance with each other and with the theoretical core of the theory. Thus, the concepts have a sort of independence that is not to be found in Kant's philosophy. This means that while, for Kant, subjects "determine" objects in a rather one-sided fashion, for Hegel, objects are *self*-determined according to the self-determination or self-unfolding of the various conceptions of objectivity.[8] Hegel calls this the "self-supporting activity of thought."[9] Objects steadily enrich themselves in accordance with ever more sophisticated criteria or concepts, and the role of the subject is merely to think the concepts through or to combine them in a single apperceptive consciousness such that they can be compared for consistency. We will have to see in more detail exactly what is involved in this notion of an inner logic, but for the moment a simple understanding of it as thought's self-determination and development is adequate for our purposes.

Also unlike Kant, on Hegel's view, the conceptions of objectivity that develop in the dialectical movement necessarily imply certain dynamic conceptions of the subject as well.[10] Admittedly, for Kant, objectivity implies what he calls an "apperceptive subject" in whom the various representations of the manifold are necessarily united.[11] In other words, the various perceptions must necessarily be united in a single subject if they are to be cognized and perceived as a single object in the first place, since we would not have an objective representation if its various elements were scattered among several subjects. Hence, a certain account of subjectivity is implied by the conception of objectivity constituted by the categories and the forms of sensible intuition; however, this account of subjectivity is both static and formal. In other words, the apperceptive "I," for Kant, is merely an unchanging logical precondition for understanding and is nothing that we might consider a self-conception or self-image, for example. In the *Encyclopaedia Logic*, Hegel writes, referring to Kant's transcendental unity of apperception,[12] "In an awkward expression which Kant used, he said that I *accompany* all my conceptions—sensations, too, desires, actions, etc. 'I' is in essence and act the universal: and such partnership is a form, though an external form, of universality."[13] But this conception of the subject as something that mechanically accompanies our representations is, says Hegel, "wholly *abstract*."[14] For Hegel, by contrast, the inner logic of the dialectic of objectivity is also the inner logic of subjectivity. As our accounts of objects change, so also do our accounts of ourselves as subjects. Thus, in the dialectic of the *Phenomenology* we are presented with a multitude of self-conceptions as well as conceptions of objectivity. First, these self-conceptions, in a fashion parallel with the account of objectivity, are not static as for Kant, but rather replace and modify one another in the course of the dialectic. Second, these accounts of subjectivity can be seen as playing an important role as a necessary condition for the possibility of certain sorts of action or political arrangements, and thus they are much richer in content than Kant's mere apperceptive "I" and can be truly considered self-images or self-conceptions.

Kant and Hegel on Transcendental Philosophy

Kant research has gone much the same way as Hegel research in a certain respect. Kant has traditionally been criticized as a metaphysician for his problematic claims about the status and nature of the thing-in-itself, but recent interpretive trends have emphasized his transcendental philosophy in an attempt to minimize the metaphysical sounding expressions he sometimes uses.[15] Hegel as well, with his talk of absolute Spirit and absolute knowing, has traditionally been criticized as a precritical or romantic metaphysician. In recent years, however, Hegel research has gone some distance toward correcting this misconception with a number of studies emphasizing Hegel's relation to Kant and his development of Kant's transcendental philosophy.[16] I wish to analyze two different passages in which Hegel discusses his philosophical methodology, in order to show that what he there describes is indeed a form of transcendental argument akin to the arguments found in Kant.

The strategy of a transcendental argument is to begin with certain facts about experience that are unproblematically accepted and then to try to show how certain other conditions must exist as necessary presuppositions for them. The form of a transcendental argument is something like the following: given that X is the case, a, b, and c must also be the case as necessary presuppositions for X. For example, we all agree that competitive games exist as a fact of human existence and experience. The concept of a game necessarily presupposes competitors who participate in it (leaving aside for the moment games that one can play alone or which imply a dummy opponent); moreover, a game necessarily presupposes an agreed upon set of rules as well as an agreed upon understanding of what would constitute winning or losing. These all necessarily belong to the concept of a game per se. Kant began with certain obvious features of our human experience and perception and applied arguments of this sort in order to unearth the universal characteristics that were necessarily presupposed in all human cognition. In this way, he deduced the categories and the forms of intuitions which are necessarily presupposed in every perceptual act and thus are necessary for objectivity and meaningful perception per se. Thus, a transcendental argument is one that exposes the necessary conditions for the possibility of something, in this case of objective thought.

Hegel discusses this methodology in the *Philosophy of Right*.[17] There, he is concerned to analyze forms of social and political life, and he indicates that his procedure is to take an institution and to unpack or deduce its necessary presuppositions. He writes,

> In a more speculative sense, a concept's determinacy and its mode of
> existence are one and the same thing. But it is to be noticed that the
> moments, whose result is a further determined form of the concept,
> precede it in the philosophical development of the Idea as determinations
> of the concept, but they do not go in advance of it in the temporal
> development as shapes of experience. Thus, for instance, the Idea
> determined as the family, *presupposes* the determinations of the concept
> from which the family will later on in this work be shown to result.[18]

What Hegel indicates here with this admittedly dense language is that
when we analyze a particular concept, here for instance the family, what
we are doing is making clear its necessary presuppositions and then
drawing the logical conclusions therefrom. Institutions, like concepts,
are analytically bound together, and when we investigate one institution
or concept, in analyzing its conceptual structure and presuppositions, we
simultaneously bring into the analysis other related institutions and concepts. The task of the philosopher is to examine the rational development
of these concepts. This deduction of the necessary preconditions or presuppositions behind institutions resembles Kant's procedure of deducing
the necessary conditions of the possibility of objective experience.

   In a passage in the opening section of the *Encyclopaedia Logic*, Hegel
describes the role of the *Phenomenology* as preparing the way for science,
and in his description he makes clear that the methodology employed by
the *Phenomenology* is that of a transcendental argument. He writes,

> In my *Phenomenology of Spirit* . . . the method adopted was to begin with the
> first and simplest phase of mind, immediate consciousness, and to show
> how that stage gradually of necessity worked onward to the philosophical
> point of view, the necessity of that view being proved by the process. But
> in these circumstances it was impossible to restrict the quest to the mere
> form of consciousness. For the stage of philosophical knowledge is the
> richest in material and organization, and therefore, as it came before
> us in the shape of a result, it *presupposed* the existence of the concrete
> formations of consciousness, such as individual and social morality, art
> and religion. In the development of consciousness, which at first sight
> appears limited to the point of form merely, there is thus at the same time
> included the development of the matter or of the objects discussed in the
> special branches of philosophy.[19]

In this rich and problematic passage, Hegel indicates that the development of the forms of consciousness that we see in the *Phenomenology*
proceeds by means of uncovering the necessary presuppositions involved

in each individual account or moment of consciousness. We begin with the "first and simplest" form, and we learn that in it the other forms are already implicitly contained. The process does not stop until consciousness arrives at absolute knowing or philosophical knowledge, which constitutes the most sophisticated and encompassing phase of knowing. Thus, the various moments along the way, "individual and social morality, art and religion," are the gradually revealed individual presuppositions or necessary conditions for knowledge-claims.[20] Here Hegel enriches the Kantian notion of a transcendental argument by including an account of these elements which are not usually thought to be relevant for the determination of truth-claims.

Hegel's dialectic in the *Phenomenology* is a transcendental account, insofar as it uncovers the necessary conditions for the possibility of specific actions, institutions, conceptions of subjectivity, and the truth-claims bound up with them. For example, what we will see in the dialectic of "Force and the Understanding" is that any account of objectivity necessarily presupposes an account of the human subject and thus human subjectivity. What we learn in the "Self-Consciousness" chapter is that in order to give an account of the human subject, we must also give an account of other human subjects, since the recognition of others is necessarily implied in the self-conception of the individual. But then, in the "Reason" chapter, we find out that any account of several independent human subjects is necessarily bound up with an account of a concrete historical community with specific institutions and practices which form and shape what formerly appeared as independent agents. Thus, at each stage we have a transcendental account, since each stage gives us an analysis of the necessary conditions for the possibility of specific conceptions of objectivity and subjectivity that are analyzed in the dialectic. This resembles, to some extent, Kant's transcendental philosophy, which attempts to give an account of the necessary conditions for the possibility of understanding and objectivity per se. However, Hegel's transcendental philosophy goes farther, since it goes beyond the individual subject and its cognitive faculties in its account of the necessary conditions of objectivity and subjectivity. Thus, Hegel's philosophy has the advantage of giving a richer and less formal account of subjectivity than Kant's philosophy, although they can both be seen as transcendental projects.

For Hegel, the determination of objectivity has a broader meaning than for Kant, for whom such a locution would only apply to the formation of representations.[21] The determination of objectivity applies not just to the sensuous representations but also to conceptions of things which Hegel calls "Notions."[22] Hegel wants to show, for instance, that the conception of the divine of a certain people is something governed by the same inner logic as the conception of an object as a thing with properties. In other words, the pantheistic Notion according to which various plants or animals are seen as deities is something which comes about in the process of conflicting Concepts or Notions of the divine. Hegel thinks that if we can reconstruct this process, then we can come to understand conceptually why certain peoples hold certain claims to be true. This broad social or historical aspect of the determination of objectivity is something wholly foreign to Kant and marks one of Hegel's most important innovations.[23] Thus, for Hegel, the self-development of our conceptions of objectivity and subjectivity is as broad and diversified as the themes in the *Phenomenology*.[24]

It is in the course of the dialectical development or self-determination of the various conceptions of subject and object that Hegel's philosophy takes on what looks like a historical element.[25] We need, however, to be careful, if we are to understand this correctly. The Notion is not historical in the sense that our conceptions of objects and of ourselves as subjects are shaped by historical influences. Of course, empirically our conceptions are so shaped, and Hegel admits as much, but to give an account of these influences is the task of the historian and not of the speculative philosopher. Hegel speaks to this issue of the difference between philosophy and history in a number of different places. In the *Philosophy of Right* he distinguishes between the philosophical approach to law, which examines the rational development of the concept of legal right, and the historical approach, which examines the historical development of legal right in the form of law.[26] In the *Encyclopaedia Logic*, he distinguishes between the history of philosophy, which is a survey of the development of the idea externally, and philosophy itself, which involves a survey of the development of the idea internally, i.e., in the realm of thought itself.[27] In the introduction to the *Lectures on the Philosophy of History*, Hegel clearly distinguishes between the empirical types of history writing and philosophical history writing, the latter of which consists of an analysis of the logic of the idea in history.[28] This conception is, moreover, not historical in the sense that social interactions gradually form our Notions of, for instance, ourselves as subjects. This is an empirical study which is consigned to the sociologist[29] and not to the philosopher. Hegel is interested in analyzing the self-development of thought and is thus less concerned with these empirical influences on our cognition. Hegel's student Gabler tells us that Hegel himself avoided illustrating the dialectical movement via specific historical examples. According to Gabler's account, Hegel preferred to work through the inner development of the Notions themselves. He writes, "The oral exposition of it [the *Phenomenology*] as well caused us great difficulties since the historical figures presented were treated only according to their inner thought and were not characterized further according to their external, historical existence."[30] Hegel's analysis in the *Phenomenology* can be understood as "historical" only in the sense that the concepts develop themselves in time into ever more complex forms. The important point to keep in mind, however, is that this "historical" development of the categories is in a sense a priori, that is, it has its own inner logic and does not appeal to specific empirical, historical, or sociological factors. Our various conceptions of objects and subjects can of course be manifested in determinate historical forms, but their rational *development*, according to Hegel, follows purely logical laws. Thus, certain conceptions of the family or specific institutions are embodied in specific historical moments, although their logic and their development are seen to some extent in abstraction from these incarnations.[31]

A second important difference between Hegel's project and a sociological account of how truth-claims arise is that a sociology of knowledge tends to eliminate truth in a weighty sense by reducing it simply to its historical or cultural context. There is thus a relativism at the heart of a sociology of knowledge which sees all truth-claims as culturally conditioned and ultimately ethnocentric once their origins have been laid bare. For Hegel, on the other hand, truth in the weighty sense is still retained in the concept of scientific truth or absolute knowing. According to his account, the results of a rigorous speculative philosophy do in some final sense represent the truth in a way that is not historically or culturally relative.

The reason why so much of the Hegel literature has failed to understand his project in the *Phenomenology* is because of the work's innovative account of the necessary logic of social relations in the categories by which we know and understand. In the "Consciousness" chapter we see analyses that we can at least vaguely recognize as having something to do with knowledge as we have always understood it, but in the "Self-Consciousness," "Reason," "Spirit," and "Religion" chapters the terms used are unfamiliar to those looking for a theory of truth or objectivity. Hence, it is Hegel's own innovative genius that is the original source of the misunderstanding. By enriching our conceptions of truth and objectivity with this demonstration of the logic of the Notions of subjectivity vis-à-vis other subjects and communities in the formation of this truth, Hegel has so shaken our conventional sense of what we mean by these terms and how we are accustomed to analyzing them that we are in danger of perceiving him as doing something entirely different where this vocabulary and analysis seem more appropriate.

Kant's Thing-In-Itself

Another major intentional departure from the philosophy of Kant is Hegel's claim that the Absolute or, in Kant's language, the thing-in-itself is intelligible. On Kant's view, as we have seen, our cognitive faculties— the forms of sensible intuition and the categories—determine objectivity and render the appearances coherent. However, we only have access to the appearances or representations, since we cannot abstract from our cognitive faculties and gain access to the things-in-themselves. We can never know how these objects really are apart from the determinations of our cognitive faculties, e.g., what a nonspatial object would be like. As we have seen, this then gives rise in Kant to the distinction between the thing-in-itself (*Ding-an-sich*) and our representations.

The thing-in-itself has been a major stumbling block in Kant's philosophy ever since his own time. How we are to understand the status of the thing-in-itself is a much debated issue.[32] Hegel's phenomenological methodology, which I will outline in more detail in the next chapter, is an attempt to reshuffle the basic epistemological presuppositions in Kant so as to obviate the problem of the thing-in-itself. Kant's basic dualism, consisting of a representation or object for consciousness and a thing-in-itself apart from consciousness, is, for Hegel, an absurdity. When we examine the issue, we see that the thing-in-itself is also an object for consciousness in a certain sense, namely, in the sense that it is merely the abstraction from what is given in perception. It is thus an abstract object of thought. It is never a thing apart from consciousness in any meaningful sense, but rather is merely an abstracted criterion of truth that we have posited and to which our representations must correspond. Fichte writes, "the thing-in-itself is a pure invention and has no reality whatever."[33] In a passage from the *Encyclopaedia Logic,* which is quite similar to Fichte's, Hegel writes,

> The thing-in-itself . . . expresses the object when we leave out of sight all that consciousness makes of it, all its emotional aspects, and all specific thoughts of it. It is easy to see what is left—utter abstraction, total emptiness, only described still as an "other-world"—the negative of every image, feeling, and definite thought. Nor does it require much penetration to see that this *caput mortuum* is still only a product of thought, such as accrues when thought is carried on to abstraction unalloyed.[34]

The point here is that when we abstract from our cognitive faculties to imagine the thing-in-itself, then we simultaneously do away with objectivity itself, since it is these faculties which determine objectivity in the first place. Thus, we are left with an "utter abstraction" that has no content.

In a difficult passage from the Introduction to the *Phenomenology*, Hegel redefines Kant's terminology in a way that makes his own phenomenological method clear. He writes, "If we designate *knowledge* as the Notion, but the essence or the *true* as what exists, or the *object*, then the examination consists in seeing whether the Notion corresponds to the object."[35] This option is the Kantian option (on the unofficial view) or the view of the correspondence theory of truth. According to this picture what is really true is the object "as what exists" or as it is in itself independent of our understanding or representations. We require a Notion or a conceptual scheme before we can have any perception or comprehension at all. The Notion serves as a way of carving up the world and making it intelligible or determinate in the first place. For Kant, the fixed cognitive faculties would thus form a Notion. Hegel's term "the Notion" can be understood when we think of contemporary concepts such as a conceptual scheme, a scientific paradigm,[36] or a worldview, all of which are meant to refer to a network of beliefs. To determine what is actually the case, we must try to match up our Notion or our theory (or on Kant's view our representation) of what a thing is with the thing-in-itself. However, this leads to an uneasy agnosticism, since we can never really get hold of the thing-in-itself to see if it matches our representations. Thus, Hegel suggests that we reshuffle the variables to avoid this skeptical problem: "But if we call the *essence* or the in-itself of the *object* the *Notion*, and on the other hand understand by the *object* the Notion itself as *object*, viz. as it exists *for an other*, then the examination consists in seeing whether the object corresponds to its Notion."[37] Hegel suggests that we conceive of our Notion or our theory, conceptual scheme, etc., as the in-itself and as the benchmark for truth and not the thing-in-itself as it exists *independently* of us. The object then is what appears as an object given our conceptual scheme, or, put differently, it is the scientific phenomenon inside of our scientific paradigm. The object is thus already conditioned by our understanding and is not an abstracted thing-in-itself. We can illustrate Hegel's term, the "Notion," by means of a familiar example that Descartes uses in the *Meditations* toward a different end. Descartes observes that there are two different concepts of the sun based on two different sets of criteria. He writes,

> For example, there are two different ideas of the sun which I find within me. One of them, which is acquired as it were from the senses and which is a prime example of an idea which I reckon to come from an external source, makes the sun appear very small. The other idea is based on

astronomical reasoning, that is, it is derived from certain notions which are innate in me (or else it is constructed by me in some other way), and this idea shows the sun to be several times larger than the earth.[38]

We need not insist on Descartes's distinction between innate ideas and empirical knowledge to see the larger point that he makes in this passage. We have two different ideas of the sun, one as a small yellowish circle in the sky smaller than the earth, and one as a massive gaseous sphere many times larger than the earth. These two conflicting ideas originally stem from two different conceptions or criteria for truth. The first idea of the sun is based on a Notion, according to which what is real and true is what appears directly to the senses. Given this Notion, the sun, understood as a small, yellowish object, is produced. However, if we change our Notion, then this object conception will no longer make sense. If we take as our criterion for truth what results from our calculations derived from mathematics, physics, and astronomy based on a wide range of data instead of merely what appears directly to our sensory apparatus, then a new idea of the sun is produced, namely, the idea that we have of it via the natural sciences. For Hegel, all of our truth-claims must be understood inside of a larger Notion of truth as a whole.

According to this view, we must merely examine the object of our representations and compare it to our conceptual scheme or Notion to see if it is consistent. Is the object consistent with what the conceptual scheme dictates? Is it at odds with other elements of the scheme? Is the object so described by the scientific paradigm that it is in agreement with the general framework or presuppositions of the paradigm? Thus, for Hegel, a phenomenology involves an examination and comparison of an object for consciousness with the Notion or theory which is also for consciousness. He writes, "the essential point to bear in mind throughout the whole investigation is that these two moments, 'Notion' and 'object,' 'being-for-another' and 'being-in-itself,' both fall *within* that knowledge which we are investigating."[39] The comparison of object and Notion is then possible, since both are for consciousness, and one of the terms is not separated and abstracted into another realm such that a genuine comparison would be impossible. Hegel continues, "Consequently, we do not need to import criteria, or to make use of our own bright ideas and thoughts during the course of the inquiry."[40] Hegel thus employs Ockham's razor to eliminate unnecessary aspects of the explanation. With a phenomenology we do not need to posit a thing-in-itself in a Kantian sense in order to explain how truth or our representations are possible. Thus, we can simply eliminate it from our account. Hegel notes that since both of these objects—the thing-in-itself or criterion for truth and the representation—are for the same consciousness, we are perfectly free to analyze their relation to one another. Thus, a "phenomenology" is an account or study (a λόγος) of the interrelations and movements of the *phenomena* (φαινόμενα) or appearances themselves without any reference to something beyond or behind them which is more real or more true.[41]

Since, for Hegel, it is absurd to try to compare our set of categories or, in more modern terminology, our conceptual schemes, with something outside or extraconceptual (since this is the origin of the problem of the thing-in-itself), he must provide us with other internal criteria for truth. If truth is not the correspondence of a statement or a representation with a real object, then what is it? Hegel, with his phenomenological method, provides us with *internal* criteria for truth: the standard for the correctness or the truth of the internal categorial determinations of objectivity is at once (1) internal consistency, (2) completeness, and (3) the necessary lack of alternatives. These are self-contained criteria which have no reference to anything beyond consciousness or the human capacity to represent objects.

1. The epistemological task of the *Phenomenology* is to examine various accounts of objects and of subjects, i.e., various self-determinations of thought, in order to see if they are internally consistent and thus, on this coherence theory, true. As we saw above, for Hegel, individual truth-claims have their meaning and value only in relation to a larger network of truth-claims. This larger network can be seen as a worldview or a scientific paradigm, and this network as a whole sets the standard for truth and validity. When new or unexpected information or phenomena arise that must be accounted for by the theory, then individual truth-claims must at times be juggled or even abandoned in order to keep the theory as a whole intact. The individual claims must be in harmony with one another, since no worldview or scientific paradigm can continue to exist if it is fraught with contradictions. Thus, it is incumbent on those who wish to maintain the theory to keep the individual truth-claims mutually consistent. If a particular worldview or account of objectivity is contradictory and cannot be consistently held, then it must be given up and replaced by a new account which reorders the important elements in a more consistent fashion. But internal consistency is only a formal criterion. If it were the only criterion, then the dialectic would not have the cumulative or waxing effect that it evinces, since internal consistency simply shows that something is logically consistent or inconsistent and does not imply any particular further development. If this were the only criterion, then we would see merely one paradigm replacing another with no apparent developmental progress.

2. Hence, what is needed is the second criterion: completeness. Certain Notions or conceptual schemes implicitly rely on hidden presuppositions which must first be explicated. As we saw, the transcendental account of the *Phenomenology* involves the postulation of an account of objectivity or subjectivity or both, and what is demonstrated is that such a view is in itself contradictory without another account, e.g., an account of an individual subject necessarily implies an account of other mutually recognizing subjects. It is here that the cumulative effect of the dialectic is to be seen. Each account gradually becomes richer and more comprehensive. This might also be illustrated by an analogy with the natural sciences. The goal of a scientific theory is to be able to explain exhaustively the phenomena of the universe. When specific phenomena stubbornly resist being incorporated into a theory, and the theory cannot account for them, then the theory is incomplete. A new theory which could account for the unexplained phenomena in addition to the same phenomena already explained by the old theory would then be seen as more successful, and we would expect that after a short period of transition this new theory would come to enjoy a position of hegemony in the sciences. The theory of scientific development at work here implies that new scientific theories must account for more and more phenomena and thus gradually become richer than their predecessors. This is what Hegel sees as the gradual enriching of the dialectic. The new theory or Notion is, according to Hegel's way of speaking, "higher and richer than its predecessor."[42] Hence, in contrast to Kant, for Hegel, truth and objectivity have a "historical" aspect (although not an empirical one) and thus must be traced in a historical fashion. For Kant, on the other hand, the objectivity of our representations is assured by their universality, and this universality is something static and fixed. But what if there are two new Notions that historically arise as successor theories? Could the dialectic then split and move along two or more separate paths?

3. Hegel believes that the dialectic is necessary, insofar as the forms that it generates afford no alternatives. When one form of consciousness is overcome or sublated, the next form comes about naturally and necessarily, and equally plausible alternative forms are simply not possible. This doctrine is difficult for even the staunchest defenders of Hegel to support.[43] However, we can by means of an analogy with the natural sciences at least make this claim somewhat plausible. When a scientific worldview or paradigm is in crisis and on the verge of collapse due to internal contradictions and unexplained phenomena, other theories or paradigms come to the fore, each claiming to be the true successor theory. At this point, the acceptance of a successor theory, although perhaps not a purely rational matter, is nevertheless governed by certain general

rules and criteria, e.g., simplicity, success in explanation of unexplained anomalous phenomena, internal consistency, etc. Thus, the adoption of a new theory cannot be considered a purely arbitrary affair in which all new contending theories have a perfectly equal chance to become the successor theory. Some new theories by virtue of their differences in the above criteria will be eliminated from the running summarily, while other pretenders will have varying chances at becoming the successor by virtue of their relative strengths vis-à-vis the criteria. Seen in this way, Hegel's claim for the lack of alternatives can be made at least somewhat plausible. Although theoretically there are, of course, alternatives, practically in concrete situations there are specific criteria for choosing an alternative theory that render the process rational in some measure and not wholly arbitrary.

With these three internal criteria, Hegel thinks we have all that we need to account for truth and objectivity. These criteria imply a "historical" development of the Notion or of the categorial determinations which work their way toward completeness and consistency. Truth-claims thus change and develop through time, and it is this development that Hegel hopes to reconstruct. In the development of the various relations of the in-itself and phenomena, truth is possible at any given stage, insofar as each given stage posits an in-itself moment as the criterion for truth. These moments, however, prove to be contradictory in the course of the dialectic until we reach the ultimate in-itself or truth, i.e., absolute knowing. At this point, at the level of what Hegel calls "science," there is no distinction between the criterion for truth, the in-itself, and the appearances or representations. Absolute knowing is the complete development or unfolding of the transcendental preconditions for subject-object thought. Since the philosopher can work through these various moments and unpack their preconditions, absolute knowing is accessible and in principle intelligible to all by an examination of the appearances themselves and not by appeal to something otherworldly beyond them.

3

Hegel's Introduction

The Justification of Science

Before we analyze the Introduction to the *Phenomenology* in detail, it will be useful to say a few words about what Hegel takes to be the goal of his philosophical system. This will allow us to understand more easily a number of the difficult concepts that he casually makes use of in the Introduction. On numerous occasions, Hegel tells us flatly that the goal of philosophy is the truth. For instance, in the Introduction to the *Encyclopaedia Logic*, he says that philosophy shares the characteristic with religion of having truth as its object.[1] But this general statement in itself does not really tell us much. Surely, other philosophers and other philosophical systems also had truth for their object; the question is specifically what kind of truth Hegel has in mind and how this differs from any other conception of truth.[2]

For Hegel, philosophical truth is bound up with what he calls "science" (*Wissenschaft*) and system, terms for which he is well known.[3] We need now explore in a preliminary fashion what he means by "science." To appreciate fully Hegel's notion of science, we must first take a brief glance at his puzzling notion of absolute knowing. This is, of course, the title of the ultimate chapter of the *Phenomenology* and the moment in the *Phenomenology* when philosophical truth is finally reached. I will try to understand this difficult idea of absolute knowing as the final and thus complete and adequate self-determination of objectivity and subjectivity. In other words, only here is our Notion of the subject-object relation fully and consistently self-determined so as not to be in need of further dialectical adjustments. It is here that the in-itself and representation correspond. As we saw in the previous chapter, for Hegel, we can know the Absolute or the thing-in-itself, insofar as we can completely reconstruct all the transcendental conditions for it. Scientific knowledge is that type of knowing which takes into account all the necessary conditions for all of our possible subject-object Notions. It then gives the totality of conditions for truth-claims. The levels of knowledge preceding this stage do this only partially, taking into account only a few specific elements in the entire process of the construction of such claims. In the following passage, Hegel describes scientific or absolute knowing that is produced by tracing the Notion through its various forms: "True thoughts and scientific insight are only to be won through the labor of the Notion. Only the Notion can produce the universality of knowledge which is neither common vagueness nor the inadequacy of ordinary common sense, but a fully developed, perfected cognition."[4] Absolute knowing involves a universality that is possible only after a complete account of the various Notions has been given, and thus scientific knowledge can only make its appearance at the level where this subject-object Notion, taken as a whole, is fully determined.

The important point for the distinction between science and common sense, or what Schelling calls the "common outlook,"[5] is that the former recognizes the essential unity of the subject and the object, which is the result of the complete self-determination of thought, while the latter does not. Hegel writes, "The standpoint of consciousness which knows objects in their antithesis to itself, and itself in antithesis to them, is for science the antithesis of its own standpoint."[6] When we say that science is knowledge of the Absolute, we mean precisely this, i.e., the Absolute is the monistic truth of subject-object identity. The opposite or antithesis of this identity would then be to see the subject and object as autonomous and independent of each other. In the *Encyclopaedia Logic*, Hegel describes the position of common sense in the following way: "Common sense, that mixture of sense and understanding, believes the objects of which it has knowledge to be severally independent and self-supporting."[7] Common sense presupposes a dualism between the subject and the object domain, insofar as it sees objects as independent of the subject. In other words, the objects do not require a thinking subject for their existence. In the *Science of Logic*, Hegel contrasts this view of common sense with his own concept of absolute knowing:

> Absolute knowing is the *truth* of every mode of consciousness because, as the course of the *Phenomenology* showed, it is only in absolute knowing that the separation of the *object* from the *certainty of itself* is completely eliminated. . . . Thus, pure science presupposes liberation from this opposition of consciousness. It contains *thought in so far as this is just as*

34

much the object in its own self, or the object in its own self in so far as it is equally pure thought.[8]

In this passage, Hegel discusses the split between the object and its representation, which he characterizes here as the "separation of the object from the *certainty of itself.*" In other words, the representation lies on the side of the subject which is *certain* of its truth; however, in the course of the dialectic this certainty or this representation invariably turns out to be self-contradictory. Science is that way of thinking which avoids the dualisms of subject and object, representation and thing-in-itself, and presupposes a unity from the start. The self-contradictory nature of the standpoint of common sense is crucial for Hegel's distinction between this standpoint and that of science, which he believes to be internally consistent.

Inconsistencies inevitably appear in the various views of common sense because, in contrast to science, they each posit some form of dualism which cannot be reconciled and which invariably leads to contradictions in the various conceptual accounts of the world. In the course of the dialectic, the essential unity of the object with the subject comes to the fore, since it is only by means of such a unity that the contradictory accounts can be rendered consistent. This unity does not imply that the object simply inheres in the subject alone; indeed, this is precisely the point of the view criticized in the "Self-Consciousness" chapter. Instead, this unity involves extensive mediating elements beyond both the subject and the object. The attempt to determine objectivity only in terms of the object itself (as in the "Consciousness" chapter) or in terms only of oneself as subject (as in the "Self-Consciousness" chapter) without relation to the complex social-historical network, which is a necessary precondition for the determination, turns out to be contradictory. Subject and object are related to one another through an intricate mediation of social, historical, and political factors. Science and absolute knowing represent the complete account of these diverse factors, of which a monism is the inevitable result, since these factors form a complex network in which both subject and object are embedded.

In the Preface to the *Phenomenology*, Hegel explains that given the intellectual climate of his time, he cannot simply begin with the system of science itself, but rather this system must be prepared or justified in some way beforehand. He writes,

> Since I hold that science exists solely in the self-movement of the Notion, and since my view differs from, and is in fact wholly opposed to, current ideas regarding the nature and form of truth, both those referred to

above and other peripheral aspects of them, it seems that any attempt to
expound the system of science from this point of view is unlikely to be
favorably received.[9]

It would, on Hegel's view, be imprudent simply to hand down his philosophical system *ex cathedra* without any preliminary justification or introduction to the so-called philosophical sciences.[10] Therefore, he says of
the *Phenomenology*, "I may hope, too, that this attempt to vindicate science
for the Notion, and to expound it in this its proper element, will succeed
in winning acceptance through the inner truth of the subject-matter."[11]
Thus, the task of the *Phenomenology* is somehow "to vindicate" or justify
science in a way that we have yet to explore.

To be sure, science must be justified ahead of time for the sake of
Hegel's philosophical contemporaries and their purported hostility to his
approach, but also there is something about the very nature of philosophy
as a discipline which requires justification. In the Introduction to the
Phenomenology, Hegel is once again concerned to distinguish science from
common sense, indicating that the relation between them implies the
need for a "phenomenology." In a number of places he discusses the
unique role of philosophy among the academic disciplines; for instance,
in the Introduction to the *Encyclopaedia*, he writes, "Philosophy misses
an advantage enjoyed by the other Sciences. It cannot like them rest
the existence of its objects on the natural admissions of consciousness,
nor can it assume that its method of cognition, either for starting or
for continuing, is one already accepted."[12] Philosophy, since it cannot
make presuppositions like other disciplines, must begin from the ground
up and be able to justify itself instead of relying on justification from
the outside. Philosophy is then a sort of "first philosophy," which serves
to justify or ground the other sciences. More importantly, nonscientific
understanding requires that science justify itself. "Only what is completely
determined is at once exoteric, comprehensible, and capable of being
learned and appropriated by all," Hegel writes. "The intelligible form
of science," he continues, "is the way open and equally accessible to
everyone, and consciousness as it approaches science justly demands
that it be able to attain to rational knowledge by way of the ordinary
understanding."[13] Science must be able to justify itself to common sense
in a way that does not fall back on any question-begging assumptions.
If one is already a thoroughgoing Hegelian, then there is no need for
a justification of science since, with the main presuppositions granted,
it is "exoteric" and "comprehensible" to all. The problem is, however,
to convince those who have not already granted these presuppositions.[14]
Common sense demands of science that it give an account of itself. Hegel

tries to do just this in the *Phenomenology*, and his procedure is to try to show that all accounts of the world based on common sense fail on their own terms and for this reason must be given up.

Later in the Preface to the *Phenomenology*, Hegel expresses this same thought about the need to justify science to common sense in the following way: "Science on its part requires that self-consciousness should have raised itself into this aether in order to be able to live—and [actually] to live—with science and in science. Conversely, the individual has the right to demand that science should at least provide him with the ladder to this standpoint, should show him this standpoint within himself."[15] Just as he wrote in the passage cited previously, here Hegel says again that the nonscientific standpoint requires a justification of science not in terms of science itself but rather on its own terms, i.e., in terms of common sense itself. This is the task of the *Phenomenology*, which begins with common sense and proceeds by exposing the inner contradictions in it until we are led via the dialectic to the level of science. However, the truly interesting thing about this passage is the metaphor that Hegel employs to describe the justification of science. He says that science must provide us with a *ladder* by means of which we, at the level of common sense, can reach the level of science. The metaphor suggests a vertical ascent to a higher level or standpoint. This image squares with what was suggested in the previous chapter when we compared Hegel's vertical account of truth and objectivity with Kant's horizontal account. There are, on Hegel's view, various views of the world rendered by the various "Concepts" or "Notions" which are given at ascending stages in the dialectic, whereas for Kant there is, so to speak, only one "Notion," i.e., one fixed set of categories and forms that determine the world. Kant's account thus remains on a single plane, while Hegel's takes on a multidimensional character. Specifically, the dialectic in the *Phenomenology* operates between two planes, that of absolute knowing or science and that of the most naive form of common sense. The course of the dialectic is thus the ascension up the ladder from the most rudimentary form of common sense to science.

In his Introduction, Hegel tells us the goal of the *Phenomenology*, and in so doing takes up just the question of truth with which we started. The goal of the *Phenomenology* is, says Hegel, to justify the scientific standpoint. This claim is explained at the end of the Introduction thus: "In pressing forward to its true existence, consciousness will arrive at a point at which it gets rid of its semblance of being burdened with something alien, with what is only for it, and some sort of 'other,' at a point where appearance becomes identical with essence, so that its exposition will coincide at just this point with the authentic science of Spirit."[16] Here

Hegel tells us that the task of the dialectic is to press on until the forms of dualism collapse entirely. This is what he means with the phrase about consciousness "being burdened with something alien . . . and some sort of 'other.'" The "other" is any object understood as something individual and existing on its own apart from the subject. This subject-object dualism in its various forms is what the *Phenomenology* tries to overcome. Hegel says more directly in the Preface to the *Phenomenology*, "It is this coming-to-be of *science as such* or of *knowledge*, that is described in this *Phenomenology of Spirit*."[17] The goal of the *Phenomenology* is then, by means of the dialectic, to reach this authentic science of Spirit, which is constituted by a complete monism of subject and object.

In his Introduction to the *Science of Logic*, Hegel explains the role of the *Phenomenology* this time in terms of a deduction: "The Notion of pure science and its deduction is therefore presupposed in the present work in so far as the *Phenomenology of Spirit* is nothing other than the deduction of it."[18] How precisely Hegel means for us to take this notion of "deduction" is a matter of some debate.[19] It is clear that he is playing on Kant's "Transcendental Deduction" from the *Critique of Pure Reason*, which tried to prove the objective validity of the categories. By "deduction," Hegel, like both Kant and Fichte before him, does not mean something like "demonstration" or "proof" in the strict sense of, for instance, analytical geometry. He means rather an explication of the necessary conditions of experience, i.e., what must be the case given that experience is as it is. We can thus say that the *Phenomenology* is a deduction of a science, i.e., of the complete and consistent self-determination of subject and object, in that it demonstrates and thus justifies the scientific standpoint in the course of the dialectic by demonstrating the necessary categorial determinations for our being able to conceive of objects and ourselves as subjects in the first place, independent of any reference to something other than consciousness which might play a role in the determination. The process of the justification of the scientific standpoint, which we find in the *Phenomenology*, is a synthetic or cumulative account, since at each stage new conditions for the various subject-object Notions are discovered and absorbed in the process. In the *Science of Logic*, on the other hand, at the level of scientific knowing itself, the analysis is analytic. Here nothing new is added to the account from "outside," but rather the scientific subject-object Notion itself is analyzed and broken down with the result being the full array of categories. The passages cited above show that at the end of the *Phenomenology* we allegedly reach the scientific standpoint, but we need to know in more detail how such a standpoint is justified. In what sense is this a true deduction?

In order to justify the scientific standpoint, the *Phenomenology* must conclusively demonstrate that scientific knowledge is somehow superior to or a necessary presupposition for any other kind of knowing. Hegel takes up this problem in the Introduction to the *Phenomenology*. It is here that he introduces the contrast between "science" and "common sense," the latter of which is, as we have seen, a way of thinking characterized by some form of dualism. The problem is how science can justify itself with respect to this other kind of knowing. Science cannot simply dismiss it "as an ordinary way of looking at things, while assuring us that its science is a quite different sort of cognition for which that ordinary knowledge is of no account whatever."[20] This would beg the question, since science would be attempting to justify itself by the mere fact that it is science, without first giving an account of what that amounts to. Hegel also tells us, "nor can it [science] appeal to the vulgar view for the intimations it gives us of something better to come."[21] This also involves a kind of question-begging, in that it presupposes that science will bear future fruits while common sense will not. Hence, we must find a way to justify science without resorting to these problematic arguments.

For Hegel, science is justified by demonstrating systematically that the nonscientific accounts are inconsistent and incomplete. Consistency and completeness are, as we have seen in the previous chapter, important features of Hegel's dialectic. Thus, Hegel's claim is in a way dependent on his definition: science is science because it is an internally consistent account, and common sense is not science because it is contradictory. After all views have been examined for consistency and the inconsistent ones have been rejected, what remains is science. In discussing the role of the *Phenomenology* in his Introduction to the *Science of Logic*, Hegel says the following of the complete or scientific view:

> The path of this movement goes through every form of the *relation of consciousness to the object* and has the notion of science for its result. This notion therefore (apart from the fact that it emerges within logic itself) needs no justification here because it has received it in that work; and it cannot be justified in any other way than by this emergence in consciousness. . . . but a definition of science—or more precisely of logic—has its proof solely in the already mentioned necessity of its emergence in consciousness.[22]

The *Phenomenology*, Hegel claims, examines all possible subject-object Notions or Concepts. In other words, all possible ways of conceiving of an object and of its relation to the thinking subject are examined for consistency in the dialectic. Only by going through each and every one of these multiple subject-object relations or conceptions and by showing that they are contradictory can Hegel show that his science is true and thus provide it with a proper justification. Only with the elimination of all possible alternatives as performed in the *Phenomenology* can science be said to be justified. Hence, by the mere fact that science has survived the dialectic while the other views have not, it is justified and requires no independent proof other than that provided in the *Phenomenology*. In the actual course of the dialectic, it is the criterion of completeness that separates the accounts of common sense from the road leading to science. At each stage in the *Phenomenology*, the proposed conception of the object or the subject or both is found necessarily to imply a larger account. As was outlined in the previous chapter, the account of the individual subject in the "Self-Consciousness" chapter, for example, is shown necessarily to presuppose an account of other mutually recognizing self-conscious agents. Thus, the road to science follows the enumeration and uncovering of the various transcendental conditions for the possibility of our Notions of the various subject-object relations.

So how does Hegel show that the nonscientific accounts are inconsistent? He does so by means of a dialectical examination of these various nonscientific accounts. He shows that there are essential elements lacking in the various accounts of objectivity that render them inconsistent, and thus the analyses must be expanded into new areas in order to include the new factors. All views fall under the scrutiny of the Hegelian dialectic, and only the final consistent one, i.e., the scientific one, stands the test, while the nonscientific views fall by the wayside since they give an incomplete account of the factors involved in the reconstruction of the criteria of subject and object, and because their dualisms lead to internal inconsistencies. The question of Hegel's use of dialectic is an extremely large and problematic issue in the literature which I intend to steer clear of. For the purposes of this study a fairly simplistic view of the dialectic will suffice. There are three aspects of the Hegelian dialectic which can be distinguished—the negative aspect (*negare*), the positive aspect (*conservare*) or what Hegel describes as "at once a *negating* and a *preserving*,"[23] and what we might call the enriching aspect (*elevare*). These three aspects are captured by the German word *aufheben*, which is often desperately translated as "to sublate" or "to supersede." Unfortunately, there is no single English word that adequately captures the various meanings of this most Hegelian of terms.[24] To complicate matters further, in his translation, Miller renders it inconsistently.[25] The foreignness of "to sublate" in contemporary English at least serves the function of flagging the problematic term for the English reader, and admittedly it is etymologically connected to the Latin word *tollere*, which shares the variety of meanings with the German *aufheben*. The literal meaning of *aufheben* is "raise up" or "elevate," i.e., *auf* + *heben*. However, it also means "to preserve" in the sense of preserving after dinner leftovers, for instance. Finally, it also means "to negate," "destroy," or "do away with."

The dialectic, understood in the negative sense (*negare*), can be seen simply as a series of *reductio ad absurdum* arguments. When Hegel wants to show, for instance, that objects are not predetermined and determinately given to passive subjects, he begins the dialectic as in a *reductio* by assuming just the opposite, i.e., that objects in the world are predetermined. Given this assumption, the task for the defender of common sense is to try to see if such an account of objectivity can be thought consistently. Seen from the other side, that is, from the side of the critic, the task of the *reductio* is to take this assumption and to show that it leads to contradictions or absurd results. If a consistent account cannot be given with this presupposition, then it must be given up and replaced by a new one. In other words, when the dialectic is applied to the various dualistic or nonscientific views of common sense, it shows how these views are internally inconsistent and must be abandoned. The task of the dialectic in this first aspect is merely negative or critical. Hegel writes of this first aspect, "First, such reasoning adopts a negative attitude towards the content it apprehends; it knows how to refute it and destroy it."[26] Hegel consistently associates this negative aspect of the dialectic with the dialectic of Plato.[27] Plato's early dialogues are often described by the Greek word ἀπορία, which means being at a loss or in a state of confusion.[28] This is indicative of the general understanding that Plato's dialectic and the Socratic ἔλεγχος, in contrast to Hegel's dialectic, are purely negative and critical. After long discussions, carefully formulated definitions, elaborate comparisons, and examples, dialogues such as the *Euthyphro* nevertheless end up without a definitive conclusion. Hegel characterizes the Platonic sense of dialectic as follows:

> Even the *Platonic* dialectic, in the *Parmenides* itself and elsewhere even more directly, on the one hand, aims only at abolishing and refuting limited assertions through themselves, and, on the other hand, has for result simply nothingness. Dialectic is commonly regarded as an external, negative activity which does not pertain to the subject matter itself, having its ground in mere conceit as a subjective itch for unsettling and destroying what is fixed and substantial.[29]

Here as elsewhere Hegel characterizes the negative form of the dialectic as displaying the conceit or arrogance involved in the sort of sophomoric fault-finding that takes pleasure in criticizing all possible assertions regardless of their content and in the absence of any positive or constructive criticism. In the *Philosophy of Right* as well, Hegel distinguishes his form of dialectic from the Platonic form:

> The concept's moving principle, which alike engenders and dissolves the particularizations of the universal, I call "dialectic," though I do not mean that dialectic which takes an object, proposition, etc. . . . and explains it away, confuses it, pursues it this way and that, and has as its sole task the deduction of the contrary of that with which it starts—a negative type of dialectic commonly appearing even in Plato.[30]

Hegel here indicates that what he understands by "dialectic" is more than this merely "negative type of dialectic" that simply refutes all truth-claims and propositions.

There is, then, also a positive moment in the Hegelian dialectic. "The exposition of the untrue consciousness in its untruth," he writes, "is not a merely *negative* procedure."[31] In the same passage in the *Philosophy of Right* cited above, Hegel says, contrasting his dialectic to the Platonic dialectic, "The loftier dialectic of the concept consists not simply in producing the determination as a contrary and a restriction, but in producing and seizing upon the positive content and outcome of the determination, because it is this which makes it solely a development and an immanent progress."[32] The "loftier dialectic" is then, for Hegel, the dialectic which is not merely negative but which finds something positive in the falsity. In the *Phenomenology*, after any given position has been rendered inconsistent, we are not left to start over again at the beginning, but rather somehow from the inconsistent view something remains or is preserved (*conservare*) with which we can continue. Thus, there is a waxing quality or a cumulative effect in the series of reduced positions. This is referred to as Hegel's doctrine of determinate negation (*bestimmte Negation*).[33]

Hegel describes this controversial doctrine in a number of different places. For instance, in the Preface to the *Phenomenology* he writes,

> On the other hand, in speculative [*begreifenden*] thinking, as we have already shown, the negative belongs to the content itself, and is the *positive*, both as the *immanent* movement and determination of the content, and as the whole of this process. Looked at as a result, what emerges from this process is the *determinate* negative [*bestimmte Negative*] which is consequently a positive content as well.[34]

In the Introduction to the *Phenomenology* he describes this concept in a similar fashion:

> For it is only when it is taken as the result of that from which it emerges, that it is, in fact, the true result; in that case it is itself a *determinate* nothingness, one which has a *content*. The skepticism that ends up with the bare abstraction of nothingness or emptiness cannot get any further from there, but must wait to see whether something new comes along and what it is, in order to throw it too into the same empty abyss. But when, on the other hand, the result is conceived as it is in truth, namely, as a *determinate* negation [*bestimmte Negation*], a new form has thereby immediately arisen, and in the negation the transition is made through which the progress through the complete series of forms comes about of itself.[35]

The key idea behind this doctrine that is illustrated in these passages is that although any given position has been negated and rendered inconsistent, nevertheless something remains left over and provides a starting point or ground for a new position. In the *Encyclopaedia*, Hegel writes, "The result of dialectic is positive, because it has a definite content, or because its result is not empty and abstract nothing, but the negation of certain specific propositions which are contained in the result—for the very reason that it is a resultant and not an immediate nothing."[36] Perhaps his clearest statement of this issue comes from the *Science of Logic:*

> All that is necessary to achieve scientific progress . . . is the recognition of the logical principle that the negative is just as much positive, or that what is self-contradictory does not resolve itself into a nullity, into an abstract nothingness, but essentially only into the negation of its *particular* content, in other words, that such a negation is not all and every negation but the negation of a specific subject matter which resolves itself, and consequently is a specific negation [*bestimmte Negation*]. . . . Because the result, the negation, is a *specific* negation it has a *content*. It is a fresh Notion but higher and richer than its predecessor; for it is richer by the negation or opposite of the latter, therefore contains it, but also something more, and is the unity of itself and its opposite.[37]

From this passage it is clear that contradiction is not a pure or complete negation, but rather in the negation something determinate remains. As early as Hegel's *Habilitationsschrift*, the little-known *On the Orbits of the Planets* of 1801, this notion is to be found. Along with the main text, Hegel had to defend a number of individual theses, the first of which was as follows: "Contradiction is the rule of the true, noncontradiction is the rule of the false."[38] Contrary to common sense, for Hegel, truth is to be found in contradiction, or, put differently, truth springs forth out of contradiction. Contradictory propositions do not merely negate one another but rather form the basis of a higher truth.

Hegel's doctrine of determinate negation is important for the interpretation at hand. In an examination of the various determinations of the subject-object Notion that we find in the *Phenomenology*, we can observe a tendency toward ever more sophistication and determination. When the shortcomings of a given criterion are exposed, we do not need to return every time to the most basic criterion (pure being), but instead we move forward with ever more sophisticated and complex criteria, and accordingly the object for consciousness or the conception of the subject becomes ever more determinate until we reach absolute knowing, which is the final and complete determination. The key to Hegel's controversial notion of determinate negation I take to be something like the following: whenever a particular network of beliefs gets called into question, there is always some experience, belief, or datum that stands in contradiction to it and which is the original source of the skepticism. If this experience or belief is persistent, the network of beliefs itself may come into such difficulties that it must be given up as implausible in favor of a new explanation. In this sense, the old network is "negated," but in the negation something is left over, i.e., the anomalous belief that originally contradicted the network of beliefs, and it is this belief which forms the basis of the new belief system. This belief can thus be seen as a *determinate* negation. With respect to the broader interpretation of the *Phenomenology* which I want to propose, I wish merely to note that this notion of determinate negation fits nicely with my interpretation that the cumulative effect of the dialectical movement corresponds to a transcendental account of the self-determination of the subject-object Notions, which gradually uncovers more and more presuppositions and necessary conditions for those conceptions until it reaches the adequate self-determination which is represented by absolute knowing.

Finally, by means of the determinate negation, the old view is raised to a higher level which can be expressed with the Latin word *elevare*. With a new network of beliefs based on the datum or experience that contradicted the old belief system, the dialectic is raised to a higher level, since the new belief system is able to account for more phenomena than the old. The new belief system can presumably account for all the same phenomena as the old system *in addition to* the set of facts or experiences which proved contradictory to the old system. In the *Philosophy of Right*, the description of the content of the dialectic is as follows: "It merely becomes continually richer in itself, and the final determination is therefore the richest."[39] By incorporating the new content, the dialectic is able gradually to become more sophisticated until it ultimately reaches absolute knowing, which it the richest possible account.

With this account of the role and dialectical methodology of the *Phenomenology* and its relation to science per se, we are now in a position to attain an overview of Hegel's philosophical system in its most basic outline form. The key to Hegel's system lies in a correct understanding of two of his four books:[40] the *Phenomenology of Spirit* and the *Encyclopaedia of the Philosophical Sciences*. The latter represents an exhaustive account of the philosophical sciences, which consists of three parts: the *Logic*, the *Philosophy of Nature,* and the *Philosophy of Mind*. Each of these disciplines is a genuine philosophical science, and each presupposes a subject-object monism. On the other hand, the *Phenomenology* is, as we have just seen, the justification of this standpoint or the deduction of science. It provides the ladder from the level of common sense to science. We can represent this relation with the diagram in figure 3.1. The vertical arrow on the left represents the material covered by the *Phenomenology,* which starts at the level of common sense and proceeds to absolute knowing, i.e., the standpoint of science. The bracketed material on the right represents a single plane at the level of science which is exhausted by the three books of the *Encyclopaedia*.

Hegel's two other published works, the *Science of Logic* and the *Philosophy of Right,* can be seen simply as elaborations on specific parts of this basic scheme. First, the *Philosophy of Right* overlaps with the material covered in the second of the three sections of the *Philosophy of Mind* from the *Encyclopaedia*. This is confirmed in the Preface to the *Philosophy of Right,* where Hegel writes, "This compendium [the *Philosophy of Right*]

Figure 3.1

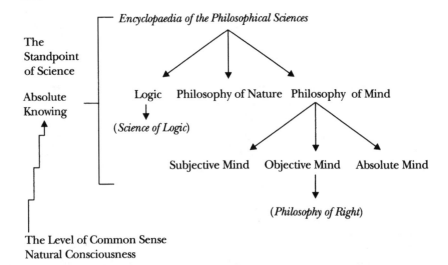

is an enlarged and especially a more systematic exposition of the same fundamental concepts which in relation to this part of philosophy are already contained in a book of mine designed previously for my lectures— the *Encyclopaedia of the Philosophical Sciences.* "[41] Second, the *Science of Logic* corresponds rather unproblematically to the *Encyclopaedia Logic,* which is a more concise and clear exposition of the former. Due to the differences in length and detail of analysis, the former is often referred to by scholars as the *Greater Logic* and the latter as the *Lesser Logic.* With this account we can thus trace the general outline of the system in terms of Hegel's published works, and we can begin to come to terms with the role of the *Phenomenology* in that system.

The Criteria of Subjectivity and Objectivity

The negative aspect of the dialectic implies that there are certain internal contradictions in the dualistic subject-object Notions which are crucial for the movement of the dialectic. Now we need to know specifically how the contradictions arise in the course of the dialectic. Hegel discusses these contradictions in terms of certain criteria for truth and objectivity not being met. He says, "If this exposition is viewed as a way of *relating science* to *phenomenal* knowledge, and as an investigation and *examination of the reality of cognition,* it would seem that it cannot take place without some presupposition which can serve as its underlying *criterion* [*Maßstab*]."[42] As Hegel goes on to explain, an examination amounts to testing things against a preestablished standard or criterion in order to see if they match up. That standard is thus accepted as the benchmark for truth, or as Hegel says, playing on Kant's language, as "the *in-itself.*"[43] This wordplay comes about since it is the thing-in-itself on Kant's "unofficial view" which seems implicitly to be the criterion against which the representations are "mere" representations, i.e., are somehow less true. As we have already seen, we cannot presuppose any "scientific" standards or criteria yet; instead, we must start with what Hegel considers common sense and examine its standards for consistency. This dualism of common sense is thus the view to be examined in all its various forms, and it is to be contrasted with science which represents, as we have seen, just the opposite, i.e., a monism of subject and object.

Hegel's representative of this view of common sense is what he calls "natural consciousness" (*natürliches Bewußtsein*).[44] Natural consciousness is, so to speak, Hegel's phenomenological actor, who goes through the various dialectical movements while we, the philosophical audience, look on. There are thus two different perspectives to keep in mind throughout the course of the dialectic: the first-person perspective of natural consciousness, which personally experiences the movements of the dialectic, and the third-person perspective of the reader, i.e., the philosophical audience, which observes the errors of natural consciousness.[45] It is important to be aware of the shift between these two perspectives in order to understand the course of the various arguments. On the one hand, Hegel tends to refer to natural consciousness simply with the word "consciousness" or in connection with the title of the individual section, for example "understanding consciousness" for the natural consciousness of "Force and the Understanding," or "observing consciousness" for the natural consciousness of "Observing Reason." On the other hand, he tends to use the expression "for us"[46] to refer to the perspective of the philosophical audience. When he uses this expression, it usually means that he is stepping back from the details of a given argument in order to gain a more general perspective or to indicate a change in the argument that we, the philosophical observers, can see but which natural consciousness cannot.

For Hegel, natural consciousness represents a sort of universal consciousness which embodies all the general prejudices of common sense. This is confirmed in his Preface, where he writes: "The task of leading the individual from his uneducated standpoint to knowledge had to be seen in its universal sense, just as it was the universal individual, self-conscious Spirit, whose formative education had to be studied. As regards the relation between them, every moment, as it gains concrete form and a shape of its own, displays itself in the universal individual."[47] In other words, natural consciousness is not any particular individual who thinks through the various subject-object Notions, but rather a universalized, ideal type. With this conception of natural consciousness, the autonomy of the dialectical movement of thought itself is underlined, since it does not matter who the natural consciousness actually is. The point is that thought determines itself in accordance with its own rules, and a subject, any subject, is needed to think through the various conceptions, though it need not be any particular subject, since the self-determination of thought is in a sense autonomous.

Natural consciousness represents the ideas of common sense, which Hegel accordingly calls "natural ideas."[48] It begins with the familiar prejudices of common sense which the dialectic must examine and expose as fallacious. Hegel writes of this uncritical attitude,

> Quite generally, the familiar, just because it is familiar, is not cognitively understood. The commonest way in which we deceive either ourselves

or others about understanding is by assuming something as familiar and accepting it on that account; with all its pros and cons, such knowing never gets anywhere, and it knows not why. Subject and object, God, nature, understanding, sensibility, and so on, are uncritically taken for granted as familiar, established as valid, and made into fixed points for starting and stopping. While these remain unmoved, the knowing activity goes back and forth between them, thus moving only on their surface.[49]

The task of the dialectic is to break through the surface and to question these fundamental, "natural" assumptions.[50] All of natural consciousness's positions are in one way or another dualistic ones prior to absolute knowing. Hegel's term "natural" is simply meant to denote the intuitive or widespread nature of the dualistic notions of common sense.[51] They represent our "natural," prephilosophical understanding of the world. It is through natural consciousness and its dualistic forms that we then uncover the various criteria for the subject-object Notion.

We can perhaps best understand Hegel's conception of natural consciousness by a quick comparison with Schelling. The first basic conviction of common sense, for Schelling, is "that there not only exists a world of things outside and independent of us, but also that our representations are . . . coincident with it."[52] Hence, for Schelling as for Hegel, the most fundamental claim of common sense is that there are independent, external objects. The task of philosophy, for Schelling, is then "to explain how our representations can absolutely coincide with objects existing wholly independently of them."[53] For Hegel, on the other hand, the task of the dialectic is to show common sense that this assertion of independent external objects is itself contradictory when one looks closely at the account that common sense gives of these objects. Hence, for Hegel, natural consciousness is simply a naive realist who represents our unreflective view of the world based on common sense.

Let us now turn to the question of the standards or criteria for the self-determination of objects and subjects. For Hegel every relation of subject to object implies some sort of a general conception of what both are. Without such a conception, the subject would be unable to pick out a thing as an object or to distinguish itself as a subject. As we saw in the previous chapter, this conception is what Hegel calls the "Notion." In order for us to conceive of anything, we must rely upon certain Notions which carve up that world for us in ways that render it intelligible.[54] As was suggested, the term the "Notion," for Hegel, corresponds roughly to what Kuhn calls a "scientific paradigm," to what Davidson calls a "conceptual scheme," or to what Dilthey calls a "worldview." Each of these terms is meant to capture a network of beliefs that together provide us with the cognitive apparatus which makes the sum total of experience intelligible and thus possible in the first place. Each of these terms is also intended to represent something dynamic and developmental instead of something static and eternal. For Hegel, the Notion gives us a way of viewing the world by providing us with specific categories which order and determine the subject-object relation. This Notion is then examined until the internal contradictions are found in it, at which time a new Notion must be introduced to replace the old contradictory one. This movement corresponds roughly to the way in which one scientific paradigm replaces another after a period of scientific revolution according to Kuhn's theory of the development of knowledge in the sciences. In the dialectic of the *Phenomenology*, the world is broken up into categories such as "living," "nonliving," and "consciousness" and "nonconsciousness," which are examples of much broader general categories running throughout the book. These are the criteria for objects and subjects at different levels, since they provide us with a basis upon which we can recognize and distinguish objects and subjects as such. In other words, each given criterion represents an account of what an object or a given subject-object Notion is. The "Notion" that Hegel analyzes in the course of the dialectic may have precedents in the history of philosophy, but usually he describes the dialectic in a way that suggests that he is not criticizing individual thinkers or theories but rather families of related theories or general tendencies in thought which he sees as flawed,[55] in a fashion analogous to Kant's conception of the necessary errors of reason. Thus, the Notions are to be treated as idealized types and not as specific examples of theories gone wrong. In this sense the Notions discussed are like natural consciousness itself.

Natural consciousness posits various accounts of objectivity and subjectivity, and then examines for consistency the objects that result from them. Hegel attempts to clarify this issue of consistency and contradiction when he says, "This contradiction and its removal will become more definite if we call to mind the abstract determinations of truth and knowledge as they occur in consciousness."[56] These abstract determinations of truth and knowledge which natural consciousness continually erects are the results of the criteria that Hegel has been discussing, and it is through the examination and subsequent breakdown of these criteria as manifested in their objects that the dialectic moves.

As we saw in the previous chapter, the important thing to keep in mind is that these self-determinations of the various subject-object Notions are in *consciousness itself.* Hegel says, "Consciousness provides its own criterion from within itself, so that the investigation becomes a comparison of consciousness with itself."[57] In other words, since the subject is always bound up with its objects, the world itself does not provide us with prepackaged rules for determinations of objectivity as Aristotle held. If it did, then we would have to match up our understanding to the world since our understanding would then be something additional or extra that would have to be compared to what was real and necessary. Likewise, the human mind does not give us criteria for objectivity a priori in the form of eternally fixed categories of the understanding or forms of intuition as Kant held; this would give rise to the suspicion that the world is somehow different *in-itself* from how we come to determine it even if there is a universality of representations among all perceiving subjects. Hegel tries to resolve this problem by putting the criteria for objects and subjects inside consciousness and by trying to avoid the presupposition of an independent external other in any sense. Hence, Hegel says, "we do not need to import *criteria*, or to make use of our own bright ideas and thoughts during the course of the inquiry."[58] I take Hegel to mean something like this with the following oft quoted passage from the Preface to the *Phenomenology:* "In my view, which can be justified only by the exposition of the system itself, everything turns on grasping and expressing the true, not only as *substance*, but equally as *subject*."[59] Truth is understood as both subject and object, because in the course of the dialectic the various Notions of the object influence our Notions of the subject. Hegel wants not only to claim that consciousness provides its own criteria for the Notions but also that those criteria are not wholly a priori, eternal, or ahistorical as Kant held. As we shall see, they are posited and worked out at least in part with respect to certain intersubjective social relations which are normally not considered to have any epistemological significance.

In his Introduction, Hegel, by means of two metaphors for cognition, tries to show the problem with this essentially Kantian position by exposing its presuppositions. Understanding can be "regarded either as the instrument to get hold of the Absolute, or as the medium through which one discovers it."[60] We will not concern ourselves with the details of the actual historical positions that these metaphors are intended to refer to, be they Kant's transcendental idealism or Locke's empiricism.[61] What is important for our purposes is what Hegel sees to be problematic about the views that these metaphors represent and what he perceives as the hidden premise that they contain. Hegel discusses the instrumental nature of cognition in the *Encyclopaedia.* There he writes, "The categories may be viewed in two aspects. On the one hand it is by their *instrumentality* that the mere perception of sense rises to objectivity and experience."[62] The categories of the understanding are here considered as an instrument that orders the perceptions. From the universality of the categories, i.e., the instrument, arises the objectivity of our representations. Hegel shows that with this view the very notion of truth itself is jeopardized, since (1) if our understanding is an instrument, then that instrument reshapes whatever is given in such a way that it does not remain what it is, i.e., the truth in itself. Likewise (2) if our understanding is a medium through which we perceive what is given, then surely the truth itself is somehow changed in passing through this medium. Hence, what results in both cases is not the truth but something that has been reshaped and artificially manipulated. Yet the claim is that truth is nevertheless still meaningful for these two models. If cognition is an instrument, then one need only familiarize oneself with the instrument of cognition and thus abstract from it and, by so doing, leave the naked truth behind.[63] Hegel writes, "If we remove from a reshaped thing what the instrument has done to it, then the thing—here the Absolute—becomes for us exactly what it was before this superfluous effort."[64] On the other hand, if we conceive of cognition as a medium, we need only subtract from the end-product or representation the activity of the medium and thus arrive at the same result. The problem with this attempt as well is that what is left behind is not the pure truth itself but rather nothing at all: "Or, if by testing cognition, which we conceive of as a *medium*, we get to know the law of its refraction, it is again useless to subtract this from the end result. For it is not the refraction of the ray, but the ray itself whereby truth reaches us, that is cognition; and if this were removed, all that would be indicated would be a pure direction or a blank space."[65] By eliminating the determining elements of cognition, we simultaneously eliminate objectivity itself. These attempts simply point to an empty absolute that was presumably there before the introduction of the instrument or the medium, but what this absolute *is* still cannot be explained.

Hegel traces the flaw in these models of cognition back to their presuppositions. He claims that these views render truth impossible, since they presuppose a strict subject-object split. Hegel summarizes the presupposition of these views collectively as a single Notion. This Notion, he claims, takes "for granted certain ideas about cognition as an *instrument* and as a *medium*, and assumes that there is a *difference between ourselves and this cognition*. Above all, it presupposes that the Absolute stands on one side and cognition on the other, independent and separated from it, and yet is something real."[66] These models at bottom presuppose a subject-object dualism. Hegel, in his attempt to avoid this subject-object split and the problems of truth that follow from it, posits the criteria for objectivity within the subject. By this means he can claim that truth is generated from this dialectical process, since the terms of the dialectic are intimately connected with each other and are not sundered, with the result being problematic terms such as inner and outer, and subjective and objective. The terms for the subject-object Notion itself thus lie within the realm of the subject although, as we have seen, in a way very different from the Kantian picture, according to which there is a sort of unilateral determination issuing from the subject alone.

The dialectic moves by a comparison of the given criterion for objectivity with the object (or subjectivity with the subject) which is necessarily bound to that criterion. Consciousness makes this comparison since "it is for this same consciousness to know whether its knowledge of the object corresponds to the object or not."[67] When there is a contradiction between the object and its criterion, then a new criterion is produced: "If the comparison shows that these two moments do not correspond to one another, it would seem that consciousness must alter its knowledge to make it conform to the object."[68] This is when consciousness introduces a new criterion: "the criterion for testing is altered when that for which it was to have been the criterion fails to pass the test; and the testing is not only a testing of what we know, but also a testing of the criterion of what knowing is."[69]

To illustrate this issue of testing criteria, let us suppose that our Notion or our conceptual scheme consists of, for example, five mutually consistent beliefs. Then in the course of experience, we come across a new phenomenon or datum that stands in contradiction to these five beliefs and thus to our Notion in general. The reaction might be to reject the new datum, since it does not match up to our criteria, but this might lead to absurdities if the new datum or experience were so prevalent that it could not be avoided or ignored. Or we might reject those beliefs that stood in contradiction to the new phenomenon while, where possible, maintaining the other beliefs. But if the phenomenon was so prevalent and so thoroughly contradicted our entire belief system that it could not be ignored, then the only other possibility would be to call into question our five background beliefs and ultimately reject them in favor of the new datum. This datum would then serve as the basis of a new Notion or network of beliefs. Here we can see with some clarity what Hegel means by determinate negation. Although the five background beliefs are "negated" and overturned, there is still something positive or determinate which remains, namely the new datum which caused the crisis in the belief system in the first place. Thus, we are not obliged to start over again at the beginning, but rather we have the basis for a new conceptual scheme. Moreover, in the passage cited above, Hegel makes it clear that there are two things at stake here—both the criterion for the subject-object Notion and the ensuing subject-object Notion itself. If our object does not match up to our criterion, then a new criterion is posited, but with this the subject-object constellation itself changes as well, since these criteria determine what is to count as subject and as object.[70] This is, of course, not to say that when a new criterion is posited the world itself changes and supplies us with a new object. First, the very conception of a world in itself is a Kantian notion. Moreover, the world for consciousness remains the same, but rather the way in which we carve it up and separate entities as individual objects has changed, and in this sense what counts for an object has changed. For instance, we could define a single object as a thing with properties or as an unseen force which produces certain appearances. How this object appears to us or how we as subjects appear to ourselves is dependent upon which description or criterion we choose to give. Hence, there is a necessary dialectical relation between the criteria themselves and the subject-object Notions that they posit.

In his Introduction, Hegel outlines in an uncharacteristically straightforward fashion how his dialectic is to proceed and what that means with respect to a "phenomenology" and "science" in general. It is clear that he is interested in examining ever more sophisticated criteria for the determination of the subject-object Notion in order to expose their internal contradictions. Hegel's innovation is to have shown that the criteria for objectivity are not entirely a priori or fixed but are, in fact, dynamic and fluid. This theme of the determination of subject and object forms the key to understanding the continuity of Hegel's *Phenomenology*.

4

Consciousness

I. Sense-Certainty: The "This" and the "I" (§§90–110)

The dialectic of "Sense-Certainty" introduces the knowledge problematic in relatively clear and straightforward terms. Natural consciousness gives an account of truth and objectivity which must be dialectically examined for consistency. Here, consciousness is *natural*, that is, it is a naive advocate of common sense, since it has as yet no dialectical experience and holds fast to the *natural* belief in a subject-object dualism. As we saw above, the path of natural consciousness is the road from these prejudices of common sense to scientific knowledge. The dialectical experiences of natural consciousness must in principle be able to be repeated from the beginning by anyone at the level of common sense, and for this reason we must start at the beginning and presuppose nothing. Natural consciousness begins with the belief of common sense in a fixed external world which is immediately accessible to the human subject. The claim that will dominate the "Consciousness" chapter is that there are external things or objects independent of the knowing subject which are given or predetermined. Each of the objects of "Consciousness" is thus a form or version of a realist metaphysics which makes claims about the independent reality of the external world. The initial claim in "Sense-Certainty" is the minimalist assertion that there is an external something.

The Notion: The "This" and the "I" (§§90–93)

At the beginning of the dialectic, we must be careful not to be misled by Hegel's terminology. When he speaks of the object of sense-certainty, he is not talking about the object of some sort of sense-data theory as we have come to use the term today. That notion corresponds more closely to the next chapter on perception. In fact, Hegel tells us outright at the beginning of the "Perception" chapter, "The wealth of sense-knowledge belongs to perception, not to immediate certainty, for which it was only the source of instances."[1] By "immediate certainty" here in this passage he means to refer to the "Sense-Certainty" section which analyzes the subject's immediate relation to objects. Hegel uses the term "sense-certainty" not to denote the variety and manifoldness of sense experience, but rather in a much narrower sense, namely to designate the most fundamental and undifferentiated form of existence given to us in sense. He tells us here we are not concerned with an object that we can distinguish "in virtue of a host of distinct qualities."[2] Moreover, we are not concerned with an object containing "a rich complex of connections, or related in various ways to other things,"[3] since Hegel says, "neither of these has anything to do with the truth of sense-certainty."[4] Rather, the dialectic here deals with what we are immediately aware of. He writes, "The knowledge or knowing which is at the start or is immediately our object cannot be anything else but immediate knowledge itself, a knowledge of the immediate or of what simply *is*."[5] Hegel thus begins his *Phenomenology* with the most simple and basic criterion for objectivity—what immediately exists. Natural consciousness' first criterion for objectivity is what it is immediately aware of, and objectivity is then thought to be determined solely by reference to this criterion.

But how specifically are we to understand this talk of an immediate given? Hegel gives us two hints. First, he tells us that at this stage we are not concerned with properties or relations of a thing, but rather with something pure and undifferentiated. The criterion for thinghood is thus not a collection of properties (since this will come later in the "Perception" chapter), but rather simple existence: "the thing *is*, and it *is*, merely because it *is*. It *is*; this is the essential point of sense-knowledge, and this pure *being*, or this simple immediacy, constitutes its *truth*."[6] Second, from this negative point of what sense-certainty is not, we can also derive an explanation of what it is: pure being. Hegel says of natural consciousness: "All that it says about what it knows is just that it *is*; and its truth contains nothing but the sheer *being* of the thing [*Sache*]."[7] Being is thus the general concept for anything autonomous and external which exists on its own, apart from a subject. Pure being is the first and most fundamental category that natural consciousness uses to determine objects. The subject indicates the autonomously existing pure being simply as a "This." By this strange locution, Hegel means to point out the mere existence of the thing, i.e., *this* is, and not to pick it out as a thing per se by calling the object a chair or a tree, etc., since that would require further determination. Hegel's discussion here of universal terms such as "This," or "I," which in contemporary Anglo-American philosophy have come to be known as indexicals or demonstratives, has made for a point of contact between Hegel and this essentially anti-Hegelian philosophical tradition.[8]

One important result of the object's complete determination is the implicit subject model which this conception espouses. Here, the subject is a mere passive observer which plays no role in shaping or forming the data. The object is fully determined on its own terms, and the subject merely observes what is the case without adding anything or ordering the data in a new way. In the Introduction to the *Science of Logic*, Hegel discusses the various prejudices of common sense and in so doing describes just this view: "First it is assumed that the material of knowing is present on its own account as a ready-made world apart from thought. . . . [T]he object is regarded as something complete and finished on its own account."[9] Since the object is predetermined, consciousness need only passively receive the information about its existence through the senses. The antithetic terms of the dialectic in the *Phenomenology* itself are set up as follows: "One of the terms is posited in sense-certainty in the form of a simple, immediate being, or as the essence, the *object;* the other, however, is posited as what is unessential and mediated."[10] Thus, the relationship of the object to consciousness is considered not to be essential with regard to the nature of the object itself. The object exists in and of itself, regardless of whether consciousness perceives it or not. Again in the *Science of Logic*, Hegel writes, "thought, on the other hand, is regarded as defective because it has to complete itself with a material and moreover, as a pliable indeterminate form, has to adapt itself to its material."[11] Thus, cognition is what is unessential, and the object is what is fundamentally true and real. This then represents Schelling's first standpoint, according to which one begins with the object as primary and then tries to determine how our representations can correspond to it. "Truth is," Hegel writes, "the agreement of thought with the object, and in order to bring about this agreement—for it does not exist on its own account—thinking is supposed to adapt and accommodate itself to the object."[12] Thus, the object is what is the essential, while the perception of it is merely accidental or secondary. Two particulars—the knowing subject and the object—are thus thought to stand in this asymmetrical relationship.

The Experience of Consciousness

The In-Itself Moment: The "This" (§§94–99)

The task is now to apply the dialectic to see if pure being can be consistently thought in accordance with this Notion of the object, i.e., as something predetermined and external. This is precisely what the dialectic does; namely, it examines the criterion for the determination of the subject-object Notion for consistency against what it finds in experience. Thus, the consistency is internal, since natural consciousness merely matches up *its* conception of objectivity with *its* actual experience of it. There is then no external term. After having set up this first Notion of objectivity, Hegel then steps back and addresses the philosophical audience: "The question must therefore be considered whether in sense-certainty itself the object is in fact the kind of essence that sense-certainty proclaims it to be; whether this Notion of it as the essence corresponds to the way it is present in sense-certainty."[13] Natural consciousness has already established the terms of the dialectic and in this case has already picked out the first criterion for objectivity: pure being. The job of the dialectic is now to compare this criterion with what we actually see in consciousness. The question is as follows: Is the picture of the object of consciousness consistent with our criterion for the subject-object Notion? Is the object really so determined?

The natural consciousness of "Sense-Certainty" tries to assert the particularity of this object, claiming, "This is," i.e., this is pure being; this particular exists as something independent and objective in the world. Hegel seems to assume that the demonstrative character of the object is somehow intrinsically bound up with this criterion for objectivity. If something is pure being, then it is able to be designated by being pointed out as a "This." The "This" is composed of the "Now" and the "Here"— its two aspects.[14] By this curious and unnatural language, Hegel seems to mean that to point out an object simply means to assert that it is here now, i.e., it is a singular object located in a particular spatiotemporal position. In the corresponding section in the *Encyclopaedia*, Hegel refers to the "Here" and "Now" as "spatial and temporal singleness."[15] Thus, natural consciousness again attempts to assert the particularity of the object by claiming, "This is Here, Now," which we can translate simply as "This is a particular independent being."

Hegel then proceeds to analyze each of the aspects of the "This" in turn. He begins with an examination of the truth of the "Now":

> To the question: "What is Now?," let us answer, e.g. "Now is Night." In order to test the truth of this sense-certainty a simple experiment will suffice. We write down this truth; a truth cannot lose anything by being written down, any more than it can lose anything through our preserving it. If *now, this noon*, we look again at the written truth we shall have to say that it has become stale.[16]

Hegel's argument seems to be roughly as follows: in our attempt to assert that an object exists now, what we mean (*meinen*) by "now" is that at this *particular moment* it exists. But when we assert this, it becomes apparent that "now" is a universal term which can in principle refer to any point on the temporal continuum. No sooner do we say "now" than the particular moment that we meant has already passed. Hence when we say that an object exists now, we have not really picked out any particular temporal moment. We do not say what we mean. Natural consciousness attempts to assert something particular about the object, but by its use of a universal term, the truth of the particular is not able to be captured and thus disappears in the universality.

The second point to note (in addition to that of universality and particularity discussed immediately above) is the issue of immediacy and mediation. The original claim was that the object was *immediately* given as fully determined, but in the course of the dialectic we discover that it is in fact mediated. The argument here is as follows: our truth that the object is here now is through the "Now" bound up with the truth "now is night." But when we examine this truth we realize that it is mediated by other terms, e.g., "day." The temporal terms that are more specific, "night," "day," "morning," etc., are all complimentary terms which *mediate* one another and cannot be made sense of in isolation. We would not know what "day" was, unless we could contrast it with "night"; likewise, we would not know what "morning" was, unless we could contrast it with "afternoon" and "evening." In the *Encyclopaedia Logic*, Hegel writes, " 'Now' has no meaning except in reference to a before and a hereafter."[17] All these terms necessarily presuppose the universality of thought (i.e., a network of concepts), and contradict natural consciousness' claim about the immediacy of the object. Hence, when we attempt to avoid the universal term "Now" and to make our truth more specific by using one of the more specific terms, we still lose the immediate truth that was originally asserted since even these "specific" terms are universals. Moreover, these terms have no immediate meaning, but rather have their truth value only in relation to the network of other terms by which they are mediated.

The same movement is experienced by the second term, the spatial term, the "Here." "Here," like "Now," is a universal and not a particular term, and thus it is useless in any attempt to pick out a particular spatial location. The corresponding argument is as follows: " 'Here' is, e.g., the tree. If I turn round, this truth has vanished and is converted into its opposite: 'No tree is here, but a house instead.' "[18] I use the same word "Here" to designate different locations, at first where the tree is located and then where the house is located. Since the "Here," qua universal, can refer to any particular place where any number of objects exist, trees, houses, etc., it cannot serve our purposes of picking out our specific object of sense-certainty. "Here" can refer in principle to anywhere. We mean (*meinen*) a particular place, e.g., where the tree is located, but we cannot capture this with the term the "Here." The suppressed second argument here about immediacy and mediation is that more specific spatial terms, e.g., "to the left," "above," etc., are all relational and thus mediated, and once again we have lost the immediate quality of sense-certainty.

The problem with the picture presented is that although consciousness claims that the object presents itself as immediately given and fully determinate, in order to describe it one must rely on certain presuppositions about cognition. In other words, the terms with which consciousness attempts to describe the object, in fact, turn out to be universal terms, which, moreover, rely upon or logically imply other universal terms. But yet these universal terms are not found in experience since experience is by its very nature particular. As Hegel writes in the *Encyclopaedia Logic:* "Sense-perception as such is always individual."[19] In the case of pure being, these universal terms that are used to describe it ("This," "Here," "Now") are not met with in experience and thus must rather belong to our cognition per se; hence, the attempt to describe the object as fully determined in itself, with the subject playing only a passive role as the receiver of information, fails since the subject must make use of certain cognitive capacities, e.g., universals or the distinction between universal and particular, in order to describe it. In the *Encyclopaedia*, Hegel summarizes this conclusion as follows: "If I say, 'the individual,' 'this individual,' 'here,' 'now,' all these are universal terms. Everything and anything is an individual, a 'this,' and if it be sensible, is here and now."[20] Although the object was originally the essential element in the relation, its description necessarily refers back to and thus implies the subject and its cognitive faculties of judgment by means of universal concepts. The subject must play some active and essential role in the determination of the subject-object relation and cannot remain passive as natural consciousness thought. However, this is the conclusion that we, the philosophical audience, reach. Natural consciousness, on the other hand, believes that the Notion of pure being can be salvaged with some minor dialectical adjustments to the Notion itself.

The For-Itself Moment: The "I" (§§100–2)

Natural consciousness now tries to juggle the variables in its conceptual scheme in order to reach a consistent account of the object. The second strategy of natural consciousness involves a reversal of the roles of the subject and the object. Instead of considering the object to be the essential term in the relationship, since this proved fruitless, natural consciousness comes to consider the essence of the object to be *in its relationship* with the knowing subject. Hegel says, "When we compare the relation in which knowing and the object first came on the scene, with the relation in which they now stand in this result, we find that it is reversed. The object, which was supposed to be the essential element in sense-certainty, is now the unessential element."[21] The immediate given still determines objectivity but only insofar as it is related to a subject. Hence, the truth of the object "is in the object as *my* object, or in its being *mine;* it is, because *I* know it."[22] In other words, it is the knowing subject that plays the crucial role, and objects of sense-certainty are necessarily related to it: "The force of its truth thus lies now in the 'I,' in the immediacy of my *seeing, hearing,* and so on."[23] Because natural consciousness sees the object, hears it and perceives it, the object is confirmed as real. It is thus dependent upon the fact of its being perceived by the subject. The being of the "I" as the subject replaces the being of the object. Pure being and singularity are no longer on the side of the object but rather on the side of the subject.

Although here consciousness recognizes the necessary role that it plays as an observer, we still have a long way to go before we reach "Self-Consciousness." Here, at this second level of the dialectic of "Sense-Certainty," natural consciousness still holds to the realist position that there are external objects independent of perceiving subjects. Natural consciousness has at this point only realized that it plays a small epistemic role in this truth-forming process, insofar as it must be present to perceive the object which is true for it. Hence, the tree that falls in the forest when no one is around still exists in itself even without an observer; natural consciousness has merely admitted that for it to be a particular object for us, we must perceive it, but this does not draw into question the original ontological status of the object on its own terms. The role of the subject is in no way constitutive of the object at this point. The more radical realization that natural consciousness comes to in the transition to "Self-Consciousness," although this by no means represents the whole story, is that there are, in fact, no objects independent of itself as subject. At this latter stage, natural consciousness sees itself as playing a *constitutive* and not merely a formal role in the determination of objectivity. In the "Self-Consciousness" chapter, we thus examine the inconsistencies in this claim that objects are fully determined by subjects without reference to a further social sphere. But this analysis will have to wait until later.

Hegel then steps back and tells us that with the Notion so determined we must now see if our experience corresponds to it: "We have now to see what experience shows us about its reality in the 'I.' "[24] The dialectic is now applied to the "I," just as formerly it was applied to the "This." Once again the question is whether this model of the object squares with our experience of it. Not surprisingly, the "I" breaks down in a manner similar to that of the "This." It turns out that the "I" just like the "This" is a universal—it refers to all "I's," not just to this particular one: "The 'I' is merely universal like 'Now,' 'Here,' or 'This' in general. . . . When I say 'this Here,' 'this Now,' or a 'single item,' I am saying all Thises, Heres, Nows, all single items. Similarly, when I say 'I,' this singular 'I,' I say in general all 'I's.' "[25] In the *Encyclopaedia Logic*, Hegel writes even more clearly, "Similarly when I say 'I,' I *mean* my single self to the exclusion of all others, but what I *say*, viz. 'I,' is just every 'I,' which in like manner excludes all others from itself."[26] Hegel's argument here is that at this point at the level of pure being there is no single fixed quality or mark that could serve to determine the "I" in a meaningful way aside from the fact that it is the "I" that knows the object, i.e., it sees it, it hears it, etc. Everyone uses "I" to refer to himself or herself, and therefore it is not a particular but rather a universal.[27] Elsewhere in the *Encyclopaedia Logic*, Hegel writes, "By the term 'I' I mean myself, a single and altogether determinate person. And yet I really utter nothing peculiar to myself, for everyone else is an 'I' or 'ego,' and when I call myself 'I,' though I indubitably mean the single person myself, I express a thorough universal."[28] Pure being has no internal differentiation or properties. There is then further Hume's problem of an enduring self-unified subject. The idea is then that the "I" that perceives the object at time T is not the same "I" that perceives the object at time T + 1 since there is nothing enduring to constitute it; and the perceptions themselves are too manifold in nature and thus must be attributed to individual "I's." But this is perhaps more relevant for Hegel's account in the "Perception" chapter, where we are concerned with the problem of substance, properties, and internal differentiation. The important point for our purposes is that the analysis once again refers back to the constitutive role of the cognitive structures or conceptual schemes in the determination of the subject-object Notion. The universal "I" is a part of our cognition and is never found in experience. But yet it is implied in the realist's claim that the "I," i.e., this specific "I," plays a necessary epistemic role vis-à-vis the independent object. Hence, once again the realist's claim breaks down in a way that points to the human cognitive faculty.

The In-and-For-Itself Moment: The Point of Contact (§§103–8)

Natural consciousness then tries to render its Notion of objectivity determinate by considering the essence of the object, i.e., its unity and singularity, to lie neither in the object itself nor in the knowing subject but rather in the combination of the two: "Sense-certainty thus comes to know by experience that its essence is neither in the object nor in the 'I,' and that its immediacy is neither an immediacy of the one nor of the other. . . . Thus we reach the stage where we have to posit the *whole* of sense-certainty itself as its *essence*, and no longer only one of its moments."[29] Here the particular essence of the object lies in the precise moment of contact or point of interaction between the subject and the object. This becomes the new "Here" and the new "Now." The particularity is not in the object itself (since the "This" is a universal) or in the subject itself (since the "I" is a universal), but rather in the moment when the subject comes into contact with the object and becomes aware of it. This unique moment is now thought to be the particular. Natural consciousness concentrates and fixes on this moment and does not compare it to other Heres and Nows: "I, *this* 'I,' assert then the 'Here' as a tree, and do not turn round so that the Here would become for me *not* a tree."[30] Natural consciousness tries to keep this instant or point of contact always in view. Hegel then steps back and, again addressing the philosophical audience, tells us that the Notion of objectivity is fully determined and that we must now merely apply the dialectic to see if our experience corresponds to the object: "Let us, then, see how that immediate is constituted that is pointed out to us."[31]

First, Hegel examines the new "Now," i.e., the specific temporal instance of the point of contact. The problem is then how to pick out this moment of contact linguistically as a unique singular moment. This temporal point of contact is referred to again as the "Now." Like the earlier "Now" and the "This," this new "Now" is superseded since it never endures beyond the moment: it always becomes something that has already past. He describes the movement as follows: "The Now, as it is pointed out to us, is Now that *has been*, and this is its truth; it has not the truth of *being*. Yet this much is true, that it has been. But what essentially *has been* [*gewesen ist*] is, in fact, not an essence that *is* [*kein Wesen*]; *it is not*, and it was with *being* that we were concerned."[32] The argument here seems to be parallel to the ones we saw before. We cannot pick out the specific moment of contact between the subject and the object with the word "Now." The inability of the "Now" to stand fast through time evinces its universal character and renders it useless as an attempt to pick out a particular. The result is that the "Now" becomes an infinite succession of "Nows"—it becomes the "Now" that always is. Every moment is in principle a "Now."

Hegel then turns to the sublation of the spatial term of the point of contact, the new "Here." Likewise, the "Here" of the immediate inter-action between subject and object becomes a plurality of "Heres." Again the particular has turned out to be a universal which is an element of thought: "The *Here pointed out*, to which I hold fast, is similarly a *this* Here which, in fact, is *not* this Here, but a Before and Behind, an Above and Below, a Right and Left. The Above is itself similarly this manifold otherness of the above, below, etc."[33] Natural consciousness is unable to keep the individual moment of contact in focus, since one moment replaces the next. Once again there is no singularity. Natural consciousness' attempt to think pure, individual being has again collapsed in a way that points back to or presupposes the subject's role as constitutive in the self-determination of the subject-object Notion. But consciousness does not yet realize this. Natural consciousness instead believes that the problem is in the attempt to think its object as *immediately* given. This problem can be solved, according to natural consciousness, if we simply introduce new criteria which will mediate the object and determine it more fully. Natural consciousness now realizes that it is fruitless to attribute to pure being any single determinate expression or to distinguish it from another, since it always collapses back into the universality of pure being.

Concluding Remarks (§§109–10)

The important point here in "Sense-Certainty" is that the dialectic has exposed the contradiction of using "pure being," which always implies some thought or something cognitive, as the criterion for objectivity. Pure being remains forever in its undetermined universality. As Hegel says in the *Jena Metaphysics*, "this singularity goes aground in its own totality."[34] In short, the particular or determined "This" always collapses into the seamless totality of pure being. Every spatiotemporal moment is overcome by another. Hegel writes, "And what consciousness will learn from experience in all sense-certainty is, in truth, only what we have seen, viz. the This as a *universal*, the very opposite of what that assertion affirmed to be universal experience."[35] Natural consciousness asserted the particularity of the "This" as its "universal experience," but the "This" turned out to be a universal instead. Hegel explains this most clearly with his example of a piece of paper:

> They *mean* "this" bit of paper on which I am writing—or rather have written—"this"; but what they mean is not what they say. If they actually wanted to *say* "this" bit of paper which they mean, if they wanted to *say* it, then this is impossible, because the sensuous This that is meant *cannot be reached* by language, which belongs to consciousness, i.e. to that which is inherently universal.[36]

Here it is clear that one means or intends (*meinen*) an individual object, but one is unable to pick it out with only the category of pure being, since the linguistic descriptions of it always rely on universal terms.

In this passage we also see the implicit role of consciousness when Hegel says that language "belongs to consciousness, i.e. to that which is inherently universal." The role of the subject in the determination of objectivity has been indicated by the constant return of universals in the dialectic. Since universals do not appear in experience, natural consciousness has been given a clear indication of the importance of the subject's cognitive structures as shaping and mediating experience, but consciousness fails to see this. The dialectic has also shown us that this pure being is always mediated and not immediately given. We thus need a new criterion for objectivity, which takes this mediation into account. We need more categories besides pure being in order to determine the subject-object Notion more precisely. We need internal differentiation and distinction by means of which we can pick out an individual object and distinguish it from other objects. To be sure, objectivity will still be determined by categories, but not by the single category of sense-certainty which produces only indeterminate objects, but instead by the categories determined and mediated by perception. This constitutes the dialectical movement of the next section.

This issue of mediation is key, since it is through this idea that Hegel will demonstrate the necessity of a social determination of the subject-object Notion. In the next two chapters—"Perception" and "Force and the Understanding"—mediation is introduced into the criteria of objectivity themselves. In "Perception" the object is no longer unmediated being but rather a thing mediated or determined by properties. In "Force and the Understanding" the true object is mediated by the appearances of the sensible world which is thus accessible to the perceiving subject. At both of these levels the objects are not immediately grasped but must be perceived indirectly through something else, i.e., properties or appearances. Mediation thus involves this indirect or *mediated* access to the object. As we shall see, in the "Self-Consciousness" and "Reason" chapters, mediation must be extended into the social sphere as a result of the contradictions and inconsistencies discovered in natural consciousness' attempt to think consistently an object as already determined in itself or to think of itself as determined without reference to other subjects. In short, there must be more to the determination of our subject-object Notion than what the realist or the solipsistic idealist thinks. Not just objects themselves or even pure subjects are responsible for the determination of the Notion, but rather a complex network of social relations must be unraveled before we reach the complete determination.

In an interesting passage at the end of "Sense-Certainty," Hegel foreshadows the first section in the "Self-Consciousness" chapter entitled "The Truth of Self-Certainty."[37] As I will argue below in greater detail, these two sections parallel one another in their employment of the same category—pure being—in the objective and the subjective spheres respectively. Hegel makes it clear that he here refers to the "Self-Consciousness" chapter when he writes, "With this appeal to universal experience we may be permitted to anticipate how the case stands in the practical sphere."[38] In the "Consciousness" chapter, we operate in the theoretical sphere in which we examine different Notions of the object. In the "Self-Consciousness" chapter we then move to the "practical" sphere and various accounts of the subject. In what follows Hegel discusses "the ancient Eleusinian mysteries of Ceres and Bacchus," which at first glance seem to be a topic entirely irrelevant to what we have learned in this chapter; however, when we examine the point that he makes here more closely, we can see that Hegel draws a parallelism between this section and "The Truth of Self-Certainty" in the "Self-Consciousness" chapter. He writes,

> For he who is initiated into these Mysteries not only comes to doubt the being of sensuous things, but to despair of it; in part he brings about the nothingness of such things himself in his dealings with them, and he sees them reduce themselves to nothingness . . . for they [sc. animals] do not just stand idly in front of sensuous things as if these possessed intrinsic being, but, despairing of their reality, and completely assured of their nothingness, they fall to without ceremony and eat them up.[39]

What Hegel describes here is in fact the level of self-consciousness and self-certainty. There the self-conscious subject sees *itself* as pure being and views the world of objects as ephemeral. It affirms this by destroying or consuming the world around it. There Hegel writes that self-consciousness "preserves itself by separating itself from this its inorganic nature, and by consuming it."[40] Although we will have more to say about this parallelism later, here it is already clear that Hegel intends this opening section of "Consciousness" to refer to "The Truth of Self-Certainty," the opening section of "Self-Consciousness."

In addition to this parallelism between the particular sections by virtue of the category of being, here in "Sense-Certainty" Hegel introduces general terms or categories which will run through all the arguments in the *Phenomenology*. First, the dialectic of universal and particular is absolutely fundamental to Hegel's dialectical method and appears in each of the following arguments in some form. In "Sense-Certainty" the problem is quite clear-cut: the object which we know or intend (*meinen*) is a particular, yet we cannot capture this particularity, since we can use only universal terms to describe it. In what follows, this dialectic of universal and particular will be reinterpreted not just to refer to the relation between individual objects and universal terms of language, but also to refer to the relation between phenomena and noumena, man and God, individual and society, etc. Second, the dialectic of mediation and immediacy is also fundamental for Hegel. Here, the object had at first been thought to be immediately given, but then we discovered that in fact it was mediated by other concepts.[41] This dynamic of mediacy and immediacy will also be reinterpreted and will take on a multitude of forms throughout the text. By following these categories or terms throughout the *Phenomenology*, we will be able to take another step toward establishing the unity of the text as a whole.

II. Perception: The "One" and the "Also" (§§111–31)

The "Perception" chapter continues the knowledge problematic that was initiated in "Sense-Certainty" but with a different category. Natural consciousness here tries to give a new account of objectivity, this time seeing the object in terms of a thing with properties or what in the history of philosophy is often referred to as substance and accident. With the further determination and mediation of the object through a category more determinate than pure being, natural consciousness believes that it will be able to give a successful account of objectivity and to pick out individual entities and thus distinguish them from one another. However, since consciousness still considers the object to be an external predetermined other and since it still fails to see the role of the subject in the determination of the subject-object Notion, it is still unable to give a consistent account. The failure of "Perception" will again presuppose an account of the constitutive role of human cognition in the determination of the subject-object Notion, just as the failure of the "Sense-Certainty" section did, but consciousness will still not be in a position to realize this. Only in the final section of the "Consciousness" chapter does consciousness come to this realization that the dialectic has been pointing to all along. The important point here is that at each stage of the "Consciousness" section we see the realist's failure to give a consistent and complete account of objectivity, since there is always lacking an account of subjectivity which any such account of objectivity implies. Later, we will try to understand the task of the "Self-Consciousness" chapter as an attempt to provide just such an account of subjectivity. Let us now turn to the specifics of the dialectic of "Perception" itself.

The problem with natural consciousness' first criterion of objectivity was that it posited a particular, an immediate given, which continually collapsed into a universal of thought, a this, here, now. This criterion ended up being entirely empty, since it was unable to designate any particular thing as an object of experience. The point for the philosophical audience was that the inevitability of universal terms in consciousness' account implied the essential and constitutive role of the subject in the determination of objectivity. But, for consciousness, which fails to see the full import of universality, the problem can be remedied simply by finding a more specific or determinate category. In order to create this new criterion, natural consciousness must make its Notion of an object more precise and more determinate so as to stop it from slipping into an empty universal. In order to define a thing specifically and thus distinguish it from something else, one must enumerate its unique set of properties which one perceives empirically. Thus, the new criterion for objectivity—the one and the many—and a corresponding new object—a thing with a set of properties[42]—is given in perception. The key category here can be seen conceptually in different ways—unity and plurality, one and many, etc. The key issue in this chapter is the self-identity of the object as opposed to the plurality of its properties. Once again, the important point is that natural consciousness still believes that the object is independent and fully determined in itself, in this case, as self-identical, without natural consciousness itself playing any role in its determination.

In this section, Hegel uses uncharacteristically clear language to describe the criterion for knowledge that is relevant here. He says of natural consciousness, "His criterion [*Kriterium*] of truth is therefore *self-identity*, and his behavior consists in apprehending the object as self-identical."[43] Here Hegel unambiguously designates the key role that the criterion for truth and objectivity plays here. By "self-identity," he seems to mean the unity that makes an object an object despite the various properties that are attached to it. We will have to examine this in greater detail below. It is against this standard of self-identity of the object with properties that natural consciousness will measure its perception of the object.

The Notion: The Thing with Properties (§§111–16)

We begin the dialectic of "Perception" just as we began the dialectic of "Sense-Certainty," namely, with the two terms, subject and object, opposed to one another. It is the object here, as in the "Sense-Certainty" chapter, that originally takes priority in the relationship, since the object is autonomous and self-determined. This understanding of the object as fundamental or true is, as we have seen, what is referred to as the in-itself moment. Hegel describes the relation as follows: "One of them [sc. subject and object], the object, defined as the simple [entity], is the essence regardless of whether it is perceived or not; but the act of perceiving, as a movement, is the unessential moment, the unstable factor which can as well be as not be."[44] Hence, in accordance with the Notion of the entire "Consciousness" chapter, the as yet undefined object is again considered to be the essential element in the relation. Once again, natural consciousness, qua naive realist, has not yet fully recognized the role that it plays in the determination of objectivity, and thus it still attempts to think objects as already determined in themselves. Thus, it sees itself once again as a passive observer playing no role in the formation of truth or objectivity: "consciousness is determined as percipient in so far as this thing is its object. It has only to *take* it, to confine itself to a pure apprehension of it, and what is thus yielded is the true. If consciousness itself did anything in taking what is given, it would by such adding or subtraction alter the truth."[45] The thing exists on its own whether it is perceived or not, and consciousness does nothing to shape it. Hegel here plays on the German verb *wahrnehmen,* which means "to perceive." Literally, *wahr + nehmen* means "to take to be true," which, on Hegel's interpretation, implies the passive reception of sense-data (as on the classic empiricist model) without the subject adding to or reordering the information received. The object is thus predetermined. This is what is presupposed throughout the "Consciousness" chapter regardless of the specific object models that are examined.

The dialectic of "Perception" pursues the truth problematic by an attempt to think consistently the relationship of a thing with a plurality of properties. The properties arise out of natural consciousness' attempt to determine its object more specifically. At the end of the dialectic of "Sense-Certainty," we ended up with no immediate particulars but rather mediated and empty universals. We begin in "Perception" at just this point. From the "This" of "Sense-Certainty," we, with the new Notion of objectivity, are now able to pick out a universal, a property. The object according to this new Notion is what Hegel refers to as the "thing" with properties.[46] Hegel describes the origin of properties thus: "Being, however, is a universal in virtue of its having mediation or the negative within it; when it *expresses* this in its immediacy it is a *differentiated, determinate* property. As a result *many* such properties are established simultaneously, one being the negative of another."[47] Although, to be sure, the language here is dense, the argument seems to be something like the following:

from the empty universality of the object of "Sense-Certainty," we are able to derive a universal property. In "Sense-Certainty" we were concerned with undifferentiated, pure being, and at that point this was ipso facto impossible. But here in "Perception" being is differentiated, or as Hegel says, "perception contains negation, that is, difference or manifoldness, within its own essence."[48] So for the first time we are able to pick out a property from this pure being. But from the mere fact that the one property is determinate, other properties are generated which compare to and contrast with it and thus constitute the determination of this particular property as a property. So now we have a number of contrasting and mutually determining properties.

But we cannot have a number of properties which are not properties of some thing. It does not make sense to talk of the property "red" without talking about the object to which it belongs, i.e., the red wagon or the red balloon. The object then arises as the simple universality which is the medium of these numerous properties: "This abstract universal medium, which can be called simply 'thinghood' or 'pure essence,' is nothing else than what Here and Now have proved themselves to be, viz. a *simple togetherness* of a plurality."[49] Hence, the object arises out of the properties and serves the function of unifying them. Hegel refers to this conception of the object with another strange neologism, the "One." The object is a "One" abstracted from the particular properties. This Notion of a thing as a "One" is contrasted to the idea of a thing as being merely a collection of properties which Hegel calls the "Also."[50] The object is an "Also" since it is made up of and is essentially nothing more than the various properties. Hegel uses the example of a piece of salt: "This salt is a simple Here, and at the same time manifold; it is white and *also* tart, *also* cubical in shape, or a specific weight, etc."[51] The Notion of the "Also" thus emphasizes the plurality of properties (the manifold) of the object, while the "One" emphasizes the unity of the object abstracted from the properties. (Hegel occasionally refers to the properties here,[52] as in the "Force and the Understanding" section, as "matters" [*Materien*].)[53] The "One" and the "Also" are then the two aspects of the thing with properties or substance-accident on this model of objectivity, just as the "Here" and the "Now" were the two aspects of the "This." At this point, the properties exist in and of themselves and are not dependent on the subject (as we usually consider, for instance, secondary properties to be). The properties belong to the object itself, and the subject plays no role in the relation between them. Natural consciousness thus perceives a more determinate object than in the previous section, but it fails to see that its Notion of a property and a thing makes specific cognitive presuppositions and that a property or a thing per se is never given in experience.

The Notion of the "One" and the "Also" can be illustrated by means of the basic Hegelian categories of identity and difference. In order for an object to be determinate it must have these two aspects: it must be *identical* with itself and *different* from other things. Every determinate object has a self-relation, i.e., one of identity; in other words, it is just what it is. This is what Hegel calls the "One": "The One . . . is . . . quite simply a relation of self to self and it excludes an other."[54] But every determinate object also has a relation of difference to other things; in other words, by virtue of the given object's being what it is, it is *not* the same as other things. This is what Hegel calls the "Also." The "Also" represents the object in its aspect of the plurality of existing properties; the object distinguishes itself in this way from other things. For example, we can distinguish a book from a balloon by saying that the balloon is red and the book is not. This distinction of the object from other objects that it is not determines thinghood: "White is white only in opposition to black, and so on, and the thing is a One precisely by being opposed to others."[55] This book is thus just this book (identity), but it is not this chair (difference). All objects are determined by the dialectical relation between these categories.

The Experience of Consciousness

The In-Itself Moment: The Thing (§117)

Hegel signals that the Notion of objectivity here in "Perception" is complete when he writes, "In these moments, taken together, the thing as the truth of perception is completed, so far as it is necessary to develop it here."[56] The combination of the two aspects, the "One" and the "Also," constitute entirely the Notion at the level of "Perception," which Hegel refers to as "thinghood." He writes, "it is this relation of the universality to the pure essential moments which at last completes the thing."[57] The object here is considered as a thing, by which Hegel means a substance with accidents, or an object with properties. The "universality" refers to the unity of the object, the "One," and the "essential moments" refer to its properties, the "Also." With the object model complete, we step back and examine it for consistency by comparing the Notion of objectivity with natural consciousness' experience of the object. Hegel writes, addressing the philosophical audience, "Let us see now what consciousness experiences in its actual perceiving. *For us*, this experience is already contained in the development of the object, and of the attitude of consciousness towards it given just now. It is only a matter of developing the contradictions that are present therein."[58] This passage parallels the one from "Sense-Certainty,"[59] where Hegel announces to the philosophical audience the completion of the Notion and the beginning of the critical or dialectical analysis of it. The task is now to apply the dialectic and to see if our experience of the object coincides with this Notion of objectivity.

By examining its experience of the object, natural consciousness soon discovers that its conception of the "One" and the "Also" cannot be consistently thought. We start with the obvious problems with the "One," i.e., the simple self-identity which exists behind the properties. Here the notion of a pure "One" or an essential unity whose properties are only accidental or inessential is indeterminate. Hegel writes, "The object which I apprehend presents itself purely as a *One;* but I also perceive in it a property which is *universal,* and which thereby transcends the singularity [of the object]."[60] As in "Sense-Certainty" we want to be able to pick out an individual thing, e.g., a particular balloon. In this particular balloon I notice a universal property such as "red." Red is universal since it can apply to any number of other things, e.g., red cars, red wagons, etc., and thus it "transcends the singularity of the object" since it does not help us to pick out this individual red balloon. Hegel continues, "The first being of the objective essence as a One was therefore not its true being. But since the *object* is what is true, the untruth falls in me; my apprehension was not correct."[61] In the in-itself moment of the dialectic, the object is always the essential and the true, whereas the subject is something unnecessary and superfluous. Therefore, the subject simply made an error in understanding the object and its relation to its property. This is the element of "deception" (*Täuschung*) that appears in the subtitle of this section. Hegel writes, "Since the object is the true and the universal, the self-identical, while consciousness is alterable and unessential, it can happen that consciousness apprehends the object incorrectly and deceives itself. The percipient is aware of the possibility of deception."[62] Thus, "deception" is not meant in the sense of some intentional trickery or deceit but rather refers to the simple fact of perceptual error.

The object and its property are still the true, but some adjustment must be made. Hegel then claims, "On account of the *universality* of the property, I must rather take the objective essence to be on the whole a *community.*"[63] The universality of the property "red" establishes implicitly a group or "community" of objects which share this property. The particular red balloon is in this large group, but it still cannot be picked out since all we have done is narrowed down the field to all objects possessing this property. He writes, "I now further perceive the property to be *determinate, opposed* to another and excluding it."[64] This community of objects is to some extent exclusive, insofar as it is opposed to other groups of objects with properties that conflict with "red," e.g., the group of objects with the property "green." (Let us assume for the moment that green and red are mutually exclusive and cannot occur in the same object in the way that cubical and spherical are, strictly speaking, mutually exclusive.) Hegel continues, "Thus I did not in fact apprehend the objective essence correctly when I defined it as a *community* with others, or as a continuity; on account of the *determinateness* of the property, I must break up the continuity and posit the objective essence as a One that excludes."[65] Thus, to view the group of objects possessing the property "red" with only the category of identity or community is an error, since there would not be "red," were there not other conflicting and exclusive properties, e.g., green, that contrasted with it. (In a universe of only red objects, there would be no "red," since there would be no concept of color at all. Red is mediated by the other colors which compare and contrast to it. Likewise our conception of individual numbers is determined by other numbers. We would have no conception of the number five without a conception of the numbers four and six. In a universe with only one number, the concept of number would not exist.) Thus, the balloon, like the other objects of the group, excludes from its essence properties that conflict with "red."

Hegel continues, "In the broken up One I find many such properties which do not affect one another but are mutually indifferent."[66] In the object, the balloon, I find other properties such as "spherical," "light," etc., that do not conflict with "red." Only certain properties, viz., other colors in this case, are contradictory, but the rest are mutually indifferent, and there is no logical contradiction in their inhering in the same object. "Therefore," Hegel writes, "I did not perceive the object correctly when I apprehended it as exclusive."[67] The object is only exclusive vis-à-vis contradictory properties, but there is no contradiction involved with all of the other properties which could coexist in harmony. He continues, "on the contrary, just as previously it was only continuity in general, so now it is a universal *common medium* in which many properties are present as sensuous *universalities*, each existing on its own account and, as *determinate*, excluding the others."[68] Our "object" has now become the universal medium of the sum total of all noncontradictory universal properties (including "red"). The properties remain determinate since they exclude their contraries, but it is clear that the "object" so conceived is indeterminate and unimaginable. "But this being so," Hegel writes, "what I perceive as the simple and the true is also not a universal medium, but the *single property* by itself, which, however, as such, is neither a property nor a determinate being; for now it is neither in a One nor connected with others."[69] We cannot conceive of an object in this sense, and thus we simply pick out any given random property to associate with the object. But here the unity of the object is no longer present. It is clear that with such a vague conception of objectivity the object simply falls away, and we are left with a plurality of determinate universal properties.

We then move to Hegel's dialectical analysis of the "Also," the conception of the object in terms of its individual properties and abstracted from its unity. He writes, "Only when it belongs to a One is it a property, and only in relation to others is it determinate."[70] As we saw above, we need distinct and contradictory properties in order for them to be determinate, but as soon as they become determinate, this leads to the falling away of the object. Yet, a property is only a property when it belongs to or inheres in an object. It does not make sense to talk of a free-floating property that is not a property of some thing, but that is precisely what we end up with. If properties are inessential, then the "One" could have any set of properties. But if this is so, then it is not determinate since it is not *this* "One" but could be any "One." Hence, the "One" has no real properties and without properties is indeterminate since without properties or marks it cannot be contrasted with other "Ones." This amounts to the same thing as the pure being of "Sense-Certainty" that ended up in indeterminacy: "As this pure relating of itself to itself, it remains merely *sensuous being* in general, since it no longer possesses the character of negativity; and the consciousness which takes its object to be a sensuous being is only 'my' *meaning*."[71] Since the "One" has no properties, it has only self-relation (and no relation to other objects); thus, it is merely a "sensuous being *in general*" and cannot be picked out as an individual object. But consciousness again means or intends the individual object. Thus, we move again to the subject. The "Also" collapses as well, since if it is the properties which are fundamental and essential, then the difficulty lies in finding the unity or the "One" which unites them. If the thing is merely the collection of properties x, y, and z, then we have no real essential thing but rather a collection of properties. To put it another way, to say that a thing is simply the collection of properties x, y, and z is not to tell us what a thing actually *is*: the statement repeats what we already know, namely, that the thing, whatever it is, has certain properties. Hence, from any given set of properties, one cannot derive a unitary thing that is meaningfully and not tautologically defined.

In the breakdown of this first stage of "Perception," we, the philosophical audience, see once again the self-reference back to the role of the subject and its cognitive capacities in the self-determination of the subject-object Notion. An object in this sense of object with properties is never per se given in experience, but rather in perception we find only a group of properties juxtaposed in a certain way. The Notion of an object or substance as self-unified is part of our intellectual capacity and is not something that can be inferred from any number of properties. In an infinite set of perceived properties, one will never find unified thinghood, since it is a universal concept and not a single perception. Moreover, the very ability to pick out properties such as "red," "spherical," etc., also implies universal terms. In order to pick out the property "red," one must have a concept of it against which one can measure the red in the given perception. Hence, a necessary condition for the mere identification of individual properties is a set of universal categories or concepts by means of which one can pick out and order individual perceptions. Natural consciousness, however, does not yet realize this. For natural consciousness, the external object still exists (and thus self-unified thinghood is not a mental concept but rather an objective thing), and the problem is simply a perceptual one. Certain properties, especially secondary properties, seem to be dependent on the subject, and thus to this degree the subject plays a role in forming the complete list of the properties of a thing, but the Notion of an independent, self-determined thing with properties is not questioned. Hence, natural consciousness tries to solve the problem by switching over to the subject as the unifier of the properties.

The For-Itself Moment: The Perceiving Subject (§§118–22)

Now at the second stage, although the individual external object still exists, the essential moment of the relationship is the subject. Hegel tells us that the dialectical movement that we have just seen repeats itself: "Consciousness, therefore, necessarily runs through this cycle again, but this time not in the same way as it did the first time."[72] This time, the object of perception is, as Hegel puts it, "reflected back into the subject." In other words, now the subject plays a key role in the relationship, and it is what is thought to make perception possible. Hegel writes, "we have now in the case of perception the same as happened in the case of sense-certainty, the aspect of consciousness being driven back into itself."[73] This passage parallels the passage from "Sense-Certainty," where Hegel writes, "Sense-certainty, then, though indeed expelled from the object, is not yet thereby overcome, but only driven back into the 'I.' "[74] There natural consciousness attempted to see *itself* as the source of the particularity and singularity of the object. Here in "Perception" likewise it is thought that "the truth, qua truth of *perception, falls* of course *within consciousness*."[75] Natural consciousness alternately posits one of the two conflicting aspects of the object—the "One" and the "Also"—within itself, qua subject, as the essential feature of the object in an attempt to render the Notion of objectivity consistent.

Natural consciousness first perceives the object as a "One."[76] Then it notes that it has no meaningful way to attribute universal properties to any one thing. Natural consciousness reconciles this contradiction by attributing the properties to itself: "the thing is white only to *our eyes, also* tart to *our* tongue, *also* cubical to *our* touch, and so on."[77] The perceiving subject is thus thought to be the medium in which the individual properties inhere: "We are thus the *universal medium* in which such moments are kept apart and exist each on its own."[78] These passages parallel the passage in "Sense-Certainty" where Hegel writes, "The force of its truth thus lies now in the 'I,' in the immediacy of my *seeing, hearing,* and so on."[79] The perceptual faculties of the subject are considered essential for getting hold of the object. The object is in and of itself a "One," and the various properties fall within the realm of the subject and are not essential to the "One" as a unity. The unity remains despite the apparently conflicting properties. We are the universal medium which contains the individual properties that exist independently of one another.

Once again, this positive moment is negated. A thing is determinate only when it has a set of properties to oppose it to another thing with a different set of properties. Hegel's argument is as follows: "it is through its *determinateness* that the thing excludes others. Things are therefore in and for themselves determinate; they have properties by which they distinguish themselves from others."[80] The problem is that when the properties of the "One" are attributed to the perceiver and not to the object, then the object itself is stripped of the very thing that it needs for determination. Hegel eloquently puts the result thus: "the fact that it is a One rather makes it like all the others."[81] Without any properties to distinguish it, the "One" is another empty universal like the This. Once again, with the breakdown of the dialectic we are thrown back to the necessary presupposition of the role of the subject in the self-determination of the subject-object Notion. The thing which exists as a unity deprived of properties is clearly a conceptual construct and not an object of experience. Natural consciousness thus ought to appeal to the constitutive role of itself as subject to account for the object, but this is precisely what it is not allowed to do given its premise that the object is predetermined.

Now exactly the opposite strategy is taken up, and natural consciousness must once again attribute the properties to the object in order to preserve it. The new object is now the "Also," the medium with many properties. But now the perceiver must attribute the unity of the medium to itself and not to the object, since in the chaos of properties no unity can actually be perceived. Hegel describes this process in the following passage: "this moment is the *unity* of the thing with itself, a unity which excludes difference from itself. Accordingly, it is this unity which consciousness has to take upon itself; for the thing itself is the *subsistence of the many diverse and independent properties.*"[82] The properties are thus attributed to the object in itself, but the unity of the object must inhere in the subject. What we are left with again is simply the mutually exclusive universal properties; the thing is only a given universal property: "*insofar* as it [the thing] is white, it is not cubical, and *insofar* as it is cubical and also white, it is not tart, and so on."[83] It is therefore only the work of consciousness which posits a unity of these independent and diverse properties, and thus the properties are, in fact, independent and external; this unity, postulated by the subject, is not essential. The thing thus collapses, and we are left with the diversity of properties. Once again, the key is the presupposition of an autonomous external world. Even though here consciousness admits that the subject plays a role in the self-determination of the subject-object Notion, it fails to see this role as a constitutive one and clings to the view that there are independent external properties apart from the subject.

At this point natural consciousness reflects upon the last two stages and realizes that they are the exact mirror image of one another. At first, the object was the true unity, and the properties existed only for the perceiving subject, and when this was shown to be inadequate, then the properties became the essential and the oneness or unity was imposed by the subject. Put differently, at first the "One" was a fact about the world, and the "Also" was what the subject imposed, and when this proved untenable the "Also" was a fact about the world, and the "One" was on the side of the subject. Hegel describes this realization as follows: "If we look back on what consciousness previously took, and now takes, responsibility for, on what it previously ascribed, and now ascribes, to the thing, we see that consciousness alternately makes itself, as well as the thing, into both a pure, many-less *One*, and into an *Also* that resolves itself into independent 'matters.' "[84] When consciousness reflects on this mirror image of the last two movements, it realizes that the unity of the thing and its properties cannot be separated, with one member on the side of the subject and the other on the side of the object. Consciousness now believes that it sees a way out of the dilemma by positing both terms—the unity of the thing (the "One") and its properties (the "Also")—between the subject and the object, with neither having priority in the relationship.

The In-and-For-Itself Moment: The Moment of Perceptual Contact (§§123–29)

This realization marks the third stage of the dialectic, since here natural consciousness realizes that it stands in a relation to the object of perception and that its perception is bound up with that relation. Hegel puts this conclusion as follows: "Our experience, then, is this, that the thing exhibits itself *for the consciousness apprehending it*, in a specific manner, but is *at the same time* reflected out of the way in which it presents itself to consciousness and back into itself."[85] Now we reach the third stage, which Hegel signals by saying, "Thus consciousness has got beyond this second type of attitude in perceiving, too."[86] Now, natural consciousness at the third stage realizes that objectivity is determined not just by a thing in the world or by itself as a subject but by the interplay of the two. As Hegel puts it, "The object is now for consciousness this whole movement which was previously shared between the object and consciousness."[87] This moment parallels the third stage of the "Sense-Certainty" chapter, in which natural consciousness came to see the relation of both aspects of sense-certainty as the realm of truth: "Thus we reach the stage where we have to posit the *whole* of sense-certainty itself as its *essence*, and no longer only one of its moments."[88] Hence, in this final stage of "Perception," as in the final stage of "Sense-Certainty," both moments collapse into a unity.

This conception of the thing with properties also breaks down in a way that points to the role of the subject as a presupposition for the complete self-determination of the subject-object Notion. Now the "One," i.e., the essential unity of the thing, and the "Also," the plurality of properties, are both of equal importance, neither having any priority over the other. Nevertheless, the Notion itself of an independent, predetermined object is contradictory. Just as we saw earlier, the "One," as the more essential concept of the two, breaks down due to its indeterminacy, so also here the "One," as a concept on the same footing as the "Also," breaks down in the same way. The "One" is thought to exist on its own account, yet we see that just as in "Sense-Certainty," the "One," like pure being, has no way to distinguish itself from anything else since it has no properties and is not determinate. Any given object can only be defined in contrast to other things that stand in relation to it: "But it is only a *thing*, or a One that exists on its own account, insofar as it does not stand in this relation to others."[89] Since the "One" is without properties, it must stand alone without relation to others. But when the propertyless "One" stands opposed to other objects, its difference is not established but rather its *identity* or *continuity* with the other objects. The "One" without properties lacks the means by which it might differentiate itself from others. Thus, the thing or the "One" vanishes, and we are left with a number of properties.

It does not matter if the "One" is considered the essential or the inessential member of the dualism. Regardless of how natural consciousness juggles the variables, the "One" remains a contradictory Notion so long as natural consciousness clings to the belief that it is a predetermined external other. Consciousness can never make sense of the "One" until it sees itself as playing the constitutive role in forming the concept of the "One" in the first place. The dialectic has shown that although the universal "One" is never met in experience, its constant return implies that it is a necessary part of human thinking and thought's self-determination. This, however, is precisely what natural consciousness fails to see. That the self-identical unity of substance or thinghood is a mental concept and not the result of an object of perception is thus the realization only of the philosophical audience and not of natural consciousness.

The concept of the "Also" or of the plurality of properties suffers the same fate. It is not a question of whether the "Also" is given precedence in the relationship or not. The point is that the ability to recognize an empirical property itself presupposes specific universal concepts. These universal concepts of, for instance, red, spherical, etc., form the necessary condition for the possibility of finding something "other" in perception that possesses these properties. Hence, these universal properties are constitutive of experience, and there is no "other" in the sense of there being a predetermined, independent property that is simply given to the perceiver. Natural consciousness fails to see this as well and is still insistent that there is an external other.

Concluding Remarks (§§130–31)

The result of the "Perception" chapter is the breakdown of the one and the many as the criterion for objectivity. The result here, as in "Sense-Certainty," is undifferentiated and indeterminate universality, which is precisely the opposite of the singularity of the object that natural consciousness thought it could achieve by attributing properties to it. "The truth which is supposed to be won by this logic of the perceptual process," Hegel writes, "proves to be in one and the same respect the opposite [of itself] and thus to have as its essence a universality which is devoid of distinctions and determinations."[90] Thus, the one and the many do no better than pure being at determining objectivity. Natural consciousness' naive view of fully determined, autonomous objects with properties breaks down, since it implies universal concepts (e.g., self-united thinghood), which are, in fact, not the objects of perception. These concepts that perceptual experience presupposes thus point back to the constitutive role of the subject in the self-determination of the subject-object Notion. But yet, natural consciousness still fails to grasp this implication and continues to hold on to the idea of an individual self-determined object. When this becomes problematic, natural consciousness ascribes to itself a merely formal role in the shaping of the empirical data without calling into question the ontological existence of the object itself. In order to form a consistent view of the realist claim, something beyond perception is now produced as a new criterion. This comes about in the all-important "Force and the Understanding" chapter, when a ground for the experience is posited which determines the objects of perception as ground and consequence.

Here in "Perception" as in "Sense-Certainty," the dialectic of universal and particular is fundamental. As we saw in "Sense-Certainty," the particular was the object of sense which could only be described by universal terms, i.e., the "This." In "Perception," the dialectic of universal and particular is reinterpreted in terms of substance and accident. On the one hand, the substance is thought to be a particular determined by a set of properties or matters which are particulars, but on the other hand the properties themselves are also universal terms—red, spherical, etc. As universal properties, they cannot define or determine any individual object since they, qua universal, are held in common by a number of objects. There are many objects which are red, and thus to say that object X has the property red is not to pick it out as a particular. Yet, abstracted from these properties, the object, having nothing to determine it, becomes a universal as well. It becomes an empty unity with nothing to distinguish it from other unities. Thus, the dialectic of universal and particular continues.

The dialectic of mediation and immediacy is also present. The belief here is that objects are mediated or determined by their properties, which are immediately present in them. However, as we have seen, the individual properties (e.g., red), like the individual terms of "Sense-Certainty" (the "Here" and the "Now") are in fact mediated, in this case by other contrasting properties. The property of red would not be possible without the existence of opposing properties such as green and blue, etc., just as the "Now" is not possible without a before, a later, etc. Once again, a universe with only the color red would not have the concept of color in the first place, and thus it would be impossible to use red, qua property, to determine any object in such a universe. Moreover, the issue of mediation also refers back to the perceiving subject. The universal properties, qua universals, are not met with in experience. In experience we perceive a patch of red, but it is only because we possess the concept of red in our intellectual apparatus that we can recognize the patch as red in the first place and can order it into the group of things which falls under the general concept red. Thus, the properties cannot simply be immediately in the objects themselves, but rather they are conceptual, and as conceptual they imply a constitutive role in the knowing process for the perceiving subject. This is the insight that natural consciousness once again fails to see.

III. Force and the Understanding: "Force" and "Law" (§§132–65)

One can say without exaggeration that the "Force and the Understanding" chapter of the *Phenomenology* is one of the most opaque pieces of philosophical argumentation in the entire tradition of German idealism. Here Hegel seems to move from one topic, or, more exactly, from one metaphor, to another, apparently with little concern for the dialectical structure that he elsewhere insists upon. The historical references, which form the background to the positions that are here presented and consequently criticized, are also rather elusive, as is evinced by the extraordinarily long list of names and theories mentioned in the literature, which are supposedly the targets of criticism here. Of all the confusion that surrounds this section, the most perplexing problem that remains open today is surely that of the transition between the "Force and the Understanding" section and the "Self-Consciousness" chapter. In the "Force and the Understanding" section, Hegel gives an analysis of supersensible forces and scientific laws, whereas in what follows in the "Self-Consciousness" chapter the set of themes and issues appears entirely different. The problems that Hegel treats in "Self-Consciousness" seem to have little to do with the epistemological questions of the "Consciousness" chapter. Despite Hegel's almost pathological concern for the symmetry, fit, and organic unity of his system, here he passes over this incoherence apparently without explanation. As indicated earlier, I will try to sketch the link between these two sections specifically in terms of the continuity in the criteria of the subject-object Notion in the context of the attempt to give an adequate account of the self-determination of that Notion.

It is convenient to divide this chapter, like the preceding ones, into three sections. In the first, Hegel introduces the Notion of force as a ground for experience or as the independent object of consciousness. This is natural consciousness' new criterion, and it then leads to the concept of the supersensible world. In the second section, the move is again from objective to subjective in the sense that the subject is thought to play a formal role in the determination of the subject-object Notion, although the independent object still exists on its own. In other words, the criterion of ground remains, but the concrete example changes from force to a natural scientific mode of explanation, the explanatory terms of which are universal laws that purport to explain the phenomena that make up the world. The explanatory laws thus fall on the side of the subject. In the third section, natural consciousness reaches a point where its Notion of law invokes an inversion according to which that which appears is in fact the opposite of what really is. Thus, in this third section, Hegel gives his famous account of the inverted world, which in the literature has been a source of at once great interest and at the same time great confusion. In each of these three sections we see at work the category of ground which determines the object at the level of understanding.

Natural consciousness here, as in "Sense-Certainty" and "Perception," still clings to the belief in a fully determined, independent object. Here the form of the object changes from hidden forces to the supersensible world, to objects explained by scientific law, and finally to the inverted world. Only in the final section here does natural consciousness come to give up its naive realist claim and to realize that it must give an account of itself in its attempt to elucidate exhaustively the self-determination of the subject-object Notion. Let us now turn to Hegel's text and try to analyze the movement of natural consciousness in an attempt to understand the puzzling "Force and the Understanding" section and the all important transition to "Self-Consciousness."

The Notion: "Force" and "Matters" (§§132–36)

In order to understand the role of the "Force and the Understanding" chapter in the self-determination of subject and object, we must first understand the nature of the object here and how it differs from the object of "Perception." In "Force and the Understanding," the object for consciousness is still an independent, self-determined other as it was in "Perception," but there is a significant difference. The object in perceiving consciousness is grasped through, naturally enough, the faculty of perception. In "Force and the Understanding," the object is accessible only through thought or the understanding. The transition from "Perception" makes this clear. At the end of the "Perception" chapter, natural consciousness had reached the stage where its conception of the object was the unconditioned universal. The object is unconditioned since it has no properties and thus is without relation to anything else. It had to be purged of all properties, since the inconsistencies and contradictions in the relationship between the object and the properties and the relationship between the properties themselves proved to be overpowering. We ended up with merely a universal conception of unity which we could not find in perception. But once the object is extricated from its properties it becomes an unconditioned universal, since it has no determining qualities. Without determining qualities, the object is no longer an object of perception. "In the dialectic of sense-certainty," Hegel says, "seeing and hearing have been lost to consciousness; and, as perception, consciousness has arrived at thoughts, which it brings together for the first time in the unconditioned universal."[91] This passage tells us explicitly that the transition from "Perception" to "Force and the Understanding" is marked by a change in the nature of the object for consciousness. In a similar passage from the *Encyclopaedia Logic*, Hegel writes, "This universal which cannot be apprehended by the senses counts as the true and essential. . . . The universal is neither seen nor heard, its existence is only for the mind."[92] In "Perception," the object is able to be perceived in the sense that we can observe its properties, but in "Force and the Understanding" the object is not an object of perception, but rather an object of thought. Of the object of "Force and the Understanding" Hegel says, "Thus the truth of force remains only the *thought* of it."[93] This contrast between the faculties of perception and understanding is precisely what Hegel indicates by the term "understanding" in the title of this section.

This Notion of an object of understanding in contrast to an object of perception is what corresponds to Hegel's conception of "force," which is something beyond the realm of sense and perception and which is accessible only by means of the faculty of thought, i.e., it is the thought of consciousness in its attempt to explain the phenomena.[94] Force is thus the ground of experience or the *super*sensible (*übersinnlich*). By "supersensible" Hegel means here the realm beyond or behind that of sense or perception (which we have just examined in the "Perception" section). The supersensible is the transcendent sphere, which cannot be reached by sense. Although the nature of the object has changed to an object of understanding, it nevertheless remains an independent external other just as in "Sense-Certainty" and "Perception." This conception of objectivity is thus the theme of the entire "Consciousness" chapter.

We must be careful to conceive the object of understanding correctly. When we say that the object of understanding-consciousness is an object of thought, we do not mean to imply that the object exists only in thought or is in itself determined by the subject or by thought. Rather, we mean that the object, which is independent and has its own external existence, is only accessible to consciousness via the understanding. The object at this level can be understood as something similar to Kant's thing-in-itself. For Kant, we perceive only representations (*Vorstellungen*) or phenomena which are representations of a thing-in-itself which we, limited as we are to our forms of human cognition, cannot perceive. Concerning this issue, Kant writes, "But our further contention must also be duly borne in mind, namely, that though we cannot *know* these objects as things-in-themselves, we must yet be in a position to *think* them as things-in-themselves; otherwise we should be landed in the absurd conclusion that there can be appearance without anything that appears."[95] Thus, for

Kant although we never perceive things-in-themselves directly, we know cognitively that they must exist as the cause of the representations which we do perceive. Thus, understanding, like perception, is merely a faculty for getting hold of an object.

Natural consciousness is still unaware of its role in the determination of subject and object, although this is clear to the philosophical observers, given the results of the previous dialectical moments which pointed unambiguously back to the subject. The implicit reliance on universal concepts implied in natural consciousness's assertions about the nature of the object up until this point indicates that there are certain important cognitive presuppositions in even the most basic claims about objects: "*For us*, this object has developed through the movement of consciousness in such a way that consciousness is involved in that development, and the reflection is the same on both sides, or, there is only one reflection."[96] But at this point in the dialectic, natural consciousness fails to recognize this: "since in this movement consciousness has for its content merely the objective essence and not consciousness as such, the result must have an objective significance for consciousness; consciousness still shrinks away from what has emerged, and takes it as the essence in the *objective* sense."[97] In this passage, Hegel indicates that natural consciousness still understands the true nature or reality of the object to be in the objective sphere, i.e., independent of and abstracted from the subject. The objects are assumed to be external and independent and thus not bound up with the subject. Since natural consciousness does not see the role that it plays in this determination of the subject-object Notion, it still sees the determinations as purely objective or somehow given as facts about the world. The object as the unconditioned universal is not the result of natural consciousness's own doing, but rather is still a real essential thing in its own right.

The dialectic of "Force and the Understanding" begins with this conception of the object, i.e., the unconditioned universal. However, now it takes place in its new realm—in the understanding. Hegel describes the object in familiar terms: "But because this unconditioned universal is an object for consciousness, there emerges in it the distinction of form and content . . . on one side, a universal medium of many subsistent 'matters,' and on the other side, a One reflected into itself, in which their independence is extinguished."[98] Here we meet once again the terms of perception—the subsistent matters or properties and the "One" reflected into itself. We must now examine more closely how this old distinction applies to this new level of understanding. It is clear that the conception of a medium of universal matters remains the medium of perception, but there is an important change in Hegel's notion of "matters" here. No longer are the matters properties which in some unexplained way hang together in an object, but rather now they are empirical manifestations which result from something behind experience, which serves as the ground for experience.

Since the thing of "Perception" with its properties has proved to be contradictory in the realm of perception, it now falls behind the scenes into the realm of understanding. The line of reasoning is something like the following: in "Perception" natural consciousness is convinced that there is a single unified object of perception that possesses the manifold of properties, but it never meets with this object in perception. Instead of giving up on the Notion entirely, natural consciousness grants that the object is not empirically perceived qua unitary object, but it insists that the object still exists *unperceived.* How else are we to explain its properties that do appear? Clearly they must belong to some unified object that we do not and cannot perceive. Hegel refers to this object behind the appearances as "being for self,"[99] i.e., the object as it is for itself without any relation to another or to the thinking subject. The properties of "Perception" become here reinterpreted as the results or consequences of the objects behind the scenes. The object in its empirical aspect, as representation or appearance, Hegel calls "being for another,"[100] since it is in this aspect that the object reveals itself to the subject. These are then considered two aspects of the same object, just as the thing-in-itself and appearance are, for Kant, two aspects of one thing. Thus, the object as it is in itself is at this level not objective in the sense that it is not an empirical object. "Thus the movement which previously displayed itself as the self-destruction of contradictory Notions here has," Hegel writes, "*objective* form and is the movement of force, the outcome of which is the unconditioned universal as something *not* objective, or as the *inner* being of things."[101] The object here is not empirical but rather conceptual; it has an "inner being" which is transcendent and accessible only by an act of intellectual abstraction from the world of perception.

The "One" which grounds appearance "appears as the essence,"[102] while the individual "matters" are simply its manifestation. These matters are, however, noncontradictory. As Hegel puts it, "they mutually interpenetrate, but without coming into contact with one another because, conversely, the many diverse 'matters' are equally independent."[103] There is thus an immediate interaction and play between the unity that exists behind the scenes and the matters that we see in appearance: "the 'matters' posited as independent directly pass over into their unity, and their unity directly unfolds its diversity, and this once again reduces itself to unity."[104] The "One" and the "Also" of "Perception" are taken over here in "Force and the Understanding" by the Notion of force. Force, qua the "One," is thus the unitary structure which, although inaccessible to perception, produces the wealth and variety of things and events, i.e., the "Also" given in perception, but force itself is accessible only through the intellect and is itself never an object of experience per se. Force is the first dialectical candidate for the principle of ground, which replaces the Notion of the thing of "Perception." The important point for our purposes about the Notion of force is that it represents the third object for natural consciousness. Like pure being and the thing with properties before it, force is also considered to have an independent existence. It is something fully determined in itself, even though it is not directly accessible to sense. Hence, the naive realism still remains, and the role of the subject in the determination of objectivity is still unrecognized.

The distinction between "force" and "matters" Hegel tries to capture with a distinction between the "*expression* of force" and "force *proper*,"[105] since they are merely two aspects of the same thing. When force is expressed, it manifests itself in the world of sense in various ways which are perceivable. This corresponds to the "Also" of "Perception" or to representation or phenomena for Kant. On the other hand, force proper (i.e., as it is in itself) is a simple, unitary structure which is available only to the understanding or intellect and is never given in sense. This is what Hegel called the "One" reflected into itself and, of course, corresponds to the "One" of "Perception" and to the thing-in-itself for Kant. Hegel summarizes this as follows: "But this movement is what is called *force*. One of its moments, the dispersal of the independent 'matters' in their [immediate] being, is the *expression* of force; but force, taken as that in which they have disappeared, is force *proper*, force which has been *driven back* into itself from its expression."[106] The idea seems to be that a plurality of properties must be tied to some common source for them to be properties of some determinate thing. But yet, as on Hume's account, all that we ever experience is a set of successive perceptions, which in itself does not supply any necessity for a given conjunction of properties. The realist alternative is that there is some sort of causal power behind the scenes, which binds the properties together even if we cannot perceive it. As one might already suspect, this distinction between force expressed and force proper will lead to the breakdown of the concept of force as the criterion for the subject-object Notion. Already we can see that the idea of knowing an object by means of the faculty of understanding is an important step toward recognizing the role of the subject in the self-determination of the subject-object Notion. Natural consciousness must admit that it never perceives force per se, but rather only its manifestations. Thus, the force itself is a cognitive postulation based on an abstraction from empirical phenomena. The key point is that natural consciousness still sees force not as a cognitive or epistemic postulation but rather as an ontological fact, i.e., there is still an independent external object called force which corresponds to natural consciousness' conception of it. This is the position to be overcome.

Although these two elements—the expression of force and force proper—both seem to belong to force, natural consciousness knows that force itself is in fact actually a unity, just as in "Perception" the "One" and its properties were supposed to constitute a unity. As Hegel says, "*in themselves,* they are not supposed to be different."[107] So consciousness posits this difference in the realm of thought and attributes the unity to the true substance of the force. The dichotomy arises again at the level of substance: "Force as such, or as driven back into itself, thus exists on its own account as an *exclusive One,* for which the unfolding of the [different] 'matters' is *another* subsisting essence."[108] Thus, just as in the "Perception" chapter the essence of a thing was posited over and against its properties, so also here in "Force and the Understanding," force in its unity is considered to be somehow essential or substantial, while its matters are merely results or accidents of its being. The matters are merely "vanishing" moments with no independent being of their own; clearly, if there were no force, there would be no expression of force. Hegel says, "Force, as thus determined, since it is conceived *as* force or as *reflected into itself,* is one side of its Notion, but posited as a substantial extreme and, moreover, with the express character of a One."[109] This essential unity or essence is said to express itself and to give rise to its empirical manifestations through what Hegel calls the process of "solicitation." Hegel signals the end of the construction of the Notion of force and the beginning of the dialectical experience when he writes, "It is therefore this movement of the two moments in which they perpetually give themselves independence and then supersede themselves again which we are now to consider."[110]

The Experience of Consciousness

The In-Itself Moment: Mutual Solicitation and the Supersensible World (§§137–48)

In this first dialectical movement of "Force and the Understanding," Hegel discusses two related dialectical figures—first that of the mutual solicitation of individual forces, and then that of the supersensible world. We must examine each of these in turn. For natural consciousness, a force must be solicited (*sollizitiert*) by a subject (*das Sollizitierende*) in order to display its manifestations. "Since it is necessary that *force itself* be this *subsistence,* or that it *express* itself," Hegel writes, "its expression presents itself in this wise, that the said 'other' approaches *it* and solicits it."[111] Since force itself is only the unseen origin of a set of empirical manifestations, a perceiving subject must be present to perceive the various matters of a given force. It thus "solicits" the force which, without a subject to perceive its matters, would be imperceptible. Force is thought to have its own independent existence as ground apart from a human subject, and it just so happens to manifest itself with objective properties in the world when it is solicited by another.

That the opposing term (*das Sollizitierende*) is in fact a subject is by no means an uncontroversial claim. Indeed, as we shall see in a moment, Hegel talks of this "other" as a force itself, and this is admittedly a curious way to refer to a perceiving subject. I base my reading on a passage where Hegel seems to indicate that the dialectic of force operates at this point between an external force and a perceiving subject. He says, "In general, it is clear that this movement is nothing else than the movement of perceiving, in which two sides, the percipient and what is perceived, are indistinguishably one in the *apprehension* of the True, and yet each side is at the same time equally *reflected into itself,* or has a being of its own. Here, these two sides are moments of force."[112] Hegel unambiguously associates his terms "force proper" and "force expressed" with what is perceived (not the empirical content but the thing itself) and the percipient, and he explains their interaction in terms of a dialectic of perceiving. And in the last sentence quoted, he clearly associates these two terms with the two moments of force (the solicited and the soliciting), which he introduces in the next paragraph. On the strength of this evidence, I interpret Hegel's talk of a soliciting other as the perceiving human subject.

But then a curious reversal comes about. Now force, understood as its manifestations, is thought to solicit the perceiving human subject. Hegel articulates this as follows: "Force is rather itself this universal medium in which the moments subsist as 'matters'; or, in other words, force *has expressed itself,* and what was supposed to be something else soliciting it is really force itself."[113] He puts the same point in this way: "What appears as an 'other' and solicits force, both to expression and to a return into itself, directly proves to be *itself force.*"[114] Here force expressed is at issue. Expressed force, understood as the perceptual medium or as a manifold of empirical manifestations, is thought to confront or solicit the subject. In order to make some sense out of this manifold, the perceiving subject posits a nonempirical force behind these manifestations. Although force (i.e., expressed force) is still thought to determine objectivity, it is here the subject as synthesizer of the various empirical manifestations that creates the Notion of force (i.e., force proper) in order to explain those "given" manifestations.

The details of this dialectic are less important for our purposes than the simple point that natural consciousness is compelled to make these various dialectical adjustments because of its stubborn insistence that there are in fact independent forces existing on their own, which, it is assumed, can be understood to play an epistemologically determinate role in the formation of perceptual qualities. The contradictions of the dialectic have shown unambiguously that force itself is not so unproblematic an object as natural consciousness thinks. It appears rather to be a concept of natural consciousness, who has simply abstracted from experience and posited a unity. This would imply that an account of the subject itself is necessary before we can give an adequate account of the Notion of objectivity. But natural consciousness must reject this solution, given its overriding presupposition in this chapter of the existence of independently existing external objects.

The result of this dialectic is a breakdown in the Notion of force, since natural consciousness comes to see with the play of forces how both sides of the dialectic mutually determine one another. Hegel describes this dissolution of the Notion of force in various ways. "The interplay of the two forces," he says, "thus consists in their being determined as mutually opposed, in their being for one another in this determination, and in the absolute, immediate alternation of the determinations."[115] By this Hegel means that the ambiguity in the Notion of force itself (force expressed and force proper) as the criterion for objectivity causes two different and contradictory accounts of that determination. On the one hand, force (force proper) is thought to determine objectivity as the ground of phenomena (force expressed), yet, on the other hand, force (force expressed) is thought to determine objectivity, insofar as it is merely a representation of *what really is*—force proper.[116] Hence, the Notion of force is itself contradictory and breaks down in the dialectic. Here again the breakdown points back to the role of the subject in the determination of the subject-object Notion. Force expressed is what is given in experience, i.e., phenomena are seen as the results or consequences of something else. But this something else, i.e., force proper, is never given in sense per se (although it is considered the true and the real in accordance with this first in-itself moment). It is instead posited by the understanding in order to explain the origin of phenomena. This Notion of force, as force proper or as ground, is then a universal concept found in the understanding but not in sense. But yet the empirical concept of force, i.e., force expressed, relies on and implies precisely this concept, as the dialectic has shown. Hence, once again, this time with force expressed, we are led back to intellectual, nonempirical concepts which constitute experience. We now move to the second phase of this first dialectical movement, namely that of the supersensible world.

Instead of individual forces behind the scenes, we are concerned with an entire realm behind the world of appearances. In order to avoid having these two contradictory conceptions of force, natural consciousness now posits two opposed forces. From the single original force arises yet another force, and the two together reify and condition each other. Now a new dichotomy arises. We have, on the one hand, not simply determinate matters stemming from a single force, but rather the "*totality of show*," i.e., a world of appearances. We have, on the other hand, not just one force behind the scenes, but a plurality of forces which thus constitute "the inner of things." This realm corresponds to the realm of noumena, in Kant, which is beyond or behind the realm of sense and phenomena. Hegel describes this as follows: "there now opens up above the *sensuous* world, which is the world of *appearance*, a *supersensible* world which henceforth is the *true* world, above the vanishing *present* world there opens up a permanent *beyond*."[117] Hence, we move to another more complex level, where the understanding posits the supersensible world as ground for the world of appearance, which Hegel, using his syllogism analogy, says serves as the middle term (between understanding and the supersensible). But the problem is not remedied, since the supersensible world is every bit as conceptual and thus subject-produced as the Notion of force. All of the same problems simply repeat themselves again, since natural consciousness fails to see that the supersensible world is the result of its own positing and determination.

Hegel discusses how this new supersensible world that natural consciousness has erected remains hollow and undetermined. "It is *empty*," he says, "for it is merely the nothingness of appearance, and positively the *simple* or *unitary* universal."[118] Natural consciousness is thus in the curious position of having posited the supersensible world in order to explain experience without being able to say anything more about it other than that it is the ground of experience. We have no knowledge of this inner world, not because, as according to Kant, our understanding is limited to certain forms and categories, but rather, says Hegel, "just because this inner world is determined as the *beyond* of consciousness."[119] In other words, the supersensible world is empty simply because according to this Notion of objectivity it was posited to explain the content of our sensibility, and as the ground of experience, it must be somehow beyond or behind sensibility and its content in order to ground it. We cannot know this world beyond consciousness simply because according to this Notion it is precisely what is *beyond* consciousness and *cannot* be known.

In this role of the ground of sensibility, the supersensible world comes into difficulties. The supersensible world was posited to explain appearances, or as Hegel says, "The inner world, or the supersensible beyond, has, however, *come into being:* it *comes from* the world of appearance which has mediated it."[120] In other words, one posits the supersensible world only to explain the world of experience, but without this world of appearance it is nothing. The Notion of objectivity here is one that dictates that natural consciousness posit an object behind the scenes as something more true than the appearances. The supersensible world is simply the truth of the world of appearance or the appearance as it really is. Hegel puts it in the following way: "The supersensible is therefore *appearance qua appearance.*"[121] This is not to imply that somehow the supersensible is, strictly speaking, the world of appearance that we perceive, but rather it is only posited because of the existence of the sensible world. From this movement we see that, like the two forces before, the supersensible and the world of appearances collapse into one another. The supersensible is thought to be the ground of appearance and thus to determine it, but yet appearance itself is the ground or reason for positing the supersensible, and thus appearance determines it. Hence, the supersensible world and the world of appearance depend on and condition one another; the result is again a collapse into a unity. The collapse of the supersensible world parallels the dialectical movement of force. The supersensible world, like force proper, represents a universal concept and not something sensible. This would pose no problem if the supersensible were only thought to be a mental construct, but for natural consciousness it has objective reality. The supersensible as objective is implied by the phenomenal description that natural consciousness insists on. Hence, natural consciousness' naive realism is still inconsistent and still relies on universal concepts and categories that experience cannot account for on its own terms.

The upshot of the account of objectivity via the supersensible is that the supersensible realm can only be posited as an explanation of what we find in experience. But yet this explanation itself is simply an abstraction from experience, and abstraction brings with it certain cognitive or epistemic presuppositions. Consciousness admits that it is through cognition or understanding that it knows the object, but it fails to see that this sort of abstraction from experience is a necessary condition for the very possibility of there being an object or this conception of an object per se; moreover, it fails to see that any such empirical object in the world could never possibly have this universal character. Thus, natural consciousness is still convinced of the independent existence of the external other. Consciousness does, however, realize that, given the contradictions of the dialectic, the principle of explanation cannot come from something outside (as with force), but rather must come from itself. This then constitutes the transition to the next stage, at which point the Notion flips over to the side of the subject.

Natural consciousness is now left with the flux or manifold of what were thought of as manifestations of force and which are now conceived as inexplicable facts given in perception. It realizes that it cannot use force or the supersensible world as a ground for the appearances. Now natural consciousness sees that what is essential about this manifold is not some determinate thing or *content* behind the scenes, but instead it is the *form* behind the scenes which determines objectivity. The unseen or intellectually grasped *form* of this manifold is law. Thus, the new Notion of "law" is introduced and becomes the new example of ground which is, of course, the general criterion for objectivity throughout this section.[122] Here scientific law, like the unseen force, is thought to explain phenomenal reality.

The For-Itself Moment: Law and the Notion of Law (§§149–56)

In this section we find what we might regard as Hegel's first version of a philosophy of science and his critique of scientific explanation in the *Phenomenology*. The distinction between law and its appearances now takes the place of the earlier distinction between force and matters. We observe the manifold of natural phenomena, and we have the intellectual curiosity to try to seek the unity behind them. The project of the natural sciences is then the outgrowth of this natural human desire. In the *Encyclopaedia*, Hegel writes,

> We find the same thing exhibited in our study of natural phenomena. For instance, we observe thunder and lightning. The phenomenon is a familiar one, and we often perceive it. But man is not content with a bare acquaintance, or with the fact as it appears to the senses; he would like to get behind the surface, to know what it is, and to comprehend it. This leads him to reflect: he seeks to find out the cause as something distinct from the mere phenomenon.[123]

The belief is that, through thought and reflection, we can go further toward discovering the truth of the matter than if we were to remain at the level of perception. According to this conception, the truth of the phenomena is thought again to lie beyond the realm of sense, this time not in the realm of supersensible forces but rather in the sphere of scientific laws. Since the scientific laws are located, in contrast to force, on the side of the subject, this represents the for-itself moment of "Force and the Understanding." The point of this account of law and explanation is similar to the conclusion of the discussion of force. Specifically, law is considered to be the ground of empirical experience, yet law per se is never discovered in experience. One seeks a universal law by means of which one can understand the specific empirical phenomena. Again in the *Encyclopaedia*, Hegel writes,

> Once more we find the inside or the force identified with the universal and permanent: not this or that flash of lightning, this or that plant—but that which continues the same in them all. The sensible appearance is individual and evanescent: the permanent in it is discovered by reflection. Nature shows us a countless number of individual forms and phenomena. Into this variety we feel a need of introducing unity: we compare, consequently, and try to find the universal of each single case.[124]

It is the human mind that, seeking the universal, thus binds the manifold phenomena under an orderly heading. Yet the universal itself is never an object of sense. There must, however, be some sort of correspondence between law and experience if we are going to be able to say that law grounds or explains experience. But yet law is a universal issuing from thought, while experience is always particular. The dialectical conundrums arise precisely because of the irreconcilability of this universal-particular relationship. Once again, the problem arises because natural consciousness believes that there is an independent law-governed nature apart from itself, which natural science seeks to understand by positing laws. The problem is that it is impossible to conceive of nature in itself as law-governed without appealing to certain epistemic presuppositions, namely about universals. In short, how can we attribute universality to nature, which we always perceive in its particularity? How many particular instances of a given phenomena do we need to observe in order to justify making a universal law? For the philosophical observers, it is clear that the laws are simply the result of consciousness's positing, but this is what natural consciousness only gradually discovers in the inverted world. Although natural consciousness considers the laws as formal and posited by a subject, they are still nevertheless objective and externally existent in the sense that there is an external reality which embodies them. In this way, scientific law is analogous to the other objects of the "Consciousness" chapter which we have already examined.

Although experience appears chaotic, in fact there is a unitary and stable law behind the scenes, which is accessible to the understanding, i.e., a law or ground which determines these appearances: "This difference is expressed in the *law,* which is the *stable* image of unstable appearance. Consequently, the *supersensible* world is an inert *realm of laws* which, though beyond the perceived world—for this exhibits law only through incessant change—is equally *present* in it and is its direct tranquil image."[125] The law remains "stable" and "tranquil" behind the flux of experience. It thus becomes the thing which determines certain regularities in the objects of experience. The Notion of a scientific law has replaced the Notion of force as the ground of experience. Strictly speaking, we never actually perceive a law of nature per se in phenomena (and thus the law remains somehow behind the scenes, just like force before it), but nevertheless we believe that the phenomena are somehow examples of our scientific laws, and in this way law is indirectly manifested in our experience. Hegel explains the complicated relation between law and the phenomena that it purports simultaneously to ground and to explain as follows: "This realm of laws is indeed the truth for the understanding, and that truth has its *content* in the law."[126] The phenomena or experience itself would be chaotic without scientific laws to explain them. Experience would appear as a constant flux lacking stability. For this reason, law is the truth of appearance, and it is the essential element in the relation.

The dialectic in this section operates with two different conceptions of law. First, law is individual and specific, and thus able to match up to the specific phenomena that it is meant to explain. There are thus many separate laws: "However, insofar as it is not law in general, but *a* law, it does contain determinateness; consequently, there are indefinitely *many* laws."[127] In other words, for a law to be said to determine anything it must be specific, just as certain specific forces caused specific phenomenal appearances. The law must be determinate and particular in order to explain effectively a particular phenomenon. The problem is that if we conceive of law in this way, i.e., as particulars, then the laws become as manifold as the appearances which they are meant to explain. This, of course, undercuts natural consciousness's overriding goal of finding something "stable" or "tranquil" which determines appearances without itself changing. As Hegel puts it, this plurality of laws "contradicts the principle of the understanding for which, as consciousness of the simple inner world, the true is the implicitly universal *unity.*"[128] The goal was to find something stable and enduring, but with such a plurality of laws we are no better off than if we simply had a plurality of phenomena without any explanation. The point here is that a plurality of laws cannot render anything determinate, since it does not categorize or systematize anything. The point of a scientific law is to be able to describe a set of phenomena by means of a single principle. Thus, the phenomena are rendered determinate in the relation of similarity to other phenomena in their set and dissimilarity to other phenomena outside of this set. But if there is one law for one phenomenon, then there is no determination, since each set of phenomena has only one member and no meaningful comparison or contrast can be made in the phenomenal chaos. The result of this is that natural consciousness must reduce this plurality of laws into a single all-encompassing law that endures throughout the flux of appearance: "It must therefore let the many laws collapse into *one* law."[129] This is then the second conception of law.

Now a problem arises with the revised Notion of law. According to this version, the single law is general and tries to encompass a broad spectrum of phenomena: "The law becomes more and more superficial, and as a result what is found is, in fact, not the unity of *these specific* laws, but a law which leaves out their specific character; just as the *one* law which combines in itself the laws of falling terrestrial bodies and the motions of the heavenly bodies, in fact expresses neither law."[130] The problem with this general law is that it becomes too vague to be of any use as an explanatory tool. In other words, although the unitary law purports to be an aggregate of other more specific laws, in fact, it loses all of the concrete character of those laws and with it all of its explanatory power. Insofar as law is able to explain anything it must explain distinct processes; the problem is how to account for the fact that a *universal* law can explain or ground *particular* events. Hegel criticizes the scientific attempt to reduce all phenomena to a single universal law. The more general or encompassing a law becomes, the less able it is to describe phenomena accurately in their individual details. For Hegel, a fully universal law is always ultimately hollow or devoid of content and thus is inadequate for explaining the particular phenomena. Hegel's way of expressing this is as follows: "This defect in the law must equally be made manifest in the law itself. What seems to be defective in it is that while it does contain difference, the difference is universal, indeterminate."[131] The law is the universal, and as such it is indeterminate and cannot be said to render anything determinate. This universality and with it indeterminacy render law ineffective at explaining the difference or the variety and particularity of experience. Once again the dialectic leads us back to universality which belongs to cognition and indicates the observer's role in the determination of objectivity. Natural consciousness, qua realist, still cannot consistently make sense of objects given its purely empiricist premises, since it keeps running up against universals and the problem of the necessary presupposition of its own role in the determination of the subject-object Notion.

Hegel's example of the law which has become too general and thus too universal is the law of universal attraction. He explains, "Universal attraction merely asserts that *everything has a constant difference in relation to other things.*"[132] This law does not really explain anything, but merely repeats what we have already assumed, namely, that everything in experience stands in a relation (that of attraction) to everything else, a relation which is able to be explained by law. Hegel continues, "The understanding imagines that in this unification it has found a universal law which expresses universal reality *as such*; but in fact it has only found the *Notion* of *law itself,* although in such a way that what it is saying is that *all* reality is *in its own self,* conformable to law."[133] The dialectic has produced no specific laws that explain any particular thing but only the "*Notion* of *law itself,*"[134] i.e., the idea that phenomena are in principle able to be explained by law.

The dialectic then turns to various problems in scientific explanation. These problems will prove to be important for the transition to the inverted world and thus for consciousness's realization that it plays a constitutive role in the determination of the Notion. Hegel's first account is of the claim for necessity in scientific laws. This account, however, is less important for our purposes than the second criticism about the tautological nature of scientific explanation. Hence, I forgo an account of the first criticism that appears in §§ 151–53 and turn now to the second, which provides the basis for the transition to the inverted world dialectic.

As we have just seen, the "Notion of law" means that the phenomenal world is in principle reducible to scientific law and that law can explain what is given in phenomena. The key to this Notion is, for Hegel, "difference." There must be a difference between the *explicans,* i.e., the law, and the *explicanda,* its phenomenal manifestations. When we posit a law we claim that it gives us a way to order or make sense of the phenomena that somehow goes beyond how the phenomena appear. This is the Notion of law itself. Hegel's dialectic shows that this Notion of law and explanation is tautological. The problem with explanation is that it contains no difference, i.e., it turns out not to be different from the phenomena that it purports to explain. In Hegel's language, it is a difference that is not a difference. Hegel says, "This process is called '*explanation.*' A *law* is enunciated; from this, its implicitly universal element or ground is distinguished as *force;* but it is said that this difference is no difference, rather that the ground is constituted exactly the same as the law."[135] Law posits a relation between forces and their manifestations, i.e., law explains things in terms of forces. For instance, we could say there is a law which states that opium induces sleep due to the somnifacient property of a force which it contains. This is both a law (opium induces sleep) and an explanation (*because* of its somnifacient property). As a law it tells us how a force—opium—causes certain results. The problem is that the law tells us no more than the force itself; since the force opium has a somnifacient property, which we have already observed, the law adds nothing new by saying that opium induces sleep. Hence, Hegel claims, *"Force is constituted exactly the same as law*; there is said to be no difference whatever between them."[136] Hence, natural consciousness discovers what we, the philosophical observers, have known all along—namely, that law and force are both identical with ground.

Hegel uses the example of lightning and electricity to explain his point: "The single occurrence of lightning, e.g., is apprehended as a universal, and this universal is enunciated as the *law* of electricity; the 'explanation' then condenses the *law* into *force* as the essence of the law."[137] According to this example, one observes a single particular phenomenon, the consequence of a force, and from this one forms a universal law—from a single occurrence of lightning one abstracts to a general law of electricity. But this does not mean that law explains the phenomena, but rather the law and the force collapse into a unity. In other words, the law and the phenomenon amount in the end to the same thing, since it was from the single example of force that the general law was derived in the first place. The law is nothing more than a single instance in its abstraction. Hence, when Hegel says, *"Force is constituted exactly the same as law,"*[138] he seems to mean that law, or at least this conception of law, has as its essence a particular instance of force, and that the Notion neither of force nor of law is able to render an effective or satisfying explanation, since they collapse into one another. Put differently, they are in the final result identical, and thus there is no element or moment of difference between them. With this moment of difference lacking, a true explanation remains impossible.

For this reason, Hegel believes that the very Notion of law gives rise to tautologies. More specifically, the scientific account of explanation must be more thoroughly examined: "It is an explanation that not only explains nothing, but is so plain that, while it pretends to say something different from what has already been said, really says nothing at all but only repeats the same thing."[139] The tautology lies in the essential identity of the law and force. The law, since it is simply an abstraction from a single force, is merely a restatement of the force in question. This, however, leaves the true explanation still wanting. This experience for understanding-consciousness compels it to rethink its Notion of explanation. It must find a way to explain and ground phenomena such that difference does not collapse into identity and thus into an empty tautology. The inverted world provides understanding-consciousness with the solution.

The In-and-For-Itself Moment: The Inverted World
(§§157–62)

The section in the "Force and the Understanding" chapter that has come to be known as "the inverted world"[140] is one of the most difficult and controversial in the entire Hegelian corpus. Its location in the *Phenomenology*, immediately before the "Self-Consciousness" chapter, signals the reader that there is something very important about it as a transition in the overall scheme; yet that something has been slow to come to the surface. Formerly, this section was ignored[141] or derided;[142] however, recently there has been some light shed on the subject by a number of commentators interested specifically in the problematic it presents.[143] The strategy of most of these commentators has been to try to pinpoint the historical target of Hegel's criticism in this section and then to explore and evaluate the criticism. Hyppolite, for example, sees the inverted world as an allusion to the Gospels,[144] while Gadamer reads it as a renewed debate between Plato and Aristotle,[145] while Flay sees in it resonances of Leibniz and Kant.[146] I will simply put to one side whatever historical references there may be here in order to see what role the so-called inverted world plays in the dialectic and the overall scheme of the *Phenomenology*. My claim is simply that the inverted world is the third and final candidate for the ground of experience and that, with the inversion of the relevant terms, consciousness finally comes to realize the role that it plays in the self-determination of the subject-object Notion and comes to see the need for an account of the subject for the complete development of the Notion.

The important point about the inverted world is that it posits what I will call a principle or law of inversion in which things are turned into their opposites or are at least different in a meaningful way from the phenomena that they are meant to explain. This principle of inversion is at once paradoxical and enlightening. It is paradoxical since it brings to a head all of the dialectical contradictions we have seen heretofore concerning law and explanation. Natural consciousness here ends up with an account of explanation according to which it paradoxically must explain a thing by an appeal to its opposite—a result which naturally seems absurd. On the other hand, the principle of inversion is enlightening, since it forces natural consciousness to reverse all the key terms and categories of the dialectic. It is with this reversal that natural consciousness trades roles with the independently existing external object and comes to see the need to give an account of itself in the complete account of the determination of the subject-object Notion.

The inverted world begins when a second law is posited. The reader will recall where we left off the dialectic: the Notion of law broke down when natural consciousness realized it was a tautological redescription and not a true explanation. This first law was a law of sameness or of difference that was no difference.[147] In other words, there is no difference between the *explicans* and the *explicanda;* this is why the "explanation" is simply a redescription. What originally appeared as different collapses into identity. Presumably a true explanation would give an account of phenomena in a way that avoids simply redescribing in different terms what was happening. In order to avoid this tautology, natural consciousness posits a second law, but this time it is a law not of identity but of difference: "And thus we have a second law whose content is the opposite of what was previously called law, viz. difference which remains constantly selfsame; for this new law expresses rather that *like* becomes *unlike* and *unlike* becomes *like.*"[148] This second law posits something different from the phenomena in order to explain the phenomena. For instance, we can understand explanation as an account of the causes of any given phenomenon. The explanation of why X happened by enumerating the factors that caused it to happen must be made in a way such that the causes are different from the phenomenon to be explained. This would thus be a very different sort of explanation from the tautological account that claims opium induces sleep because it has a somnifacient property, where the cause is synonymous with the effect. Hence, the law of inversion states that whatever there is in phenomena must be truly in itself quite different from how it appears. In other words, something very different behind the scenes produces and grounds the phenomena.

In this way, the first supersensible world, i.e., the set of laws which mirrored the phenomena is replaced by a second supersensible world which does not mirror the phenomena but, in fact, is the opposite of them or is at least something sufficiently different from them to explain or ground them. In Hegel's words, "Through this principle [sc. that of difference], the first supersensible world, the tranquil kingdom of laws, the immediate copy of the perceived world, is changed into its opposite."[149] The second supersensible world now becomes the criterion for the subject-object Notion. Its principle is that the phenomena do not appear in the way that they are in themselves but rather as just the opposite of the way in which they truly are. Thus, the real supersensible world is an inversion of the phenomenal world. Hegel describes it thus: "*This second supersensible world* is in this way the *inverted* [*verkehrt*] world and, moreover, since one aspect is already present in the first supersensible world, the inversion of the first."[150] The inverted world is then an inversion of the first supersensible world by the simple principle of transitivity. Since the first supersensible world is a copy of the phenomenal world, and since the inverted world is an inversion of the phenomenal world, it follows that it is also an inversion of the first supersensible world.

Hegel emphasizes that the problem with the first supersensible world was that it lacked a principle of change. By this he means that in the first supersensible world there was no change or difference between the phenomenon and the explanation. Lacking any difference, they appeared identical. As we have seen, this Notion of law collapses into tautology. Now, in the inverted world, natural consciousness has adopted a principle of change which it uses to explain phenomena. Hegel says, "For the first supersensible world was only the *immediate* raising of the perceived world into the universal element; it had its necessary counterpart in this perceived world which still retained *for itself the principle of change and alteration.* The first kingdom of laws lacked that principle, but obtains it as an inverted world."[151] Hence, what is crucial about the inverted world is this concept of change or difference. It is this concept which moved natural consciousness beyond the dialectic of law and will bring it to the complex concept of "life."

Hegel describes the inverted world and its principle of change with a number of provocative examples which sound like paradoxes or outright contradictions: "what in the law of the first world is sweet, in this inverted in-itself is sour, what in the former is black is, in the other, white. What in the law of the first is the north pole of the magnet is, in its other, supersensible in-itself, the south pole: but what is there south pole is here north pole."[152] However, Hegel best articulates the inverted world with the simple principle which is its law: "what is *like* in the first world is *unlike* to itself, and what is *unlike* in the first world is equally *unlike to itself,* or it becomes *like* itself."[153] In sum, the law of the inverted world is a law of difference. Everything is turned into something different and appears as different from how it really is in itself. It is precisely this concept of difference or what we might call a principle of inversion that the secondary literature on this section has been unable to do much with. As a result, these strange formulations of the principle of inversion are quite often simply ignored. But we cannot ignore this principle of inversion if we are going to understand the transition to "Self-Consciousness," since precisely this principle plays the key role. Here I take Hegel quite literally to mean that at this stage the key point is that a difference arises between the terms of the dialectic. This is the absurd and paradoxical result of the breakdown of explanation, but, moreover, it compels natural consciousness to reverse the subject-object relation which it has hitherto been working with, and this reversal allows natural consciousness to see the need for giving an account of itself for the complete determination of the subject-object Notion.

Concluding Remarks (§§163–65)

Heretofore the object of consciousness as pure being, a thing with properties or a force, was thought to be independent of the subject. This relation to the world of objects without reference to the subject per se is what characterizes "Consciousness." Here when natural consciousness posits a law, it is able to see itself in the world and to recognize itself in the sphere of objects. Thus, consciousness becomes an object for itself, and this is what we call "self-consciousness." In considering a scientific law, consciousness realizes the law is not an independent object like the other objects of this chapter, but rather the object is dependent upon consciousness itself, which posits or formulates it: "the ego in its judgement has an object which is not distinct from it—it has itself. Consciousness has passed into self-consciousness."[154] This distinction found in the "Consciousness" and "Self-Consciousness" chapters between immediate awareness of objects and awareness of the self is found in various theories of childhood development such as, for instance, that of Piaget. According to this theory, children at an early age are able to perceive and recognize objects, but have no awareness of themselves as distinct and autonomous entities. They lack the ability to abstract and to see themselves from an external perspective. This is precisely what consciousness achieves at this point, since with the concept of law it recognizes itself in the external world and thus relates that world to itself. For the first time consciousness is able to see itself as an object.

Natural consciousness comes to recognize via the law of inversion or the law of difference that it has posited the object and that the object is not a fact about the world: "I put the 'opposite' here, and the 'other' of which it is the opposite, there."[155] Natural consciousness realizes that it is itself the ground of its experience. When natural consciousness comes to see this, it discovers simultaneously that in the determination of the Notion it plays a heretofore unseen role which presupposes an account of subjectivity which has not yet been considered. It realizes that in this mode of explanation it gives an account of things with this principle of difference. Natural consciousness only comes to discover the importance of difference or infinity with the concept of "explanation":

> Infinity, or this absolute unrest of pure self-movement, in which whatever is determined in one way or another, e.g. as being, is rather the opposite of this determinateness, this no doubt has been from the start the soul of all that has gone before; but it is in the *inner* world that it has first freely and clearly shown itself. Appearance, or the play of forces, already displays it, but it is as "*explanation*" that it first freely stands forth; and in being

finally an object for consciousness, as *that which it is*, consciousness is thus *self-consciousness*.[156]

In this crucial passage, Hegel discusses the role of infinity and explanation in the transition of consciousness to self-consciousness. In the concept of infinity or difference, which the inverted world introduces, consciousness for the first time sees itself in the process of determining the subject-object Notion, since it is only with the concept of difference that the law of inversion is generated, and from the law of inversion consciousness sees itself suddenly as the ground of objectivity. It is thus the paradoxes involved in explanation that bring about this self-realization. In fact, all along consciousness has played this epistemic role, but only here does it realize what the philosophical audience has long since known, namely, that consciousness plays a constitutive role in the determination of the criteria of the subject-object Notion, and thus an account of the subject itself must be given.

This crucial dialectical movement can best be understood by a comparison with the previous dialectic of law. It turned out that scientific law collapses into a tautological redescription of the phenomena, and, as we have seen, the inverted world is the solution to this problem, since its explanation is not a redescription of the phenomena but rather a contradiction or inversion of them. This is the key point, since it is here that natural consciousness's realism must finally be given up. Applying the principle of opposites or of difference characterized by the inverted world, natural consciousness realizes that the object which it took for something external is in fact a part of itself; likewise, what it took to be independent is thus dependent, and so forth. Thus, in the inverted world the object moves into, so to speak, the realm of the subject. The same dialectic of inversion occurs with the concept of "explanation." Up until this point "explanation" meant giving an account of something other and external, but now explanation is simply natural consciousness's account of itself and its own internal determinations. Explanation thus no longer refers to something other or beyond itself in the realm of experience, but rather, as the philosophical audience has known all along, it refers back to the subject. As we saw in the passage above, this was the upshot of everything which has happened up until this point, since we always ended up with universals, which natural consciousness could not explain by reference to experience. But only now through the concept of explanation does consciousness realize that it, in fact, plays a constitutive role in the determination of the subject-object Notion. Thus, "explanation" is not just an account of what appears in the phenomena, but it also implies an account of the principles of cognition of the self-conscious subject. Hegel expresses this as follows: "The understanding's 'explanation' is primarily only the description of what self-consciousness is."[157] "Explanation" thus indicates the role of the self-conscious subject in the determination of subject and object via the principles of cognition.

Hegel continues in the same vein, however, using different terms to describe this dual nature of the Notion of "explanation": "The reason why 'explaining' affords so much self-satisfaction is just because in it consciousness is, so to speak, communing directly with itself, enjoying only itself; although it seems to be busy with something else, it is in fact occupied only with itself."[158] Natural consciousness in the process of experience seems to busy itself simply with the *explicanda;* however, in the inverted world, it comes to realize that the scientific laws or the *explicans* are not facts about the world but rather issue from itself as subject. Thus, natural consciousness sees itself as playing a role in the process of the determination of the subject-object Notion.

Yet another important inversion for both this chapter and the next is that of the infinity of perceptions or the manifold, which were hitherto conceived as a part of the world. Now with the inversion, natural consciousness sees the infinity of the manifold as a part of itself: "This apprehension of the difference as it is *in truth,* or the apprehension of *infinity* as such, is *for us,* or *in itself* [i.e., is merely implicit]."[159] In other words, the truth of infinity is that it belongs to the self-conscious subject who plays a role in determining the Notion of objectivity and is not something given to the subject from outside. The infinity of difference is not simply found in the world but is at least in part a result of consciousness's positing. This is the universal infinity of "life" that Hegel will take up in the next chapter, "Self-Consciousness."

Once natural consciousness has, by means of the inverted world, made this realization about its role in the process of the self-determination of subject and object, then the dualism of the inverted world falls away of its own accord. In other words, there is no longer any reason to attribute something substantial to the realm behind the appearances, since natural consciousness recognizes itself as the ground of appearances: "This curtain [of appearance] hanging before the inner world is therefore drawn away, and we have the inner being [the 'I'] gazing into the inner world."[160] In short, now natural consciousness recognizes itself on both sides of the former dualism, i.e., on the side of appearances (as it had formerly seen itself) and now on the side of the ground of appearances. Consciousness sees itself in the world of appearances for the first time as an object and thus becomes self-conscious: consciousness "posits itself as an inner being containing different moments, but for which equally these moments are immediately *not* different—*self-consciousness.*"[161] Thus, the dualism collapses into the unity of the self-conscious subject who is now both subject and object.

What the "Consciousness" chapter has shown is the futility of attempting to give an account of objectivity with the presupposition that the categories are in the empirical manifold itself. Every realist attempt to give an account of objects turns out contradictory and points back to the role of the subject. An account of the subject is necessarily presupposed in any account of objectivity. This is precisely the point of the "Consciousness" chapter; namely, all attempts to give an account of the determination of objectivity without reference to the subject's formative and substantive role in that determination are necessarily contradictory and incomplete, since such an account necessarily presupposes an account of the subject. In order to give an account of objectivity, one must first come to terms with the constitutive role of the subject which that account presupposes. Hegel writes, "The *necessary advance* from the previous shapes of consciousness for which their truth was a thing, an 'other' than themselves expresses just this, that not only is consciousness of a thing possible only for a self-consciousness, but that self-consciousness alone is the truth of those shapes."[162] Thus, the forms of consciousness implicitly imply a self-conscious subject. All realist accounts must of necessity fail, since they cling to the notion of an independent external object, and thus they never recognize the constitutive role of the subject. Yet their account necessarily presupposes an account of subjectivity which they fail to see. Up until this point the various principles of cognition—being, the one and the many, and ground—have all been applied directly to the objects in the world. Now we have arrived at the reflexive turn where consciousness, now self-consciousness, turns these same categories onto itself in an attempt to determine itself consistently as a self-conscious subject. In the last sentence of the "Consciousness" chapter, Hegel writes, "it will be equally evident that the cognition of *what consciousness knows in knowing itself,* requires a still more complex movement, the exposition of which is contained in what follows."[163] An account must be given of consciousness's knowledge of itself in order for the Notion to be completely determined.

The dialectic of universal and particular here in the "Force and the Understanding" section is easy to recognize. At first, the universal is the force that operates beyond the world of sense; this universal unseen force produces a plurality of empirical manifestations which are the particulars. When the dialectic proves this dualism to be untenable, the universal force then is interpreted as a scientific law that explains the world of sense. The laws of science are universals that order the various empirical phenomena, i.e., the particulars, under organized headings. The issue of immediacy and mediation is also present here in "Force and the Understanding." At first force is considered to be the unmediated universal; it is immediately determined on its own apart from human understanding. Yet this turns out to be contradictory, since in order to be recognized as individual in the first place, force must be mediated by a plurality of empirical manifestations by means of which consciousness has access to it. Thus, the force is mediated by its matters or manifestations. So also with the scientific laws. Without the various empirical phenomena, there would be no general law. Thus, law is mediated by the natural phenomena that it is meant to explain.

The individual sections of the "Consciousness" chapter parallel one another with respect to structure, although they each operate with a different category and a different Notion of the object. We can represent this movement graphically as in table 4.1. At each stage a more sophisticated category is applied to the object domain in order to determine the object completely. However, as we have seen, each of the object-Notions here in "Consciousness" proves to be internally contradictory and incomplete. Insofar as the categories become more sophisticated, the movement of the dialectic is an ascending one. This parallel structure of in-itself, for-itself, and in-and-for-itself in the "Consciousness" chapter is a model case for the later chapters, where this movement is often more difficult to locate. Nonetheless, this parallelism helps us to see the unitary plan and, with the repeating categories that we will see in the subjective sphere in "Self-Consciousness," forms a strong argument for the unitary structure of the *Phenomenology* as a whole.

Table 4.1

Category	Section	In-Itself	For-Itself	In-and-For-Itself
Ground and Consequence	Force and the Understanding	Force and Matters (Force Proper and Force Expressed)	Law	The Inverted World
One and Many	Perception	Thing with Properties (The One and the Also)	Perceiving Subject (The One and the Also)	Moment of Perceptual Contact (The One and the Also)
Being	Sense-Certainty	The This (The Here and the Now)	The "I"	The Point of Contact (The Here and the Now)

5

Self-Consciousness

The importance of the "Self-Consciousness" chapter for an understanding of the *Phenomenology* is beyond doubt. It is the most read and most quoted section of the book,[1] and many commentators such as Kojève[2] use it as a foundation for an interpretation of the *Phenomenology* as a whole; moreover, Hegel himself dubbed this chapter the "turning point" in his argument.[3] The philological evidence as well seems to support the claim for the importance of this section of text, since Hegel carefully reworked the material found here throughout the Jena period. Yet precisely here in the sequence of the dialectic Hegel seems to introduce a wholly new theme. The discussion seems to move away from the epistemological issues that have been examined up until this point and to take up issues of intersubjective human relations. As was mentioned above, this apparent change in content gives rise to questions about the continuity of these first two chapters. As one commentator puts it, "In short, this is as important a transition as any in Hegel, and it is unfortunately as opaque, if not more so, than any other."[4] As I have indicated, this chapter is continuous with the "Consciousness" chapter in its goals and methodology. Once again, criteria for the subject-object Notion are posited and tested just as they were in the preceding section. The crucial difference here at the level of self-consciousness is that consciousness has become aware of the need to give an account of its own self-determination in order to account for possible knowledge of objects. It realizes not only that an adequate Notion of the subject must be found, but also that such a subject-Notion changes with the object-Notion. In an attempt to give an account of the subject and thus of the object domain, natural consciousness here applies to itself as self-conscious subject the categories which in the "Consciousness" chapter were applied to the other as object. Thus, as I have indicated earlier, the categories, which were applied to the empirical manifold or, more exactly, to the object of consciousness in the "Consciousness" chapter, reappear here at a higher level in the same order, paralleling the earlier movement.

The important point is that at the level of self-consciousness the independent, self-determined object has disappeared.[5] Unlike in the "Consciousness" chapter, natural consciousness no longer believes in an independent other of thought or something substantial which is external to itself and which could function as some sort of privileged epistemic ground. Natural consciousness now sees itself as playing a constitutive role in the determination of the object-Notion. This then, as we have seen, implies an account of itself as subject. What is immediate and true is no longer the object but rather the self-conscious subject. This is the Notion that in its various forms is presented throughout the "Self-Consciousness" chapter. We will analyze natural consciousness' attempt to follow through with this Notion by trying to match it up consistently with its experience.

We will discover that the attempt to determine the subject-object Notion only by an account of the individual subject without reference to other subjects leads to contradictions. These contradictions point to the role of the social community and historical relations in the determination of the Notion in the same way that the object models of "Consciousness" broke down while pointing to the role of the subject in a complete account of the self-determination of the Notion. The key is that the account of the purely subjective determination of the subject-object Notion which portrays the subject as purely atomic is self-contradictory and necessarily presupposes an account of the subject in a wider social and historical context. Thus, what Hegel intends to show in this section is that the determination of the subject-object Notion by the self-conscious subject presupposes certain social practices and institutions which in traditional epistemological theories are usually not considered to play any meaningful role. In the "Reason" chapter, just these sorts of things come to be included in the account.

Here in the "Self-Consciousness" chapter, the formal categories that were set out so clearly in the "Consciousness" chapter are still operative, yet they are reinterpreted in what we might call a subjective context, i.e., without reference to an external object or to the wider social and historical context. The initial category of being comes to be understood in the "Self-Consciousness" chapter as the self-conscious subject itself constituted by "desire." In the "Lordship and Bondage" section, the account of recognition represents in its concrete social form the dialectical play of the category of the one and the many. Finally, the "Freedom of Self-Consciousness" section provides us with different examples of the category of ground at the level of self-consciousness. Hence, the categories for the determination of the subject-object Notion repeat themselves here in the "Self-Consciousness" chapter, but this time on the side of the subject. The "Consciousness" chapter on the whole can be seen as the in-itself moment, since each of the Notions examined there involved the belief in the truth of independent external objects. On the other hand, "Self-Consciousness," with its claim for the truth of the subject and the relegation of the objective sphere to a secondary position, can be seen as the for-itself moment. "Consciousness" thus represents an ontology of objects, while "Self-Consciousness" represents an ontology of subjects.

In my analysis, I will occasionally make use of the term "natural consciousness," although, strictly speaking, this term is no longer applicable at this stage, since natural consciousness has given up the "natural point of view," i.e., that there are independent, external objects. By "natural consciousness," I mean at this level simply to refer to the phenomenological actor in contrast to the philosophical audience. I want to continue using this term in this sense and do not mean to imply that here in "Self-Consciousness" we are still examining the view held in the various stages of the "Consciousness" chapter.

I. The Truth of Self-Certainty: "Self-Consciousness" and "Life" (§§166–77)

This section, which immediately precedes the most famous and most read section of the *Phenomenology*—the lordship-bondage dialectic—is, along with the chapter "Force and the Understanding," among the most opaque in the Hegelian corpus. As a result, there is little agreement in the literature concerning what Hegel expects it to accomplish or how the dialectic is supposed to work. Some commentators[6] see this first section of the "Self-Consciousness" chapter, entitled "The Truth of Self-Certainty," as a simple introduction to the substantive philosophical issues which follow in the "Lordship and Bondage" section. Other commentators[7] see this section as incomplete or as presupposing some of the dialectical moves that we find in some of Hegel's other Jena writings. The original source of confusion stems from Hegel's own outline. When one looks at the "Self-Consciousness" chapter in the table of contents, one notices straightaway a certain asymmetry. Whereas Hegel in the rest of the book orders his chapters into three sections, here we seem to have only two sections, "A. Lordship and Bondage" and "B. Freedom of Self-Consciousness," that fall under the heading of "IV. The Truth of Self-Certainty." Because of this asymmetry, there is some confusion about the status of the section "The Truth of Self-Certainty." The main problem is that Hegel wrote a second table of contents with the Latin letters (A, B, C, etc.) in addition to the original table of contents, which was ordered only according to Roman numerals. My thesis is that the material in the "Self-Consciousness" chapter preceding the "Lordship and Bondage" dialectic, which is purportedly only introductory, is in fact expected to do philosophical work and thus is not merely intended as an introduction. Specifically, I wish to argue that this section, in fact, forms the first argumentative step in the "Self-Consciousness" chapter, and that it forms the first of a three-step argument that is complemented by "Lordship and Bondage" and the "Freedom of Self-Consciousness." I refer to this material for the sake of simplicity as "The Truth of Self-Certainty," although this title originally was apparently intended to cover the dialectical movements of "Lordship and Bondage" and the "Freedom of Self-Consciousness." Thus, I propose to read the "Self-Consciousness" chapter with the following structure: (1) The Truth of Self-Certainty (§§ 166–77), (2) Lordship and Bondage (§§ 178–96), and (3) Freedom of Self-Consciousness (§§ 197–230).

There are three important arguments that speak in favor of this view and against the thesis that "The Truth of Self-Certainty" constitutes only introductory material or forms something distinct from the course of the argumentation of the rest of the "Self-Consciousness" chapter. First, when Hegel reworked the same material in the *Encyclopaedia*, he removed the apparent asymmetry in the "Self-Consciousness" chapter and used the material that I am calling "The Truth of Self-Certainty" as the first part of a three-step argument in precisely the way I have indicated above. In the *Philosophy of Mind*, which constitutes the third part of the *Encyclopaedia*, the "Self-Consciousness" chapter is organized as follows:

B) Self-Consciousness
   α) Appetite
   β) Self-Consciousness Recognitive
   γ) Universal Self-Consciousness

From the contents of this chapter it is clear that "Appetite" corresponds to "The Truth of Self-Certainty" where the key term is "desire." It is likewise obvious that "Self-Consciousness Recognitive" corresponds to "Lordship and Bondage," where the key category is recognition (*Anerkennung*), and finally that "Universal Self-Consciousness" corresponds to "Freedom of Self-Consciousness."

Second, in addition to Hegel's account of "Self-Consciousness" in the *Encyclopaedia*, we also have his analysis from *The Philosophical Propaedeutic*, written during the Nüremberg Period from 1808 to 1811, shortly after the *Phenomenology*. "Self-Consciousness," according to the discussion there, likewise contains three different moments:

Self-Consciousness has, in its formative development or movement, three stages:

(1) Of *Desire* insofar as it is directed to other things;

(2) Of the relation of *Master and Slave* insofar as it is directed to another self-consciousness unlike itself;

(3) Of the *Universal Self-Consciousness* which recognizes itself in other self-consciousnesses and is identical with them as they are identical with it.[8]

In the course of this discussion Hegel likewise leaves no ambiguity about the fact that the material preceding the "Lordship and Bondage" dialectic in the *Phenomenology* corresponds to the first stage, i.e., that of "desire," in the *Propaedeutic.*

The third argument that speaks against the thesis that the material preceding "Lordship and Bondage" forms only an introductory section concerns the subject matter of the section itself. When we examine the text closely, we see that the argument here parallels the argument that was given in "Sense-Certainty," the first section of the "Consciousness" chapter. In "Sense-Certainty" we are concerned with the pure being of the object, which at the beginning of "Self-Consciousness" becomes reinterpreted as the pure being of the subject. Moreover, "Lordship and Bondage" parallels the "Perception" section in a similar fashion. In "Perception," a second object is introduced, and the categories of identity and difference become relevant for the determination of objectivity. So also in "Lordship and Bondage" we see a second self-consciousness introduced for the first time which forms a standard for comparison and contrast for the other, and it is this standard which then serves to determine the self-conscious subject. Finally, the "Freedom of Self-Consciousness" parallels the "Force and the Understanding" section. Instead of forces operating behind the scenes causing the world of experience to appear as in "Force and the Understanding," in the "Unhappy Consciousness" section it is a self-conscious other, God, or what Hegel calls "the unchangeable,"[9] which constitutes the otherworldly reality which is responsible for the mutable mundane sphere. This structural parallelism of the two chapters indicates that this material at the beginning of "Self-Consciousness" is intended as an independent argument in its own right, just as "Sense-Certainty" was an independent argument at the earlier stage.

Here in the opening section, the category of being is posited again and the accompanying dialectic with the problem of universality is repeated. In the "Sense-Certainty" section of the "Consciousness" chapter, consciousness posited being, qua criterion for the object, as the other of consciousness; however, here self-consciousness considers itself as pure being and considers the rest of the world as inessential. As Hegel says, it negates the other. We will see in the course of the dialectic how the category of being again breaks down due to its universality and at the abstract categorial level how it is unable to distinguish one thing (here itself as a self-conscious subject) from another. Thus, at first the category of being was applied to the sphere of objects, and now it is applied to the self-conscious subject. We will further see here at the social level self-consciousness' need for mediation of its determinations through other self-conscious subjects. Hence, despite the change in the language, the procedure remains the same, and the pursuit of truth and a consistent subject-object Notion remains the overriding goal. As one commentator has put it, "The project of the relation between self and objects/others can be named knowledge in general; the project of the relation of the self and itself can be named self-knowledge. These projects can appear to be separate; but in the [*Phenomenology*] they are fused."[10]

This initial section of the "Self-Consciousness" chapter, to which I have transferred the title "The Truth of Self-Certainty," indicates the shift in the Notions of truth and certainty from the object to the subject. At the corresponding stage in the "Consciousness" chapter, we were concerned with sense-*certainty*, i.e., consciousness was certain of the other which was immediately given in sense; however, here we are concerned with self-*certainty*, since consciousness has become its own object and has given up the idea of an independent other. The goal of this section is to give an account of the subject, given that we have determined that it is essentially and necessarily bound up with subject-object determinations in ways that we did not suspect in the "Consciousness" chapter. In other words, self-consciousness' relation to itself as object makes it self-certain and not merely certain of the truth of external objects.

Hegel states that a new conception of "certainty" arises which we have not seen before. He says, "But now there has arisen what did not emerge in these previous relationships, viz. a certainty which is identical with its truth; for the certainty is to itself its own object, and consciousness is to itself the truth."[11] What Hegel means by this must be shown with respect to the conclusions obtained from the "Consciousness" chapter. There, when the criteria for subject and object were thought to be external and independent of consciousness, truth and certainty were domiciled in those objects which consciousness saw as facts in the world and not as issuing from itself. In "Sense-Certainty," for instance, a thing was "true" if it was an immediate this, here, now, regardless of the role of consciousness. Natural consciousness was certain of its object qua object; however, the outcome of the "Consciousness" chapter was that knowledge of objects necessarily presupposed the role of the subject.

This means that apart from the subject there can be no truth or certainty as before. Now when Hegel says, "the certainty is to itself its own object, and consciousness is to itself the truth," he means natural consciousness now realizes that it, as subject, constitutes, in part, the criteria for certainty and that in this way consciousness is to itself the truth. Consciousness is certain of *itself* qua object.

The result of consciousness' realization of its own role in the self-determination of the subject-object Notion is that consciousness now comes to see itself as the object of the inquiry and tries to articulate itself consistently as a knowing subject. Hegel expresses this succinctly in his Jena lectures: "the I has become the object."[12] This act of consciousness reflecting upon itself is the beginning of self-consciousness. As I have indicated, consciousness does so by using the same categories, albeit interpreted in a different context, by which formerly objects were thought to be determined. Here at the beginning of the "Self-Consciousness" chapter, Hegel makes clear what he takes the difference between consciousness and self-consciousness to be. He explicitly characterizes the "Self-Consciousness" chapter as "knowing of itself," and contrasts this conception with the "Consciousness" chapter, which he describes as "the knowing of an other."[13] Here in the "Self-Consciousness" chapter, we must examine the self-conscious subject's self-determination as a necessary presupposition for the determination of the object-Notion.

For Hegel, although self-consciousness is necessary for an account of objectivity, it is not per se an ultimate epistemological foundation. Hegel wants to show that although this view is an improvement over the naive realism of the "Consciousness" chapter, an account of the determination of the subject-object Notion *only* by means of an account of the faculties of knowing of the individual self-conscious subject is necessarily inadequate and implies a further account of the relevant intersubjective relations and determinations. In the *Philosophy of Right*, Hegel writes, "in Fichte . . . the ego, as that which is without limitation, is taken (in the first proposition of his *Science of Knowledge*) purely and simply as something positive and so as the universality and identity of the understanding. The result is that this abstract ego by itself is supposed to be the whole truth."[14] This view, for Hegel, is one-sided and thus incomplete, since it stops short of giving an account of the individual in society or of the society in history and how these factors shape the process of the determination of the Notion.

According to the object-Notion examined in the "Consciousness" chapter, objects—the immediate given, the thing with properties, and the explanatory forces—were considered to be essentially independent and distinct from the subject. These subject-object Notions, as we have seen, at that level proved to be inadequate. Hegel expresses this in the opening lines of the "Self-Consciousness" chapter: "In the previous modes of certainty what is true for consciousness is something other than itself. But the Notion of this truth vanishes in the experience of it."[15] What Hegel means by this is that according to this subject-object Notion, the criteria were always applied to these objects which were the independent other of consciousness, but in the course of the dialectical experience this account of subjectivity and objectivity proved contradictory. The Notion did not match our experience of it: "What the object immediately was *in itself*—mere being in sense-certainty, the concrete thing of perception, and for the understanding, a force—proves to be in truth, not this at all; instead, this *in-itself* turns out to be a mode in which the object is only for an other."[16] We discovered that these conceptions were not part of the object domain itself as preconstituted, but rather that these were object-Notions posited by a subject. These conceptions are not part of the objects in themselves, but rather they are for natural consciousness: "The [mere] *being* of what is merely 'meant' [in 'Sense-Certainty']; the *singleness* and *universality* opposed to it of perception, as also the *empty inner* being of the understanding, these are no longer essences, but are moments of self-consciousness."[17] The dialectic of the inverted world completed this sequence of criteria by showing the inconsistencies involved in attributing the categories to something other or distinct from consciousness and demonstrated via the account of explanation that natural consciousness is bound up in the process of establishing the criteria for truth. Now these same criteria must be applied to the subject which is now considered the ground of all knowing. We must now examine in some detail what follows from this conclusion.

At the end of "Force and the Understanding," we saw how the category of ground broke down in the inverted world and how natural consciousness at that point finally eliminated the ground-appearance dualism. Natural consciousness, through the principle of inversion, saw itself as the ground; the appearances, with which it had formerly associated itself, simply become insubstantial parts of itself. Now neither ground nor appearance is something foreign or external, but rather both belong to the sphere of the subject. Hence, the ground-appearance dualism collapses into pure subjectivity. This is the first dialectical stage of "Self-Consciousness."

The Notion: "Self-Consciousness" and "Life" (§§166–68)

Hegel signals the beginning of the construction of the Notion in this opening section when he writes, "We have now to see how the shape of self-consciousness first makes its appearance."[18] We start here in "Self-Consciousness" with a subjective monism that is the immediate result of what has come before. Here at the beginning of the "Self-Consciousness" chapter, consciousness has two objects—itself and the insubstantial object. "Consciousness, as self-consciousness, henceforth has a double object," Hegel writes, "one is the immediate object, that of sense-certainty and perception, which however *for self-consciousness* has the character of a *negative*; and the second, viz. *itself*, which is the true *essence*."[19] The object of the earlier dialectic still remains but only in a negative, inessential sense. In other words, the external object is not perceived to have its own independent existence. Formerly, consciousness only contemplated the object together with the inconsistencies and incongruities of its Notion, but now that it has realized the role it plays in the subject-object Notion, it must also contemplate itself contemplating the object. Self-consciousness thus involves a self-awareness that was not present at the level of consciousness, where we were concerned with consciousness' simple awareness of the object sphere. The self-conscious subject represents the essential and the positive in this relationship since the account of subjectivity is a necessary precondition for an account of objectivity.

Now, self-consciousness as the dominant member in this subject-object relationship denies the essential, external reality of the other which Hegel refers to as "life."[20] Hegel says, "In this there is indeed an otherness; that is to say, consciousness makes a distinction, but one which at the same time is for consciousness *not* a distinction."[21] What Hegel means by this curious oxymoron is that at this initial level, self-consciousness does not recognize objects as independent and thus does not distinguish itself from others. Self-consciousness is pure being, and it thus engulfs all otherness. In the *Encyclopaedia Logic*, he writes:

> We may say "I" and thought are the same, or, more definitely, "I" is thought as a thinker. What I have in my consciousness is for me. "I" is the vacuum or receptacle for anything and everything: for which everything is and which stores up everything in itself. . . . In other words, it is not a mere universality and nothing more, but the universality which includes in it everything.[22]

The object sphere is absorbed in the universality of the subject. Since at this level pure subjectivity is thought to be a necessary condition for an account of objectivity, the objects themselves have no autonomous reality apart from the subject-Notion. Thus, when self-consciousness sees an object, it does not see an independent other but rather its own thought determination. This seems to imply a curious sort of pantheism, in which self-consciousness sees its objects and nature as a whole as something living and participating in its own subjectivity. This aspect of the dialectic we will pursue further below. Hegel gives another characterization which is a bit more illuminating: "Opposed to an other, the 'I' is its own self, and at the same time it overarches this other which, for the 'I,' is equally only the 'I' itself."[23] Not only is there obvious and simple self-identity of the self-conscious subject, but the object is also bound up with the subject as well—it too "is equally only the 'I' itself." By "overarching" here Hegel means that the object sphere is thought to be dependent on the self-conscious subject or is merely for the use and enjoyment of self-consciousness.

Hegel claims that the objects of "Sense-Certainty," "Perception," and "Force and the Understanding" have disappeared, since at this point they are simply continuous with the being of the subject. They exist, but only in an insubstantial sense:

> If we consider this new shape of knowing, the knowing of itself [self-consciousness], in relation to that which preceded, viz. the knowing of an other [consciousness], then we see that though this other has indeed vanished, its moments have at the same time no less been preserved, and the loss consists in this, that here they are present as they are in themselves.[24]

Since one realizes that the subject plays a role in the determinations of objects, these objects "are present in themselves," i.e., we finally realize them (at least partially) for what they are, i.e., determinations of the subject. What has vanished is the belief that the object is an independent substantial other: "Thus it seems that only the principal moment itself has been lost, viz. the *simple self-subsistent existence* for consciousness."[25] Objects are now connected to consciousness and are necessarily bound up with it. They are thus in themselves insubstantial, while self-consciousness represents the essential element as pure being.

Hegel discusses the universality of self-consciousness with an allusion to Fichte: "As self-conscious, it is movement; but since what it distinguishes from itself is *only itself as* itself, the difference, as an otherness, is *immediately superseded* for it; the difference *is not*, and it [self-consciousness] is only the motionless tautology of: 'I am I.' "[26] In the *Philosophy of Right*, Hegel describes this aspect of self-consciousness in a similar fashion: "The subjectivity of the will means therefore (a) the pure form of the will, the absolute unity of self-consciousness with itself (a unity in which self-consciousness, as I = I, is purely and simply inward and abstractly self-dependent), the pure certainty, as distinguished from the truth, of individuality."[27] Here self-consciousness does not recognize anything essential or substantial that is external to itself. What Hegel calls here the "motionless tautology" is in fact Fichte's first proposition in the *Science of Knowledge.*[28] By the phrase "I am I" Fichte tries to capture the unity of self-consciousness with its representations or with the objective sphere in general. Thus, "I am I" means that the objects qua representations are just as much a part of the subject as the subject itself. The world consists merely of the subject's determinations.

In the *Phenomenology,* Hegel tells us explicitly that the "I" represents the category of universal being here at the level of self-consciousness. Hegel, in considering this moment, characterizes it as "*immediate* unity," or as that "unity expressed as a [mere] *being.*"[29] Clearly, the "I" here in "The Truth of Self-Certainty" parallels the "This" of "Sense-Certainty" since, as we have seen, the "This" was also the immediate given which was determined by the category of being. In another passage, Hegel indicates the enriched nature of this Notion of being at this new level in reference to the same Notion at the level of sense-certainty: "*Being* no longer has the significance of *abstract* being, nor has their pure essentiality the significance of *abstract* universality; on the contrary, their being is precisely that simple fluid substance of pure movement within itself."[30] The being of "Sense-Certainty" was, as we have seen, abstract universality which could not be made particular. Here Hegel indicates that this Notion has been preserved at this level, yet reinterpreted as the bizarre concept of fluid substance, which is associated with Hegel's equally bizarre concept of "life" which we will examine below. In any case, the parallelism between the two sections is clear: the category of being once belonged to the object as a "This" and now to the subject as an "I." It is no longer abstract but rather is bound up with the problematic concepts of "life" and desire.

Hegel now introduces without any preliminary explanation his difficult and disputed concept of desire (*Begierde*), which on the face of it seems to have nothing to do with the knowledge problematic. He says, "this unity [of self-consciousness with itself] must become essential to self-consciousness, i.e. self-consciousness is *desire* in general."[31] It is certainly difficult to see how Hegel's *id est* clause is meant to clarify what comes before it.[32] In the passage immediately preceding this, Hegel discusses the unity of appearance with the self-conscious subject; this is what he means by the unity of self-consciousness with itself, i.e., the unity of appearances produced by self-consciousness with self-consciousness itself is tantamount, à la Fichte, to the unity of self-consciousness with itself. Since self-consciousness is bound up with the criteria for objectivity and appearances, and since self-consciousness perceives itself as pure being without division or separation, self-consciousness and these appearances are united. The pure being of self-consciousness is manifested empirically in terms of universal, unmediated, unbroken desire which forms self-consciousness' immediate relation to objects.

Desire as well plays a role in the self-determination of the subject-object Notion. Since self-consciousness attempts to give an account of itself alone without the mediation of other subjects and without reference to historical or social institutions, the criterion for the Notion of subjectivity must be entirely subjective in the strictest sense. The first account of the subject involves the subject in its immediate or natural state, and in this element simple, immediate desire is its most important characteristic. The criterion must belong to the subject's immediate desire, which is subjective in this way. Objects for self-consciousness are simply objects of its desire. Desire is thus an extension of the first abstract criterion for objectivity, or, put differently, it is a manifestation of being at the level of self-consciousness, and this is why Hegel takes the claim that "self-consciousness is *desire* in general" to be an explanation of the claim that the unity of self-consciousness with itself is essential to self-consciousness. In other words, unity is possible through desire as an extension of the criterion for objectivity applied to the subject. As one commentator has put it, "The dialectic of knowledge and the dialectic of desire are not separate dialectics."[33] Desire is pure being's universal negation of objects for self-consciousness, and thus an object is always an object of desire: "Self-consciousness . . . is simply *for itself* and directly characterizes its object as a negative element, or is primarily *desire*."[34] And an object of desire is hence always related to self-consciousness; so it follows that there must be a unity of self-consciousness with its appearances or with itself as Hegel claims. Not only is Hegel's claim about desire an explanation of what precedes it, but indeed, the two statements are tautological. To say that the desire of self-consciousness plays a role in the criterion for the subject-object Notion is also to say that objects are essentially bound up with the self-conscious subject.

In the *Philosophy of Right*, Hegel characterizes the immediate subject determined by desires as the "natural will." He writes, "The specific characteristics of the difference which the self-determining concept sets up within the will appear in the natural will as an immediately existing content, i.e. as the impulses, desires [*Begierden*], inclinations, whereby the will finds itself determined in the course of nature."[35] Hegel indicates that this is the most basic model of the subject, i.e., the subject in its immediacy with given natural desires as its most important element. Just as we began in "Sense-Certainty" with the most basic conception of objectivity, so also here in "The Truth of Self-Certainty" we begin with the most basic conception of a subject: a natural subject determined by natural desire.

This reference to the natural will affords us an occasion to step back from the dense epistemological language we have just examined and look at a concrete example. We have seen here that Hegel intends to portray the "natural will" of self-consciousness in its most rudimentary condition. Empirically, the most basic or immediate state of human consciousness is that of infancy. The human infant is characterized primarily by desires, since its higher faculties are not yet developed. Hegel's description of the natural will as a bundle of "impulses, desires, inclinations," etc. could be used as an accurate description of human infants. This example not only helps us to understand Hegel's discussion of desire, but also his earlier account of the universality of self-consciousness, which "overarches" or "negates" the object sphere. As we know from child psychology, children only gradually learn to distinguish themselves from their environment, and only later develop the ability of abstraction that allows them to see themselves as objects. Originally, they cannot discriminate, and they view the world simply as an extension of their own being. Thus, Hegel's attempt to describe the natural will or the most basic form of self-consciousness can be quite reasonably understood apart from the terse language employed here.

Now that we have seen the same criterion for the Notion posited again at a higher level, i.e., at the level of subjectivity, we must try to understand how the dialectic operates here. The important point to keep in mind is that we are still concerned with what I have been calling "the problem of truth." The "Self-Consciousness" chapter just like the "Consciousness" chapter pursues the goal of attaining the satisfactory or complete self-development of the Notion of the subject and object by a dialectical examination of internally inconsistent criteria. Hence, although the criterion has now switched to the side of the subject and thus differs from the criteria that preceded it, nevertheless the problem and the method for its solution remain the same. These two chapters are indeed engaged in the same project, and the break between them is not as great as some authors would have us believe.

The terms of the dualism in the Notion at this stage are self-consciousness and life, as Hegel says in the following passage: "and this Notion sunders itself into the antithesis of self-consciousness and life."[36] Like all of the Notions examined heretofore, this one is composed of two elements which hang together in an uneasy relation and which prove ultimately to be its undoing. Here self-consciousness represents the subjective side, while "life" represents the objective side. In his Jena lectures, Hegel discusses this identity of the two: "The two sides are so identical to one another that here too what they are in themselves falls apart into two equivalent aspects. The universality as such is only the one; being, however, is the reality itself, subsistence as multiplicity."[37] Hegel underlines the importance of the universal term "being," which represents the self-consciousness in which all other reality loses its independence. He indicates that the Notion is complete and that the dialectical experience of consciousness is about to begin when he writes that despite self-consciousness' assertion of its independence and control over objects, it will nevertheless "on the contrary, learn through experience that the object is independent."[38] Here Hegel briefly summarizes the Notion and looks ahead to its dialectical sublation.

The Experience of Consciousness

The In-Itself Moment: "Life" (§§169–72)

We begin with an analysis of the inessential objective sphere and its immediate continuity with consciousness, which Hegel characterizes with the concept of "life,"[39] and later we will examine the subjective aspect of this Notion. Hegel says that "life" is a conception of the object sphere that appears for the first time in the "Self-Consciousness" chapter. He claims the object of desire has "life": "the object of immediate desire is a *living thing*."[40] Although this at first seems puzzling, we can understand what Hegel means here by an analysis of a parallel passage from the *Philosophy of Right*. There, he defines the term "life" in an illuminating way: "The comprehensive sum of external activity, i.e. life, is not external to personality as that which itself is immediate and a *this*. The surrender or the sacrifice of life is not the existence of *this* personality but the very opposite."[41] By "life" Hegel means the inessential objective sphere here at the level of self-consciousness, toward which self-consciousness directs its desires. As this passage indicates, this sphere differs from the "This" of "Sense-Certainty," insofar as the former is bound up with the self-conscious subject, while the latter was thought to be independent. Thus, objects are not considered "living" in any truly vitalist sense, but rather they are merely the objects of desire. Desire amounts to the individual's desire to preserve his own identity and individuality by negating other insubstantial objects and by reinterpreting the world by means of this criterion. The world is appropriated in accordance with the needs and desires of the self-conscious subject in the pursuit of its self-identity, and the concept of "life" functions as an abstract category for the world of nature that self-consciousness makes use of.[42] The important point to note about this concept of "life" is that it is the manifestation of the inessential universality of being at the level of self-consciousness. In the next section, Hegel makes exactly this connection, referring to the "being of *life*."[43] He tries to describe this concept with terms such as "fluidity," "flux," "fluent continuity," "movement," etc., all of which are meant to signify the universality at the level of self-consciousness. He, for instance, characterizes "life" as "the universal fluid medium" or as "the *universal* substance."[44]

Hegel refers to three discrete stages that "life" works through and which culminate in its sublation. First, it is "*essence*" or "the *supersession* of all distinctions."[45] Hegel describes this aspect as follows: "as the first moment, the subsistence of the independent shapes, or the suppression of what diremption is in itself, viz. that the shapes have no being in themselves, no enduring existence."[46] By this Hegel means to refer to the object sphere's immediate continuity and universality. According to the Notion, the world of objects is an unbroken continuity that stands opposite consciousness. There are originally no individual objects that stand out in this continuity. Such individual entities have been "overcome" or "superseded."

At the second stage, this continuity in the object sphere is broken by activity of objects in the external sphere that set them apart from the continuity. Some objects, e.g. animals, seem to have an independent existence: "it comes forward in antithesis to the *universal* substance, disowns this fluent continuity with it and asserts that it is not dissolved in this universal element, but on the contrary preserves itself by separating itself from this its inorganic nature, and by consuming it."[47] Here Hegel refers back to the passage in "Sense-Certainty," cited above, in which he claimed that this destruction of the objective sphere was the form of sense-certainty at the level of self-consciousness. Once again, he claims that animals, "do not just stand idly in front of sensuous things as if these possessed intrinsic being, but, despairing of their reality, and completely assured of their nothingness, they fall to without ceremony and eat them up."[48] The universality or self-identity of "life" or the object sphere thus contains an aspect of particularity or difference which stands apart from the universality.

In the third moment, these differences are overcome and the original unity and continuity of the object sphere is reestablished. According to the Notion, the object sphere is inessential and indeterminate, and thus individual objects should not be able to be differentiated. Distinctions cannot be made in seamless being: "The *difference*, however, *qua* difference, of these members with respect to one another consists in general in no other *determinateness* than that of the moments of infinity or of the pure movement itself."[49] In other words, there is no genuine moment of difference to be discerned in nature. "Life" is an abstract universal that encompasses everything including the seeming difference at the second stage. Both are living and exist in the medium of "life." Thus, the individual moments cease to exist and the dualism disappears: "With this, the two sides of the whole movement which before were distinguished, viz. the passive separatedness of the shapes in the general medium of independence, and the process of life, collapse into one another."[50]

With the dualism overcome, we now have a new form of unity with the object; however, this unity is no longer immediate like the first unity, but rather it is a unity that is mediated by the movement we have just examined. It is mediated by the awareness of the differences or of the individual objects that must be overcome:

> Since we started from the first immediate unity and returned through the moments of formation and of process to the unity of both these moments, and thus back again to the original simple substance, this *reflected* unity is different from the first. Contrasted with that *immediate* unity, or that unity expressed as a [mere] *being*, this second is the *universal* unity which contains all these moments as superseded within itself.[51]

Here Hegel makes it clear once again that we are concerned with the same category as before—pure being—but this time at a higher, richer level. Here the category of being is still at work, but it is not immediate undifferentiated being as before; rather, here we analyze the unity of being of self-consciousness, which has already overcome the difference represented by individual objects. The being of self-consciousness is the mediated unity of self-consciousness in the objective sphere. Being at this level implies a self-conscious subject: "Life points to something other than itself, viz. to consciousness, for which life exists as this unity, or as genus."[52] The new concept of "life" as a universal that overcomes and contains the differences is an abstract concept, which is not found in nature itself but rather which requires a self-conscious subject. Hegel indicates this with his use of the term "genus" (*Gattung*). Animals can perceive objects of sense such as immediate being of sense-certainty and perception; however, here the concept of being has become enriched and is no longer the immediate object of sense. Here being has become an abstract concept or "genus," as Hegel says. Only the human conceptual apparatus with its ability to abstract from the sensible particulars can think this Notion. Thus, the Notion of "life," qua genus, that we have arrived at implies or points to the self-conscious subject. This then completes the sublation of "life" and signals the transition to the subjective side of the Notion.

The For-Itself Moment: The Pure "I" (§§173–77)

After the sublation of "life," the objective element, we now move to examine the other aspect of the Notion, the side of the subject. Now we need to determine the self-conscious subject as a specific individual entity. Hegel signals the shift from the analysis of "life" to the analysis of the self-conscious subject when he writes, "In the course of its experience which we are now to consider, this abstract object will enrich itself for the 'I' and undergo the unfolding which we have seen in the sphere of life."[53] Here he indicates that this development and sublation of the self-conscious subject parallels that of "life." This development, like the last one, goes through three stages.

In the first stage, "the pure undifferentiated 'I' is its first immediate object."[54] Just as the analysis of "life" began with an account of the continuity of "life" with consciousness and the universality of the two, so also we begin here with the universality of consciousness, which sees only itself and its representations in the object sphere. It is the only thing that is essential and independent. Consciousness forms an unbroken continuity for which there is no independent or essential other. The world of objects is an inessential extension of self-consciousness itself.

In the second stage, self-consciousness perceives seemingly independent objects which it must negate: "it *is* only as a supersession of the independent object, in other words, it is desire."[55] Here the sphere of objects in the experience of self-consciousness appears as something different and independent. As Hegel writes in the *Philosophy of Right*, "Matter offers resistance to me—and matter is nothing except the resistance it offers to me—that is, it presents itself to my mind as something abstractly independent only when my mind is taken abstractly as sensation. . . . In relation to the will and property, however, this independence of matter has no truth."[56] The world does not come ready made for us. In order to make use of objects of nature, we must first remove them from their natural context and then destroy and negate them or later (as in "Lordship and Bondage") form and reshape them in a fashion appropriate to our end. Since objects of nature are not already prepared for our use and consumption, they seem to offer resistance to our will. They appear independent of us, since they are indifferent to our goals and purposes. However, self-consciousness cannot accept this, since this experience contradicts its Notion that it, as subject, is independent and the world of objects dependent on it.

Self-consciousness must establish itself and confirm its own self-identity apart from the object, as other, which in its particularity and independence poses a threat to the universality of the self-conscious subject.

Self-consciousness thus tries to understand itself as universality and as pure being. It does this by negating the other, e.g., the illusory object for self-consciousness. Hegel says, self-consciousness "comes forward in antithesis to the *universal* substance, disowns this fluent continuity with it and asserts that it is not dissolved in this universal element, but on the contrary preserves itself by separating itself from this its inorganic nature, and by consuming it."[57] He makes it clear once again that everything is posited for self-consciousness. First, self-consciousness posits the other as a negation, since self-consciousness is pure being, and what is other than itself is nothing. It sees itself as a unity and the other as an insubstantial difference. But in order to confirm its own essentiality and unity, self-consciousness must negate the other, thus proving the latter's dependence and contingency. In the text that is now known as the *First Philosophy of Spirit*, Hegel articulates this negation of the other in the following terms: "For consciousness [in] itself, as active, as negative, as cancelling the being of its other-being, is consciousness as one side of it only; it is subjective consciousness, or consciousness as absolute singularity."[58] Consciousness is thus aware of itself as a unity or "absolute singularity" and negates the other in an attempt to deny its independent being. In the *Jena Metaphysics*, Hegel describes the other as follows: "Despite reflection and negation, it is a part of the world, a part posited in negated form, but thereby a dominant negative."[59] The point here is that self-consciousness must assert and demonstrate its own individuality and dominance over the object which it does by appropriating or destroying it. Self-consciousness is satisfied only by the negation of the other, since through this act self-consciousness certifies its own universality as being and maintains the assertion that the world is for it and not independent. Hegel writes, "the individuality which maintains itself at the expense of the universal, and which gives itself the feeling of its unity with itself, just by so doing supersedes its antithesis to the other by means of which it exists for itself."[60]

The assertion of the self-unity and its consequent universality of self-consciousness shows the contradiction at this level. In short, as pure being or universal "I," the self-conscious subject is indeterminate. The problem at this point is the same as we saw earlier at the level of sense-certainty. There the *object* of consciousness was the universal pure being which could not be made particular; likewise, here the "I" is the universal at a higher level which cannot be made particular. As Hegel says in the corresponding section in the *Jena Metaphysics*, "the I has determined itself only as universal."[61] Self-consciousness, through negation of the other, attempts to determine or confirm itself as pure being, but in fact it remains *in*determinate. As Hegel says, with everything else negated, the "I" is "the simple universal,"[62] and as such it cannot distinguish itself from anything else, since everything else is insubstantial. The "I" is a unity with the world as a fluidity of "life" and thus cannot establish itself as a particular "I" over and against something else.

This indeterminacy of the self-conscious subject can perhaps best be understood by an account of the categories of identity and difference. For Hegel, all entities are determined by these two relations. Every object has a self-relation, i.e., it is identical to itself and has a relation to other objects; namely, it is different from other objects. The problem here, as in "Sense-Certainty," is that the Notion involves only the self-relation of identity and is thus lacking the aspect of difference. Since the "This" was pure, undifferentiated being without properties in the dialectic of "Sense-Certainty," it could not be determined in contrast with other objects. There was no difference. So also here in "The Truth of Self-Certainty" the subject is considered universal, which it confirms by negating the inessential objects around it. Once again, we are left with simple identity without difference, since there is no meaningful or essential other with which self-consciousness can contrast itself. The aspect of difference is lacking now at this new level of self-consciousness, and thus the self-conscious subject remains indeterminate. In his lectures, Hegel explains self-consciousness's need for others in order to determine itself and to avoid empty universality:

> The *essence of consciousness* is that there is absolute unity of the antithesis immediately in an aetheric identity. It can only be this *in as much as immediately, so far as it is opposed,* both terms *of the antithesis are consciousness itself,* [and are] *in themselves, as terms of the antithesis, immediately the opposite of themselves,* [i.e.,] they are the absolute difference cancelling itself, they are the superseded difference, they are simple.[63]

Self-unity and universality are contradictory and antithetical terms, since self-unity implies particularity and individuation. Self-consciousness must stand opposed to something else in order to be a determinate particular. It cannot be determinate as the universality of being. Only as opposed to one another can both elements be "simple" and particular and hence determinate. Such opposition is necessary for self-consciousness's determination: "it only is consciousness so far as it *opposes* itself as an *other*."[64] One's own desire does not adequately constitute self-consciousness since there is no determinate other.

Hegel describes this abstract epistemological point in terms of dependence and independence. Self-consciousness believes that it is determinate and independent, just as before consciousness believed that the object was in itself determinate and independent. Now, however, in the course of this attempt to prove that the world is dependent on it as a universal "I," we see this curious reversal come about: "experience makes it aware that the object has its own independence."[65] By the destruction of the object, self-consciousness realizes that instead of the other depending on it for its existence, rather self-consciousness is dependent on the object. The negated object is the object of desire. Once the object is negated, the desire returns and shapes and molds the self-conscious subject in a way that self-consciousness had not formerly seen: "Desire and the self-certainty obtained in its gratification, are conditioned by the object, for self-certainty comes from superseding this other: in order that this supersession can take place, there must be this other."[66] As Hegel says, for self-consciousness to determine itself, there must thus be a substantial, independent other opposed to it, which it desires and by which it can compare and contrast itself and thus establish its particularity. Its own desire is not sufficient as a criterion. Hegel expresses this dialectical interaction between self-consciousness and its object in different ways in different places, although the point is the same—the universal "I" is unable to determine itself without opposition or contrast: "These extreme [poles], however, are at the same time simply related to one another: identical to one another in their indifference or universality, each related to itself but also for the other—since each itself is what it is only in opposition to the other."[67] Now it appears that the object of desire as other must condition the subject: "The I has the other only as something passive determining it."[68] Through this experience, self-consciousness realizes the independence of the object and its own dependence upon it—an exact reversal of the original situation where self-consciousness believed that it was independent and the object dependent as the object of its desire. Self-consciousness needs the other in order to determine itself as an individual "I" and not as a universal.

The problem is that there is something missing. Once self-consciousness has destroyed and negated everything, there is still desire and need. As Hegel says in his lectures, "the will is *being-for-self* which has extinguished all foreign content within itself. But thus it is left without an *other*, without content—and feels this lack."[69] Self-consciousness, by determining itself only vis-à-vis the object of desire, has determined itself as an object and not as a self-conscious subject. Self-consciousness knows itself to be in possession of other essentially human characteristics, but yet it is defined in the same way as an animal, i.e., in terms of the objects of its desire. Thus, it lacks the essentially human element in its self-determination which, for Hegel, can only come about as the result of interaction with other human beings and not merely in concourse with objects. Self-consciousness must now overcome this lack. Without the other, the problem of self-identity arises again. Self-consciousness has negated all of its objects and has still not achieved satisfaction of its desire in identity. Now the object must change; specifically, it must become enriched. But the problem now is how to establish its self-identity with respect to another self-consciousness.

Finally, at the third stage, we see the need for a second self-consciousness: "But the truth of this certainty is really a double reflection, the duplication of self-consciousness."[70] We are now concerned with two self-conscious subjects. In order for self-consciousness to achieve satisfaction or, in our terms, determination, the other must not be destroyed. Instead, it must negate itself: "On account of the independence of the object, therefore, it can achieve satisfaction only when the object itself effects the negation within itself."[71] But objects cannot negate themselves; only free subjects can. By this Hegel means that humans, unlike animals, stand in a mediated relation to their natural desires and drives.[72] Animals are determined by nature and have no choice but to act on the basis of their desires. Humans, on the other hand, can abstract from their desires and even negate them. Only humans are capable of denying their natural desires by, for example, fasting, remaining chaste, staying awake on vigils, committing suicide, etc. Only humans can negate their desires and by so doing "negate themselves." This self-imposed internal negation of the other self-conscious agent is now the only way for self-consciousness to achieve satisfaction; hence, Hegel's famous statement, "*Self-consciousness achieves its satisfaction only in another self-consciousness.*"[73] Hegel claims here that the truth of self-certainty and the existence of self-consciousness can only come about in a dynamic relationship with another self-consciousness and not with an object. With the imposed self-negation, the other is no longer independent and thus serves to certify self-consciousness. However, the insight that another self-conscious agent is necessary to mediate the self-conception of oneself is comprehended by the philosophical audience, but it remains unrecognized by self-consciousness itself. Self-consciousness continues to deny the reality of the other, insisting again on the universality of its own ego. It is still unwilling to admit the truth and validity of anything external to itself. Thus, although it sees the need for another self-consciousness, it does so only by seeing the other self-consciousness as something negative and inessential. This will ultimately prove to be the contradiction in the next section. Only in the final section of the "Self-Consciousness" chapter does self-consciousness realize the positive meaning of other self-conscious agents in the determination of the subject-object Notion.

Concluding Remarks

Strictly speaking there is here no in-and-for-itself moment in the sense of a fully developed and worked out dialectical step; however, the unity of the two self-conscious subjects that clearly forms the transition to the next section parallels the subject-object unity we have heretofore come to know as the in-and-for-itself moment. With the sublation of the Notion of "life" and of the individual autonomous self-conscious subject, natural consciousness realizes the need for a new unity, this time not between a subject and its sphere of objects, but rather between two self-conscious subjects. We see this Notion posited here at the end of "The Truth of Self-Certainty," but we must wait until the next section to see its articulation and sublation. This is confirmed by the opening sentence of the "Lordship and Bondage" section: "Self-consciousness exists in-and-for-itself when, and by the fact that, it so exists for another."[74] In order to reach the "in-and-for-itself" moment we need to consider a second self-conscious subject. This then forms the new Notion in the next section.

At the end of "The Truth of Self-Certainty," Hegel foreshadows the sections on "Spirit" by claiming that there the voluntary self-negation is mutual and that both self-conscious subjects certify themselves. He writes, "A self-consciousness, in being an object, is just as much 'I' as 'object.' With this, we already have before us the Notion of *Spirit*."[75] By this, Hegel means that here for the first time we have the mediation of truth-claims by two self-conscious subjects. This communal or group consciousness is what Hegel refers to with his celebrated concept of "Spirit" (*Geist*). But self-consciousness must pass through the various asymmetrical relationships before it can reach the mutual recognition of the egalitarian level of Spirit in which both parties "enjoy perfect freedom and independence: 'I' that is 'We' and 'We' that is 'I.' "[76] He here means that the goal of our inquiry is to achieve a universal concept (the "We") in which the individual is able to recognize himself and his own individual will (the "I"). Likewise, the goal, for Hegel, of political philosophy is to achieve a universally valid state with which one, qua individual, can identify, but in which one at the same time can maintain one's individuality.[77] At this stage, we have only the foreshadowing of Spirit and not yet its articulation and development.

The point of all this is to show that the seemingly "practical" terms of this section can be best understood by epistemological categories and analyses. The discussion of "life" and desire, when understood correctly, fits into the story of the self-development of the subject-object Notion which we have been following. Self-consciousness is here still trying to give a consistent account of the subject-object Notion, just as it did in the "Consciousness" chapter, but here since self-consciousness realizes that it must first give an account of itself as subject, it has recourse to its own "subjective" aspects, e.g., desire, in order to understand the subject-object relation. Moreover, as should be clear by now, this objective self-determination also amounts to the self-determination of self-consciousness as subject. What the dialectic has shown in the analysis of desire is that such a consistent account of subjectivity necessarily presupposes interaction with other self-conscious subjects. Self-consciousness cannot give an account of itself as subject consistently with only an account of its relation to objects. Other self-conscious subjects must thus be introduced into the account, since otherwise self-consciousness's desire would remain unfulfilled. In the next section, the notion or category of desire, which was here understood as the most basic impulse for the consumption or destruction of the other, gets interpreted in the context of what we might call a more social view. There, desire becomes desire for recognition. This will prove to be the key for the next attempt to give a consistent account of subjectivity. Thus, the purely formal categories that we saw before are interpreted in terms of different aspects of subjectivity, where they nevertheless serve the same function of determining the subject-object Notion.

The epistemological issues that we have been following throughout the "Consciousness" chapter appear once again here in "Self-Consciousness" and help to form a link which unifies the two chapters. The dialectic of universal and particular appears here with the self-conscious subject. At first self-consciousness asserts its own truth and independence over the object sphere. This truth and essentiality take the form of a universal continuity with and preeminence over the world of objects. Like the "This," self-consciousness here remains undetermined, since it has only self-certainty, or, put differently, it operates only with its own conception of itself. However, this conception lacks objectivity, since it is a mere assertion which has not been validated or mediated. The self-conscious subject tries to fix and determine itself by negating objects, but by this negation it simply remains universal. Like the "This," the self-conscious subject lacks something different and other than itself in contrast to which it can determine itself. A universe with only one object is unimaginable, since the object would remain indeterminate in the absence of other contrasting objects. This is the account we find in "Sense-Certainty." Here in "The Truth of Self-Certainty," natural consciousness imagines that it is the only self-conscious agent in the universe. Since it is the only one and lacks other contrasting self-conscious agents, natural consciousness remains indeterminate.

Here in "The Truth of Self-Certainty," the categories of immediacy and mediation come into play once again as well. Self-consciousness first attempts to see itself as an immediate existent, but in the course of the dialectic it learns that only with the aspect of difference or, in this case, only with the mediation of another self-conscious agent can the self-conception of the self-conscious subject rise above self-certainty and become truth. Only by means of this "double relation" of identity and difference can the self-conscious subject become determinate— (1) as relation of identity with its self-conception, and (2) as a relation of difference or variation in this self-conception from the appraisal given to it by another. The terms of universality and particularity as well as mediacy and immediacy, which we have followed throughout the "Consciousness" chapter, appear here again, this time applied to the self-conscious subject.

We have also seen the first parallel with the "Consciousness" chapter in terms of the repetition of the category of being here at the higher level of self-consciousness. We have seen the way in which the new Notion introduced in this chapter with its terms "life" and the pure "I" is simply a reinterpretation of the "This" of "Consciousness. Thus, the "Truth of Self-Certainty" parallels the "Sense-Certainty" section of the previous chapter at the categorial level by virtue of its repetition of the abstract category of being here applied in a richer ontological context than before, i.e., to the self-conscious subject and no longer to the independent object of consciousness. In our analysis of the next two sections, we will demonstrate the further parallel analyses between the two chapters.

II. Lordship and Bondage: The Struggle for Recognition (§§178–96)

The master-slave parable has come to be the best-known part of Hegel's philosophical corpus, due largely to the interpretations of Marx and Kojève. Although these interpretations have been important in making Hegel's philosophy famous, they have also done no small amount of damage to our understanding of it. The problem is that most Marxist and many existentialist interpreters tend to view the whole of Hegel's philosophy only in terms of this short section, since it lends itself to their own philosophical agenda. They thus tend to interpret this section without much sensitivity to Hegel's overall system. I, however, will attempt to read this section in terms of the general theme that I have been pursuing—the problem of truth and the self-development of a consistent subject-object Notion. I will argue that the category of the one and the many that we saw in "Perception" is reintroduced and reinterpreted here at the level of self-consciousness. This interpretation will allow us not only to understand this section in its proper context, but also to reconstruct an important part of the system.

Although most commentators would agree that this section is quite clear and cogent compared to the difficult ground which we have just covered in "Force and the Understanding" and "The Truth of Self-Certainty,"[78] and, to be sure, Hegel's lucidity here has been one important reason for the popularity of this section, nevertheless despite all this there is still little consensus as to what is really being proved. The most common views are that Hegel is giving an ontological theory of selfhood in accordance with the model of Descartes,[79] or that he is showing us the dialectical road to freedom.[80] There has recently been some impressive work done on this section that indicates the importance of the prominent concept of recognition (*Anerkennung*).[81] However, most of these studies do not go far enough in explicating the epistemological issues involved. In this section, Hegel's true goal is to examine the problem of truth with, for the first time, two self-conscious subjects.

What is important is that here we see the faint beginnings of an account of the social determination of truth and the subject-object Notion. In "Lordship and Bondage," a second self-consciousness is introduced as a result of the previous dialectic. But yet the original self-consciousness still considers the object realm to be purely its own and sees the other as something inessential. Thus, insofar as self-consciousness denies the other a role in the account of subjectivity and objectivity and thus fails to allow its own determinations to be mediated and conditioned by the other, we are still at the level of pure subjectivity, and have not yet truly advanced to the social level. I propose to interpret the "practical" or "social" actions and relations of this section in these epistemological terms, which accord with the knowledge problematic.

We saw in "The Truth of Self-Certainty" that the subject-object Notion could not be adequately established just with self-consciousness' self-affirmation and negation of its object. This proved inadequate, since the universality of self-consciousness proved to be indeterminate (just as the universal "This" proved to be in the "Consciousness" chapter). What was lacking was a means by which self-consciousness could distinguish itself from another and thus render itself determinate. This distinction and determination is made possible in "Lordship and Bondage" by the key concept of recognition. With recognition by an other, self-consciousness is rendered determinate and its account of subject and object becomes mediated. Self-consciousness realizes the need for the recognition of its truth-claims by the other self-consciousness. In this way, we take yet another step along the dialectical path toward unearthing all of the transcendental presuppositions in any subject-object Notion. Without recognition, the account of subject and object still remains "subjective" in the sense that it is simply the one-sided account of self-consciousness; self-consciousness has here what Hegel calls self-certainty, but, without the recognition of the other, it still does not have truth. With self-certainty, self-consciousness has only its own self-conception but no means of testing it, since there is no other Notion to contrast it with. In short, there is identity but no difference. But when another self-consciousness recognizes and mediates those same criteria, the determination takes on a larger aspect. Then self-consciousness has a dialectical relation between its view of itself (identity) and the other's view of it (difference). Hence, another self-consciousness is necessary in order for self-consciousness's account of subject and object to become mediated. Recognition, as the reinterpretation of the category of the one and the many, serves an epistemological purpose which most of the recent work on this concept has failed to see.

Hegel's "Lordship and Bondage" dialectic appears in many places and takes many forms throughout his corpus. Prior to the *Phenomenology*, its epistemological significance is sketched in the *Jena Metaphysics*. It also occurs more clearly in the sets of Jena lecture notes of 1802–3, 1803–4, and 1805–6. There, Hegel's account is more difficult to understand, since it includes many other dialectical moments, e.g., the family, the tool, property, etc., which do not survive in the 1807 *Phenomenology*, although they do show up later in different forms in the *Philosophy of Right*. After Jena, the master-slave dialectic also appears in the so-called *Nüremberg Propaedeutic* and in the editions of the *Encyclopaedia*. Although we have a large body of material upon which to base our interpretation, new problems arise about why Hegel changed his account. That, however, is not the central task of this interpretation.

Before we turn to the actual text, let us once again briefly review the dialectic as it now stands. In the "Consciousness" chapter, natural consciousness believed that the criteria for the subject-object Notion were independent of itself; however, in "Force and the Understanding," natural consciousness realized that it played a constitutive role in this self-determination of the criteria of subject and object, and thus before it could give an account of these criteria it had to give an account of itself as a necessary presupposition for the former. This it tried to do in the section "The Truth of Self-Certainty." There, consciousness realized the universality and thus the hollowness of its own determinations and realized that in order to give an account of its role in the determination of the subject-object Notion, it needed to give an account of itself with relation to other self-conscious agents. The mediation of other self-conscious agents is thus presupposed in any account of the subject-object Notion. This is where the "Lordship and Bondage" dialectic begins.

The Notion: "Recognition" (§§178–84)

Hegel immediately makes known to us in the passage cited above that it is the concept of recognition (*Anerkennung*) that will play the key role in this section: "Self-consciousness exists in and for itself when, and by the fact that, it so exists for another; that is, it exists only in being acknowledged [*als ein Anerkanntes*]."[82] This concept of recognition, however, is not static, but instead changeable; hence, Hegel calls this the *process* of recognition: "The detailed exposition of the Notion of this spiritual unity in its duplication will present us with the process of recognition."[83] This dynamic between two reciprocally recognizing self-conscious subjects is the parallel argument in "Self-Consciousness" to the dialectical play between the one and the many that we saw in the "Perception" chapter.

In "Perception," the dialectic, working with the categories the one and the many, moved back and forth between two conceptions of an object with properties. At first, as a "One," the unity of the object was emphasized and the properties interpenetrated and dwelt in the unity. Then, as an "Also," the properties themselves had priority in the relationship and were considered the essential. Here in "Lordship and Bondage," we see a parallel movement reinterpreted in terms of recognition. The play here is between one self-consciousness, which considers itself to be the unitary and the essential, over and against another self-consciousness, which is perceived as a mere "infinity" belonging to the fluid notion of nature which depends on the first self-consciousness. By "infinity," Hegel means the inessential, just as the "Also" represented the properties which were inessential to the true unity of the object in "Perception." Here as before, Hegel associates plurality with the inessential side of the dialectic. This is illustrated in the following passage from the Jena lectures: "Consciousness is the ideality of the universality and infinity of the simple in [the] form of opposition; as universal it is undistinguished unity of both [universality and infinity]. But as infinity [it is] the ideality in which its opposition *is*."[84] Here the terms of the dialectic are parallel to those seen earlier in "Perception." At this level, self-consciousness is at once an essential unity which encompasses the infinity of the other, just as the "One" is the element in which the many properties interpenetrate. But at the same time self-consciousness is also this infinity or many which is the inessential element dependent on an other since, as universal, it cannot determine itself. Once again the dialectic moves back and forth between two self-conscious agents, between the "One" and the "infinity," in an attempt to render consistent this picture of self-consciousness, as determined by the categories the one and the many.

Hegel draws this parallel with "Perception" fairly clearly in the "Lordship and Bondage" section itself when he writes, "We have now to see how the process of this pure Notion of recognition, of the duplicating of self-consciousness in its oneness [*Einheit*], appears to self-consciousness."[85] Here he repeats the key term from "Perception": the essential self-consciousness is considered a unity and a "One," just as in "Perception" the independent object was essentially considered a "One." The contrasting concept in both cases is the many or plurality, which here represents the inessential other. It may seem at the level of lordship and bondage that, since we are concerned with only two self-conscious subjects, the appropriate category would be the one and the other, and not the one and the many. How can a single self-conscious subject be conceived as a many? The answer is not difficult when we recall the issue in the "Perception" chapter. On the one hand, a self-consciousness in its abstract moment is a unity or totality: "The single individual is a whole and everything distinguishable in him is posited in this wholeness."[86] On the other hand, the individual self-consciousness is composed of a plurality of individual properties and relations, a "totality of single aspects."[87] A self-consciousness can be conceived as lacking unity and as only existing by virtue of its individual characteristics, relations, or properties. In "Perception" we were concerned with the inessential plurality of properties, the "Also." Here in "Self-Consciousness" the inessential self-consciousness that forms the other is not perceived as a unity but rather as a plurality: "The other is an *immediate* consciousness entangled in a variety of relationships, and it must regard its otherness as a pure being-for-self or as an absolute negation."[88] The other self-consciousness is considered in its plurality as unreal and inessential. It exists as the plurality of its "variety of relationships" and lacks the unitary core that constitutes the essential self-consciousness. In this way we can understand Hegel's talk of a plurality as something meaningfully applied to a self-conscious subject.

Since we are dealing with two self-conscious agents, the desire for recognition and self-certification takes place on both sides: "this action of the one has itself the double significance of being both its own action and the action of the other as well."[89] For the first time, the dialectic operates in a parallel or reciprocal fashion between two self-conscious subjects. In "The Truth of Self-Certainty" the relation was always one-sided, since self-consciousness dominated the object sphere. There was no parallel development, since only the subject could negate the other and certify its own unity. Now that there are two self-conscious subjects, which are internally differentiated infinities, we have two stories to examine.

Each self-consciousness posits its own account of the subject-object relation as determined according to the criterion of its own desire. According to the Notion, each self-consciousness then desires that its own account be mediated by the other: "The middle term is self-consciousness which splits into the extremes; and each extreme is this exchanging of its own determinateness and an absolute transition into the opposite."[90] In the other, self-consciousness perceives an account or conception different from its own. According to this Notion, the self-conscious subject realizes the need for recognition of the other in order to confirm its own account of self-certainty. Self-consciousness must find a way to win the recognition of its subject-object account from the other. The Notion here involves the confirmation of self-consciousness's self-certainty via the recognition of the other. Only with this recognition can self-consciousness determine itself as subject. This model of mutual recognition completes the Notion at this level, which Hegel indicates in the passage examined above: "We have now to see how the process of this pure Notion of recognition, of the duplicating of self-consciousness in its oneness, appears to self-consciousness."[91] We now turn to the experience of consciousness to see how this recognition comes about.

The Experience of Consciousness

The In-Itself Moment: The Lord (§§185–92)

In experience, consciousness perceives at first only an inessential other, a self-consciousness that it does not recognize. Specifically, each self-consciousness has a conception of itself as independent and autonomous while its object remains dependent and inessential. But when confronted by the other, each self-conscious agent realizes that the other's account differs from its own:

> Self-consciousness is, to begin with, simple being-for-self, self-equal through the exclusion from itself of everything else. For it, its essence and absolute object is "I"; and in this immediacy, or in this [mere] being, of its being-for-self, it is an *individual.* What is "other" for it is an unessential, negatively characterized object. But the "other" is also a self-consciousness.[92]

Self-consciousness sees itself as an individual unity and the other as plurality and as something inessential. However, since this movement is reciprocal, with each self-conscious subject viewing the other as inessential, the problem of self-certainty is here raised again. Neither self-consciousness can claim self-certainty for its own account so long as there is an other who seems to deny it: "Each is indeed certain of its own self, but not of the other, and therefore its own self-certainty still has no truth."[93] The other does not reflect back to self-consciousness an affirmation of self-consciousness's account, as it should according to the Notion; it does not yet recognize self-consciousness's assessment of the subject-object Notion. The element of self-identity is present, but the element of difference is still lacking since the recognition of the other is not granted.

Self-consciousness comports itself toward the other self-consciousness just as it did toward its object earlier. Self-consciousness once again tries to overcome its own universality, or as Hegel says in the Jena lectures, its own "exclusive totality,"[94] and this means negating the other. Again this involves self-consciousness attempting to deny the other its independence and by so doing certifying the certainty of itself. Self-consciousness sees the other as inessential, i.e., as its own simple determination and not as something independent, and attempts to reduce it to the status of an object. Self-consciousness tries to understand itself as an individual, but by denying the real existence of the other it remains a universal. We are thus left with pure indeterminate subjectivity. Now we begin at the same place, but this time with self-consciousness confronted not just by an object but by another self-consciousness.

At this point, self-consciousness must prove to itself its own self-certainty by pure abstraction from and negation of the world. As Hegel says in his Jena lectures, self-consciousness' natural state is one in which it is dependent on nature: "it is at first in [a] negative relation with nature, and in this negative relation it exists as tied to nature itself within the relation."[95] By this Hegel means that we are all originally dependent on nature for our survival, but this contradicts self-consciousness's Notion according to which it is independent and essential. Hence, in order to demonstrate its freedom and independence, self-consciousness must detach itself from nature. Self-consciousness shows that it is detached from the world and from the determinations of others by holding its own natural existence at naught: "The presentation of itself, however, as the pure abstraction of self-consciousness consists in showing itself as the pure negation of its objective mode, or in showing that it is not attached to any specific *existence*, not to the individuality common to existence as such, that it is not attached to life."[96] Self-consciousness proves that it does not value its existence in a struggle to the death with the other. Self-consciousness tries to validate its own Notion of subject and object by the destruction of the other. Hegel illustrates this conception of freedom as follows:

It is the freedom *of his privacy* [*obstinacy, Eigensinn*]; the single being can make himself into this point, he can abstract from everything absolutely, he can give everything up; he cannot be made dependent on anything, or held to anything; every determinacy by which he should be gripped he can cut away from himself, and in death he can realize his absolute independence and freedom [for] himself as absolutely negative consciousness.[97]

Dependency on nature is conquered by self-consciousness's risking its life in a struggle to the death. In such a struggle self-consciousness's freedom is proved, or, in terms of our interpretation, self-consciousness's subject-object Notion becomes mediated. Each thus "seeks the death of the other"[98] in order to destroy the other's universal determination and to assert its own lack of attachment to natural existence.

The key point of this struggle to the death is that it is an attempt to overcome the apparent subjectivity of self-consciousness's subject-object Notion in the face of another self-consciousness's conflicting Notion. Self-consciousness must risk its life, since not doing so would be implicitly to acknowledge the essentiality and validity of something external which could pose as a threat to be avoided. Insofar as one avoids or flees something threatening, one simultaneously recognizes its existence as something real. In order to prove that the other self-consciousness is not a true existent and is not a threat and in order not to recognize the foreign other, self-consciousness must risk its life in a struggle. The other self-consciousness represents a challenge to the absolute subjectivity of the first self-consciousness. In the other, self-consciousness sees something independent and external, which thus poses a threat to its absolute determination. "They must engage in this struggle," Hegel says, "for they must raise their certainty of being *for themselves* to truth, both in the case of the other and in their own case."[99] The other must be made to accept self-consciousness's subject-object Notion, and by so doing it mediates this Notion and makes it objective. If this is done, then the other effects a self-negation which affirms self-consciousness's pure subjectivity and absolute determination. Through self-negation the other admits its dependence on self-consciousness and its determinations. Thus, the account of the first self-consciousness is confirmed by the second. This then results in the beginning of recognition and of a communal like-mindedness, albeit based on power relations and not rational institutions or just practices.

One possible result of this struggle is the death of one of the combatants. This result leads to a stumbling block. If one party is dead, then there remains no one to recognize the conquering party's truth-claims, and the desired goal has not been achieved: "death is the *natural* negation of consciousness, negation without independence, which thus remains without the required significance of recognition."[100] By destroying the other, self-consciousness destroys the means of asserting its own account of truth as valid. The result is the same as in the previous section, when self-consciousness destroyed individual objects to assert its self-certainty. Natural consciousness remains at the level of self-certainty where it validates its own truth-claims, but, as we have seen, this appears hollow, since there is no intersubjective agreement or mediation about its determinations. Self-consciousness remains an abstract universality. Although it maintains its natural existence, it loses what was really important—a valid account of the determination of itself and the world. It still cannot individuate itself from other things. Self-consciousness now realizes that the life of the other is essential for its own recognition: "In this experience, self-consciousness learns that life is as essential to it as pure self-consciousness."[101]

The other result of the struggle is that one party submits to the other out of fear of death. By doing so, the self-consciousness that yields proves that it has not wholly detached itself from its natural existence, and thus it gives up its claim to determine the subject-object Notion independently. By submitting, the one self-consciousness recognizes the existence of the other as a threat to itself. Hegel refers to the epistemological aspects of the result of this struggle thus: "If in his own case he stops short of death, he only proves to the other that he will accept the loss of a part or the whole of his possessions, that he will risk a wound but not life itself; then for the other he is immediately not a totality, he is not absolutely for himself, he becomes the slave of the other."[102] Hence, by submitting, self-consciousness gives up its claims to the individuality and determination of its subjectivity and becomes a mere inessential "infinity" for the other self-consciousness. In other words, it gives up the claim that the world is merely the insubstantial result of its determinations and grants that there is something substantial and essential which is other than itself, i.e., the other self-consciousness. The defeated self-consciousness must then live by and recognize the other's desires and consequent determinations as objective. Hegel says, "they exist as two opposed shapes of consciousness; one is the independent consciousness whose essential nature is to be for itself, the other is the dependent consciousness whose essential nature is simply to live or to be for another. The former is the lord, the other is the bondsman."[103] By winning the struggle, the self-consciousness, having become the lord, asserts himself as that which truly and essentially exists, while the bondsman has his existence only in the other. The other thus believes that he has achieved individuation and determinacy from the former universality.

The master then in this first moment is the essential and the "One," and the slave is the negative "infinity" or plurality which is dependent on the "One." Hegel explains the epistemological aspects of this situation as follows:

> I am absolute totality in that the consciousness of the other as a totality of singularity is in me only as cancelled; but likewise my own totality *of singularity* is *one* that is cancelled in others; singularity is absolute singularity, it is infinity, the immediate contrary of itself, the essence of Spirit, which is to have infinity within itself in an infinite way, so that the antithesis immediately cancels itself.[104]

Here the "I" of the master is clearly associated with the singularity and the "One" that we saw in the "Perception" chapter. The master is the essential, objective in-itself. The "One" cancelled the diverse properties that dwelled in it and existed primarily as a unity, just as the master is a one that cancels the infinity, which is the other who depends on the master. Thus, since it is a totalizing unity, the master has the "infinity within itself" in a way that makes clear its essentiality and the bondsman's dependency.

The master's desire and his account of the subject-object Notion become *true* now, since not only does the master assert it as true, but also the slave recognizes it as true: "Here, therefore, is present this moment of recognition, viz. that the other consciousness sets aside its own being-for-self."[105] The lord in his hegemonic position has overcome mere self-certainty. This Notion, no longer simply asserted by one self-consciousness, is now mediated by an other in a way that we have not seen before: "The lord is the consciousness that exists *for itself*, but no longer merely the Notion of such a consciousness. Rather, it is a consciousness existing *for itself* which is mediated with itself through another consciousness, i.e. through a consciousness whose nature it is to be bound up with an existence that is independent, or thinghood in general."[106] Through the mediation of the slave, the validity claims of the lord take on an aspect of truth and transcend the lord's subjectivity. For the first time in the dialectic, truth-claims are mutually determined by two self-conscious subjects. This is confirmed in the respective actions of the lord and the bondsman.

First, with respect to labor, the lord is freed from the labor of self-determination that he was obliged to engage in. The lord no longer has to negate the objects of nature in order to make use of them as in "The Truth of Self-Certainty." Now, the lord has the immediate enjoyment of the objects of nature, which the bondsman is compelled to provide for him.

The bondsman, on the other hand, must labor without the satisfaction of the negation of the object of nature, which is reserved for the master. The bondsman is thus alienated from the fruit of his labor. Moreover, the lord, like the condescending bourgeoisie, looks down on the base labor of the bondsman, which he considers beneath himself. The bondsman, on the other hand, is relegated to a menial position and stands in an immediate relation to nature, upon which he is obliged to work.

Second, with respect to the relation to nature, the lord daily demonstrates his independence over nature by his negation or consummation of the products provided by the slave: "For the lord . . . the *immediate* relation becomes through this mediation the sheer negation of the thing, or the enjoyment of it."[107] The lord can thus enjoy the product without having to work for it, and at the same time nonetheless symbolically announces his independence over nature. On the other hand, it was originally the slave's dependence on nature that brought him into a position of servitude in the first place. The slave was not able to overcome the fear for his own person and is now via his servitude reminded daily of his dependence on nature: "for it is just this which holds the bondsman in bondage; it is his chain from which he could not break free in the struggle, thus proving himself to be dependent, to possess his independence in thinghood."[108]

The problem with this arrangement which leads to its sublation is that the recognition given by the slave, which is all-important for certifying the truth-claims of the master, is not meaningful. The subject-object Notion is in a sense socially mediated, but only in an asymmetrical fashion. The lord asserts truth-claims with his account, and the slave by recognizing them and thus mediating them validates their truth. However, by regarding the slave as unessential and as a thing or a mere object, the lord himself undercuts the possibility of the meaningful recognition of his truth-claims:

> it is clear that this object does not correspond to its Notion, but rather that the object in which the lord has achieved his lordship has in reality turned out to be something quite different from an independent consciousness. What now really confronts him is not an independent consciousness, but a dependent one. . . . his [the lord's] truth is in reality the unessential consciousness and its unessential action.[109]

The validation of the other is only meaningful if it is freely given from an independent agent. The bondsman, however, is a *dependent* consciousness, and its recognition is not meaningful. The recognition of a slave simply does not count. Herein lie the seeds of the sublation of this in-itself moment. Recognition makes sense only if it is freely given among equals. As Hegel says in his Jena lectures, "Neither can prove this [its own totality] to the other through words, assurances, threats, or promises."[110] If recognition is compelled, then it is not genuine, and if it comes from something which is less than human, then it is meaningless. Hence, for Hegel, "The outcome is a recognition that is one-sided and unequal."[111] The master has merely asserted his own account of the subject-object Notion in a dogmatic fashion and has compelled the other to assent to it. Hence, he has not really mediated his truth-claims meaningfully or validated his own being as self-certainty.

The For-Itself Moment: The Bondsman (§§192–96)

The slave mediates between the master's desires and the objects of desire. Now it is the slave who negates the objects in the world and who collects and fashions things for the master's desire. The master gives up his immediate relation to nature, and it devolves upon the slave to work on it and negate it for him. The master depends on the work and the products of the bondsman, without which he would perish. The master receives the satisfaction of the product that he desires, while the slave merely works to produce such products. The slave now appears as independent, while the master appears as the dependent consciousness. The master is dependent on the slave to recognize and validate his truth-claims, and thus the master needs the slave for whatever little truth-value his claims will have. Hence, for Hegel, "The *truth* of the independent consciousness is accordingly the servile consciousness of the bondsman."[112] On the other hand, the slave through his work grows ever more independent of the master. Now the slave slowly becomes the "One" and the essential while the master slips back into the inessential.

The slave originally submitted to the master, since he was unable to free himself from his natural existence. Out of fear of death, he became the servile consciousness. Now in the course of his service to the master, the slave truly does rid "himself of his attachment to natural existence."[113] A harsh discipline is bred into the slave, which far outweighs the original one-time fear of death that the struggle represented. Now at every moment of servitude, the slave fears death. Hence, Hegel says, quoting scripture, "the fear of the lord is indeed the beginning of wisdom"[114] although the slave is not yet aware of it. Through this daily experience, the bondsman disciplines his fear and overcomes it, which allows him to break his bond with nature and become independent.

Now the essentiality of the bondsman is asserted over that of the lord. No longer is the lord's subject-Notion the true and the essential one while that of the bondsman is unessential, but rather now the roles are reversed. Labor is the key by which the slave is transformed: "Through work, however, the bondsman becomes conscious of what he truly is."[115] In the earlier dialectic, the problem with desire was that once the thing, i.e., the object of desire, was negated, the desire always returned. The result is that satisfaction of desire is always ephemeral, since after the negation of the object the desire always returns: "Desire has reserved to itself the pure negating of the object and thereby its unalloyed feeling of self. But that is the reason why this satisfaction is only a fleeting one, for it lacks the side of objectivity and permanence."[116] Through work, however, the slave creates objects which endure and which reflect the slave's unity and personality in themselves. The slave still negates the object by taking it out of nature and transforming it, yet this kind of negation is not destruction or annihilation, but rather the object remains: "Desire does not come to its satisfaction in its nullification, and the object continues to subsist even as it is nullified."[117] Satisfaction is no longer fleeting but remains in the permanence of the product. "Work," Hegel writes, "is desire held in check, fleetingness staved off; in other words, work forms and shapes the thing. The negative relation to the object becomes its *form* and something *permanent*, because it is precisely for the worker that the object has independence."[118] Hence, through the activity of work, the slave fulfills his own desires in a more meaningful and less fleeting way than the master.[119] The slave negates the infinity of the objects in its transformation of the object through work. As a product of the slave's labor, the object remains a part of the totality and unity of the slave. The bondsman identifies with the object of his labor and thus externalizes himself and confirms himself in the world: "consciousness, *qua* worker, comes to see in the independent being [of the object] its *own* independence."[120]

Through the creation of things (instead of through their destruction as before), the slave comes to see itself in the world, and the world thus reflects the slave's oneness and unity. Moreover, the master, through his use and consumption of the products of the bondsman's labor, recognizes the products and in so doing validates the slave's subject-object Notion. The lord gradually becomes dependent on the products of the bondsman for his very existence, and thus his Notion sinks into the background the more he comes to depend on the bondsman and to accept his Notion. By recognizing the product of the slave, the master unwittingly recognizes the slave himself as an independent existence. The slave's own criteria are asserted in the world in a new way. The other that used to be a pure negative has now become something positive—a reflection of itself. Now the slave realizes that it is an independent existence: "in fashioning the thing, he becomes aware that being-for-self belongs to *him*, that he himself exists essentially and actually in his own right."[121] The bondsman sees himself via his product reflected in the world and thus realizes his own essentiality: "Now, however, he [sc. the bondsman] destroys this alien negative moment, posits *himself* as a negative in the permanent order of things, and thereby becomes *for himself*, someone existing on his own account."[122] Self-consciousness determines its own self-identity and oneness with reference to the products of its labor or the many.

However, this Notion also represents an unsatisfactory result. The bondsman finds his independence in his object or product. He has become a "One" by reshaping the infinity of nature. The problem with the scenario is that although the bondsman appears to be independent—through his product—nevertheless he relies on something physical and external, namely, the product itself. The object of the struggle was to overcome one's natural existence, yet the bondsman appears bound to it once again in order to certify his own self-identity. In other words, the slave as an essential "One" needs the "infinity" of nature in order to create products which certify his self-unity and oneness. This is where Hegel leaves us at the end of the master-slave section. In order to overcome this problem of being bound to the physical or natural existence, self-consciousness must withdraw itself from the physical world and posit the new criterion in the realm of thought so as to prove its independence. Here, Hegel reintroduces the criterion of ground in the next section, "Stoicism, Skepticism, and Unhappy Consciousness."

Concluding Remarks

As before in "The Truth of Self-Certainty," there in no in-and-for-itself moment at this level. At first, the category of unity, the "One," was applied to one self-conscious subject—the lord—which created the in-itself moment. Then the same category was applied to the other self-conscious subject and thus formed the for-itself moment. Self-consciousness, despite its dialectical experience does not yet see the need for the genuine mediation of its subject-Notion, which would constitute a genuine unity of the two self-conscious subjects. At this level, we remain with a unity that is compelled by the self-consciousness that happens to be the stronger.

The key to the lordship-bondage dialectic is that through the Notion of recognition we have the beginnings of a social account of truth and of the subject-object Notion, even though natural consciousness does not yet realize it. The concept of recognition indicates the inadequacy of the pure, subjective account of subjects and objects which ignores the accounts of others. The master must be recognized as the master if his status is to have any meaning. In this recognition the slave acknowledges and validates the master's account of the subject-object Notion. But there is here another level. Recognition must be freely given and not extracted by force. Hence, recognition must be mutual and granted by equal parties in order for its result to represent a true account. The ultimate account of subject and object can only take place in a just society with egalitarian institutions among citizens of free and equal status such that no coercion or power-claims enter into the relationship. Lacking this, the determination remains "merely subjective," in the sense that it is simply imposed by a single self-consciousness, and the social mediation is in this case only a meaningless show; it is not mediation but rather coercion or compulsion. Thus, a new goal is posited for the dialectic. Once the pure, subjective account has been overcome, we must try to give an account of the subject-object Notion as mediated by other subjects on an equal social footing. But at this point, self-consciousness still stubbornly refuses to realize the necessity of the mediation of his account via other subjects and continues to insist on the claim that he, as pure subjectivity, determines everything.

Here in "Lordship and Bondage," the categories that we have been following can be seen once again. The categories of universal and particular are divided between the lord and the bondsman. The lord asserts his own particularity and essentiality, which is mediated by the recognition of the bondsman. The bondsman in turn recognizes the lord's particularity and has himself no determination or identity outside of his relation to the lord. However, with the reversal of roles, the particularity of the lord turns out to be indeterminate, since the recognition of the bondsman does not count for genuine or valid. With the lord's dependence on the labor of the bondsman, the former slips back into the inessentiality and universality of nature. The bondsman, on the other hand, finds his individuality and particularity reflected in the product of his labor. However, recognition through a product is not intersubjective recognition and remains fixed on an object. Thus, this moment as well proves untenable.

The categories of mediation and immediacy are also at work here in the dialectic of "Lordship and Bondage." At first, the respective subject-object Notions of the two self-conscious agents are immediate: they are simply asserted and not validated by another. In other words, they have merely self-certainty. However, after the struggle for recognition and the establishment of the relationship between lord and bondsman, the subject-object Notion is mediated. At first the lord's Notion or self-certainty is mediated by the bondsman, who recognizes without being recognized. The lord asserts a validity claim which he then sees reflected and affirmed by the bondsman. This reflection amounts to mediation. Then, by contrast, the lord implicitly mediates the Notion of the bondsman by implicitly recognizing the value of his labor of which the lord is the beneficiary.

The categorial parallelism with the "Perception" chapter is also present here. Just as the category of being for "Sense-Certainty" was repeated in "The Truth of Sense-Certainty," so also the category of the one and the many from "Perception" is here repeated in "Lordship and Bondage." The unity and essentiality that was first assigned to the object sphere is here at the level of self-consciousness first applied to the lord. The plurality of properties of the object of "Perception" here takes the form of the plurality of relations and properties of the inessential self-conscious subject, namely, the bondsman. This relation then gets turned around, and the bondsman becomes the one with his unity with the product of his labor, while the lord becomes the plurality, here in the sense of the plurality of his desires and drives which make him dependent on the slave and consequently once again on nature. Thus, the same categories that were formerly used in the attempt to determine the object are now applied to the realm of self-conscious subjects.

III. The Freedom of Self-Consciousness (§§197–230)

The third section of the "Self-Consciousness" chapter has become famous for its discussion of what Hegel calls the "Unhappy Consciousness." Studies on this section have tended to concentrate solely on this discussion and have generally ignored its systematic role as the third Notion in the "Self-Consciousness" chapter.[123] Moreover, they have failed to see the importance of this account as the key step in the transition to "Reason." I wish to establish the systematic importance of this section as a whole by following up on the parallelism with the "Consciousness" chapter that we have been examining.[124] Specifically, I will argue that in this final section of the "Self-Consciousness" chapter, the category of ground is reintroduced, this time at a higher level which parallels the section "Force and the Understanding." The important feature of both sections is the dialectical play between the supersensible beyond, this time not a force as at the level of consciousness, but rather as pure thought itself or thought reified as a personified other—God. The sensible world is this time not the world of appearances understood as objects, but rather the world containing the various self-conscious human subjects and forms of human activity. Just as force and the supersensible were thought at the level of objectivity to ground appearance, so also here what Hegel calls "pure thought," "God," or the "unchangeable" at the level of subjectivity is thought to ground human existence. With respect to the transition to "Reason," I will argue that, with the breakdown of the Notion here in the discussion of the unhappy consciousness, the self-conscious subject finally comes to realize the futility of giving an account of the subject-object Notion only with reference to itself as an isolated, individual subject. It realizes that its account of itself presupposes a wider social sphere as a necessary condition for any such account. Hence, natural consciousness ultimately escapes from its own pure subjectivity and moves to the realm of human communities and institutions which mediate and condition the truth-claims of the individual.

This section has been problematic in the literature for a couple of different reasons. First, the organization of this section is difficult to make sense of. In the discussions of the "Consciousness" and "Self-Consciousness" chapters examined above, each section seemed to contain a single dialectical Notion that was examined for consistency. In this section, however, we seem to be confronted with three different Notions, as is evinced by Hegel's subtitle: "Stoicism, Skepticism, and the Unhappy Consciousness." I will argue that, in fact, these constitute three aspects of the same Notion and not three different Notions. This division thus fits nicely into the schema consisting of in-itself, for-itself, and in-and-for-itself that we have been following so far.

The second problem has been that of the alleged introduction of actual historical forms or Notions here. Heretofore we have examined only various abstract idealized forms of an idealized subject, natural consciousness. However, now it seems that Hegel introduces concrete historical movements of thought, which break with and transcend the idealized forms we have examined. It has been pointed out that in his account of Stoicism, Hegel has in mind the late Roman stoics—Seneca, Epictetus, and Marcus Aurelius.[125] Likewise, his discussion of Skepticism is allegedly an allusion to Pyrrhonian skepticism, as represented by Sextus Empiricus—a movement which, in fact, historically succeeded Stoicism. Finally, it is claimed, the unhappy consciousness represents a medieval Christian worldview, according to which the believer is eternally separated from the divine.

What evidence is there for the claim that Hegel is now treating specific historical Notions? After setting up the Notion at this level, Hegel writes, "This freedom of self-consciousness when it appeared as a conscious manifestation in the history of Spirit has, as we know, been called Stoicism."[126] The question is how we are to take this reference to "the history of Spirit." I wish to argue that Hegel alludes to the historical movements of Stoicism and skepticism only as a manner of illustration, and does not mean to imply that we will at this point begin to study actual historical forms. He is simply alluding to historical moments that his audience is familiar with in order to illustrate better the movement of the dialectic. He gives us no indication in the passage cited above that he intends to shift gears here and to move to a historical analysis. Moreover, such a movement is not dictated by the course of the dialectic. There is no reason to introduce particular historical forms here when we are analyzing forms of self-conscious subjectivity. This is confirmed by the abstractness and the level of generality with which Hegel describes these movements. He is in fact so vague in his treatment of the unhappy consciousness, for instance, that commentators are divided about the real target of his criticism. This, however, presupposes that he in fact had in mind a real historical target. At this point we are still at the level of abstract forms of consciousness and have not yet reached the point where actual historical forms are introduced. Thus, although the dialectic here has certain affinities with given historical moments, nevertheless it is in no way to be construed as representing a historical analysis. This section on Stoicism no more represents the actual Stoicism of Seneca or Epictetus than the master-slave dialectic actually represents some concrete historical event.

The Notion: The Freedom of Self-Consciousness (§197)

This dialectic follows from and can be construed as a continuation of Hegel's account of the lordship-bondage scenario. The master conceives of himself as independent of the slave and his products. The true or essential part of the master is what is abstracted from the other: "For the independent self-consciousness, it is only the pure abstraction of the 'I' that is its essential nature."[127] The slave, on the other hand, regards itself as independent since it sees itself reflected in the product of its labor. Hence, it seems that the slave has a relation to an external object, i.e., he has two objects—itself and its object: the slave has "these two moments—*itself* as an independent object, and this object as a mode of consciousness."[128] But as it turns out, these are not two separate things, but rather one and the same, and their "*intrinsic* being is consciousness."[129] The product or the object for self-consciousness is grounded in the thought of self-consciousness. Thus, both the master and the slave retreat to the realm of thought.

The slave, having attained a measure of independence through his labor, withdraws into the realm of thought. The idea is that although in the real world he is still a slave, nevertheless in thought he is free. For instance, the master cannot compel the slave to think something. With this freedom, the slave negates the world and dwells in the purely cognitive sphere which he alone determines. Truth and objectivity reside in the realm of his own "subjective" thought and not among concrete entities in the world. Thought is what is real and essential, whereas the physical world is transitory. This at first seems to stand in contrast to the previous state, where truth was found in the slave as a result of the product of his labor, yet it in fact comes about as a direct result of that state. The slave comes to realize that he not only physically forms the object of his labor but also mentally shapes it in accordance with an idea or plan. The product of the slave's labor is primarily the result of his thought. Hegel expresses this in a rather elliptical fashion: "the moment of intrinsic being or thinghood which received its form in being fashioned is no other substance than consciousness."[130] In other words, the object which self-consciousness fashions reflects the plan and will of self-consciousness, and thus it is identical with consciousness or "is no other substance than consciousness." Just as in "Force and the Understanding" the Notion of force had two aspects—force expressed and force proper—so also here we have rational thought in itself and how it expresses itself in work and in a product. Hence, it is not the product itself, outside of the slave, which is the key for the slave's independence and self-realization, but rather it is the slave's thought, since this is what produces the product in the first place. With an appeal to the realm of thought, self-consciousness hopes once again to overcome its dependence on natural existence. It tries to show that it is aloof from the world and dependent only on its thoughts; thus it reenacts, in part, the earlier moments of the "Self-Consciousness" chapter in which the self-conscious subject tried to prove its independence.

Hegel indicates the introduction of the new Notion at this level and characterizes it in the following passage: "We are in the presence of self-consciousness in a new shape, a consciousness which, as the infinitude of consciousness or as its own pure movement, is aware of itself as essential being, a being which *thinks* or is a free self-consciousness."[131] Here Hegel indicates straightaway that the essential feature of the freedom of self-consciousness is thought and abstraction. Thought functions like force, as something unseen working behind the scenes that serves to explain various empirical appearances, here understood as human action and labor. Hegel continues with his analysis of thinking: "For *to think* does not mean to be an *abstract* 'I,' but an 'I' which has at the same time the significance of *intrinsic* being, of having itself for object, or of relating itself to objective being in such a way that its significance is the *being-in-itself* of the consciousness for which it is [an object]."[132] Self-consciousness is able to see itself in the object of its labor and thus as an object. As in all of the moments of the "Self-Consciousness" chapter so far, self-consciousness sees itself as the essential element in the subject-object relation.

At this point, we have a new moment in which freedom and thought are linked. What is essential to self-consciousness is that it thinks. In the realm of thought, self-consciousness asserts its independence from the other: "In thinking, I *am free*, because I am not in an *other*, but remain simply and solely in communion with myself, and the object, which is for me the *essential* being, is in undivided unity my being-for-myself."[133] In thought self-consciousness depends only on itself and is thus autonomous, needing nothing from outside. Here the criterion of ground is reinterpreted in terms of thought. Thought, which is identified with and reflected in the object, is what is essential and unified, while the world of objects per se is an inessential appearance. The object for self-consciousness is the product of its labor to which it relates itself. Its truth, however, is not in its thinghood but rather in the thought of the self-conscious subject.

Despite the previous lordship-bondage dialectic, which broke down in a way that showed the inadequacy of an entirely subjective account of the subject-object Notion by indicating the need for social mediation, self-consciousness still remains firm in its insistence on the purely subjective Notion. Self-consciousness still sees itself as being the sole factor in the account of subject and object. The world can be accounted for solely with reference to the subject and its cognition. Likewise, objects or the products of the slave's labor, which were so important before, are now considered inessential, while pure subjective thought takes over the leading role. For self-consciousness, the pure subjectivity of its thought is what is most real and essential. Hence, self-consciousness is cut off from the world and from other self-conscious subjects which might otherwise be thought to play a role in mediating this thought and consequently this account of the determination of the Notion. Just as in "The Truth of Self-Certainty," here natural consciousness negates everything that is other, not physically as before but rather mentally or in thought. Self-consciousness recognizes only its own subjective thought and cognition as valid and sees no other factors as relevant for the complete account of the subject-object Notion.

In "Force and the Understanding," we saw a single pair of categories at work, namely, ground and consequence; however, this pair of categories has a number of instantiations. First, it was conceived as a force, then as a supersensible world, then as a realm of scientific laws, and finally as an inverted world. Here, in "Self-Consciousness" we see the same thing. The dialectic operates with the category of ground at the level of self-consciousness, but this category takes on a number of different forms with the same general Notion. This Notion, which Hegel calls the "freedom of self-consciousness," we have just characterized by the belief that what is essential and real is the thought of self-consciousness. This thought is then the ground of human activity and the human sphere, which is considered inessential. This basic Notion will be repeated in different forms in Stoicism, skepticism, and the unhappy consciousness.

With "Force and the Understanding" we broke with the level of perception and sensibility, and we moved to the level of thought. Forces are not things or objects that one perceives directly, but rather they are conceived and posited by thought as something behind the scenes which explains the empirical phenomena. Similarly, here in this parallel section in "Self-Consciousness," we are no longer concerned with the immediate object of sense or desire as before. Now the analysis turns again from sense perception to thought, this time in the realm of self-consciousness. Hegel writes,

> Essential importance no longer attaches to the difference as a specific *thing*, or as a consciousness of a specific *natural existence*, as a feeling, or as desire and its object, whether this is posited by myself or by an alien consciousness. What alone has importance is the difference posited by *thought*, or the difference which from the very first is not distinct from myself.[134]

Hence, here all of the discussions will operate at the abstract level of thought, i.e., with the highest cognitive faculty, and not at the level of simple perception.

The Experience of Consciousness

The In-Itself Moment: Stoicism (§§198–201)

After setting up the new Notion at this level, Hegel turns to the first experience of consciousness, which he calls "Stoicism."[135] He says of Stoicism, "Its principle is that consciousness is a being that *thinks*, and that consciousness holds something to be essentially important, or true and good only insofar as it *thinks* it to be such."[136] Here we have a quite clear account of this new version of the criterion for the subject-object Notion, which is, as we have seen, ground construed this time as thought. Hegel later says this explicitly when he claims, "Stoicism, therefore, was perplexed when it was asked for what was called a 'criterion of truth as such,' i.e. strictly speaking, for a *content* of thought itself."[137] This is one of Hegel's clearest assertions that he is interested in a self-developing account of the subject-object Notion via these criteria for truth (contrary to interpretations claiming that he is interested only in freedom in this section).

In the earlier dialectical movements of "Self-Consciousness," what was essential was the relation to a specific thing, i.e., the object posited by self-consciousness as a result of desire. Since thought is the new criterion, what is essential is not the empirical object but rather the object of thought. Thought is here understood to be abstracted from the natural world and from desire, which were so important in the previous dialectic. The key point here is that thought is still not considered as mediated or produced in the social sphere, but rather it is still wholly subjective. Self-consciousness is still thought to determine the subject-object Notion alone and without the mediation of other self-conscious agents.

The result of this emphasis on thought is that material conditions are unimportant. Pure thought abstracts from the empirical world of appearances. Objectivity can be determined in pure thought regardless of one's position or social status. Hegel captures this with an allusion to the two great Roman stoics, Marcus Aurelius and Epictetus: "whether on the throne or in chains, in the utter dependence of its individual existence, its aim is to be free, and to maintain that lifeless indifference which steadfastly withdraws from the bustle of existence, alike from being active as passive, into the simple essentiality of thought."[138] We see in this passage the categories of the ground and consequence reinterpreted at the level of self-consciousness. Ground or the supersensible realm of thought is portrayed as the stable and unchanging "lifeless indifference," i.e., unity and universality, which exists in the "simple essentiality of thought." The consequence on the other hand is portrayed as "the bustle of existence," i.e., the inessential empirical world seen in daily life. In the one case, the slave can only be free in the realm of thought, where he is abstracted from his real material condition. By retreating into thought, the slave denies or negates his own wretched condition, which is considered inessential and belonging to the inessentiality of his petty daily existence. Here as before the empirical world is negated, while something positive is posited as its ground, namely, thought itself. But the passage also alludes to Marcus Aurelius the master. The emperor or the master must reject the riches and comforts of this world and seek the true freedom which lies in the mind of each man and not in the material conditions which surround him. Hence, thought or the account of the subject-object Notion is fully subjective and is withdrawn from the world and other subjects which it considers insubstantial and negates.

This freedom, however, in its abstraction begins to break down in the experience of consciousness. Since self-consciousness claims to exist purely in the realm of thought, it seems to have no connection to actuality: "Freedom in thought has only *pure thought* as its truth, a truth lacking the fullness of life."[139] In other words, for this freedom to be fully consummated it would have to thrive not just in the realm of thought but also in the realm of activity. But here we see freedom only in terms of thought or as a withdrawn unity which has no connection with daily life. In terms of our categories, ground becomes simply empty and indeterminate, since it has no relation to the consequence. The consequence is inessential and unreal. An abstract freedom is always a limited freedom, i.e., limited to thought, and thus this freedom is in a sense not actual: "Hence freedom in thought, too, is only the Notion of freedom, not the living reality of freedom itself."[140] In short, the Notion contradicts the experience.

In the *Philosophy of Right*, Hegel describes this contradiction of the withdrawal into pure thought in terms of the mind-body dualism. On the one hand, it is possible to abstract from everything corporeal: "I can withdraw into myself out of my bodily existence and make my body something external to myself; particular feelings I can regard as something outside me and in chains I can still be free."[141] However, on the other hand, I am in fact still connected with the things from which I abstract: "If my body is touched or suffers violence, then, because I feel, I am touched myself actually, here and now."[142] Despite my best efforts mentally to abstract from my body and my material condition, nonetheless I remain ultimately in both.

Moreover, the Notion proves indeterminate. This freedom, set apart in the realm of thought, lacks meaningful content, since it has no worldly instantiations. It is an empty ground undetermined by any meaningful relation to the consequence. The slave, even lost in the realms of thought, is still a slave. Lacking content, this Notion becomes empty and useless: "To the question, *what* is good and true, it again gave for answer the *contentless* thought: the true and the good shall consist in reasonableness."[143] Although thought at first appeared to be a useful criterion for the subject-object Notion, insofar as it moved us out of the master-slave dialectic, now it appears to be no criterion at all, since it is so abstract that it cannot determine the Notion. Hegel says, "this self-identity of thought is again only the pure form in which nothing is determined."[144] A criterion that determines nothing is thus no criterion. Ground has again become an indeterminate universal.

The breakdown of Stoicism once again implies the need for an account of the wider social community in the complete and adequate determination of the subject-object Notion. We need an account of a community in which the resolution of the problem of recognition is both determinate and rational in a way that the subject-object Notion could be generally recognized as true. Since the account of the subject-object Notion is considered to concern self-consciousness itself and to be without relation to the world or other self-conscious subjects, that account is still found wanting since it lacks a validation or mediation. The sort of freedom that is only in thought is hollow, since it cannot find itself in the world of other self-conscious agents. The slave, although perhaps free in thought, comes up every day against the empirical truth of the servitude which constitutes his existence. This servitude is socially recognized and thus validated (although, to be sure, in a way that is based on power-claims), while self-consciousness's thought appears purely subjective. Once again the dialectic breaks down in a way that shows that pure subjectivity presupposes a social competence and certain social relations which must first be accounted for.

Stoicism, for Hegel, represents "the incomplete negation of otherness,"[145] insofar as self-consciousness by withdrawing into the realm of thought implicitly negates the other mentally, i.e., the world as an independent existence, since it regards thought as the true and the real. This is an incomplete negation, since it implicitly negates the other, while confidently asserting its own freedom. This, as we have seen, was incapable of rendering anything determinate, since it remained purely subjective and lacked intersubjective mediation and determination. Now self-consciousness tries to overcome this by a total or complete negation in the realm of Skepticism.

The For-Itself Moment: Skepticism (§§202–6)

In the moment of Skepticism, self-consciousness universally negates all determinations and denies all validity. Nothing is true or objective; hence, there exists simply a chaotic plurality of inessential appearance. Here, as in Stoicism, the attempt is made to negate whatever is other and thus to assert one's own subjectivity. Hegel characterizes Skepticism thus:

> In Skepticism, now, the wholly unessential and non-independent character of this "other" becomes explicit *for consciousness*; the [abstract] thought becomes the concrete thinking which annihilates the being of the world in all its manifold determinateness, and the negativity of free self-consciousness comes to know itself in the many and varied forms of life as a real negativity.[146]

The external world of appearances is negated and considered inessential. Stoicism tried to withdraw from the world, which was considered an inessential appearance, in order to solve this problem of truth, but Skepticism negates or denies the world by adopting a critical negative attitude toward it. This negation of the world gives the slave a tool with which to criticize the master's existence as valueless or at least as not being any better than his own. The slave denies the validity of the master's account of subject and object by denying the validity of all such accounts. Thus, the slave can avoid recognizing his own lowly status by slipping into a form of nihilism. Yet, by doing so, the slave in his actions and thoughts implicitly asserts his own account as the true, thus contradicting the very heart of his own skeptical attitude.

By adopting the negative attitude toward otherness, the skeptical self-consciousness realizes the negation that Stoicism implied in its withdrawal from the world. Hegel writes, "*Skepticism* is the realization of that of which Stoicism was only the Notion."[147] He continues, "It is clear that just as Stoicism corresponds to the *Notion* of the *independent* consciousness which appeared as the lord and bondsman relationship, so Skepticism corresponds to its *realization* as a negative attitude towards otherness, to desire and work."[148] Stoicism, as we have seen, represents the Notion of the freedom of consciousness, since it involved a withdrawal from the world into pure thought and an implicit negation or disavowal of the reality of the empirical world. In Skepticism we see the realization of this Notion, since here in the sophistry of its relativism, skeptical self-consciousness actively negates the world in thought. This skeptical attitude also completes the negation that self-consciousness tried to effect through desire in the master-slave dialectic. There desire and work were unable to negate the other, since self-consciousness perceived its other as an independent totality to be negated. Here at the level of Skepticism, all determinations are negated, and nothing is true or independent in the world of chaotic appearances.

At this point in the dialectic, objects or determinations are made to vanish by self-consciousness. By negating these determinations, self-consciousness implicitly establishes itself as truth and freedom. Thus, despite its claims to being pure negation with no positive content, self-consciousness implicitly affirms its own account of subject and object by categorically denying the validity of all others. Hegel says, "consciousness itself is the *absolute dialectical unrest*, this medley of sensuous and intellectual representations whose differences coincide, and whose identity is equally again dissolved, for it is itself determinateness as contrasted with the non-identical."[149] Hence, thought, which for Stoicism was considered a calm ground behind the scenes over and against an empirical world, is here considered to be just a part of the appearances or a "medley of sensuous and intellectual representations." Hegel makes this clear when he says, "But it is just in this process that this consciousness, instead of being self-identical, is in fact nothing but a purely casual, confused medley, the dizziness of a perpetually self-engendered disorder."[150] Self-consciousness, attempting to think this Skepticism consistently, must occasionally have recourse to denying the truth of everything; however, seeing that this implicitly contradicts its own truth-claims, self-consciousness withdraws from the radical and contradictory skepticism only to come back to it when convenient. Skeptical consciousness is aware of this confusion and thrives in it.

In "The Truth of Self-Certainty" and "Lordship and Bondage," self-consciousness tried to negate the other as an immediate object of sense in order to confirm its own self-certainty. At first, it negated other objects and then, in "Lordship and Bondage," the object of negation was another self-conscious subject. These negations, corresponding to "Sense-Certainty" and "Perception," involve objects of sense and perception. However, here in Stoicism and Skepticism we see explicitly the negation of the other as object of *thought*. Opinions, points of view, theories, and all sundry Notions are negated in a wild relativism. Hegel writes,

> What Skepticism causes to vanish is not only objective reality as such,
> but its own relationship to it, in which the "other" is held to be objective
> and is established as such, and hence, too its *perceiving*, along with firmly
> securing what it is in danger of losing, viz. *sophistry*, and the truth it has
> itself determined and established. Through this self-conscious negation
> it procures for its own self the certainty of its freedom, generates the
> experience of that freedom, and thereby raises it to truth.[151]

This negation of the other at the level of thought corresponds to the object of thought in "Force and the Understanding." There the Notion involved a cognitive act, a positing of some mental construct behind the phenomena. Accordingly, here we see the negation of the products of thought.

This form of freedom of self-consciousness breaks down due to an inner contradiction in its Notion that leads to the indeterminacy of self-consciousness: "But equally, while it takes itself in this way to be a single and separate, contingent and, in fact, animal life, and a *lost* self-consciousness, it also, on the contrary, converts itself again into a consciousness that is universal and self-identical."[152] In other words, although it mercilessly criticizes all traditions, beliefs, perceptions, etc., self-consciousness must nevertheless hold on to something as true in this negativity, i.e., its own subject-object Notion. While denying that anything is true, the skeptic affirms the single truth that nothing is true; while denying the validity of all ethical principles, the skeptic yet affirms those principles in his daily practice. Hegel says, "It pronounces an absolute vanishing, but the pronouncement *is*, and this consciousness is the vanishing that is pronounced. It affirms the nullity of seeing, hearing, etc., yet it is itself seeing, hearing, etc. It affirms the nullity of ethical principles, and lets its conduct be governed by these very principles."[153] A full-fledged skepticism or relativism without distinctions is a logical impossibility, since it precludes any action or thought. Everything that skeptical self-consciousness does or says refutes the relativism it affirms intellectually. Self-consciousness thus cannot claim validity for its own account of the subject-object Notion. It is this contradiction which completes the moment of Skepticism and compels us on to the moment of the unhappy consciousness which combines the two preceding moments.

Here self-consciousness remains indeterminate as well. Despite its attempts to determine itself by negating the opinions of others, here consciousness remains "universal and self-identical." The reason for this is that when everything is meaningless and false except one's own opinions, then once again there is only a relationship of self-identity and no relationship of difference. Self-consciousness has thus only its own self-relation, but since it has refuted all possible counterpositions or opinions contradicting its own view, it remains indeterminate. With every negation and refutation of opposing positions, self-consciousness becomes ever more universal and indeterminate until the last "other" is eliminated, at which point self-consciousness itself simultaneously becomes indeterminate.

The very beliefs and values that self-consciousness holds contradict the universal skepticism that it asserts. These beliefs and values, however, did not arise in a subjective vacuum, but rather were the result of self-consciousness's interaction with a broader social sphere. Self-consciousness, however, still fails to recognize that such beliefs and values have their validity in the context of the social order as a whole. Hence, the breakdown of Skepticism with the contradiction of self-consciousness's own beliefs and its universal skepticism points once again to the wider social community and shows the inadequacy of a purely subjective determination of the subject-object Notion.

The In-and-For-Itself Moment: The Unhappy Consciousness (§§207–30)

The discussion of the "Unhappy Consciousness" is of crucial importance, since it is here that self-consciousness finally abandons the attempt to give an account of the subject-object relation solely with reference to itself and its own subjectivity. In this section, self-consciousness finally sees the necessary role of human institutions and interaction in this determination. The unhappy consciousness, in its attempt to mediate between two self-conscious extremes, namely, itself and God, comes to the realization that this mediation exists in the institution of the church and in the practices of the religious community. This community will then serve as a basis for further dialectical adjustments in the attempt to give a complete account of subject and object via social mediation.

The unhappy consciousness, qua in-and-for-itself moment, begins with a combination or synthesis of the two previous movements. The duality of the absolutely free, self-identical stoic and the nihilistic, all-denying skeptic is here combined in a single consciousness. Hegel says, "the duplication which formerly was divided between two individuals, the lord and the bondsman, is now lodged in one."[154] Yet in order for consciousness to be aware of this contradiction, it must reflect on itself; hence, the unhappy consciousness is (1) the interaction of two essentially opposed and contradictory forms of self-consciousness—Stoicism and Skepticism—and (2) the unity of these disparate elements—the unhappy consciousness. Once again, as in "Force and the Understanding," we see another form of an otherworldly account with ground as the operative category. These then become the terms of the dialectic of the section "Unhappy Consciousness."

Here self-consciousness posits God, which is referred to here as "the unchangeable,"[155] as pure subjectivity which determines reality. This is the moment of Stoicism that has been carried over. The account of the subject-object relation is thought to come from the subject alone with no other social or historical factors playing a role, but this time subjectivity is the personified subjectivity of God. Thus, this absolute subjectivity remains behind the scenes, like force, and determines all human existence; however, the human world, as the determination or consequence of something else, is thus less real and appears insubstantial. The unhappy consciousness sees itself separated from the unchangeable God and on the side of the transitory appearances. This is the moment of Skepticism, which Hegel refers to here simply as "the changeable." This is clear when he writes, "the simple unchangeable, it [the unhappy consciousness] takes to be the *essential* being; but the other, the protean changeable, it takes to be the unessential . . . it identifies itself with the changeable consciousness, and takes itself to be the unessential being."[156] These constitute the terms of the dualism of pure thought and the empirical world at this third stage of the "Freedom of Self-Consciousness." The criterion for truth for the unhappy consciousness is ground newly interpreted as the unchangeable that dwells in the beyond. The world of the sensible is transitory and ephemeral, whereas the beyond is stable and enduring, just as before the forces were what was truly real and the phenomena mere consequences. The unhappy consciousness is eternally unhappy, since when comparing objects of this world to those of the beyond, the former inevitably come up short and appear unreal and unable to match up to the divine standard. The unhappy consciousness, hence, operates in a world of falsity with a criterion of truth from the beyond.

The unchangeable or God is not to be understood here in the ontological sense of some real, independent being existing apart from the self-conscious subject. Instead, here God is understood merely as the product of the unhappy consciousness's thought or imagination. Just as in "Force and the Understanding," consciousness itself posited the forces to explain the phenomena, so also here with the unhappy consciousness, self-consciousness posits God as the ground for human existence. The unhappy consciousness represents a higher stage of the dialectic than the former, since here we are concerned not with forces and representations as objects but with God, i.e., as a determination of thought and a self-conscious subject. By at once positing the unchangeable in thought and yet at the same time dwelling in the realm of the transitory, the unhappy consciousness forms a link between the two extremes: "The unhappy consciousness *is* this contact; it is the unity of pure thinking and individuality."[157] Yet this unity remains unknown to the unhappy consciousness until the final stage of this section: "But what it [the unhappy consciousness] does *not* know is that this its object, the unchangeable, which it knows essentially in the form of individuality, is *its own self*, is itself the individuality of consciousness."[158] Insofar as the unchangeable is a result of the unhappy consciousness's thought, it has for the philosophical observers no independent external existence; however, self-consciousness, like all true believers, has faith in the true ontological existence of its object of thought. Here the account of the subject-object Notion determined by the subject alone continues, yet this time the subject is absolute subjectivity, i.e., God, who determines all human existence. Here self-consciousness simply recognizes and accepts the divine determinations.

The problem with the attempt to understand the Notion in this way is that the God-man relationship represents an extreme form of the master-slave relation. Here God, like the master, is thought to give the complete and ultimate account of subjects and objects which must be merely accepted by self-consciousness. Yet, the unhappy consciousness, like the slave, finds itself on the wrong side of the essential-inessential dualism, i.e., it dwells in the fleeting human world and not with the timeless other. Hence, this account must be mediated by some middle term such that the unhappy consciousness can have genuine equal participation in the other sphere. The story of the attempts at mediation between these two unequal elements is the story of the unhappy consciousness. The futility of these attempts will ultimately lead us to a social mediation of the subject-object Notion.

The terms of the dialectic make clear this parallelism between the sections, "Force and the Understanding" and the "Freedom of Self-Consciousness," as do the parallel passages cited below, the first of which is taken from "Force and the Understanding" and the second from this section of "Self-Consciousness":

> Certainly, we have no knowledge of this inner world as it is here in its immediacy; but not because reason is too short-sighted or is limited, or however else one likes to call it—on this point, we know nothing as yet because we have not yet gone deep enough—but because of the simple nature of the matter in hand, that is to say, because in the *void* nothing is known, or, expressed from the other side, just because this inner world is determined as the *beyond* of consciousness.[159]

> Just as, on the one hand, when striving to find itself in the essence it takes hold only of its own separate existence, so on the other hand it cannot lay hold of the "other" as an *individual* or as an *actual* being. Where that "other" is sought, it cannot be found, for it is supposed to be just a *beyond*, something that can *not* be found.[160]

As we have seen from our analysis of "Force and the Understanding," the force behind the scenes or the supersensible world is unable to be conceived or determined simply because it is posited by consciousness as the beyond of consciousness which grounds appearances. Likewise, at the higher level of self-consciousness the same dialectic occurs. The unchangeable or God cannot be found, simply because it is conceived of as beyond the finite human subject. Hence, the dialectic of ground at first was played out at the level of objects with a ground as a thing, i.e., a force conceived by consciousness as the other and the beyond, and now it plays itself over again, this time at the level of self-consciousness, with self-conscious subjects. The other is this time a personified self-consciousness posited as a "beyond" by self-consciousness and which stands over and against the individual human subject. These passages help to make the dialectical parallelism clear.

The terms of this dualism, the unchangeable (God) and the changeable (man), pass through three steps, which Hegel characterizes as follows: "The movement in which the unessential consciousness strives to attain this oneness is itself threefold in accordance with the threefold relation this consciousness will have with its incarnate beyond: first, as pure consciousness; second, as a particular individual who approaches the actual world in the forms of desire and work; and third, as consciousness that is aware of its own being-for-self."[161] In the end, self-consciousness recognizes the truth of the religious community which is mutually determined and validated by the members of the congregation, and thus comes to realize the need for an account of the social sphere in the determination of the subject-object Notion. God corresponds to the realm of pure thought and the truths therein; this we saw before in the supersensible realm of unseen forces in "Force and the Understanding."[162]

In the first stage (§§ 215–17), consciousness conceives of the unchangeable in its transcendent form. Initially, God, or the unchangeable, appears as a beyond to which the believer tries to attain. Here consciousness is painfully divided, and this division requires a reconciliation by a unification of the unhappy consciousness with the unchangeable in its abstract form. The suffering of the believer is at its pinnacle, since the unhappy consciousness is at an infinite distance from God: "What we have here, then, is the inward movement of the pure heart which *feels* itself, but itself as agonizingly self-divided."[163] Here the relation to the unchangeable, due to the division between the unhappy consciousness and the unchangeable, is primarily emotional, often characterized by the expression "the pure heart," and not conceptual: "This infinite, pure inner feeling does indeed come into possession of its object; but this does not make its appearance in conceptual form."[164]

This division leads to an attempt at reconciliation between the two extremes. The unchangeable as universal becomes something individual or particular—Christ. God condescends to allow His Son to become an actual, individual, historical being in order to redeem man. This gives the world a new meaning and seems to render the insubstantial human world into something essential. Man thus should be able to attain to this particular incarnation of the universal and play a meaningful role in the account of the determination of subject and object, yet we are still unable to reach God: "When sought as a particular individual, it is not a *universal* individuality in the form of thought, not a *Notion*, but an individual in the form of an object, or an *actual* individual; an object of immediate sense-certainty, and for that very reason only something that has already vanished."[165] Christ is not an object of sense for us, but rather he is something that we can only imagine in the realm of thought. The attempt to bridge the transcendent gap between man and God with Christ fails, since a spatial-temporal gap is created in its place. We are historically separated from Christ and spatially separated from

Jerusalem. The unhappy consciousness remains separated from God and still is not thought to play a role in the account of the determination of the subject-object Notion. The believer attempts to locate his essence in the unchangeable but is doomed to failure, since the unchangeable is never able to be located.[166] The unhappy consciousness remains without the reconciliation that it originally sought. The point here is that the unhappy consciousness plays no role in the account of the subject-object Notion, and according to the account of the other, the unhappy consciousness inhabits a world which is inessential and insubstantial.

In the second stage (§§ 218–22), the unhappy consciousness tries a new strategy in order to give its life meaning and to attain the unchangeable. The believer must content himself with living a Christian life by imitating the life and works of Christ. Just as the slave reached a measure of independence by seeing himself in the products of his labor, so also the believer hopes to become one with the unchangeable through Christian acts. In the absence of Christ's physical being in the world, the believer must imitate his actions in order to associate himself with the divine: "In this return into self there comes to view its second relationship, that of desire and work in which consciousness finds confirmation of that inner certainty of itself which we know it has attained, by overcoming and enjoying the existence alien to it."[167] Here Hegel signals the beginning of the second stage by mentioning the "second relationship." We see the key terms of "desire" and "work" from the master-slave dialectic used again here. The inner certainty which indicates an overcoming of the dualism of the unchangeable and the changeable comes about in the believer through Christian acts.

The unhappy consciousness, however, does not find fulfillment in its work, since it attributes it not to itself but rather to the unchangeable: "Instead, therefore, of returning from its activity back into itself, and having obtained confirmation of its self-certainty, consciousness really reflects this activity back into the other extreme, which is thus exhibited as a pure universal, as the absolute power from which the activity started in all directions."[168] Yet the believer in his humble renunciation wishes to attribute all his works and activities to God, since they are the result of God's grace and were given as a free gift to man. Hence, a seeming unity is achieved through a reciprocal renunciation in which "the unchangeable consciousness *renounces* and *surrenders* its embodied form, while . . . the particular individual consciousness . . . *denies* itself the satisfaction of being conscious of its *independence*, and assigns the essence of its action not to itself but to the beyond."[169] This unity breaks down since the individual can never completely rid himself of his personal agency. "For though consciousness renounces the *show* of satisfying its feeling of self," Hegel writes, "it obtains the *actual* satisfaction of it; for it *has been* desire, work, and enjoyment; as consciousness it has *willed, acted* and *enjoyed.*"[170] The unhappy consciousness cannot at the same time purge itself of its own personal agency and reach a noncontradictory relation to work. Although it understands its skills and achievements merely as gifts of God and not of its own doing, nonetheless the unhappy consciousness cannot avoid the fact that it was the one who carried out the act and gained satisfaction from it. The contradiction is most clear in the act of giving thanks: "Similarly, even its *giving of thanks,* in which it acknowledges the other extreme as the essential being and counts itself nothing, is its *own* act which counterbalances the action of the other extreme, and meets the self-sacrificing beneficence with a *like* action."[171] In giving thanks, the unhappy consciousness implicitly recognizes that it is in possession of a skill or ability that is worthy of thankfulness. This then implies that the unhappy consciousness is not so entirely inessential and unworthy as it had supposed. Moreover, the act of thanksgiving itself ineluctably confirms the agency of the unhappy consciousness, since the act of giving thanks cannot be attributed to God. The believer must ultimately accept that even his most humble act—giving thanks—is his own, since the unchangeable would not give thanks to itself.

Finally, the unhappy consciousness reaches the third stage (§§ 223–30). Here the church emerges as the mediator between the unchangeable consciousness and the unessential consciousness. Hegel writes,

> This mediated relation is thus a syllogism in which the individuality, initially fixed in its antithesis to the *in-itself,* is united with this other extreme only through a third term. Through this middle term the one extreme, the unchangeable is brought into relation with the unessential consciousness. . . . This middle term is itself a conscious being [the mediator], for it is an action which mediates consciousness as such.[172]

The mediator, for Hegel, is the priest who (in the Catholic tradition) forms the link between God and the common believer. Only with the intercession of the priest and the church, the institution which he represents, can the unhappy consciousness overcome its dualism. The mediator, being thought to have direct access to both moments, represents the moment of unity. The believer is able to find reconciliation in the church in that he can now renounce his actions and surrender his will to the church and thus to God, and in this way, through his actions, the believer is concretely identified with God. The unhappy consciousness can remain humble about its own will and actions by simply performing the religious rituals and activities required by the priest:

In the mediator, then, this consciousness frees itself from action and enjoyment so far as they are regarded as its own. As a separate, independent extreme, it rejects the essence of its will, and casts upon the mediator or minister [priest] in its own freedom of decision, and herewith the responsibility for its own action. This mediator, having a direct relationship with the unchangeable being, ministers by giving advice on what is right.[173]

Self-consciousness thus overcomes the contradiction (in the second stage) of attributing actions to itself, although it was supposed to be meaningless and inessential. Here the unhappy consciousness need not take responsibility for its actions, since it is a mere servant of the priest or the church. Moreover, the unhappy consciousness surrenders its fulfillment from its action as well: "These [its labor and enjoyment] therefore, it rejects as well, and just as it renounces its *will*, so it renounces the *actuality* it received in work and enjoyment."[174] The church as the middle term "is the unity directly aware of both and connecting them, and is the consciousness of their unity."[175] Thus, the unity of the unchangeable and the unessential comes about.

Ultimately, this attempt to surrender one's will and to make contact with the divine through the mediation of the church and its officers remains unsuccessful. The church absorbs the individual believer in its universality, but only in principle and not in fact. The individual renounces his will but is unable to recognize it reflected in the universality of the church: "The surrender of its own will, as a *particular* will, is not taken by it to be in principle the positive aspect of universal will."[176] The individual remains alienated from the church and the universal will that it represents. Thus, the actions of the individual have only a "negative meaning"[177] in themselves. The church promises salvation and deliverance from misery, but this must always remain a promise, since it does not refer to life in the Christian community of the present but rather to an indeterminate time in the future when Christ will establish his kingdom of heaven. Until that time the suffering of the believer remains just what it is. Therefore, the unhappy consciousness' "misery is only *in principle* the reverse, i.e. its action brings it only *in principle* self-satisfaction or blessed enjoyment."[178] In fact, the unhappy consciousness is still alienated from the divine, and its renunciation of its will brings it no satisfaction. In short, everything remains as it was for the unhappy consciousness, and its joy and salvation are always deferred to the future: "But *for itself*, action and its own actual doing remain pitiable, its enjoyment remains pain, and the overcoming of these in a positive sense remains a *beyond*."[179] There is thus still a separation and an alienation from the divine. Despite this negative result of the third phase of the unhappy consciousness, there is also a positive insight, which is reached in the interaction of the unhappy consciousness with the community of the church.

The unhappy consciousness comes to realize that it must give an account of the social whole and its own relation to it in order for its account of the subject-object Notion to be complete. The important realization is that the unhappy consciousness can renounce its will and can find meaning in its own actions and works, understood as the activities of the believer, i.e., vigils, fasting, praying, etc. In these activities the believer is united with God through the church, which serves as the mediator. What the unhappy consciousness realizes is that the activities that it performs in this fashion have no merely arbitrary significance. Instead, they are essentially bound up with the life of the church. For such activities to make sense in the first place, there must first be the institution of the church which they presuppose. Without this institution such activities have only the arbitrary meaning that each individual assigns to them. Such activities are therefore not objective. Thus, the unhappy consciousness comes to see that what it essentially is as a human being is necessarily bound up with a social community and a human institution, since only through these things can its activity be understood as meaningful. Hence, the unhappy consciousness' truth-claims, likewise, must be understood in a social context, since the attempt to think such truth-claims as purely subjective is contradictory. Now the unhappy consciousness realizes that it must examine the constitution of the community and its relationship to the individual in order to arrive at a consistent subject-object Notion.

The unhappy consciousness ultimately comes to see that God's determinations lie not in the beyond but in the human world and in a human institution—the church. Here self-consciousness finally realizes that the determination of subject and object cannot be accounted for by an account solely of itself as subject or of God as subject. At each stage of the dialectic, the purely subjective attempt at determination broke down in a way that pointed to the community as a mediator of determinations. In order to make a truth-claim, self-consciousness must already be inside of a larger social community with institutions and norms about what counts as a truth-claim in the first place. Any account of self-consciousness in abstraction from the wider social community is necessarily incomplete, since self-consciousness is essentially a social creature, created and shaped in a social environment. Now at last self-consciousness realizes the need for this mediation and gives up its own pure subjectivity as the sufficient condition for an adequate subject-object Notion. Its own subjectivity is mediated by its participation in human institutions, and thus it is shaped and formed by this mediation as are its determinations. In the experience of servitude, self-consciousness has also learned that an adequate subject-object Notion is not the result of just any institution, since human relations in many institutions are based on power-claims, and, as a result, the ensuing subject-object Notion is not a rational one. Thus, the goal is to arrive at an account of human interaction in which human agents mutually recognize one another in a free environment such that an adequate subject-object Notion results from their mutual self-determination.

Concluding Remarks

The conception of a community of individuals that forms the necessary mediation is the important concept for our theme. The idea that satisfaction can be achieved among a group of people represents a significant improvement over the solution of the master-slave dialectic. For the first time, truth is not determined by atomic individuals and their desires, but rather by the individual in a community as a whole in the context of shared beliefs and practices. The dialectic of "Self-Consciousness" has taken us all the way to a transcendental theory of truth in the social sphere, whereby truth is determined by a network of self-conscious agents mutually interacting and participating in shared practices. In the next chapter we must try to understand how the same criteria for truth are carried through at the level of communities in the "Reason" chapter.

The dialectic of universal and particular that we have been tracing all along takes many forms here in the "Freedom of Self-Consciousness." At first, the Stoical self-consciousness tried paradoxically to determine itself as a particular via the universal medium of thought. This particularity disappeared as soon as the emptiness of pure thought as a criterion was recognized. The skeptical self-consciousness tried to determine itself as an individual by negating all other individual beliefs and opinions. But by this very action it left itself with no "other" or competing point of view of any merit which could serve to contrast with its own view and thus determine it. Skeptical self-consciousness thus became a simple relation of self-identity without difference. Finally and most obviously, the unhappy consciousness, dissatisfied with its impoverished individuality, desired to unite with the unchangeable and become a part of the universal. The manifold ways in which these attempts failed we have just examined.

Likewise, immediacy and mediation appear here in the "Freedom of Self-Consciousness," at first as Stoicism's mediated relation to the realm of thought via the object in which the Stoical self-consciousness sees itself. As we have seen, this contradicts Stoicism's immediate relation to its environment, which invariably reminds the stoical self-consciousness of its facticity and relation to the real world. In Skepticism, self-consciousness rejected and negated the other views which appeared to it as unmediated but which might otherwise have served to mediate its own account of objectivity. The unhappy consciousness is unhappy precisely because it has only an immediate relation to the unessential world while it desires an immediate relation to the unchangeable. Finally, the unhappy consciousness attains at least a mediated relation to the unchangeable through the priest and the church, designated appropriately enough as "the mediator."

The general outline of the "Self-Consciousness" chapter corresponds to that of "Consciousness." At first, in the "Consciousness" chapter the general Notion is that there are independent objects which are true and determinate in and of themselves apart from human subjects. Thus, the three categories—being, one and many, ground and consequence—are introduced and applied one after another to the sphere of objects. This then produces the various Notions that appear in that chapter. Given the contradictions produced by these various models, natural consciousness is compelled to give up its basic presupposition that there are individual self-determined objects. At this point the self-conscious subject is considered the true and the real, since it is what is thought to determine objectivity. Thus, in "Self-Consciousness" the same categories are applied to the sphere of subjects, and herein consists the parallelism. Table 5.1 represents the ground we have covered so far. The failure of "Self-Consciousness" to produce a consistent Notion demands once again that consciousness give up its basic premise that the single, atomic, isolated self-conscious subject determines objectivity. Now new elements must be introduced which shape the individual self-consciousness and its

Table 5.1

Category	Being	One and Many	Ground and Consequence
"Self-Consciousness"	"The Truth of Self-Certainty" Self-Consciousness	"Lordship and Bondage" Lord and Bondsman	"Freedom of Self-Consciousness" Pure Thought, Thought as Negation, the Unchangeable
"Consciousness"	"Sense-Certainty" This	"Perception" One and Also	"Force and the Understanding" Force, the Supersensible World, Law, the Inverted World

determinations. These new elements provide new material and a number of new contexts to which the categories can once again be applied. This parallelism of categories will continue in the coming chapters as well, and will allow us to establish the systematic unity of Hegel's text.

Hegel's transcendental argument develops roughly as follows: the task in the "Consciousness" chapter was to give a complete account of the determination of objectivity with reference to the object sphere itself. However, this proved inadequate. As a necessary presupposition for the determination of objectivity, the subject sphere had to be taken into account as well. The task of the "Self-Consciousness" chapter was to fulfill the original goal—to give a complete account of objectivity— but this time with reference to the subjective sphere. This too proved inadequate, since the self-conscious subject is not an isolated atomic entity, but rather is ontologically bound up with other self-conscious subjects. Thus, an account of the interaction of one self-consciousness with other self-conscious subjects must be given in a way that demonstrates how the social whole serves to shape the determination of objectivity in its interaction with the individual self-consciousness and vice versa. This is the task of the "Reason" chapter that we must now examine.

6

The Dialectic of Reason

General Introduction (§§231–39)

The "Reason" chapter of the *Phenomenology* and particularly its first section, entitled "Observing Reason," is one of the least known and least frequently taught parts of the entire book. The reasons for this are varied. First, this chapter strikes one immediately as disproportionately long in comparison to the two previous chapters, which renders it somewhat unwieldy to treat carefully either in the classroom or in a written discussion. Therefore, not surprisingly, a number of commentators devote to it only the briefest analysis and seem to do so only in order to get it out of the way before moving on.[1] At first glance, the size of the "Reason" chapter seems to be inordinately long. In the Miller translation, the "Consciousness" and "Self-Consciousness" chapters *together* take up some eighty pages, whereas the "Reason" chapter alone amounts to some 125 pages. This apparently disproportionate length, along with the uncertain organization and purpose[2] of "Reason" and the remaining chapters in the *Phenomenology*, has caused some scholars to question the thematic and structural unity of the work as a whole. In fact, the "Reason" chapter is precisely the locus in the text that is pointed to as the place where Hegel lost control over his creation and where it grew into something disunified. As one writer puts it, in this chapter Hegel "got carried away entirely."[3] For these reasons, it is here that the tenability of Hegel's purportedly organic system is most difficult to defend.

The second reason for this chapter's obscurity has to do with its extremely heterogeneous subject matter. The long first section of "Reason," which bears the title "Observing Reason," represents Hegel's philosophy of nature in the *Phenomenology* (which corresponds roughly to his treatment of the sciences in the second part of the *Encyclopaedia*). After this tedious discussion of scientific theory, Hegel discusses a number of different relationships of the individual to others and to the community in "Pleasure and Necessity," "The Law of the Heart and the Frenzy of Self-Conceit," etc. Finally, he seems to analyze a position that roughly corresponds to Kant's ethical theory in "Reason as Law-Giver" and "Reason as Testing Laws." In comparison with the chapters examined so far, where the discussions have been fairly continuous, the "Reason" chapter, with this strange mixture of natural science, ethics, and social analysis, seems to be extraordinarily heterogeneous and difficult to bring under a single theme or argument.

In my treatment of this chapter, I will attempt to show how the originally metaphysical categories that we have examined up until now are interpreted once again in terms of social relations and forms, this time at a level higher than that of "Self-Consciousness." These social relations will be shown to play a role in the development of the subject-object Notion just as did the purely objective metaphysical concepts (i.e., those in the object sphere) in "Consciousness" and the subjective concepts (i.e., those in the sphere of the subject) in "Self-Consciousness." Specifically, the "Reason" chapter represents natural consciousness's attempt to take into account the role of human institutions and social life in the collective establishment of mutually satisfying, epistemic, and ethical criteria of evaluation. A quick review will perhaps put the project of the "Reason" chapter into perspective. The upshot of the "Consciousness" chapter was that the subject-object Notion cannot be predetermined by the object sphere, but rather consciousness itself plays a crucial role in its determinations. The upshot of the "Self-Consciousness" chapter was that the Notion is not satisfactorily developed with an account of the abstract, individual subject alone, but rather it was learned that the subject's determinations must be socially mediated by other self-conscious subjects in the context of a wider community in order for self-consciousness's determinations to have truth and validity. "Reason" is the story of the various accounts of the social mediation of the subject-object Notion. At the end of the "Self-Consciousness" chapter, we saw how self-consciousness's attempts to give an account of the subject-object Notion only by means of its own subjective determinations and categories broke down in a way that indicated the need for an account of social institutions and the role of the community. We saw how, for the unhappy consciousness, the church represented just such a communal account of truth. In the church, the unhappy consciousness found its own truth-claims validated and objectified just as it validated the claims of its fellow believers. Hence, a specific subject-object Notion was found to be formed in a communal setting that went beyond the arbitrary claims of the individual. Now in "Reason" we go on to examine the various forms that this account of the role of the community takes in its relation to the individual for the development of the subject-object Notion.

At the end of "Self-Consciousness," the unhappy consciousness finally finds its fulfillment in the community of the church. The truth of the beyond, it discovers, is to be found merely in the shared practices and beliefs of the congregation. This truth is thus socially mediated via the institution of the church and the community of believers. The individual saw himself reflected in the socially accepted practices of the community and thus found himself in the world. Here, at the beginning of "Reason," this idea of a communally formed belief or truth continues, but this time not in the form of a religious community but rather in the form of a scientific community. The truth of the world is, on this view, simply the scientific account of the world, i.e., that which is agreed upon by a community of researchers. The scientific observer likewise finds himself reflected in the objects of observation, insofar as they are governed by regular laws that are accessible to reason.

At the beginning of the "Reason" chapter, Hegel once again explains the result of the dialectic of the unhappy consciousness in order to make clear the transition to "Reason."[4] He writes,

> In grasping the thought that the *single* individual consciousness is *in itself* absolute essence, consciousness has returned into itself. For the unhappy consciousness the in-itself is the beyond of itself. But its movement has resulted in positing the completely developed single individual, or the single individual that is an *actual* consciousness, as the *negative* of itself, viz. as the *objective* extreme; in other words, it has successfully struggled to divest itself of its being-for-self and has turned it into [mere] being.[5]

The unhappy consciousness posited God and thus true being and reality in a realm beyond this world. For the unhappy consciousness, "absolute essence" was something otherworldly that could never be observed directly in the mundane sphere. However, through the work of the priest and the mediation of the church, self-consciousness comes to realize that absolute essence lies in itself as a single individual and not in some ephemeral beyond. This realization comes through an understanding of the role of the church as the mediating institution between God and man, in which self-consciousness can realize or actualize itself in the world of objects and implicitly in the external social sphere. The result of this dialectical movement of the unhappy consciousness is "an *actual* consciousness [*wirkliches Bewußtsein*], as the negative of itself, viz. as the *objective* extreme." The key point here is what Hegel means by "an *actual* consciousness." Throughout the "Self-Consciousness" chapter we saw abstract, theoretical forms of self-consciousness. The lordship and bondage relation showed that each self-consciousness had its own self-relation, but relation to an other, understood as meaningful recognition, was precluded by the unequal status of the two parties. Thus, the self-relation or self-image of each self-conscious agent remained abstract, since it could not be actualized or realized in the world through the mediation or the recognition of an other. So also in "Stoicism, Skepticism and the Unhappy Consciousness," the self-image of the individual remained abstract and separated from the real world. Only at the end of the "Unhappy Consciousness" section did self-consciousness actualize or realize itself through its work as mediated by the church. Through its work in this social context, self-consciousness externalizes its own self-image and posits itself in the actual world. This is what Hegel means by "an *actual* consciousness" in the passage above. Self-consciousness is actual since it can be seen and recognized as an object of the real world in its work as opposed to remaining a mere abstract idea as in, for example, "Stoicism." The slave in the lordship and bondage dialectic tried to externalize himself through work, but the necessary egalitarian social context that would have provided meaningful recognition was missing, and thus he remained a slave. In the sphere of the unhappy consciousness, however, we witness for the first time true self-externalization and thus true realization of the individual. The self-externalization fundamentally involves recognizing oneself in the sphere of objects or as Hegel puts it "as the *negative* of itself, viz. as the *objective* extreme." Only as something objective in the real world can the abstract will of a self-conscious subject become a possible object of recognition by other self-conscious agents.[6] Formerly, the objective sphere was something foreign and other, which stood in opposition and contradiction to the self-conscious agent. It was thus something to be negated and destroyed as in, for instance, "The Truth of Self-Certainty." Now, however, since self-consciousness has realized itself through the process of externalization, it sees the external world of objects, and it recognizes itself in them. Thus, Hegel writes, self-consciousness "has also become aware of its *unity* with this universal."[7] Self-consciousness as an individual, by recognizing itself in the realm of objects, is united with that universal sphere and thus overcomes its own subjectivity by making possible intersubjective recognition and interaction in the process of the production of truth-claims.

By this externalization, which appears at this crucial transition to "Reason," self-consciousness is reconciled with external reality, and this reconciliation appears in the form of a subject-object unity. It is precisely the unity of subject and object that is characteristic of "Reason." Hegel describes this as follows:

> Now that self-consciousness is Reason, its hitherto negative relation to otherness turns round into a positive relation. Up till now it has been concerned only with its independence and freedom, concerned to save and maintain itself for itself at the expense of the *world*, or of its own actuality, both of which appeared to it as the negative of its essence. But as Reason, assured of itself, it is at peace with them, and can endure them; for it is certain that it is itself reality, or that everything actual is none other than itself; its thinking is itself directly actuality, and thus its relationship to the latter is that of idealism.[8]

The subject-object split that has dominated the dialectic up until now is in a sense overcome here with "Reason." As Hegel tells us in this passage, the object is not an independent other, as it was in the "Consciousness" chapter, and it is not something threatening which has to be negated, as in the "Self-Consciousness" chapter; now, the other or the world of objects is simply a reflection of the self-conscious subject. This implies that self-consciousness makes its peace with the external world by declaring itself to be identical with it. By the claim that the world is merely a self-reflection of self-consciousness itself, Hegel, at the level of "Observing Reason" which we are about to examine, means that the world is conceived as something that is intelligible via scientific theory. The theory of the sciences, both natural and social, is of course abstract and operates at the level of thought, and thus it falls on the side of the subject; however, this theory is also thought to depict the external world accurately, and thus it mirrors or reflects the world in itself. Therefore, since self-consciousness is associated with thought and scientific theory which it finds evidence for in the world, it sees itself reflected in the world, insofar as it can recognize law-governed phenomena in the natural order. The task then of scientific theory is to seek out the rational in nature, since precisely this aspect of nature represents its truth and can be grasped by the human intellect. The external world is not negated as before in "Self-Consciousness," since it is no longer anything foreign or threatening. Thus, "Reason" is the standpoint where self-consciousness sees itself as all reality in the sense that it recognizes the fundamental structures of thought, here understood as the laws and principles of scientific theory, in the external world. This is the position which Hegel refers to as "idealism."[9] As the paragraphs in this introductory section attest,[10] Hegel has at least in some measure the idealism of Fichte in mind here.

A parallelism with the preceding chapters can be seen predictably enough with respect to Reason's relation to its object.[11] Here the issue is the *certainty* of Reason, and this is the key to our comparison with "Consciousness" and "Self-Consciousness." In the first section of the "Consciousness" chapter, natural consciousness thought that it had *sense*-certainty, i.e., it thought that what was immediately given as a propertyless "This" was true and thus was the object of certainty. In the first section of the "Self-Consciousness" chapter, we saw a new sort of certainty arise, i.e., the truth of *self*-certainty. Here natural consciousness, after realizing that it plays the crucial role in the account of the determination of the subject-object Notion, deems itself the true and the certain, whereas whatever was other than the self it considered nonbeing and something inessential. The category of being thus moves from the objective to the subjective realm between these two chapters. Here in the "Reason" chapter, Hegel explains this relation between "Consciousness" and "Self-Consciousness" as follows:

> There appeared two aspects, one after the other: one in which the essence or the true had for consciousness the determinateness of *being*, the other in which it had the determinateness of being only *for consciousness*. But the two reduced themselves to a single truth, viz. that what *is*, or the in-itself, only *is* insofar as it is *for* consciousness, and what is *for* consciousness is also *in itself* or has *intrinsic* being.[12]

The first aspect mentioned in this passage is, of course, "Consciousness," and the second "Self-Consciousness," which come together in the third, i.e., "Reason." Now here at the level of "Reason" we are concerned with the *certainty* of Reason. The certainty of Reason differs from self-certainty in the following respect: in self-certainty the self, qua individual "I," is considered the true and the real, whereas in the certainty of reason, the certainty is of the union of the self with the external world and of the universal with the particular. In other words, self-consciousness is certain that it sees itself reflected in the natural order in the form of abstract scientific laws. Thus, in these laws and in the λόγος of nature it sees itself objectified in the external sphere, and it thus overcomes its merely abstract and theoretical self-image that it leaves behind at the level of self-consciousness. Insofar as self-consciousness realizes itself and objectifies its will in the external world, it overcomes its subjectivity. It now becomes something objective and as such becomes a possible object of recognition and validation. Thus, the subject of reason is no longer the abstract, subjective "I" of self-consciousness, but rather is a universal "I" that is continuous with the natural order and which recognizes itself in that order. Hegel expresses this as follows: "Reason appeals to the *self*-consciousness of each and every consciousness."[13] With respect to natural scientific inquiry, the individual with his own characteristics and idiosyncrasies is not what is important. A scientific experiment must in principle be able to be carried out by a universal subject, and in this sense science is impersonal. Hence, at the level of "Reason," the subject-object Notion is socially determined by a group whose members are parts of a larger social whole, whereas in "Self-Consciousness" it is precisely the isolated individual who determines the truth.

In addition to these statements about the necessity of working through the dialectical forms of consciousness and self-consciousness, Hegel gives a clear explication of the way in which the coming section, "Observing Reason," is to fit with what has come before, and these hints will be a great help in the attempt to reconstruct the systematic unity of the work as a whole. He writes, "Since Reason is all reality in the sense of the abstract 'mine,' and the 'other' is for it something indifferent and extraneous, what is here made explicit is that kind of knowing of an 'other' by Reason, which we met with in the form of 'meaning,' 'perceiving' and the 'understanding,' which apprehends what is 'meant' and what is 'perceived.' "[14] Here Hegel indicates that the dialectical movements that we have examined from the "Consciousness" chapter, i.e., "Sense-Certainty," "Perception," and "Force and the Understanding" will be repeated here at a higher level, i.e., at the level of "Reason." Thus, the "Observing Reason" section will correspond as a whole to the "Consciousness" chapter, while its three sections will correspond to the individual sections of the "Consciousness" chapter.[15] Using this as a guide, we end up with the following parallelism:

Consciousness	Observing Reason
1. Sense-Certainty	1. Observation of Nature
2. Perception	2. Observation of Self-Consciousness in Its Purity and in Its Relation to External Actuality
3. Force and the Understanding	3. Observation of Self-Consciousness in Its Relation to Its Immediate Actuality

I do not want to insist strictly on this parallelism since, as we shall see, there is some overlapping and some combining of themes from the individual sections. However, the general parallelism between "Consciousness" and "Observing Reason" is quite unproblematic given the evidence at hand. In the course of our analysis, we must try to get clearer about in what respect specifically the parallelism exists and in what respect the corresponding sections differ.

A quick glance back at the table of contents will confirm this parallel structure. Hegel revised his table of contents after the *Phenomenology* was already completed. I take Hegel's second version to be his considered opinion about the structure of the text, and, in my view, this second version squares with the argumentative course of the work as well. Let us then cast a glance at this second version of the table of contents in order to see how the "Reason" chapter fits with the two chapters we have just examined.

The Second Scheme

A. Consciousness

B. Self-Consciousness

C. (AA.) Reason

A. Observing Reason

B. The Actualization of Rational Self-Consciousness through Its Own Activity

C. Individuality Which Takes Itself to Be Real In and For Itself

(BB.) Spirit

A. The True Spirit. The Ethical Order

B. Self-Alienated Spirit. Culture

C. Spirit That Is Certain of Itself. Morality

(CC.) Religion

A. Natural Religion

B. Religion in the Form of Art

C. The Revealed Religion

(DD.) Absolute Knowing

The key question here is what the single and the double letters are supposed to indicate about the structure of the text. In my view, which I think is supported by the text internally by virtue of the corresponding arguments in the relevant chapters, the single and double letters are meant to indicate the parallelisms among the various parts of the text. "Consciousness" and "Self-Consciousness" are meant to form independent units that build upon one another (hence the A and B). Then comes "Reason," which also forms an independent unit (hence the C), but here something is different. By inserting the AA in front of the "Reason" chapter, Hegel means to indicate that the dialectic at this point goes back to the original position (represented by A) and works through the same forms of consciousness again, but at a different level. This is precisely what the passage cited above indicates, i.e., that the "Consciousness" chapter corresponds to the first section of the "Reason" chapter. Likewise, "Spirit" and "Religion," which are also represented with double letters (BB and CC) thereby showing their parallelism with "Reason," return to the beginning of the cycle as well and work through each of the figures again under their own aspect. This then gives us an important clue into the architectonic of the work as a whole, which we will have to try to test in the course of our analysis vis-à-vis Hegel's further statements about the structure and plan of the work as well as the internal development of the argument itself. As we shall see later, this hypothesis is expressly supported by Hegel's comment[16] that with "Reason" we in a sense revert from self-consciousness back to consciousness.

When seen in this light, the apparently disproportionate length of the "Reason" chapter begins to make sense. This chapter must be longer than the "Consciousness" and the "Self-Consciousness" chapters, since it is intended to work through the same material found there, and in addition it even adds a third section which is supposed to complete the sequence. When we see that "Consciousness" is supposed to correspond to "Observing Reason" and not to the entire "Reason" chapter, then the disparity in length becomes nominal. The former consists of forty-five pages in the English translation while the latter has sixty-five pages—a difference which is hardly significant. The second section in "Reason," which then corresponds to the "Self-Consciousness" chapter, is in fact shorter than its correspondent. With this structure in mind, we are now prepared to turn to our analysis of the individual sections of "Observing Reason."

A. The Repetition of "Consciousness": Observing Reason (§§240–346)

General Introduction (§§240–43)

As was mentioned above, the section entitled "Observing Reason" is probably the least known section in the entire book, yet it is extremely important for a number of different reasons.[17] The length of this section alone is intimidating enough for most students; however, it is its content which discourages most otherwise enthusiastic readers. In this section, Hegel analyzes the scientific understanding of the world, and in order to do so he draws, naturally enough, on the scientific theory of his day.

The remoteness of the scientific theories which he discusses has led one commentator to remark that this is "the most foreign section of the *Phenomenology*."[18] For anyone who is not a historian of science, this long section can, indeed, be very difficult to understand. Hence, this section of the *Phenomenology* is relatively unknown for the same reason that the second book of the *Encyclopaedia*, i.e., *The Philosophy of Nature*, is relatively unknown; namely, they both treat largely obsolete scientific theories which are generally inaccessible to most modern readers. Moreover, in this section Hegel draws heavily on Schelling's *Naturphilosophie*, to which he is reacting and which he is in part rehashing. Since Schelling's philosophy is for most modern students entirely unknown, this section is all the more difficult.

The thesis outlined above that "Observing Reason" corresponds to and in some way repeats the phenomenological movement of the "Consciousness" chapter is confirmed in Hegel's brief introductory discussion of this section. Of "Observing Reason," he writes, "It is true that we now see this consciousness, for which being [*Sein*] means what is its own [*Seinen*], revert to the standpoint of 'meaning' and 'perceiving'; but not in the sense that it is certain of what is merely an 'other.' "[19] Hegel tells us explicitly in this passage that the dialectic that we are about to examine will "revert to" or go back to the level of "Sense-Certainty" (i.e., "meaning") and "Perception" (i.e., "perceiving"). However, it is clear that we have already traversed precisely this dialectical terrain, and we thus cannot expect that the dialectic will simply go back to the beginning and start over again. What does Hegel mean then with this claim that we will return to "Sense-Certainty"? In what respect will we return and in what respect will we remain here at a different conceptual level in "Reason"? I will argue that the parallelism and continuity in these sections lies in the common categories that are used to determine the subject-object Notion at the different levels. Specifically, the dialectic will run through the same sequence of categories again, and in this we can see that the dialectic reverts to the beginning; it will parallel these moments at the higher level of "Reason." In the passage cited above, Hegel mentions explicitly the category of "being" that we began with in the "Sense-Certainty" section. But as he makes clear, being is not conceived of here in "Reason" as something external and independent of consciousness as it was then. Now, in the first section of "Observing Reason," being becomes reinterpreted as the scientific structure of the natural order which reflects self-consciousness' thought and thus self-consciousness itself. This is the key to the play on words that Hegel uses in this passage. The German word *Sein*, meaning "being," is strangely similar to the possessive adjective used here in its substantive form (*Seinen*). Hegel uses this wordplay to emphasize the fact that being, at the level of "Reason," is not an independent other but rather is something which belongs to self-consciousness itself or in which self-consciousness sees itself. There is thus a unity of subject and object (captured by this wordplay) that did not exist at the stage of consciousness. It is precisely this that distinguishes the level of "Consciousness" from the level of "Observing Reason." Hegel continues, "Previously, its perception and *experience* of various aspects of the thing were something that only *happened to* consciousness; but here, consciousness *makes its own* observations and experiments."[20] In the "Consciousness" chapter, natural consciousness considered the truth to lie in the objective, external world. This world was passively received by consciousness, who added nothing to it. Here, on the other hand, the self-conscious subject takes an active role in examining the natural order. In "Observing Reason," consciousness examines and observes nature according to the scientific method, and by so doing comes to recognize itself in the natural order.

In these few paragraphs prior to the "Observation of Nature" section, Hegel outlines in some detail the general Notion of the section "Observing Reason." He takes here the Notion of these three sections together and later dilates upon the individual concepts or forms of the Notion in more detail in their respective sections. There is in principle a single Notion that is treated in these three sections: namely, that scientific observation and theory can determine truth. Similarly, as we saw above, there is in principle a single Notion in the "Consciousness" chapter— namely, that external objects are independent and are determinate in themselves. Thus, it is not surprising that Hegel outlines this general Notion here, prior to the individual sections in question, and explains later what the variants of it are in the individual cases.[21]

At this level, the supposition of self-consciousness is that the world is a cosmos, i.e., that it is rule-governed and conforms to universal patterns, in short, that it is rational and therefore comprehensible; thus, it can be explored and examined with the tools of the natural sciences. The scientific theories order the manifold phenomena into structures comprehensible to reason. Thus, in the world of scientific theory and law, one recognizes the structure of nature, and in nature one recognizes the vestige of rational self-consciousness, which is able to find the order in the chaos of the natural world: "Reason now has, therefore, a universal *interest* in the world, because it is certain of its presence in the world, or that the world present to it is rational. It seeks its 'other,' knowing that therein it possesses nothing else but itself."[22] In seeing the other, i.e., the world of nature, self-consciousness simultaneously sees itself by being able to recognize the rationality in the natural order. As we shall see in more detail later, this position is roughly that of Schelling, who argues that the task of the natural sciences is to make nature into something mental (*Vergeistigung*). The idea is that one so thoroughly orders the various phenomena found in nature into mental categories and theoretical constructs such that nothing escapes being a part of the mental process or model.

As we have already seen, the category of being again comes to play the crucial role even at this social level. Here the universal structure of the scientific account of nature (purportedly found in nature) or the communal account of truth is reified and considered as the true. Hegel states the role of being at this level as follows: "It is the first *positivity* in which self-consciousness is *in its own self* explicitly *for itself*, and 'I' is therefore only the *pure essentiality* of the existent, or is the simple *category*. The category, which formerly had the meaning of being the essentiality of the existent . . . is now the essentiality or simple *unity* of the existent only as a reality that thinks."[23] Here being is attached to the "reality that thinks," i.e., to the scientific account generated by the community of rational observers. The social whole in the form of a community of scientists is now thought to play the key role in the determination of the subject-object Notion. In other words, at this level it is the group which sets the standards for what counts as a proper experiment or theory. Moreover, it is the group which dictates what counts as reliable investigative methods and how experience is to be interpreted. By the determination of these standards, the community simultaneously determines the object domain of what will count as objective and valid. For the phenomenological actor, this scientific account is not arbitrary or idiosyncratic, but rather it represents a true and accurate account of the world. Thus, the being that we are concerned with here is simultaneously being on the subject side of scientific observers and on the object side of the natural order. And with this account of objectivity, an account of subjectivity is also implicitly given. This social whole is made up of individual agents in their universal form, i.e., as any scientific observer. Thus, the individual is abstracted from his individuality. To be counted as a scientist one must first be socialized in a certain way. This socialization can be seen as a process of both abstraction from one's individuality and affiliation with the scientific enterprise as represented by the currently successful scientific theory.

Although, to be sure, truth is here considered to issue from the results of scientific analyses, and there is no independent, external other, nevertheless, as in "Self-Consciousness" the subject-object dualism is in a sense still present here, as Hegel is quick to point out once again with a reference to Fichte:

"*I am I*, my object and my essence is *I*"; and no one will deny Reason this truth. But in basing itself on this appeal, Reason sanctions the truth of the other certainty, viz. that there is for me an "other"; that an other than "I" is object and is essence for me, or, in that I am object and essence to myself, I am only so by drawing back from the "other" altogether, and taking my place as an actuality *alongside* it.[24]

The claim that the world is simply what the scientific account of the world says it is (i.e., as it is for the universal "I" as scientific observer) tends to reify science's own subject matter and to give it some sort of independent existence. The scientific account must be an account of *something*, and this something is thus the new other of thought. This does not necessarily imply that the scientific account corresponds to something preexisting. Rather, it means that there is some sort of raw material with which science works, although, to be sure, truth-claims are verified by the norms of verification which are defined by the scientific group, and thus this process is a predominantly social enterprise. Hence, the dialectic in the first section of "Reason" operates between the new subject-object split, i.e., the scientific community and the subject matter of its inquiry. "Observing Reason" is the story of the various forms that this subject matter takes along with its various relationships to the scientific observer.

Finally, Hegel signals that the general discussion of the Notion of "Observing Reason" is here complete, and that it is now time to turn to the individual forms of the Notion in order to test them for internal consistency: "This *action* of Reason in its observational role we have to consider in the moments of its movement: how it looks upon nature and Spirit, and, lastly, upon the relationship of both in the form of sensuous being, and how it seeks itself as actuality in the form of immediate being."[25] In this passage, not only does Hegel signal that we are now about to begin with the experience of consciousness, but he also provides us with the relevant differences in the Notion that will be treated in the individual sections of "Observing Reason." At first consciousness will observe "nature," i.e., "Observation of Nature." Then it will observe itself or "Spirit," i.e., "Observation of Self-Consciousness in Its Purity and in Its Relation to External Activity." Finally, it will combine these two or will observe "the relationship of both in the form of sensuous being," and this combination will be treated in the final section, "Observation of Self-Consciousness in Its Relation to Its Immediate Actuality." With this outline, we are now prepared to turn to the first dialectical experience of consciousness represented by the "Observation of Nature."

I. Observation of Nature: The Natural Sciences (§§244–97)

In this first section, "Observation of Nature," Hegel treats the truth-claims of the various natural sciences, e.g., biology, anatomy, and physics. In the next section, by contrast, he treats psychology, which he takes to be representative of the social sciences. In his day the social sciences were, of course, only in their incipient phase and were developed only in their most rudimentary forms. Since Hegel compresses his treatment of all the natural sciences into this one section, the task of the student of the *Phenomenology* here is to pull apart the various discussions and to give them some sort of order. At times, this requires reconstructing some of the science of Hegel's own day. Hegel tries here to outline the conceptual movement of natural scientific thinking in order to show that it too is not immune from self-contradictions and paradoxes.

The Notion: Observation of the Natural World

As we have seen, Hegel has already outlined the basic thesis of "Observing Reason" as a whole, and thus he does not do so again in any great detail here. We saw that observing consciousness believes that truth lies in its observation and scientific analysis of the world. As we also saw,[26] Hegel then breaks down this general Notion into three more determinate Notions corresponding to three different object domains: nature, Spirit, and then a combination of both. Here in "Observation of Nature," we begin with the first object domain—the natural order. Thus, the Notion at this stage amounts to a claim about the truth of scientific analysis of objects of nature. Of all the Notions that Hegel discusses, this one is among the most plausible and intuitive for the modern reader, since our commonsense belief in the natural sciences tells us that what biology, chemistry, and physics say about the world is in fact true. Hegel wants to question precisely this naive or "natural" belief by examining the logic of scientific analysis which, on his view, invariably leads to contradictions and absurdities.

As we indicated earlier, the Notion here in "Observation of Nature" parallels at the categorial level the Notion that was examined in the "Sense-Certainty" section of the "Consciousness" chapter. Specifically, the first category that was examined in the "Consciousness" chapter was pure being, which was considered the most immediate categorial determination possible. So also here in the first section, "Observation of Nature," we begin with the category of immediate being:[27] "Reason, as it *immediately* comes before us as the certainty of consciousness that it is all reality, takes its reality in the sense of the *immediacy of being*, and similarly, the unity of the 'I' with this objective being in the sense of an *immediate unity*, in which it has not yet divided and reunited the moments of being and the 'I,' or which has not yet discerned them."[28] Just as in "Sense-Certainty," the object domain is considered immediate being, and the subject is thought of as an immediately unified "I." These two terms form the basis of the new subject-object split once again, and it is this dualism that must be overcome. The naive belief of observing consciousness at this first stage is that it sees the world of nature as something that can be captured by scientific theory. It understands the world in terms of "Notions" or scientific theories, which it believes correspond to the external world of objects. It fails to see that these "Notions" in fact constitute the world and are necessarily bound up with it. Earlier we tentatively put forward the thesis that there is a parallelism between the "Consciousness" chapter and the "Observing Reason" section. According to this thesis, the individual categories of the various sections of the "Consciousness" chapter ought to find their correspondents here. This, I wish to argue, is precisely what we find.

The objects of scientific observation become the new other of thought. Hegel summarizes the dualism of "Observing Reason" thus: "Reason, therefore, in its observational activity, approaches things in the belief that it truly apprehends them as sensuous things opposite to the 'I.' "[29] What Reason does not realize is that in the course of scientific observation and explanation, it organizes its subject matter in such a way that it no longer remains an autonomous subject matter or other of thought. Hegel continues, "but what it [sc. Reason] actually does, contradicts this belief, for it apprehends them [sc. the sensuous things opposite to the 'I'] *intellectually*, it transforms their sensuous being into *Notions*, i.e. into just that kind of being which is at the same time 'I,' hence transforms thought into the form of being, or being into the form of thought."[30] In scientific classification and schematization, the original chaos of nature is given an order and structure by thought in order to make it comprehensible. As such it is no longer, or put better, it never was nature as it is in itself, but rather it is the product of thought, and so observing consciousness sees that the world is like itself. This is the realization of self-consciousness at the end of "Observing Reason" after it has run through the various dualisms at this level: "Self-Consciousness found the thing to be like itself, and itself to be like a thing; i.e., it is aware that it is *in itself* the objectively real world."[31]

Hegel has in mind here in this section the philosophy of nature of his friend and colleague Schelling, who conceived of the idea of the task of the natural sciences as unifying the various natural laws and making them more and more abstract. In his *System of Transcendental Idealism,* Schelling writes,

> The necessary tendency of all *natural science* is thus to move from nature to intelligence. This and nothing else is at the bottom of the urge to bring *theory* into the phenomena of nature.—The highest consummation of natural science would be the complete spiritualizing of all natural laws into laws of intuition and thought. The phenomena (the matter) must wholly disappear, and only the laws (the form) remain. Hence it is, that the more lawfulness emerges in nature itself, the more the husk disappears, the phenomena themselves become more mental, and at length vanish entirely. . . . The completed theory of nature would be that whereby the whole of nature was resolved into an intelligence.[32]

The task of the natural sciences, for Schelling, is to begin with the empirical phenomena and to reduce them to fundamental laws of thought or to the "Notion," in Hegel's terms. The goal is the complete comprehension of nature via the abstract laws of mathematics and physics, and it is in this way that the natural scientist ultimately tries to free the sciences from their empirical aspect. Thus, we go beyond the empirical phenomena and reach a level of necessity and truth. Hegel writes, "This essential nature of theirs, to pass over immediately into a neutral product, makes their *being* into a being which is implicitly superseded or universal." One begins with a specific concrete being, and, through the natural scientific understanding of it, one is able to go beyond this particular being and to understand it as universal being. Schelling's account, just as here in "Observing Reason," emphasizes the role of the subject in the positing of the abstract universal laws of nature. For Schelling there is a correspondence between mind and nature, insofar as the scientist discovers the universals in nature. So also at this point in the *Phenomenology,* observing consciousness sees itself in the world of empirical phenomena, and the abstract laws are the mediating element between the two.

One important point here is that any scientific claim that we make about the world necessarily presupposes a set of institutions and a community of researchers with agreed upon methods and theories (roughly in the sense of a Kuhnian paradigm). In other words, any scientific claim about the world is not so much a claim about some external other, but rather it is more a claim about the scientific framework or paradigm within which one is working. The very concepts, to say nothing of the object models which science uses to understand nature, are historically mutable, since they are bound up with the network of meaning that forms any given scientific theory. Thus, it is an illusion to think that one can make an isolated, individual claim about the world without relying on a larger structure of shared meaning which makes up scientific theory.

The essence of Hegel's point here can be fruitfully illuminated by considering some of Kuhn's work on the relation between science, truth, and the social community. In this section, Hegel has anticipated many of Kuhn's insights, although we must be sure to note that Hegel's account is supposed to be nonempirical in the way we have tried to indicate earlier, whereas Kuhn's account could be seen as both empirical and sociological. As Kuhn has so aptly shown, the network of scientific meaning is not a wholly rational construction. Behind hegemonic scientific theories lies a whole set of practices and institutions which are in fact all too transitory. For instance, the education of young scientists can be seen, as Kuhn points out, simply as indoctrination into the practices and truth-claims of the ruling paradigm. In such an atmosphere, the first premise about whether or not the dominant paradigm is true is never seriously challenged. The scientific enterprise is necessarily carried on by a social group with a shared set of core doctrinal beliefs as well as a common idea about how to pass those beliefs on to others. The point of all this is simply that the project of scientific inquiry implies a common set of beliefs and practices among the members of a social group, and any purportedly scientific claim about the world is necessarily a reflection of this whole background of presuppositions. This is what observing consciousness comes to realize in the end.

The Experience of Consciousness (§§244–97)

The In-Itself Moment: Observation of Objects of Nature (§§244–54)

Classification (§§244–47)

This section on the "Observation of Nature" begins with an account of scientific description and classification. The classification of organic and inorganic objects involves, for Hegel, typically enough, the movement from particular to universal. For instance, one perceives with the senses a particular animal. This particular becomes a universal, insofar as one categorizes it under a specific genus or species. These general categories have no specific content but rather are universals. Thus, in the observation of nature, we are not concerned with what is particular to each individual plant or animal, but rather with what is universal in the particular entities. Hegel writes,

> This universal is thus, to begin with, only what remains *identical with itself*; its movement is only the uniform recurrence of the same action.

Consciousness, which thus far finds in the object only *universality* . . . must take upon itself the movement proper to the object and, since it is not yet the understanding of the object, must at least be the remembrance of it, which expresses in a universal way what is actually present only as a single item.[33]

What the scientific observer looks for in the object is that which "remains identical with itself," i.e., some form of continuity that connects different plants or animals under the same aspect. Thus, one looks for the commonality in things and ignores the superficial differences which are not relevant for scientific classification. These differences are then the empirical particulars, while the commonalties which serve as the basis for the categories of genus, species, etc., form the universals. "What enables things to be intelligently apprehended," Hegel writes, "is more important to it [sc. the self-conscious observer] than the rest of the complex sensuous properties which, of course, the thing itself cannot dispense with, but which consciousness can do without."[34] The object in itself has a number of properties, all of which belong to it and which it "cannot dispense with." However, observing consciousness must select certain properties as relevant for purposes of categorization, and it must separate these from the irrelevant ones. For instance, the color of a particular bear's pelt is not relevant with respect to its being a mammal, whereas other characteristics are essential to it, i.e., that it nurses its young, that it is born live without feathers, etc. As observers, we abstract from the empirical particulars in order to be able to categorize the given empirical entities under universal headings. This is what Hegel refers to as "the activity of *describing* things,"[35] and the plurality of the natural world provides us with an endless supply of material to be described and classified.

On this view, our scientific ordering is not a mere construct that is useful for distinguishing certain things from others, but rather it corresponds to the reality of the world itself. This is in fact the very standpoint of Reason: "*Differentiae* are supposed, not merely to have an essential connection with cognition, but also to accord with the essential characteristics of things, and our artificial system is supposed to accord with nature's own system and to express only this. This follows necessarily from the Notion of Reason."[36] According to this view, observing consciousness constructs a model of the universe which is not an idiosyncratic or "artificial system" imposed on reality but rather one which accurately mirrors the world or "nature's own system." Thus, the characteristics of plants and animals which the observer selects as relevant vis-à-vis the process of categorization are also the truly relevant and essential categories, while the other categories are simply inessential: "The distinguishing marks of animals, e.g., are taken from their claws and teeth; for in point of fact it is not only cognition that thereby distinguishes one animal from another, but each animal itself *separates* itself from the other thereby."[37] The distinctions are not merely in our theories or, as Hegel says, "in cognition," but rather they are distinctions which lie at the heart of reality itself.

Description and classification become problematic, since the diversity of the empirical world puts the scheme of classification under such great stress that it merely reduces to a simple description of the individual entities. In other words, in the best system of classification of the natural order there are a number of gray areas between the categories, and there are overlapping and conflicting properties which belong in some cases to one group and in some cases to another. Every rule has an exception, since the manifold of the natural world defies any clear-cut order. Hegel describes this as follows:

> Observation, which kept them [the essential and inessential characteristics] properly apart and believed that in them it had something firm and settled, sees principles overlapping one another, transitions and confusions developing; what it at first took to be absolutely separate, it sees combined with something else, and what it reckoned to be in combination, it sees apart and separate.[38]

The anomalies and exceptions in the scheme of classification compel observing consciousness to back down from its claims about the universality and necessity of the general categories. The more complex the scheme becomes in order to take into account more objects and entities and consequently more exceptions, the more the scheme reduces to a simple description of individual objects lacking any universal feature. He writes,

> So it is that observation, which clings to passive, unbroken selfsameness of being, inevitably sees itself tormented just in its most general determinations—e.g. of what are the *differentiae* of an animal or a plant—by instances which rob it of every determination, invalidate the universality to which it had risen, and reduce it to an observation and description which is devoid of thought.[39]

What is left is a simple description of individual objects in the absence of any real scheme of classification at all. The observation is thus "devoid of thought," since it no longer contains any real universal structure or scheme of classification. The observed entity remains rather at the level of empirical description.

Explanation: Law and Experiment (§§248–54)

Having fallen back into the plurality of particularity, observing consciousness seeks a new way to order the chaos of the natural order and to bring
together the discrete empirical elements under some universal form. It
once again seeks the rational order of things which it identifies with itself.
It then tries to order things according to scientific laws; hence, we move
from classification to law. Hegel describes this transition when he writes,

> Since Reason now reaches the stage of looking for the determinateness as
> something which essentially is *not* for itself, but which passes over into its
> opposite, it seeks for the *law* and the *Notion* of the determinateness. True,
> it seeks for them equally as an actuality in the form of *immediate being*,
> but this will, in fact, vanish for it, and the aspects of the law become pure
> moments of abstractions.[40]

Since classification failed to determine individual species adequately,
observing consciousness hopes to find the determination of the object in
law. Just as before, the scheme of classification that corresponded to the
natural order was considered to be pure being, so also here "immediate
being" is bound up with the scientific law which mirrors the natural order.
It becomes the new universal that tries to capture the apparently isolated,
individual phenomena. Thus, we remain with the same category of pure
being that we saw in "Sense-Certainty."

Just as before the classificatory scheme was not an artificial system
but was actually a fact about the world, so also here, for observing
consciousness, scientific law has its true reality and justification in the
empirical world where this abstract law is confirmed by various empirical
phenomena: "To the observing consciousness, the *truth of the law* is found
in *experience*, in the same way that sensuous being is [an object] for
consciousness."[41] If the actual empirical phenomena were to contradict
the law, then we would be compelled to give it up and replace it with a
new one. Thus, the true reality of the law is in fact to be found in the
natural phenomena: "The law is valid as a law because it is manifested in
the world of appearance, and is also in its own self a Notion."[42]

However, this view of law proves to be problematic since it raises
what has come to be known as the problem of induction that was treated
by Hume.[43] Hegel describes the problem in terms of justifying the law of
gravity by means of the example of dropping rocks and watching them fall:

> The assertion that stones fall when raised above the ground and dropped
> certainly does not require us to make this experiment with every stone;
> it does perhaps mean that the experiment must have been made with

at least a great number, and from this we can then *by analogy* draw an inference about the rest with the greatest probability or with perfect right. But analogy . . . does not give a perfect right.[44]

As Hume showed, the necessity of scientific laws cannot ultimately be justified by a large number of empirical experiments of this kind. Although in the past every stone that was raised and dropped happened to fall, this in no way justifies the claim that *of necessity* the next stone that is raised and dropped must fall. There is no logical contradiction in the thought that a dropped stone does not fall in the way that there seems to be a necessary contradiction in the concept of a four-sided triangle. We can perhaps approach necessity by dropping ever more stones and by making ever more experiments, but ultimately we cannot justify laws of this kind empirically. The best we can do is to weaken the claims about necessity and retreat to a notion of strong probability. We can say that the next stone that is dropped will *in all probability* fall, although there is nothing in principle that speaks against the possibility that our future experience might radically contradict our experience heretofore, and thus we cannot guarantee the necessity of its falling. Thus, observing consciousness is compelled to reduce "the truth of the matter itself to the level of probability."[45]

By means of experiment, observing consciousness hopes to separate out the relevant from the irrelevant aspects of the phenomena in order to arrive at what Hegel calls the "pure law." The goal is to overcome the various specific empirical aspects of the phenomena and to end up with a purely abstract law:

> The law as it first appears exhibits itself in an impure form, enveloped in single, sensuous forms of being, and the Notion constituting its nature is immersed in empirical material. In its experiments the instinct of Reason sets out to find what happens in such and such circumstances. . . . The inner significance of this investigation is to find the *pure conditions* of the law; and this means nothing else . . . than to raise the law into the form of Notion, and to free its moments completely from being tied to a specific being.[46]

What Hegel means here by raising "the law into the form of Notion" is that a scientific law must be a universal in order for it to be a law. Hegel uses the word "Notion" here to mean something conceptual, such as an abstract universal law that stands in contrast to the manifold of empirical reality. It cannot remain at the level of the particular phenomena that it wishes to describe. It would be absurd to have a plurality of individual scientific laws that corresponded to every individual empirical phenomenon. Thus, the goal of science is to capture the manifold of the natural world with as few laws as possible. This can be seen in the attempt in contemporary physics to derive some kind of a unified theory that would combine the results of relativity theory and quantum mechanics, thus bringing under a single law phenomena at the macrolevel with those at the microlevel.

As we have seen earlier in our discussion of Schelling, the object of science, on this view, is to eliminate the empirical elements entirely and to end up with a universal law. Hegel expresses this as follows: "This essential nature of theirs [sc. of natural objects], to pass over immediately into a neutral product, makes their *being* into a being which is implicitly superseded or universal."[47] The individual being of, for instance, a falling rock is superseded by the abstract law of gravitation. As an instance of a law, the rock no longer has sensuous being but rather is something conceptual. To the way of thinking of observing consciousness, experiment performs the function of raising empirical being to the conceptual level.

The problem with this conception of pure law involves, predictably enough, the universal-particular split. Specifically, the abstract relations which are determined by scientific law, such as acid and base or positive and negative electrical charge, have their meaning only at the abstract conceptual level. "But these separated detached things," Hegel writes, "have no actuality; the power which forces them apart cannot prevent them from at once entering again into a process, for they are only this relation. They cannot, like a tooth or a claw, remain apart on their own and as such be pointed out."[48] At the level of classification, entities were distinguishable at the sensible level by characteristics such as the teeth or claws of animals. Now at this level the distinctions are purely conceptual and no longer have any relation to the empirical element. These conceptual distinctions "have no reality" in the sense that they cannot be experienced. "The result of the experience," Hegel writes, "is in this way to cancel the moments or activated sides as properties of specific things, and to free the predicates from their subjects."[49] In other words, experimenting consciousness divorces the predicate of the falling rock from the sensible entity and places it in a purely conceptual law. This divorce then leaves both the sensible entities and the universal laws indeterminate, since the former no longer have any meaningful properties and the latter have no existent actuality. Being understood at the level of universality is what Hegel refers to as "matter" or "matters": "*Matter*, on the contrary, is not an *existent thing*, but is being in the form of a *universal*, or in the form of a Notion."[50] The specific object, a table, a stone, a fruit, is irrelevant, since at the conceptual level at which science operates they are all referred to as matter or as individual matters. Hegel refers to this as "*pure law*"[51] as well.

We have here the important transition from inorganic to organic being. On Hegel's view, as we have seen, the relation that we have just examined of a plurality of inorganic beings that are connected through an external universal law is inadequate. In other words, the universal-particular dialectic takes place between general laws which encompass a number of phenomena and objects and the discrete entities themselves. Now observing consciousness looks for a single entity which has this universal-particular relationship within itself, i.e., that does not have to appeal to other objects to find its universal side. Organic nature is full of such objects. Hegel expresses this as follows:

> The inorganic thing has determinateness for its essential nature, and for that reason constitutes the moments of the Notion in their completeness only together with another thing, and therefore is lost when it enters into the process; in the organic being, on the contrary, every determinateness through which it is open to an other is controlled by the organic simple unity.[52]

Organic nature has a universal within itself as an individual organism. This universal is its end, and this stands in contrast to its particular sensible form. The dialectic of the teleology of organic nature is thus the next step that observing consciousness explores.

The For-Itself Moment: Observation of Organic Nature (§§255–87)

Teleology (§§255–65)

Observing consciousness now backs down from the conception of "pure law" or matters and tries to see the law in individual organic entities. Hegel describes this shift as follows: "This which is in truth the result and essence [of its activity], is now present to this consciousness itself, but as an *object* . . . it presents itself to consciousness as a *particular kind* of object, and the relation of consciousness to it appears as another kind of observation."[53] This new object is an "organism" or "organic being" in general,[54] and the new law becomes a law of ends or teleology. By teleology here, Hegel understands something like the following: plants and animals and the organic sphere in general adapt themselves in manners appropriate to their surroundings. The natural environment is thus the end toward which the individual organic entities aim. For instance, according to this view, it is the end of animals that live in the sea to have fins and gills, while it is the end of animals that live in cold climates to have warm pelts. These general teleological principles become the new universals which correspond to law in the previous analysis and to classification before that.

Teleology understood in this fashion fails for two reasons: first the laws that issue from it fail to capture the plurality of the natural order. Hegel describes this by saying, "But laws of this kind: animals belonging to the air have the nature of birds, those belonging to water have the nature of fish, animals in northern latitudes have thick hairy pelts, and so on—such laws are seen at a glance to display a poverty which does not do justice to the manifold variety of organic nature."[55] These teleological laws are too general and are thus unable to distinguish between specific types of organic entities. In other words, it is well and good to say that animals "belonging to water have the nature of fish," since this helps us to distinguish fish from say reptiles or mammals; however, this sort of law is entirely too general to help us to distinguish specific types of fish. This kind of law stops at a very general level and is unable to penetrate further and to explain the full spectrum of organic life in its rich detail.

The second reason why this type of teleological explanation is inadequate is that it fails to provide the element of necessity which it purports to contain in its laws. When the matter is examined more carefully, we find that in fact there is no necessary relation whatever between the individual characteristics found in the various plants and animals and the natural environment:

> In the Notion of acid lies the *Notion* of base, just as the Notion of positive electricity *implies* that of negative; but often as we may find a thick, hairy pelt associated with northern latitudes, or the structure of a fish associated with water, or that of birds with air, the Notion of north does not imply the Notion of a thick, hairy pelt, the Notion of sea does not imply the Notion of the structure of fish, or the Notion of air that of the structure of birds.[56]

Simply because animals that live in the water tend to have fins, there is no strict necessity that links water with fins. Likewise, though there may be a great many animals living in northern extremities that have thick furs, there is no necessity in this law. It is rather an empirical observation of the type which Hume called a "constant conjunction." In other words, all we can really say is that we have enumerated a number of experiences in which this conjunction of characteristics is present, i.e., "living in the north" and "having a thick pelt." However, as we know from Hume, even an extremely large number of such empirical observations will never supply the strict necessity requisite for a law if the given characteristic is

not already contained in the very nature of the concept itself in the way
that "three-sided" necessarily belongs to the concept "triangle."

There are, however, two kinds of teleological concepts.[57] In the analysis just discussed, the end of an organism is in the natural environment
and thus is something external to the organism itself. The organism
aims to adapt itself to conditions that are external to it, and in this
adaptation lies its essence. There is, however, another sense of teleology
according to which an organism develops not in accordance with some
external arbitrary standard but rather internally, according to its own
nature and principle. On this view, the end is not something external
but rather is essentially bound up with the organism itself; this is what
Hegel calls the "real end,"[58] and it is this notion of teleology that Hegel
much prefers. Here Hegel refers back to the notion of the "end in itself"[59]
(*Zweck an sich selbst;* sometimes *Endzweck*), which was an important idea
in the teleological theories current in German philosophy before his
day.[60] This was an influential concept above all in moral theory, which
considered human beings as true ends in themselves, which means that
humans have an absolute worth and ought not to be used as a means
toward some other end. In the *Critique of Judgment,* Kant makes use of this
term in his treatment of nature, and it is his account that Hegel most
likely has in mind. To say that nature is an end in itself means merely
that the development of nature ultimately serves no other purpose than
self-development. This idea of an immanent development was extremely
attractive to Hegel. Observing consciousness, on the other hand, views the
ends in nature as essentially external to the organism: "But firstly, the end
is for that instinct *outside* of the thing presenting itself as end. Secondly,
this end, *qua* end, is also *objective,* and therefore does not fall within the
observing consciousness itself, but in another intelligence."[61] Observing
consciousness sees the ends in nature as external to itself. Its attempt
to understand the end of nature through laws or classificatory schemes
merely confirms the dualism between its own theoretical construct and
a preexistent reality.

Observing consciousness then realizes that it needs to move from
the conception of an outer teleology to that of an inner one. Specifically,
the problem confronting observing consciousness is that it desires to stay
at the empirical level of observation, but yet in its observation it is unable
to perceive the end of the organic entity, which seems to be something
nonempirical. Hegel describes this as follows:

> As instinct, Reason also remains at the level of [mere] *being* and a state of
> *indifference,* and the thing expressing the Notion remains for it something
> other than this Notion, and the Notion other than the thing. . . . But this

> observing consciousness does not recognize in this being the Notion of
> end, or that the Notion of end exists just here and in the form of the
> thing, and not elsewhere in some other intelligence.[62]

Thus, a split comes about again between the empirical and the conceptual, the particular and the universal. Since observing consciousness cannot discern the teleology of the organism in its empirical, undifferentiated being, it must appeal to some other form of teleology that operates at the conceptual level beyond the realm of sense: "this unity of universality [sc. the ends] and the activity [sc. the observed empirical activity of the organism] does not exist for this *observing* consciousness, because that unity is essentially the inner movement of the organism and can only be grasped as Notion."[63] As we have just seen from the examination of the environment, nothing necessarily follows about the teleological nature of the entities with respect to the environment they inhabit. The end or teleology of the organism can only be made sense of when we abstract from the empirical observations and try to conceive of the organism apart from its empirical element or according to its "Notion" or its true inner side.

The Inner (§§265–82)

This split between the empirical and the conceptual naturally gives rise to another split between the inner and the outer. The inner represents the side that is hidden from the world of appearance, which contains the true τέλος or end, while the outer is precisely the form in which the object presents itself to experience:

> In this way, the organism appears to the observing consciousness as a
> relation of two *fixed* moments in the form of *immediate* being—of an
> antithesis whose two sides, on the one hand, appear to be given to it in
> observation, and on the other hand, as regards their content, express the
> antithesis of the organic *Notion* of *end* and actuality. . . . Thus we see the
> Notion taken to mean roughly the *inner*, and actuality the *outer*; and their
> relation produces the law that *the outer is the expression of the inner*.[64]

Since the end of the organism cannot be seen in its immediate activity or being, observing consciousness concludes, it must be present in the organism's "inner aspect." This inner side is expressed only indirectly in the empirical or external side which can be observed. However, the inner and the outer aspects of the organism are not considered to be essentially distinct since both belong essentially to the same organism and express the same thing.

The inner-outer split is intended by Hegel to capture a distinction between two different sorts of biological explanation.[65] The first, which belongs to anatomy, tries to understand the organism in terms of specific structures or systems, namely the nervous system, the muscular system and the intestinal system. Hegel refers to the organism so understood as the outer presumably because these systems are part of an organism's outer morphology. As we will see, consistent with his general insistence of systematic thought, Hegel is critical of this kind of explanatory strategy, since it tries to understand individual systems in isolation from one another as a whole. As one commentator writes, "The underlying theme of the *Phenomenology*—the truth is the whole—is never stronger than it is recorded in Hegel's account of biological phenomena."[66] The second kind of explanation is that based on function and belongs to the field of physiology. Here three capacities or functions are isolated for study: sensibility, irritability, and reproduction. This represents the inner aspect of the organism.

As Hegel tells us,[67] we must now examine the structure of both the inner and the outer aspect of the organism in order to see if their correspondence can be consistently thought. The unity of the inner and outer aspects of the organism is expressed in the unity of the three structures—the nervous, muscular, and intestinal systems—with the three functions: sensibility, irritability, and reproduction.[68] With respect to the latter, Hegel is referring to the theory of physiology of the gifted Albrecht von Haller (1708–77), as described in his *Elementa physiologiae corporis humani* (*The Elements of the Physiology of the Human Body*), published in eight volumes from 1759 to 1766. There Haller correctly distinguished between nerve impulse, which he called "sensibility," and the contraction of muscles, which he dubbed "irritability."[69] This theory was popular in Germany during Hegel's time due to Schelling's criticism of it and one of its adherents, John Brown (1735–88), in the former's work *On the World-Soul*.[70] For the concept of irritability, Haller relied heavily on the work of Francis Glisson (1597–1677), who examined the expansion and contraction of organs such as the heart and intestines. Glisson noted that a light stimulus was sufficient to produce the contraction, and he called this capacity for contraction "irritability" in response to stimuli. Haller took up Glisson's notion of irritability and distinguished it from what he called "sensibility," which was the same quality for contraction, but which was a force in the nerves instead of in the muscles. The three organic capacities were put together in a system by the biologist Karl-Friedrich Kielmeyer (1765–1844), whose lectures in 1793, "On the Relation of the Organic Powers," were decidedly influential for Schelling, among others.[71]

These two capacities of irritability and sensibility along with reproduction express, on the one hand, the inner or universal structure of
the organism, insofar as they are universal properties common to all
organisms and, on the other hand, the outer, insofar as they can be
concretely observed in terms of the corresponding natural systems and
organs of each individual organism. Although sensibility is a universal
property or capacity, we can see it manifested empirically in the nervous
system of each individual organism.[72] Likewise, we can observe irritability
in the muscular system of the organism. Thus, these three properties unify
the dual nature of the inner and the outer of the organism: "The laws
peculiar to organism accordingly concern a relationship of the organic
moments in their twofold significance, once as being a *part* of the organic
structure, and again as being a *universal fluid* determinateness which
pervades all those systems."[73] In other words, every individual organism
has as a part of its organic structure certain systems, e.g., the reproductive
system, the nervous system, etc., but these systems, although found in
individual organic entities, are in fact, qua systems, universals. Thus, the
law of organic nature is simply that it is characterized by these universal
systems, which are found empirically in the individual organic entities:
"Thus, in formulating such a law, a specific sensibility, e.g., would find its
expression, *qua* moment of the *whole* organism, in a specifically formed
nervous system, or it would also be linked up with a specific *reproduction*
of the organic parts of the individual."[74] Thus, the universal systems are
purportedly the inner aspect of the organic life in general, which can be
perceived by observing reason in its outer aspect as a particular system
in a particular organism. In this way the inner is thought to mirror the
outer, and a law is thought to connect the two aspects.

The law that connects the aspects of inner and outer, however,
becomes problematic.[75] We begin first by analyzing the concept of the
inner, which proves to be a complex concept which has a plurality of
characteristics: "the aspect or the inner is, on its own account, also a
relationship of several aspects."[76] Before we can determine whether or not
the law is able to connect the inner and the outer, we must first analyze the
various aspects of the inner, i.e. sensibility, irritability, and reproduction,
so as to know precisely what it is that the outer must correspond to:
"Whether such a law [sc. connecting the inner and the outer] is possible
must be decided from the nature of such a property [sc. the properties
constituting the realm of the inner]."[77] The problem that observing reason faces is how to formulate a law that satisfactorily distinguishes the two
capacities of sensibility and irritability. Before Haller's time they in fact
were not distinguished. When observing reason examines the capacity of
sensibility, it notices that it stands in a law-governed relation to irritability.

Specifically, it realizes that the two properties stand in an inverse relation to one another: when sensibility increases, irritability decreases. This, however, cannot truly be considered a law, since it amounts to a simple tautology, as Hegel illustrates with the following example:

> Should, however, a specific content, as given to this law, say, that the size of a hole *increases*, the more what it is filled with *decreases*, then this inverse relation can equally be changed into a direct relation and expressed in this way, that the size of the hole *increases* in direct ratio to the amount taken away—a *tautological* proposition, whether expressed as a direct or as an inverse ratio.[78]

The reciprocal relationship of the two aspects or properties of the organism, i.e., sensibility and irritability, indicates the unitary nature of the two aspects which were thought to be distinct universals which, along with reproduction, characterized organic life. Thus, since the two aspects are essentially identical, it does not matter which of them one chooses to analyze when examining organic life: "it is a matter of indifference whether an organic phenomenon is considered as irritability or as sensibility."[79]

These two aspects of organic life thus collapse into one another, and we are left with reproduction, the third characteristic of organic life. Reproduction, however, is not in a reciprocal relationship as the other two were, and it resists being characterized by laws:

> Lastly, if instead of sensibility and irritability, reproduction is brought into relation with one or the other of them, there is no longer even the occasion for making laws of this kind; for reproduction does not stand in an antithetical relation to those moments as they do to one another; and since this law-making is based on such an antithesis, here even the show of its being practiced is absent.[80]

Here the process of formulating laws cannot even get off the ground, since reproduction is considered something different and distinct from the other two aspects of organic life. In order for there to be a law, one object or element must stand in some regular relationship to another. Lacking this relationship, we are left merely to describe the individual entity, and we cannot generate a general law.

Next, all of these functions or capacities are considered to be merely properties, which in principle are independent of one another or, as Hegel says, which are "equally indifferent towards one another."[81] Each property is autonomous, and each organic being must be examined in terms of the three properties distinctly in order to be analyzed correctly.

Sensibility, irritability, and reproduction all exist independent of one another in the same entity just as the properties of white, round, and salty can simultaneously exist in the same entity without any contradiction. However, the organism viewed in this way becomes indeterminate, since it contains within it three mutually existing and independent characteristics, but these are in no way bound together in a single unit or organic system. They seem, on the contrary, to be indifferent to one another: "because those simple moments are pervasive fluid properties, they do not have in the organic thing such a separate, real expression as what is called an individual system of the shape."[82] With nothing to unite these properties, the organism remains indeterminate. However, as we know, the truth of the organism lies in its interconnections and its complete structure and not in the individual parts seen in isolation from one another:

> Since the *being* of the organism is essentially a universality or a reflection-into-self, the *being* of its totality, like its moments, cannot consist in an anatomical system; on the contrary, the actual expression of the whole, and the externalization of its moments, are really found only as a movement which runs its course through the various parts of the structure, a movement in which what is forcibly detached and fixed as an individual system essentially displays itself as a fluid moment.[83]

Anatomy, by studying only the organism from its outer aspect as an inanimate dead entity fails to grasp the organism in its living truth. In other words, anatomy can, on Hegel's view, only examine the various organs in isolation and perhaps make speculations about how the various organs work together; however, the truth of an organic entity is in its living form as a living and developing structure. The task of the natural scientific community is then to grasp this living structure as such and not to abstract from it and analyze it in its dead, inanimate form after the fact. Here it becomes clear, after our analysis of the various components of the inner sphere, that the law between the inner and the outer sphere that we were searching for is rendered impossible: "In this way the idea of a *law* in the case of organic being is altogether lost."[84]

One problem raised by commentators of this section is that Hegel here simply repeats the same discussion of the one and the many from "Perception" and of force and matters from "Force and the Understanding." How can Hegel claim that his work has a systematic structure when he repeats the same material in various sections? This repetition seems to be a sign of careless composition indicative of the fact that Hegel paid little attention to the overall structure of the work. However, this reproach badly misunderstands the systematic structure of the work which we have been following. To start with, as we have seen above, this first section in "Reason" corresponds to the first section in "Consciousness," i.e., "Sense-Certainty" and not to "Perception" or "Force and the Understanding." Moreover, Hegel himself addressed precisely this problem and tells us explicitly the ways in which this discussion is intended to differ from those discussions. Not surprisingly, the difference lies in the level of sophistication of the Notion that we are examining.[85] Hegel writes,

> If, namely, we look back to the movement of perceiving and to that of the understanding, in which the latter reflects itself into itself, and thereby determines its object, we see that the understanding does not, in that movement, have before itself in its object the *relation* of these abstract determinations of universal and individual, essential and external: it is itself the transition, which does not become objective to it. Here, on the contrary, the organic unity, which is just the relation of those opposites, this relation being a pure transition, is itself the *object*.[86]

The key difference between the moments of "Consciousness," taken together here as "Perception" and "Force and the Understanding," lies in the fact that the universal and the particular are split, with only one side being domiciled on the side of the object. In "Perception," the universal is thought to be the "One" or the unity in the manifold of empirical properties, and it is alternately placed on the side of the subject and the object. Or in "Force and the Understanding," for instance, the particular was seen as the various empirical manifestations that natural consciousness perceived, whereas the universal was in the force behind the scenes that caused these manifestations. But with the interaction and solicitation of forces, it became clear that the human subject could also be seen as a force. In any case, the universal and the particular were split up, the one being on the side of the subject and the other on the side of the object. This is what I take Hegel to mean when he says in the passage above "we see that the understanding does not . . . have before itself in its object the *relation* of . . . universal and individual." Now, however, in the present section, "Observing Reason," the universal and particular are united in the object. As Hegel puts it above, "Here, on the contrary, the organic unity, which is just the relation of those opposites . . . is itself the *object*." Now the two aspects are not split up between the subject and the object, the mind and the world, but rather inhere together in the object domain. This is precisely what is meant by the equivalence of the inner and the outer. The inner is the hidden universal and the outer is the empirical form, but both are thought to reside on the side of the object, and they are thought to parallel one another.

Hegel continues with his comparison of "Consciousness" and "Observing Reason" by comparing the objects of both with respect to the question of sensible properties. He writes,

> *Immediate* sensuous being is immediately one with the determinateness as such, and therefore expresses a qualitative difference in that being, e.g. blue as against red, acid as against alkali, and so on. But organic being that has returned into itself is completely indifferent towards an other, its existence is a simple universality, and it denies to observation any lasting sensuous differences.[87]

Here Hegel takes "Sense-Certainty" (sc. *immediate* sensuous being) and "Perception," the conception of an object as a thing with properties, together. As we saw earlier, the object for this consciousness is one that is essentially determined by the comparison and contrast of its properties with other objects. Thus, the object of "Perception" has its determination in an other, so to speak. However, for "Observing Reason" these properties are not relevant or essential for the determination of its object domain. It does not matter if a dog is black or gray, since according to the conceptual scheme of observing consciousness these are not essential characteristics in the determination of what it is to be a dog. Thus, dogness is "a simple universality," or, as Aristotle says, a natural kind. With this example we can see fairly clearly that the level of sophistication of the conceptual scheme here in "Observing Reason" is considerably higher than that of "Perception." In the former we have an elaborate conceptual framework of inner and outer law, classificatory schemes, and theories of the muscular, nervous, and reproductive systems, whereas in "Perception" the conceptual scheme amounts to nothing more than saying that an object is simply a thing with properties. Hegel illustrates this with a few examples of an object as understood by "Consciousness" and as understood by "Observing Reason." He writes, "something which perception takes to be an 'animal with strong muscles' is defined [here in "Observing Reason"] as an 'animal organism of high irritability,' or what perception takes to be a 'condition of great weakness' is defined as a 'condition of high sensibility,' or if we prefer it, as an 'abnormal affection.' "[88] The Notion of "Perception," according to which an object is a thing with properties, understands the animal in which a well-developed musculature is found as an animal with the property of "strong muscles." On the other hand, the same empirical phenomenon is described differently by observing consciousness, who interprets the musculature in terms of the physiological functions of sensibility, irritability, and reproduction that characterize all organic life. Thus, it defines the same animal as an "organism of high irritability."

Hegel, however, does not think that the new way of conceiving entities that comes about here in "Observing Reason" is any more effective at determining the object or, in this case, the organism than were the Notions involved in the "Consciousness" chapter. According to the dialectical movement here, explanations and determinations of this kind in fact leave the object indeterminate. "Though the indefiniteness of the expressions 'force,' 'strength,' and 'weakness' was thereby eliminated," he writes, "there now arises equally futile, vague floundering-about between the antitheses of higher and lower sensibility and irritability as they increase and decrease relatively to one another."[89] Thus, although it seems that consciousness has won some explanatory advantages by getting rid of the mysterious, unseen forces as the determining factors, nonetheless new explanatory principles are employed which are equally ad hoc, vague, and in need of revision and precision. What is really meant by "higher" or "lower sensibility"? Is there anything more to their interaction than a simple tautologous inverse relation? These terms in the final analysis fail to determine the organism just as the concepts in "Consciousness" failed to determine their objects.

The Outer (§§283–87)

As Hegel tells us explicitly,[90] we now turn to an examination of the outer aspect of organic being. Typically, the outer is considered the inessential element. "The *outer*," Hegel writes, "considered by itself, is the *structured shape* in general, the system of life articulating itself in the *element* of being, and at the same time essentially the being *for an other* of the organism—objective being in its *being-for-self*. This *other* appears, in the first instance, as its outer inorganic nature."[91] In this difficult passage, Hegel sets up the new dualism that is operative in this analysis. The dualism consists of two distinct aspects of organic nature: first, organic nature understood as the outer is seen as mere being, as something inorganic. By this Hegel seems to mean that from the outside, organic entities often cannot be distinguished from inorganic ones. The true organic nature of the entity, consisting for instance of sensibility and irritability, is something internal and not readily visible from the outer shell. The inner is thought of as a numerically single entity or as an "infinite One,"[92] whereas the outer aspect consists of the plurality of external properties such as color, shape, texture, etc. Understood only by virtue of its inner aspect, the entity "can only be that which is expressed in *number*."[93] In other words, the only thing that can be said about the entity is that it is a numerically identical organic entity in its inner being since the qualities of its outer being do not count as essential for its determination: "That which in the former, the *inner*, would be expressed *numerically*, the outer would have to express in accordance with *its* mode as a multiform actuality, viz. as its manner of life, color, etc."[94] Thus, where the inner failed to determine the entity, the outer here seems to succeed.

However, this Notion runs aground again on precisely the inner-outer relation. This conception of the relation of the inner to the outer in organic beings amounts simply to saying that in fact there is no such relation. In other words, the outer properties and characteristics seem indifferent to the numerical unity of the entity since the former are qualitative, concerning color, texture, shape, etc., while the latter are quantitative, i.e., numerically singular. Thus, the qualitative cannot be translated into the quantitative. For Hegel, this reduces organic being to inorganic being:

> But to consider the *shape* of the organism as such, and the inner, *qua* inner, merely of the shape, is in fact no longer to consider organic being. For the two aspects which were supposed to be related are posited as merely indifferent towards each other, with the result that the reflection-into-self which constitutes the essence of the organism is done away with.[95]

By seeing the inner of an organism as a mere number or as a numerical identity and not as a living and developing entity, we in fact see the organism as a lifeless thing.

The In-and-For-Itself Moment: Organic and Inorganic Nature (§§287–97)

At this point the dialectic goes back and reintroduces inorganic nature in order to analyze both organic and inorganic nature together.[96] Hegel describes this return to lifeless nature as follows:

> But to consider the *shape* of the organism as such, and the inner, *qua* inner, merely of the shape, is in fact no longer to consider organic being. For the two aspects which were supposed to be related are posited as merely indifferent towards each other, with the result that the reflection-into-self which constitutes the essence of the organism is done away with. What really happens here is that the attempted comparison of inner and outer is transferred to inorganic nature.[97]

As we have seen above, for Hegel the main characteristic of inorganic being is that it is an individual or particular which is separated from the universal, or which has the universal outside of itself in, for instance, pure laws. Here we find just such a constellation. The inner is merely a numerical unity, which is an abstract concept. This concept stands in opposition to the manifold of properties and characteristics displayed by outer existence. The numerical identity has no relation to the external properties.[98] Hegel thus concludes that the inner and the outer stand in a relation that only truly applies in the sphere of inorganic life. We now must turn to this analysis: "This relation of inner and outer has thus still to be considered in its own proper sphere."[99] By "its own proper sphere" Hegel means the sphere of organic and inorganic life, and it is to this sphere that we now turn.

Specific Gravity and Cohesion (§§288–91)

The first concept that is analyzed is that of "specific gravity," which forms the inner aspect of inorganic nature.[100] The first thing to get straight about is what Hegel means by this concept. In physics, specific gravity is that ratio that is expressed by the mass of a specific volume of substance compared with the mass of the same volume of some standard substance such as water. Thus, we could say that the specific gravity of a given object is two times more dense than that of water. With respect to the dialectical movement that we are following, the suggestion is made here that we understand the specific gravity of an entity to be its true inner substance or essence and its other qualities to be merely accidental. The specific gravity is thus the object's true inner being, whereas its shape and color, etc., form its superficial, nonessential outer being.[101]

Observing consciousness is now obliged to think through the relation between the inner and the outer with this conception of specific gravity as the inner. Since the inner must somehow reflect the outer or run parallel to it, we must examine the outer to determine how it corresponds to specific gravity. It is precisely here that this conception fails. In the manifold of external properties that constitute the outer, there is nothing that can be said to correspond to the inner. Hegel uses the example of a series of entities which are determined to stand in a specific numerical relation to one another according to their specific gravity. Let us imagine three objects which have a regularly increasing degree of specific gravity. The problem is that the relation of these three objects is in no way reflected by the outer relation of properties: "This being so, then a series of bodies in which the difference is expressed as a numerical difference of their specific gravities by no means runs parallel to a series in which the difference is that of the other properties."[102] When we examine the outer properties we find absolutely nothing at all resembling the numerical relation of specific gravity of the three objects. In fact, we even find qualitative differences which cannot in principle be expressed by a quantitative or numerical relation. Thus, the relation of the inner to the outer with the inner understood as specific gravity fails.

In contrast to this inner being or specific gravity we have the concept of cohesion,[103] which forms the outer aspect of the inorganic entity: "If this plurality itself is concentrated into the simplicity of the antithesis, and determined, say as *cohesion,* so that this cohesion is a *being-for-self in otherness* (just as specific gravity is a *pure being-for-self*), then this cohesion is in the first place pure determinateness posited in the Notion in contrast to that other determinateness."[104] But yet the individual properties such as white, hard, and salty are indifferent to the simple gravity of the entity. In other words, cohesion as a whole is independent of the very essence of the entity, and thus they "are Notions completely indifferent towards each other."[105] Cohesion has two sides, the one or the unity of the entity, and the plurality of properties.[106]

The Organic Universal (Genus) and the Determinate Universal (Species) and the Universal Individual (the Earth) (§§292–94)

This then leads us to the dialectic of genus and species.[107] Here we meet once again Hegel's term of art "genus," which we saw earlier in "The Truth of Self-Certainty." Just as there genus was associated with the universal continuity of life, so also here genus is what Hegel calls "the *universal life,*"[108] which he contrasts to the more specific term "species." The dialectic of universal genus and species is the beginning of the last attempt to come up with a determinate scheme which will capture the diversity of nature. The attempt amounts to ordering nature into a universal scheme involving the terms genus and species. Hegel introduces and contrasts the two terms in the following passage:

> But now, though pure negativity, the principle of the process, does not fall outside of the organism, which therefore does not have it in its *essence* as a determinateness, the single individual being itself intrinsically universal, yet in the organism the moments of this pure individual are not developed and actual as moments which are themselves *abstract* or *universal.* On the contrary, this their expression appears outside of that universality, which falls back into the *inwardness* of the organism; and between the actual existence or shape, i.e. the self-developing individual, and the organic universal or the genus, there comes the *determinate* universal, the *species.*[109]

Genus is the more universal or abstract of the two terms. Species is also a universal but its scope is not as wide as genus, and thus it is ordered under genus. Finally, there are determinate individual organisms which fall under any given species. Thus, genus is the abstract universal, whereas species is what Hegel calls the "*determinate* universal." What he seems to indicate here is that although species is also a universal it is not so encompassing as the other universal, genus. There are many different species which can be determined with respect to the various qualities and properties that characterize them vis-à-vis other species. The determinate universal of species is thus a sort of halfway house between the genuine universal of genus and the genuine particular that is simply the individual organism. This scheme is then thought to be able to capture the plurality of nature.

Typically, the scheme of genus and species breaks down and leaves its object domain indeterminate. The problem seems to be the indifference of the relationships of individual to species and species to genus. Hegel describes this in the following extremely dense passage:

> True universality, as we have defined it, is here only an *inner essence;* as *determinateness of the species* it is a formal universality, and, over against this, the true universality takes its stand on the side of the single individual, which is thereby a living individual, and in virtue of its *inner being* takes no account of its *determinateness as species.* But this individual is not at the same time a universal individual, i.e. one in which the universality would have an outer actual existence as well; the universal individual falls outside of the living organism.[110]

What Hegel seems to mean here is that a given individual organism is in the final analysis an individual, which is indifferent to the abstract determinations or characteristics of its species. The indifference has to do with the fact that the organism is, qua species, determined only in its inner sphere, i.e., only abstractly in thought. This determination cannot, however, be immediately recognized from the side of the empirical or the outer. Ultimately, for Hegel the distinctions between individual and species or genus are arbitrary. When we observe certain forms of insect life such as ants, for example, one can make a strong case that the entire colony constitutes a single organism and the individual ants perform functions analogous to the various systems in the body, i.e., nourishment, waste disposal, etc. Examples like this call into question the distinction between individual and genus by demonstrating that certain aggregates, e.g., ant colonies, can in fact quite plausibly constitute an individual entity. Thus, although taxonomists might be able to understand differences between an individual entity and species or a species and genus at the conceptual or inner level, these systems lose their plausibility in the empirical or outer sphere. What is needed is an account of the organism that is characterized by a universal that is reflected in both its inner and outer spheres.

Observing consciousness' response to this dilemma is to introduce the idea of the earth as the universal individual that displays its universality in the outer sphere. Here Hegel conceives of the earth as a single huge organic entity in the same sense that a colony of ants constitutes a single organism. The earth is thus the most extensive and all-encompassing notion available of a single organic unit. What Hegel seems to mean by this idea is that the earth is, on the one hand, a particular, i.e., there is only one earth per se, yet, on the other hand, as universal, it contains the manifold of species and individuals within itself. This extremely strange notion of the earth as the universal individual plays an important role in the Jena philosophy of nature manuscripts of 1803–4.[111] Hegel introduces the concept of the earth in contrast to genus as follows:

> The genus which divides itself into species on the basis of the *general determinateness* of number, or which may adopt as its principle of division particular features of its existence, e.g. shape, color, etc., while peacefully engaged in this activity, suffers violence from the universal individual, *the earth*, which as a universal negativity preserves the differences as they exist within itself—their nature, on account of the substance to which they belong, being different from the nature of those of the genus—and in face of the systematization of the genus.[112]

Genus contains differences within itself, namely the individual species, which it tries to order and distinguish by their general characteristics, e.g., "shape, color, etc." In this sense, genus is sublated or overcome by species, which is the next further mode of determination. The earth, on the other hand, contains precisely these same individual species and organisms within itself, but it is not sublated by them. In other words, the earth as a concept can preserve itself in the plurality of the natural world. The differences or individual entities that compose it rest in it indifferently.

The problem with this attempt to understand nature with the concept of the earth as the universal individual is that in fact, when all is said and done, the individual entities are still not determinate, since they are in fact indifferent to one another in the universal individual. In the final analysis, Hegel thinks that the plurality of nature resists organization, classification, or lawlike rules. "It follows from this," he writes, "that in existence in its structured shape, observation can encounter Reason only as *life in general*, which, however, in its differentiating process does not actually possess any rational ordering and arrangement of parts, and is not an immanently grounded system of shapes."[113] Reason cannot find itself in nature again as it had hoped, since it is unable to find in nature the logical and rational structure of its own thought. Every attempt to find such structures in nature has only led to contradictions and absurdities.[114]

Concluding Remarks (§§295–97)

In his final remarks, Hegel interestingly enough compares the notion of earth with that of Spirit and self-consciousness, which to his mind forms some sort of a parallel.[115] He writes,

> It is thus that *consciousness*, as the middle term between universal Spirit and its individuality or sense-consciousness, has for middle term the system of structured shapes assumed by consciousness as a self-systematizing whole of the life of Spirit—the system that we are considering here, and which has its objective existence as world-history. But organic nature has no history; it falls from its universal, from life, directly into singleness of existence, and the moments of simple determinateness, and the single organic life united in this actuality, produce the process of becoming merely as a contingent movement, in which each is active in its own part and the whole is preserved.[116]

Both Spirit and nature share the characteristic in common of having a plurality of individual things or moments within themselves. In the case of Spirit, it is the individual moments of world history which are bound together as a whole. As we have seen, in nature it is the plurality of species and individuals that constitute the natural order. In this passage, Hegel tells us that the two differ in one fundamental respect; namely, nature in the final analysis is "merely . . . a contingent movement." In other words, there is no necessity or genuine law in the natural order. On the other hand, the movement of Spirit and the movement of human thought and history are necessary and evince genuine universal laws. This is Hegel's extremely counterintuitive conclusion to this section.

In his final observations, Hegel reminds us once again of the parallelism with "Sense-Certainty," which distinguished between the particulars which natural consciousness meant (*meinen*) and the universals which it said. He writes,

> Since, then, the *universality of organic life* falls, in its actuality, directly into the extreme of singleness without a genuine mediation of its own, the thing before the observing Reason is only something "meant"; and if Reason can take an idle interest in observing this "meant" thing, it is

restricted to the description and narration of the "meanings" and fanciful conceits it finds in nature.[117]

Observing consciousness means to capture the fullness and diversity of the empirical natural order with its science, but as we have seen, this collapses into the "universal individual" which is in fact an indeterminate, inchoate natural mass. Observing consciousness fails again and again to find ways of breaking down this mass and of determining the individual entities in it and in their connections and relationships to one another. However, all of its attempts to order this subject matter end up useless, and observing consciousness is unable to provide a truly necessary system of laws for understanding the objective world of nature. Its laws remain always at best merely probable: "But, as regards law and necessity, when observation connects the organic with the merely given differences of the inorganic, the elements, zones, and climates, it does not get beyond the idea of a 'great influence.' "[118] We can talk vaguely about the various influences of natural factors on one another, but we can never get beyond this to the true necessity of nature which observing consciousness wants to explain.

The dialectic of universal and particular is quite straightforward in this section. At the beginning, the universal was the general scheme of classification which tried to order the particular entities of the natural world. When the classificatory scheme failed, observing consciousness tried to understand the universal as a pure law which brought a number of specific organic entities together in terms of a specific relation. When pure law failed, the analysis shifted over to organic entities in which a universal aspect was to be found in their end. After the analysis of the teleology of nature, observing consciousness turned to an account of the inner of the organism, which it took to be the various corresponding systems—the nervous system, the muscular system, the reproductive system. These capacities or systems formed the universal aspect of the individual organic entities. Finally, observing consciousness examined the dialectic of genus and species and reached the idea of the earth as the universal individual.

It is once again worthwhile to point out that Hegel's criticism here contradicts many of our naive modern intuitions about the truth-value of the natural sciences. In contemporary culture, modern physics is often considered to be the ultimate benchmark for truth in the sciences. The social sciences, being able to apply the scientific method only imperfectly to their subject matter, fall far behind according to the common view. The humanities disciplines can hardly even be mentioned when we are talking about truth, since the reigning opinion is that the humanities disciplines have given up the idea of truth altogether and are wallowing in a freewheeling relativism. Thus, it is claimed, the ad hoc and idiosyncratic theories of, for instance, history, theology, or philosophy simply cannot compete with the modern natural sciences in their claims about the nature of the universe. Hegel would find our modern view repellent. According to his view, as we have just seen, the material of the natural sciences is "merely . . . a contingent movement"[119] lacking necessity. It is, on the contrary, philosophy where necessary truths exist. For Hegel, philosophical truth is the highest form of truth, which is followed by religious truth. The truths of history that are examined in the "Spirit" chapter come next. Only after the truth-claims of these disciplines can we come to speak of truths in the natural sciences which, on Hegel's view, pale by comparison.

II. Observation of Self-Consciousness in Its Purity and in Its Relation to External Actuality: Psychology (§§298–308)

This relatively unknown section contains another account of Kant's epistemology or logic, as well as Hegel's treatment of the science of psychology.[120] First Hegel treats the so-called laws of thought, which are considered to form the cognitive capacity of the self-conscious subject. The paradoxes involved in this view lead us to the science of psychology. Hegel's idea of psychology, although not entirely disparate from our own, is very specific. He sees the central task of psychology as understanding the societal influences on the individual; more precisely, psychology examines how the external influences shape and determine the individual personality. On the basis of empirical observation, psychology tries to formulate necessary laws to account for the interaction of the individual with his or her environment. In the course of the dialectic, we come to see that in fact these stimuli never wholly determine anything, but rather their influence is always indeterminate. The laws, with their claims to necessity, fail due to their inability to account for the freedom of the individual vis-à-vis the environmental influences.

According to the schematic structure of the work that we have been following, this section corresponds to the "Perception" section in the "Consciousness" chapter. Although it would be a mistake always to insist on a one-to-one correspondence especially in this case since, as we have seen, some of the material in the previous section which officially corresponds to "Sense-Certainty" spills over into some of the material that parallels the "Perception" section, nevertheless the correspondence between the present section and "Perception" is striking when we look at the categorial parallelism. The one and the many, the categories operative in "Perception," are repeated here at the level of the self-conscious subject. The unity of self-consciousness is juxtaposed to the plurality of mental faculties. The task of the psychologist is to try to bring this unity and plurality into a harmonious whole, just as natural consciousness tried to reconcile the "One" with the "Also" in the "Perception" section.

The Notion: Observation of the Self-Conscious Subject (§298)

Since Hegel has already discussed the general Notion of "Observing Reason" earlier,[121] at this point he merely distinguishes another variant of that Notion from the variant which we have just explored in "Observation of Nature." At this point we are no longer concerned with observing the other or the object of consciousness, but rather now we turn to examine the self-conscious subject itself as an object of scientific examination. Hegel begins here by explaining how the results of the previous section, "Observation of Nature," lead us to the next step of observation of the individual. He indicates that the observation of organic and inorganic nature proved to be conceptually inadequate. First, of inorganic nature, he writes, "Observation of Nature finds the Notion realized in inorganic Nature, laws whose moments are things which, at the same time, have the character of abstractions; but this Notion is not a simplicity that is reflected into itself."[122] What Hegel reminds us of here is that in the dialectic of classification and categorization inorganic nature collapsed into a plurality of individual moments that observing consciousness was unable to bring together into any meaningful unity. According to this account, the plurality of nature defied the classificatory schemes of the rigid natural sciences and ended up being a mere description of individual entities. Thus, the being of inorganic nature proved to be manifold. Since it was a manifold without any dialectical relation to a singularity or unity, the world of inorganic nature remained indeterminate.

Hegel then turns to sum up the results of the analysis of organic nature: "The life of organic Nature, on the other hand, is only this introreflected simplicity; the antithesis within it of universal and individual does not sunder itself in the essence of this life itself."[123] Here Hegel indicates that organic nature, in opposition to inorganic, manifests itself as a unity or, as Hegel says, as an "introreflected simplicity"; however, here organic nature lacks the moment of plurality. Organic nature, like the pure being of "Sense-Certainty," collapses into a seamless one without any distinguishing traits; thus, it too remains indeterminate. What is needed is an object that maintains its oneness or unity, like organic nature, but at the same time possesses properties or characteristics that can distinguish it from other things, like inorganic nature. As we saw in "Perception," what was needed was a conception of an object that maintained the moment of both the "One" and the "Also," unity and plurality. Observing consciousness believes that it has found just such an object in the individual human subject. This subject is a unity with a plurality and as such is the proper object of study for observing reason. Hegel expresses this as follows: "Observation finds this free Notion, whose universality contains just as absolutely within it developed individuality, only in the Notion which itself *exists* as Notion, i.e. in self-consciousness."[124] We therefore turn to the observational study of the self-conscious human agent. Unlike the objects of organic and inorganic nature studied so far, a human subject contains within the unity of self-consciousness a number of intellectual capacities and faculties. Only in the human subject are the one and the many brought together.

The Notion at this point is simply the idea that a scientific under-standing of the human subject via observation can ultimately determine truth. Once again, when we look back to where Hegel outlines the stages of "Observing Reason,"[125] we realize that we are at this point at the stage where observing consciousness observes what Hegel there calls "Spirit." In this context, Hegel simply means reason observes itself, qua self-conscious subject, as an object of investigation. Humans differ from the rest of nature by virtue of their capacity for self-consciousness. Precisely this distinction is what Hegel hopes to capture with his distinction between nature and Spirit in the passage in question. We have just seen the dialectic of the observation of nature, and now we move to the observation of Spirit.

The Experience of Consciousness (§§299–308)

The Laws of Thought (§§299–301)

Observing consciousness, in its examination of the self-conscious subject, observes straightaway the universal structures of human thought. These structures it conceives as necessary "laws of thought." By the term "laws of thought," Hegel is self-consciously referring to the formal logic of his day, as well as to the epistemology of Kant. According to traditional logic, the laws of thought are the principles of identity, contradiction, and excluded middle. These laws were thought to serve as the very criteria for truth. To these we can also add the categories which, on Kant's view, correspond to these formal laws and principles. As we have seen earlier, on the Kantian picture, this brings about a split between content and form. The logical

208

rules and categories supply the formal or universal aspect of thought, but the content of thought is something different. This gives rise to an ambivalent position with respect to the pretensions to truth of the laws of thought. The laws are only formal and have no truth in themselves: "To say that they have no *reality*, means, in general, nothing else than that they lack truth. They are indeed, not supposed to be the *entire* truth, but still *formal* truth."[126] The laws of thought are supposed to be true in some sense, namely for the human subject, but since they, according to Kant, are only subjective and formal, they lack content and the full truth. This then, as Hegel mentioned in his Introduction,[127] gives rise to two standards of truth, that is, truth for the human subject and truth in itself or in reality. But this dual standard serves only to undercut truth for the subject, since this subjective truth clearly seems to be the weaker of the two. Indeed the very existence of a truth in itself raises the problem of skepticism for the concept of subjective truth. As we have seen, on Hegel's view there is no form-content split. The universal structures or rules of thought have within themselves a content, and this is the very principle of a phenomenology.

Since, according to the Kantian view, these laws are a part of the subjective apparatus, they are not considered to be laws about things or objects themselves, but merely to be laws about the way human beings structure reality. Thus, these are laws of knowing and not laws of being: "In their truth, as vanishing moments in the unity of thought, they would have to be taken as a knowing, or as a movement of thought, but not as *laws* of being."[128] Hegel notes here that his philosophy, or speculative knowing in general, refuses to distinguish between thought and being in this sense. As he puts it, the whole relation between the two terms is a "movement of thought, *knowing* itself."[129] The basic idea here is one which we have seen before. Any talk about "reality" amounts in the final analysis to our "thought" about reality. There is no getting behind thought or language to get at reality in itself; thus, the comparison, if it is to be a meaningful one, cannot be between thought and an external independent reality but rather between two different modalities of thought.

Since observing consciousness has discovered only "laws of knowing" and not "laws of being," this first variant of the Notion of "Observation of Self-Consciousness" fails. In other words, observing consciousness itself must make use of these laws of thought in its analysis of the self-conscious subject; however, since these laws are merely subjective or are laws of knowing (and not of being), then the truth-value of the results of observing consciousness' investigation is undermined. This Hegel expresses in the following obscure passage: "But *observing* is not *knowing* itself, and is ignorant of it; it converts its own nature into the form of *being*, i.e. it grasps its negativity only as *laws* of knowing."[130] The observer comprehends its object domain (its negativity) "only as laws of knowing." The key here is the word "only," which clearly implies the contrast with laws of being which are thought to be more true and more real.

In the dialectical movement at this stage, the categories of the one and the many or the "One" and the "Also" that we know from "Perception" are clearly visible. At this point, the "One" is simply the self-conscious subject itself, which is considered to be a unified living organism. The many, on the other hand, are the various laws of thought or intellectual faculties that each individual possesses. Hegel makes this clear in a couple of different passages: "This absolute truth of fixed determinatenesses, or of a number of different laws, contradicts, however, the unity of self-consciousness, or of thought and form in general."[131] Even more explicitly he writes,

> Observational psychology, which in the first instance records its perceptions of the *general modes* coming to its notice in the active consciousness, comes across all sorts of faculties, inclinations, and passions; and since, while recounting the details of this collection it cannot help recalling the unity of self-consciousness, it must at least go so far as to be astonished that such a contingent medley of heterogeneous beings can be together in the mind like things in a bag, more especially since they show themselves to be not dead, inert things but restless movements.[132]

Here the categories of the one and the many are explicit. Observing consciousness empirically observes and analyzes the various human faculties but has no way in terms of theory to bring them together into a single self-conscious agent. They are not adequately mediated. The faculties seem to be independent atomic units, which each have their own function. How this plurality is united with an underlying unity is thus a question of "astonishment" for the observing consciousness.

Hegel describes[133] the transition between two variants of the Notion at this level. Observing consciousness conceives of the unitary subject differently in order to escape the contradictions implied by the laws of thought. The subject is no longer conceived as an inert or passive knower in possession of a number of cognitive laws, but rather the subject is thought of as living and acting in the real world as an "*active consciousness.*"[134] By considering the self-conscious subject as active, observing consciousness hopes to put the laws of thought on one side and to see the subject as determined by the number of relations he has to the external world via his action. Hegel writes, observing consciousness "supposes that thought, in its laws, remains over on one side, and that, on the other side, it obtains another being in what is now an object for it, viz. the active consciousness."[135] Psychology is then the new field that observes active consciousness in its determination.

Psychology (§§302–8)

The field of empirical psychology is the new discipline, the study of which observing reason embarks upon.[136] This field has as its object the examination of the individual subject and his faculties in his relation to the world or to his external environment. Psychology tries to establish laws for how the environment affects the individual and for how the individual responds to various stimuli from his environment. These laws then replace the laws of thought that we have just examined. The environment and the individual are then the two aspects whose interaction must be explored: "The moments constituting the content of the law are, on the one hand, the individuality itself, on the other hand, its universal inorganic nature, viz. the given circumstances, situation, habits, customs, religion, and so on; from these the specific individuality is to be comprehended."[137] The individual subject is thus understood in one sense as the result of these environmental influences. In other words, an individual in an environment where a certain religion is dominant or particular customs prevail will in all probability take up this religion and adopt precisely these customs. This is the type of law formulated by empirical psychology. The problem is that psychology does not want to admit that it is a question of probability at best and instead insists on the necessity of these sorts of laws.

When we observe a bit closer, however, we see that in fact there are exceptions to this sort of psychological law about the necessity of environmental influence on the individual. Indeed, it is true that in any given society most individuals, as a result of their upbringing and cultural influence, share the same religion and customs; however, there are also in every society those who do not share the dominant religion and the accepted customs despite their socialization in them. There thus seems to be two possibilities: one can simply absorb the dominant cultural elements into one's own personality, or one can assert one's individuality and freedom and reshape those cultural aspects as one wishes:

> Since, on account of this freedom, the actual world is capable of having this twofold meaning, the world of the individual is to be comprehended only from the individual himself; and the *influence* on the individual of the actual world, conceived as *existing* in and for itself, receives through

the individual the absolutely opposite significance, viz. that the individual either *allows* free play to the stream of the actual world flowing in upon it, or else breaks it off and transforms it.[138]

Once one realizes that individual freedom plays a role in this interaction between environment and individual, then it is difficult to make sense out of the pretense to the necessity of the psychological laws. If the individual can always reject any given aspect of "the stream of the actual world flowing in upon" him, then it is clear that observing consciousness cannot assert that one necessarily simply accepts and internalizes everything that comes from the external environment. Hegel writes, "Therefore, *what* is to have an influence on the individuality, and what *kind* of influence it is to have—which really mean the same thing—depend solely on the individuality itself."[139] Since the whole issue turns on the nature of the individual subject, general psychological laws cannot be formulated. We simply have to see how the individual reacts to his environmental influences in each individual case. We cannot ultimately come up with laws that separate environmental influence from human character or original nature. Thus, Hegel concludes, "'psychological necessity' becomes an empty phrase."[140]

Concluding Remarks

In the dialectic at this level, the universal is represented at first by the unified self-conscious subject who, like the "One" of "Perception," seems to be an empty unity. The particular in this dialectic is represented by the laws of thought and the various cognitive faculties which seem, like the independent, isolated properties of the "Also," to be free-floating and not to be hooked up in any meaningful way with the self-conscious subject. The dialectic of immediacy and mediation likewise has affinities with the dialectic of "Perception." The single self-conscious agent is immediate, but he lacks the level of mediacy, since he has no faculties or properties which could serve as distinguishing marks. On the other hand, the free-floating faculties mediate and determine one another, but they lack the moment of immediate unity.

Observing consciousness now searches for something else that it can fix on as an object of study which forms the key to the character of the individual subject. The study of psychology proved that the environmental influences were entirely intangible and indeterminate and thus could not be of any service in fixing the character of the person. Observing consciousness now casts around for something more tangible and determinate, for something that is immediate to observation. It finds this in the face and the cranium or skull of the individual subject itself. The face and the skull of the person are thought to be immediate and accurate representations of the individual's true inner nature. Observing consciousness now switches from psychology to the dubious sciences of physiognomy and phrenology and from the categories of the one and the many to the inner and the outer.

III. Observation of Self-Consciousness in Its Relation to Its Immediate Actuality: Physiognomy and Phrenology (§§309–46)

In this section, observing consciousness withdraws from the claim to know the individual subject by its being determined outwardly by nature and the social environment. Now the object of study becomes concrete outward manifestations, which are thought to mirror something inner that is otherwise empirically inaccessible. As the scheme we have been following implies, this section corresponds to the "Force and the Understanding" section of the "Consciousness" chapter. The dialectic here returns to the relation of inner and outer that we saw in "Force and the Understanding" in the form of the dialectic of forces and their empirical manifestations. This time the inner and the outer are not understood as a relationship in the realm of objects as a force behind the scenes with an empirical manifestation, but rather as a relationship of two aspects of the human subject. In this section, the outer appearance of the subject, in particular the face or skull of the individual, is thought to mirror his inner nature.

The esoteric nature of the sciences of physiognomy and phrenology that Hegel treats here has been largely responsible for the obscurity of his account as well as for the fact that this section has received little treatment in the literature. Although this section has been fairly neglected, and the disciplines of phrenology and physiognomy are no longer in mode, it would be a mistake to think that Hegel's discussion here is irrelevant or meaningless for the modern reader. Instead, as an important essay by Alasdair MacIntyre has pointed out,[141] the issues treated here are still very much alive in the debates of contemporary philosophy of mind. Some of the central theses of physiognomy and phrenology, far from having fallen into desuetude, are in fact alive and well in their modern dress. MacIntyre's thesis is that a number of contemporary materialist doctrines, which from the present perspective appear wholly legitimate and respectable, do not differ in their essentials from these two ill-reputed sciences that every self-respecting scientist has long since abjured. Moreover, despite the difficulty of this section, which issues from the foreignness of the pseudosciences involved, this analysis counts as one of Hegel's most lively, due to the merciless and seldom recognized satire that he uses as a weapon in his criticism of these positions.

The Notion: Observation of the Self-Conscious Subject in Its Objective Aspect (§§309–11)

Typically enough, Hegel begins by telling us how the formation of the new variant of the Notion here is the result of the failure of the variant examined in the previous section. Specifically, the failure of psychology to provide laws of genuine necessity to describe how the world or the environment influences the individual subject leads back to the determinate person of the subject himself as the object of investigation. "Psychological observation," Hegel writes, "discovers no law for the relation of self-consciousness to actuality, or to the world over against it; and, through the mutual indifference of both, it is forced to fall back on the *peculiar determinateness* of real individuality which exists *in and for itself.*"[142] Observing consciousness now examines the individual himself and attempts to abstract from the environmental influences since they proved to be indeterminate.

A new dualism in the conception of the subject appears at this point. The individual is, on the one hand, the external person and activity that is observable in the empirical world and, on the other hand, the internal self that is nonempirical. Hegel expresses this as follows: "In his own self, therefore, there emerges the antithesis, this duality of being the movement of consciousness, and the fixed being of an appearing actuality, an actuality which in the individual is immediately his *own.*"[143] Each individual expresses himself in the external sphere through words and actions; this is the public side of his character that is available to all. However, he also has another side that is private. This side consists of his intentions, thoughts, and so forth. These are not originally accessible to other self-conscious agents unless the individual expresses them and purposely makes them public. It is our commonsense belief that the external side accurately mirrors the internal side; in other words, like observing consciousness, we tend to believe, unless we have reason to be suspicious, that an individual's words and actions are a reflection of his true self or his inner being. These things function like a sign indicating the nature of the inner individual.

This conception of the individual differs from the conception that was operative in the previous mode of consciousness, i.e., in psychology. The idea at work there was that the external influences entirely shape the individual; in other words, the individual is determined solely from without. Thus, in order to know what an individual is, we first need to know what sort of culture he is from and what sort of environment he inhabits. Here, on the other hand, the belief is that there is in each individual an inner being that is expressed through his own person and activity independent of the environment. Hegel describes this as follows:

> To the outer whole, therefore, belongs not only the *original being*, the inherited body, but equally the formation of the body resulting from the activity of the inner being; the body is the unity of the unshaped and of the shaped being. . . . This whole, which contains within it the specific original fixed parts and the lineaments arising solely from the activity, *is*, and this *being* is the *expression* of the inner being, of the individual posited as consciousness and movement.[144]

Here the outward appearance of the body or of human activity is not considered something merely accidental or what Hegel calls "the *original being*." Rather, the body is seen as an essential expression of the inner aspect of the person. The body and its activity are determined and fixed things which can be observed. They express the inner nature and fix its inner indeterminacy.

One important thing to note here is the obvious parallelism with the section "Force and the Understanding." There, the true nature of the object was thought to be the unseen forces that were domiciled in the unseen, nonempirical sphere behind the appearances. The forces had two sides, just like the individual here. Force, qua in itself, was seen as something beyond the empirical world, which Hegel called "force proper." But force was also considered in its "for another" aspect, which Hegel called "force expressed," i.e., force as it appears through the manifestations in the empirical world.[145] Just as force had two aspects in "Force and the Understanding," so also here the individual has two aspects which are couched in precisely the same language. The individual, qua in itself, is called "inner being." But the individual manifests himself in the world by means of "expression," which consists of his body and his activities. The sphere of the inner and the outer that we saw in "Force and the Understanding" is likewise repeated here at the level of the self-conscious agent. Here, instead of the nonempirical sphere of forces, the inner sphere is considered to be the intentions, will, and thoughts of an individual, self-conscious subject. The outer sphere is then the sum total of outward manifestations of the self-conscious agent. The operative belief in both sections is that there is a sort of mapping between the inner and the outer, i.e., between the appearances and the forces themselves or in this case between the external and internal sides of the individual.

As Hegel notes in his outline of "Observing Reason,"[146] this section is supposed to be a combination of the two preceding ones. We begin with the world of objects in "Observation of Nature," and then we move to the realm of subjects with the discipline of psychology in "Observation of Self-Consciousness in Its Purity and in Its Relation to External Activity," and it is in this section that subject and object are supposed to come together. The present section, "Observation of Self-Consciousness in Its Relation to Its Immediate Actuality," represents a combination of the subject and the object in the following way: first, the object of study is still the human subject, and thus the subjective element is still present. However, the actual object of study is only the outer aspect of the human subject—the face or the skull. These elements belong, properly speaking, to the realm of objects or dead things, as Hegel says.[147] Thus, the inner-outer distinction provides the clue for how the present section contains the previous two sections: the outer, i.e., the skull or the face, represents the object side, while the inner, which the outer presumably reflects, represents the subject side.

After setting up the terms of the object-Notion, Hegel then signals the turn to the experience of observing consciousness: "We have then to consider here how to determine the relation between these two sides and what is to be understood by this 'expression' of the inner in the outer."[148] By addressing the philosophical audience ("we") here in this way, Hegel indicates that at this point the examination of the Notion will begin. We need to examine precisely what the relationship is between the inner and the outer in order to see if in fact the relationship of the outer mirroring the inner can be made sense of conceptually. Just as the last section treated the science of empirical psychology, this section will treat the relevant sciences that operate with this conception of the individual. In what follows, Hegel discusses the so-called sciences of physiognomy and phrenology, which were in his day much more in mode than in our own. Despite the historical distance of these dubious fields, we can attain a basic understanding of the point that Hegel wants to make in his analysis of them without too much in depth study of their historical development and significance. Let us then turn to his dialectical analysis of this variation of the Notion.

The Experience of Consciousness (§§312–40)

Physiognomy (§§312–23)

Physiognomy was in Hegel's time a more or less reputable science. It is a discipline which ultimately traces its roots back to Aristotle and had no mean following in the Middle Ages. In Hegel's day it enjoyed something of a renaissance through the work of the Swiss theologian Johann Kaspar Lavater (1741–1801), whose *Physiognomische Fragmente zur Beförderung der Menschenkenntnis und Menschenliebe* (*Physiognomical Fragments for the Promotion of the Knowledge and Love of Man*), published in four volumes from 1775 to 1778, was effective at reviving this more or less dormant discipline. This dubious science was based on the belief that there is an intelligible correlation of some sort between the size and shape of the body, especially the face, and personal character. The word "physiognomy" comes from the Greek φὔσιογνώμονια, which means a judging (γνώμων) of the character or nature (φύσις) of an individual. Thus, physiognomy is the science which allows the observer to determine the true inner character of observed subjects through certain outward traits and properties. For instance, a gaunt body might be indicative of an intellectual proclivity, whereas a heavy-set body might designate a lustful character, and so on. Certain folds or lines on the face might be indicative of a morally wicked character or an avaricious one. The task of the physiognomist was then to establish these correlations on the basis of empirical evidence.

According to the first version of physiognomy which Hegel explores, the true nature of the individual consciousness can be determined by examining the individual's actions and the organs used to effect them. In other words, the hand, the mouth, the legs, etc., are the physical means of expression of the true inner nature in activity. Observing consciousness thus first recognizes external activity as the essential expression of the inner person. Through activity the person makes his true self visible to the external world. Activity transfers the being-for-himself of a person to being-for-another. It is an expression of one's inner intentions and desires manifested in the social world. This expression of the inner takes place via specific bodily organs, which function as the vehicle of the activity. Hegel writes,

> This outer, in the first place, acts only as an *organ* in making the inner visible or, in general, a being-for-another; for the inner, in so far as it is in the organ, is the *activity* itself. The speaking mouth, the working hand, and, if you like, the legs too are the organs of performance and actualization which have within them the action *qua* action, or the inner as such.[149]

Through these key bodily organs, the individual realizes himself in the external world. His true essence is no longer something that he keeps in his own mind, but rather it is an object in the public realm due to this action.

There is, however, a problem with this conception, insofar as activity of this sort does not necessarily reflect the inner nature of a person. There are a couple of different ways in which the external action could fail to be an accurate reflection of the inner person:

> Not only do the results of the actions, through this externality of the influences of others, lose the character of being something constant in face of other individualities, but since, in their relationship to the inner which they contain, they behave as a separated, indifferent externality, they can, *qua* inner, *through the individual himself*, be something other than they appear to be: either the individual intentionality makes them appear to be other than what they are in truth; or else he is too clumsy to give himself the outer aspect he really wanted, and to establish it so firmly that his work cannot be misconstrued by others.[150]

First, the individual can dissemble his true self by his actions. In other words, the individual can intentionally deceive others about his true desires and motivations through strategically calculated actions presented in the public sphere to a carefully selected audience. In this case, the external action would clearly not be a true reflection of the inner nature of the person, and observing consciousness would be deceived. Second, the individual might simply be incompetent, and this incompetence might stand in the way of his performing the actions that he actually wanted to perform. He might through his own incompetence unintentionally be the cause of an unfortunate event, although his will was benevolent. In this case, we would not say that the person is wicked, since he clearly did not intend the negative consequences that in fact issued from his action, although this would be the logical result if we were judging the character, like observing consciousness, on the basis of observation alone. Here once again observation would be misleading, since the outer is not a true reflection of the inner. Thus, Hegel concludes, observing consciousness cannot fix its judgment of the inner character based merely on the action of an individual, since that action is ultimately inconclusive: "The action, then, as a completed work, has the double and opposite meaning of being either the *inner* individuality and *not* its *expression*, or, *qua* external, a reality *free from* the inner, a reality which is something quite different from the inner."[151]

Observing consciousness must now find something else to examine and investigate, which more accurately reflects the inner character of the person. It then comes to see the body as a whole as just such a possible object of study. Although one might use disguises or similar ruses, nevertheless ultimately one cannot dissemble the nature of one's own body in the way one can dissemble one's true character or intentions through action. We cannot so readily manipulate the body, which seems to be simply a natural given, in the way that we can manipulate our actions to fit the circumstances. Thus, observing consciousness comes to see the body and in particular the face, as an object of study, and sees it as the true reflection of the inner nature of the individual. This then is the fundamental premise of the discipline of physiognomy.

The next thesis of physiognomy involves a withdrawal from the claims about action, which seem ultimately external, and concentrates instead on the bodily parts that are relevant. In this respect, in the mind of observing consciousness, the discipline of physiognomy enjoys an important advantage over pseudosciences such as astrology and palmistry. These studies operate with the premise that there is some causal connection between external factors. For instance, astrology assumes that there is some important correlation between one's character or one's fate and the given constellation of heavenly bodies that happened to be in the sky at the precise moment of one's birth. Palmistry likewise assumes a causal connection between the folds and lines of the hand and the character and destiny of the individual. These connections are in a deep sense "external" to the individual himself (although the lines on the hand can perhaps be seen as something that is not external), and thus the causal connection seems all the more capricious. As Hegel puts it, "Being externalities, they are indifferent towards each other, and lack the necessity for one another that ought to lie in the relation of an outer to an inner."[152] These factors seem to have in principle nothing to do with one another. They are not obviously causally related in a way that we can confirm.

Physiognomy, on the other hand, claims for itself a more intuitive correlation of factors than the two disciplines just mentioned. Body size and type as well as facial characteristics are thought to reflect the inner nature of the individual and to function as a sort of mediating element between the inner nature of the self and its externalization or realization. Here there is no "external" correlation to test our credulity. On the contrary, it is quite intuitive that there is some connection between an individual's inner character and his bodily characteristics. For instance, individuals with a robust stature tend to be athletic. Individuals with a frail bodily composition tend to be less athletic and more bookish. Indeed, we make character judgments of this sort every day based on the outward appearance of individuals. When we make such judgments, we are not concerned with individual organs, as in the previous stage, but rather with "the movement and form of countenance and figure [of the body] in general."[153] The body as a whole thus shares in both the inner nature of the individual and his externalization.

Just as in "Force and the Understanding" the forces had two aspects, one behind the scenes and one expressed in the real world, so also here the individual has two aspects, a true nature behind the scenes and its expression in the empirical world via the middle term of the body. Thus, we have here a constellation similar to the world of appearances and things-in-themselves and the appearances from "Force and the Understanding" which Hegel refers to as follows: "Observation accepts this antithesis in the same inverted relationship which characterizes it in the sphere of appearance [sc. "Force and the Understanding"]. It regards as the *unessential outer* the *deed* itself and the performance, whether it be that of speech or a more durable reality; but it is the being-within-self of the individual which is for it the *essential inner*."[154] The action or deed of the individual is the inessential external form of the true inner nature of the individual which is not accessible to the public world. Intention and desire form the true inner nature of an individual which is expressed as an inessential action: "the intention is supposed to have its more or less *unessential* expression in the deed, but it has its true expression in the shape of the individuality. The latter expression is the immediate sensuous presence of the individual spirit; the inwardness which is supposed to be the true inner is the particularity of the intention and singleness of the being-for-self."[155] The intention of the individual constitutes the inner side of the relation while activity or body shape or form represents the outer.

Hegel refers to the inner-outer relation in both sections as "reflection." The specific empirical characteristics "reflect" or refer back to the inner nature of the force or the self. The different aspects of the body thus form "signs,"[156] which indicate the true nature of the individual within. These signs serve the function of making the otherwise invisible true inner being of the person visible. Hegel expresses this with the oxymoron the "visible invisible."[157] In other words, the body or face makes visible the inner nature of the self, which is empirically invisible. However, these external signs are themselves ultimately inconclusive. "In this appearance," Hegel writes, "the inner is no doubt a *visible* invisible, but it is not tied to this appearance; it can be manifested just as well in another way, just as another inner can be manifested in the same appearance."[158] In other words, any given sign is in a sense arbitrary. In different countries, the sign indicating a one-way street is different; there is nothing about the nature of a one-way street that ultimately determines how the street sign representing it should look. Likewise, the signs or bodily characteristics expressing any given character trait are in a sense arbitrary and are not necessarily tied to the character trait in question. The result is "a sign indifferent to what is signified, therefore truly signifying nothing."[159]

The laws of physiognomy thus amount to simple generalizations that lack all semblance of necessity. It is in the final analysis what Hegel calls "idle chatter."[160] Here Hegel shows a sense of humor that he is little known for: "As regards their content, however, these observations [of physiognomy] are on a par with these: 'It always rains when we have our annual fair,' says the dealer; 'and every time, too,' says the housewife, 'when I am drying my washing.' "[161] These idle observations at bottom mindlessly imply that there is some causal connection between the fair or doing the wash and rain. Hegel goes on to analyze a passage from the German physicist Lichtenberg (1742–99), who was famous for his satirical criticism of Lavater's physiognomy. Hegel writes, quoting Lichtenberg, "If anyone said, 'You certainly act like an honest man, but I see from your face that you are forcing yourself to do so and are a rogue at heart'; without a doubt, every honest fellow to the end of time, when thus addressed, will retort with a box on the ear."[162] Our basic commonsense understanding of action, intention, and human character is utterly offended by statements of this kind that seem to ignore every relevant factor that constitutes human character and reduces it merely to the external appearance of the face. Hegel notes with a touch of irony that the box on the ear is the appropriate response to claims of this sort:

> Should this idle thinking want to set its sterile wisdom to work, with the aim of denying the doer the character of Reason, and so ill-using him as to declare that not his deed, but his face and lineaments are his real being, then it may expect to get the retort spoken of above, a retort which demonstrates that the face or outward appearance is not the individual's *in-itself* but, on the contrary, can be an object for handling.[163]

The response of a box on the ear is appropriate, since by striking someone on the face one alters the appearance of the other, perhaps in a radical way. This would then seem to imply that one's face or appearance is not something eternally fixed but rather is something more or less malleable. By striking someone in the correct way and by issuing the proper new lines or black eye or whatever on the face, one could turn the very tools of physiognomy against it by claiming that after the beating it is clear from the now changed face of the advocate of physiognomy that he is in fact a rogue. To carry this example to its most absurd extreme, we could imagine physiognomists giving each other scientifically planned out strategic blows in order to produce the desirable and positive character traits that would correspond to the new facial configuration.

Hegel refers back[164] to the two previous dialectical movements and contrasts them to the dialectic of phrenology, which we are about to explore. Thus, this passage forms a transition between the analyses of physiognomy and phrenology. He writes,

> In psychology it is the *external reality of things* which is supposed to have its self-conscious *counterpart* in spirit and to make spirit intelligible. In physiognomy, on the other hand, spirit is supposed to be known in its *own* outer aspect, as in a being which is the *utterance* of spirit—the visible invisibility of its essence. There remains the further determination of the aspect of reality, viz. that the individuality expresses its essence in its immediate, firmly established, and purely existent actuality.[165]

With the reference to "Psychology," Hegel is referring back to the previous section, where the external world or "the external reality of things" was thought wholly to determine the individual self-consciousness. Then Hegel refers to physiognomy, the dialectic which we have just examined. He then contrasts physiognomy with the next stage:

> This last relation is thus distinguished from the physiognomic by the fact that this is the *speaking* presence of the individual who, in expressing himself in *action*, at the same time exhibits himself as inwardly *reflecting* and *contemplating* himself, an expression which is itself a movement, features in repose which are themselves essentially a mediated being. In the determination yet to be considered, however, the outer aspect is lastly a wholly *immobile* reality which is not in its own self a speaking sign but, separated from self-conscious movement, presents itself on its own account and is a mere thing.[166]

In physiognomy the true inner reality was revealed in the individual bodily organs and their corresponding external activities. In phrenology, on the other hand, the inner is not revealed in dynamic activity but rather in "a mere thing," namely the skull-bone.

Phrenology (§§324–40)

Observing consciousness then casts around in order to come up with a satisfactory conceptual relationship between the inner and the outer. The original premise that there is some causal connection between the two must at all costs be maintained.[167] The considerations take up a form most familiar in contemporary debates in philosophy of mind. If we conceive of the inner as something mental (*geistlich*), translated by Miller as "spiritual," then we must imagine that there is a causal interaction between something mental, the inner, and something physical, the outer.[168] This is, of course, one of the classic philosophical problems of the tradition, often referred to as the problem of interaction, which takes perhaps its clearest form in the work of Descartes, with his distinction between extended things (*res extensa*) and thinking things (*res cogitates*). How is this relationship to be construed? How can we account for the fact that these two elements are found in the same entity and seem to interact and work together?

The reasoning of the phrenologist in response to these questions goes something like the following: the most obvious seat for the mental is the brain. What organs or objects stand in a physical relation to that brain, such that the latter could influence or interact with them? Observing consciousness infers that the skull-bone, by virtue of its immediate physical relation to the brain, qualifies for just this special relationship. The brain is thought to shape the skull physically:

> For the relation of those processes and functions to the skull, which as a dead being does not have spirit dwelling within it, there presents itself, in the first instance, the external mechanical relation established above, so that the organs proper—and these are in the brain—*here* press the skull out around, *there* widen or flatten it, or in whatever other way one cares to represent this action on it.[169]

On this view, the brain physically shapes and forms the skull-bone, thus clearly indicating a causal relation between the two: "But since the determination of *being-for-self* falls on the side of the brain, but that of *existence* on the side of the skull, there is *also* to be established a causal connection between them within the organic unity—a necessary relation between them as external for one another."[170] The brain thus represents the inner while the skull-bone is seen as the outer which reflects this inner. Observing consciousness must now examine the skull in order to glean the essence of the inner nature of the individual, and in this we recognize the basic premise of the discipline of phrenology.

Phrenology, like physiognomy, is an antiquated discipline, which was popular in Hegel's day. This ancient science was revived in Hegel's time by Franz Joseph Gall (1758–1828),[171] who is accounted as its modern founder. Gall gave lectures on phrenology in Vienna in 1796, and after the authorities there forbade him to continue propagating his theory, he went with his able student John Caspar Spurzheim (1776–1832) to France and England to win adherents for the new doctrine. The guiding belief behind this science was the claim, which still enjoys respectability today, that the faculties of the mind can be localized in parts of the brain. A highly developed part of the brain was then thought to correspond to a highly developed mental faculty. Hence, the phrenologists also believed that by a study of the shape of the skull-bone, they could draw conclusions about the development of the various mental faculties, due to the skull-bone's close proximity to the brain. In other words, bumps in a particular place were thought to be indicative of an industrious character, while folds in another place were indicative of a pernicious one. Phrenology was thus a λόγος or rational study of the φρήν, the mind or, in this case, the skull or the head. Spurzheim classified the twenty-seven faculties isolated by his mentor Gall, which included "benevolence," "wit," and "combativeness," and these classifications were then located and graphically represented on the cerebral charts which were popular even into the beginning of the twentieth century.

According to this conception, the brain forms the inner side of the person and the true self. It is, however, essentially related to his outer sphere, which is represented in the form of the skull-bone: "But the other aspect of self-conscious individuality, the aspect of its outer existence, is *being qua* independent and subject, or *qua* a 'thing,' viz. a bone: the *actuality and existence of man is his skull-bone.*"[172] By this, observing consciousness means that the essential inner character of an individual, as determined by the brain, can be discerned by the shape and form of the skull-bone, which stands in a causal relation to it; however, by formulating the basic premise of this field of study in this way, Hegel hopes to draw attention to the obvious absurdity inherent in it. The basic idea is that certain human character traits have their locus in parts of the brain and then accordingly in the corresponding parts of the skull. When the brain is particularly developed in one region or another, this, it was thought, will be apparent in the corresponding area of the skull-bone. Hegel explains the logic of phrenology as follows:

> Just as, e.g., some people complain of feeling a painful tension somewhere in the head when they are thinking hard, or even when thinking at all, so too could stealing, committing murder, writing poetry, and so on, each be accompanied by its own feeling, which besides would necessarily be localized in its own special place. This area of the brain which would in this way be more moved and activated would probably also develop the adjacent area of the skull-bone.[173]

By a careful examination of various cases, the phrenologist thinks he can establish laws for these correlations between character traits, which correspond to more or less developed regions of the brain, and the shapes of the skull.

However, the problem is an obvious one: there is in all likelihood no relation whatever (let alone a necessary one) between the size and shape of the head and various character traits. As Hegel puts it, these two things are "indifferent" to one another, i.e., they stand in no necessary relation. He uses the example of a murderer to make the obvious case against phrenology:

> The skull of a murderer has—not this organ or even sign—but this bump. But this murderer has as well a multitude of other properties, just as he has other bumps, and along with the bumps also hollows; one has a choice of bumps and hollows. And again, his murderous disposition can be related to any bump or hollow, and this in turn to any mental property; for the murderer is neither merely this abstraction of a murderer, nor does he have only one bump and one hollow.[174]

Phrenology must ultimately begin by assigning character traits to various bumps or hollows or folds in the skull. This in itself seems to be an entirely arbitrary practice since, as we have just noted, there seems to be no connection whatever between the two. Why is a bump on the right side necessarily indicative of a murderous disposition and one on the left side of an avaricious one? Thus, in principle, a given bump or fold can represent any given trait we please. Hegel notes[175] that we can well imagine that there might be some correlation between these things, but this simple power of imagining is not enough to make it so, since after all we can imagine a number of clearly ludicrous things.

The phrenologist tries to save the situation in the face of these problems by backing down from the claims of necessity somewhat. He claims that a given bump on the head does not necessarily correspond to a specific character trait which is manifested in action. Instead, he argues that a given bump or hollow in the skull is characteristic of certain proclivities or dispositions which may or may not be developed according to a number of other factors. Thus, when the phrenologist concludes that an individual has a murderous disposition due to a certain bump and is informed that nonetheless the man is in fact a morally upright individual, then the phrenologist can still argue that the man has the essential disposition of a murderer, but this disposition has thankfully not been able to be realized due to, for instance, certain social influences. Hegel explains this point as follows: "So too when observing the skull, it might be said that this individual *really ought* to be what, according to the law, his skull proclaims him to be, and that he has an *original disposition,* but one that has not been developed: this quality is not *present,* but it *ought to be present.*"[176] But argumentation of this kind moves us further and further away from empirical science, since it is impossible to refute or amend this conception of an original disposition with empirical evidence. It does not matter how badly the facts of the matter contradict the supposed "original disposition" of the individual based on the phrenological study, the results still hold fast and are considered legitimate. It is, to borrow a term from the philosophy of science, unfalsifiable. As in the discussion of physiognomy, this conceptual form corresponds to the inverted world of "Force and the Understanding." Just as the phenomena there are seen as inversions of the true forces or things in themselves behind the scenes, so also here one's actions may well in fact be an inversion of one's original disposition. The contradiction between the two is counted as meaningless.

This sort of talk reduces to the absurdity of discounting all other evidence such as action, intention, etc., and considering the true nature of the individual to be his skull-bone. Hegel humorously discusses this absurdity in the following passage:

> When, therefore, a man is told "You (your inner being) are this kind of person because your skull-bone is constituted in such and such a way," this means nothing else than, "I regard a bone as *your reality*." To reply to such a judgement with a box on the ear, as in the case of a similar judgement in physiognomy mentioned above, at first takes away from the *soft* parts their importance and position, and proves only that these are not true *in-itself*, are not the reality of spirit; the retort here would, strictly speaking, have to go the length of beating in the skull of anyone making such a judgement, in order to demonstrate in a manner just as palpable as his wisdom, that for a man, a bone is nothing *in itself*, much less *his* true reality.[177]

In this apparently tongue in cheek passage, Hegel in fact makes a philosophical point with humor. The result of boxing someone about the ears is usually that a few new bumps appear on the skull. These new bumps then would have to be taken seriously by the phrenologist as important character traits in their own right. However, it is absurd to imagine that such new character traits as important as the ones we have seen treated above, e.g., a murderous disposition, can arise as quickly as a bump on the head arises as a result of a blow. According to the phrenologist's reasoning, we would be compelled to conclude that an individual who had just suffered a thorough beating had radically changed his character by virtue of the fact that the shape of his skull had changed due to the various new swellings. Thus, Hegel's point here is not entirely flippant. This constitutes in its essentials the dialectical sublation of the claim of the phrenologists that the essence of the individual self-conscious subject is to be found in the shape of the skull or as Hegel puts it "that the *being of spirit is a bone.*"[178]

Concluding Remarks (§§341–46)

The dialectic of universal and particular is quite obvious in this section. The universal is, for the sciences of physiognomy and phrenology, the inner character of the individual. It has the form of certain universal types or characteristics, such as benevolence or avarice. These universals are then presumably reflected in the particular empirical appearances—the individual lines or folds on the face, for the physiognomist, and the particular bumps and hollows of the skull, for the phrenologist. The dialectic of mediacy and immediacy is likewise evident. As the title of this section indicates, observing consciousness at this point tries to understand the true nature of the self-conscious agent "in its relation to its immediate actuality." In other words, given the inner-outer mirroring that observing consciousness works with in this section, the inner character is manifested in the outward appearance, and this outward appearance is something that is immediately actual for observing consciousness. The skull-bone or the face is something that is immediately able to be perceived. The absurdity arises when we take the skull, qua immediately given, to represent the essence of the individual's character. If observing consciousness were to admit that the character was only given mediately through the skull-bone, then there would be room for contingency and interpretation, and the claim for the necessity of the phrenological laws would have to be given up.

In his conclusion to this long section, Hegel provides us with a very helpful summary of the dialectical movements examined here as well as a brief overview of the dialectic as it now stands in relation to the previous chapters of "Consciousness" and "Self-Consciousness." His account breaks down in the following way: § 341 (*PhG*, p. 189) is a summary of "Observation of Nature; § 342 (*PhG*, pp. 189–90) is a summary of the short section "Observation of Self-Consciousness in Its Purity and in Its Relation to External Actuality"; § 343 (*PhG*, p. 190) is a summary of the results of the present section, "Observation of Self-Consciousness to Its Immediate Actuality."

Now Hegel discusses two results of the dialectic of "Reason" that we have examined so far.[179] These paragraphs are extremely helpful for us in our attempt to reconstruct Hegel's intended structure of the work, since it is here that he steps back from the details of the dialectical analysis and reflects on the general movement of the book. Thus, it is worthwhile to analyze these passages in some detail. Perhaps the most important single thing about Hegel's comments here is that they unambiguously confirm the thesis that we tentatively put forth at the beginning of this chapter about the structure of "Reason." The reader will recall that there we argued, based on a brief discussion of the table of contents and the changes it went through, that the "Reason" chapter is intended in a sense to go back to the beginning of the dialectic and to repeat the dialectic of "Consciousness" at a higher level. In this passage, Hegel says precisely this:

> One [of the results of the "Reason" chapter so far examined] is its true meaning, insofar as it is a completion of the outcome of the preceding movement of self-consciousness. The unhappy self-consciousness renounced its independence, and struggled to make its *being-for-self* into a *thing*. It thereby reverted from self-consciousness to consciousness, i.e. to the consciousness for which the object is something which merely *is*, a thing; but here, what is a thing is self-consciousness; the thing is, therefore, the unity of the "I" and being—the *category*.[180]

Here Hegel says expressly that the unhappy consciousness at the conclusion of the "Self-Consciousness" chapter reverts "from self-consciousness to consciousness," and it is at this point that the "Reason" chapter begins. Thus, the first section of the "Reason" chapter, "Observing Reason," returns to a treatment of the object sphere, and precisely in this respect it overlaps with the "Consciousness" chapter. However, "Observing Reason" is no mere repetition of the "Consciousness" chapter; despite this important similarity and parallelism, there is also an important difference. This time the object is not thought to be something independent and external to the subject, but rather here in "Observing Reason" the object is self-consciousness itself. In the "Observation of Nature" the object sphere was considered important only insofar as it mirrored certain laws or classificatory schemes of the self-conscious subject, and in this self-consciousness saw itself in the objective sphere. By seeing lawlike patterns in nature, self-consciousness recognized itself in the external sphere. In the next two sections, self-consciousness was explicitly the object of scientific investigation, first by the discipline of empirical psychology (in "Observation of Self-Consciousness in Its Purity and in Its Relation to External Actuality") and second by the dubious sciences of physiognomy and phrenology (in "Observation of Self-Consciousness to Its Immediate Actuality"). Here the self-conscious subject is quite straightforwardly the object.

Another point that Hegel emphasizes in this passage is the overlap in the categories involved. In the "Consciousness" chapter, the external sphere of objects was considered, and there we began with being as the purest, most unmediated category. This same category is at work here in "Reason," but it has been developed to a higher stage:

> The *pure* category, which is present for consciousness in the form of *being* or *immediacy*, is the object as still *unmediated*, as merely *given*, and consciousness is equally unmediated in its relation to it. The moment of that infinite judgement is the transition of *immediacy* into mediation, or *negativity*. The given object is consequently a negative object; consciousness, however, is determined as *self*-consciousness over against it; in other words, the category which, in the course of observation, has run through the form of *being* is now posited in the form of being-for-self: consciousness no longer aims to *find* itself *immediately* but to produce itself by its own activity. It is *itself* the end at which its action aims, whereas in its role of observer it was concerned only with things.[181]

This longish passage is crucial for our understanding of the development of the overall argument of the book. Here Hegel summarizes the movement from "Consciousness" to "Self-Consciousness," as well as the movement from "Observing Reason" to the next stage, "The Actualization of Rational Self-Consciousness through Its Own Activity." At first, that is in "Consciousness," the category of being was considered in its immediacy as something "merely *given*." In the course of the dialectical movement of "Consciousness," natural consciousness realized that in order for an object to be determinate it must involve "negativity" or difference, i.e., it must be distinguishable from other objects. This led us to the dialectic of "Self-Consciousness" which began by trying to determine itself as something negative over and against the sphere of objects. In the passage cited above, Hegel then immediately shifts over to a description of the movement of "Reason," indicating that the movement from "Consciousness" to "Self-Consciousness" corresponds to the movement here in "Reason" from "Observing Reason" to "The Actualization of Rational Self-Consciousness through Its Own Activity." As he puts it, "Observing Reason" has just run through the dialectical movement that corresponds to the simple "form of being." Now, however, the moment of negation or otherness is introduced as in "Self-Consciousness." At this point, we will see different forms of the individual self-conscious subject in its attempt to determine itself by distinguishing itself from others. Both in the "Consciousness" chapter and in "Observing Reason," consciousness "was concerned only with things," but now we will as in "Self-Consciousness" be concerned with the sphere of the self-conscious subject.

The parallelisms between "Consciousness" and Observing Reason," for the sake of simplicity, have been represented in table 6.1. The gen-

Table 6.1

Category	Consciousness	Observing Reason
Ground and Consequence (Inner and Outer)	Force and the Understanding (Force and Matters)	Observation of Self-Consciousness in Its Relation to Its Immediate Actuality (Physiognomy: Inner Being and the Face and Body. Phrenology: Inner Being and the Skull-Bone)
One and Many	Perception	Observation of Self-Consciousness in Its Purity and in Its Relation to External Actuality
	(The One and the Also)	(Unity of Self-Consciousness and the Plurality of Mental Faculties)
Being	Sense-Certainty (The This)	Observation of Nature (Being of Organic and Inorganic Nature)

eral thesis that "Consciousness" corresponds to "Observing Reason" is confirmed by the parallelisms of the respective categories. The category of pure being that we begin with in "Sense-Certainty" finds its analogue in the being of organic and inorganic nature, which observing consciousness constantly fails to capture or determine with laws or classificatory schemes. The categories of the one and the many that were introduced in "Perception" reappear at a higher conceptual level in Hegel's account of psychology in the second section of "Observing Reason." There the dialectic of unity and plurality is instantiated in a unified human subject with a plurality of cognitive faculties. Finally, the categories of ground and consequence or the inner and the outer that we first saw in "Force and the Understanding" reappear, predictably enough, in the third and final section of "Observing Reason." There the inner and the outer are conceptual terms introduced by the adherents of the pseudosciences, phrenology and physiognomy, in order to understand the relation between the hidden character of the individual and the outward appearances of, for instance, his face or skull. The categories are thus repeated at a level that is conceptually richer than before.

In his concluding remarks to this section, Hegel uses humor once again in his criticism of the disciplines of physiognomy and phrenology. In a passage which reminds us, as Miller notes, of a passage from the *Philosophy of Nature* in the *Encyclopaedia*,[182] Hegel compares a curious natural unity of opposites to the ambivalent nature of these pseudosciences which unknowingly combine insight with foolishness:

> The *depth* which spirit brings forth from within . . . and the *ignorance* of
> this consciousness about what it really is saying, are the same conjunction
> of the high and the low which, in the living being nature naïvely expresses
> when it combines the organ of its highest fulfillment, the organ of
> generation, with the organ of urination. The infinite judgement, *qua*
> infinite, would be the fulfillment of life that comprehends itself; the
> consciousness of the infinite judgement that remains at the level of
> picture-thinking behaves as urination.[183]

There is, in other words, a certain depth of judgment in observing
consciousness's attempt to know itself and to see itself in its object;
however, on the other hand, the attempts of observing consciousness
to learn about itself simply become more and more absurd. We thus
have a strange juxtaposition of, on the one hand, profound insight and,
on the other hand, absurd scientific inquiries, a juxtaposition which
Hegel likens to the juxtaposition in nature of the organ of reproduction
being the same (at least in some animals) as the organ of urination.
On this rather unhappy comparison, the sciences of physiognomy and
phrenology would then correspond to urination.

B. "Self-Consciousness" Repeated: The Actualization of Rational Self-Consciousness through Its Own Activity (§§347–93)

General Introduction (§§347–59)

This section is generally more accessible than the difficult terrain that
we have just covered in "Observing Reason," and it is for this reason that
it has been more popular in the secondary literature and more often
taught in courses on the *Phenomenology*. Here Hegel criticizes what we
might call various forms of individualism, that is, forms of consciousness
according to which the individual self-conscious agent is the essential,
and the world of objects or the community is the inessential. Here the
individual is considered to be an atomic unit opposed to the social whole.
This section is particularly lively because of the ironical or satirical tone
that runs throughout it. This tone is often explained by the fact, which
commentators have often noted, that various contemporaries of Hegel
are the targets of his criticism in this section. As is clear both here and
in the *Philosophy of Right*, Hegel was an ardent opponent of various forms
of romanticism and the accompanying forms of individualism which
were popular in his day.[184] His criticism of the forms of subjectivity is

particularly polemical in this section, due perhaps more to personal than philosophical motives.

Hegel begins here[185] by discussing the transition from "Observing Reason" to the present section. The alleged break between "Observing Reason" and "The Actualization of Rational Self-Consciousness through Its Own Activity" has been no less problematic than the purported break, examined above, between the "Consciousness" and "Self-Consciousness" chapters. What do the forms of practical self-consciousness of this section have to do with the scientific views treated in "Observing Reason"? This problem can be easily resolved when we analyze the overall argument of the work. Just as the "Self-Consciousness" chapter can be seen as a logical continuation of the argumentative structure that began in the "Consciousness" chapter, so also this second section in "Reason" can be seen as a continuation of the problematic begun in "Observing Reason." Hegel begins by reminding us of the fundamental premise of "Observing Reason": "Self-consciousness found the thing to be like itself, and itself to be like a thing; i.e., it is aware that it is *in itself* the objectively real world."[186] In the course of the previous section, observing consciousness, working with this basic belief, continually tried to find itself in the world of nature. However, as we have just seen, this attempt led to tautologies and paradoxes. Now the phenomenological actor must find itself in the world in a different sense. Hegel writes,

> It [self-consciousness] is no longer the *immediate* certainty of being all reality, but a certainty for which the immediate in general has the form of something superseded, so that the *objectivity* of the immediate still has only the value of something superficial, its inner being and essence being self-consciousness itself. The object, to which it is positively related, is therefore a self-consciousness.[187]

Here Hegel begins by referring back to the failed attempts of phrenology and physiognomy to find the true essence of the subject in his immediate being, i.e., in the bumps and hollows of the head or in the lines and lineaments of the face. This constituted the last attempt to find true essence in the sphere of objects. Thus, the objective sphere of nature remains "superficial" or inessential. Now, with this transition, the phenomenological actor tries to find the essence of the individual, in this case himself, not in his external being but rather in another self-conscious subject. Thus, self-consciousness is no longer concerned with objects but rather with other self-conscious subjects. This dialectical movement gives us a strong reason to believe that this transition parallels that from "Consciousness" to "Self-Consciousness," where the movement was from the external sphere of objects to self-conscious subjects. Moreover, the issue of self-certainty and truth is also raised again here[188] in a way that hearkens back to the beginning of the "Self-Consciousness" chapter and to "The Truth of Self-Certainty," and this gives us additional support for the supposition about the parallelism with "Self-Consciousness." Here as before self-certainty amounts to self-consciousness's own account of the subject-object Notion, while truth amounts to something agreed upon by a wider social community beyond the individual. Self-consciousness recognizes itself and the other as free and independent, but only in principle and not yet in praxis. The various figures that we will examine in this section will all be attempts to assert and implement this freedom and to bring it into the external sphere via the efforts of the self-conscious subject. This seems again to indicate an affinity between the "Self-Consciousness" chapter and the present section.

This supposition is confirmed when we analyze the place and role of this section in the *Phenomenology* as a whole. Hegel here in these introductory paragraphs[189] gives us a fairly thorough discussion of the structure of the "Reason" chapter, to which we can now turn. Since, as we have seen, the "Observing Reason" section parallels the "Consciousness" chapter, we can infer that the present section, following "Observing Reason" as it does, must then correspond to "Self-Consciousness." Hegel confirms this structure rather straightforwardly at the beginning of the present section when he writes: "Just as Reason, in the role of observer, repeated, in the element of the category, the movement of *consciousness*, viz. sense-certainty, perception, and the understanding, so will Reason again run through the double movement of self-consciousness, and pass over from independence into its freedom."[190] Here by "Reason, in the role of observer," it is clear that Hegel means to refer to the section "Observing Reason" as a whole. In this passage he makes clear once again that the three sections of "Observing Reason" correspond to the three sections of the "Consciousness" chapter. Then, referring implicitly to the present section, which he is here introducing, he says that Reason, just like self-consciousness, will "pass over from independence into its freedom." Here Hegel indicates that the present section, "The Actualization of Rational Self-Consciousness through Its Own Activity," corresponds to the "Self-Consciousness" chapter, which included first the "Independence and Dependence of Self-Consciousness," here referred to simply as "independence," and then the "Freedom of Self-Consciousness," here referred to as "its freedom." Hegel's formulation of the overlapping structures here is particularly important. He says specifically that the sections overlap "in the element of the category." By this he seems to mean that although the content of the various dialectical movements changes and becomes gradually richer, nevertheless with respect to the form of the dialectic, certain categorial elements remain the same and in fact are repeated at the various levels. We have tried to indicate how in the previous section the categories from the various stages of "Consciousness" were repeated in "Observing Reason." Now we will expect to see the categories and forms of consciousness examined in "Self-Consciousness" turn up once again in the present section. This brief explanation by Hegel of his systematic plan helps us to see an important part of the overlapping structure of the work as a whole and to appreciate the enriched dialectical level at which we currently find ourselves. We can schematically represent the outline of the "Reason" chapter implied by Hegel's remarks here in figure 6.1. As we have seen earlier, the fundamental categories developed in the "Consciousness" chapter are repeated at the level of "Self-Consciousness." These two units then form the basic structures first of the object sphere and then of the subject sphere, units which are repeated here at the level of "Reason." Now the task of the "Reason" chapter is to unify the subject

Figure 6.1

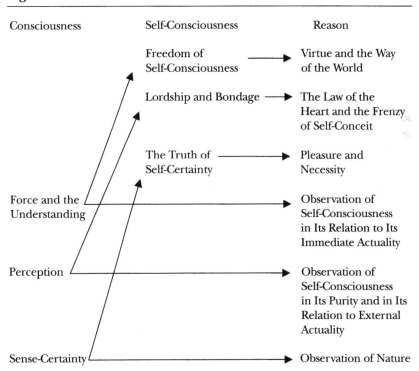

and the object and to overcome the dualism that has plagued the dialectic up until this point. New forms of subject and object appear here in the first two sections of "Reason" before they are presumably unified in the third section.

Hegel goes on in the same passage first to explain the overlap here with the "Self-Consciousness" chapter, and then to discuss the last section of the "Reason" chapter:

> To begin with, this active Reason is aware of itself merely as an individual and as such must demand and produce its reality in an "other." Then, however, its consciousness having raised itself into universality, it becomes *universal* Reason, and is conscious of itself as Reason, as a consciousness that is already recognized in and for itself, which in its pure consciousness unites all self-consciousness.[191]

In the first sentence, Hegel makes clear the parallelism with "Self-Consciousness." In that chapter, the individual self-consciousness was certain of itself and had to negate the other in order to validate its own self-certainty. The lordship and bondage relation showed us the need for mutual recognition in intersubjective relations. Here as well, the self-consciousness "must demand and produce its reality in an 'other.' " In the second sentence of this passage, Hegel refers to the final section in the "Reason" chapter, "Individuality Which Takes Itself to be Real in and for Itself." This stage is characterized by what Hegel calls "universal Reason," which involves an overcoming of private subjectivity and the move to a universality of wills.

After orienting us again with respect to the plan of the work, Hegel then[192] introduces two of the most important concepts that will form the guiding threads for the rest of the book. Most importantly, we find here Hegel's first real treatment of his key term of art "Spirit" (*Geist*).[193] We have seen this term employed earlier in "Observing Reason," where it was simply used to refer to "self-consciousness" as opposed to "nature," but here we see the term in its true context. However, we must be careful to note that we have not yet arrived at the level of Spirit per se, and his use of this term here is not yet meant to represent the full-blown version of it that appears there. Here Hegel gives us a preliminary indication of what he means by this all-important term:

> It [self-consciousness] is in the form of thinghood, i.e. it is *independent*; but it is certain that this independent object is for it not something alien, and thus it knows that it is *in principle* recognized by the object. It is Spirit which, in the duplication of its self-consciousness and in the independence

of both, has the certainty of its unity with itself. This certainty has now to be raised to the level of truth.[194]

Here "Spirit" is characterized as self-consciousness relating itself to another independent self-conscious subject. Spirit involves finding oneself and one's identity in the other and in the unity of the social whole. This notion stands in marked contrast to the "Lordship and Bondage" dialectic in which self-consciousness, when at first confronted by another self-conscious agent, refused to recognize the validity of the other's value and worth. The result was the asymmetrical lord-bondsman relation, which was a relation of dependency. Here, on the other hand, self-consciousness recognizes the other as precisely something independent. Hegel also refers to "Spirit" here as "universal self-consciousness."[195] Likewise in the *Philosophy of Right*, he says that Spirit "is the nature of human beings *en masse* and their nature is therefore twofold: (i) at the one extreme, explicit individuality of consciousness and will, and (ii) at the other extreme, universality which knows and wills what is substantive."[196] By this definition, he seems to indicate the unity of self-conscious subjects, but it is more than this. Spirit is not a simple aggregate of self-conscious agents; rather, in Spirit human subjects share common values and culture, and it is these things that weld individuals into a universal self-consciousness. I do not wish to explore this concept further here, since we will have occasion to treat it in some detail below. We do, however, need to flag this term in order to see how Hegel uses it here and how it can be applied to the dialectical movements prior to the "Spirit" chapter.

Hegel, in his discussion of his term "Spirit," indicates that at this point we, qua philosophical observers, have already reached the moment of Spirit, i.e., the communal determination of the subject-object Notion, although self-consciousness is still not able to see it. He writes,

> If we take this goal—and this is the *Notion* which *for us* has already appeared on the scene—in its reality, viz. the self-consciousness that is recognized and acknowledged, and which has its own self-certainty in the other free self-consciousness, and possesses its truth precisely in that "other"; in other words, if we look on this still *inner* Spirit as substance that has already advanced to the stage of having an *outer* existence, then in this Notion there is disclosed the *realm of ethical life*. For this is nothing else than the absolute spiritual *unity* of the essence of individuals in their independent *actual existence*.[197]

As usual, in this passage Hegel indicates the perspective of the philosophical observer by introducing the issue with the expression "for us." Here, we are able to see that self-consciousness has its truth and validity only insofar as its truth-claims match up to the universal truth-claims of the other. This is the point of "universal Reason." The "goal" of our dialectical movement is to reach this level of universal mutual recognition, but this is only a goal that we, the philosophical observers, have perceived; the philosophical actor is as yet unaware of his identification with a larger social whole and of this dialectical goal. This goal of identification and self-fulfillment among self-conscious agents indicates the crucial importance of the notion of recognition for Hegel's philosophy as a whole. Often in discussions on Hegel, the term "recognition" is used only to refer to the lordship and bondage dialectic; however, as we can see here, the story of recognition is still a long way from being complete. Hegel worked out this notion carefully during his Jena years,[198] and thus it comes as no great surprise that it plays a crucial role in the development of the overall argument of the *Phenomenology*.

The ability to identify oneself and one's truth-claims with the social whole can only take place in the forum of what Hegel calls "ethical life" (*Sittlichkeit*). This term is another one of Hegel's most important bits of philosophical jargon, which is particularly significant in his political philosophy. Sadly, it is notoriously difficult to translate.[199] The German word *Sittlichkeit* is etymologically related to the word *Sitte*, meaning "custom." The substantive ending *-keit* in German is a common ending for abstract nouns (e.g., *Wirklichkeit* [reality]; *Notwendigkeit* [necessity]; *Möglichkeit* [possibility]) and is similar to the *-itas* ending in Latin. A similar etymological connection exists in English, although it is somewhat more hidden than its German correspondent. Our words "morality" and "moral" have their origin in the Latin word *mos*, meaning "custom"; in other words, to the noun *mos* is added the ending *-itas* to produce the Latin word *moralitas* from which our word "morality" ultimately stems. The point of discussing the etymology is simply to indicate that *Sittlichkeit* refers to the concrete realm of customs and values and not to the abstract realm of philosophical discussions of morals. In the *Philosophy of Right*, Hegel, by means of a play on words, makes clear the connection between everyday customs and ethical life in its philosophical sense:

> But when individuals are simply identified with the actual order, ethical life [*das Sittliche*] appears as their general mode of conduct, i.e. as custom [*Sitte*], while the habitual practice of ethical living appears as a second nature which, put in the place of the initial, purely natural will, is the soul of custom permeating it through and through, the significance and the actuality of its existence. It is mind [*Geist*] living and present as a world, and the substance of mind [*Geist*] thus exists now for the first time.[200]

With this juxtaposition of words, the important etymological connection between *Sittlichkeit* and *Sitte* is made obvious. This helps to make clear that with the term *Sittlichkeit* Hegel means to refer to a wide and heterogeneous range of moral and legal practices and phenomena, and not merely to an abstract ethical code or theory. But, moreover, Hegel in this passage connects "ethical life" with "Spirit," translated here as "mind."

Hegel explicitly introduces his term "ethical life" in order to make a self-conscious contrast with what he in the *Philosophy of Right* calls "morality" (*Moralität*).[201] He frequently associates "morality" in this context with Kant and criticizes it as something overly abstract which fails to capture the true nature of ethical actions in everyday life of individuals interacting in a society. In the *Philosophy of Right*, he writes,

> "Morality" [*Moralität*] and "ethical life" [*Sittlichkeit*], which perhaps usually pass current as synonyms, are taken here in essentially different senses. Yet even commonplace thinking seems to be distinguishing them; Kant generally prefers to use the word "morality" and, since the principles of action in his philosophy are always limited to this conception, they make the standpoint of ethical life completely impossible, in fact they explicitly nullify and spurn it.[202]

For Hegel, since Kant's ethical theory requires that one abstract from the concrete situation with all its interests and specifics and that one attempt to formulate a general law, it renders true morality, or better, ethical action impossible. Hegel brings out the one-sidedness of the Kantian view in the present section when he writes, "This ethical *substance*, taken in its abstract universality, is only law in the form of *thought;* but it is no less immediately actual *self-consciousness*, or it is *custom*."[203] Here Hegel grants that an important aspect of morality and ethics consists in the abstract ethical laws and principles which inform moral action, referred to here as "law in the form of *thought*"; however, this for Hegel is not the whole story. Ethics is not merely acting in accordance with abstract ethical principles, but rather it primarily involves the realm of custom and concrete ethical situations. The key point for our purposes is that the forms of consciousness that we will examine in this and the next section are all abstract in some sense, and it is not until this abstractness becomes obvious in "Reason as Lawgiver" at the end of the "Reason" chapter that we realize that something more concrete is required.

Hegel, in his discussion of the terms "Spirit" and "ethical life," intends to draw a contrast with the present section. Spirit is characterized here as unity of the social whole, which Hegel refers to as "substance," and which stands in contrast to the subjectivity or individualism in this section. He uses a simile to illustrate the identification of the individual with the social whole:

> Reason is present here as the fluid universal *substance*, as unchangeable simple thinghood, which bursts asunder into many completely independent beings, just as a light bursts asunder into stars as countless self-luminous points, which in their absolute being-for-self are dissolved, not merely *implicitly* in the simple independent substance, but *explicitly for themselves.*[204]

Thus, Spirit will be at once the one or the harmonious collectivity of all the members of a community and at the same time the many individual self-conscious agents which make up that community and the truth and values for which it stands. It is the perfect balance of individuality and identification with the social whole. The simile employed in the passage above reminds us of the universal-particular dialectic that we have been following all along. Here the universal is reinterpreted as the community or the social whole, while the particular is represented by the individual social agent in his interaction with the community. Hegel characterizes this moment once more in terms of the identification of the individual with the universal social whole as follows:

> This unity of being-for-another or making oneself a thing, and of being-for-self, this universal substance, speaks its *universal language* in the customs and laws of its nation. But this existent unchangeable essence is the expression of the very individuality which seems opposed to it; the laws proclaim what each individual is and does; the individual knows himself in them, or knows them as *particularized* in his own individuality, and in each of his fellow citizens.[205]

The initial stage of Spirit is one of immediate identification with the social whole. One follows a blind and unreflective patriotism or ethnocentrism in favor of one's own culture. The customs and laws of one's own society reflect one's own true being. This conception of ethical life can only come about, according to Hegel, in the actual historical development of individual peoples. The dialectic, however, has not yet advanced this far. He writes: "It is in fact in the life of a people or nation that the *Notion* of self-conscious Reason's actualization—of beholding, in the independence of the 'other,' complete *unity* with it, or having for my object the free thinghood of an 'other' which confronts me and is the negative of myself, as my own being-for-*myself*—that the Notion has its complete reality."[206] We have not yet reached this level of Spirit where self-consciousness is fully immersed in the ethical substance of its culture. The complete unity with other self-conscious subjects has not yet taken place. The dialectic does not yet operate at the level of nations or historical peoples or communities. The key aspect of history comes for the first time in the "Spirit" chapter.

In what follows,[207] Hegel briefly sketches, by way of anticipation, the dialectical movement of the "Spirit" section. It begins with an immediate unreflective harmony in the Greek *polis*, but this unreflective state is destroyed by an alienation that separates the individual from the social whole and its various institutions. This alienation gives rise to social isolation and individualism. Only in the modern world is it possible for Spirit to become aware of itself, i.e., for the individual to enjoy a principle of subjectivity but yet at the same time reflectively to be a part of a unified social whole. However, all of this is sketched by Hegel merely by way of preview, and thus we need not examine his account here in great detail. He tells us at this point that consciousness has not yet reached this stage of unity and identification. In other words, although self-consciousness is implicitly in the realm of Spirit and potentially can enjoy the unity with the social whole that we have just sketched, nonetheless it does not yet see this, and it remains at the level of alienation and separation from the social whole. Hegel emphasizes this point once again in his description of the stage that results from "Observing Reason":

> self-consciousness has *not yet* attained *this happy state* of being the ethical substance, the Spirit of a people. For having turned back from its role of observer, Spirit, at first, is not yet as such realized through itself; it is established only as an *inner* essence or as an abstraction. In other words, Spirit is, at first, *immediate*; but existing immediately, it is separate and individual.[208]

Self-consciousness at first is "immediately" only realized through itself and its own activity and is unable to find itself reflected in the social whole. Thus, each of the three stages in this section will involve an attempt by self-consciousness to realize itself or its subject-object Notion by some activity. The self-consciousness is then still a separate individual although its activity is social. It, qua individual, is the essential and the true while the social whole is thought to be the unessential. Hegel continues, "If, then, *for us* the truth of this rational self-consciousness is the ethical substance, here, *for that self-consciousness*, it is the beginning of its ethical experience of the world."[209] In this passage, Hegel makes the distinction between the two perspectives perfectly clear. We, the philosophical observers, can grasp the true meaning of the dialectical movement of this level against the background of Spirit and ethical life. For the self-conscious subject, on the other hand, this remains as yet unperceived.

This difference in perspective between the philosophical observers and the self-conscious subject also helps to bring out the transcendental nature of the argument. In other words, we can see that there is a whole realm of ethical life that underlies the actions of the individual and serves as a necessary precondition for those actions. The task is to examine the Notion here in order to see what is necessarily contained in it or presupposed by it. We, as readers, can anticipate the results, whereas self-consciousness cannot. Hegel makes this clear when he writes,

> The ethical substance has sunk to the level of a predicate devoid of self, whose living subjects are individuals who themselves have to provide the filling for their universality and to fulfill their essential nature through their own efforts. Taken in the former sense, then, those forms are the coming-to-be of the ethical substance and precede it; in the latter, they succeed it and reveal to self-consciousness what its essential nature is.[210]

Since self-consciousness is unable to find its identity in the established customs and values of society, it must give itself meaning and validity through its own action which stands in contrast to the status quo of society. These actions form the "coming-to-be of ethical substance"; in other words, they serve as a transcendental justification for the unity of ethical substance later. The self-conscious subject abstracts from the social whole, or, as Hegel says in "Pleasure and Necessity," "it has lifted itself out of the ethical substance."[211] Only after one has pursued an identity and individuality which stands in abstraction from the social whole does one later come to see the true value and meaning of the established customs and values of society.

After examining the ideas of Spirit and ethical life and anticipating the basic movement of "Spirit," Hegel then[212] turns to examine at a general level the Notion that will be at play in this section. The general Notion of this section involves seeing the self-conscious agent as an individual fundamentally at odds with the social whole. In this we can see the clear contrast with "Spirit" as described above. Hegel writes,

> In other words, Spirit is, at first, *immediate;* but existing immediately, it is separate and individual. It is the *practical* consciousness, which steps into its world which it finds already *given,* with the aim of duplicating itself in this distinct form of something separate and individual, of producing itself as *this* individual, as this existent counterpart of itself, and of becoming

conscious of this unity of its own actuality with the objective being of the world.[213]

We thus begin with the individual self-conscious agent, which finds the world or the social order as something "already *given*" over and against itself. It attempts to find itself in other self-conscious agents, just as it tried to find itself in the sphere of natural objects before. This involves trying to find oneself reflected in the other via the process of recognition. Since the individual self-conscious agent fails to see its unity with the social whole, it needs to try to establish its own identity on its own without reference to the society or the state. It must try to create itself by its "own efforts."[214] Thus, the self-conscious agent must try to realize itself "through its own activity" as is indicated by the title of this section. Self-consciousness, here as in the "Self-Consciousness" chapter, thus begins by seeing itself as the essential and the true. "Self-consciousness," Hegel writes, "which is at first only the Notion of Spirit, enters on this path with the characteristic of holding itself to be, as a particular spirit, essential being; and its aim, therefore, is to give itself as a particular individual an actual existence and to enjoy itself as an individual in it."[215] The dualism at this stage is then between the individual and the society.

Finally, Hegel sketches the structure of this section by briefly outlining its three dialectical movements.[216] At first he characterizes in a general way the common feature of all of the various forms of consciousness at this level: "In holding itself to be, *qua being-for-self*, essential being, it is the *negativity* of the 'other.' In its consciousness, therefore, it appears as the positive in contrast to something which certainly *is*, but which has for it the significance of something without intrinsic being."[217] Each of the three following forms will be characterized by a contrast with the individual and the social whole. The individual is thought to be the essential, and thus the task is to negate the other and the social whole. In a reference to the first form of consciousness at this level, i.e., "Pleasure and Necessity," Hegel writes, "Its primary end, however, is its *immediate* abstract *being-for-self;* in other words, seeing itself as *this particular individual* in another, or seeing another self-consciousness as itself."[218] As we shall see in our analysis, the self-consciousness of "Pleasure and Necessity" tries to negate the other unessential self-consciousness in an attempt to unite itself with it. The result of this dialectic is an inner law which Hegel refers to as "The Law of the Heart": "The experience of what the truth of this end is raises self-consciousness to a higher level, and from now on it is itself its own end, insofar as it is at the same time universal and has the law directly within it."[219] Finally, Hegel refers to the final discussion of this section entitled "Virtue and the Way of the World": "In carrying out this law of its heart, however, it learns that the individual, in doing so, cannot preserve himself, but rather that the good can only be accomplished through the sacrifice of the individual: and self-consciousness becomes *virtue.*"[220] The conclusion that consciousness reaches from these various figures Hegel expresses as follows: "Having discovered this, self-consciousness thus knows itself to be reality in the form of an individuality that directly expresses *itself,* an individuality which no longer encounters resistance from an actual world opposed to it, and whose aim and object are only this expressing of itself."[221] Hegel here only sketches very briefly the outline of this section and does not dwell on the details of the dialectical movement that we are about to explore; thus, we need not examine these passages in depth, since they serve only as a general outline. We are now ready to turn to an analysis of the first of these forms of practical self-consciousness.

I. Pleasure and Necessity (§§360–66)

This first dialectical stage of "The Actualization of Rational Self-Consciousness through Its Own Activity" corresponds to the first stage of the "Self-Consciousness" chapter, namely "The Truth of Self-Certainty." There the category of pure being from "Sense-Certainty" was reinterpreted at the level of self-consciousness as desire (*Begierde*). Likewise, here self-consciousness is considered "*immediate simple* being,"[222] which is reinterpreted as "*desire,*"[223] and which in turn leads to the key concept of pleasure. This categorial overlap is important if we are to understand the unity of the work as a whole and the role of the "Pleasure and Necessity" section in particular. The important difference that appears in the Notion at this level is that self-consciousness is no longer concerned with abstract theory, as observing consciousness was in the previous section. The Notion at this level is something that is grounded in the world of experience and action: "The shadowy existence of science, laws and principles . . . vanishes like a lifeless mist which cannot compare with the certainty of its own reality."[224] The transition from the theoretical to the practical, so to speak, corresponds once again to the transition from "Consciousness" to "Self-Consciousness."

Some commentators[225] take the reference to Goethe's *Faust*[226] in this section as a conclusive proof that the form of consciousness that is analyzed here is in fact the protagonist of that famous work. However, this single reference is by no means enough to make this case. Merely by virtue of Hegel's quotation of Schiller's *Die Freundschaft* in "Absolute Knowing,"[227] we would hardly be tempted to argue that there he means to use a concept or character in that work as prototypical for his concept of absolute knowing. Instead, it seems more likely that there, as here with the quotation from *Faust*, Hegel is simply using well-known literary passages to illustrate key concepts that he wishes to discuss. The citation is illustrative and not, strictly speaking, referential. I thus agree with Kaufmann in his contention that with this passage from *Faust*, Hegel merely "characterizes a type."[228] It would perhaps be different if Hegel had analyzed the passage in some depth or discussed in detail some direct parallel between *Faust* and the form of self-consciousness examined here in "Pleasure and Necessity"; however, this is not what we see. Instead, Hegel seems to cite the passage to illustrate a single point and then moves on without explanation, never to mention it again. Thus, we need not take this quotation too much to heart as being absolutely crucial for the actual content of the analysis in this section. I will argue that, just as is the case with the rest of the forms of consciousness, the target of criticism here in this section is not nearly so concrete as this.

The Notion: Pleasure (§§360–62)

This stage differs from the previous one, "Observing Reason," since here we are concerned with self-consciousness finding itself in another independent self-consciousness and not in the sphere of objects. Hegel describes this in the following way:

> Insofar as it has lifted itself out of the ethical substance and the tranquil being of thought to its being-*for-self*, it has left behind the law of custom and existence, the knowledge acquired through observation, and theory. . . . For the latter is rather a knowledge of something whose being-for-self and actuality are other than those of this self-consciousness.[229]

In "Observing Reason," as in its corresponding chapter (i.e., "Consciousness"), the object domain was the external world of independent objects. Here in the "Actualization of Self-Consciousness," the object domain is other self-conscious subjects, just as in the "Self-Consciousness" chapter. Hegel expresses this same point later when he writes, "Nevertheless it [this form of self-consciousness] no longer has the form of *immediate simple* being, as it has for Reason in its observational role where it is abstract *being* or, posited in the form of an alien being, is *thinghood* in general."[230] Thus, the object for observing reason was something objective and "other" than self-consciousness, whereas here in "Pleasure and Necessity" the object will be coordinate with self-consciousness, i.e., another self-conscious subject. Now we (as in "Self-Consciousness") once again analyze the various attempts of the self-conscious subject to determine itself with respect to other self-conscious agents.

The description of this form of consciousness begins just as the "Self-Consciousness" chapter began; namely, the self-conscious subject believes that it is the real, the essential, and the true, but, since the other of consciousness appears to be something independent, it must prove its reality to itself and see itself in the world around it in order to validate itself. Hegel writes,

> Self-consciousness which, on the whole, knows itself to be *reality*, has its object in its own self, but as an object which initially is merely *for self-consciousness*, and does not as yet possess [objective] being which confronts it as a reality other than its own; and self-consciousness, by behaving as a being-for-self, aims to see itself as another independent being.[231]

Self-consciousness's self-certainty remains subjective, that is, it is "merely for self-consciousness." In other words, self-consciousness has intentions and desires which are merely subjective and have to be realized in the world. The task for self-consciousness at this stage is to make itself objective or to give itself, by means of its own activity, an external form that can be recognized in the objective social sphere. Only by doing so can self-consciousness raise its subjective, internal self-certainty to an objective truth.

At the stage of "Pleasure and Necessity," self-consciousness attempts to assert its individuality and to contrast it with the community in the self-certification that it, qua individual, gains through the other: "This *primary* end is to become aware of itself as an individual in the other self-consciousness, or to make this other into itself."[232] Here, unlike in the master-slave scenario, self-consciousness recognizes the necessity of mediating its truth-claims through the other. It attempts to do so through the mediation of desire, since in its desire for the other the self-conscious agent believes itself to be unique and capable of fully developing its independence. In other words, the other is not objectified as in the master-slave scenario, but rather self-consciousness realizes that it needs the other in order to determine its own individuality.

Here, as in the corresponding section ("The Truth of Self-Certainty"), the task of self-consciousness is to define itself as a discrete, autonomous individual entity. At this level, self-consciousness believes that its individuality lies in its own activity, and only through its activity can it determine itself as such. For the self-conscious agent at this level, "true actuality is merely that being which is the actuality of the *individual* consciousness."[233] Thus, the dialectic of universal and particular is at work again. Self-consciousness attempts to determine itself through its activity as an individual agent only to discover that the result of its activity is only indeterminacy and universality. The activity of self-consciousness at this level (as at the level of "The Truth of Self-Certainty") is dictated by desire and pleasure which, as some commentators have pointed out,[234] seems to associate this view with hedonism. Self-consciousness tries to prove that the object of its desire, now a self-conscious agent, is not truly an independent other: "It does not aim at the destruction of objective being in its entirety, but only at the form of its otherness or its independence, which is a show devoid of essence."[235] The act of seduction that self-consciousness undertakes here does not represent a complete destruction of the other in contrast to the dialectic of "The Truth of Self-Certainty," where self-consciousness tried utterly to destroy everything that seemed independent. By enjoying the pleasure, self-consciousness is able, so it thinks, to determine itself as an individual and to secure the recognition of the other: "the enjoyment of desire puts an end to this [sc. independent] existence so far as it belongs to the object of desire. . . . It attains therefore to the enjoyment of *pleasure*, to the consciousness of its actualization in a consciousness which appears as independent, or to the vision of the unity of two independent self-consciousnesses."[236] By seducing the other, self-consciousness implicitly wrings from the other an admission of dependence and a form of intersubjective recognition. In the satisfaction of desire, self-consciousness finds its identity. Some commentators find here a criticism of the romantics' emphasis on the importance of individual emotion or feeling in contrast to reason. On this view, the faculty of reason is something universal that is shared by all human subjects, and, therefore, by virtue of this universality, one cannot express one's individuality or particularity by using this faculty. When one works out a problem in mathematics, for instance, one is not expressing anything particular about oneself. Feeling, on the other hand, is something unique and subjective. Only when one expresses one's feelings and emotions, does one, on this view, express something unique about oneself.

It is important to note that the individuality of the self-conscious agent that is derived from the satisfaction of desire and from pleasure is not one that involves self-consciousness in its isolation. Rather here self-consciousness purportedly attains its individuality only in relation to and via the mediation of another: "For it is not as *this particular* individual that it becomes an object to itself, but rather as the *unity* of itself and the other self-consciousness, hence as an individual that is only a moment, or a *universal*."[237] This implies the interdependence of self-conscious subjects that is bound up in Hegel's concept of Spirit; moreover, the failure to recognize this interdependence foreshadows the breakdown of the Notion that appears in the experience of consciousness. Here consciousness is unable to determine itself as an individual in this activity, but rather becomes merely a part of an undetermined universal together with the other self-consciousness. Since, according to its Notion here, self-consciousness sees itself only as the desiring self-consciousness, when this desire renders it universal, there is no other mark of its individuality. What self-consciousness will learn from this is that desire cannot form the basis for meaningful social interaction. A new social medium must be found, and certain social institutions must be created through which individuals can at the same time meaningfully participate in a larger civil unit without losing their individuality. All of this, however, is merely an anticipation of the experience of consciousness that begins here.[238]

The Experience of Consciousness (§§363–65)

Hegel indicates quite clearly the positive and the negative sides of the dialectic when he announces the beginning of the experience of consciousness. He writes,

> The pleasure enjoyed has indeed the positive significance that self-consciousness has become objective *to itself;* but equally it has the negative one of having reduced *itself* to a moment. And since it grasped its realization in the former sense only, its experience is of a contradiction in which the attained reality of its individuality sees itself destroyed by the negative *essence* confronting it, which is devoid of reality and content.[239]

Desire has a positive side insofar as it becomes externalized and consummated in the external world of objects. In this way, self-consciousness becomes "objective *to itself.*" Precisely this was the intention of the self-conscious subject. Only by becoming an individual in the objective sphere can self-consciousness come to determine itself. There is, however, a negative side to the dialectic which self-consciousness failed to see, and it is this negative side which constitutes the sublation of the Notion at this stage.

The sublation appears when self-consciousness is unable to find anything lasting in the pleasure that it takes from the other self-consciousness. By defining itself only in terms of the satisfaction of desire, self-consciousness is able to determine itself but only for a finite period of time. However, desire returns, and self-consciousness is compelled to return again and again to take its pleasure if it is to continue to determine itself. Thus, self-consciousness has "reduced *itself* to a moment," since it exists as a determinate entity only for a moment, namely for the moment of pleasure and the satisfaction of desire. Hegel analyzes the problem with this form of consciousness with the term "necessity." While self-consciousness is trying to establish its individuality and its independence through pleasure, it proves just the opposite of what is intended, namely its dependence. Self-consciousness is compelled to return again and again to take its pleasure in order to determine itself. It cannot free itself from the obsession of this dependency: "The *object*, then, that is for self-consciousness as it takes its pleasure . . . is the expansion of those empty essentialities of pure unity, of pure difference, and their relation; beyond this, the object which the individuality experiences as its *essence*, has no content. It is what is called *necessity*."[240] The necessity drives self-consciousness and hinders it from becoming truly autonomous. The individuality that self-consciousness strives after has no lasting content since pleasure is always fleeting.

The other aspect of necessity is that it reduces the self-conscious subject to an object. In other words, we usually speak of necessity when we speak of, for instance, the natural order. Animals are not free but rather are determined by the necessity of their natural impulses and drives. Human beings, however, have an intellectual faculty which they can, so to speak, place between themselves and their natural drives; thus, humans can fast, thus denying the impulse to eat, or they can stay awake on vigils, thus denying the impulse to sleep, or they can be celibate, commit suicide, etc. Precisely by virtue of this faculty, humans are free.[241] Now self-consciousness at this level has associated itself wholly with the pleasure obtained by satisfying the natural drives. It has thus removed the aspect of rational mediation. It therefore pursues the satisfaction of its natural drives just as animals do, i.e., out of necessity. Self-consciousness in this way becomes a mere object characterized by the necessity of nature, and thus it undermines its own freedom.

Concluding Remarks (§366)

In the final paragraph of this section, Hegel reflects briefly on the conclusion of this form of consciousness and on the transition to the next stage:

> The final moment of its existence is the thought of the loss of itself
> in necessity, or the thought of itself as a being that is absolutely *alien*
> to it. However, self-consciousness has *in itself* survived this loss; for
> this necessity or pure universality is *its own* essence. This reflection of

consciousness into itself, the knowledge that necessity is *itself*, is a new form of consciousness.[242]

Self-consciousness realizes that the universality of desire via the dialectic of necessity has undermined its individuality and its determination. However, self-consciousness tries to find something positive in this necessity and universality. It comes upon the idea that it has within itself a law that is necessary and universal and is valid for all others as well. This is then the Notion of the next section, "The Law of the Heart."

The movement here, as in both "Sense-Certainty" and "The Truth of Self-Certainty," is once again a movement from particular to universal. Self-consciousness tries to determine itself as a particular, individual being via the particularity of its own desire and the pleasure that follows from its satisfaction, but in the course of the dialectic it turns out that this pleasure renders self-consciousness an indeterminate universal. Hegel expresses this as follows: "The transition is made from the form of the *one* or unit into that of *universality*, from one absolute abstraction into the other, from the purpose of pure *being-for-self* which has thrown off all community with others, into the sheer opposite which is thus equally abstract *being-in-itself*."[243] Later, he writes in a similar vein, "The *abstract necessity* therefore has the character of the merely negative, uncomprehended power of universality, on which individuality is smashed to pieces."[244] This sublation of the individual parallels the movements we have seen earlier. In "Sense-Certainty," natural consciousness thought it referred to an individual object with the term "This"; however, the "This" collapsed into universality. In "The Truth of Self-Certainty," consciousness tried to determine itself as an individual vis-à-vis the objects of desire, but it turned out to be a universal, since there were no other self-conscious subjects to form a contrast and to supply the moment of difference. Likewise, here self-consciousness also tries to determine itself in another with the concept of desire. As we have seen, this once again renders the self-consciousness indeterminate.

II. The Law of the Heart and the Frenzy of Self-Conceit (§§367–80)

At the second level of this section, "The Law of the Heart and the Frenzy of Self-Conceit," an attempt is made once again to establish individuality vis-à-vis an implicit community or society, which Hegel calls "the universal order." In his analysis here, Hegel's sarcastic tone comes forth even stronger than before. Here, as in the corresponding sections,

"Perception" and "Lordship and Bondage," the category of the one and the many comes to play the key role. Self-consciousness interprets itself as an individual, as a one, and sees itself as opposed to the community or the social order which it regards as an inessential plurality. Here the attempt to assert individuality comes from an inner law, or what Hegel calls "the law of the heart." In the two dialectical moves at this stage, the individual law of the heart is first contrasted with the status quo or the universal order taken abstractly, and then it is contrasted with the various private laws of other individuals. Here the categories of the one and the many are most apparent.

The doctrine criticized here as "the law of the heart" apparently has its origins in the Enlightenment in writers such as Shaftesbury and Hutcheson, who promulgated ethical theories based on benevolent feelings and moral sentiment.[245] These thinkers are referred to as "the pre-Kantian philosophers" in the following passage from the *Philosophy of Right:* "This doctrine is rooted in the 'benevolence' [*guten Herzens*, literally 'the good heart'] of the pre-Kantian philosophers and constitutes, e.g., the quintessence of well-known touching dramatic productions."[246] The doctrine was then taken and developed further by Hegel's contemporaries in the romantic movement. He continues, "but today it has been resuscitated in a more extravagant form, and inner enthusiasm and the heart, i.e. the form of particularity as such, has been made the criterion of right, rationality, and excellence."[247] For Hegel, the manifestation of this doctrine of benevolence that was popular in his time was a form of romantic individualism that places the self and the individual's arbitrary feelings above the legitimate social order. It is, however, important to note that we are exploring here a conceptual moment and not a historical one. In other words, this particular view of the romantics is not understood or analyzed here in its historical context; rather, it is taken merely as a form of thought.

The transition from "Pleasure and Necessity" comes about when the concept of necessity from the previous dialectic becomes reinterpreted as the inner necessity of the law of the individual: "What necessity truly is in self-consciousness, it is for this new form of self-consciousness, in which it knows its own self to be the principle of necessity."[248] The necessity from "Pleasure and Necessity" that seemed to reduce the individual to an animal or a thing and to deprive him of both his freedom and his individuality here becomes reinterpreted as something positive. Self-consciousness sees necessity not as something having come from the outside but rather as a part of itself. Necessity and universality become the foundation of self-consciousness' inner law. Self-consciousness uses the idea of necessity to claim universality for its law, although it is only a subjective, inner law, that goes unrecognized by other self-conscious subjects.

The Notion: The Inner Law (§§367–68)

After discussing the transition from "Pleasure and Necessity," Hegel briefly sketches the Notion at this level. The self-righteous individual sees himself as the source of the true universal moral law: "It knows that it has the universal of law *immediately* within itself, and because the law is *immediately* present in the being-for-*self* of consciousness, it is called the *law* of the *heart*."[249] Self-consciousness here shares with the previous form of consciousness the belief in its own truth and reality; the Notion at this point is also a form of subjectivity. However, what is new here is the element of necessity which it sees as issuing from its own side: "This form takes *itself* to be, *qua* individuality, essence like the previous form; but the new form is richer because its *being-for-self* has for it the character of necessity or universality."[250] In other words, in "Pleasure and Necessity" self-consciousness pursued the objects of its own desire, but this activity aimed only at its own pleasure and not at that of others; thus, the active consciousness seeking pleasure lacked universality. Here, on the other hand, self-consciousness seeks the universal, since the law of the heart, although present only in the breast of the individual, is universal and leads to "the universal pleasure of all hearts."[251] The end of self-consciousness's action is thus a universal one.

Self-consciousness possesses this law in its own heart, but, as was the case in "Pleasure and Necessity," it must realize this law in the external world through its own activity. "The law," Hegel writes, "therefore, which is immediately self-consciousness' own law, or a heart which, however, has within it a law, is the *end* which self-consciousness proceeds to realize."[252] By means of its activity self-consciousness tries to save humanity from its deluded and oppressed state. The realization of the law of the heart is seen by self-consciousness as the only possible salvation for the destitute world, and it is for this reason that self-consciousness must with all its energy try to implement it for the sake of all mankind. As self-consciousness takes upon itself this epic task of correcting the ills of the world, we begin the first experience of consciousness.

The Experience of Consciousness (§§369–80)

The Law of the Heart (§§369–75)

The Notion at this level goes through two perturbations in the experience of consciousness. First we examine the breakdown of the law of the heart and then that of its new form, "the deranged consciousness" that results from it. Hegel announces the dialectical experience of consciousness at this level when he writes, "We have now to see whether its [self-consciousness'] realization corresponds to this Notion and whether in that realization it will find that this its law is its essential nature."[253] The dialectical task at this point consists in comparing self-consciousness's Notion of the law of the heart (and its purportedly positive effects on the welfare of humanity) with self-consciousness's own activity, with which it tries to actualize the law of the heart and to give it an objective form. In this dialectical examination the movement from particular to universal will play a central role. The self-conscious subject believes that it is determined, qua individual, by virtue of the law of the heart. Its lofty mission to save humanity from oppression sets it apart from the rest of mankind, which self-consciousness sees as living in a deluded state, unable to see the true ills from which it suffers. Thus, the law of the heart is a form of individualism or subjectivity, or, as Hegel says, "its essential nature is . . . to be for its own self."[254] As we shall see in the course of the dialectic, the determination of self-consciousness as an individual collapses predictably into universality.

In contrast to the benevolent inner law, the society and the community, i.e., "the universal order," is viewed by self-consciousness as unjust and oppressing. The corrupt world appears to the individual as something which is other than what it should be: "This heart is confronted by a real world; for in the heart the law is, in the first place, only for its own self, it is not yet realized, and is therefore at the same time something other than what the Notion is. This other is thereby characterized as a reality which is the opposite of what is to be realized, and consequently is the contradiction of the law and the individuality."[255] The law is something which is internal to the individual and as such it is not yet realized in the world. It implicitly contains a vision of the world as it should be. Thus, the world as it really is appears as something which contradicts this inner law. The individual is hopelessly alienated from the social order at large precisely because it sees this order as "the contradiction of the law and the individuality." The individual must attempt to follow its own inner law and actively combat the injustice and oppression of the world. The real world for the self-conscious subject is characterized as follows: "This reality is, therefore, on the one hand a law by which the particular individuality is oppressed, a violent ordering of the world which contradicts the law of the heart, and, on the other hand, a humanity suffering under that ordering, a humanity that does not follow the law of the heart, but is subjected to an alien necessity."[256] Humanity is viewed by self-consciousness as being held captive in the yoke of tradition, absolutism, and despotism. Although humanity is originally good, it suffers from the corruption of society and civilization. This thesis strongly resembles that of the *Discourse on the Origin of Inequality* of Rousseau, whom Hegel greatly admired in his youth.

The task for self-consciousness at this level is then to implement its inner law and to realize it in the real world, i.e., to actualize itself through its own activity, in order to combat the corruption of the world. "This individuality," Hegel writes, "therefore directs its energies to getting rid of this necessity which contradicts the law of the heart, and also the suffering caused by it."[257] This causes then a self-righteous tone that we did not see in the previous form of consciousness. Here self-consciousness not merely flippantly tries to achieve its own pleasure and to indulge itself as in "Pleasure and Necessity," but rather now self-consciousness sees itself as invested with a lofty mission to rid the world of its oppression: "And so it is no longer characterized by the levity of the previous form of self-consciousness, which only wanted the particular pleasure of the individual; on the contrary, it is the earnestness of a high purpose which seeks its pleasure in displaying the *excellence* of its own nature, and in promoting the welfare of mankind."[258] In "Pleasure and Necessity," self-consciousness displayed a frivolous self-indulgence, referred to here by Hegel as "levity," by pursuing only its own desire and pleasure. Now in "The Law of the Heart," self-consciousness casts aside this selfishness and takes a stand for humanity at large. It believes itself to be fighting the injustices that plague humanity. It strives self-righteously for the "welfare of mankind." Thus, at this level self-consciousness appears at least to itself to have a much higher purpose than before.

The rest of mankind, unenlightened by the law of the heart, lives under the arbitrary and perverse oppression of the human laws that are thought to crush individuality and freedom. Hegel characterizes the law that governs the social order and the status quo as follows:

> The law, on the other hand, which confronts the law of the heart is separated from the heart, and exists in its own right. Humanity which is bound by this law does not live in the blessed unity of the law with the heart; but either lives in their cruel separation and in suffering, or at least dispenses with the enjoyment *of itself* in obeying the law, and lacks the consciousness of its own excellence in *transgressing* it.[259]

In other words, the other human agents in their oppression are not even able to see the nobility and liberation involved in breaking the laws of the status quo. They are deluded by the ideology of the establishment and are coerced by its totalitarian system and forced to accept its laws and standards.

The contradiction in this Notion arises as the individual attempts to act in accordance with its law in order to implement its social reform in the real world. Hegel describes this contradiction as follows: "The individual, then, *carries out* the law of his heart. This becomes a *universal* ordinance, and pleasure becomes a reality which absolutely conforms to law. But, in this realization, the law has in fact escaped the individual; it directly becomes merely the relation which was supposed to be got rid of."[260] By actually realizing its goal and bringing its own personal law to the light of day, the individual implicitly makes its law something universal and available to all. This, however, contradicts the individuality which was the key aspect of the law of the heart. Now, since the law is something objective, it is no longer indicative or characteristic of the individual self-conscious subject. Such actions cannot be satisfying or fulfilling as an expression of self-consciousness's individuality since, once realized, they form a universal law. As a universal law, it is something which any morally virtuous person could act in accordance with, and thus the moral agent loses his individual character. Hegel expresses this as follows: "The law of the heart, through its very realization, ceases to be a law of the *heart*. For in its realization it receives the form of an [affirmative] *being*, and is now a *universal* power for which this particular heart is a matter of indifference, so that the individual, by setting up his own ordinance, no longer finds it to be his own."[261] The universality of the law contradicts precisely the individuality that the action in its fulfillment was supposed to establish. The determination of the self-conscious subject is undermined by the actualization of the law: "By his act he places himself in, or rather posits himself as, the universal element of existent reality, and his act is supposed to have, even according to his own interpretation, the value of a universal ordinance. But he has thereby *freed* himself from himself; he goes on growing *qua* universality, on his own account and purges himself of his particularity."[262] One might illustrate Hegel's point here about the collapse of particularity into universality with the example of a fad. In the beginning a new innovation is considered to be something interesting and exciting that does credit to the small circle of individuals who participate in it. It represents a concrete expression of their individuality and personality in the external world. However, as soon as the innovation catches on and becomes a fad, everyone comes to participate in it. But when everyone jumps on the bandwagon, then the original innovation becomes debased and loses its meaning. It is no longer able to express the particularity of the individuals who participate in it, since they are simply too numerous and too heterogeneous. Likewise, the law of the heart must remain ultimately esoteric and individual if it is to have meaning, but if it remains thus, then it cannot be actualized and made real.

As soon as self-consciousness is aware of the fact that by the very implementation of its law it becomes universal and is no longer particular, it tries to reevaluate its Notion in order to maintain its individuality. Hegel says of self-consciousness, "His deed, *qua actuality*, belongs to the universal; but its content is his own individuality which, as this particular individuality, wants to preserve itself in opposition to the universal."[263] In order to preserve its individuality, self-consciousness must pass over into a new form, which Hegel appropriately calls "the deranged consciousness" or simply "self-conceit." In short, in order to separate itself from other subjects, self-consciousness must come to despise the individual laws of all others in favor of its own. Hegel writes,

> Consequently, others do not find in this content the fulfillment of the law of *their* hearts, but rather that of someone else; and precisely in accordance with the universal law that each shall find in what is law *his* own heart, they turn against the reality *he* set up, just as he turned against theirs. Thus, just as the individual at first finds only the rigid law, now he finds the hearts of men themselves, opposed to his excellent intentions and detestable.[264]

At first, self-consciousness saw its own inner law of the heart as the universal law that all humanity would ascribe to if it were not deluded by the universal order. The individual law of the self-conscious subject was thought to be beneficial to all humanity. Now, however, since this law ultimately destroyed the individuality of the self-conscious subject, the phenomenological actor must distinguish its law from the fallacious laws of others. However, this inner law still has for self-consciousness a necessity which distinguishes it from the inner laws of other individuals. Self-consciousness guards against the encroachment of other laws by setting up its law of the heart as the true and infallible law. The laws of others are at best trivial and inessential and at worst corrupt and malicious. This might be illustrated by the internal divisions of political movements or parties. The internal disputes among, for instance, communists, environmentalists, or feminists are often much more heated and bitter than the official disputes with their declared opponents. Not everyone can be allowed to possess the law of the heart with its plan to reform the world. Such positions are in a deep sense exclusive. The generally recognized social order along with all laws of other individuals are now placed in opposition to the "true" individual law of self-consciousness, as if the former had no legitimacy whatsoever. Hegel writes, "The law of *this* particular heart is alone that in which self-consciousness recognizes itself."[265] The arrogance of consciously placing one's own inner law on a par with that of the social whole leads to the next dialectical movement "the deranged consciousness" or the "frenzy of self-conceit."

The Deranged Consciousness (§§376–80)

We now begin our analysis of the second dialectical movement at this stage. Hegel introduces this new form in the experience of consciousness as a perversion or madness, which compares unfavorably even with the previous form of consciousness: "In giving expression to this moment of its self-conscious downfall as the result of its experience, it reveals itself to be this inner perversion of itself, to be a deranged consciousness which finds that its essential being is immediately nonessential, its reality immediately an unreality."[266] Similarly, in the next paragraph Hegel describes with an unusual literary flair the paranoia and self-indulged nature of the worldview of the deluded self-consciousness:

> The heart-throb for the welfare of humanity therefore passes into the ravings of an insane self-conceit, into the fury of consciousness to preserve itself from destruction. . . . It therefore speaks of the universal order as a perversion of the law of the heart and of its happiness, a perversion invented by fanatical priests, gluttonous despots and their minions, who compensate themselves for their own degradation by degrading and oppressing others, a perversion which has led to the nameless misery of deluded humanity.[267]

Here self-consciousness comes to see individual self-interest as the dangerous and oppressing force of mankind: "In this its derangement, consciousness declares individuality to be the source of this derangement and perversion, but one that is alien and accidental."[268] By implementing individual, private laws, the "fanatical priests" and "gluttonous despots" are able to subject all of mankind to an alien necessity which contradicts natural human freedom.

The first interpretive question that we must raise is why this form of consciousness represents a kind of perversion or "madness in general."[269] For Hegel, it is a kind of madness because it combines within itself two entirely contradictory notions. On the one hand, as a universal consciousness aware of the social order, it realizes that this order with its laws and customs is valid for all self-conscious subjects. In the course of the dialectic just examined, self-consciousness comes to see that what it perceived as the dead social order is in fact something living and something which has won the assent and recognition of individual social agents that compose it:

But that in which it does not recognize itself is no longer a dead necessity, but a necessity animated by the universal individuality. It took this divine and human ordinance which it found as an accepted authority to be a dead authority in which not only its own self . . . but also those subject to that ordinance would have no consciousness of themselves; but it finds that this ordinance is really animated by the consciousness of all, that it is the law of every heart.[270]

Self-consciousness in this experience sees to its surprise that the social order is not viewed as oppressive by his fellow citizens but rather that they live in it happily and spontaneously. On the other hand, self-consciousness excepts itself from this universal order and withholds its assent. By so doing it hopes to maintain its individuality. Hegel describes this moment as follows in the *Philosophy of Right:*

Such a law may claim its authority from God or the state. It may even have behind it the authority of tens of centuries during which it was the bond which gave men, with all their deeds and destiny, coherence and subsistence. And these are authorities which enshrine the convictions of countless individuals. Now if I set against these the authority of my single conviction—for as my subjective conviction its sole validity is authority—that at first seems a monstrous self-conceit, but in virtue of the principle that subjective conviction is to be the measuring-rod, it is pronounced not to be self-conceit at all.[271]

Self-consciousness honoring its inner subjective side arrogantly puts its own private law ahead of the entire sphere of the social order and human history. These two aspects are then combined in a single consciousness: the awareness of the legitimacy of the universal order and the stubbornness of not granting assent to it and of insisting on one's own arbitrary law. In this we see the madness of this form of consciousness. Hegel sums up: "since they both are fixed [in my consciousness], this is a unity which is madness in general."[272]

This madness leads to a form of relativism. Self-consciousness holds up its inner law in contrast to the laws of others which it views with contempt. It criticizes what it perceives as the purely subjective laws of others that are handed down by the leaders of the social order, i.e., priests, princes, etc. These laws are a perversion of the inner law of the individual. Both the law of the objective order and the self-interestedness of the individual are perversions based on pure subjectivity.[273] However, the law of self-consciousness is likewise subjective. It might just as well be the case that self-consciousness itself is a despotic priest or prince whose individual law oppresses humanity. Both laws have an equal value. This realization that the subjectivity of the law undermines its humanitarian appeal forms the sublation of the Notion of the deranged consciousness.

This insight that all laws are only of subjective worth naturally leads self-consciousness to the view that it is self-interest and subjectivity itself which are the source of the sufferings of mankind. The evil forms of self-interest that play the key role in the next section are foreshadowed here:

> What seems to be the public *order*, then, is this universal state of war, in which each wrests what he can for himself, executes justice on the individuality of others and establishes his own, which is equally nullified through the action of others. It is the "way of the world," the show of an unchanging course that is only *meant* to be a universality, and whose content is rather the essenceless play of establishing and nullifying individualities.[274]

Here the social order is cynically considered to be nothing more than the forum for the play of naked self-interest. This Hegel refers to with the expression "the way of the world" (*Weltlauf*). Here everyone tries to impose his law on everyone else, and the competing self-interests simply negate one another. These forms reappear in the next section "Virtue and the Way of the World."[275]

Concluding Remarks

The dialectic of universal and particular is quite obvious in this section. Here the individual self-consciousness tries to determine itself as a particular via the law of the heart, which has universal validity. This particularity is contrasted with the universal order which represents the social whole of mankind at large, but whose law has no validity in the eyes of the individual self-consciousness. The law of the heart, however, becomes a universal in its actualization, since once it is actualized it is no longer something that is characteristic of the particular consciousness; instead, in the social sphere it becomes the common property of all. In order to preserve itself as something individual, self-consciousness then stubbornly insists on its own individuality in contrast to the plurality of the other particular laws and the individual social forces of the community. Here as well the Notion is unsuccessful, since self-consciousness simply collapses into a relativism of various laws with its own law having no more validity than the others.

The dialectic of immediacy and mediation is also to be found here. At first, self-consciousness sees the law of the heart "as *immediate*."[276] It immediately knows the law within its own breast to be necessary and universal. This immediacy is, however, undermined by the fact that it is actualized in the world. In its actualization it becomes mediated by others in the social sphere, and due to this self-consciousness loses its privileged position with respect to the law. Then, in the frenzy of self-conceit, self-consciousness tries to hold on to the validity of the individual law in its immediacy in the face of the contradiction that the valid social order presents to it. In the final analysis, the immediacy becomes meaningless, since everyone has an immediate relation to his own self-interested law.

In "Perception" the one and the many were interpreted metaphysically as an object (the one) with many properties (the many). In "Lordship and Bondage" the same category was applied to two self-conscious subjects who mutually determined one another in an asymmetrical fashion. In "The Law of the Heart," the one and the many are interpreted as the individual self-conscious subject (the one) and the plurality of other self-conscious subjects (the many) that constitute the social order. The one is represented by the individual and the law of the heart, and the many by the rest of society with their plurality of laws. The upshot of the analysis here, that we the philosophical audience can see, is that the particular law, the one, cannot be consistently determined without relation to the many or the social whole. Here we can begin to see in quite concrete terms the emerging form of Hegel's theory of the social determination of the subject-object Notion.

III. Virtue and the Way of the World (§§381–93)

With "Virtue and the Way of the World" we finally reach the third and final stage of active self-consciousness. Here the two previous dialectical movements come together to constitute one final form of consciousness that contains the previous ones within itself. According to the scheme we have been following, this stage corresponds to the dialectical movements of at once "Force and the Understanding" from "Consciousness" and at the same time "Stoicism, Skepticism, and the Unhappy Consciousness" from the "Self-Consciousness" chapter. The category here as there is that of ground and consequence. In this section, virtue represents a vague otherworldly abstraction that is contrasted with this world in a fashion similar to the concept of force in "Force and the Understanding" and to the concept of the unchangeable in the "Unhappy Consciousness," to which Hegel here directly refers.[277] The inner-outer dualism appears here again when the otherworldly virtue is characterized as the "*inner* essence"[278] or the "*inner* principle."[279]

The Notion: Virtue (§§381–83)

Hegel tells us that the Notion of "Virtue and the Way of the World" comes from and is the direct result of the two previous dialectical movements of active consciousness. At the beginning of this section, he compares the three forms of active reason:

> In the first shape of active Reason [sc. "Pleasure and Necessity"], self-consciousness took itself to be pure individuality, and it was confronted by an empty universality. In the second [sc. "The Law of the Heart"], the two sides of the antithesis each had both moments within them, law *and* individuality; but one side, the heart, was their immediate unity, the other their antithesis.[280]

In "Pleasure and Necessity," the self-conscious subject saw itself as something determined and particular, which it confirmed in the satisfaction of its desire. Just as the object in "Sense-Certainty" was thought to be a pure particular without any universal element, so also the self-consciousness of "Pleasure and Necessity" thinks of itself as a pure individual. This individuality, however, turns into a universality, and we move to "The Law of the Heart," where the universal, i.e., the law, and the particular, i.e., the self-conscious subject, were bound together in the same self-consciousness. This stage parallels, for instance, the "One" and the "Also," the universal and particular aspects of the object that were thought to be found in a single object in "Perception." Hegel then describes the configuration in the present section: "Here, in the relationship of virtue and the 'way of the world,' the two members [sc. universal and particular] are each severally the unity and antithesis of these moments, or are each a movement of law and individuality towards one another, but a movement of opposition."[281] Here once again the universal and the particular aspects are both present in each member of the dualism.

In describing the dualism of "Virtue and the Way of the World," Hegel explains that this form of consciousness is the result of the two previous forms, each of which give it one side of the dualism. At first, from "Pleasure and Necessity" the concept of "the way of the world" is generated: "The 'way of the world' is thus . . . the single individuality which seeks its [own] pleasure and enjoyment."[282] On the other hand, the concept of virtue issues from the dialectic of the "Law of the Heart": "The other moment of the 'way of the world' is the individuality which claims to be law in its own right, and in its own conceit disturbs the existing order." The concept of the deranged consciousness that has a universal law inside of itself is still present here and is still "madness."[283] Thus, the way of the world and virtue form the two competing sides of the dialectic in this section. We now have to see how Hegel characterizes these two sides.

In contrast to the dialectic of "Pleasure and Necessity," at this stage self-consciousness gives up the bid for individuality and posits the true and the good in the universality of the community, i.e., the common good. Hegel sets up this dialectic in the following way: "For the virtuous consciousness law is the essential moment, and individuality the one to be nullified. . . . [O]ne's own individuality is to be brought under the discipline of the universal, the intrinsically true and good."[284] In this instance the whole, which is represented by the community, is the standard of truth, and the individuals are to be dissolved in it. Virtue views the world as being dominated by corruption, manipulation, and oppression caused by uncontrolled individual desires, greed, and self-interest. The mortal enemies of virtue are individualism and self-interest, which destroy the natural goodness of humanity. The job of virtue is then to combat this evil by struggling against the naked self-interest which perverts mankind: "It is from virtue now that the universal is to receive its true reality by nullifying individuality, the principle of perversion."[285] But in order to combat self-interest and individuality it must "sacrifice . . . [its] entire personality as proof that individual peculiarities are in fact no longer insisted on."[286] Anything less than the complete sacrifice of individuality would be insufficient in self-consciousness' attempt to save humanity from the corrupting influence of self-interest.

The Experience of Consciousness (§§384–91)

The key to understanding virtuous consciousness's conception of virtue or the good is to see it as something abstract, an "essenceless abstraction."[287] In the corresponding section in "Self-Consciousness," the concept for Stoicism was also an empty abstraction which lacked all content.[288] Thus, it was not able to be actualized in a meaningful way in the real world. So also here, the good or the universal is something abstract and, in the final analysis, lacking in content. In this section, the knight of virtue, as Hegel sarcastically calls him, must try to bring virtue into reality through the martyrdom of his own self-interest, since the real world in itself is, in the eyes of the knight of virtue, devoid of virtue due to the self-interested strivings of individuals. Hegel describes these differences between, on the one hand, virtue and the way of the world and, on the other hand, actuality and abstraction in the following passage:

> For virtue as yet only *wills* to accomplish the good, and does not, to begin with, claim that it is reality. . . . [T]he good, in making its appearance in

the conflict with the "way of the world," thereby presents itself as being for an *other*, as something that does not have a being of its own, for otherwise it would not want to make itself true by conquering its opposite. That it is, to begin with, only for an *other*, means the same as was shown in the opposite way of looking at it, viz. that it is, to begin with, an *abstraction* which has reality, not in its own right, but only in its relation to the "way of the world."[289]

Here Hegel designates the concept of virtue as "being for an other." By this he means that the concept of virtue itself has no meaning in itself when taken in isolation from other concepts. Rather the concept of virtue is determined only in its relation, i.e., its negative relation, to the way of the world. It is the opposite of the corrupt world. Specifically, virtue is an abstraction from the way of the world. Consciousness observes the ills of individualism and self-interest in the real world and simply abstracts from this, positing a concept that stands over and against these principles. This concept is by no means entirely determinate and remains rather vague, since it has no positive content; it is merely a negative abstraction from actuality. Here we can see clearly the parallelism with "Force and the Understanding" and the "Unhappy Consciousness." Just as the concept of virtue is an abstraction from the world of self-interest, so also force is a metaphysical entity posited by abstracting from empirical manifestations. Likewise, God or the unchangeable is in the "Unhappy Consciousness" section merely an abstract self-consciousness posited by abstracting from the individual self-conscious subject.

The knight of virtue sees individual abilities and capacities as being a part of the abstract and intangible good. Human beings are endowed with a number of capacities, but unfortunately these capacities are often corrupted and misused in society toward the wrong ends. Thus, abilities can be good or bad depending upon the end to which they are put. Hegel writes,

> This universal is put to *good* use by the principle of individuality, insofar as this principle lives in the virtuous consciousness, but is *misused* insofar as it clings to the "way of the world"—a passive instrument which, controlled by a free individuality which is indifferent to the use it makes of it, can also be misused for the production of an actual existence which destroys it.[290]

Humans are, for instance, given strength that they might use to combat any number of evils, but instead they use it toward personal gain and toward the oppression of others. In this cynical, self-interested struggle for life and wealth, nothing is sacred and nothing is respected. Whether one's abilities are put to good or bad use is a matter of indifference to the way of the world, which subordinates everything to the single criterion of self-interest, profit, and personal gain.

The contradiction at this level comes about due to the abstract and indeterminate nature of virtue itself. First, virtue, qua principle contrasted to individuality and self-interest, cannot be made real without contradiction, since the principle of reality or the way of the world is precisely its contrary, i.e., self-interest. Hegel writes,

> Virtue, therefore, is conquered by the "way of the world" because its purpose is, in fact, the abstract, unreal *essence*, and because its action as regards reality rests on distinctions which are purely nominal. It wanted to consist in bringing the good into actual existence by the sacrifice of individuality, but the side of reality is itself nothing else but the side of individuality.[291]

Since the concept of virtue is abstract and contentless, it cannot in principle be made real or concrete any more than the Stoics' empty doctrine of reason in the earlier dialectic could be. Moreover, individual self-interest is a concrete principle of social reality. It has content and is actual. This content cannot be replaced by the empty slogans of the virtuous consciousness.

Self-consciousness assumes that the real world is devoid of anything human or good, and thus these elements must be introduced from without; however, self-consciousness begins to feel the hint of a contradiction when it notices that in the real world, supposedly driven by mad self-interest, there are in fact instances of the good. Hegel writes,

> The virtuous consciousness, however, enters into conflict with the "way of the world," as if this were something opposed to the good; what the conflict offers to it is the universal, not merely as an abstract universal, but as a universal animated by individuality and existing for an other, in other words, the *actual good*. Therefore, wherever virtue comes to grips with the "way of the world," it always hits upon places which are the actual existence of the good itself which, as the *in-itself* of the "way of the world," is inextricably interwoven in every manifestation of the "way of the world."[292]

To the surprise of the knight of virtue, the apparently heartless, dog-eat-dog realm of, for instance, economic life, in fact, produces from within itself examples of the good. In satisfying one's own needs, the individual is brought into cooperation with others, and in their cooperative work, groups of individuals simultaneously satisfy the needs of still others. This produces a social interdependence that links individuals in a community by virtue of their common needs and the common means of satisfying them. This represents a concrete good, which is contrasted to the knight of virtue's abstract concept of the good.

Individuality, far from being a purely negative force that stands in contrast to virtue, is instead the very means of implementing virtue in the real world in the first place. It is the very vehicle by which virtue is realized at all. Hegel writes,

> The "way of the world" was supposed to be a perversion of the good because it had individuality for its principle; only, individuality is the principle of the *real* world; for it is precisely individuality that is consciousness, whereby what exists *in itself* exists equally *for an other;* it does pervert the unchangeable, but it perverts it in fact from the *nothing of abstraction into the being of reality.*[293]

Here Hegel unambiguously associates "the unchangeable" that we know as the universal God from the "Unhappy Consciousness" with the abstract and illusory, universal realm of virtue. Far from corrupting or perverting virtue, individuality in fact gives it a real existence and by so doing takes it out of the abstract realm where it dwells for the knight of virtue. Thus, Hegel uses the word "perverts" ironically in this passage, since if virtue were not realized or *perverted,* then it would remain merely the abstract and empty concept that it is for the knight of virtue.

Virtue necessarily collapses into hollow and self-righteous moralizing, since it can only appeal to an abstract and self-contradictory good and cannot satisfy itself in action. Hegel describes this with his little recognized literary flair:

> [The knight of virtue] glories in this pompous talk about doing what is best for humanity, about the oppression of humanity, about making sacrifices for the sake of the good and the misuse of gifts. Ideal entities and purposes of this kind are empty, ineffectual words which lift up the heart but leave reason unsatisfied, which edify, but raise no edifice.[294]

The knight of virtue is left to wallow in hollow self-aggrandizing slogans. Such empty moralizing can have a profound effect on the emotions of the audience, but when the content of the moral caveats is examined by reason, it is exposed immediately as worthless and merely rhetorical. The conception of virtue remains abstract and contentless, and the preaching, inveighing, and sloganizing of the knight of virtue serves only to unmask its own self-conceit and self-congratulation.

Hegel contrasts the ancient notion of virtue with the modern notion in order to show the poverty of the latter. For Hegel, the ancients, specifically the ancient Greeks, had a very concrete notion of virtue that involved immediately living in accordance with the customs and laws of the community. He describes this as follows: "Virtue in the ancient world had its own definite sure meaning, for it had in the *spiritual substance* of the nation a foundation full of meaning, and for its purpose an actual good already in existence. Consequently, too, it was not directed against the actual world as against something *generally perverted*, and against a 'way of the world.' "[295] The ancient Greeks, on Hegel's interpretation, lived in immediate harmony with their community, its religion, customs, and mores. The principle of the modern, on the other hand, is one of alienation. As moderns, we are alienated from our culture, our communities, our laws, etc. As a result, we are obliged to posit virtue in another sphere, since we do not find it in the real world that we are familiar with: "But the virtue we are considering has its being outside of the spiritual substance; it is an unreal virtue, a virtue in imagination and name only, which lacks that substantial content."[296] Because we posit a virtue in contrast to the real world, our concept of virtue remains empty and abstract. It is merely a negative abstraction from the real world.

As a result of this dialectic and the recognition of the positive aspects of self-interest, the knight of virtue comes to be reconciled with the way of the world. It comes to see that individualism and self-interest are not necessarily purely evil principles, but rather it realizes that in the pursuit of individual self-interest, one serves the interests of all. Hegel writes, "The result, then, which issues from this antithesis consists in the fact that consciousness drops like a discarded cloak its idea of a good that exists [only] in principle, but has as yet no actual existence. In its conflict it has learnt by experience that the 'way of the world' is not as bad as it looked; for its reality is the reality of the universal."[297] The real world "is not as bad as it looked," since self-interest and individualism are dialectical concepts which also have a positive side. Now virtue is something with a substantive content to be found in the real world. Self-consciousness now gives up the idea of fighting individuality and bringing virtue into the world from the outside, so to speak. It recognizes virtue in the actual sphere:

> The individuality of the "way of the world" may well imagine that it acts only for *itself* or in its own interest. It is better than it thinks, for its action is at the same time an implicitly universal action. When it acts in its own interest, it simply does not know what it is doing; and when it avers that

everyone acts in his own interest, it is merely asserting that no one knows what action is.[298]

In a social community, individuals are bound together in thousands of different ways. By working and seeking to satisfy their own desires, they simultaneously satisfy the desires of others. Here we see Hegel's version of Adam Smith's "invisible hand" that takes care that everything in the economic sphere works to the benefit of all despite the general appearance of chaos and disorder. Out of the chaos and the play of pure self-interest comes a rational and universal system for meeting the needs of all the members of a community. Hegel discusses this in some detail in the *Philosophy of Right* in the section entitled "The System of Needs." There he writes, "When men are thus dependent on one another and reciprocally related to one another in their work and the satisfaction of their needs, subjective self-seeking turns into a contribution to the satisfaction of the needs of everyone else."[299] No individual can satisfy his desires alone, but rather, for the satisfaction of our desires we are dependent upon one another. This dependence gives rise to a "dialectical advance" according to which "subjective self-seeking turns into the mediation of the particular through the universal, with the result that each man in earning, producing, and enjoying on his own account is *eo ipso* producing and earning for the enjoyment of everyone else."[300] This is the implicit rationality in, for instance, the economic sphere. On the face of it, it appears to be the chaotic play of self-interests, but to the philosopher who can recognize the inner logic and truth behind this chaos, there is a deep dialectical truth that connects the interests and desires of the individual with those of the community at large.

Concluding Remarks (§§392–93)

The forms of "Reason" that we have seen in "Pleasure and Necessity" and "The Law of the Heart" have shown the contradictions involved in the attempt to understand the subject-object Notion (here interpreted in terms of, for example, what social justice or the good is) by means of the individual alone and at the same time by wholly denying or negating the validity of the social whole. In "Virtue and the Way of the World" the opposite strategy is also denied. In other words, here we are shown the contradiction of trying to attribute all validity to an abstract principle at the expense of the individual. This is a simple point which many commentators, who have accused Hegel of providing the philosophical justification for totalitarianism in which individuality is crushed, have not appreciated.[301] Thus, once again the goal is to strike the difficult balance between the ethical life or commonality of the community and the freedom or fulfillment of the individual.

With the realization that the real world can contain virtue, the dualism between virtue and the way of the world collapses. Just as the unhappy consciousness was reconciled with the unchangeable via the church, so also here the virtuous consciousness is reconciled with the way of the world. The unhappy consciousness could see the universal that it formerly associated with God in the concrete institutions of the church. Likewise, here virtuous consciousness perceives concrete instantiations of virtue in the social sphere. In this way the abstract and ultimately empty concepts of God and virtue are brought into the sphere of actuality. Moreover, the self-conscious agent now no longer sees itself as opposed to the world of objects or the social sphere as it exists, qua given. Rather, by finding virtue in the world, self-consciousness is able to recognize itself and its will in the social sphere. Thus, just as at the end of "Self-Consciousness," so also here the subject-object dualism is overcome, this time at a conceptually higher level.

The dialectic of the universal and the particular is evident here in the opposing terms of virtue and the way of the world. The underdetermined concept of virtue constitutes the universal. It is the empty, abstract good that will save humanity. On the other hand, the way of the world represents the plurality of particulars that constitute social life. It is the aggregate of individual self-interest of each and every self-conscious agent. The concept of virtue remains abstract and universal, since it has no particular content. It thus reduces to empty moralizing. The way of the world, on the other hand, although originally the play of particulars, in fact contains a universal aspect. Also implicitly bound up in the pursuit of individual self-interest is the pursuit of the interest of all. In satisfying my needs, I simultaneously work toward the satisfaction of the needs of others. Thus, the way of the world forms a dialectical concept containing both a universal and a particular aspect.

C. The Final Moment: Individuality Which Takes Itself to Be Real In and For Itself (§§394–437)

General Introduction (§§394–96)

In this third and final section of the "Reason" chapter, self-consciousness finally comes to realize what we, the philosophical audience, have known all along, namely, the unity of subject and object. We can therefore speak in a certain sense of the "absolute knowing" of the "Reason" chapter, insofar as here the subject-object split is closed at least initially. What self-consciousness learned from "Virtue and the Way of the World" is that the world is not an evil, external other that stands in contradiction to the individual subject or the moral sphere: self-consciousness, "being now absolutely certain of its reality, no longer seeks only to realize itself as end in antithesis to the reality which immediately confronts it."[302] On the contrary, the world is in harmony with the individual and allows him to fulfill his needs cooperatively with others. The individual is now able to identify himself with the external sphere and to see himself in it by means of his work and activity. In this self-recognition in the world of objects, the various dualisms such as universal and particular come together. Here we have "the interfusion of *being-in-itself* and *being-for-itself*, of universal and individuality."[303] Self-consciousness, in viewing the world implicitly, views itself, since it sees its own individuality expressed in the external sphere: "it starts afresh from *itself*, and is occupied not with an *other*, but with *itself*."[304]

In making this point about the closure of the dualisms explored heretofore, Hegel indicates the overall structure of the "Reason" chapter and simultaneously locates the present section with a reference to the first two sections that we have just discussed. He writes,

> With this Notion of itself, therefore, self-consciousness has returned into itself out of those opposed determinations which the category had for it, and which characterized the relation of self-consciousness to the category in its observational [sc. "Observing Reason"] and also active [sc. "The Actualization of Rational Self-Consciousness through Its Own Activity"] roles.[305]

Both of the two previous forms of consciousness represented "opposed determinations," i.e., subject-object Notions which posited an opposition or split. At first, in "Observing Reason" as in "Consciousness," priority was given to the object sphere, and the subject was considered something secondary. Then, in "The Actualization of Rational Self-Consciousness through Its Own Activity" as in "Self-Consciousness," the individual self-conscious agent was given priority, and the world stood opposed to it. Here finally this dialectic seems to come to an end, since the subject-object split is apparently overcome. From Hegel's hints about the structure of the "Reason" chapter here, we can also draw some inferences about the structure of the work as a whole and the relation of this chapter to the "Consciousness" and "Self-Consciousness" chapters. The reconstruction I wish to give below is illustrated graphically in figure 6.2. First, it is clear that this final section, "Individuality which takes itself to be real in and

Figure 6.2

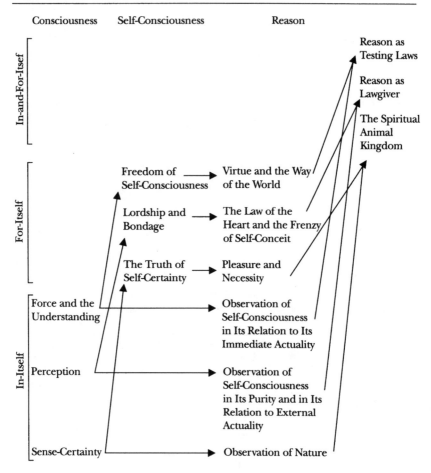

for itself" is meant to form a third discrete unit which brings together the two preceding sections. "Observing Reason," like "Consciousness," represented the object side of the Notion or the "real in itself." With respect to the role of "Reason" in the work as a whole, we can see that "The Actualization of Rational Self-Consciousness through Its Own Activity" parallels "Self-Consciousness" in its emphasis on the subject side of the Notion or the "for itself." Here in this third section, these two moments come together as the "real in and for itself," where there is no longer any opposition. Thus, this section forms the apex of the pyramid consisting of "Consciousness," "Self-Consciousness," and the sections in "Reason" which run parallel to them. With respect to the categorial analyses that we have been following, Hegel makes it clear in a few key passages that they are still present here as well. As we shall see in the course of our analysis, the first section, "The Spiritual Animal Kingdom," operates with the category of being and thus parallels "Sense-Certainty" and "The Truth of Self-Certainty."[306] The second section, "Reason as Lawgiver," parallels "Perception" and "Lordship and Bondage." The third and final section, "Reason as Testing Laws," parallels "Force and the Understanding" and "Stoicism, Skepticism, and the Unhappy Consciousness."

I. The Spiritual Animal Kingdom (§§397–418)

This has been a much neglected section in the secondary literature, despite its important place in the architectonic scheme of the work. Most commentators see the discussion in this section as one concerning the question of intellectual or artistic originality and integrity.[307] Although in its essentials, this interpretation is on target, nevertheless this is hardly the whole story. Most problematic, it leaves untouched the key issue of subject-object identity, which is the important point for the argument of the entire work up until this point. It also fails to recognize the sublation of the Notion of individuality which takes place here when self-consciousness realizes the commonalities between itself and other self-conscious agents in the pursuit of their projects. Thus, we here move from individuality to universality and to an identification with the social whole. This is the key dialectical step which must stand at the fore of any interpretation of this section.

That this section reverts back to the beginning of the dialectic with respect to the category it analyzes and that it therefore corresponds to the sections, "Sense-Certainty" and "The Truth of Self-Certainty," can be seen from the following passage in which Hegel makes a direct reference to "Sense-Certainty": "A movement corresponding to that from sense-certainty to perception will run its course here."[308] Moreover, self-consciousness is here referred to as "an immediate consciousness of its substance"[309] just as natural consciousness was immediately aware of pure being. In the next section, "Reason as Lawgiver," Hegel begins by summarizing the dialectic of "The Spiritual Animal Kingdom" by writing, "Spiritual essence is, in its simple being, *pure consciousness*, and *this self*-consciousness."[310] In this passage, he refers to the "pure self-consciousness" of "The Truth of Self-Certainty" and the "simple being" of the "This" from "Sense-Certainty." Thus, the category of being that we saw there will play the important role here as well. But the Notion of being in this section is not the same as the being of the pure object, as in "Sense-Certainty," or of the pure subject, as in "The Truth of Self-Certainty." Rather being is here conceived as the unity of individuality with, on the one hand, its intentions and plans and, on the other hand, its realization through work and activity in the real world. Thus, a new Notion of being is formed, which unifies the subjective and the objective aspects which Hegel calls "an absolute interfusion of individuality and being."[311]

The Notion: Original Determinate Nature (§§397–404)

The construction of the Notion in this section can for the sake of convenience be broken into two parts. In the first part,[312] Hegel examines the Notion of an inner human nature from its abstract or implicit side, i.e., human nature as ideal but not yet real. Here we view the essence of the individual self-consciousness as "an *abstract, universal* reality lacking filling and content."[313] In the second part,[314] Hegel analyzes this Notion with respect to the realization of its essence through the action of the individual self-consciousness. In this discussion he isolates three distinct aspects of action which belong to the complex Notion at that level.

Concerning the first point, every human being is according to this Notion in possession of something unique and special which makes him or her an individual. It may be a particular talent or capacity that singles out the individual and determines him as someone special and unique. Hegel calls this true human essence the "original determinate nature" or sometimes "*implicit* being."[315] It is implicit or potential since it is as yet not realized through an action. The inner essence is at first simply a latent ability which has not yet been developed: "it has not yet set forth its movement and reality."[316] Here we can immediately recognize the categorial parallelism that we have been following up until now. By characterizing the true inner human nature of each individual as "implicit being" or "mere being," Hegel reminds us that we return again to the beginning of the categorial development here at the beginning of this section, i.e., back to the first category from "Sense-Certainty," which is characterized in the same way.

If it is not to remain merely potential and abstract, this true inner nature must express itself and must act in the real world. This introduces the second half of Hegel's construction of the Notion. "Consciousness must act," he writes, "merely in order that what it is *in itself* may become explicit *for it.*"[317] It must give itself a reality in the external world which mirrors its inner nature. This then gives rise to a relation between the inner character of the individual and its expression or manifestation in the world. This relationship of the "mere being" of true inner nature and its expression in action brings about three distinct moments of the Notion which Hegel proceeds to discuss. Although these three moments are discussed individually, they are supposed to form a single unitary Notion.[318]

The first moment Hegel describes as follows: "Action is present at first in the form of *object*, an object, too, as pertaining to consciousness, as *end*, and hence opposed to a reality already given."[319] This first moment concerns the intention of the self-conscious agent; therefore, by the words "object" or "end," Hegel here means something like "objective" or "desired result." A desired result, for consciousness, is an idea or plan which is not yet real. Given that each individual has a unique capacity or talent in himself that can be realized only through action, the action must begin with an intention on the part of the individual to perform a certain work that reflects the particular genius of the individual. For example, let us suppose that someone has a hidden capacity for painting. This person must then come to have the intention to paint and pursue artistic endeavors in order for this capacity to be realized.

The second moment of the realization of the inner human nature concerns the activity itself by means of which the original intention is actualized. Hegel writes, "The second moment is the *movement* of the end conceived as passive, and realization conceived as the relation of the end to the wholly formal actuality, hence the idea of the transition itself, or the *means*."[320] This is the moment of the work itself. Here the individual, working in accordance with his intentions and plans, selects a means to produce an object representative of his ability. In short, the painter paints his masterpiece, which before was only an intention. Hegel calls this "means" since how the work gets done can take many forms. Since there are many means by which we can transform an idea into reality, Hegel sometimes refers to this simply as the "how."[321]

The third moment is the finished product as an object or artifact in the public world, which results from the intention and the work of the individual. Hegel describes this by saying, "The third moment is, finally, the object, which is no longer in the form of an end directly known by the agent to be *his own*, but as brought out into the light of day and having *for him* the form of an 'other.' "[322] The object then represents the individual and his ability in the objective, public sphere. In the painting we recognize the skill and talent and consequently the individuality of the artist. In the absence of an actual object or product, the talent and with it the individuality of self-consciousness remain only potential. Hegel characterizes this third moment as "work done."[323] The object, qua real and existing in the real world, is, however, something other or detached from the individual agent, and it is precisely at this point that a new subject-object dualism will creep in again.

We can see with this analysis the difference between this third section and the previous one. Formerly self-consciousness acted in opposition to the world which it saw as something negative and opposed to the individual law of the heart or virtue. Here, on the contrary, the individual sees himself and his own individuality in the world in the form of his action and his products. "There is nothing," Hegel writes, "*for* individuality which has not been made so *by* it, or there is no reality which is not individuality's own nature and doing."[324] Since these products express his true inner character and his unique personality, the individual is united with the world, and the external, objective sphere no longer appears as something foreign or negative. Thus, the subject-object dualism appears to be overcome for the moment.

The final point that Hegel makes about this Notion is that value-judgments and terms such as "good" and "bad" cannot be relevant here, since all works are ultimately expressions of one's true inner essence. Every work, since it mirrors the individual personality, must be positively evaluated. All aesthetic criteria collapse into a relativism, since everything is an expression of a personality. Likewise, "feelings of exaltation, or lamentation, or repentance are altogether out of place."[325] To exalt at a successful finished product would imply that the product was simply a matter of chance or luck which just happened to mirror the individual personality successfully and to reflect the individual's talent, which it might not have done had circumstances been different. But if all works reflect one's true individuality, then it makes no sense to be happy or sad about the final product because, once again, all products successfully represent the inner nature and special talent of the individual.

The Experience of Consciousness (§§405–18)

Hegel at this point signals the reader that the Notion with its various moments is now complete and the task is now to examine it for consistency: "This is the Notion which consciousness forms of itself. . . . Let us see whether this Notion is confirmed by experience, and whether its reality corresponds to it."[326] Here universal and particular come together in the essential being and action of the self-conscious agent. The inner nature is expressed directly in the work and in the product of self-consciousness. This unity of action and human nature is what Hegel, alluding to "Sense-Certainty," calls "the qualityless void of being."[327] Likewise, alluding to "The Truth of Self-Certainty," Hegel states that self-consciousness is "universal consciousness"[328] when seen from the side of its essential nature.

In the experience of this Notion, self-consciousness comes to learn that in fact there are distinctions that must be made in this unity of human nature and action. The complex Notions of intention, means, and action cannot be held together as a complete unity. Above all, there is what Hegel calls "the antithesis of doing and being,"[329] by which he means to indicate the gap that is so often present between, on the one hand, our plans and intentions (sc. "being") that form our true inner nature on this view, and, on the other hand, our action and its products (sc. "doing"). Hegel then goes back through the three aspects of the Notion and analyzes how contingency can act upon each of them and render them ineffective at expressing the true nature of the individual.

First, with respect to intentions, in order to express our true nature, we must have the intention of undertaking the appropriate work. However, it might well be the case that we pursue some contingent purpose which does not express our true nature. When the master painter has as his purpose preparing a meal or playing the piano, we would have to consider these purposes nonessential, since they have nothing to do with his true inner nature, qua genius for painting. The painter is simply out of his element when his purpose involves doing something else: "It is accidental if the purpose has a truly essential nature, or if the in-itself is made the purpose."[330] It is therefore a matter of contingency whether or not the purpose or intention is one that will mirror the individual's inner nature.

Second, in order to express our nature, we must select the appropriate means for realizing it. However, in pursuing his purpose, the individual may select the wrong means. It might be, for instance, that an individual who has a genius for acting continually gets bad roles with which he is unable to develop his ability properly. In this case, the individual would still implicitly be a great actor, but he simply cannot make this explicit or realize his talent effectively, due to the poor choice of means at his disposal. When the wrong means are selected, the true talent of the individual is simply wasted. Thus, according to this second kind of contingency, "it is accidental if a *means* is chosen which expresses the purpose."[331]

Third, not only can the purpose and the means be contingent, but the relation between the action or the product and the real world is also contingent: "And finally the entirety of these inner moments . . . is again in an accidental relationship to *reality* in general."[332] It may be that the historical circumstances are simply not right for a certain genre or a particular work of art. Once a work of art becomes an artifact in the real world, fortune plays an important role in its reception, and this cannot be allowed to count as a reflection of the inner being of its author. Certain things become fads, others are ignored, yet others become long-lasting, and this is largely contingent upon historical circumstances. Thus, contingency touches the actual product or action of the individual as well.

For Hegel, the individual, acting in accordance with the Notion, nevertheless tries to see himself, in the face of all these contingencies, as enduring in the contingent object. The object itself may vanish or never reach completion, yet consciousness with its hopes and expectations remains. In the complex aggregate of intention, action, product, means, etc., self-consciousness selects one element which counts as essential and truly representative of its own inner self. This element is called the "heart of the matter" or sometimes "the matter in hand" (*die Sache selbst*) in the Miller translation. We can abstract from the accidental circumstances of an action, but the heart of the matter is the essential and important part of the action that we are truly interested in and which truly mirrors the inner character of the individual. "This unity is the true work," Hegel writes, "it is the very heart of the matter which completely holds its own and is experienced as that which *endures*, independently of what is merely the *contingent* result of an individual action, the result of contingent circumstances, means, and reality."[333] The heart of the matter is the essential and enduring aspect of the constellation of elements that constitute action.

Given the analysis above, each of the moments in the constellation of the action of self-consciousness can be taken as contingent: "the moments of his end, of the means, of the action itself, and of the reality, all these are, on the one hand, single particular moments for this consciousness, which . . . it can abandon and surrender."[334] Since there is room for luck and since the product does not necessarily immediately represent the inner nature of the individual, we are dependent upon self-consciousness's own self-description of how his intentions match up to his action. We must examine carefully what self-consciousness takes responsibility for as a part of its inner essence of human nature and what it rejects as coincidence and accident. Since consciousness determines the various moments of the matter in hand, it is able to display them selectively along with its actions, which are by nature already public. Thus, consciousness is able to deceive others with respect to, for instance, the motives of its actions. The possibility of deception implies that the social realm is inevitably tied to action. There are many possibilities in this constellation.[335] First, if the self-conscious subject is unable to do anything, he can make purpose alone the heart of the matter and claim that he tried to do it, ignoring the other aspects of action. Thus, intention was the key, and the means and the action are nothing. Or the individual might not even try or might do nothing at all, in which case he could claim that it was impossible. The matter in hand is just the intention and the fact that it is impossible to be realized. Or something might present itself purely by chance to the individual which he himself did nothing to obtain, but yet for which he could still claim responsibility, abstracting from the intention and means and concentrating solely on the object and end-result of its labor. Thus, self-consciousness can manipulate the various elements of the action-constellation to present the picture most favorable to itself: "it makes one meaning after another the subject of this predicate, and forgets them one after another."[336]

This division between, on the one hand, the self-interpretation of self-consciousness and its selective designation of the matter in hand and, on the other hand, the legitimacy of each of the elements of action leads to deception. Hegel describes the deception as follows: "An individuality sets about carrying out something; by so doing it seems to have made something *its own* affair; it acts and in acting becomes involved with others and seems to itself to be having to do with *reality*. The others therefore take its action for a sign of interest in the 'matter in hand' as such."[337] When we see the painter engaged in painting, we assume right away that he is engaged in this activity out of a pure love of art. He would paint if he were rich or poor, famous or unknown. But, in fact, the painter is dissembling in this appearance of high purpose. Instead, "it is its [self-consciousness'] *own* action and its *own* effort that constitute its interest in the 'matter in hand.' "[338] In another passage, Hegel describes this as follows: "While, then, it seems to him that his concern is only with the 'matter in hand' as an *abstract* reality, it is also a fact that he is concerned with it as his own doing. But just because he is concerned merely with being active and busy, he is not really in earnest about it."[339] The deception then is essentially in the claim to be interested only in the activity itself for its own sake and to have abstracted entirely from one's individuality, whereas in fact one is more concerned with giving the impression of being busy with a serious and important project: "It is, then . . . a deception of oneself and of others if it is pretended that what one is concerned with is the *'matter in hand' alone*."[340] Each individual is not so much concerned with the matter in hand but rather with one's own attitude and opinion about it. The goal of deception is to produce a favorable attitude in an other toward one's action and to gain social recognition by pursuing a meaningful project. Hence, the matter in hand, like all action, becomes public in that it is subject to public scrutiny. Action then ceases to be that which is done by an individual agent, since it always has significance for a wider community.

The deception is particularly clear when we see how self-consciousness reacts to others who pursue the same project. Self-consciousness sees how avid others are to jump on the bandwagon and to busy themselves with its matter in hand once it has become fashionable: "A consciousness that opens up a subject-matter soon learns that others hurry along like flies to freshly poured-out milk, and want to busy themselves with it; and they learn about that individual that he, too, is concerned with the subject-matter, not as an *object*, but as his *own* affair."[341] Wherever there is an innovator, there is also a crowd of followers that attach themselves to the innovation. This causes the innovator to try to distance himself from the crowd, but this attempt merely shows that he is not interested in the innovation per se, but is only interested in maintaining his own identity and individuality, qua innovator.

The experience of deceit and jealousy is important for the sublation of the Notion of the matter in hand which now takes place. When the self-conscious agent observes others who pursue the very activity that was supposed to determine it as an individual, it comes to an important realization about the social nature of activity itself. Hegel writes, "it is learned by all parties that they all regard themselves as affected and invited to participate, and instead of a mere 'doing,' or separate action, peculiar to the individual who opened up the subject-matter, something has been opened up that is for others as well, or is a subject-matter on its own account."[342] Self-consciousness finally recognizes the validity of the interest of others in its project and of their pursuit of the same project. It no longer regards its work or its art, for instance, as its own private property, which mirrors its own private inner sphere. Now self-consciousness recognizes that its own project—music, acting, writing, etc.—represents a subject matter in its own right which others are free to explore. In this experience, self-consciousness "learns what the *nature of the 'matter in hand'* really is."[343] Specifically, it realizes that its project or matter in hand is not something particular, but rather something universal. It is no longer the particular matter in hand, but rather the *"universal matter in hand"*[344] which everyone has an interest in.

This social process then fundamentally changes the nature of the matter in hand and ultimately sublates the Notion of individuality so determined. First, the matter in hand is no longer something for the individual himself; rather, it is something, like a fad or a school of thought, for everyone. It is now the universal matter in hand. The matter in hand is "such that its *being* is the *action* of the *single* individual and of all individuals and whose action is immediately *for others*, or is a 'matter in hand' and is such only as the action of *each* and *everyone:* the essence which is the essence of all beings, viz. *spiritual essence.*"[345] The truth of the matter in hand is that it is something which everyone participates in. It is simply the action of everyone in the social order which Hegel calls here "*spiritual essence.*" This, however, destroys the individuality of self-consciousness which was asserted in the Notion. In short, as in "Sense-Certainty" and "The Truth of Self-Certainty," so also here particularity collapses into universality.

Concluding Remarks

The realization that the matter in hand is something universal and not particular marks the end of this analysis and leads self-consciousness to the concept of the universal law, which is the theme of the next two sections which complete the "Reason" chapter. When self-consciousness sees that its action and its project are essentially the same as the action and projects of others, it sees itself for the first time as a member of a wider social community. Self-consciousness realizes now that it participates in the common customs and mores that it shares with other self-conscious agents. This then leads self-consciousness in the next section to the belief in an implicit and immediately understood set of moral laws which form the socially binding force of the community. Self-consciousness then goes on to try to articulate these laws, and this forms the subject matter of the next dialectical movement.

The dialectic of universal and particular is present in this section originally in the opposition between the two main aspects of the Notion, i.e., the original determinate nature and the object. The former represents the universal, since it is a potential genius or talent which has not yet been realized. As potential it remains universal and indeterminate. In a sense everyone is *potentially* a talented painter, writer, etc. For this reason self-consciousness here characterized as "universal consciousness."[346] The product or object created by the work of self-consciousness is, on the other hand, the aspect of particularity. It is a concrete, particular object in the real world. This particular object reflects the otherwise merely abstract talent and individuality of its creator; however, how it reflects it is not determined. This is where the dialectical twisting and turning begins. The indeterminate relation between the inner nature of the individual and the product leads to deception and ultimately to the sublation of individuality. The dialectic of universal and particular also takes place with respect to the Notion of the matter in hand, which was originally particular and was intended to determine the particularity of the self-conscious agent. Just as in "Sense-Certainty" and "The Truth of Self-Certainty," the particularity that is intended from the beginning is sublated by a reference to the social world. Self-consciousness tries to determine itself as an individual in the particular matter in hand of its action, but as we have seen, this turns out not to be particular but rather the universal matter in hand.[347]

II. Reason as Lawgiver (§§419–28)

This section has been neglected in the secondary literature, although it forms an absolutely crucial phase in the transition from the individual, atomic self-consciousness to the realm of ethical life and Spirit. The shift in the previous section from the individual matter in hand to the universal matter in hand represents the sublation of the isolated and abstracted individuality of the self-conscious agent. Hegel sums this up as follows: "The originally *determinate* nature of the individual has lost its positive meaning of being *in itself* the element and the purpose of its activity; it is merely a superseded moment, and the individual is a *self* in the form of a universal self."[348] The individual now becomes a genuine part of the social whole. It too works toward the universal matter in hand and no longer sees itself as an atomic subject in opposition to others as in the previous sections.

Moreover, the dialectic here still operates at the level of the in-and-for-itself, i.e., of the subject-object unity, as in "The Spiritual Animal Kingdom." Hegel expresses this at the beginning of this section thus: "The category is *in itself*, or implicit, as the universal of *pure consciousness;* it is equally *for itself* or explicit, for the *self* of consciousness is equally a moment of it."[349] Here the universality of the matter in hand with which the individual identifies itself forms something in the external world and thus is something in itself. On the other hand, this world reflects the self-conscious individuals who share this common matter in hand, and thus this is also a part of the subject or is for itself. The combination of the two, qua universal matter in hand, is therefore the "authoritative in and for itself."[350] We have once again the subject-object closure that we would expect throughout this third section of the "Reason" chapter. The dualisms are overcome once again: "It is the *absolute* 'matter in hand,' which no longer suffers from the antithesis of certainty and its truth, between universal and individual, between purpose and its reality, but whose existence is the *reality* and *action* of self-consciousness."[351]

The unity of the universal subject and the world is what Hegel here refers to as "absolute being."[352] By this he means the self-awareness of a group or social whole that the external world is their creation and that they are thus a part of the objective sphere. With this terminology of "absolute being," we can see once again the sense in which we can talk of the "absolute knowing" of the "Reason" chapter that comes about with the subject-object unity. As we have seen, self-consciousness ceases to be the individual self-consciousness and becomes the universal in accordance with the universal "heart of the matter." Once again the social whole is given precedence in the relationship, this time in the form of universal laws or moral imperatives: "Thus what is object for consciousness has the significance of being the True; *it is* and it is *authoritative*."[353] The objective side of this universality involves the shared customs and values of the community which Hegel here refers to as "*ethical substance*."[354]

The subjective side, which represents self-consciousness' self-awareness of its unity with these universal customs and values and thus with this external ethical sphere, Hegel calls "the *ethical* consciousness."[355] Natural consciousness is at this stage ethical consciousness.

With respect to the categorial analysis that we have been following, this section operates with the category of the one and the many and therefore parallels "Perception," "Lordship and Bondage," and the corresponding sections that we have already discussed in "Reason." Here the one is represented by the universal matter in hand or the universal sphere of ethics. In order to determine this sphere more precisely, self-consciousness tries to articulate its immediate ethical understanding into individual moral laws or precepts. As Findlay writes, "But just as the immediate deliverances of sense-certainty become articulate in perception, so the deliverances of moral sense become articulate in various well-known precepts."[356] These moral laws then constitute the many at this level. As it turns out, the ethical maxims cannot be rendered determinate, and this leads to the sublation of the Notion here.

The Notion: The Moral Law (§§419–23)

In the unity of the universal ethical substance and ethical consciousness, self-consciousness distinguishes "'masses' or spheres which are the *determinate laws* of the absolute essence."[357] By this Hegel seems to mean that in the public sphere there are any number of agreed upon social mores and customs which make social life possible in the first place. These can be isolated and abstracted from the universal sphere of ethics in general by a simple act of reflection. These laws are intuitive to every member of a given society. Entirely immersed in the daily ethical life of a community, no one thinks to ask about the validity or legitimacy of certain customs and values: they are simply so. They exist necessarily in the moral law, which is domiciled in every rational moral agent: "We cannot ask for their origin and justification, nor can we look for any other warrant."[358] Hegel seems to have in mind here the Kantian idea that every rational agent necessarily has the moral law within himself. Therefore, everyone who is capable of exercising his or her faculty of reason has access to the moral law. Access to the moral sphere comes about above all in the form of specific moral maxims or precepts, the universal validity of which everyone can immediately recognize and understand. The fundamental claim of the Notion here is that every socially competent individual who participates in the universal matter in hand has immediate access to this ethical sphere and can explain its laws when asked. Hegel formulates the Notion here as follows: "sound reason knows immediately what is right and good."[359]

Hegel refers directly to the "Sense-Certainty" and "Perception" chapters here in order to indicate the parallelism as well as to signal the end of the construction of the Notion at this point: "Just as in the case of sense-certainty, we had to examine the nature of what it immediately expressed as *being*, so here, too, we have to see how the being expressed by this immediate ethical certainty, or by the immediately existing 'masses' of the ethical substance, is constituted."[360] We saw in "Sense-Certainty" how pure being, in order to be determinate, had to be further articulated in "Perception" by means of properties. So also here in "Reason as Lawgiver" the immediate ethical certainty must be articulated by concrete instances or ethical precepts. Hegel in this passage indicates the beginning of the comparison of the Notion with the experience of consciousness when he writes "we have to see how the being expressed by this immediate certainty . . . is constituted."

The Experience of Consciousness (§§424–28)

The experience of consciousness here consists above all in the analysis of two ethical maxims, which are supposed to represent the universal and necessary realm of ethical certainty. Hegel analyzes the moral law, "Everyone ought to speak the truth,"[361] and then goes on to treat the Biblical commandment, "Love thy neighbor as thyself."[362] Although both laws are supposed to be immediately accessible and intuitive to every moral agent, upon closer analysis, they turn out to be not nearly so obvious and unproblematic as self-consciousness supposed them to be.

Let us then begin with Hegel's analysis of the first ethical maxim: "Everyone ought to speak the truth." Hegel indicates that we cannot take this maxim at face value, since it implies a number of things which are not explicit. Above all it implies the presupposition that the one speaking the truth is, in fact, in possession of it and can recognize it. Thus, according to Hegel we must qualify this absolute, necessary moral law with the conditional, "if one knows the truth, then one ought to speak it." But precisely this qualification undermines the universality of the law itself: "But with this correction, what the proposition wanted to enunciate as universally necessary and intrinsically valid, has really turned round into something completely contingent. For speaking the truth is made contingent on whether I can know it, and can convince myself of it."[363] The problem is that in order for this maxim to make sense, it must be qualified to the point where it loses its universal validity, i.e., everyone ought to speak the truth, provided that he or she knows it and is convinced of it. It is easy to see that this imperative, thus stated as a conditional, is a contingent fact. From this contingency would seem to issue a new ethical imperative: one ought to know the truth. But this implicitly contradicts the original maxim: "Sound reason was at first supposed to possess *immediately* the capacity to speak the truth; now, however, it is said that it *ought to know*, that is to say, that it does not *immediately* know what is true."[364] Knowing in general has, however, nothing in principle to do with speaking the truth. The problem with this ethical law is that it ultimately proves to have no content. After being examined carefully, the law seems not to say anything. Every attempt to give it a real content simply reduces the law to contingency and undermines its universal validity.

Let us turn to Hegel's second example of an intuitive moral maxim: "Love thy neighbor as thyself." This purportedly universal moral maxim is problematic, since it too implies more than what it directly says. The command to love one's neighbor seems in practice to mean actively helping and doing beneficial things for others. But before I can help someone else, I must first know what he or she needs help with. My good will might be counterproductive or even destructive if I try to help someone with respect to something with which he or she needs no help. Hegel describes this by saying that in order to help someone, "I have to distinguish what is bad for him, what is the appropriate good to counter this evil, and what in general is good for him; i.e. I must love him *intelligently*. Unintelligent love will perhaps do him more harm than hatred."[365] Precisely here come a number of qualifications that render this law contingent as well. For instance, my being beneficent is contingent upon whether or not I know what is beneficial for the other person. It also depends on the external circumstances of my action: "Chance determines not only the occasion of the action but also whether it is a 'work' at all, whether it is not immediately undone and even perverted into something bad."[366] In the face of the manifold of these contingencies, we can no longer speak of the necessity of this maxim as an imperative.

These maxims need to be qualified, interpreted, and given a definite content if they are to be serviceable. But once they have been so qualified, it becomes clear that they are no longer universal and necessary. These commandments as such remain only formal, since any attempt to make them more determinate will inevitably come up short. The very idea of a "universal, absolute content"[367] is contradictory, since any content draws the law into contingent relations, and this compromises the element of universality. In the absence of any determinate content we are left with "the mere form of universality"[368] which, like the "One" from the dialectic of "Perception," is indeterminate.

Concluding Remarks

Since they do not have determinate content, the most that these commandments can have is internal consistency. We can then no longer expect Reason to be able to produce for us determinate laws with a specific content but rather to help us test certain laws for truth: "Reason as the giver of laws is reduced to a Reason which merely *critically examines* them."[369] In the end, we must forsake universality in the content of moral maxims and try to preserve it in their form. The job then for self-consciousness becomes merely to examine the moral laws for consistency.

In this dialectical movement the universal and the particular take the form of abstract universal ethical maxims and contingent ethical acts. The ethical maxims that ethical consciousness formulates constitute the universal at this level, since they are seen as universally valid for all rational agents. However, these universal maxims are ultimately empty and indeterminate. In order to give them meaning, ethical consciousness must make them individual and contingent. The qualified ethical laws, formulated as conditionals, then represent the particulars at this level. But as particulars, they lose their universal and necessary validity. With respect to immediacy and mediation, ethical consciousness begins with the belief that it is immediately aware of the truth of the universal ethical maxims. Everyone intuitively knows what it means, for instance, to love one's neighbor. However, this meaning turns out not to be immediate or intuitive at all. On the contrary, it is mediated by a number of other contingent factors which ethical consciousness must make itself aware of.

III. Reason as Testing Laws (§§429–37)

Despite the absolutely crucial role of "Reason as Testing Laws" as the transition from "Reason" to "Spirit," this section has attracted considerably less attention in the secondary literature than the other transitions, such as "Force and the Understanding" and the "Unhappy Consciousness." Here ethical consciousness shifts from finding and recognizing ethical laws to testing them. As a parallel passage from the *Philosophy of Right* indicates, Hegel in this section continues his critique of Kant's moral theory, which he refers to as an "empty formalism."[370] Specifically, Hegel criticizes Kant's claim that all rational agents can adequately test individual maxims in order to determine if they have moral worth. In the *Philosophy of Right* he says, "Kant's further formulation, the possibility of visualizing an action as a *universal* maxim, does lead to the more concrete visualization of a situation, but in itself it contains no principle beyond abstract identity and the 'absence of contradiction.' "[371] As we shall see, the problem with this Notion is that the absence of contradiction still leaves the moral law abstract and does not enjoin any particular action.

Predictably enough, the categories operative in this section are ground and consequence, as in "Force and the Understanding" and "Stoicism, Skepticism, and the Unhappy Consciousness." Just as forces were thought to ground individual appearances in "Force and the Understanding," so also here ethical laws are thought to be the ground for ethical action. However, just as forces could not be thought consistently and remained indeterminate, so also here ethical laws evaluated only by the criterion of consistency remain indeterminate and do not translate unambiguously into any particular ethical action. Here Hegel writes about the ground of the maxim that is to be tested: "the essence of ethics consists just in law being identical with itself and through this self-identity, i.e. through having its ground in itself."[372] Here, as in "Force and the Understanding," the result of ground is not something different from ground itself, but rather it is simply another aspect of the same phenomenon, just as force and appearance were earlier. Ethical action cannot be judged by its results which, as we have seen, may be contingent. Rather, the ground of ethical action is thought to be its own internal consistency with itself.

The Notion: Testing Moral Laws (§429)

In this final section of "Reason," the self-conscious subject gives up its attempt to generate laws based on pure reason as in the previous section. Here it sticks to the less ambitious claim that reason can adequately test ethical laws for moral worth, regardless of their origin. Thus, here self-consciousness attempts to test moral principles for consistency. Hegel tersely summarizes the Notion here in comparison to the Notion of the previous section:

> Laws are no longer given, but *tested;* and for the consciousness which tests them they are *already* given. It takes up their *content* simply as it is, without concerning itself . . . with the particularity and contingency inherent in its reality; it is concerned with the commandment simply as commandment, and its attitude towards it is just as uncomplicated as its being a criterion for testing it.[373]

Here ethical consciousness is concerned neither with the origin of the ethical laws nor with the fact that they are contingent as was discussed in the previous section. Internal consistency is the criterion against which the laws are tested. However, as we shall see, with the sole criterion of consistency, self-consciousness is unable to reach any determinate conclusions since any two contradictory positions can always be rendered internally self-consistent.

The Experience of Consciousness (§§430–31)

In his discussion, Hegel indicates that the criterion of internal consistency is insufficient when taken on its own, since any given institution can be proved to be contradictory or noncontradictory, depending on the presuppositions involved. His analysis treats the logical consistency of the institution of private property vis-à-vis communism. He writes, "Suppose the question is: 'Ought it to be an absolute law that there should be property?' "[374] Ethical consciousness then tries to find ethical maxims which answer this question consistently. His discussion breaks down into four parts. First he treats the noncontradictoriness of (1) the institution of property and then (2) its absence. Then he indicates how both (3) the institution of communism and (4) property-holding can be shown to be contradictory.

First, all institutions, such as the communal sharing of property or the holding of private property, when taken in abstraction and without any further presuppositions are noncontradictory: "Property, simply as such, does not contradict itself; it is an *isolated* determinateness, or is posited as merely self-identical. Non-property, the non-ownership of things, or a common ownership of goods is just as little self-contradictory."[375] The criterion of internal consistency alone does not help us to adjudicate between the two positions. In the *Philosophy of Right*, Hegel expresses the same point as follows: "The absence of property contains in itself just as little contradiction as the non-existence of this or that nation, family, etc., or the death of the whole human race."[376] Both institutions of property and nonproperty are internally consistent in this sense. In order to generate a contradiction, we need to make other presuppositions; however, since we have tested and analyzed these institutions in the abstract, i.e., since we have abstracted from all other institutions and presuppositions, there can be no contradiction.

On the other hand, all institutions taken in their concrete nature and given specific presuppositions can be shown to be contradictory. Again in the *Philosophy of Right*, he claims, "But if it is already established on other grounds and presupposed that property and human life are to exist and be respected, then indeed it is a contradiction to commit theft or murder; a contradiction must be a contradiction of something, i.e. of some content presupposed from the start as a fixed principle."[377] Anything can be proven contradictory if examined in the concrete context of other presuppositions and background beliefs which are at odds with it. For instance, with respect to communism, if the distribution of goods is regulated according to the needs of each individual, such that each individual obtains as much as he requires, then grave inequalities will arise, since some people simply require more than others. This would then contradict the implicit assumption about "the equality of individuals,"[378] i.e. that everyone, qua equal, ought to receive the same share of goods. On the other hand, if the goods in a society were uniformly distributed and each individual received exactly the same allotment of goods as the others, then the result would be a disproportion with respect to need. Some individuals would be able to live quite well with their allotment, but this same share would seem to consign others to utter poverty. The concrete context tells us that individuals have varying needs, and this would then contradict the principle of this version of communism.

Hegel then turns to the contradiction with respect to property-holding when he writes, "The same applies to [the notion of] property, if this is resolved into its moments."[379] The contradiction involved in property-holding concerns the contradictory nature of the universal and the particular aspects of thinghood per se. On the one hand, a given piece of property, as an object, is a universal which is shared by all self-conscious subjects, in the sense that it is an object for all in the objective sphere. On the other hand, qua piece of private property, the object is particular and unique with respect to its special relationship to its owner. Hegel expresses this as follows: "What I possess is a thing, i.e. something which is for others in general and is only for *me* in a quite general, undefined way; that *I* possess it, contradicts its universal thinghood."[380] With the idea of private property alone, there is no contradiction; rather, the contradiction arises only when the object of private property is put in its determinate context as an ontological object. Thus, Hegel concludes, "Consequently, property is just as much an all-around contradiction as non-property; each contains within it these two opposed, self-contradictory moments of individuality and universality."[381]

Concluding Remarks (§§432–37)

The problem in these last two sections was that ethical laws are considered as something abstracted from the social context from which they originally sprung. "That law-giving and the testing of laws have proved to be futile," Hegel writes, "means that both, when taken singly and in isolation, are merely unstable moments of the ethical consciousness."[382] These imperatives are understood by ethical consciousness as something abstracted and "in isolation" from the ethical mores of everyday life, and for this reason they appear "unstable" and contradictory. In fact, they presuppose an ethical background of daily life from which they were originally abstracted. What ethical consciousness finally learns is that ethical commandments are not something abstract, but rather are already present in the fabric of everyday life: "Spiritual being is actual substance through these modes being valid, not in isolation, but only as superseded [moments]."[383] As a result of this, self-consciousness is already immediately in touch with these ethical laws just as immediately as one is in touch with one's own culture. Here we find once again Hegel's crucial distinction between morality (*Moralität*) and ethical life (*Sittlichkeit*). Morality involves an abstract understanding of moral commands and moral obligation, as was examined in the last two sections. From this perspective, ethics is understood only as something abstracted from all concrete relations to culture and community, and is discussed above all in abstract theoretical terms. Ethical life, on the other hand, involves the concrete ethical basis of a given community. Here ethical commands are analyzed in their particular historical and communal context. This forms the subject matter of the "Spirit" chapter.

This relation of the immediate unity of the individual with the ethical substance of the community marks the move to "Spirit." Hegel claims, "Ethical *self*-consciousness is *immediately* one with essential being through the *universality* of its *self*."[384] There is thus a new kind of harmony, this time between the universality of the individual's own ethical action and the universality of the ethical sphere in general. This is where the true realm of ethics lies. Ethics is not something to be debated among philosophers or something to be evaluated abstractly; instead, it is something to be found in actuality among a community of individuals with their laws, institutions, customs, and mores in the realm of Spirit. It is just this ethical sphere of Spirit where we have finally arrived. Thus, moral laws cannot be handed down *ex cathedra*, nor can they be determined merely formally. Formal commands cannot be the true ground of morality or the ethical life of a people. The "Reason" chapter then ends with the claim that ethical substance always exists immediately in communal life. It has immediate validity and is recognized on all hands as such. It requires no grounding or tests for consistency: "The law is equally an eternal law which is grounded not in the will of a particular individual, but is valid in and for itself; it is the absolute *pure will of all* which has the form of immediate being."[385] Thus, all the members of the community immediately play a role in the development of the Notion or ethical substance. At this stage, we have surpassed the levels of lordship and bondage and of the particular matter in hand in which subject and object were thought to be determined by particular individuals in conflict with others. Here the harmony of the whole forms the ethical life of individuals.

The dialectic of "Reason" shows the various attempts to render the communal account of the subject-object Notion valid by means of attaining a satisfactory integration of the individual in the social whole. Thus, the terms of the dialectic always involve greater or lesser degrees of alienation or identification of the individual with the community. Only when the individuals are integrated in the community in a free, fulfilling, and meaningful way can the result of their communal determinations be said to be valid and not based on unjust institutions or power-claims. Hence, the "Reason" chapter can be interpreted as playing a role in the story of the development of the Notion that we have been following. In order for terms such as "alienation" and "integration" to make sense in the first place there must already be some sort of commonality or shared set of beliefs which forms the background against which one can react when alienated and with which one identifies when one is well-integrated. In other words, in order to be alienated one must first have internalized certain beliefs or customs from which one feels alienated. These background beliefs cannot be expressed directly or cognitively by formal moral laws or ethical principles. Instead, they are in the everyday fabric of life and are thus always immediately present, since they form a necessary presupposition for the very notion of individuality and with it of alienation in the first place.

7

The Dialectic of Spirit

General Introduction (§§438–43)

We must now address the question of the import of our reading of the "Consciousness," "Self-Consciousness," and "Reason" chapters for the rest of the book. With each chapter a new element or account is introduced into the process of the self-development of the Notion. As was seen in some detail, "Consciousness" was the stage at which objects were considered external and predetermined. The important shift that the "Self-Consciousness" chapter effected was that consciousness saw *itself* as being the ultimate source of subject-object determinations. Thus, it attempted to give an account of itself as a necessary precondition for an account of the Notion. At the end of "Self-Consciousness," the realization was made that the individual alone cannot determine the subject-object Notion. Rather, the Notion is formed in an intersubjective social forum with other self-conscious agents. Then the "Reason" chapter introduced social and intersubjective factors into the account of subject and object. Here the truth-claims of the individual are not purely subjective but are rather intersubjective and thus mediated in a sense by a larger social group and by self-consciousness's relation to it. At the end of the "Reason" chapter, the subject-object split was closed when self-consciousness came to see itself in the rationality of the object sphere.

The question that remains is what the "Spirit" and "Religion" chapters have to add to this story. With the introduction of the social community in the "Reason" chapter are not the relevant elements in the account of the self-determination of the subject-object Notion already exhausted? Given that the dualisms of subject and object have been resolved, what further could "Spirit" and "Religion" tell us about the knowledge problematic? This line of questioning seems to support the thesis that the *Phenomenology* was actually intended to end with the "Reason" chapter, which according to Hegel's original plan culminated in absolute knowing.[1] According to this argument, Hegel lost control over his creation and in haste added the chapters "Spirit" and "Religion," which in fact did not fit into the argumentative scheme of the book as he had originally planned it. This would represent a serious problem for my thesis since, although my ultimate goal is to put a small stone into place in the large mosaic of the Hegelian architectonic, nevertheless it appears that the results of my interpretation support the patchwork thesis. In short, it might appear that the result of my attempt to save Hegel and to begin to demonstrate a coherent structure in this work by showing the coherence of the first three chapters ("Consciousness," "Self-Consciousness," and "Reason") has been to eliminate the two chapters that follow ("Spirit" and "Religion"). In order to render a part of Hegel's philosophy coherent, my interpretation seems to render another part incoherent, and thus it appears that the cure I am proposing is at least as bad as the disease.

Fortunately, this is not the case, and one can easily understand the rest of the *Phenomenology* in terms of my interpretation without doing damage to its systematicity. Before we examine specifically what "Spirit" and "Religion" have to add to the argument we have been following, let us briefly take account of the architectonic structure as it now stands. At the beginning of the "Spirit" chapter, Hegel gives us an extremely helpful review of the ground covered so far, and in this discussion he indicates how the "Spirit" chapter is supposed to fit into the story. Referring to "Observing Reason," he writes, "In Reason as *observer*, this pure unity of the *I* and *being*, of being *for itself* and being *in itself*, is determined as the *in-itself* or as *being*, and the consciousness of Reason *finds* itself."[2] As we have already seen, "Observing Reason" corresponds to "Consciousness" in its emphasis on the object sphere. As Hegel here says, these sections determine objectivity as "being" or as the "in-itself" moment. In the course of both dialectical movements, consciousness was led from the object sphere back to itself as subject. As he writes, "Reason [qua observer] *finds* itself." This then leads us to "Self-Consciousness" and "The Actualization of Rational Self-Consciousness through Its Own Activity," respectively. This Hegel describes as follows: "The *intuited category*, the *found thing*, enters consciousness as the *being-for-self* of the 'I,' which is now aware of itself as the *self* in objective being. But this determination of the category, of being-for-self opposed to being-in-itself, is equally one-sided and is a moment that supersedes itself."[3] With this second large dialectical step we move from the object to the subject or the "I." This forms the "being-for-itself" side of the dialectic. Here the subject is considered to be the essential in the relationship. Finally, we reach the apex of the pyramid with the third section of the "Reason" chapter, "Individuality Which Takes Itself to Be Real In and For Itself." This brings together the two moments of substance and subject, in-itself and for-itself: "The category is therefore determined for consciousness as it is in its universal truth, as a being that is *in* and *for itself*."[4] This section brings the subject-object dualism to a close, and at this point the triad of "Consciousness," "Self-Consciousness," and "Reason" is complete. The question, then remains about what work there is still left to do.

In the celebrated "Spirit" chapter, the longest of the book, Hegel begins with his account of the Greek *polis* and its demise, which he sees represented in Sophocles' drama *Antigone*. He then, proceeding roughly historically, analyzes the forms of life of the Roman world in "Legal Status." Following the account of Rome comes the dialectic of Medieval court culture in the longish section, "Culture and Its Realm of Actuality." Leaping somewhat in the historical sequence, Hegel examines the collision of religion and the critical thinking characteristic of the Enlightenment. In the section "The Struggle of Enlightenment with Superstition," he analyzes Diderot's *Nephew of Rameau* as a work which captures the inner tensions and contradictions of this period. The French Revolution and the Reign of Terror are then treated in "Absolute Freedom and Terror." In the final section, Hegel begins with a discussion of Kantian morality and continues with an account of various moral positions from the romantic movement, which he sees as the logical conclusion of Kant's moral theory. These views Hegel takes to be the most recent forms of Spirit in his own day. This then forms the contents of the "Spirit" chapter. What is the status of these discussions vis-à-vis "Consciousness," "Self-Consciousness," and "Reason"?

After the brief summary of the first three chapters discussed above, Hegel proceeds to answer this question about the role of "Spirit" and to justify the rest of the work. In a very important passage, he writes, referring to this third and final section of "Reason,"

> This still *abstract* determination which constitutes the "matter in hand" itself is at first only spiritual essence, and its consciousness [only] a formal knowing of it, which busies itself with all kinds of content of the essence. This consciousness, as a particular individual, is still in fact distinct from substance, and either makes arbitrary laws or fancies that in simply knowing laws it possesses them in their own absolute nature. Or, looked at from the side of substance, this is spiritual essence that is in and for itself, but which is not yet *consciousness* of itself. But essence that is *in* and *for itself*, and which is at the same time actual as consciousness and aware of itself, this is *Spirit*.[5]

Here Hegel makes the distinction between the level of "Reason" and that of "Spirit." In "Reason" self-consciousness had only a "formal knowing" of spiritual essence. It was abstracted or alienated from its immediate ethical relations. As he says later, "Spirit is thus self-supporting, absolute, real being. All previous shapes of consciousness are abstract forms of it. . . . This isolating of those moments *presupposes* Spirit itself and subsists therein."[6] In "Reason" an account of the community and the social whole was given, but this account was always abstract.[7] It was never any particular community. Likewise, the account of self-consciousness was always abstract. For instance, in the final two sections, "Reason as Lawgiver" and "Reason as Testing Laws," we were not concerned with a particular human subject in a particular community, but rather with any rational moral agent at all. These abstracted analyses "presuppose" a concrete social and historical community from which they were originally abstracted. This then forms the next major step in our transcendental argument. Now in order to give an account of the Notion, we must include an account of concrete historical communities.

From this analysis we can see that the key point is that "Spirit" introduces history into the account of the self-development of the subject-object Notion.[8] In order to move beyond the formal account of morality examined in "Reason," we need to examine concrete social situations, and this is only possible by an examination of particular historical communities. As Hegel says of Spirit in the "Absolute Knowing" chapter, "The movement of carrying forward the form of its [Spirit's] self-knowledge is the labor which it accomplishes as actual history."[9] In the *Philosophy of Right*, Hegel says, "the history of this genuine formation of ethical life is the content of the whole course of world-history."[10] The role of the community in "Reason" was static and abstract, whereas in "Spirit" it moves through history, and this movement shapes the truth-claims of its people in a way that the "Reason" chapter could not account for. Hegel confirms this interpretation that in "Spirit" history is introduced into the dialectic: "Only the totality of Spirit is in time, and the 'shapes,' which are 'shapes' of the totality of *Spirit*, display themselves in a temporal succession."[11] We now view historical communities not in the abstract but rather in the concrete way in which they move and develop in time. Hegel says of the forms and movement in "Spirit": "These shapes, however, are distinguished from the previous ones by the fact that they are real Spirits, actualities in the strict meaning of the word, and instead of being shapes merely of consciousness, are shapes of a world."[12] Hegel's point is that we are now concerned with the actual historical development of communities or as he says "actualities in the strict meaning of the word." The problem is that in "Reason," human communities were considered abstract and thus static, but yet they have historical origins which must be investigated. In order to give an account of how communities mediate truth-claims, we must first give a historical account of how a given community developed and how it came to hold certain truths or values. Such a historical account is thus presupposed in any abstract account of the role of the community in the self-determination of truth-claims. In other words, the abstract accounts of morality or individuality from the "Reason" chapter are abstracted from concrete historical communities which they presuppose. The role of the "Spirit" chapter is to provide just this account and thus to add yet another dimension which was missing in "Reason" to the account of the ultimate self-development of the subject-object Notion.

The question that this explanation raises for us is how these real or historical forms of "Spirit" fit with our analysis of the architectonic of the work given so far. The most obvious hint is that Hegel divides his abbreviated version of world history here in the "Spirit" chapter into three major sections as follows:

A. The True Spirit. The Ethical Order.
B. Self-Alienated Spirit. Culture.
C. Spirit That Is Certain of Itself. Morality.

This would seem to imply a correspondence with the three sections of "Reason" and their corresponding sections in "Consciousness" and "Self-Consciousness." In other words, this would seem to imply that "A. The True Spirit" corresponds to "Consciousness," and "Observing Reason." Similarly, "B. Self-Alienated Spirit" would then correspond to "Self-Consciousness" and "The Actualization of Rational Self-Consciousness through Its own Activity." Finally, the third section, "C. Spirit That Is Certain of Itself" would form the apex, corresponding to "Individuality Which Takes Itself to Be Real In and For Itself," the third and final section of the "Reason" chapter. For the sake of simplicity we can graphically represent the parallelisms that are implied by this reading in figure 7.1. There are three important pieces of evidence that support this thesis about the parallel sections.

First, this correspondence is indicated by the double Latin letters "BB" of the "Spirit" chapter which are intended to parallel the double letters "AA" of "Reason." In other words, "Spirit" will return to the beginning of the dialectic and will then go through all of the same stages as "Reason." These two chapters run parallel to each other as wholes or complete units. This implies that the "Spirit" chapter will have ipso facto the same parallelisms with "Consciousness" and "Self-Consciousness" as the "Reason" chapter before it.

Figure 7.1

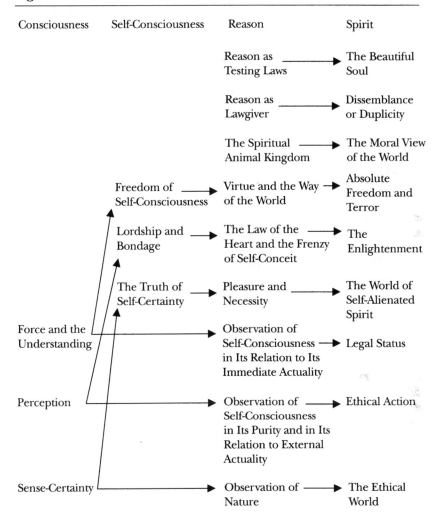

Consciousness	Self-Consciousness	Reason	Spirit
		Reason as Testing Laws ———▶	The Beautiful Soul
		Reason as Lawgiver ———▶	Dissemblance or Duplicity
		The Spiritual ———▶ Animal Kingdom	The Moral View of the World
	Freedom of ———▶ Self-Consciousness	Virtue and the Way ———▶ of the World	Absolute Freedom and Terror
	Lordship and Bondage ———▶	The Law of the ———▶ Heart and the Frenzy of Self-Conceit	The Enlightenment
	The Truth of ———▶ Self-Certainty	Pleasure and ———▶ Necessity	The World of Self-Alienated Spirit
Force and the Understanding		Observation of ———▶ Self-Consciousness in Its Relation to Its Immediate Actuality	Legal Status
Perception		Observation of ———▶ Self-Consciousness in Its Purity and in Its Relation to External Actuality	Ethical Action
Sense-Certainty		Observation of ———▶ Nature	The Ethical World

Second, Hegel indicates this parallelism explicitly in a couple of different places, above all in § 440, which was cited above. Later, in the "Religion" chapter, he writes, "But the moments are *consciousness, self-consciousness, Reason,* and *Spirit*—Spirit, that is, as immediate Spirit, which is not yet consciousness of Spirit. Their totality, *taken together,* constitutes Spirit in its mundane existence generally; Spirit as such contains the previous structured shapes in universal determinations, in the moments just named."[13] Here is it clear that the dialectical movements that we have examined in the first three chapters repeat themselves again here in "Spirit." The forms of consciousness in the first three chapters represent what Hegel here calls "universal determinations." In other words, they constitute universal patterns of thought which can take a number of different forms. These same universal forms are all contained in "Spirit" in their historical manifestations as Hegel indicates here.

Third, these parallelisms are confirmed by the actual contents of the individual sections of the "Spirit" chapter which we are about to explore. The first section represents the in-itself moment of the dialectic. Here in the discussion of *Antigone*, the ethical order is considered to be something objective. It is a fact about the world that stands over and above all human opinions and authority. Hegel writes, citing *Antigone*, "Thus, Sophocles' *Antigone* acknowledges them [sc. ethical laws] as the unwritten and infallible law of the gods. 'They are not of yesterday or today, but everlasting, / Though where they came from, none of us can tell.' "[14] The moral laws are ontological facts about the world according to this view. This then clearly corresponds to "Consciousness" and "Observing Reason," where priority is given to the object sphere at the expense of the subject. Hegel writes explicitly, "Spirit, then is consciousness in general which embraces sense-certainty, perception, and the understanding, insofar as in its self-analysis Spirit holds fast to the moment of being an objectively existent actuality to itself, and ignores the fact that this actuality is its own being-for-self."[15] From this passage it is, moreover, clear that the individual sections inside of these chapters and subsections also correspond.

The second section of "Spirit," "Self-Alienated Spirit," represents the break and the move to the for-itself moment. Here the historical subject, epitomized for Hegel by the nephew of Rameau in his alienation, rejects the accepted traditions and ethical order. He accepts only his own ethical views as valid and negates those of the tradition which he sees as contradictory or hypocritical. Here we can clearly see the for-itself aspect with its rejection of the objective sphere and its insistence on the truth and validity of the individual subject. This then corresponds to "Self-Consciousness" and the second section in "Reason." Hegel also indicates that "Spirit" has an aspect of self-consciousness when he writes, "If, on the contrary, it [Spirit] holds fast to the other moment of the analysis, viz. that its object is its own *being-for-self,* then it is self-consciousness."[16]

Finally, in the third section, "Spirit That Is Certain of Itself," the triad comes to a close with the in-and-for-itself moment. Here the dualisms of the two previous dialectics are overcome: "Here, then, knowledge appears at last to have become completely identical with its truth; for its truth is this very knowledge and any antithesis between the two sides has vanished."[17] In this third section of "Spirit" the moment of alienation has been overcome and with it the dualism between the inner private law and the external world of nature or culture. In "The Moral View of the World" nature is not an obstacle to morality; instead, it is thought to be conducive to moral life, since obeying moral laws is thought to lead to happiness. Likewise, the beautiful soul's appeal to conscience as the criterion for moral living unites the universally valid moral law with the individual. Thus, the third section represents the reconciliation of the two previous sections. Hegel explains this as follows: "But as immediate consciousness of the being that is *in and for itself*, as unity of consciousness and self-consciousness, Spirit is consciousness that *has Reason*."[18]

A. The Repetition of "Consciousness": The Ancient World— the True Spirit (§§444–83)

General Introduction (§§444–45)

Hegel begins his chronological treatment of world history, understandably enough, with an account of the ancient world. In this first section of the "Spirit" chapter, called "The Ethical Order," he analyzes the two major ancient civilizations of the Western tradition, namely, the Greek and the Roman world. It might be noted that this scheme deviates slightly from his later *Lectures on the Philosophy of History*, which begin not with "The Greek World" but rather with "The Oriental World." This apparent asymmetry disappears when one read Hegel's somewhat dismissive comments about the oriental world. Although he includes an analysis of Near and Far Eastern civilizations, for Hegel, true history begins with the Greeks. In the *Lectures on the Philosophy of History*, he says, "China and India lie, as it were, still outside world's history, as the mere presupposition of elements whose combination must be waited for to constitute their vital progress."[19] Later in the same lectures he claims, "the proper emergence, the true palingenesis of Spirit must be looked for in Greece first."[20] By this, Hegel is not denying that there were peoples, rulers, wars, and empires in the East prior to the birth of Western civilization with the Greeks; instead, with the concept of history, he has something very specific in mind, which on his view is characteristic of true history, yet which is absent from Eastern cultural development. As we will see in our analyses of the "Spirit" chapter as a whole, for Hegel, history is characterized by the dynamic dialectical movement of subjective and objective freedom. By "subjective freedom," Hegel means the conception of the subject which allows one to see oneself as an individual apart from the community and to dissent from the whole when necessary. There are a host of subjective freedoms in the social, economic, and political spheres which Hegel outlines in the *Philosophy of Right.* "Objective freedom" is simply the identification of the individual with the social whole with respect to religion, custom, etc. Regarding China and other Eastern civilizations, Hegel writes, "the contrast between objective existence and subjective freedom of movement in it, is still wanting, every change is excluded, and the fixedness of a character which recurs perpetually, takes the place of what we should call the truly historical."[21] Given the fact that, for Hegel, Eastern civilizations are lacking the dialectical principle of subjective and objective freedom and for this reason fall outside the realm of history as defined above, his treatment of "The Oriental World" in the *Lectures on the Philosophy of History* can be seen as a mere antehistorical supplement to the account of world history, strictly speaking. For this reason its omission in the *Phenomenology* is neither surprising nor vexing.

For the purposes of our reconstruction of the *Phenomenology* as a unitary whole, the section "The Ethical Order" appears somewhat problematic with respect to its content. Although regarding the apparent structure of the section, there seems to be no conflict with the basic interpretation I have been developing, since the section is conveniently composed of three separate sections which one would expect to correspond to the three sections of the "Consciousness" chapter and to the three sections of "Observing Reason," there are, however, two problems which stand in the way of a straightforward parallelism of this kind. To begin with, the first and the second sections in "The Ethical Order"—namely, "The Ethical World" and "Ethical Action"—do not treat two different Notions but instead seem to develop the same Notion, which Hegel sees as characteristic of the Greek world. Moreover, there does not seem to be any breakdown or sublation of the Notion in the section "The Ethical World," and thus the dialectical movement presented there seems incomplete. For these reasons, it is difficult to see exactly how the first two sections here can correspond straightforwardly to "Sense-Certainty" and "Perception" from the "Consciousness" chapter and to the first two sections of "Observing Reason," as one would expect them to do.

I propose to remedy this problem by taking "The Ethical World" and "Ethical Action" together as a single dialectical movement, the former representing the construction of the Notion and the latter its sublation in the experience of consciousness. Together, these two sections form a single Notion which compresses the respective Notions of "Sense-Certainty" and "Perception" into one. This might at first appear to be merely an ad hoc and self-serving solution to the problem, but when we go to the text, we see that this is precisely what Hegel indicates in his own opening remarks on the section. He writes,

> The simple substance of Spirit, as consciousness, is divided. In other words, just as the consciousness of abstract sensuous being passes over into perception, so also does the immediate certainty of a real ethical situation; and just as for sense-perception simple being becomes a thing of many properties, so for ethical perception a given action is an actual situation with many ethical connections.[22]

In this passage Hegel directly draws a parallel between the opening sections here in "Spirit" and the dialectical movements of "Sense-Certainty" and "Perception" from the "Consciousness" chapter. Just as "Sense-Certainty" was characterized by an immediate relation of the subject to its object, so also here the ethical subject is immediately related to the ethical law, which exists as immediately given, and indeed this proves ultimately to be its undoing. This is the situation portrayed here in the first section, "The Ethical World." Just as in "Perception" the Notion is characterized as a thing with properties, so also here a concrete ethical action has many different aspects and can be interpreted in many different ways. This is what characterizes the second section, "Ethical Action." Thus, the parallelism with the first two sections of the "Consciousness" chapter, in fact, finds support in Hegel's own remarks.

In "Perception" the conception of a thing as a medium of a given set of properties breaks down, since consciousness cannot reconcile the unity of the thing with its properties, which are themselves considered things. Likewise, in Spirit, the ethical substance, manifested in any given action, breaks down into two conflicting moments—divine law (individuality) and human law (universality). For sense perception, Hegel claims, "the superfluous plurality of properties concentrates itself more into the antithesis of individuality and universality; and still more for ethical perception . . . does the plurality of ethical moments become the duality of a law of individuality and a law of universality."[23] Hence, the cause of the breakdown is the same—an inability to reconcile the universal and the particular—in the case of "Perception," the universal thing with its particular properties, and in the case of "Spirit," the universal with the particular law. Hence, the universal-particular dualism is still operative in the "Spirit" chapter, and can be used to illustrate the parallelism between the movement of the dialectic here and in the "Consciousness" chapter.

There is another apparent disanalogy between "Consciousness" and "Spirit" which needs to be addressed briefly. In "Consciousness" an important part of what made the dialectic move was the fact that both moments—the universal and the particular—were united in a single consciousness. Natural consciousness was then always the agent which tried to overcome the contradictions caused by this perpetual dualism. How then can the same dialectical movement be operative in the realm of Spirit in which there is no single consciousness to unify the two moments and hence to realize the contradictions and attempt to overcome them? Hegel makes it clear that here in the "Spirit" chapter there is some sense in which we can consider ethical substance to be conscious: "Spirit is, in its simple truth, consciousness."[24] Hence, Spirit is originally conceived as a conscious unity. Yet, for Hegel, this unity is sundered: "*Action* divides it [Spirit] into substance, and consciousness of the substance; and divides the substance as well as consciousness."[25] The problem recurs anew: if consciousness of ethical substance is divided, then how can the contradiction between the two moments occur in a single consciousness? Hence, although ethical substance is somehow split, nevertheless "each of these divisions of substance remains Spirit in its entirety."[26] What then is the nature of this simple consciousness of ethical substance?

Although in Spirit there is no one all-seeing consciousness in a literal sense, there is a sense, for Hegel, in which the simple system of Spirit as ethical substance can be thought of as unitary and self-correcting. In this sense, it is conceived as a complex, multilayered system in which various subsystems (divine law and human law) come into conflict and consequently pass over into new forms. The individual parts of Spirit can be seen as mutually interacting with one another, constantly pushing and pulling, stretching and twisting their way through history. Although there are antagonistic and contradictory elements, these are all united dialectically in a single organic system. In this manner, the substance of Spirit is a type of metaphorical spirit of the age which, having split up into its various component parts, moves along on its dialectical path. Just as the various moments of the dialectic before were unified in a single consciousness—thus making possible a comparison of consciousness with itself—so also here in "Spirit" the various moments are unified in a closed self-correcting system of ethical substance.

I. The Ethical World and Ethical Action: The Greek World (§§446–76)

In Hegel's initial section in "Spirit," he examines individuals or individual types, which are unreflectively immersed in ethical substance as it is manifested in one of its moments. For his account of the Greek world in these first two sections, Hegel analyzes Sophocles' tragedy *Antigone*. It would seem that the fundamental tension presented in that drama represents, for him, the basic contradiction at the heart of the Greek world which caused its downfall. Hegel thus makes use of a literary text in order to give a historical analysis. Of course, he did not think that the events of *Antigone* were historical per se. Given the considerations above, I propose to analyze these first two sections of "Spirit" together, taking "The Ethical World" to be Hegel's construction of the Notion that characterizes the Greek world, and "Ethical Action" as its dialectical experience and subsequent sublation.

The Notion: The Ethical World—Human Law and Divine Law (§§446–63)

For Hegel, Greek tragedy captures the unreflective nature of Greek public life, which does not have the conceptual resources at the early stages of Spirit to bring a resolution to the collision of the divine and human laws. These laws are both universal and essential to true ethical life. "Spirit is the *ethical life* of a nation," Hegel notes, "insofar as it is the *immediate truth*— the individual that is a world."[27] The initial nature of Spirit is an ethical life—a society of customs, laws, and obligations—in which the members unreflectively identify with and engage in the goals and customs of the society. Here Spirit is a community of individuals who immediately find themselves absorbed in an unreflective harmony in their society. This simple ethical harmony is not a product of reflection or thought, as a social contractarian view might understand the origins of communal life, but rather it is a community in which the intense communal identification is based on spontaneous love of or affinity with one's own culture. This immediate relation to the community, of course, corresponds to natural consciousness' immediate relation to its object in "Sense-Certainty." Here custom takes over the role of pure being in "Sense-Certainty," and the immediately existing object of "Observing Reason."[28] Hegel's historical exemplification of such a stage in Spirit's development—its advancing from what it is immediately to a state of reflective, abstract apprehension of itself, to a knowledge of itself which is a mediated immediacy—is the Greek city-state or *polis*. For Hegel, the *polis* can be seen as a society that unites its citizens through feeling. Without participating in the civil duties and adhering in an immediate way to the socially recognized moral standards, an individual cannot function, since precisely what it is to be an individual is to be defined by the activities of the *polis* that the individual finds himself already engaged in. Hegel discusses the Greek *polis* and its decline in his *Lectures on the Philosophy of History*. There he characterizes the freedom of the Greek Spirit in much the same way as he does here in the *Phenomenology*. He describes the immediate identification of the individual with the ethical life of the state as follows:

> Of the Greeks in the first and genuine form of their freedom, we may assert, that they had no conscience; the habit of living for their country without further [analysis or] reflection, was the principle dominant among them. The consideration of the state in the abstract—which to our understanding is the essential point—was alien to them. Their grand object was their country in its living and real aspect—*this actual* Athens, this Sparta, these temples, these altars, this form of social life, this union of fellow-citizens, these manners and customs.[29]

According to Hegel, the Greeks were unreflectively immersed in the ethical life of their *polis*. They followed spontaneously and without reflection the customs and mores of Greek society. They thus lived in a spontaneous freedom or harmony with the social whole.

To begin the construction of the Notion, Hegel says of Spirit, "As *actual substance*, it is a nation, as *actual consciousness*, it is the citizens of that nation."[30] Spirit thus represents a sort of collective consciousness of a community as in the Greek *polis*. Hegel claims that this general consciousness has two domains: the governmental order or state, known as the self-conscious human law typified by man, and the family, known as the unconscious yet implicit divine law typified by woman. Thus, Hegel's first claim is that the simple ethical substance splits into two moments: the human law and the divine law.[31]

The human law, or what Hegel calls "the law of universality," is ethical substance that is conscious of itself, i.e., its action is conscious action. The human law, as represented by the state, the government, and its laws, is known and publicly displayed for all to understand and accept: "Its truth is the authority which is openly accepted and manifest to all."[32] Because the laws and practices of the *polis* are actual and concrete, they are self-consciously recognized by the citizens. In being public and explicit, they are at the level of self-consciousness in general, with the nation being conceived as a self-consciousness made up of individual consciousnesses. As Hegel notes, "human right has for its content and power the actual ethical substance that is conscious of itself, i.e. the entire nation."[33] Because the individuals are defined by, and have their identity in, the *polis*, they maintain themselves by maintaining these laws, for apart from the *polis*, they are nothing, and exile is the worst possible punishment.

The divine law, on the other hand, is ethical substance that is manifested in immediate action. This law is unknown and unconscious, since it is not available to public view, but instead is only immediately accessible to the individual. While human law is grounded in the community and its laws and customs, the divine law has its roots in the family. Hence, both moments of ethical substance are represented by basic human institutions. Like "pure being" in "Sense-Certainty," the divine law "has the form of immediate substance or substance that simply is."[34] The community is conscious of what it does, but the family—the other ethical domain—expresses the ethical realm in a simple immediacy: "the law of the family is an implicit, inner essence which is not exposed to the daylight of consciousness, but remains an inner feeling and the divine element that is exempt from an existence in the real world."[35] As an element of the *polis*, the family stands opposed to the state. The laws of the *polis* are actual existents, and any familial claims or rights which might clash with the public laws of the *polis* would appear unjustified. The two types of laws are interdependent and are not irreconcilable antithets.

Hegel uses the metaphor of the union of man and woman to signify the relationship between these ethical powers. For this reason many feminist interpreters have directed their attention to this analysis for an account of Hegel's views on women generally.[36] Hegel writes, "Nature, not the accident of circumstance or choice, assigns one sex to one law, the other to the other law; or conversely, the two ethical powers give themselves an individual existence and actualize themselves in the two sexes."[37] Hegel represents the human law by man, the one who has to become involved in the government and thus becomes self-conscious in his involvement with the process of making and maintaining laws in the *polis*. In the *Philosophy of Right*, Hegel writes, "man has his actual substantive life in the state, in learning, and so forth, as well as in labor and struggle with the external world."[38] Similarly, the woman represents the divine law in her immersion in the family: "Woman, on the other hand, has her substantive destiny in the family."[39] The woman thus represents the unconscious, immediate force of Spirit, which stands in potential conflict with the self-conscious laws of the *polis*—laws which explicitly represent the universal; in other words, she stands in potential conflict with man, since her law is universal as well.

Hegel points out the perfect manifestation of the divine law or the essential duty of the family: the burial of its dead. For Hegel, the ethical principle of the family is not that of love, but rather concerns the end of the individual's actions in relation to the family as a whole. The deeds and actions of an individual are then interpreted as his deeds and actions qua family member. Hence, the deeds of the dead are appropriated and extolled by the family. Therefore, the essential duty of divine law, and hence of the family, is the burial rites and consequent honoring of the dead. The family tries to keep the dead relatives—*di penates*—from becoming purely natural beings by keeping them alive through recounting their exploits, prayer, and sacrifice to their souls, etc. In this way, the true power of the divine law is thought to lie in the other world, the nether world. Hegel then wants to show that in order for the relationship among family members to be truly ethical, there can be no accidental relationship between members; actual deeds aimed at assisting the individuals have only limited content and are contingent in that these deeds produce only a particular, and not a universal, effect. The living individual can be seen as a "long succession of disconnected experiences," and it is only when the individual has died—has been freed from the contingency of the sensuous—that he can become a single, complete shape, i.e., a universal. It is the duty of the member of a family to ensure the completion of the deceased family member by burying him and making him "something *done.*"[40] This is the way the family tries to overcome the purely natural. If the deceased are not buried, they become subject to the forces of nature which continually transform them; unburied, the deceased individual is not complete and thus is not a universal, since he is still being transformed by the material elements of existence—storms, birds of prey, and other animals. The burial of the family member thus gives the person a final rest, completion, and meaning which is universal and which symbolizes what those who bury this person are—blood relatives, who are able to transcend the sensuous contingency of brute nature and become universal, imperishable individuals when they die. As Hegel says, "This last duty thus constitutes the perfect *divine* law, or the positive *ethical* action towards the individual."[41] Thus, the human law has for its power and content the actual *polis* or nation that is conscious of itself, while the divine law has for its power and content the individual.

In the family there are three kinds of relationship: husband and wife, parents and children, and brothers and sisters.[42] For Hegel, the first two display certain asymmetries, whereas only the third represents a kind of harmony among equals. Brother and sister alone reach "a state of rest and equilibrium."[43] The relation of husband and wife is based on desire and mutual recognition, which are unstable and transitory. For Hegel, the essence of the relation of husband and wife lies ultimately in their offspring. The parents have their true being in their children, and in them they perish as individuals. The relation of child to parent is one of dependency: the child is wholly dependent on the parents and thus has his entire being in them. But yet in the natural death of the parents, this is lost forever. The truly stable and harmonious family relationship, for Hegel, is that of brother and sister. Brothers and sisters do not desire one another as husbands and wives nor do they owe their existence to one another as do parents and children; instead, "they are free individualities in regard to each other."[44] Here Hegel clearly has in mind the brother-sister relation of Polyneices and Antigone in Sophocles' drama. The sister cannot recognize herself in her parents since, although she owes her existence to them, they will nevertheless perish. Nor can the woman find her identity through her husband or her children, since her relation to them involves contingent desire; moreover, she sees them as something evanescent, and thus her children could be any children and her husband any husband. Therefore, the woman can only recognize herself through her brother—the lone unmixed relationship she possesses. Thus, Hegel's claim is that the sister, representing the family by having her identity bound up in the identity of the brother, the prominent family member, overcomes her merely natural being and takes on ethical significance. The brother takes on ethical significance by going out into the social world and creating his identity. He, then, represents both the community, wherein his identity lies, and the human law, which he has left the family to find.

Both moments of ethical substance—divine law and human law—are necessarily interrelated, and neither is valid without the other; instead, there is an essential interdependence between both orders. In his *Lectures on the Philosophy of History*, Hegel indicates this reciprocity: "the divine receives its honor through the respect paid to the human, and the human in virtue of the honor paid to the divine."[45] The family has its identity in the laws and practices of the community, and conversely, the community possesses in the family the formal, divine law concerning the burial of the dead, which is essential to the community, since it is composed of individuals who essentially and implicitly have this divine right. Hegel puts the relationship between the two succinctly: "human law proceeds in its living process from the divine, the law valid on earth from that of the nether world, the conscious from the unconscious, mediation from immediacy—and equally returns whence it came. The power of the nether world, on the other hand, has its actual existence on earth; through consciousness, it becomes existence and activity."[46] Because the community is comprised of individuals who are part of a family, the basis of the community is the unconscious divine law of the family, and the divine law of the family only finds expression on earth, where governments or some kind of social regulation is necessary in order to sustain families. The laws and customs of the *polis* thus are the objective universals in which individuals of a family find themselves absorbed. The family must have a community, since it is into a community that the brother (the family's representative) must go in order to gain his identity, which in turn the family makes immortal, thus creating its own identity as a family. Likewise, the community must have families in order to produce individuals who are able to direct, defend, and govern it; in short, it must have individuals if it is to exist at all. Therefore, Hegel concludes, "Neither of the two [sc. the community or the family] is by itself absolutely valid."[47] They are mutually dependent, and each needs the other for its own validation and authority. Both together constitute ethical substance. Divine and human law are harmoniously united in the union of man and woman, with man representing self-conscious action, and woman, immediate, unconscious action. A harmony or stable equilibrium thus comes to exist between these two moments.

The Experience of Consciousness: Ethical Action (§§464–76)

The harmony is broken by an individual deed, which brings the two elements into conflict. This conflict originates in an *act* or deed perpetrated by a particular individual, which ruptures the peaceful harmony of these two essences and forces an irresolvable opposition between them. It is thus ethical *action* that we are concerned with in this section. At this initial stage of ethical life in which there is an unreflective immersion in the laws of the *polis*, there is no recognition of the valid and essential nature of the individual action, which appears to be a transgression of the objective, legitimate, and universal laws of the community. What results is an absolute decision between mutually exclusive options in which a reconciliation or resolution (or a mediation) is impossible. Those who take the side of the human laws claim that any challenge to these laws is only a capricious, arbitrary expression of individual *pathos*, whereas those who challenge the human laws claim the universal validity of the divine law which, though not explicit and thus not actual, is the implicit universal which is valid. Seen from this side, the human law is just an expression of an ethical law, which is grounded on the arbitrary and contingent decree of a human ruler, rather than on a necessary, absolute standard which would give the human law true legitimacy.

Ethical consciousness thus splits into two powers, which assume a rigid and uncompromising position, each of which is unable to overcome the positivity of the other because neither can accept "that both have the same *essential* nature."[48] Both individuals involved perceive only one law and see the legality of their action only in terms of that one law. Both become conscious of only one law, while they subordinate and fail to recognize the validity of the other law. By doing so, each party is guilty in terms of the law he or she denies and falls into an implicit self-contradiction by denying the law that necessarily complements his or her own law. For this reason, "the opposition between them appears as an *unfortunate* collision of duty merely with a reality which possesses no rights of its own."[49] Hegel's choice of the word "unfortunate" reveals the somber pessimism of Greek tragedy;[50] given the unmediated nature of the *polis*, no resolution is possible, although both sides are in the right. The issue of this conflict is not the success of one side or the other, but a "dreadful fate which engulfs in the abyss of its single nature divine and human law alike, as well as the two self-consciousnesses in which these powers have their existence."[51] The tragic outcome is that the lack of a possible resolution leads to the destruction of both sides of the true ethical order. Given the preceding framework, Hegel's analysis of the drama *Antigone* should by now be apparent.

In *Antigone*, Creon, as King of Thebes, represents the side of self-conscious human law, while Antigone, the daughter of Oedipus who is betrothed to Creon's son Haemon, represents the side of divine law. Eteocles and Polyneices are Antigone's brothers. While leading a rebellion against the state, Polyneices is killed. Creon issues a decree forbidding the burial of Polyneices, for his crime against the fatherland. The point of the decree is to leave "his corpse disgraced, / A dinner for the birds and for the dogs."[52] Creon stands for the immutability and absolute legitimacy of the human or communal law; he says, "The man who is well-minded to the state / From me in death in life shall have his honor."[53]

Antigone, on the other hand, defies Creon's decree and gives her brother burial in accordance with the demands of the law of the family. Representing the unconscious divine law, Antigone appeals to the universal nature of the unwritten law: "Death yearns for equal law for all the dead."[54] She claims that Creon's edict carries no legitimacy since Creon has audaciously placed his own particular will over the "unwritten" yet universal law of the gods, the divine law of the family. Antigone says to Creon:

> For me it was not Zeus who made that order.
> Nor did that justice who lives with the gods below
> mark out such laws to hold among mankind.
> Nor did I think your orders were so strong
> that you, a mortal man, could over-run
> the gods' unwritten and unfailing laws.
> Not now, nor yesterday's, they always live,
> and no one knows their origin in time.[55]

The positions of Creon and Antigone, in Hegel's eyes, must remain resolute. Hegel notes, "the ethical essence has split itself into two laws, and consciousness, as an undivided attitude towards law, is assigned only to one."[56] Each side knows immediately its duty: "In it there is no caprice and equally no struggle, no indecision . . . on the contrary, the essence of ethical life is for consciousness immediate, unwavering, without contradiction."[57] Creon, as King of Thebes and sustainer of objective, human law, must forbid the burial of Polyneices in order to support the supremacy and authority of the state. Creon says,

> There is no greater wrong than disobedience.
> This ruins cities, this tears down our homes,
> this breaks the battle-front in panic rout.
> If men live decently it is because
> discipline saves their very lives for them.[58]

Justice in this system is then conceived of as the force that stabilizes the equilibrium when the whole becomes unbalanced by the actions of certain individuals. This justice or human law exacts vengeance on individuals whom it persecutes; by denying them proper burial rites and thus an ongoing existence, justice reduces such individuals to mere natural beings. Hence, a harmony is maintained by suppressing rebellious individualism. The city is what makes humans human and distinguishes them from savage, uncivil animals. Thus, Creon must take action against those who try to destroy the *polis*, which is the bastion of civilization's overcoming mere nature; for this reason, Polyneices cannot be allowed to receive a proper burial. As Hegel notes, "He who wantonly attacked the Spirit's highest form of consciousness, the Spirit of the community, must be stripped of the honor of his entire and finished being, the honor due to the Spirit of the departed."[59] The community attempts to establish its former equilibrium by repressing individualistic spirits, but by denying the validity of the divine law, the community destroys itself. Although it looks as though the community has the upper hand, since it has its power in this world while the divine law has the root of its power in the nether world, nevertheless by denying the family its sacred burial rites and not recognizing the divine law, the community, which itself depends on divine law, destroys itself. The community is now vulnerable to other communities, which, no longer fearing destruction, rise up to gain vengeance for the one who has been denied rites.

Antigone is just as resolute and intractable as Creon: "Polyneices knows the price I pay / for doing final service to his corpse. / And yet the wise will know my choice was right."[60] For Antigone, one must obey the higher law. By insisting on the actual realm of human law, Creon has unwittingly removed the presupposition of its existence, the divine law. Hegel says, "The self-certainty and self-assurance of a nation possesses the *truth* of its oath, which binds all into one, solely in the mute unconscious substance of all, in the waters of forgetfulness."[61] Antigone is unwavering in bringing these waters to consciousness.

The unfortunate collision of the divine and human, of right and right, leads to the destruction of both sides.[62] The confrontation leads to a suffering or guilt in the individual consciousness, which ultimately leads to the destruction of both. The intentions of these ethical agents, as we know, are not particular but represent genuine and legitimate universals, and herein lies the aspect of tragedy: "for neither power has any advantage over the other that would make it a more essential moment of the [ethical] substance."[63] Both sides are essential, and without this recognition—a mediation—the tragic destruction of both is inevitable.

The outcome of *Antigone* bears out the mutual destruction of each law and the respective destruction and suffering of each consciousness representing these laws. Antigone, in challenging the state by making actual the implicit divine law through her deed of burying Polyneices, loses her life. Her disobedience vitiates her citizenship and identification with the city, and thus she has lost an essential part of her being, the community. Her alienation from the community ends in her permanent alienation of herself via the community: she hangs herself symbolically outside the city in a natural setting. The chorus says to Antigone, "Your self-sufficiency has brought you down."[64] Her self-sufficiency was her disobedience of the community. Antigone's deed leads to her guilt since her action makes her a criminal, "for as simple, ethical consciousness, it has turned towards one law, but turned its back on the other and violates the latter by its deed."[65]

Creon, on the other hand, in upholding the public, objective laws of the *polis*, loses himself as well, because he ironically loses his family, the very thing that he neglected and that Antigone fought to preserve. Creon's son Haemon falls on his sword in anguish over Antigone's suicide, and Creon's wife in turn kills herself in grief over Haemon's suicide. In losing his family, Creon loses that essential ethical domain which constitutes one aspect of full ethical consciousness. He too is now alienated in the absence of his family, and he must suffer guilt: "This is my guilt, all mine. I killed you [Haemon], I say it clear. / Servants, take me away, out of the sight of men. / I who am nothing more than nothing now."[66] Creon loses himself in doing his duty because this required the sacrifice of his family. For both Antigone and Creon, their guilt and suffering are universal. Antigone suffered for her violation of the universal communal law as well as ultimately for her being a member of the Labdakos family, the tragically destined family of Oedipus. As the chorus says to Antigone, "Perhaps you are paying your father's pain."[67] Creon likewise suffers for keeping the communal universal, for doing right.

Through this cycle the community succumbs to individuality, and the harmony is disrupted. Hegel claims, "This ruin of the ethical substance and its passage into another form is thus determined by the fact that the ethical consciousness is directed on to the law in a way that is essentially *immediate*."[68] In other words, it was divine law, the feminine, the immediate, the particular, which through its deed initiated the conflict with the community, the universal. This immediacy—the family—was found to be contradictory due to its conflict with self-conscious mediation—the community—which it was essentially bound up with. Now that the harmony of the community is dissolved and the immediacy has been overcome, a new form appears: mediated individuals. The community now is "shattered into a multitude of separate atoms,"[69] each in possession of its own rights and obligations; this is the stage of Roman law.

Concluding Remarks

The failure of the Greek ethical community implicitly suggests what would be a successful ethical community—one in which both orders of ethical life do not stand opposed, but instead recognize the ineliminable dependence of one on the other such that a peaceful integration of the two is achieved. The successful ethical community is one in which there is a harmonious unity between the divine and the human orders. Each order does not appear as one element standing in opposition to another, but is somehow an embodiment of the other. In Hegelian terminology, the subject is object; the community is a manifestation of those participating in it. The true ethical substance is one where the laws of the community are both divine and human—human insofar as they are products of human beings, and yet divine in that they are not laws of any particular, finite human being but of all humans and for this reason are truly objective and universal. Now this unreflective absorption in the community has gone through a historical development in which Spirit becomes a new social form—the Roman Empire.

For Hegel, the sublation of the moment of immediacy is required for the development of freedom in history. As he says in his lectures, "The history of the world is none other than the progress of the consciousness of freedom."[70] He conceives of freedom as autonomy, i.e., the ability of the individual to give a law to himself and to act on the basis of his or her own decisions free of any adventitious authority. In "Ethical Action," individuals are not autonomous in this sense. Due to the fact that they immediately identify with the given ethical laws, they have no moment of reflection, which is required for a genuinely autonomous decision. An autonomous decision is one that results from critical reflection and critical assessment of the pros and cons of a particular situation. By contrast, here in "Ethical Action," Antigone and Creon simply accept without reflection or mediation the respective ethical laws. Thus, the sublation of this Notion of an immediate relation to one's own ethical life is a necessary step on the way to the historical development of a genuine conception of freedom as autonomy. For Hegel, it is not an unfortunate contingent fact that humans must leave the harmonious Garden of Eden in which they are at home in the world;[71] instead, it is conceptually necessary that this moment of immediacy be overcome.

II. Legal Status: The Roman World (§§477–83)

After finishing his account of the destruction of the Greek *polis* which came about as a result of the conflict between divine and human law, Hegel goes on, following the historical sequence, to examine the Roman world. The section "Legal Status" is Hegel's portrayal of the Notion represented by the Roman Spirit. This sequence follows his account in the *Lectures on the Philosophy of History*, where the Roman world is given a much fuller treatment than here in the *Phenomenology*. In fact, Hegel's analysis of Roman civilization in the *Phenomenology* is limited to the Roman Empire and constitutes only the third stage in Roman history according to the scheme outlined in the *Lectures on the Philosophy of History*.

With respect to the categorial parallelisms that we have been following, this section, as the third section in the sequence here, corresponds explicitly to the third sections of "Consciousness" and "Observing Reason," respectively, and implicitly to the third section of "Self-Consciousness." Although I have been unable to represent the relation adequately in my diagrams, it should nevertheless be clear that, as we said earlier, in respect to the categorial aspect of the respective Notions, the chapters "Consciousness" and "Self-Consciousness" and their individual sections correspond to one another. Thus, the third section of each of these accounts in "Self-Consciousness" (and not just the third section in "Consciousness") corresponds to "Legal Status." In fact, throughout this section Hegel constantly refers to the dialectical movement of "Stoicism, Skepticism, and the Unhappy Consciousness," which, of course, constituted the third Notion in "Self-Consciousness."[72] He says explicitly that what appeared there was merely the abstract movement of consciousness, whereas here we are concerned with actual historical realities: "What was for Stoicism only the *abstraction* of an *intrinsic* reality is now an *actual* world. Stoicism is nothing else but the consciousness which reduces to its abstract form the principle of legal status."[73] He goes on to indicate the parallel movements through the forms of Skepticism[74] and finally the unhappy consciousness:[75] "Now, just as the *abstract* independence of Stoicism exhibited [the process of] its actualization, so too will this last form of independence recapitulate the process of the first form."[76] As we have seen, the third Notion in each of the dialectical movements always involves objects of thought, such as force, in contrast to the sensible objects of perception. So also here, the Notion—abstract personhood of the individual—is not something empirical, but rather is a legal construct based on abstract concepts of thought. This Notion contrasts with the conception of ethical action explored in the previous section in that, as we have seen, ethical action is something empirical and corresponds to the empirical spheres of "Sense-Certainty" and "Perception." In contrast to the Greeks, the Romans, according to Hegel, dwelled in the realm of thought and not in the sphere of sensibility: "The Roman had always to do with something *secret*; in everything he believed in and sought for something *concealed*; and while in the Greek religion everything is open and clear, present to sense and contemplation . . . among the Romans everything exhibits itself as mysterious, duplicate."[77] The Romans grasp the world with understanding and not with the senses, and this gives rise to a split between appearance and reality or to a duplication of the object— one seen and one unseen, just like force proper and force expressed. With this categorial parallelism clarified, we need now to examine more closely the nature of the Notion presented here in "Legal Status."

The Notion: Abstract Personhood (§§477–81)

The Roman Empire as a form of human society differed radically from the Greek *polis*. The Empire was an enormous multinational institution, which brought together vastly differing peoples, languages, and customs. It was a cosmopolitan world, which contrasted sharply with the more homogeneous Greek states. Historically speaking, this difference can be explained by the contrasting ways in which the Romans and the Greeks dealt with conquered enemies. For the Greeks, conquered states always maintained their subordinate status, and little effort was made to integrate them into the social or political order of the hegemonic states, such as Athens or Sparta. By contrast, the less xenophobic Romans from their earliest history attempted to co-opt defeated enemies into their own state. By extending Roman citizenship to defeated states, Rome saw those states gradually lose their own self-identity and become a part of the Empire. The result of this process over the centuries was a huge, heterogeneous empire consisting of different peoples, languages, and customs. To use Hegel's language, the Empire enjoyed no unitary ethical substance, as was the case in the Greek *polis*. As he says in his lectures, "There does not exist therefore a substantial national unity—not that beautiful and moral necessity of united life in the *polis*."[78] There were no obvious, immediate, universally accepted customs or standards, and thus there was no common basis of ethical substance. Instead, there was simply a plurality of individuals in a vast empire. Given that there was no common ethical substance, emphasis was placed on the individual, who was conceived of as a self-sufficient monadic entity among others. In the absence of universally recognized customs, individuals were separated from one another in a way unknown to life in the Greek *polis*. Hegel uses the metaphor of individual atoms to describe the isolated and alienated individuals in the expansive empire in contrast to the Greek absorption in the ethical life of the social whole.[79]

A new abstract, legalistic conception of the citizen as someone possessing "legal status," i.e., the much desired citizenship rights of a Roman, takes the place of the Greek conception of the individual as a concrete family member or representative of the state: "The universal unity into which the living immediate unity of individuality and substance withdraws is the soulless community which has ceased to be the substance . . . of individuals, and in which they now have the value of selves and substances, possessing a separate being-for-self."[80] Legal status is the conception of the individual in a "soulless community," since there is no common ethical basis upon which to base a more concrete notion of the individual. The Romans were not immediately absorbed in the life of the family or the state as the Greeks were. The result is the abstract status which Hegel refers to simply as "personhood": "The universal being thus split up into a mere multiplicity of individuals, this lifeless Spirit is an equality, in which all count the same, i.e. as *persons*."[81] The key characteristic of personhood is abstraction: " 'Person,' which involves the recognition of the independent dignity of the social unit—not on the ground of the display of the life which he possesses—in his complete individuality—but as the abstract *individuum*."[82] All citizens are recognized as isolated individuals by the legal institutions of Roman law.

Just as when in "Force and the Understanding" an elusive unseen force was thought to stand behind and ground a particular appearance, so also here abstract, nonsensuous personhood is thought to be the true essence of each concrete individual. An individual is precisely and essentially what he is in the eyes of Roman law, i.e., a person who is enjoined with a certain set of duties, such as paying taxes and participating in military service, and who enjoys certain rights, such as the right to hold property and to stand for public office.[83] Thus, what counts for a person is essentially an abstract Notion, which Hegel sometimes refers to as an "empty unit":[84] "For what counts as absolute, essential being is self-consciousness as the sheer *empty unit* of the person."[85] This abstract conception of the individual is lacking in all content, since it is that which can be filled by any particular individual.

Just as the individual *subject* is conceived as abstract personhood, so also the *object* or things in general are here conceived as "property," i.e., they too are conceived in terms of an abstract legal status. Hegel explains this in his lectures: "Private right, viz., is this, that the social unit as such enjoys consideration in the state, in the reality which he gives to himself— viz., in property."[86] Also in his lectures, he says explicitly, "Personality constitutes the fundamental concept of legal right; it appears chiefly in the category of property."[87] It is through the abstract legal right to possess property that the individual in the Roman Empire is thought to be valid as an individual. Thus, in his private possessions, the Roman citizen expresses his personhood in concrete form. Hegel says of consciousness, "it finds before it a manifold existence in the form of 'possession' and . . . stamps it with the same abstract universality, whereby it is called 'property.' "[88] Individual possessions take on the status of "property"; they are universally recognized to belong to particular individuals.[89] Thus, it is no accident that in the *Philosophy of Right*, Hegel treats property, along with contract, under the heading of "Abstract Right."

Opposed to the plurality of atomistic individual Roman citizens is the Roman emperor, who stands above Roman law and abstract personhood. In his lofty and unique status he is separated from the citizens, who must view him from a distance: "He is a person, but the solitary person who stands over against all the rest. These constitute the real authoritative universality of that person; for the single individual as such is true only as a universal multiplicity of single individuals."[90] It is the emperor who guarantees the validity of Roman law and the legal status of the citizens precisely in his ability to dismiss all legality whenever his arbitrary will so desires. He represents "isolated subjectivity," which leads to "caprice absolutely unfettered."[91] It is the person of the emperor that embodies the principle of unrestrained individuality that ultimately leads to the destruction of the Roman world.

The Experience of Consciousness (§§482–83)

The dissipation and destructive, irrational acts of the emperor cause fear and alienation among the citizens. Precisely as a result of the emperor's unrestrained actions, the citizens disassociate themselves from the state and come to see themselves as something essentially different from the abstract right that the emperor guarantees:

> For his power is not the *union* and *harmony* of Spirit in which persons would recognize their own self-consciousness. Rather they exist, as persons, on their own account, and exclude any continuity with others from the rigid unyieldingness of their atomicity. They exist, therefore, in a merely negative relationship, both to one another and to him who is their bond of connection or continuity.[92]

They regard themselves essentially as content, i.e., as what they are as concrete, separate individuals, and they reject the notion of themselves as form in accordance with the abstract legalistic conception, since it is this formal conception which is guaranteed by the emperor.

In a dense passage Hegel describes the key to the conceptual contradiction in "Legal Status": "This truth consists in the fact that this *universally acknowledged authority* of self-consciousness is the reality from which it is alienated. This acknowledgment of its authority is the universal actuality of the self; but this actuality is directly the perversion of the self as well; it is the loss of its essence."[93] The contradiction consists in the fact that although it is the emperor who upholds Roman law and thus guarantees the rights and legal status of individual citizens, nevertheless the emperor is also above the law and thus can trample it underfoot whenever he wants. Thus, by acknowledging the authority and legitimacy of the emperor, qua guarantor of Roman law, the citizen simultaneously acknowledges the emperor's "right" in practice to defy it, and this amounts to denying one's own existence as an individual with legal status precisely because one recognizes that this status can potentially be violated at any moment. Hegel describes this in his lectures, where he refers to the emperor abstractly as "the One":

> Individuals are thereby posited as atoms; but they are at the same time subject to the severe rule of the *One*, which as *monas monadum* is a power over private persons. . . . That private right is therefore, *ipso facto*, a nullity, an ignoring of the personality; and the supposed condition of right turns out to be an absolute destitution of it. This contradiction is the misery of the Roman World.[94]

The citizen is thus alienated not merely from both the state and its representative, the emperor, but also from his own existence as an individual which he once thought was to be found in his legal status as a citizen. It is here that the next section, "Self-Alienated Spirit," begins.

For Hegel it is the arbitrary will of the individual that brings down the Roman world.[95] First, in the struggle of the orders, individual self-interest led the patricians to exclude their fellow countrymen from all forms of genuine political participation. Then, following the Second Punic War, Rome was constantly the victim of civil strife, beginning with the reforms of the Gracchi, up through the series of civil wars that ultimately led to the establishment of the principate. Finally, arbitrary individuality takes on its highest form in the Roman Emperor, whose irrational and destructive will meets with no opposition. In his lectures, Hegel says, "the connection between the rule and the ruled is not mediated by the claim of divine or of constitutional right, or any general principle, but is direct and individual, the Emperor being the immediate lord of each subject in the Empire."[96] The failure of Rome was that, in the absence of any broader notion, its conception of right was limited to the will of an individual—the emperor. Thus, even though there were occasionally benevolent emperors, who performed beneficial services to individuals and the state, this was simply a matter of luck, which changed nothing with regard to the underlying principle:

> Thus there were emperors of noble character and noble nature, and who highly distinguished themselves by mental and moral culture. Titus, Trajan, the Antonines, are known as such characters, rigorously strict in self-government; yet even these produced no change in the state. The proposition was never made during their time to give the Roman Empire an organization of free social relationship; they were only a happy chance, which passes over without a trace, and leaves the condition of things as it was.[97]

Thus, despite the fortuitous appearance of upright emperors, the fundamental contradiction of the Roman world remained.

Concluding Remarks

With the collapse of the Roman Empire, Spirit attains the level of "Self-Consciousness" in its alienation from itself. Truth is no longer something given in the world immediately, such as was the case in the ethical law of the Greeks, or mediately, such as was the case here in legal status for the Romans. On the contrary, truth is not to be found in the world or on the side of the object at all. It dwells rather on the side of the subject, as the Roman emperor evinces with his arbitrary acts. Thus, this transition in world history from the dissolving of the Roman world into the Medieval world corresponds to the transition from "Consciousness" to "Self-Consciousness" at the purely conceptual level. We now enter into the realm of the for-itself, where historical consciousness, now having become aware of itself in its self-alienation, resolutely maintains the truth of its own will and pronouncements, however arbitrary, at the expense of the established order of culture.

B. The Repetition of "Self-Consciousness": Self-Alienated Spirit. Culture (§§484–537)

General Introduction (§§484–86)

With the move to "Self-Alienated Spirit," we advance both categorially in the conceptual movement, as well as historically in the dialectical movement of Spirit. With respect to the categorial parallelisms that we have been surveying, the section "Self-Alienated Spirit" corresponds to the "Self-Consciousness" chapter and to the second section of the "Reason" chapter. Here self-consciousness moves away from its emphasis on the object as criterion for truth and turns its attention to itself as a self-conscious subject. What this amounts to at the historical level can be seen by contrasting the material here with that just covered. For Hegel, the Greek world represented a harmonious place, where the individual was immediately at home with the customs, values, and traditions of his *polis*. There was no question but that the criterion of truth was given in the world in just those customs or traditions. Apart from the laws and customs, the individual was nothing, a mere object of nature. Antigone asserts that the laws "are not of yesterday or today, but everlasting."[98] These laws were conceived as fixed entities in the universe, which no individual human could alter. In the Roman world, this law became abstract in the form of legal recognition. Here also the criterion for truth was found in the world of objects. Every Roman citizen enjoyed legal status and counted as an abstract person with the right to hold property. This fact stood forth as a fact about the world, and no private citizen could change it. But the emperor was able to change it by an arbitrary act of will, and this is the key to understanding the movement of the criterion for truth from the objective to the subjective sphere. Roman legal status is supposed to be a fixed fact about the world—no less fixed than natural laws—but the fact that the emperor can violate it at will proves that, in reality, it is not fixed at all but rather is at the arbitrary whim of a particular individual. Thus, the criterion for truth is not a static law in the world, but rather the caprice of a particular individual. Now, as a result of the dialectical movement of "Legal Status," the criterion for truth lies on the side of the subject. While the "in-itself" moment was portrayed in "The True Spirit," the present section, "Self-Alienated Spirit," thus represents the "for-itself" moment of the "Spirit" chapter.

This middle section of "Spirit" is divided into three distinct subsections: "The World of Self-Alienated Spirit," "The Enlightenment," and "Absolute Freedom and Terror." This accords in principle with the organizational scheme that we have been tracing, since we would expect that the three sections here would correspond to the three sections outlined in our discussion of the "Self-Consciousness" chapter with respect to the three sets of categories. However, there are two slight anomalies here which are worthy of note. First, the individual subsections are numbered with Roman numerals and not with Latin letters, differing in this respect from the format of the three subsections of "The True Spirit" and "Spirit That Is Certain of Itself," the first and the third sections, respectively, of "Spirit." Given the changes in the conception of the table of contents, this slight variation can hardly be seen as troublesome. Indeed, we must recall that the subsections of the "Consciousness" chapter are all numbered with Roman numerals as well, while "Self-Consciousness" is organized with both Roman numerals and Latin letters. In short, it is best to follow the conceptual movement, as we have been doing, and to allow that movement to dictate the correspondences without becoming too preoccupied with the changing Roman numerals and Latin letters. The second asymmetry can be found in the fact that the first and second subsections here, "The World of Self-Alienated Spirit" and "The Enlightenment," themselves contain two subsections, the status of which is somewhat unclear. Are these two independent dialectical movements? In what relation do they stand to each other? I will argue that "Self-Alienated Spirit," with its two subsections, corresponds to "The Truth of Self-Certainty," while "The Enlightenment," with its two subsections, corresponds to "Lordship and Bondage." We can represent this schematically in figure 7.2. The subsections within both of these accounts thus represent two different versions of the same general categorial movement. This is likewise not particularly troublesome, since we have already seen variations of individual Notions treated and overcome in individual sections. The only difference here is that Hegel has divided his accounts into two distinct sections, perhaps for the sake of clarity, given the fact that the sections at issue are somewhat lengthy and difficult to see in overview.

Concerning the course of world history that we have been tracing, the references in this middle section are not always entirely clear. Although the second and third sections, "The Enlightenment" and "Absolute Freedom and Terror," clearly refer to the key events of the Enlightenment in Europe in the eighteenth century and the French Revolution in 1789 up through the Reign of Terror, the subject matter of the first

Figure 7.2

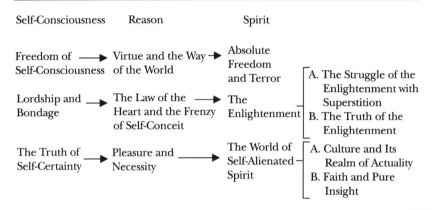

section, "The World of Self-Alienated Spirit," is far from obvious. There is, moreover, a large historical gap between the fall of the Roman world where we left off and the beginning of the Enlightenment where the next section begins. Most commentators are in agreement that the first subsection here refers to the court culture of the *ancien régime* of Louis XIV.[99] Support for this is found in Hegel's use of material from Diderot's *Nephew of Rameau*, which satirizes that culture. In a certain sense, this appears plausible, but it seems to imply that Hegel has left out the entire Medieval world from his account of world history. This would amount to a rather serious oversight of several hundred years; moreover, in his *Lectures on the Philosophy of History*, there is no such oversight, since we find therein a detailed discussion dedicated to Medieval Europe and even the Arab world. Thus, I wish to argue that, although his discussion here is intended to capture the court culture of the French kings immediately preceding the French Revolution, it is also intended as an account of the court culture of Medieval and early modern Europe that preceded it.[100] Thus, I propose to expand the current interpretation to include the earlier periods of European history following the fall of the Roman Empire. Evidence for this claim can be found in Hegel's discussion of the Reformation in the *Lectures on the Philosophy of History*, where he indicates the continuity between certain aspects of the Medieval world and early modern Europe. He states that although there were changes in certain spheres, "the entire body of private obligations and rights which had been handed down from the Middle Ages still retained validity."[101] Thus, this long time period can be treated with an account of a single Notion, due to its continuity. Although there were doubtless many important historical changes during this long, heterogeneous period, for Hegel, these are not relevant for the general Notion that is at work here. The passage just cited is taken from the section in his lectures which immediately precedes his treatment of the Enlightenment, which also constitutes the subject matter of the next section in the *Phenomenology*. As I will indicate in the course of my discussion, the claim is also supported by parallel passages in Hegel's treatment of the actual content of the Medieval world in his *Lectures on the Philosophy of History*.

I. The World of Self-Alienated Spirit (§§487–537)

Culture and Its Realm of Actuality: The Medieval and Early Modern World I (§§488–526)

As I have indicated, this subsection and the following one correspond to "The Truth of Self-Certainty" in the "Self-Consciousness" chapter. This is confirmed by a number of different passages. Just as the "I" was the fundamental category in "The Truth of Self-Certainty," where the individual tried to determine itself as individual while nonetheless denying the existence of others, so also in the present section the pure "I" plays a key role in relation to language, which is the medium in which the individual is established as an individual at this level. Hegel writes, "For it is the *real existence* of the pure self as self; in speech, self-consciousness, *qua independent separate individuality*, comes as such into existence, so that it exists *for others*. Otherwise the 'I,' this *pure* 'I,' is non-existent, is not *there*."[102] This is the analogue here at the level of Spirit to the realization in the "Self-Consciousness" chapter that "a self-consciousness exists *for a self-consciousness*."[103] Moreover, when referring to the Notion at this stage in "Spirit," Hegel uses the term "self-certainty" explicitly.[104] Thus, the categorial parallelism here is rather unproblematic.

As we have seen, this subsection represents Hegel's treatment of the Medieval world up through the Reformation. In his *Lectures on the Philosophy of History*, he discusses the conflict of the nobles with state power, which forms an important part of the content in this section of the *Phenomenology*. Hegel in his lectures points to events such as the signing of the Magna Carta as characteristic of the attempts of the nobles to curb royal power to their own advantage.[105] On the other hand, with the invention of standing armies and the old system of feudal dependency, the monarchs of Europe attempted to consolidate state power to the disadvantage of the nobles. This constitutes the historical background for the present section, which we must constantly keep in mind since, in

the course of his analysis, Hegel offers very few direct historical references
with which one might orient oneself.

The Notion: Judgment of Good and Bad (§§488–92)

We need now to examine Hegel's treatment of Medieval court culture.
The word "culture" that appears in the title of this section is the German
word *Bildung,* and in this context it is meant to indicate any of a number
of the artificial and affected customs and habits which were required
for participation in life at the court or in higher society. Culture alone
becomes the standard by which individuals are judged in this new social
order. "It is therefore through culture," Hegel writes, "that the individual
acquires standing and actuality. His true *original nature* and substance
is the alienation of himself as Spirit from his *natural* being. . . . [T]he
measure of its culture is the measure of its actuality and power."[106] For an
individual to have any social worth whatsoever, he must be attached to
the court culture, and this presupposes that he be thoroughly versed in
the diverse ceremonies and manners of the court; in short, he must be
cultured. Thus, his very being or actuality in these circles is dependent
upon his mastery of these elements of culture.

The fact that the individual must learn with patience and diligence
these customs and aspects of culture testifies to the fact that he does not
find them naturally in his own person and to this extent is alienated from
them. The world of culture amounts to a denial of the natural, since the
goal is to overcome one's natural being and rise to the realm of culture.
It is thus that we find ourselves here in the realm of "self-alienated" Spirit,
which sees itself as separated and essentially apart from the world, here
understood as the world of culture: "Although this world has come into
being through individuality, it is for self-consciousness immediately an
alienated world which has the form of a fixed and solid reality over
against it."[107] Unlike Antigone, who is immediately at home in the world
of the *polis* and the unwritten laws of the gods, self-consciousness here is
estranged from his world. In order to be anything at all, the individual
must strive to be cultured, but this attempt amounts to learning something essentially foreign to the individual's nature, and leads one to be not
merely alienated from the social order as a whole but also from oneself.

Just as the previous section began with a dichotomy between human
law and divine law which divided the ethical order in two, so also here the
world of culture is split into two principles, good and bad. Hegel indicates
this parallelism as follows: "We see that these spheres correspond to
the community and the family in the ethical world, without, however,
possessing the native Spirit peculiar to the latter."[108] Here the good and

the bad divide the world between them, and the Notion at this level of Spirit amounts to forming a judgment about them. The contrast between culture and nature, which characterizes self-alienated Spirit, gives rise to thinking in terms of dichotomies. The good and the bad are the terms of the fundamental dichotomy of this type: "Thinking fixes this difference in the most general way by the absolute antithesis of *good* and *bad* which, shunning each other, cannot in any way become one and the same."[109] Thus, the Notion at this stage is one of dualistic judgment, which amounts to ordering things under the fundamental categories of good and bad.

Hegel indicates that the experience of consciousness of this Notion of the judgment of good and bad will work through three distinct moments: "In the first sphere it [Spirit] is an implicitly universal, self-identical spiritual being; in the second it is explicitly for itself and has become inwardly divided against itself, sacrificing and abandoning itself; in the third, which as self-consciousness is subject, it possesses directly in its own self the force of fire."[110] Despite the rather abstract language here, we can recognize the stages of in-itself, for-itself, and in-and-for-itself, which are characteristic of the dialectical movement for Hegel. The beginning of the historical experience of consciousness here is indicated by a reference to the "we," i.e., the philosophical audience: "We have to consider how, in the first instance, these two members are represented within pure consciousness as thoughts, or as having only an *implicit* being; and also how they are represented in actual consciousness as having an *objective* existence."[111] Let us thus turn now to the experience of consciousness.

The Experience of Consciousness

The In-Itself Moment: State Power (§§493–97)

Hegel at first contrasts the moment at this stage of Spirit with its corresponding stage in "Self-Consciousness." At the level of pure thought, which is the level of "The Truth of Self-Certainty," the good is simply the self as independent self-consciousness: "the self-accordant, immediate, and unchangeable essence of every consciousness, the independent spiritual power of the *in-itself*."[112] The other of consciousness is then assigned the predicate "the bad" and is considered, as in "The Truth of Self-Certainty," to be unessential and something to be negated: "it is the essence that is null and invalid, the bad."[113] This was the Notion at the purely abstract level of "Self-Consciousness." Now we must see what the Notion amounts to here at the historical level, where these terms are not "*simple thoughts* of good and bad" but instead are "*actual*" historical moments.[114]

In the first moment, the good is assigned to the realm of the court and to state power in general, while the bad is thought to lie in wealth and its evils. Hegel expresses this straightforwardly as follows: "these simple *thoughts* of good and bad are likewise immediately self-alienated; they are *actual* and are present in actual consciousness as *objective* moments. Thus the first essence is *state power*, the other is *wealth*."[115] The courtiers find their identity in the state power and the realm of the court, which is the good. It is "where their separate individuality is merely a consciousness of their *universality*. . . . [I]t remains the absolute foundation and subsistence of all that they do."[116] The courtier has his true being in the state, which he serves with his noble deeds. The state is thus the universal end of the individual's actions, and in it the courtier sees himself reflected. This represents the in-itself moment, since the courtier defines himself essentially in terms of the universal, which constitutes the criterion of all truth here.

By contrast, wealth is thought to be corrupt and the source of dissipation. Wealth is the result of the labor of the individual, and although the individual gains enjoyment for it, wealth in itself is thought to be devoid of ethical value. In labor and the accumulation of wealth, the individual fails to see that he is connected with a wider social whole and thus is equally satisfying the desires of others while he satisfies his own. Instead, "each individual is quite sure that he is acting in his own interest when seeking this enjoyment; for it is in this that he becomes conscious of his own independent existence and for that reason does not take it to be something spiritual."[117] There is thus no great virtue in the accumulation of wealth. It is rather a sign of decadence and of the uninhibited pursuit of one's own private self-interest. Wealth has no essential or universal element with which one could identify oneself. It is purely individual, empty, and meaningless.

The first dialectical sublation comes as the courtier works through his conceptions of good and bad. Although he tries to see himself in the world of the court and has his identity and actuality in it, nevertheless the courtier cannot fail to recognize that this world is an artificial one from which he is in fact alienated. The court culture contradicts the courtier's true natural self. This causes an inversion in the value system: "It follows, then, that the consciousness that is in and for itself does find in the state power its simple essence and subsistence in general, but not its individuality as such; it does find there its *intrinsic* being, but not what it explicitly is *for itself*."[118] Precisely what the courtier is as an individual or as "for-itself" is overlooked and neglected in his relation to state power, which has only a universal element. Thus, the state power is not thought to be the source of self-fulfillment of the courtier, but rather it is seen as a source of oppression: "The individual, therefore, faced with this power reflects himself into himself; it is for him an oppressor and the bad; for, instead of being of like nature to itself, its nature is essentially different from that of individuality."[119] The court culture does not reflect the nature of the individual, but rather is only an artificial construct imposed on him. Thus, the individual rejects it and sees it as bad, thus inverting the original judgment.

Likewise, the status of wealth is subjected to dialectical examination and is subsequently reevaluated. In contrast to the universal aspect characterized by state power, wealth is particular and focuses on the individual, and it is precisely in this individual aspect that it has its positive side. Hegel writes, "Wealth, on the other hand, is the good; it leads to the general enjoyment, is there to be made use of, and procures for everyone the consciousness of his particular self."[120] In wealth and the pleasure derived from it, each individual becomes aware of who he truly is. Far from being the source of corruption, wealth represents the true aspect of the individual by means of which he can realize himself as an individual and gain pleasure and enjoyment. Thus, both original evaluations are reversed, and we move to the second moment.

The For-Itself Moment: Wealth (§§497–99)

In the second moment wealth is considered to be the good, while state power, as the universal oppression, is thought to be the bad. Given that wealth is particular in contrast to the universality of state power, its elevation to the level of the good in the Notion represents the for-itself moment of the dialectical movement. Now these two new judgments are in their turn the subject of dialectical analysis. First, the negative aspect of the state must be reevaluated: "the state power expresses its [consciousness's] *essence;* this power is in part the established law, and in part government and command, which regulates the particular activities within the action of the whole. . . . The individual thus finds therein his ground and essence expressed, organized, and manifested."[121] Consciousness comes to recognize that the state power represents the universal or higher aspect of the individual, in that it orders the social whole in a way that makes public life possible in the first place. It is the institution which makes virtuous public service meaningful, since only in the context of service to the state do the noble deeds of the courtier make sense. Thus, the state cannot be seen simply as a negative and oppressing force; instead, it is something much larger and fundamental than the courtier originally realized.

The positive evaluation of wealth is now reconsidered. The courtier realizes that this positive evaluation is shortsighted, since wealth can only bring about the momentary satisfaction of individual needs. Through wealth self-consciousness is able to satisfy individual desires for a time, but these desires always demand a new expenditure. In this circular movement, wealth can never gain the upper hand, since it is always finite, while desire is infinite. The individual is unable to see himself reflected in it over any extended period: "the individual, through the enjoyment of wealth, gains no experience of his universal nature, but only gets a *transitory* consciousness and enjoyment of himself *qua* single and independent individual."[122] Once again both terms must be reversed.

The In-and-For-Itself Moment: Noble Consciousness (§§500–20)

Now self-consciousness, looking back on the dialectical movement heretofore, comes to see that it has simply reversed its evaluations without result: "in the first case consciousness judges the state power to be essentially different from it, and the enjoyment of wealth to accord with its own nature; while in the second case it judges the state power to accord with its nature and the enjoyment of wealth to be essentially different from it."[123] This leads consciousness to the conclusion that, instead of the one or the other, the good must include both elements at once; it must be both wealth and state power together: "one is a relationship to the state power and wealth as to something of like nature to itself; the other as to something disparate from it."[124] Thus, this combination of the universal aspect—state power—and the particular aspect—wealth—represents the in-and-for-itself moment. This ushers in the new concept of the noble, and the new dichotomy of the noble and the ignoble consciousness.

The noble consciousness is the courtier who associates himself with both wealth and the state. First, he identifies himself with the state as his "end and absolute content."[125] The noble consciousness recognizes the authority of the state as right and august, and labors in its service. The noble consciousness furthers the ends of the state in his self-effacing virtuous service to the king:

> it adopts a negative attitude to its own ends, to its particular content and existence, and lets them vanish. This consciousness is the heroism of *service*, the *virtue* which sacrifices the single individual to the universal, thereby bringing this into existence—the *person*, one who voluntarily renounces possessions and enjoyment and acts and is effective in the interests of the ruling power.[126]

It likewise recognizes the virtues of wealth, which secure the bond between it and the court, its royal benefactor. For his service to the state power, noble consciousness receives gifts and wealth. Insofar as these are the external signs of his service and loyalty, they represent an essential aspect of the noble consciousness.

By contrast, the ignoble consciousness scorns both state power and wealth. It "sees in the sovereign power a fetter and a suppression of its own *being-for-self*, and therefore hates the ruler, obeys only with a secret malice, and is always on the point of revolt."[127] In his lectures, Hegel says, "the fidelity of vassals is not an obligation to the commonwealth, but a private one—*ipso facto* therefore subject to the sway of chance, caprice, and violence."[128] Thus, the ignoble consciousness knows no true loyalty and holds state power in contempt. Its attitude toward wealth is no different. In the enjoyment of its wealth, "it becomes conscious of itself merely as an isolated individual, conscious only of a transitory enjoyment, loving yet hating wealth."[129] Although ignoble consciousness enjoys wealth in some measure, this enjoyment makes even more clear the impoverished nature of its own existence, which gains a fleeting pleasure in it. Moreover, the relation to wealth evinces the patronizing attitude of the sovereign, who believes he can buy loyalty with trifling gifts.

The noble consciousness becomes estranged from the state power for much the same reason that the Roman citizen became estranged from the emperor. The courtier sees that state power is not grounded on any particular principle of right, but rather rests on the simple will of the individual, i.e., the king. The courtier thus becomes "the *haughty vassal*,"[130] a cynical, self-promoting servant of the state: "there was as yet no subjectivity involving unity, but only a subjectivity conditioned by a careless superficial self-seeking."[131] The courtier thus feels no genuine duty to serve the state but only does so when it appears to be in his self-interest: "The valor that now manifested itself, was displayed not on behalf of the state, but of private interests."[132] He partakes in royal counsel, being careful to rehearse pious words about "the general good,"[133] while always being certain to secure his own further advancement and to eschew genuine responsibility and truly onerous duty when possible. Hegel discusses at some length here the importance of dissembling language in creating the illusion of a monarch whose power and authority are everywhere recognized. Through the medium of language, the men of the court merely flatter and indulge the king, while constantly keeping clearly in view their own self-interest: "The heroism of silent service becomes the heroism of flattery."[134]

This dissembling leads to the sublation of the noble consciousness with respect to state power. It looks as if in his service the noble consciousness has sacrificed himself for the sake of the state, but in fact he maintains and furthers his own interests while giving the impression of pious self-denial: "While, therefore, the noble consciousness behaves as if it were *conforming* to the universal power, the truth about it is rather that in its service it retains its own being-for-self, and that in the genuine renunciation of its personality, it actually sets aside and rends in pieces the universal substance."[135] The courtier desires genuine honor for his service, but he collapses into a cynicism of self-serving flattery in which there can be no room for honor. Even when bestowed, honor is nothing but a shell, an empty word having nothing to do with true virtue. Thus, the courtier is alienated not merely from the sovereign but also from himself: "Its Spirit is a completely disparate relationship: on the one hand, in its position of honor it retains its own will; on the other hand, it gives up its will, but in so doing it in part alienates itself from its own inner nature and becomes utterly at variance with itself."[136] Thus, the noble consciousness is both alienated from the court, where he must constantly dissemble, and from himself, since he must forsake the virtue of honor by making a mockery of it, integrity no longer offering any incentive for action. Thus, the noble consciousness is transformed into the ignoble consciousness.

Now although noble consciousness is alienated from state power— one aspect of its self-conception—it still identifies itself with the wealth that it receives from the monarch. It is now to a sublation of this second aspect of the noble consciousness that Hegel turns. Noble consciousness believes that although it has become flattering and duplicitous vis-à-vis state power, it can nonetheless be the cynical beneficiary of the monarch's gifts. But this becomes problematic when the noble consciousness sees that while he depends on the monarch for his wealth, his self-conception, qua noble, is dependent on something external and contingent: "Here, however, as regards the aspect of that pure *actuality* which is its very own, viz. its own 'I,' it finds that it is outside of itself and belongs to another, finds its *personality* as such dependent on the contingent personality of another, on the accident of a moment, on a caprice, or some other utterly unimportant circumstance."[137] Noble consciousness is thus not free and independent, but rather depends on the good will of the individual monarch. Thus, he has nothing fixed when he tries to identify himself with wealth. When he receives wealth from the monarch, he "is *conscious* of not being satisfied."[138] Thus, the noble consciousness collapses and is "absolutely disrupted."[139] Once again it is transformed into its opposite— the ignoble consciousness. As Hegel says, "the distinction within its Spirit of being noble, as opposed to ignoble, falls away and both are the same."[140]

Concluding Remarks (§§521–26)

The end result of this form of historical Spirit is that noble consciousness collapses into a cynical, ironical, thoroughly self-contradictory skeptic.

Given that every Notion was transformed into its opposite—the good into the bad, the noble into the ignoble—there remains nothing firm to hold on to. In Hegel's lectures we read, "This dialectic, which unsettles all particular judgments and opinions, transmuting the evil into good and good into evil, left at last nothing remaining but the mere action of subjectivity itself, the abstractum of Spirit—*thought.*"[141] The alienated courtier becomes Diderot's nephew of Rameau, who mercilessly criticizes everything, including the senseless charade of court culture: "It exists in the universal talk and destructive judgment which strips of their significance all those moments which are supposed to count as the true being and as actual members of the whole, and is equally this nihilistic game which it plays with itself. This judging and talking is, therefore, what is true and invincible, while *it* overpowers everything."[142] But yet, the courtier nonetheless remains a part of this culture. He too plays a role in the charade of social life and is thus implicitly the victim of his own criticism. By this universal denial of the legitimacy of the entire social realm, self-consciousness itself remains indeterminate since, just as in "The Truth of Self-Certainty," it needs another in order to determine itself. Thus, just as in that section, so also here self-consciousness remains merely "the *pure 'I' itself.*"[143] Hegel continues this discussion of the pure "I" in the next subsection, "Faith and Pure Insight."

Faith and Pure Insight: The Medieval and Early Modern World II (§§527–37)

The discussion in "Faith and Pure Insight" continues the analysis of "culture" from the previous section. This is evinced by, among other things, the constant reference to "culture" that we find here. The analogue to this section is, therefore, still that of "The Truth of Self-Certainty," and thus, with respect to the category, we are still concerned with the "*pure I*"[144] or "the *self-identity* of pure consciousness."[145] Just like the "I" of "The Truth of Self-Certainty," consciousness here "seeks to abolish every kind of independence other than that of self-consciousness."[146] The historical reference here is to the end of the *ancien régime* and the Enlightenment. In this subsection, Hegel examines above all the form of religious thinking characteristic of this period. This religious thinking arises from the destruction of the noble consciousness that we saw in the previous section.

At the end of "Culture and Its Realm of Actuality," the nihilistic noble consciousness divides into two spheres, and it is here that we start in the present dialectical movement. Hegel characterizes the two aspects there as follows: "In the first case, Spirit that has come to itself has directed its gaze to the world of actuality and still has there its purpose and immediate content; but, in the other case, its gaze is in part turned only inward and negatively against it, and in part is turned away from that world towards heaven, and its object is the beyond of this world."[147] On the one hand, there is the alienated self-consciousness which Hegel refers to as "pure insight." This is the form of consciousness that, in its alienation from the court and the actual world, retreats into itself. It counts itself as the only valid criterion for truth, while it subjects everything in the actual world to merciless skepticism and criticism. It is this critical spirit that will eventually develop into the Enlightenment. Hegel describes the Notion of pure insight as follows: "objectivity has the significance of a merely negative content, a content which is reduced to a moment and returns into the self; that is to say, only the self is really the object of the self, or the object only has truth so far as it has the form of the self."[148] Pure insight is thus essentially "*negativity*, which eliminates everything objective that supposedly stands over against consciousness."[149] This concept gets its full treatment in the next section on the Enlightenment, where Hegel discusses the crusade of pure insight to universalize its critical position, operating with the maxim: "*be for yourselves* what you all are *in yourselves—reasonable.*"[150] The consciousness that escapes this world in the thought of a beyond is what Hegel refers to as "faith." It is the dialectical movement of faith which constitutes the principal object of this section.

The Notion: Faith (§§527–30)

Faith, like pure insight, is also a reaction to the alienation from the world of court culture; however, instead of retreating into the self like pure insight, the consciousness of faith retreats into a world beyond the actual. Thus, faith represents a "flight from this actuality"[151] or "from this world."[152] Faith posits God as an ontological entity in the beyond and regards that beyond as what is truly real at the expense of the actual world of court culture. For Hegel, the self-consciousness of faith belongs to the sphere of self-alienated Spirit, since it conceives of God as absolute being in another world, with which it associates itself, while it lives in the realm of actuality which is separated from the beyond: "This *pure consciousness* of absolute being is an *alienated* consciousness. . . . [T]his pure consciousness seems to have over against it only the *world* of actuality; but since it is the flight from this world and therefore has the character of an *antithesis* to it, it bears this world within itself; pure consciousness is therefore in its own self alienated from itself."[153] Thus, self-consciousness is alienated from God and from itself. The world of the beyond is essentially separated from the actual world of culture.

Hegel articulates what he means by faith by explaining that it does not dwell in the realm of the beyond conceptually or with thoughts, but rather in the form of religious "picture-thinking": "Since, however, thought is in the first instance [only] the *element* of this world, consciousness only *has* these thoughts, but as yet it does not *think* them, or is unaware that they are thoughts; they exist for consciousness in the form of *picture-thoughts*."[154] The term "picture-thinking," which plays such an important role in Hegel's philosophy of religion, is a translation of the German word *Vorstellung*, which in other contexts is usually rendered as "representation."[155] By this Hegel means to indicate that religious consciousness conceives of God and heaven primarily in terms of anthropocentric images and stories, and not philosophically or abstractly in terms of the Notion. We will have occasion to explore this distinction in more detail below in our account of the "Religion" chapter.

The dialectical experience of the Notion of faith is essentially connected with that of pure insight and is divided into three parts which Hegel clearly lays out: "First, each [faith and pure insight] is an *intrinsic being on its own account*, apart from all relationships; second, each stands in relationship with the *actual* world in an antithesis to pure consciousness; and third, each is related within pure consciousness to the other."[156] I will analyze these stages in accordance with our accustomed formula of in-itself, for-itself, and in-and-for-itself. In this subsection, Hegel is concerned above all with the sublation of faith, whereas in the next subsection he turns his attention to pure insight.

The Experience of Consciousness (§§530–37)

The In-Itself Moment: The Three Distinct Beings (§§531–33)
This first moment of faith involves the development of the conception of the Christian God. First, God is conceived as a static, eternal, absolute entity in the beyond. Then in the incarnation in Christ, God becomes man and enters into the sensible world. Finally, through his death, Christ is reunited with the absolute God of the beyond. These are, for Hegel, the three "distinct beings" of the beyond which, taken together, characterize this first moment. He describes this as follows:

> the first is the *absolute being*, Spirit that is in and for itself insofar as it is the simple eternal *substance*. But in the actualization of its Notion, in being Spirit, it passes over into *being-for-another*, its self-identity becomes an *actual*, self-*sacrificing* absolute being; it becomes a *self*, but a mortal, perishable self. Consequently, the third moment is the return of this alienated self and of the humiliated substance into their original simplicity.[157]

These three moments are considered as a whole and represented in pic-tures by the consciousness of faith: "These distinct beings, when brought back to themselves by thought, out of the flux of the actual world, are immutable eternal Spirits, whose being lies in thinking the unity which they constitute."[158] Self-consciousness takes this aggregate to be the true and the real, in contrast to the corrupt actual world of culture. But God cannot remain in the beyond. For the individual self-consciousness to have a relationship to God or the beyond, God must come into contact with the actual world or must somehow be attainable through it. If God were to remain purely otherworldly, He "would remain alien to self-consciousness."[159] In each of these three "beings" the element of the beyond is still existent in one form or another.

The For-Itself Moment: Absolute Being and Actuality (§534)

In the second moment, self-conscious recognizes that it dwells in the corrupt and hypocritical world of culture which stands in such stark contrast to the realm of the beyond. Being painfully aware of its alienation from God in each of the three forms, consciousness therefore tries to overcome the distance between itself in the corrupt, mortal world and God in the unchangeable beyond. Its effort to come into contact with God takes the form of "service and praise," which Hegel characterizes as follows: "This obedience of service and praise, by setting aside sense-knowledge and action, produces the consciousness of unity with the absolute being, though not as a unity that is actually perceived; on the contrary, this service is only the perpetual process of producing that unity, a process which does not completely attain its goal in the present."[160] Service and praise represent a process and not a fixed objective that can be fully achieved, since these acts must be constantly and interminably repeated in order to sustain the unity with God. Thus, although in service and praise one can perhaps reach into the beyond and make contact with God, so to speak, nonetheless this contact is only momentary and lapses as soon as the praising is over and the virtuous service complete. Instead, "the realm of pure thought necessarily remains a beyond of its actual world, or since this beyond, through the externalization of the eternal being, has entered the actual world, the actuality is an uncomprehended, sensuous actuality."[161]

Since God in the first instance as a God in the beyond cannot be reached, consciousness of faith tries to attain a community with Him in His sensuous form as Christ. Similarly, the attempt to reach God through the mediation of Christ is also doomed to failure. Even though in the person of Christ, God enters the world of sensuous actuality and should in principle be able to commune with other sensuous beings, nevertheless "one sensuous actuality remains indifferent to the other, and the beyond has only received the further character of remoteness in space and time."[162] Christ as a historical individual is separated from us by "space" and "time," and thus the distance between the believer and him is no less great than the original distance between the believer and God in the beyond. The gap between God and the believer thus still remains.

The In-and-For-Itself Moment: Faith in Relation to Pure Insight (§§535–37)

Finally, in the third moment faith stands in a relation to pure insight in the same consciousness, and this constitutes its true aspect. First, Hegel describes what is left over after the sublation of service and praise: "The Notion, however, the actuality of Spirit present to itself, remains in the consciousness of the believer the *inner being*, which is everything and which acts, but does not itself come forth."[163] What remains after the collapse of the effort to reach God via service and praise is the inner belief of Spirit in each individual believer, which Hegel refers to here as "the Notion." Although this inner belief is what is essential in this dialectical movement, it does not manifest itself directly. This inner conviction is the conviction of pure insight that it alone is the criterion of truth: "In *pure insight*, however, the Notion [of faith] is alone the actual; and this third aspect of faith, that of being an object for pure insight, is really the true relation in which faith here appears."[164] Thus, faith, qua inner conviction, becomes an individual self-relation, just as in "The Truth of Self-Certainty."

Pure insight has still not been worked out thoroughly at this level where it is limited to the individual or the pure "I." Hegel explains this by saying, "in the form in which the Notion of pure insight first makes it appearance, it is not yet *realized*. Accordingly, its consciousness still appears as *contingent*, as *single* and *separate*, and its essence appears for it in the form of an *end* which it has to realize."[165] The consciousness of pure insight sets as its goal the conversion of others to its own skepticism and critical thinking. Lacking this general recognition and before this Notion gains widespread acceptance, pure insight gives the impression of being simply an anarchistic radical like the nephew of Rameau. Just as in the transition from "The Truth of Self-Certainty" to "Lordship and Bondage," so also consciousness here realizes that its Notion alone has no validity without the recognition of others. In "Lordship and Bondage" each self-consciousness attempts to induce the other to accept and validate its own Notion in the hope that the result will be some form of universality based on a sort of consensus. So also here, consciousness seeks to universalize its Notion of critical thinking. The universalization of pure insight takes place in the next section, where this general worldview of scientistic skepticism becomes the intellectual movement, the Enlightenment.

Concluding Remarks

The self-identity of the self-conscious subject caused by the negating skepticism of pure insight establishes the parallelism with the analogue in the "Self-Consciousness" chapter. Pure insight ends up, just like the "I" of self-certainty, with its own "certainty of self-conscious reason that it is all truth."[166] Hegel writes,

> This last difference, however, has been effaced by the fact that in the completely disrupted state of consciousness difference changed round into an absolutely qualitative difference. There, what is for the "I" an "other" is only the "I" itself. In this infinite judgment all one-sidedness and peculiarity of the original being-for-self has been eradicated; the self knows itself *qua* pure self to be its own object.[167]

Just as formerly the individuality of self-consciousness slipped into universality in the absence of another self-consciousness as a contrasting term, so also here self-consciousness ends up "*self-identical* and universal."[168] The move to the Enlightenment and its conflict with superstition thus corresponds to the move to the "Lordship and Bondage" dialectic, and the struggle between the two self-conscious agents found there. Here at the level of Spirit, the struggle is not between individuals, but rather between two conflicting worldviews, one old and one new, which find themselves at odds with one another. In our historical survey of the Notion, we have thus reached the Enlightenment of eighteenth-century Europe.

II. The Enlightenment (§§538–81)

The Struggle of the Enlightenment with Superstition (§§541–73)

This section contains, as the title indicates, Hegel's well-known discussion of the Enlightenment, and thus the historical reference in this section is unproblematic. Here, pure insight from the previous section becomes universalized and embodied in the spirit of empirical science and Enlightenment reason.[169] Hegel outlines the development of the Enlightenment in two subsections, "The Struggle of the Enlightenment with Superstition" and "The Truth of Enlightenment," both of which correspond to this same general Notion and both of which treat the same historical period. At the categorial level, this section corresponds to the "Lordship and Bondage" dialectic of "Self-Consciousness." Just as the lord and the bondsman determined their own identity in the struggle with one another, so also here at the level of Spirit, the Enlightenment and established religion determine themselves vis-à-vis one another. Not only does Hegel describe the conflict here, just as in "Lordship and Bondage," as "a violent struggle,"[170] but also he makes clear the connection with that section when he writes, "Further, since what is object for me is that in which I recognize myself, I am for myself at the same time in that object in the form of *another* self-consciousness."[171] Here he indicates the fundamental importance of the notion of recognition between two self-conscious agents, just as was the case in the "Lordship and Bondage" section.

The transition from the previous section to the present one can be characterized in terms of pure insight's attempt to overcome its arbitrariness and the contingency of its individuality with a move to universality. Its goal is that "the individual judgment" be "resolved into the universal insight."[172] As an individual skeptic and cynic, pure consciousness can put forth only judgments with contingent force, but in order to be valid, its judgments must be recognized by others. Pure insight must make critical thinking and skepticism a general methodology for everyone:

> Since this language is that of a distracted mind, and the pronouncement only some twaddle uttered on the spur of the moment, which is again quickly forgotten, and exists as a whole only for a third consciousness, this latter can only be distinguished as *pure* insight if it brings these scattered traits into a general picture and then makes them into an insight for everyone.[173]

Pure insight takes on universal scope in its struggle with religion and superstition. It sees that even religion implicitly accepts many of its basic premises. Pure insight exploits this contradiction by constantly highlighting the inconsistent conclusions that religion draws while it tries to hold on at once to a certain rationalistic framework and at the same time to its religious belief. In dialectical interaction with religion, pure insight creates and solidifies its own self-identity as an intellectual movement: "This struggle with its antithesis, therefore, also has the significance of being the *actualization* of insight."[174]

The Notion: Faith and the Enlightenment (§§541–51)

What we know as "pure insight" from the previous section becomes here the historical movement, the Enlightenment. The fundamental idea of this movement is that the individual alone with the faculty of reason is the ultimate standard of judgment: "for pure insight is born of the substance, knows the pure *self* of consciousness to be absolute."[175] Hegel characterizes this in another passage as follows: "we have found that it is not the groups and the specific Notions and individualities that are the essence of this actuality, but that this has its substance and support solely in the Spirit which exists *qua* judging and discussing."[176] In his lectures, Hegel describes the Notion of the Enlightenment as follows: "The absolute criterion—taking the place of all authority based on religious belief and positive laws of right (especially political right)— is the verdict passed by Spirit itself on the character of that which is to be believed or obeyed."[177] This emphasis on the individual brings the Enlightenment into conflict with the established religious order or "faith," as Hegel calls it, which sees man as only one part of a much larger system. For faith, it is not man who is absolute but rather God. These two positions constitute the antagonistic poles in this dialectical movement. Hegel characterizes the difference between faith and pure insight by saying, "the essence is for faith [mere] *thought*, not *Notion*, and is therefore the sheer opposite of *self*-consciousness, whereas for pure insight the essence is the *self*."[178] The truth for faith is its thought of God posited in picture-thinking in the beyond. This is diametrically opposed to the criterion for truth of pure insight, which is the individual.

The Enlightenment regards faith as its opposite. Not only is religion thought to be wrong in itself, "to be a tissue of superstitions, prejudices, and errors,"[179] but also it is seen as an insidious entity that operates through the agency of a corrupt class of priests in legion with despotic rulers. It deceives and manipulates the general mass of people to its own advantage. Superstition is propagated by three different social units, which the Enlightenment views as its enemies: first, the ignorant mass of people; second, the corrupt and hypocritical priests; and third, the self-serving despots.[180] Of these three, it is the general mass of people which pure insight hopes to convert. The Enlightenment believes that, unlike the other two groups, the general mass of people does not have an evil will; instead, it has simply been deceived and misled into accepting superstitions. But this group can be enlightened and shown the error of its ways, since every individual is, the Enlightenment believes, implicitly rational. There exists "the *Notion* of rational self-consciousness which has its existence in the general mass but is not yet present there *qua*

Notion."[181] The goal of the Enlightenment is to awaken this dormant rationality in the mass of people in order to combat superstition.

Although Hegel has often been caricatured as an archrationalist, in this section he shows clearly that he is aware of the limitations of Enlightenment reason and of its distortions of religious doctrine.[182] Hegel describes in provocative terms the manner in which pure insight insinuates its way into the Spirit of the naive religious thinking of the masses. As we shall see, according to Hegel's analysis, faith tacitly comes to accept some of the fundamental principles of the Enlightenment, which in the final analysis prove to be contradictory when juxtaposed to traditional religious doctrine. Hegel portrays how these principles subtly and insidiously find their way into the thinking of religious consciousness. He writes,

> It is on this account that the communication of pure insight is comparable to a silent expansion or to the *diffusion*, say, of a perfume in the unresisting atmosphere. It is a penetrating infection which does not make itself noticeable beforehand as something opposed to the indifferent element into which it insinuates itself, and therefore cannot be warded off. Only when the infection has become widespread is that consciousness, which unheedingly yielded to its influence, *aware of it*.[183]

Here he uses two metaphors for reason: a perfume and an infection. Like a perfume, pure insight works its way initially unimpaired into the ways of thinking and acting that form the matrix of ethical life. Religion is simply a part of the passive and "unresisting atmosphere" which reason interpenetrates, since the former does not perceive the imminent danger that rationality presents to its most dearly held beliefs and institutions. But gradually reason, like a perfume, diffuses itself silently and insidiously into all aspects of culture.

Hegel then changes the metaphor from that of a benign diffusion of perfume in space to the clearly negative image of an infection. According to this metaphor, Spirit is conceived as an organic system which is attacked from the inside by a deleterious force, i.e., a cancerous disease. But this disease is latent and goes long undetected by spiritual doctors, and when the illness is finally detected, the disaster and the lasting damage therefrom have already taken place:

> Consequently, when consciousness does become aware of pure insight, the latter is already widespread; the struggle against it betrays the fact that infection has occurred. The struggle is too late, and every remedy adopted only aggravates the disease, for it has laid hold of the marrow of

spiritual life, viz. the Notion of consciousness, or the pure essence itself of consciousness. Therefore, too, there is no power in consciousness which could overcome the disease.[184]

Just as self-awareness comes about only after the original sin, so also awareness of the destructive nature of reason comes only after the damage has already been done. Here the remedies to save religion from the onslaught of reason are ineffectual, since religion attempts to defend itself using the very tools of reason, thus giving away the game from the start. Religion attempts to justify itself with rational argumentation and scientistic reason in order to show that it can hold up under the test of this scientistic rationality, yet this betrays that the attempt at defense or treatment has come about entirely too late, since even the defenders of religion have already unknowingly come to accept as their standard the basics of Enlightenment rationality, its methodology and its criteria for truth. Thus, the disease is only aggravated: far from erecting an effective defense, the defenders of religion unknowingly ally themselves with the enemy. By using reason as its standard, religion destroys itself, since at its heart are mystery and revelation, which are by their very nature irreducible to logical categories and rational explanation. Reason has by this time so permeated our way of thinking that we cannot imagine anything else as a viable option. As Hegel puts it, reason "has laid hold of the marrow of spiritual life." Thus, the spiritual life of religion cannot be rescued, since it has become unable to defend itself, being so infected by the foreign principle of thought. Reason here is clearly portrayed as something subtle, insidious, and destructive, and this account stands squarely in opposition to the myth of Hegel's unqualified advocation of reason. Thus, these passages indicate clearly that Hegel was not a naive *Aufklärer* or optimist who believed in the unqualified positive force of reason. We must now turn to the experience of consciousness and examine in its details the dialectical struggle of the two sides, the Enlightenment and religion.

The Experience of Consciousness

The In-Itself Moment: Faith's Negative Understanding of the Enlightenment (§§551–56)

The structure of the experience of consciousness here is one of the most complex in the entire book, and at the same time one of the most systematically sound. The analysis will consist of the usual three moments, each of which will in turn consist of three further phases. Hegel begins the first of these in his accustomed manner by addressing the philosophical audience: "Let us see further how faith experiences the Enlightenment in the *different* moments of its own consciousness, to which the view mentioned above referred to only generally."[185] Thus, the first moment will be religion's negative assessment of the Enlightenment's criticisms. As I have indicated, this dialectical movement is itself divided, typically enough, into three stages, which Hegel signals at the beginning of his analysis when he writes, "These moments are: pure thought or, as object, *absolute being* in and for itself; then its relation—as a knowing—to absolute being, the *ground of its belief;* and lastly, its relation to absolute being in its acts, or its *worship* and *service.*"[186] These three stages will be repeated in each of the following two moments as well.

Absolute Being (§§552–53). For the disabused, empirical way of thinking of pure insight, all talk of God amounts in the final analysis to the simple thought of the individual projected into the beyond. God exists only in the mind of the believer, and there can be no talk of any independent ontological existence: "Pure insight adopts a negative attitude to the absolute being of the believing consciousness. This being is pure *thought,* and pure thought posited within itself as an object or as *essence.*"[187] For the believer, on the other hand, God is no mere mental fiction, but rather one comes upon God as an independently existing entity: "in the believing consciousness, this *intrinsic being* of thought acquires at the same time for consciousness that is *for itself,* the form—but only the empty form—of objectivity; it has the character of something presented to consciousness."[188] Faith thus rejects the Enlightenment's psychologistic analysis of its belief in God, seeing God as an independently existing ontological entity.

The Enlightenment mistakenly interprets all of the objects of faith in terms of its own materialistic categories, thus largely missing the point of religious belief. For pure insight, the Eucharist, for example, is simply a material object, a piece of dough, with no further significance. This, however, is clearly not what belief understands by the Eucharist and the ceremony associated with it. Hegel writes of the Enlightenment, "in apprehending the object of faith as insight's own object, it already does faith a wrong. For it is saying that the absolute being of faith is a piece of stone, a block of wood, which has eyes and sees not, or again, a piece of dough which, having come from the field is transformed by man and returned to earth again."[189] This interpretation of religion by pure insight is, of course, a distortion of religious belief, since the objects in question—the Eucharist or the bones of the saints—are supposed to be more than simply any ordinary material stuff. They are supposed to be invested with some higher spiritual power. Thus, the "Enlightenment is completely in the wrong when it imputes this view to faith. What faith reveres, it certainly does not regard as stone or wood or dough, nor any other kind of temporal, sensuous thing."[190] Simply because the Enlightenment sees such objects as devoid of spiritual properties and to be mere matter, it does not follow that this is in fact the case or that belief views such objects in the same way. In short, the Enlightenment begs the question in this regard.

The Ground of Belief (§554). With the move to the second aspect, we now turn to the believer's understanding of the existence of God or "the absolute being," as Hegel says. This involves above all the question of how faith grounds its belief. Once again the pure insight of the Enlightenment misconstrues the nature of religious faith by interpreting it in terms of its own categories:

> it falsely charges religious belief with basing its certainty on some *particular historical evidences* which, considered as historical evidences, would certainly not guarantee the degree of certainty about their content which is given by newspaper accounts of any happening—further, that its certainty rests on the accidental *preservation* of these evidences; on the one hand, the preservation by means of paper, and on the other hand, by the skill and honesty of their transference from one piece of paper to another, and lastly, on the *correct interpretation* of the meaning of dead words and letters.[191]

For pure insight, all belief must be grounded in hard empirical evidence, and it imposes this standard on religious faith, mistakenly thinking that the believer grounds his belief on what he perceives to be solid historical evidence about Christ's life or on the rigor of the philological record which transmits his words and teachings through the ages. The Enlightenment demonstrates the many problems with the historical record and points out that this sort of evidence in no way justifies the belief that religious consciousness holds. This is, of course, a misunderstanding of religious belief, which appeals to no such evidence in support of itself. Here Hegel anticipates many of Kierkegaard's criticisms in the *Concluding Unscientific Postscript*, by showing clearly that he is sensitive to the inward nature of belief that Kierkegaard insisted on. "Faith, in its certainty," Hegel writes, "is an unsophisticated relationship to its absolute object, a pure knowing of it which does not mix up letters, paper, and copyists in its consciousness of absolute being, and does not bring itself into relation with it by means of things of that kind."[192] Once again the Enlightenment unjustly imposes its own standards of truth and verification on religious consciousness. Such standards may be entirely appropriate when we are dealing with empirical phenomena, but they make little sense when we are concerned with the supersensible realm of religion.

The Relation of Absolute Being to the Individual: Action (§§555–56). Finally, we reach the third aspect, which Hegel unambiguously notes as follows: "There still remains the third side, *the relation to absolute being of conscious-ness* as *action.*"[193] This third aspect concerns the Enlightenment's criticism of various religious practices aimed at leading a moral life. It is through righteous action that the believing consciousness tries to overcome its individuality and become united with God. The Enlightenment focuses on the disparity between the means and the ends of faith's action. In principle, the Enlightenment shares with faith the end of leading a better moral and spiritual life, but it has nothing but scorn for the means that faith employs to reach this end. The Enlightenment criticizes, for example, the abstention and poverty that it sees believing consciousness practicing: "the purpose of showing oneself to be free of pleasure and possession is not served by denying oneself pleasure and giving away a possession."[194] For the Enlightenment, the actions of religious conscious-ness are simply insufficient and even incongruent with the end that they are supposed to serve. But what this criticism seems to amount to is that any honest, well-intentioned means will be insufficient for the ends of an upright moral life. Thus, Hegel characterizes pure insight as a deception here in its criticism of faith:

> it . . . affirms as a pure intention the necessity of rising above natural existence . . . only it finds it foolish and wrong that this elevation should be demonstrated *by deeds*; in other words, this pure insight is in truth a deception, which feigns and demands an *inner* elevation, but declares that it is superfluous, foolish, and even wrong to be *in earnest* about it, to put this elevation into *actual practice* and *demonstrate its truth.*[195]

Once again the Enlightenment shows its sophistry, this time by at once acknowledging the ends of faith to be good while at the same time denying faith all possible means of actually attaining it.

The For-Itself Moment: The Positive Truth of the Enlightenment (§§557–59)

After having examined the negative side of the Enlightenment as faith perceived it, we now turn to its positive side to see if it fares any better. Hegel marks this transition by writing, the Enlightenment "at first ap-peared as a negative reality. Perhaps its *positive reality* is better constituted.

Let us see how things stand with this."[196] We need now to learn what positive truth the Enlightenment will offer to replace religion that it tries to destroy. Here we work through the same three stages as before, namely, being, the ground of belief, and the relation of the absolute to the individual, but this time under the aspect of the positive side of the Enlightenment.

Absolute Being (§557).   As we have seen, the Enlightenment criticizes faith's superstitious belief in an anthropomorphic God in the realm of the beyond. This conception of absolute being in picture-thinking has, for the Enlightenment, no independent reality, but rather is simply a fiction of faith's own making. The Enlightenment claims that all descriptions of God are ultimately subject to distorted anthropomorphic picture-thinking. Thus, it assumes a deistic position, claiming that God is simply our way of referring to the abstract concept of the infinite or absolute being. It is simply the empty *Être suprême.* The positive doctrine of the Enlightenment in this regard is, therefore, that there is an infinite vacuum which cannot be further described or articulated without falling into the superstition of picture-thinking: "The attribution of predicates to such a vacuum would be in itself reprehensible; and it is just in such a union that the monstrosities of superstition have been produced."[197] In this way, the Enlightenment clearly separates the finite realm, where its own empirical rationality is operative, from the realm of the infinite about which one can say nothing. This move gains Hegel's approbation, since he sees in it a much more dignified conception of God than that presented by faith and superstition: "To let nothing of that sort appertain to absolute being or be attributed to it, this is the prudent behavior of Reason, or pure insight, which knows how to put itself and its finite riches in their proper place, and how to deal with the Absolute in a worthy manner."[198]

Ground of Belief (§558).   The Enlightenment, begging the question as we saw, criticized the unfounded nature of religious belief in terms of its own model of truth. For the Enlightenment, empirical science is the only form of truth which has any validity, and this constitutes its second positive aspect. Hegel compares the Enlightenment's Notion of truth with that of "Sense-Certainty," which also concentrated on the empirical or on "*things of sense.*"[199] Here he indicates that, although the Enlightenment shares this empirical element with "Sense-Certainty," it is not immediate, but rather here in "Spirit" it is a whole methodology of scientific enquiry. Unlike faith, which is alienated from its object, the Enlightenment knows sensible objects to be its own, qua the objects of examination: "the positive truth of sense-certainty is in its own self the *immediate* being-for-self of the Notion itself *qua* object, and that too in the form of otherness."[200] This connection with other objects marks an improvement over faith's conception of an absolute being in a beyond from which it is eternally separated. The Enlightenment thus overcomes religion's alienation from its object.

The Relation of Absolute Being to the Individual: Utility (§§559–62). As we have come to expect from previous dialectical movements, this third stage will unite the first two: "Lastly, the third moment of the *truth of Enlightenment* is the relation of the individual being to absolute being, is the relation between the first two moments."[201] Here we examine the Enlightenment's conception of the relation of absolute being to the finite world of objects. These two realms as opposites mutually determine each other. The sensuous, finite world is what it is in contrast to the nonsensuous, infinite beyond. Each term has a self-identical positive relation to itself and a negative relation to the opposite term, and it is in this dialectical relation that both are determined: "The sensuous is therefore now related *positively* to the Absolute as to the *in-itself*, and sensuous reality is itself an *intrinsic being;* the Absolute makes it, fosters and cherishes it. Then, again, it is related to the Absolute as an opposite, as to its own *non-being;* in this relationship it is not anything in itself, but exists only for an 'other.' "[202] It is from this dialectical movement of identity and difference that the third positive truth of the Enlightenment arises, namely the concept of utility.

Both as in themselves and for another, objects are useful, and this is their essence for Enlightenment reason: "Different things are useful to one another in different ways; but all things are mutually serviceable through their own nature."[203] Thus, all objects, including human beings and religion itself, are interpreted and evaluated in terms of their utility, which is recognized as the lone standard of evaluation. The world was made for the use and enjoyment of human beings, and thus the objects of the world are all good and positive to some degree. This evaluation of objects naturally secularizes the world and robs everything spiritual of its mystical element, and it is this which belief cannot countenance. Faith cannot accept these positive aspects of the Enlightenment any more than the Enlightenment can accept the criticisms it received at the hands of belief.

The In-and-For-Itself Moment: The Contradictions of Belief (§§563–69)

Now we arrive at the point at the level of Spirit where the "Lordship and Bondage" dialectic left off at the level of "Self-Consciousness," namely with two opposing truth-claims neither of which can ultimately gain the upper hand: "two equal rights of Spirit could be left confronting each other, neither being capable of satisfying the other."[204] In this final moment, the Enlightenment points out the elements of Enlightenment reason that are hidden in certain aspects of belief's Notion. By bringing these into view and comparing them with other aspects of faith's Notion, the Enlightenment is able to generate contradictions that even belief itself must concede. The result of this final experience of consciousness is the ultimate capitulation of faith in the face of the criticisms of the Enlightenment. Although the point of this third moment is essentially to expose the contradictions of belief, Hegel nevertheless points out the one-sided nature of the Enlightenment's criticism as well, since it is the Enlightenment's Notion that will be the subject of dialectical scrutiny in the next section.

Absolute Being (§§566–67). There is an internal contradiction on the side of faith with regard to its conception of God. The question at issue is whether or not God has an independent ontological existence apart from human beings and their conceptions of Him. Hegel describes the perspective of faith as follows:

> To faith, its absolute being, while it is possessed of *intrinsic being* for the believer, is also at the same time not like an alien thing which is just *found* in him, no one knowing how and whence it came. On the contrary, the faith of the believer consists just in his *finding* himself as *this* particular personal consciousness in the absolute being, and his obedience and service consist in producing, through his own *activity*, that being as *his own* absolute being.[205]

On the one hand, the believer asserts that God exists on his own, independent of the believer, i.e., that God has "*intrinsic being.*" But, on the other hand, faith also grants that God exists only and essentially in relation to the believer. It is through the believer's service and activity that the essential relation to God is established, and this service and activity are domiciled clearly on the side of the belief. This inconsistency is pointed out by the Enlightenment, which constantly underlines the mundane side of God while firmly denying the ontological existence of the otherworldly side.

The Enlightenment's claim that spiritual objects such as the Eucharist, the cross, or the bones of the saints are merely material objects must also be in part granted by faith. The reason for this is that faith maintains a dualistic ontology that involves a conception of God in the beyond and the believer in the mundane sphere. It must grant that these objects, insofar as they constitute a part of the mundane sphere, are in fact merely material objects as pure insight asserts. Whatever spiritual properties they may possess, they are also physical objects. Once again the Enlightenment must merely remind faith of this, since faith itself "does not bring together these two thoughts of absolute being."[206]

Ground of Belief (§568). Faith is also caught up in contradictions with regard to the foundation of its belief. On the one hand, it claims to have immediate knowledge of God in its belief, and it affirms the absolute belief that is required of it. Yet, at the same time it concedes that it is but a finite, contingent consciousness with only partial knowledge. Hegel describes this contradiction as follows:

> Faith itself acknowledges a contingent knowledge; for it has a relationship to contingent things, and absolute being itself exists for faith in the form of a pictorial representation of a common reality. Consequently, the believing consciousness, too, is a certainty which does not possess the truth within itself, and it confesses itself to be such an unessential consciousness, to be of *this* world and separated from the Spirit that is certain of itself and self-authenticated. But it forgets this moment in its immediate spiritual knowledge of absolute being.[207]

Consciousness seems both to know and not to know, to be certain of God, but to acknowledge its own uncertainty and limitation. Once again it is the Enlightenment which reminds faith of this inconsistency, concentrating only on the contingent aspect of the believer.

The Relation of Absolute Being to the Individual: Action (§§569–71). Faith's pious action is no less fraught with contradictions than its previous moments. It practices a kind of poverty and denies itself the enjoyment of certain kinds of pleasures while at the same time maintaining others. Thus, "retention occurs *along with* sacrifice."[208] For this reason there is no true sacrifice, or what is performed has only outward or symbolic value. The Enlightenment sees the contradiction at work in this very conception of pious action: "Enlightenment finds it inept to throw away *one* possession in order to know and to prove that one is liberated from *all* possessions, to deny oneself *one* enjoyment in order to know and to prove that one is liberated from all enjoyment."[209] There is a clear mistake in thinking at work here in faith's understanding of the meaning of its own action. These actions can in no way be seen as a mastery of passions. The individual deeds fall far short of the universal principle that is allegedly being advanced.

Concluding Remarks (§§572–73)

This marks the end of faith's Notion, since even the believer is compelled to acknowledge the internal contradictions in it. Faith must recognize the aspects of Enlightenment reason that are implicit in its own way of thinking. The believing consciousness seems always to be operating with two different standards—one, the standard of picture-thinking native to itself, and the other, the standard of empirical perception of the Enlightenment: "faith lives in two sorts of non-*notional* perceptions, the one of the perceptions of the *slumbering* consciousness which lives purely in non-notional thoughts, the other those of the *waking* consciousness which lives solely in the world of sense."[210] The Enlightenment thus serves to wake up naive faith and to expose the fallacies of its picture-thinking for what they are as judged against the criterion of hard-headed empirical perception.

Faith, having been deprived of its content and its belief in a beyond, collapses into the same Notion as the Enlightenment. It too is now left with nothing more than a conception of "an Absolute without predicates, an Absolute unknown and unknowable."[211] But understandably this leaves faith unsatisfied, since this Notion has nothing of the richness and beauty of picture-thinking. Thus, faith becomes the "unsatisfied Enlightenment" in contrast to the "satisfied Enlightenment," which does not require anything more than an empty Absolute, since it never took picture-thinking seriously in the first place. We have now to see in the next section if the Enlightenment can remain satisfied and can sustain itself in this satisfaction.

Hegel uses the Biblical image of the serpent to describe the status of reason after the capitulation of religion. For the disabused *Aufklärer*, religion remains but a hollow husk lacking any substantial meaning and alive only in memory and in history books: "Memory alone then still preserves the dead form of Spirit's previous shape as a vanished history, vanished one knows not how. And the new serpent of wisdom raised on high for adoration has in this way painlessly cast merely a withered skin."[212] Here reason frees itself of religion and superstition just as the serpent sheds its skin. Religion is merely a dead form of Spirit that falls away when it is no longer of use. This image suggests that in fact religion and reason are in a sense the same thing, i.e., the same serpent with a new form. This new form of religion then simply replaces the old form, and its fallacies will be exposed in the next section.

The Truth of Enlightenment (§§574–81)

In this second section Hegel continues the analysis that he began in the previous section, and for this reason he forgoes any introductory discussion here. At this point the Enlightenment is no longer confronted with an external opposing principle since, as we have seen, faith has already capitulated in the face of numerous contradictions. Instead, the principle of negation arises within the Enlightenment itself, which now breaks up into two internally conflicting strains that consciousness tries to hold together. Thus, instead of a conflict between two opposing worldviews, what we see here is a factional debate between two different strands of the same basic Notion represented by the Enlightenment. At the level of the category, we are, as in the previous section, still concerned with a section which forms an analogue to the "Lordship and Bondage" dialectic, and which operates with the categories of identity and difference and thinghood as in "Perception."

The Notion: Absolute Being as the Pure Thing (§§574–75)

Now that the Enlightenment has banished faith entirely and has done away with all superstitious conceptions of the beyond, it creates a new worldview based solely on the here and now, the world of sense perception and empirical science. This is the way in which the Enlightenment "actualizes itself."[213] The world now, in the absence of any mystical or otherworldly entities, consists simply of absolute being in the empirical sphere alone, without any reference to a beyond. Hegel characterizes this as "the pure thing," recalling the corresponding Notion of thinghood from the "Perception" section of the "Consciousness" chapter. Here he introduces this empirical conception of objectivity as follows: "there has come into being the *pure thing*, the absolute being, that has no further determination whatever."[214] The object sphere is simply the empirical other of consciousness, which is the object of scientific investigation. This pure thing is the object of both Enlightenment empiricism and of what remains of religious consciousness's Notion.

Despite this mundane conception of objectivity, the Enlightenment is, however, no less self-alienated in its Notion than was faith. Although the Enlightenment has eliminated the abstract beyond, it still sees the absolute being of this world as a foreign other. It fails to recognize that it has posited this conception of being as a Notion and therefore is related to it. It thus fails to see the implicit unity of its thought with the being of the universe, and for this reason it remains self-alienated: "The self-alienated Notion . . . does not, however, recognize this *identical* essence of the two sides—the movement of self-consciousness and of its absolute being."[215] As a result, even though the supersensible other and the beyond have been eliminated, "absolute being has value for it only in the form of a beyond standing over against it."[216] In the experience of consciousness, two different interpretations of the relation to the object try to come to terms with this division.

The Experience of Consciousness

The In-Itself Moment: The Beyond of Consciousness (§576)
The Enlightenment now divides into two different interpretations of the conception of absolute being, and this begins the experience of consciousness. According to the first interpretation, absolute being is considered to be simply an object of thought: "Pure absolute being is only in pure thought, or rather it is pure thought itself, and therefore utterly *beyond* the finite, *beyond self*-consciousness, and is only being in a negative sense."[217] Here the world of being is simply an abstraction from or negation of self-consciousness. It is the other of consciousness, or, as Hegel says, "one party of the Enlightenment calls absolute being that predicateless Absolute which exists in thought beyond the actual consciousness which formed the starting-point."[218] This interpretation begins with consciousness or "pure thinking" and, by abstracting from it, arrives at a conception of being. As we shall see, the second interpretation, moves in just the opposite direction, starting with being and working its way to thought.

The negative other of thought is, however, nothing more than a simple abstraction. Ultimately, it is related to a subject that does the abstracting, and thus it is not wholly other: "But in this way, it is just [mere] *being*, the negative of self-consciousness. As the *negative* of self-consciousness it is *also* related to it."[219] Moreover, this thought is not purely thought, since it is related to matter from which it was abstracted. Hegel explains this as follows: "it is an *external being* which, related to self-consciousness within which differences and determination fall, receives within it the differences of being tasted, seen, etc.; and the relationship is that of *sense*-certainty and perception."[220] We would not be able to think this abstract concept of the other of consciousness if we did not first have the empirical relation to objects, since it is from this empirical relation that the concept is abstracted. We know the concept only because we find various empirical relations in us. In short, thought has its origin in sense. Thus, in the final analysis the conception of the other as thought reduces to a conception of pure matter.

The For-Itself Moment: Matter (§577)
For the other faction of the Enlightenment, the world represented by absolute being is simply matter. This conception of matter is derived from perception, which constitutes this Notion's starting point; in fact, this

Notion amounts to an abstraction from the distinct modes of perception. Hegel describes this as follows: "If we start from this *sensuous* being into which that negative beyond necessarily passes, but abstract from these specific ways in which consciousness is related to it, then what remains is pure *matter* as a listless, aimless movement to and fro within itself. . . . [P]*ure matter* is merely what is *left over* when we *abstract* from seeing, feeling, tasting, etc."[221] This interpretation insists on the empirical aspect of the object and does not recognize the role played by thought. Matter is fundamentally the unity of an object with a set of empirical properties.

But what consciousness fails to see is that once we abstract from all of our ways of perceiving the object, there is nothing left but a unity posited in thought, and thus we can no longer talk of an empirical entity, which in fact does not evince unity, but rather must consider the unified object an object of thought: "Matter is rather a *pure abstraction;* and so what we are presented with here is the *pure essence of thought,* or pure thought itself as the Absolute, which contains no differences, is indeterminate and devoid of predicates."[222] When we can think away the different modalities of perception, we end up with an equally abstract conception of the object as matter. Since consciousness has abstracted from all modes of perception, its Notion ultimately amounts to a mere thought. Here sense perception is changed into thoughts. Both factions of the Enlightenment see absolute being as something other and fail to recognize themselves in it.

The In-and-For-Itself Moment: Utility (§§578–80)

These two interpretations ultimately amount to the same thing, although they begin with entirely different starting points—the first with pure thought and the second with sense perception. The first interpretation fails to see that its Notion of the negative other of consciousness amounts to pure matter in the final analysis:

> For to the one, absolute being is in its pure thinking, or is immediately for pure consciousness, is outside finite consciousness, the *negative* beyond of it. If it would reflect, firstly, that the simple immediacy of thought is nothing else but *pure being,* and secondly, that what is *negative* for consciousness is at the same time related to it . . . it would come to see that this beyond, characterized as something existing *externally,* stands in a relation to consciousness and is thus the same as what is called *pure matter.*[223]

In the dialectical movement here, Hegel shows that consciousness's abstract thought ultimately reduces to empirical matter. This thought is not truly an external other, but rather is, like empirical perception, necessarily related to the knowing subject who must abstract from the empirical sphere in order to arrive at this Notion. Thus, this Notion ultimately has its origin in the empirical sphere of matter. In just the opposite movement, the second interpretation, although beginning with sense perception, ends up with the abstract concept of a negative other of thought:

> The other Enlightenment starts from sensuous being, then *abstracts* from the sensuous relation of tasting, seeing, etc., and makes that being into a pure *in-itself*, into an *absolute matter*, into what is neither felt nor tasted. This being has in this way become something simple and without predicates, the essence of *pure consciousness*; it is the pure Notion as *implicitly* existent, or *pure thought within itself.* This insight does not consciously take the reverse step from what *is*, what *simply* is, to what is thought, which is the same as what *simply* is, does not take the step from the pure positive to the pure negative.[224]

The movement here is from matter to thought. Once we have abstracted from all empirical relations to the object, there is nothing left but the thought of the object behind the empirical properties.

The first interpretation begins with pure thought and moves to a conception of being or matter. The second begins with empirical being and moves to a conception of pure thought. Thus, these two interpretations represent the mirror image of each other. Both are one-sided and fail to see the ultimate unity of being and thought. Hegel writes,

> they have not arrived at the Notion found in Descartes' metaphysics, that being and thought are, *in themselves*, the same; they have not arrived at the thought that being, *pure* being, is not something *concretely real* but a *pure abstraction*, and conversely, pure thought, self-identity or essence, partly is the *negative* of self-consciousness and therefore *being*, partly, as immediately simple, is likewise nothing else but being; *thought* is *thinghood*, or *thinghood* is *thought.*[225]

For Hegel there is ultimately no conceptual difference here in the two conceptions. It makes little difference whether one regards absolute being from the side of matter or from the side of thought. Each interpretation insists on one side of the dichotomy without acknowledging its opposite.

As we have come to expect, the final moment unites the first two moments, in this case the two strains of the Enlightenment: "the two ways of considering it [essence] merge into one."[226] The two different interpretations of the objective world are here united in the concept of utility. With the concept of utility, being and thought finally come together. On the one hand, the object is no longer pure being, but is related to the thought of the individual who makes use of it. The object of utility is thus an object seen in terms of the specific thoughts and purposes of the individual: "it is absolutely *for an other*."[227] On the other hand, it is not pure thought, since it is also an object in itself: "What is useful, is something with an enduring being in itself, or a thing."[228] The object retains its in-itself moment and can never be ultimately reduced to the ends of the subject. Thus, the object of utility displays both aspects—thought and matter.

It is only in the concept of utility that the Enlightenment overcomes the alienation from the object sphere and sees itself in the object: "it is in utility that pure insight achieves its realization and has itself for its *object*, an object which it now no longer repudiates and which, too, no longer has for it the value of the void or the pure beyond."[229] The object as something useful clearly stands in relation to the human subject for whom it is useful. The Enlightenment sees in the object sphere tools ready to be appropriated for its own end and use. Objects are already endowed with human meaning and function. Thus, this Notion replaces the conception of an object as an alien, indifferent other.

Concluding Remarks (§581)

In the final paragraph of this section, Hegel briefly summarizes the ground covered so far in the now completed first two phases of "Self-Alienated Spirit." In this review, he clearly makes reference to the corresponding sections of the "Self-Consciousness" chapter. For instance, he writes, "The first world of Spirit is the widespread realm of its self-dispersed existence and of the self-*certainty* of its individual forms."[230] The "first world," to which Hegel makes reference here, is "The World of Self-Alienated Spirit," which, as we have seen, corresponds at the historical level to "The Truth of Self-Certainty." Hegel continues, "The second world . . . is the realm of *intrinsic being* or *truth* over against that certainty."[231] This refers to "The Enlightenment," which, in its struggle with religion, tries to establish a universal truth recognized by all parties, which thus transcends individual certainty. As we have seen, this corresponds to the "Lordship and Bondage" dialectic. Now we arrive at the third and final phase, Hegel's treatment of the French Revolution, and his development of the concept of utility. As we will see, this will, predictably enough, correspond to "Stoicism, Skepticism, and the Unhappy Consciousness" and will operate at the level of abstract understanding.

At the end of the present section, self-consciousness overcomes otherness and comes via the concept of utility to recognize itself in objects for the first time. Hegel describes this as the culmination of what has come before: "What is thus lacking is obtained in utility, insofar as pure insight there acquires positive objectivity; pure insight is thereby an actual consciousness satisfied within itself. This objectivity now constitutes its *world*; it has become the truth of the entire preceding world, of the ideal, as well as of the real, world."[232] Now that the entire objective sphere is interpreted in terms of utility, a radical change in worldview comes about, and humanity sees itself in the object sphere at large in terms of its thought and intentions. In his lectures, Hegel describes the earth-shaking impact of this realization of Spirit:

> Never since the sun had stood in the firmament and the planets revolved around him had it been perceived that man's existence centers in his head, i.e. in thought, inspired by which he builds up the world of reality. Anaxagoras had been the first to say that νοῦς governs the world; but not until now had man advanced to the recognition of the principle that thought ought to govern spiritual reality. This was accordingly a glorious mental dawn.[233]

For the first time, world-historical Spirit recognizes the unity of itself and the world. We now see this played out historically in the notion of utility in the French Revolution, for it is there that "the Enlightenment will taste the fruits of its deeds."[234]

III. The French Revolution and the Reign of Terror (§§582–95)

Hegel's political philosophy has been highly disputed for any number of different reasons. Some commentators locate him on the far left of the political spectrum, emphasizing his role as the most important forerunner of Marx and Engels. By contrast, other commentators view him as a hopeless reactionary and regard the *Philosophy of Right* as a defense and theoretical justification of the Restoration and, specifically, of the repressive Prussian state. Hegel's appraisal of the French Revolution has often been seen as one of the central points of contention in this debate. The French Revolution took place while Hegel was a student at the theological seminary in Tübingen, and at that time he along with his fellow students welcomed and in a sense idolized the events that were taking place in Paris. Yet, with the transformation of the Revolution into the Reign of Terror, it appears that Hegel modified his views somewhat, although he never entirely abandoned the basic ideals of the Revolution and seems to have remained a firm advocate of the Napoleonic order throughout his life. The issue of Hegel's relation to the French Revolution has attracted some of the most famous Hegel commentators and has produced a rich body of literature.[235] The analysis of the French Revolution here in the *Phenomenology* is quite naturally of importance for this debate, since the work was written during a relatively uncontroversial time in his career, i.e., after the youthful excesses of Tübingen, yet before the Berlin period when Hegel was in the employ of the Prussian government.

For our purposes, Hegel's discussion here is primarily of importance for its role in the systematic interpretation of world history that we have been surveying. This section brings to a close his discussion of "Culture" and the Enlightenment and, according to our scheme, corresponds to "Stoicism, Skepticism, and the Unhappy Consciousness" in the "Self-Consciousness" chapter. The idea of absolute freedom, which constitutes the Notion here, is a new version of freedom that originated in "The Freedom of Self-Consciousness."[236] In accordance with the higher level of sophistication of the dialectical movement at this point, freedom here is not the freedom of the individual, as in the "Self-Consciousness" chapter, but rather of Spirit. At the categorial level we are concerned here with ground and appearance or with an abstract conception of the general will in contrast to concrete individuals. This dialectical movement thus operates in the realm of abstract understanding. Hegel confirms this in his treatment of the French Revolution in *Lectures on the Philosophy of History*, where he says the following of the principle of freedom and equality which, for him, characterizes the period: "That principle remains formal, because it originated with abstract thought—with the understanding, which is primarily the self-consciousness of pure reason, and as direct is abstract."[237] Thus, in this section both the historical reference and the categorial analogue are unproblematic.

The Notion: Absolute Freedom and the General Will (§§582–84)

At the beginning of Hegel's conceptual account of the French Revolution, he makes clear the transition from the previous section by telling us that there is a move from objectivity to subjectivity in the Notion of utility discussed above. In the previous section, the useful object was still first and foremost an object. Here, however, the subject comes to see itself as playing the primary role in the Notion of utility; now the useful is "directly nothing else but the self of consciousness."[238] Hegel expresses this somewhat more opaquely as follows: "of the *being-in-and-for-itself* of the useful *qua* object, consciousness recognizes that its *being-in-itself* is essentially a *being-for-an-other;* being-in-itself, as *devoid of self,* is in truth a passive self, of that which is a self for another self."[239] It is human beings and their interests which determine a given object ontologically as something useful. Thus, the object in itself is not what is important; on the contrary, it is the human subject which plays the essential role in the relationship, for without human beings there would be nothing for which an object could be useful. Thus, there is no separation between the subject of the Enlightenment and the object, since the object is simply synonymous with the goals, abilities, etc., of the subject. The subject sees only itself reflected in the object.

But since we are at the level of Spirit and not mere self-consciousness, this subject is not conceived as an individual subject, but rather as the universal subject, Spirit. Hegel writes,

> But the *being-for-self* into which being-for-an-other returns, i.e. the self, is not a self belonging exclusively to what is called object and distinct from the "I"; for consciousness, *qua* pure insight, is not a *single* self which could be confronted by the object as equally having a self of its own, but is pure Notion, the gazing of the self into the self, the absolute seeing of *itself* doubled; the certainty of itself is the universal subject, and its conscious Notion is the essence of all actuality.[240]

It is thus a universal subject, Spirit, which sees itself not in the individual object but rather in the object sphere in general and is thus no longer separated from it. There is no longer something essential or other located in a beyond in the way the transcendent God, for the consciousness of faith, was supposed to embody the universal will earlier. For self-conscious Spirit at this point, God is merely a projection of human reason, and Spirit sees the world, including the entire social order, as itself and as a result of its own activity. This is, for Hegel, a new insight and principle upon which the French revolutionaries tried to build an entirely rational state.[241] Social institutions are not things handed down mysteriously from above, but rather are merely the creations of human beings. Things such as social classes and the legitimacy of monarchy do not have their grounding in the natural order of the universe; instead, they are artificial and created by particular humans to serve specific human ends. Thus, institutions and societies can be consciously changed by the agency of human beings.

The insight that Spirit sees itself in the object sphere and in the world has as its result that Spirit knows itself to be absolutely free. In the object sphere there is nothing alien which could hinder Spirit from pursuing its goals and ideals and from effecting social change in accordance with them. In acting in the world, Spirit is not acting on something foreign or other, but rather is merely communing with itself. "Spirit," Hegel writes, "thus comes before us as *absolute freedom*. It is self-consciousness which grasps the fact that its certainty of itself is the essence of all the spiritual 'masses,' or spheres, of the real as well as of the supersensible world, or conversely, that essence and actuality are consciousness' knowledge of *itself*."[242] This conception of a universal subject that sees itself as absolutely free is what, for Hegel, characterizes the actual event of the French Revolution: "This withdrawal from the form of objectivity of the useful has, however, already taken place in principle and from this inner revolution there emerges the actual revolution of the actual world, the new shape of consciousness, *absolute freedom*."[243] For the first time in world history, Spirit sees itself in the object sphere and as perfectly free, but only in France does this insight get translated directly into action with world-historical repercussions.

The absolutely free Spirit must determine itself by means of its universal will. The Notion of a universal self-conscious subject which represents the will of all corresponds to Rousseau's notion of the "general will" or the *volonté générale* in *The Social Contract*.[244] The general will represents the rational will of each and every individual in a society which always aims at the good of society as a whole. Hegel writes, "It is conscious of its pure personality and therein of all spiritual reality, and all reality is solely spiritual; the world is for it simply its own will, and this is a general will. And what is more, this will is not the empty thought of will which consists in silent assent, or assent by a representative, but a real general will, the will of all *individuals* as such."[245] The general will has the power to reshape society according to rational principles in the face of the irrationality of history, custom, and religion.[246] It is also aware of its own power to destroy antiquated customs and institutions and to replace them with new ones based on just and rational principles. This self-awareness is the conviction and self-certainty of the French revolutionary.

The Experience of Consciousness (§§585–95)

The In-Itself Moment: The Abstract Universal Will (§§585–88)

The Notion of the general will is at first a mere abstract conception of a universal will. It is the rational will and the good for all in principle. This abstract thinking of the revolutionary does not recognize the traditional forms of life that separated individuals into specific groups with specific interests: "In this absolute freedom, therefore, all social groups or classes which are the spiritual spheres into which the whole is articulated are abolished."[247] Now, since the estates and classes have been done away with, the individual no longer sees himself and his interests represented by his specific class or social station; instead, all individuals see themselves in an overarching general will or universal consciousness, which encompasses all people in all classes: "the individual consciousness that belonged to any such sphere, and willed and fulfilled itself in it, has put aside its limitation; its purpose is the general purpose, its language universal laws, its work the universal work."[248] The general will is not internally divided, since it recognizes no distinctions or classes among the citizenry. It is thus simple self-identity without any moment of difference or distinction. The universal will is the rational will of each individual, and any difference between the two is only an illusory one.[249] In theory, the universal will is thus immediately consciousness' own: "in passing over into action and in creating objectivity, it is doing nothing individual, but carrying out the laws and functions of the state."[250] At this theoretical level, there is a reciprocal movement back and forth with no difference in content. There is "the immanent movement of universal self-consciousness as a reciprocity of self-consciousness in the form of *universality* and of *personal* consciousness."[251] The universal will manifests itself in the individual, and the individual sees itself in the universal will.

This universal will, however, cannot remain abstract. As an abstract universal in the realm of the ideas, it remains impotent: "It follows from this that it cannot achieve anything positive, either universal works of language or of reality, either of laws and general institutions of *conscious* freedom, or of deeds and works of a freedom that *wills* them."[252] In order to become meaningful and to have a real content, it must become real. Only with specific actions and with the agency of the individual does it enter the realm of existence. We now move from the abstract theoretical relation characterized by the transparent harmony of the individual with the general will to the realm of praxis. To be efficacious, the general will must be reflected in the concrete actions of the individual.

The For-Itself Moment: The Abstract Will Becomes Actual in the Individual (§§588–90)

The universal will must take on a concrete form for it to be actual in the world. In order to act, the universal will must have the agency of an individual at its disposal. Only through a particular individual can the universal will be transformed into concrete actions. "Before the universal can perform a deed," Hegel writes, "it must concentrate itself into the One of individuality and put at the head an individual self-consciousness; for the universal will is only an *actual* will in a self, which is a One."[253] It is the revolutionary who embodies in his person and actions the abstract general will. The revolutionary at first destroys antiquated institutions and then tries to erect new ones, thus giving the general will a concrete form. In these new institutions the general will finds its objective manifestation: "The work which *conscious* freedom might accomplish would consist in that freedom, *qua universal* substance, making itself into an *object* and into an *enduring being*."[254] Now the universal will has a specific organ in reality, which executes its commands and thus makes it real. In the action of the revolutionary, the universal will makes "itself into an *existent* substance."[255]

The individual revolutionary, however, qua individual, cannot be an adequate incarnation of the general will. Precisely by becoming real and thus individual, the universal will necessarily loses its universal character: "when placed in the element of *being*, personality would have the significance of a specific personality; it would cease to be in truth universal self-consciousness."[256] Thus, alienation is introduced for the first time between particular individuals and the universal will as a result of the fact that the universal will has become real. Now not every individual can necessarily see himself reflected in the universal will. Since the universal will is manifested in a single will, this means ipso facto that "all other individuals are excluded from the entirety of this deed and have only a limited share in it."[257] The universal will, since it is abstract and lacks content, becomes simply the arbitrary action and caprice of the individual who claims to represent it. For Hegel, the natural result of this caprice is blind destruction. In the end, it is on his own initiative that the revolutionary destroys individuals and antiquated institutions while claiming all the while that he is acting in the name of the lofty, yet altogether empty, ideal of the general will: "Now that it has completed the destruction of the actual organization of the world, and exists now just for itself, this is its sole object, an object that no longer has any content, possession, existence, or outer extension, but is merely this knowledge of itself as an absolutely pure and free individual self."[258] In the absence of any positive content from the side of the general will, the revolutionary's actions are simply blind and destructive. Such actions, lacking any deeper meaning, do little more than affirm the revolutionary's absolute freedom.

We now have the two poles of universality and particularity, which are represented by these first two moments. Hegel describes these as follows: "it [consciousness] divides itself into extremes equally abstract, into a simple, inflexible cold universality, and into the discrete, absolute hard rigidity and self-willed atomism of actual self-consciousness."[259] On the one hand, the universal will remains an indifferent universality lacking positive meaning. On the other hand, the revolutionary is a concrete individual, but is also capricious since his actions are not governed by any general principles. These two extremes come together in a third moment. According to Hegel's metaphor from logic, the third moment represents the "middle term" of the syllogism: "The relation, then, of these two, since each exists indivisibly and absolutely for itself, and thus cannot dispose of a middle term which would link them together, is one of wholly *unmediated* pure negation, a negation, moreover of the individual as a being *existing* in the universal."[260] This third term or connecting link between the arbitrary individual and the abstract general will is the government.

The In-and-For-Itself Moment: The Revolutionary Government (§§591–95)

The two previous moments are united in the form of the revolutionary government, which brings together the moments of universality and particularity. The government is, on the one hand, a universal term, since it represents the will of all the people. Contrary to the famous statement of Louis XIV, no one individual is the government. In principle, it stands for the rational good of society as a whole. But at the same time the government is a concrete institution, which executes concrete, individual actions. It has particular individuals in its service who execute its will. The government is thus both universal and particular: "The government is itself nothing else but the self-established focus, or the individuality, of the universal will."[261] The government in a sense takes the place of the individual revolutionary as the agent which transforms the universal commands of the general will into real actions.

But the revolutionary government suffers the same fate as the individual revolutionary and ultimately proves to be insufficient as a mediating force. The revolutionary government claims to represent the general will, but this is still an empty abstraction lacking content, and for this reason the government, in the final analysis, represents only itself and remains a mere particular. As a particular, it excludes other particulars, and by excluding other particulars, it can no longer lay claim to universal validity deriving from the general will: "it excludes all other individuals from its act, and on the other hand, it thereby constitutes itself a government that is a specific will, and so stands opposed to the universal will."[262] In the absence of a true universality, the government, like the individual revolutionary previously, remains a particular and amounts to a mere faction: "consequently, it is absolutely impossible for it to exhibit itself as anything else but a *faction*. What is called government is merely the *victorious* faction, and in the very fact of its being a faction lies the direct necessity of its overthrow."[263] The revolutionary government that rests its claim to power on the abstract general will that it purportedly represents ultimately is supported only by its own force of arms. The government thus necessarily collapses into a repressive state which must negate everything else. In the *Philosophy of Right*, Hegel characterizes this as follows:

> For instance, during the Terror in the French Revolution all differences of talent and authority were supposed to have been superseded. This period was an upheaval, an agitation, an irreconcilable hatred of everything particular. Since fanaticism wills an abstraction only, nothing articulated, it follows that, when distinctions appear, it finds them antagonistic to its own indeterminacy and annuls them. For this reason, the French revolutionaries destroyed once more the institutions which they had made themselves, since any institution whatever is antagonistic to the abstract self-consciousness of equality.[264]

Absolute freedom thus proves to be an abstract concept devoid of content, which leads to terror and destruction. The principle at work is merely negation or "the *terror* of death."[265] For Hegel, the Reign of Terror was no historical accident, but rather a necessary result of the abstract Notion of freedom. Because the general will is abstract, everything that is real and concrete seems ipso facto to oppose it. Every existent institution thus must be destroyed since it is hostile to the abstract idea represented by the general will.

Concluding Remarks

From the failure of the abstract general will, consciousness now tries to rework the variables in its conceptual scheme in order to constitute a new form of World Spirit. The general will in the abstract, when conceived as the essential term, proved to be empty of content, and so now consciousness conceives of itself as the essential, thus making its own will into the general will: "What vanishes for it in that experience is abstract *being* or the immediacy of that insubstantial point, and this vanished immediacy is the universal will itself which it now knows itself to be insofar as it is a pure knowing or pure will. Consequently, it knows that will to be itself, and knows itself to be essential being."[266] The emphasis now shifts from the abstract universal to the particular individual. Now "the *universal will* is its *pure knowing and willing* and *it* is the universal will *qua* this pure knowing and willing."[267] This is the Notion of the final section of "Spirit," which treats different forms of moral consciousness that result from the conceptual chaos of the French Revolution.

C. Spirit That Is Certain of Itself: German Romanticism (§§596–671)

General Introduction (§§596–98)

This final section of "Spirit" is somewhat problematic, since at first glance it does not seem to portray specific periods of history as in the previous sections of this chapter. In other words, in the "Spirit" chapter up until now we have seen a fairly straightforward account of Western history, beginning with the Greeks and working through the French Revolution and the Reign of Terror; however, it is not clear that Hegel continues his historical narrative in this final section, since the historical period per se is by no means easy to identify. Hegel sheds some light on the transition here from the second to the third part of "Spirit" in his *Lectures on the Philosophy of History*. There he says that the ideal of freedom achieved in the Enlightenment took different forms in the different countries and developed in different ways: "Among the Germans this view assumed no other form than that of tranquil theory; but the French wished to give it practical effect."[268] As we saw in the previous discussion, the ideal of absolute freedom which arose from the Enlightenment constituted the Notion for the French revolutionary. This Notion was immediately translated into political action in the French Revolution; however, it also manifested itself in other ways. Although there was no corresponding political revolution in Germany, nonetheless the German states could not help becoming a part of the Spirit of the Enlightenment. The Notion of absolute freedom did not find any direct political manifestation in Germany for reasons which Hegel discusses in *Lectures on the Philosophy of History*, but nevertheless this Notion of Spirit was very much alive in the cultural life of the German states. It found its embodiment in the movement of German romanticism, which involved some of the most celebrated names in the history of German letters. This form of Spirit represents not just well-known examples of romantic literature, but rather the whole constellation of activities and beliefs characteristic of this period, e.g., philosophy, ethics, religion, art, etc. Thus, Hegel does in fact have a concrete historical period in mind here, namely, the period in Germany from the French Revolution up until the composition of the *Phenomenology*. Now the same Notion of absolute freedom seen before in the French Revolution is taken up again and followed through its various mutations in this context. Here Hegel describes the content of this section as follows: "It [Spirit] is absolutely free in that it knows its freedom, and just this knowledge is its substance and purpose and its sole content."[269]

With respect to the structure of the "Spirit" chapter as a whole, Hegel makes clear that this third section brings together the two previous ones, i.e., "The True Spirit" and "Self-Alienated Spirit." In "The True Spirit," historical Spirit saw the truth in the object sphere, i.e., in the customs and traditions of its own culture. It thus immediately identified itself with the social whole. Then, in the next section, "Self-Alienated Spirit," estrangement set in, and the truth was thought not to be in tradition or custom but rather in the disabused, enlightened individual. In this final section, these two moments of subject and object come together at the level of Spirit: "Here, then, knowledge appears at last to have become completely identical with its truth; for its truth is this very knowledge and any antithesis between the two sides has vanished, vanished not only *for us* or *in itself*, but for self-consciousness itself."[270] As we shall see, the unity of the two spheres takes many different forms in the course of the dialectical movement here.

I. The Moral View of the World (§§599–615)

The first section of "Spirit That Is Certain of Itself" is devoted to a criticism of the basic principles of Kant's moral theory. The absolute moral duty or the categorical imperative and the so-called postulates of practical reason are here put to the rigorous test of Hegel's dialectic. Although the context might at first seem puzzling, this discussion forms a smooth and natural transition from the previous analysis of the French Revolution when we consider how strongly Kant was influenced by Rousseau and how similar Kant's moral law and Rousseau's general will are. The location of this analysis at the end of the "Spirit" chapter indicates Hegel's understanding of Kant's theory in the context of this world-historical period. It is not that the Kantian theory was, in Hegel's eyes, so influential that it became a historical figure in its own right, but rather it constituted one part of a larger historical movement. In *Lectures on the Philosophy of History*, Hegel writes, "the same principle [sc. of freedom] obtained speculative recognition in Germany, in the *Kantian* philosophy."[271] In other words, Kant's philosophy gave philosophical expression to this historical movement. Thus, what is examined here in this section is not an abstract theory of morality per se, but rather the actual form of historical Spirit which follows the French Revolution. The period in question is that of early German romanticism.[272]

This section, qua the first of three analyses, contains as its category pure being. But this being is neither the being of the in-itself of the object nor the being of the for-itself of the subject but rather being-in-and-for-itself. The Notion here involves the unity of the moral and the natural spheres. Thus, the category of being is neither on the subjective side of morality nor on the objective side of nature but rather in their unity. The unity of morality and nature is "thought of in the form of *being* that is not yet actual—a necessity not of the *Notion qua* Notion, but of *being*."[273] In this third section, "Spirit That Is Certain of Itself," all three of the categories—being, the one and the many, ground and consequence—will, of course, be interpreted as a unity of subject and object as was the case in the third section of "Reason."

The Notion: Duty and the Moral World (§§599–600)

At the end of the analysis of the French Revolution, it was seen how the Notion of the general will collapsed and how the individual came to see himself as the essential in the moral sphere. This is where we begin in "The Moral View of the World." Here it is moral duty which plays the key role: "Self-consciousness knows duty to be the absolute essence. It is bound only by duty, and this substance is its own pure consciousness, for which duty cannot receive the form of something alien."[274] The moral law is what all rational agents would will if they were not influenced by unworthy natural inclinations. The content of the moral law is the good per se: "For the subjective will, the good and the good alone is the essential, and the subjective will has value and dignity only in so far as its insight and intention accord with the good."[275] To act in accordance with the moral law is consciousness' greatest task, and to perform an action out of duty for the moral law is the primary characteristic of moral life. Morality is duty to the moral law for duty's sake and not in the hope of some other reward beyond moral action itself: "Since duty is thus abstract and universal in character, it should be done for duty's sake."[276] Consciousness sees the moral law and the duty which it enjoins as a manifestation of its own will, just as earlier its will was synonymous with the general will. Thus, consciousness' relation to the moral law and to duty is not the relation of a subject to an object, but rather consciousness is "locked up within itself."[277]

Hegel then derives what he calls "the moral view of the world" from the concept of duty. Since moral consciousness is bound up only in its relation to the abstract moral law, it has no essential relation to the empirical world. The world of nature is regarded as an inessential other without meaning for the moral consciousness. Only the moral law is real and essential, and the natural world plays no meaningful role in the moral sphere. Hegel defines the former as follows:

> From this determination is developed a moral view of the world which
> consists in the relation between the absoluteness of morality and the
> absoluteness of nature. This relation is based, on the one hand, on the
> complete *indifference* and independence of nature towards moral purposes
> and activity, and, on the other hand, on the consciousness of duty alone
> as the essential fact, and of nature as completely devoid of independence
> and essential being.[278]

The moral view of the world is thus that view which sees moral action as
the highest of all human activities and thus fundamentally interprets the
world in moral categories. In the moral world, the realm of nature has
a minimal role, since it does not lend itself to interpretation of this sort.
On the contrary, it is considered something indifferent and inessential
to the true world, which is represented by the moral sphere.

It is in this realm where the unity of subject and object takes place.
We are no longer concerned with an unreflective individual immediately
united with the social whole (as in "The True Spirit") or with a radical
revolutionary or social critic wholly alienated from it (as in "Self-Alienated
Spirit"); rather, here these two moments come together, as is typical of the
content of each of the third sections. Here this unity is characterized as
the harmony of the objective sphere of nature and the subjective sphere
of morality. Here the moral sphere is the highest realm, and the natural
world is an inessential other in harmony with it. Put differently, the world
is viewed as an entity with a moral teleology. The moral view of the world
is characterized by this belief in the unity of nature and morality. We now
turn to see how this Notion develops in experience.

The Experience of Consciousness (§§601–9)

The In-Itself Moment: The First Postulate—the Unity of Nature and Morality (§§601–2)

In accordance with the Notion, consciousness believes in the existence of
the abstract moral law or "pure duty." But moral consciousness observes
empirically that the world of nature is indifferent to the moral law. It sees
that sometimes the evil are rewarded and the good punished. It observes
that strict adherence to the moral law does not seem in every case to lead
to happiness.[279] Sometimes morally righteous individuals suffer unjustly.
Thus, there seems to be an incoherence between nature and morality,
which the moral consciousness must reconcile. Moral consciousness must
actualize its abstract duty in the real world, but this becomes problematic
if nature and the empirical world are indifferent or even hostile to moral

action. Morality offers no incentive, since it is by no means clear that it will lead to a happy life. The solution to this dilemma is to postulate the harmony of the moral and the natural world. In other words, since the harmony of the two spheres cannot be observed empirically, it must be presupposed or postulated in thought: "The harmony of morality and nature—or, since nature comes into account only in so far as consciousness experiences its unity with it—the harmony of morality and happiness, is *thought of* as something that necessarily *is*, i.e. it is *postulated*."[280] Here Hegel clearly refers to Kant's doctrine of the postulates of practical reason. In the *Critique of Practical Reason*, Kant explains this as follows: "From this solution . . . it follows that in practical principles a natural and necessary connection between the consciousness of morality and the expectation of proportionate happiness as its consequence may be thought at least possible, though it is by no means known or understood."[281] According to Kant's view, the harmony of the two spheres, although by no means an empirically established fact, must nevertheless be a postulate of practical reason. Although we cannot demonstrate the harmony of morality and nature metaphysically, due to the limits of human reason, we must postulate it in order for the moral world to make sense: "it is . . . a demand of reason, or an immediate certainty and presupposition of reason."[282] The unity of nature and morality is thus the first postulate.

This postulate of practical reason remains only an abstract idea lacking reality. It lacks actuality, since it is not an object of possible experience. Instead, it is only "the *thought* of actuality."[283] The happiness that this unity of nature and morality promises to the virtuous moral consciousness is not an actual happiness of this world but rather an abstract idea. Likewise, the harmony itself is an idea which moral consciousness can never personally experience. In the *Encyclopaedia Logic*, Hegel describes this as follows: "The harmony is then described as merely subjective, something which merely ought to be, and which at the same time is not real—a mere article of faith, possessing a subjective certainty, but without truth, or that objectivity which is proper to the Idea."[284] This harmony of the moral and the natural spheres in thought alone remains unsatisfying, due to its abstract and unreal nature.

The For-Itself Moment: The Second Postulate—the Unity of Desire and Duty (§§603–4)

Since, for moral consciousness, nature must ultimately be in harmony with the moral universe and happiness must naturally be in accordance with a moral life, it follows that the individual impulses and desires that stem from nature must also be in alignment with the moral law. But once again, empirically the individual moral subject experiences just the opposite. As "a contingent and natural existence,"[285] moral consciousness finds within himself drives and desires which lead him away from the moral law.[286] There is empirically a "conflict between reason and sensuousness"[287] in the concrete individual consciousness. Since the unity of desire and morality is not at hand empirically, it too must be postulated; thus, this constitutes the second postulate. This conflict is thought to be overcome when the moral consciousness masters nature and renounces its desires in order to act in accordance with the moral law. This is the unity of the moral and the natural spheres, which constitutes true morality, since only this combination of *actual* drives and inclinations with *abstract* duty would constitute a real moral act: "Only such a unity is *actual* morality, for in it is contained the antithesis whereby the self is consciousness, or first is an actual self in fact, and at the same time a universal."[288] But upon closer examination, there is no genuine unity or mediation here, since the natural desires are simply discarded and considered morally worthless. The true and the real is the aspect of abstract duty: "Since, of the two moments of the antithesis, sensuousness is sheer *otherness*, or the negative, while, on the other hand, the pure thought of duty is the essence, no element of which can be given up, it seems that the resultant unity can only be brought about by getting rid of sensuousness."[289] But without the natural, sensuous element, morality remains abstract, and there is no actuality and no moral action.

Moral consciousness must now try to come up with a Notion in which the natural desires are not discarded as morally meaningless, but instead have moral value in their attaining harmony with the moral law. It must then try to unify the two and to purify its natural desires such that they fall in line with the abstract moral law. This can only be done by patient education of the natural inclinations. The natural drives and desires must be cultivated such that they spontaneously accord with the moral law. Kant explains,

> In [the] will . . . the complete fitness of intentions to the moral law is the supreme condition of the highest good. . . . But complete fitness of the will to the moral law is holiness which is a perfection of which no rational being in the world of sense is at any time capable. But since it is required as practically necessary, it can be found only in an endless progress to that complete fitness.[290]

The process of training the drives is a tedious one, which in principle never ends. One is forever on the way to purifying the desires without ever reaching the goal of a perfectly harmonious will: "The consummation, therefore, cannot be attained, but is to be thought of merely as an *absolute* task, i.e. one which simply remains a task."[291] Even if morality is conceived as a task to be accomplished, since the harmony of the desires and morality is eternally postponed, the task can in principle never be achieved. Thus, morality is perpetually deferred and postponed into the infinite future. In the *Encyclopaedia Logic*, Hegel writes,

> This contradiction may seem to be disguised by adjourning the realization of the Idea to a future, to a *time* when the Idea will also be. But a sensuous condition like time is the reverse of reconciliation of the discrepancy; and an infinite progression—which is the corresponding image adopted by the understanding—on the very face of it only repeats and re-enacts the contradiction.[292]

This postponement of morality is tantamount to an admission that there is no unity in moral action itself, and that this harmony exists only in thought: "But, in that harmony, *morality qua* consciousness, i.e. its *actuality*, vanishes, just as in the moral consciousness, or in the *actuality* of morality, the *harmony* vanishes."[293] The logical result is that there is in fact no real instance of moral action, and it is impossible for any particular existent agent to be moral. These two points represent the irreconcilable contradictions at this point of abstract morality.[294]

The In-and-For-Itself Moment: The Third Postulate—God as Lawgiver (§§605–9)

Now the first two postulates come together in the third moment. The first postulate represents the unity of the objective world of nature with morality, and thus it represents the in-itself moment. The second postulate concerns the subjective consciousness and the unity of his impulses with morality, and thus it represents the for-itself moment with its emphasis on the subject. Now these two moments are united in a third:

> The first postulate was the harmony of morality and objective nature, the final purpose of the *world;* the other, the harmony of morality and the sensuous will, the final purpose of *self-consciousness* as such. The first, then, is a harmony in the form of an *implicit* being, the other, in the form of *being-for-self.* But what connects, as middle term, these postulated two extreme final purposes is the movement of *actual* conduct itself.[295]

We now examine the unity of the subject and the object in moral action itself which, according to Hegel's syllogism, forms the middle term between the two spheres. This middle term thus represents the in-and-for-itself moment in this unity. Hegel says, "The postulates arising from this now contain the harmonies both in and for themselves, whereas previously they were postulated only as separate, one being *in itself* or implicit and the other being *for itself* or explicit."[296]

Moral consciousness is now confronted with a concrete moral situation in the empirical world. Each moral situation is a complex entity full of relations and situated in a many-sided context. This complexity stands opposed to the abstract moral consciousness, which knows only the abstract moral law: "The moral consciousness as the *simple knowing* and *willing* of pure duty is, in the doing of it, brought into relation with the object that stands in contrast to its simplicity, into relation with the actuality of the complex case, and thereby has a complex moral *relationship* with it."[297] From these various moral situations various moral laws must be drawn upon, each of which is appropriate to an individual case: "Here arise, in relation to content, the *many* laws generally, and in relation to form, the contradictory powers of the knowing consciousness and of non-conscious."[298]

But this situation creates a contradiction. In principle there is only a single moral law and a single absolute moral duty, yet in the realm of actuality there appear several moral laws in accordance with the plurality of moral situations. On the one hand, only the abstract single moral law seems to be the essential, while the plurality of maxims remains inessential: "In the first place, as regard the *many* duties, the moral consciousness in general heeds only the *pure duty* in them; the many duties *qua* manifold are *specific* and therefore as such have nothing sacred about them for the moral consciousness."[299] Thus, morality stands on the side of abstraction, and concrete actuality seems to be devoid of moral content. But this moral law, qua abstract, remains empty without particular content provided by particular duties. The abstract moral law lacks the aspect of actuality: "At the same time, however, being *necessary*, since the Notion of 'doing' implies a complex actuality and therefore a complex moral relation to it, these many duties must be regarded as possessing an intrinsic being of their own."[300] Moral consciousness thus faces the contradiction involved in the split between actual and theoretical morality. It needs the plurality of moral laws in order to be actual, yet precisely this plurality of laws contradicts the singularity of the one true moral law. Moral consciousness thus searches for a way to bring the actual and the theoretical together.

In order to resolve this contradiction, consciousness must separate these two moments into two different moral agents. On the one hand, moral consciousness itself takes responsibility for the plurality of moral laws in the sphere of the actual. On the other hand, the essentiality and reality of these moral laws and their unity with *the* moral law must be found in another consciousness: "since they can exist only in a moral *consciousness*, they exist at the same time in another consciousness than that for which only pure duty *qua* pure duty possesses an intrinsic being of its own and is sacred."[301] Thus, another self-consciousness is posited to ensure the reality and moral sanctity of the plurality of moral duties: "it is postulated that it is *another* consciousness which makes them sacred, or which knows and wills them as duties."[302] This other consciousness is, of course, God, as Hegel makes clear in the *Encyclopaedia Logic*:

> The universality moulded by reason, and described as the absolute and final end or the good, would be realized in the world, and realized moreover by means of a third thing, the power which proposes this end as well as realizes it—that is, God. Thus in him, who is the absolute truth, those oppositions of universal and [particular], subjective and objective, are solved and explained to be neither self-subsistent nor true.[303]

While man with his finite cognitive capacities cannot know the unity of the plurality of moral laws with *the* moral law or the ultimate unity of nature and morality, God, who created the universe with a specific purpose in mind, knows this harmony. It is ultimately God, as "master and ruler of the world, who brings about the harmony of morality and happiness, and at the same time sanctifies duties in their multiplicity."[304] This third moment unites the previous two by bringing together the universal moral law with the plurality of particular duties: "This consciousness is consequently one in which universal and particular are simply one."[305] The unity found in God thus represents the in-and-for-itself moment here.

But by positing these individual duties in another consciousness, the moral agent has robbed himself once again of the possibility of moral action. The aspect of actuality is no longer in moral consciousness: "In the actual 'doing,' however, consciousness behaves as this particular self, as completely individual; it is directed towards reality as such, and has this for its purpose, for it wills to achieve something. Duty in general thus falls outside of it into another being, which is consciousness and the sacred law-giver of pure duty."[306] The absolute duty lies with God and not with the actual moral consciousness. This solution proves to be contradictory, since the moral consciousness can only act in accordance with the plurality of inessential moral laws and not with the essential single moral law, which resides in the realm of the divine. Consciousness thus knows itself "as the *imperfect* moral consciousness."[307] The moral view is still unable to bring together the abstract moral law with actuality.

Ultimately, morality reduces to a mere thought, since it cannot be translated into the realm of actuality and into particular moral laws by the moral consciousness. Morality can be found only in the divine sphere which lies beyond actuality. The unity of morality and nature is only a thought in God's mind which human reason can never attain: "But though its actuality is imperfect, all the same its *pure* will and knowledge hold duty to be what is essential. In the Notion, therefore, so far as the Notion is contrasted with reality, or in thought, it *is* perfect. But the absolute being is just this being that is *thought*, a being that is postulated *beyond* reality."[308] The whole idea of morality on this view is reduced to an absurdity. The moral law maintains its sublime status but at the cost of its never being able to enter the actual world. Morality remains a mere idea with no empirical manifestation.

Concluding Remarks (§§610–15)

The split between the abstract moral law and actuality proves to be overpowering for this level of Spirit. In the end there is nothing left of consciousness' moral law or duty which is tangible. Hegel indicates the end of this dialectical movement with the following summary of the previous movements:

> In this, the moral view of the world is completed. For in the Notion of the moral self-consciousness the two aspects, pure duty and actuality, are explicitly joined in a single unity, and consequently the one, like the other, is expressly without a being of its own, but is only a *moment*, or is superseded. This becomes explicit for consciousness in the last phase of the moral view of the world. That is to say, it places pure duty in a being other than itself, i.e. it posits pure duty partly as something existing only in *thought*.[309]

Duty and morality remain abstract and find no adequate concrete manifestation without collapsing into conceptual contradictions. Practical reason never truly becomes practical, since it has no content. The category of being here, which represents the unity of nature and morality, remains an abstract thought.[310] The unity continually collapses, and moral consciousness is alienated from the world, which it still sees as opposed to its moral purpose. This alienation must be overcome if Spirit is to reach a consistent and satisfying account of morality.

II. Dissemblance or Duplicity (§§616–31)

In this section Hegel continues his discussion of the different conceptions of morality that were in vogue during the period of German romanticism.

He tells us directly that his account here is a continuation of the discussion of the moral view of the world from the previous section of the same name: "this world of dissemblance is nothing else but the development of moral self-consciousness in its moments, and hence is its *reality*, its essential nature."[311] From this statement, we can begin to come to terms with the relation between these two sections, which seem strangely similar in content. In "The Moral View of the World," we considered the unity of morality and nature from the abstract level. But the postulates must be brought into actuality if they are to be valid for actual morality. Indeed, a moral code which remains purely theoretical is useless; it must be able to be translated into action. "But this practical reason," Hegel writes, "does not confine the universal principle of the good to its own inward regulation: it first becomes *practical*, in the true sense of the word, when it insists on the good being manifested in the world with an outward objectivity."[312] In the previous section, the moral consciousness fell into contradictions again and again so long as morality was conceived purely abstractly. In order to avoid this, moral consciousness now shifts to the realm of concrete action. In the present section, moral consciousness is considered above all from its actual active side or in "its essential nature."

As the second analysis in the series, the discussion here of dissemblance operates with the categories of the one and the many, and thus corresponds to "Perception." Hegel makes this explicit with a direct reference to the "Perception" section, where this category was first introduced: "For each case is a concrescence of many moral relations, just as an object of perception in general is a thing of many properties."[313] Here what is at issue is the moral situation, which has the same categorial determination as an object. In the previous section, we were concerned with the abstract unity of nature and morality, and pure being was the category that corresponded to this abstract Notion. Now we shift to the empirical sphere of concrete perception, and with this shift a new category comes on the scene—the one and the many. This category of perception now applies to the concrete moral situation.

The Notion: Duty and the Moral World from the Side of Actuality (§§616–17)

Since the account in "Dissemblance or Duplicity" is a continuation of the previous discussion in "The Moral View of the World," it shares with that discussion the same Notion. In other words, the Notion that is operative here is once again the belief that there is a harmony between the moral and the natural spheres, and between morality and natural impulses and desires. Thus, given that the Notion is the same, the corresponding phases of the experience of consciousness will also be the same in this section. Although the Notion and the moments of the experience of consciousness correspond in the two sections, the account of dissemblance is not redundant, since the analysis of the experience of consciousness here is performed from a different perspective. We are no longer concerned with morality as an abstract theoretical entity, but rather we must now explore it from the side of the actual. Thus, we see the shift from the abstract category of pure being to the concrete category of the one and the many, which is typical of perception. Examined from this side, this concept of morality will produce contradictions which evince a clear contradiction on the part of moral consciousness: "in order to assert one moment as possessing being in itself, it asserts the *opposite* as the one that possesses being in itself. In so doing it confesses that, as a matter of fact, it is in earnest with neither of them."[314] Since moral consciousness is aware of this contradiction and this switching back and forth of positions, it displays a sort of hypocrisy, which Hegel refers to as "dissemblance" or "duplicity."

As is typical of all of the Notions in "Spirit That Is Certain of Itself," the Notion of the moral worldview still operates with a subject-object unity. Moral consciousness still insists on the unity of morality and nature and thus of the for-itself and the in-itself: "we see that it neither encounters the object as something alien to it, nor does the object come before it in an unconscious manner. On the contrary, it proceeds in every case in accordance with a principle on the basis of which it posits *objective* being. It thus knows this latter to be its own self, for it knows itself to be the *active* agent that produces it."[315] The moral law produced by the rational moral consciousness has objective validity for all rational moral agents and thus is both subjective and objective. We now turn to explore the contradictions that begin to appear in the experience of consciousness.

The Experience of Consciousness (§§618–31)

The In-Itself Moment: The First Postulate—the Unity of Nature and Morality (§§618–21)

As was the case in the previous section, Hegel here begins with the postulate about the harmony of nature and morality. Consciousness can never know this unity as an object of possible experience, but, as we have seen, this unity must be postulated as a necessary assumption of reason: "It is supposed to be an *implicit* harmony, not explicitly for actual consciousness, not present."[316] What is present and observed empirically is the contradiction of the moral and the natural spheres. Nonetheless, in spite of this empirical contradiction, the theoretical belief that morality as such exists is unwavering. Yet, given this belief that morality already exists, it can only exist in the real actions of the moral consciousness. It would clearly be an absurdity to assert that morality exists but only in abstract theory and not in real actions. The very concept of existence implies actuality: "it is precisely therein that the actuality of its morality consists."[317] Yet, this very action proves that in fact the disputed unity does exist in the empirical sphere and is not just posited: "for the action is nothing other than the actualization of the inner moral purpose, nothing other than the production of an *actuality determined by the purpose*, or of the harmony of the moral purpose and actuality itself."[318] When moral action is conceived as self-consciously acting according to a moral purpose, then concrete moral actions do exist. Thus, insofar as this unity can be and in fact is realized in the sphere of action, to postulate it is superfluous: "Action, therefore, in fact directly fulfils what was asserted could not take place, what was supposed to be merely a postulate, merely a beyond."[319] This then is the first instance of inauthenticity on the part of the moral consciousness: "Consciousness thus proclaims through its deed that it is not in earnest in making its postulate, because the meaning of the action is really this, to make into a present reality what was not supposed to exist in the present."[320]

Given that moral action does in fact exist, moral consciousness now focuses on it as the key aspect of morality as a whole. Consciousness now comes to see the limitations of moral action. An individual action can in no way embody the universal purpose of reason. Indeed, individual action, however virtuous, seems insignificant in comparison to the lofty goal of reason. Hegel explains,

> In point of fact, however, the actual deed is only a deed of the *individual* consciousness, and therefore itself only something individual, and the result contingent. But the purpose of reason as the universal, all-embracing purpose, is nothing less than the whole world; a final purpose going far beyond the content of this individual deed, and therefore to be placed altogether beyond anything actually done.[321]

Seen from this point of view, concrete action always seems negligible and limited. Thus, the emphasis on action fails and gives way to a Notion of the highest good for humanity as a whole.

Now moral consciousness thinks that it is the "highest good that essentially matters."[322] But when this is thought through, it turns out that the Notion of the highest good eliminates the notion of morality altogether. The first postulate says that there is a unity of nature and morality, and this is the final purpose of the world. But if this unity is presupposed, then individual "moral action is superfluous."[323] The sublime call for moral action is no longer necessary, since morality already prevails. The highest good is achieved anyway, without the help of moral consciousness's individual actions. Thus, morality only makes sense when something is opposed to it, and it can achieve something by overcoming this opposition: "action takes place only on the assumption of a negative which is to be set aside by action."[324] The emphasis on the highest good must thus be rejected by moral consciousness, which finds itself once again in logical conundrums.

The first postulate in this way leads to one contradiction after another. The characteristic of the contradictions evinced here is what Hegel calls "a dissemblance of the facts."[325] In each case, moral consciousness begins with an idea that it does not really seriously believe, and then it moves to another one that directly contradicts it. Here Hegel reviews the three phases we have just examined:

> Consciousness starts from the idea that, *for it*, morality and reality do not harmonize; but it is not in earnest about this, for in the deed the presence of this harmony becomes *explicit for it*. But it is not in earnest even about this deed, since the deed is something individual; for it has such a high purpose, the *highest good*. But this again is only a dissemblance of the facts, for such dissemblance would do away with all action and all morality.[326]

The emphasis on the empirical split between morality and nature, on the concrete moral action, on the highest good, each in its turn proved to be conceptually incoherent. Thus, the first postulate is proven to be fraught with contradictions and dubious assumptions. This then completes the first stage of the experience of consciousness.

The For-Itself Moment: The Second Postulate—the Unity of Desire and Duty (§§622–25)

From the analysis of the first postulate, we now turn to the second postulate, which concerns the unity of natural drives with morality. In its moral acts, moral consciousness claims to have effectively purged its will of all sultry, natural motives which are devoid of moral value, and it "asserts that its purpose is pure, is independent of inclinations and impulses."[327] But this is impossible since in order to be an *actual* agent in the world, moral consciousness must be a natural individual. It is impossible to eliminate natural impulses entirely and still have a real action. Once again, the result is duplicity. "Moral self-consciousness," Hegel writes, "is not, therefore, in earnest with the elimination of inclinations and impulses, for it is just these that are the *self-realizing self-consciousness.*"[328] Self-consciousness cannot be serious about its moral objective to purge itself of natural impulses, since to do this completely would be to destroy itself as a natural being, i.e., it would amount to no less than self-destruction.

But as we saw earlier, these impulses "ought not to be *suppressed,* but only to be *in conformity with* reason."[329] Yet, if this is taken to mean that morality can function as a drive or impulse for action, then in actual action there are instances when these impulses are in accordance with reason: "And they *are* in conformity with reason, for moral *action* is nothing else but consciousness realizing itself, thus giving itself the shape of an *impulse,* i.e. it is immediately the *present* harmony of impulse and morality."[330] In this case, there is no need to posit the harmony of the two, since this harmony already exists. But this is not the same as the cultivation of natural desires, which simply are what they are:

> But impulse is not in fact merely this empty shape which could have within it a spring of action other than the one it is, and be impelled by it. For sense-nature is one which contains within itself its own laws and springs of action; consequently, morality cannot therefore be in earnest about being itself the mainspring of impulses, the angle of inclination for inclinations.[331]

The moral duty is abstract and empty, while on the contrary natural impulses are full of sensuous content. Thus, the will would naturally act in accordance with the sensuous content, but this kind of action would of course have no moral worth. The result is that "the harmony of the two is . . . merely *implicit,* merely *postulated.*"[332]

Now the harmony of the inclinations and morality is "displaced" from the realm of actuality into the realm of thought. It does not exist in fact but instead is merely postulated. It is thought that moral perfection occurs when "the struggle of morality and sense-nature has ceased, and the latter is in conformity with morality in a way that is beyond our comprehension."[333] But this Notion of moral perfection is self-contradictory, since it would destroy the very Notion of morality altogether. If our desires were spontaneously in accordance with the moral law anyway, there would be no virtue in acting in accordance with them. If there were no conflict between desire and the moral law, then the Notion of duty would be destroyed. Once again, morality requires something opposed to it in order to make sense. Thus, moral consciousness cannot be serious about really desiring to reach this goal and this notion of moral perfection.

Moral consciousness tries to maintain this difference by postponing moral perfection into an indeterminate time in the future and creating

the Notion of moral progress toward this goal. Thus, it is able to maintain
the aspect of opposition, at least temporarily. The moral project involves
training the will such that the passions are spontaneously in accordance
with the moral law. Thus, the moral agent is forever progressing toward
true morality without ever reaching it: "What consciousness really holds to
be the truth of the matter is only this intermediate state of imperfection,
a state nevertheless which at least is supposed to be a *progress towards*
perfection."[334] But when we think this through, we see that moral consciousness cannot be serious about this progress toward moral perfection,
since to attain that perfection would mean the very end of morality
per se: "for to advance in morality would really be to move towards its
disappearance. That is to say, the goal would be the nothingness or the
abolition, mentioned above, or morality and consciousness itself; but to
approach ever nearer to nothingness means to diminish."[335]

   Since moral consciousness can neither attain moral perfection nor
make progress toward this end, it ends up here in this second phase as
"the intermediate state of an imperfect morality."[336] This intermediate
state is the only thing that is certain and actual. But since consciousness
is imperfect with respect to morality, it no longer has the right to expect
to receive happiness as a result of its action. If it does receive happiness,
then it is a matter of grace or luck and not as a reward for consciousness's
virtuous action. Likewise, the empirical observation that the virtuous
often suffer no longer makes sense. If all humans are in this imperfect
intermediate state, then no one has the right to be deemed virtuous, and
thus there is no conflict if morally wretched individuals suffer. The second
postulate thus leads to a host of contradictions, and moral consciousness
is led to the third postulate as a last attempt to make the moral view of
the world consistent.

The In-and-For-Itself Moment: The Third Postulate—God as Lawgiver (§§626–30)

Now, with the third postulate, God is thought to be the guarantor of the
moral sphere. Since moral consciousness is essentially morally imperfect
and since morality is still thought to exist, it must exist elsewhere, for
example, in the divine: "Morality itself thus exists in another being than
the actual consciousness. This other being is a *holy moral lawgiver.*"[337] As
we saw earlier, moral consciousness requires God to sanctify the plurality
of individual duties, since otherwise they seem morally valueless to moral
consciousness who only heeds the one true moral law. But Hegel indicates
once again that this gesture is not authentic. As a rational moral agent,
moral consciousness must itself be able to recognize and act on moral

laws. With respect to morality, God enjoys no advantage over any other rational moral agent: "For the moral self-consciousness is its own Absolute, and duty is absolutely only what *it knows* as duty. But duty it knows only as pure duty; what is not sacred for it is not sacred in itself, and what is not in itself sacred, cannot be made sacred by the holy being."[338] If a moral agent is always obliged to defer to God in moral decisions, then his rationality alone is not sufficient for moral action anyway. For morality to make sense, duties must be universally recognizable by all moral agents. A moral duty must be a duty for an individual agent if that agent's actions are to be judged according to criteria of morality.

Moral consciousness knows only the plurality of moral laws, while the true moral law lies with God alone. The single moral law is valid only for the divine, since the pure duty which it enjoins is impossible for the actual moral consciousness to reach. But this once again posits morality in another sphere and deprives any real natural being of the chance of ever attaining it. In an actual moral agent "morality is affected and conditioned by the sense-nature, and is therefore not free and independent, but contingent on free *will.*"[339] An actual moral agent is not wholly free, since he is determined by natural impulses. God, on the other hand, lacking any natural element, is thought to be wholly free and thus the only truly moral agent: "Morality, therefore, in and for itself is in another being."[340] Moral perfection is thus achieved only by God, who is wholly free of a sensible aspect: "This other being, then, is here the purely perfect morality, for in it morality does not stand in a relation to nature and sense."[341] But this creates an internal contradiction in the notion of morality, since morality implies real action, which implies a sensuous element: "But the *reality* of pure duty is its *realization* in nature and sense."[342] Once again, if there is no sensuous element, then there is no action. Moreover, since there is no opposition in the divine will caused by natural impulses, there would once again be no morality: "But a pure morality that was completely separated from reality, and so likewise was without any positive relation to it, would be an unconscious, unreal abstraction in which the concept of morality, which involves thinking of pure duty, willing, and doing it, would be done away with."[343]

Morality is thus impossible both for the concrete moral consciousness and for the divine. Hegel summarizes the problem of the sensuous moral consciousness as follows: "In that first, imperfect consciousness morality is not realized . . . for it is associated with nature and sense, with the *reality* of being and consciousness which constitutes its content, and nature and sense are morally nothing."[344] Thus, the concrete moral agent is capable of action per se but not *moral* action, since it lacks the element of abstract morality that only God possesses. But morality is also impossible for the divine: "In the second consciousness morality exists as *perfect*. . . . But this perfection consists precisely in morality having *reality* in a *consciousness*, as well as a *free* reality, an existence in general, in being something not empty but full-filled, full of content."[345] God has the aspect of absolute morality in himself, but since he has no natural being he is incapable of action. Thus, this Notion of morality proves to be conceptually bankrupt, since it renders moral action impossible.

Concluding Remarks (§631)

The end result of all of these dialectical considerations is, for Hegel, not mere logical inconsistency but outright hypocrisy: "Consciousness comes to see that the placing-apart of these moments is a '*dis*placing' of them, a dissemblance, and that it would be *hypocrisy* if, nevertheless, it were to keep them separate."[346] Moral consciousness shifts from one position to the next with little attention paid to the logical contradictions involved in its views. Now consciousness retreats into itself in the sense that it rejects as abstruse theorizing this movement back and forth of the moral point of view. It now holds its own conscience to be the absolute moral law. This then forms the Notion that is explored in the next section.

III. Conscience and the "Beautiful Soul" (§§632–71)

Hegel completes the account of historical Spirit with his famous discussion of conscience and the so-called "beautiful soul." Here he criticizes forms of romantic moralism that arose out of the context of Kant's moral theory. In the *Philosophy of Right*, various forms of subjectivism are discussed, and Hegel indicates explicitly that his analysis there treats the same material as the discussion in this section: "What is said here may be compared with the entire section (C.), 'Conscience,' in the *Phenomenology*, especially the part dealing with the transition to a higher stage."[347] A number of Hegel's contemporaries who are well-known figures in the German romantic movement constitute the historical targets of his criticism here. Hegel mentions Goethe's *The Sufferings of Young Werther* and explicitly associates the figure of the beautiful soul with a novel by Jacobi: "we may include here the 'beautiful soul' of Jacobi's *Woldemar*. In this novel there is displayed in the fullest measure the imposture of the heart's splendor, the self-deceptive delusion of its own virtue and excellence."[348] The account here in the "Spirit" chapter leads us historically up to Hegel's own day and to the composition of the *Phenomenology* itself. However, this is not to say, as is so often claimed, that this Notion represents, for

Hegel, the apex of world history or that he sees this as the culmination of World Spirit in which all dualisms and contradictions are resolved. On the contrary, as we shall see, Hegel sees this form of Spirit as fraught with contradictions and conceptual errors, and he is by no means above the occasional use of sarcasm in his treatment of it. Thus, this form of historical Spirit, although historically the last that Hegel treats, can in no way be conceived of teleologically as the end toward which world history has been striving and which ultimately resolves all conflicts and historical confusions.

This final section, "Conscience," represents the third analysis of "Spirit That Is Certain of Itself," and, as the third analysis in the series, it operates with the categorial structure of appearance-reality or ground-consequence that was initiated in "Force and the Understanding." Here the concept of moral conscience itself takes this categorial form. On the one hand, it represents the absolute truth of abstract morality and thus can be seen as resembling the thing-in-itself or the noumenal realm. On the other hand, this morality is not merely abstract, but can at the same time be put into praxis in the empirical realm and thus can be seen in the world of appearance. There is thus a dialectical movement between the inner and the outer which is characteristic of this category.[349] The subject-object unity or the in-and-for-itself aspect typical of all the moments of "Spirit That Is Certain of Itself" is also contained in this concept: "Moral self-consciousness having attained its truth . . . therefore abandons, or rather supersedes, the internal division which gave rise to the dissemblance, the division between the in-itself and the self."[350] The objective validity of morality is no longer something other, but rather is thought to be immediately in the conscience of the individual subject. This, as we shall see, represents a conceptual advance over the unity of morality and nature from "The Moral View of the World." Finally, in the overall architectonic of the *Phenomenology*, this section, as the third analysis of the third dialectical movement of the chapter, corresponds to "Reason as Testing Laws" in "Reason." Hegel makes this clear with a direct reference to that section: "This content at the same time counts as a moral *essentiality* or as *duty*. For pure duty, as was found when testing laws, is utterly indifferent to any content and tolerates any content."[351]

The Notion: Conscience (§§632–41)

In "The Moral View of the World," the harmony of nature and morality was thought to be an objective fact about the world independent of the moral subject. This unity was ultimately posited in a beyond, in the sphere of the divine, which was in principle inaccessible to the knowing subject.

Now the dualisms and the dialectical confusions of "The Moral View of the World" are resolved, when moral consciousness realizes that the moral considerations and the contradictory movements back and forth are the movements of its own thought. It thus realizes that the unity of morality occurs in itself, qua moral consciousness:

> what appear as contradictory propositions, which the moral consciousness makes clumsy efforts first to separate and then to reconcile, are intrinsically the same, since pure duty, viz. as *pure knowing*, is nothing else than the *self* of consciousness, and the self of consciousness is *being* and *actuality*: and similarly . . . what is supposed to lie beyond *actual* consciousness is nothing else than pure thought, and thus is, in fact, the self.[352]

There is thus a shift from the objective to the subjective sphere here when moral consciousness "retreats into itself."[353] There is no longer a beyond, and moral consciousness is no longer separated from the objective sphere. This ushers in the Notion of conscience, which contains the abstract moral law in itself.

The harmony of moral duty and moral action now occurs immediately in the conscience of the individual subject. Moral duty is no longer something adventitious, but rather it issues from moral consciousness itself: "this self, *qua* a pure self-identical knowing, is the *absolute universal*, so that just this knowing, as *its own* knowing, as conviction, is *duty*. Duty is no longer the universal that stands over against the self; on the contrary, it is known to have no validity when thus separated."[354] The moral law is not a fact about the world but is in the conscience of the individual moral agent. Since moral consciousness now has the moral law immediately within itself, it is "aware of itself as absolute truth and being,"[355] and it is from this self-certainty that the entire third part of the triad of "Spirit," namely "Spirit That Is Certain of Itself," gets its name. Knowledge or conviction of one's own moral purpose thus plays the key role here. The truth of moral consciousness now lies above all in "knowing or his *own conviction*."[356] The moral consciousness must merely be convinced of its own inner moral duty for that duty to have objective reality and validity. Thus, this self-knowledge is essential for conscience: "Suppose a case of moral action; it is an objective reality for the knowing consciousness. This, *qua* conscience, knows it in an immediate, concrete manner; and at the same time *is* only as conscience knows it."[357]

Since there is no longer a split between nature and morality, moral consciousness no longer has the problem of realizing abstract morality in actual action. The moral consciousness immediately knows what its moral duty is and can immediately translate it into action: "Action *qua* actualization is thus the pure form of will—the simple conversion of a reality that merely *is* into a reality that results from *action*, the conversion of the bare mode of *objective* knowing into one of knowing *reality* as something produced by consciousness."[358] The transition from the abstract moral law to concrete moral action is simple here, since the moral law is not other but is conscience itself: "The action is thus only the translation of its *individual* content into the *objective* element, in which it is universal and recognized, and it is just the fact that it is recognized that makes the deed a reality."[359] Others recognize and respect the individual who acts according to his own conscience. The element of recognition by other self-conscious agents is thus at work in this dialectical movement. This then completes the notion of conscience which Hegel now subjects to dialectical analysis.

The Experience of Consciousness

The In-Itself Moment: Abstract Duty (§§642–47)

The first aspect of conscience is of course its universality. Since the moral law is situated in conscience itself, it is immediately known to the moral agent. Moral consciousness thus has immediate access to the universal law. Likewise, since moral consciousness is an actual subject in the real world, it has an immediate relation to moral action: "its relation to the *actual* case in which it has to act is, in the first instance, that of *knower*."[360] In order to judge the individual moral situation correctly and to be entirely certain of its knowing, moral consciousness must know all of the manifold facts about it: "Insofar as this knowing has in it the moment of *universality*, conscientious action requires that the actual case before it should be viewed unrestrictedly in all its bearings, and therefore that all the circumstances of the case should be accurately known and taken into consideration."[361] But concrete action stands in such a complex set of relations and contains so many different aspects that moral consciousness cannot hope to evaluate them all. Moral consciousness knows that it "does not possess that full acquaintance with *all* the attendant circumstances which is required, and that its pretense of conscientiously weighing all the circumstances is in vain."[362] Incomplete knowledge is nonetheless sufficient for moral consciousness, provided that this knowledge is its own. Consciousness needs only complete knowledge of its own inner duty in conscience and not of the empirical situation. Thus, the universal aspect of duty is what is most important and not the empirical contingencies.

Nonetheless, moral consciousness with its universal duty stands in relation to the manifold world of moral action. From the complexity of the empirical world issues a plurality of ethical duties: "Conscience knows that it has to choose between them, and to make a decision; for none of them, in its specific character or in its content, is absolute; only pure duty is that."[363] Moral consciousness must then find the concrete duties that are in accordance with its absolute duty, which it finds in its own conscience alone. But this duty from the conviction of conscience is abstract and lacking in content, like Rousseau's general will and Kant's moral law: "This *pure* conviction is, as such, as empty as pure *duty*, is pure in the sense that there is nothing in it, no specific content that is a duty."[364] Since conviction or conscience itself is not a principle which can offer any concrete content, moral consciousness must fall back on its own natural drives and inclinations to find this content, since after all that content must issue from the moral subject itself: "But action is called for, something must be *determined* by the individual, and the self-certain Spirit . . . knows that it has this determination and content in the immediate *certainty* of itself. This, as a determination and content, is the *natural* consciousness, i.e. impulses and inclinations."[365] Thus, in the final analysis moral consciousness, lacking any concrete content, must fall back on its own irrational drives and motivations, but these natural drives, although rich in content, are wholly devoid of moral value. Conscience reduces to the simple "caprice of the individual,"[366] since it amounts to the caprice of individual natural desires.

The problem is that conscience conceived of in its universal aspect is, like the general will or the Kantian moral law, an abstraction lacking content. As an abstraction, it cannot determine any particular content. "Morality lies in the consciousness of having fulfilled one's duty," but "the abstraction called duty" is "capable of any content."[367] To keep the duty of conscience abstract and free from content is to maintain its sublime, universal status, and this is the goal of moral consciousness. Thus, abstract duty is not tainted by contingent duties in the empirical sphere:

> It is of no use to object to this freedom, which places any and every kind of content in the universal passive medium of "duty" and "knowing," by maintaining that another content ought to have been placed in it; for whatever content it be, it contains the *blemish of determinateness* from which pure knowing is free, determinateness which pure knowing can disdainfully reject, or equally can accept.[368]

But the sublime universal nature of conscience is maintained only at the cost of its determinacy. It can enjoin no action and remains in the colorless night of abstraction: "conscience is free from any content whatever; it absolves itself from any specific duty which is supposed to have the validity of law."[369]

The For-Itself Moment: Specific Action (§§648–58)

The universal aspect of conscience remains abstract and indeterminate. Now moral consciousness must bring its inner duty to concrete action and by so doing give it a concrete form in the public sphere. This constitutes the second moment of the experience of consciousness:

> The duty which it fulfils is a *specific* content; it is true that this content is the *self* of consciousness, and so consciousness' *knowledge* of itself, its *identity* with itself. But once fulfilled, set in the medium of *being*, this identity is no longer knowing, no longer this process of differentiation in which its differences are at the same time immediately superseded; on the contrary, in *being*, the difference is established as an *enduring* difference, and the action is a *specific* action.[370]

With a concrete action, conscience must commit itself morally. A concrete action can be judged by others as right or wrong, unlike an inner duty of conscience, which remains indeterminate. Yet, an epistemological problem arises for the other moral agents, who have no access to the inner duty of conscience and thus cannot see if that duty matches up to the concrete action that they observe: "the consciousness which is explicitly aware of the action finds itself in a state of complete *uncertainty* about the Spirit which does the action and is certain of itself."[371] The action of moral consciousness can now be observed from two different sides—from the side of the moral agent, in terms of intention, and from the side of the observer, in terms of the act itself. Moral consciousness is aware of the epistemological problem and exploits it to its own advantage. While the other subjects are obliged to judge the particular action on its own terms, moral conscience can always retreat to the realm of abstract duty and present any concrete action in a positive light by portraying it through the prism of a good inner duty or intention: "What, therefore, it places before them it also 'displaces' again, or rather has straightaway 'displaced' or dissembled. For its *actual* being is for it not this duty and determinate character it has put forward, but the actuality which it has in the absolute certainty of itself."[372] What is essential is not the action itself but rather the inner duty of conscience, which only conscience itself knows: "Its *immediate* action is not the *determinate* aspect of action, not its *intrinsic* being, but solely the self-knowing *self* as such."[373]

It is through the medium of language that conscience either solves the epistemological problem by revealing its true motives and intentions to the public world or aggravates it by dissembling them:

> The content of the language of conscience is the *self that knows itself as essential being*. This alone is what it declares, and this declaration is the true actuality of the act, and the validating of the action. Consciousness declares its *conviction*; it is in this conviction alone that the action is a duty; also it is valid as duty solely through the conviction being *declared*.[374]

The action of moral consciousness is validated by its "assurance" to the public world that the action is done in accordance with its own inner duty. The act of speaking and making public one's intention is thus essential to moral consciousness, since it makes that intention universal: "The declaration of this assurance in itself rids the form of its particularity. . . . But it is essential that he should *say* so, for this self must be at the same time a *universal* self."[375]

This conception of conscience breaks down, since its abstract moments never endure. Since the assertion in speech is essential to moral consciousness, it disappears with the disappearance of its pronouncement:

> The moments of consciousness are, therefore, these extreme abstractions, none of which endures but each of which loses itself in the other and produces it. . . . The absolute certainty of itself thus finds itself, *qua* consciousness, changed immediately into a sound that dies away, into an objectification of its being-for-self; but this created world is its *speech*, which likewise it has immediately heard and only the echo of which returns to it.[376]

Just as the temporal "Now" of "Sense-Certainty" disappears into ever new temporal moments, so also here the assertion of consciousness cannot endure. When the assertion of moral consciousness' intentions disappears, the universal duty vanishes as well.

The self-certainty is an empty universal, just as pure duty was. Moral consciousness merely declares its universal intention to act in accordance with conscience, but it does not commit itself to any particular duty, and thus it fails to commit itself in the actual world: "it has declared . . . *what* it holds to be duty. But it is free from any *specific* duty."[377] Consciousness does not dare to commit itself to anything particular and enduring by performing any particular action, since this would seem to taint its sublime inner purpose: "It lacks the power to externalize itself, the power to make itself into a thing, and to endure [mere] being. It lives in dread of besmirching the splendor of its inner being by action and an existence; and, in order to preserve the purity of its heart, it flees from contact with the actual world, and persists in its self-willed impotence."[378] This position is what Hegel refers to as "the beautiful soul." The essential feature of the beautiful soul is that it is an abstract will that lacks content and thus cannot act in the real world: "A will which resolves on nothing is no actual will. . . . However 'beautiful' such a disposition may be, it is nevertheless dead. . . . Only by resolving can a man step into actuality."[379] The essential aspect of the act is moral consciousness's self-certainty that it is in accordance with this inner law, but since the inner law is abstract and empty, this self-certainty is meaningless: "This absolute *certainty* into which substance has resolved itself is the absolute *untruth* which collapses internally."[380]

The In-and-For-Itself Moment: The Beautiful Soul and the Evil Consciousness (§§659–71)

We now move to the third moment of conscience, which involves moral consciousness' relation to other moral subjects: "the antithesis of individuality to other individuals, and to the universal, inevitably comes on the scene, and we have to consider this relationship and its movement."[381] Once again moral consciousness retreats to a position where conscience determines itself above all in terms of its purpose or intent in action: "in the *purpose* of its action, a purpose with an actual content, it is aware of itself as this particular individual, and is conscious of the antithesis between what it is for itself and what it is for others."[382] The dialectical movement of particular inner intention vis-à-vis the universal moral law gives rise to two forms of consciousness—the beautiful soul and the evil consciousness. First, there is the consciousness of universal morality or the beautiful soul that acknowledges universal duty but does not act. Then there is the evil consciousness which acknowledges its own inner law, which is at odds with universal morality, and which can and does act in defiance of the universal. We thus have two moral subjects at odds with each other.

We first examine the rise and fall of the evil consciousness. Now the moral consciousness that is certain of itself has collapsed into a kind of self-worship, and its universal moral duty collapses into self-centered individuality: "this universality and duty have the very opposite significance of the specific *individuality* that exempts itself from the universal."[383] There is thus a split between the individual conscience and the universal. This individuality is the aspect that is conceived as evil: "the first consciousness counts as *evil*, because of the disparity between its *inner being* and the universal."[384] Nonetheless, the evil consciousness still recognizes the validity of universality, but claims that it is being true to itself and acting in accordance with its own inner law. This lip service to the universal thus makes the evil consciousness hypocritical: "this first consciousness declares its action to be in conformity with itself, to be duty and conscientiousness, it is held by the universal consciousness to be *hypocrisy*."[385] The evil consciousness is ultimately self-defeating and is betrayed by its own hypocritical stance: "It admits, in fact, to being evil by asserting that it acts, in opposition to the acknowledged universal, according to its *own* inner law and conscience."[386] Insofar as it is hypocritical, the evil consciousness implicitly acknowledges the validity of the universal law. Thus, it is aware of the contradiction involved in insisting on its own subjectivity over that law.

We now turn to the sublation of the beautiful soul. The consciousness of universal morality, or the beautiful soul, proves to be hypocritical in its criticism of evil consciousness. Since the beautiful soul is abstract, its criticism of the particular content of evil consciousness must be based on its own arbitrary content, which can be no better than that of the evil consciousness: "In denouncing hypocrisy as base, vile, and so on, it is appealing in such judgment to its *own* law, just as the evil consciousness appeals to *its* own law. . . . It has, therefore, no superiority over the other law; rather it legitimizes it."[387] Moreover, the consciousness of universal morality remains at the level of abstract thought, since it lacks content and is incapable of action. Thus, it too is a form of hypocrisy since it pretends its moral judgments are actual actions: "It does well to preserve itself in its purity, for it *does not act;* it is the hypocrisy which wants its judging to be taken for an *actual* deed, and instead of proving its rectitude by actions, does so by uttering fine sentiments."[388] Ultimately, the beautiful soul collapses in its own abstractions. It is "disordered to the point of madness, wastes itself in yearning and pines away in consumption."[389] In the *Philosophy of Right*, Hegel writes of the sublation of the beautiful soul, "In my *Phenomenology of Spirit* . . . I have also shown how what has been called a 'beautiful soul' . . . empties the objective of all content and so fades away until it loses all actuality."[390]

Concluding Remarks

The conclusion of Hegel's account of historical Spirit as well as the transition to "Religion" are extremely obscure. Thus, we must examine carefully the end of this section, along with the fate of the evil consciousness and the beautiful soul. By criticizing the evil consciousness, the beautiful soul puts its content alongside that of its opponent and becomes like the other. There is thus an identity of the two which the evil consciousness can recognize, since it recognizes the empirical content implicit in the other's criticism. But the result is by no means symmetrical. The evil consciousness can recognize itself in the other and confess its wickedness, but the beautiful soul of universal morality remains in its lofty sphere of moral judgment unencumbered by the burden of actual action. It "contrasts the beauty of his own soul with the penitent's wickedness, yet confronts the confession of the penitent with its own stiff-necked unrepentant character."[391]

Ultimately, the beautiful soul can collapse in the contradictions of pure universality, as we saw above, or can be compelled to recognize the other moral consciousness. Only when it recognizes itself in the other is reconciliation possible. Now both sides recognize their one-sidedness: "just as the [one] has to surrender its one-sided, unacknowledged existence of its particular being-for-self, so too must this other set aside its one-sided, unacknowledged judgment."[392] Now the moments of thought and action are seen as moments of the same complex entity: "The *self* that carries out the action, the form of its act, is only a *moment* of the whole, and so likewise is the knowledge, that by its judgment determines and establishes the distinction between the individual and universal aspects of the action."[393] The beautiful soul now sees that action is not bad but rather is good and a necessary complement to moral thought. It recognizes the impoverished nature of its own abstract moralizing. There is now "a reciprocal recognition which is capable of *Absolute* Spirit."[394] Both the beautiful soul and the evil consciousness recognize themselves in the other.

Here at the end of "Spirit" we are left with the individual self-conscious agents recognizing their own agency in the faults and one-sidedness of the other. With this, the realm of Spirit reaches a form of self-consciousness when it recognizes an absolute moral claim in the objective realm. This absolute claim represents the first appearance of God: "It is the *actual* 'I,' the universal knowledge *of itself* in its *absolute opposite*."[395] Just as in the "Lordship and Bondage" dialectic the recognition and reflection of oneself in the other was essential for self-consciousness, so also here historical World Spirit comes to see itself in the objective world in the form of an absolute moral imperative. At the level of consciousness the other is simply another conscious agent, now at the level world history the other of Spirit is God. Hegel writes, "it is God manifested in the midst of those who know themselves in the form of pure knowledge."[396] Historical Spirit has become self-conscious and has thus reached the sphere of religious consciousness, which posits itself in the form of the divine in the world. This is the first figure of the "Religion" chapter, entitled "Natural Religion."

8

The Shapes of Religion

General Introduction (§§672–83)

The "Religion" chapter has been a vastly underestimated and little explored part of the *Phenomenology* in the Anglo-American tradition. Although in the francophone world, Hegel's philosophy of religion has been taken seriously and made the subject of a handful of important studies, its influence in the English-speaking world has remained minimal. This is regrettable for a number of reasons, not the least of which is that it is here in the "Religion" chapter that Hegel gives some of the clearest indications concerning the systematic structure of the work as a whole. For this reason, we need to examine this chapter closely in light of the systematic interpretation we have been following. In the "Religion" chapter, Hegel gives a systematic survey of world religion and the development of religious consciousness. Hegel was not the first to organize religions into a conceptually or historically developmental scheme of this sort; indeed, considerably prior to the *Phenomenology*, Lessing, in his *The Education of Man* (1780), and Schleiermacher, in his *On Religion: Speeches to Its Cultured Despisers* (1799), both developed similar schemes. Hegel's originality here lies in the way in which he interprets the forms of religion in the fundamental categories of his own philosophy.

If anywhere in the *Phenomenology*, it is in the "Religion" chapter that signs of hasty composition are evident. In "Natural Religion," for instance, the analyses are hardly more than a few paragraphs long. However, this is not to say that there are lapses in the systematic unity of the work. In fact, strangely enough, Hegel's systematic intentions come out more clearly here than in some of the earlier sections in which the discussions are more thoroughly developed. The role that the individual analyses are supposed to play is more or less clear, although certain discussions need more filling out. Thus, I will, when necessary, supplement Hegel's account of the forms of religious consciousness here in the *Phenomenology* primarily with four other sources—his Berlin *Lectures on the Philosophy of Religion*, which were all held considerably after the composition of the *Phenomenology* and which constitute his most detailed statement on the subject, his *Lectures on the Philosophy of History* and *Lectures on Aesthetics*, and his so-called *Early Theological Writings*, which of course antedate the *Phenomenology*. These accounts will help us to fill in the details of the forms of religious consciousness that Hegel was only able to sketch in the *Phenomenology*. Although some commentators[1] are critical of Hegel's systematic pretensions in the "Religion" chapter, since he modifies his discussion of this material in his later lectures, it should be pointed out that there is more continuity between the *Phenomenology* and these later lectures than is generally recognized. For example, in the *Lectures on Aesthetics*, for the discussion of "Natural Religion" found here in the *Phenomenology*, exactly the same three stages are distinguished in the same order. Moreover, in the *Lectures on the Philosophy of Religion*, the three major sections of the "Religion" chapter here can be readily recognized in the same order with largely the same content.

The content of the "Religion" chapter, when taken at face value, seems to pose a difficult problem for the interpretation I am proposing. First, it appears that religion forms simply one aspect or dimension of the individual, the community, or the development of world history, and this would seem to imply that it should be fully treated in the "Self-Consciousness," "Reason," and "Spirit" chapters, respectively, instead of being given its own independent treatment in a separate chapter. Thus, there seems to be a serious structural disanalogy with respect to the nature of religion vis-à-vis the other fundamental structures that the *Phenomenology* has treated. In fact, we have already seen analyses of forms of religious consciousness in previous dialectical movements.[2] For instance, in "Force and the Understanding" we were concerned with a supersensible otherworldly realm.[3] We also saw how the "Self-Consciousness" chapter concluded with an account of the suffering religious consciousness, which Hegel called the unhappy consciousness. Likewise, in the "Spirit" chapter, forms of religious consciousness were treated in the account of *Antigone*, in the struggle of religion with the Enlightenment, and finally in the religious sentiment in "Morality."[4] Given that Hegel has already treated religion in these various forms, why does he need to do so again here in the "Religion" chapter? Clearly, this, if anything, seems to represent a break in the unity of the structure of the work.

At the beginning of the "Religion" chapter, Hegel provides us with a summary of the previous forms of religious consciousness precisely in order to answer this question. At the end of his recapitulation, he contrasts these previous forms of religion with the contents of the chapter at hand. He writes,

> In the structured forms hitherto considered which are distinguished in general as Consciousness, Self-Consciousness, Reason, and Spirit, religion, too, as consciousness of *absolute being* as such, has indeed made its appearance, although only from the *standpoint of the consciousness* that is conscious of absolute being; but absolute being in and for itself, the self-consciousness of Spirit, has not appeared in those "shapes."[5]

Here Hegel points out that the forms of religion examined so far have been treated only from a limited perspective. The issue turns on what Hegel means in this passage by saying that religion has been treated hitherto "only from the *standpoint of . . . consciousness.*" What he seems to want to indicate by this is that, in these forms of consciousness, the self-conscious subject sees the various forms of religion as something distinct and other than itself. From these previous views, religion and its object are understood as something in the object sphere, and self-conscious Spirit has not yet come to see itself in it.

This analysis helps us to understand what the "Religion" chapter adds to the transcendental argument we have been following. The movement tends to be one toward greater complexity, i.e., in "Consciousness," the emphasis was on the object, and the role of the self was unrecognized; in "Self-Consciousness," the role of the self as individual was all-important, but the role of the community remained unrecognized; in "Reason" the role of the abstract community was the key, but an account of the actual historical community was absent; and finally, in "Spirit," the role of the historically changing community was essential. Here it is clear that "Religion" likewise represents a more complex configuration than what we saw before in the "Spirit" chapter. In "Religion" Spirit becomes aware of itself. This self-awareness is what Hegel calls "universal" or "Absolute Spirit," which he introduces here for the first time.[6] He writes, "Spirit conceived as object, has for itself the significance of being the universal Spirit that contains within itself all essence and all actuality."[7] This self-consciousness is implicitly implied in Spirit's awareness of its object sphere. Thus, "Religion" represents a further unpacking of the presuppositions implied in the subject-object Notion. First, in order to give an account of the Notion we must do more than give an account of the development of the historical community. In this development is necessarily implied the self-awareness of Spirit which, for Hegel, comes about first in "Religion" and most explicitly in "Revealed Religion." Spirit becomes self-aware in the revelation of God on earth in the Christian religion. In Christ Spirit becomes aware of itself when it sees that God and the Absolute are not something otherworldly or different from man, but rather that God is man or Spirit in the world.

In his *Lectures on the Philosophy of History*, Hegel discusses at length the relation of history to religion, and thus implicitly the relation of the "Spirit" chapter to the "Religion" chapter in the *Phenomenology*. In that context he indicates that history and religion in principle cover the same material and are governed by the same principle:

> The distinction between religion and the world is only this—that religion as such, is reason in the soul and heart—that it is a temple in which truth and freedom in God are presented to the conceptive faculty: the state, on the other hand, regulated by the selfsame reason, is the temple of human freedom concerned with the perception and volition of a reality, whose purport may itself be called divine.[8]

Both the historical and the religious sphere are governed by human reason. History is the realm in which Spirit observes actual events and empirical perceptions. Religion works through similar forms not at the empirical level but at the conceptual level. Hegel thus indicates that the content of the two spheres is similar but is conceived of differently: "The process displayed in history is only the manifestation of religion as human reason—the production of the religious principle which dwells in the heart of man, under the form of secular freedom."[9] The empirical sphere of history thus presupposes as its necessary condition the abstract conceptual sphere of religion as its basis. In this way the "Religion" chapter can be seen as the next step in the transcendental argument of the *Phenomenology*.

Hegel indicates here at the beginning of "Religion" that the parallelisms that we have been following up until now will continue in this chapter. He indicates that the forms of religion will correspond to the forms of the chapters we have examined so far:

> If, therefore, religion is the perfection of Spirit into which its individual moments—consciousness, self-consciousness, reason, and Spirit—return and have returned as into their ground, they together constitute the *existent* actuality of the totality of Spirit, which *is* only as the differentiating and self-returning movement of these its aspects. The genesis of religion *in general* is contained in the movement of the universal moments.[10]

In this extremely important passage, Hegel lays out for us in large measure the architectonic of the second half of the *Phenomenology*. He first repeats what we have already learned, namely that Spirit encompasses the previous forms and runs through them once again: "Spirit as such contains the previous structured shapes in universal determinations, in the moments just named."[11] Moreover, religion will encompass all of the previous forms as well. In its development, religious consciousness will work through the same conceptual forms that we have already seen under a different aspect. Hegel indicates this in the following passage:

> In this genesis of religion, Spirit itself therefore assumes *specific* "shapes" which constitute the different moments of this movement; at the same time, the specific religion has likewise a specific actual Spirit. Thus, if consciousness, self-consciousness, reason, and Spirit, belong to self-knowing Spirit in general, similarly the specific "shapes" which were specially developed within consciousness, self-consciousness, reason, and Spirit, belong to the specific "shapes" of self-knowing Spirit.[12]

Thus, the individual dialectical movements inside of the individual chapters explored previously will, as expected, have their analogues here in "Religion."

Hegel then goes on to explain the role of the "Religion" chapter, telling us that in contrast to the forms of religious consciousness up until now, which ran their course in atemporal, purely conceptual forms, "Religion" will do the same temporally or according to its own Notion of the development of religious Spirit:

> The course traversed by these moments is, moreover, in relation to religion, not to be represented as occurring in time. Only the totality of Spirit, is in time, and the "shapes," which are "shapes" of the totality of *Spirit*, display themselves in a temporal succession; for only the whole has true actuality and therefore the form of pure freedom in face of an "other," a form which expresses itself as time. But the *moments* of the whole, consciousness, self-consciousness, reason, and Spirit, just because they are moments, have no existence in separation from one another.[13]

Here Hegel makes clear that only the forms of "Spirit" were temporal or historical, and although some religious figures made an appearance there, that was not the main subject of analysis. Now we will examine in the "Religion" chapter a historical development of different religions which represents Spirit's gradual self-awareness. In the *Lectures on the Philosophy of Religion* Hegel says,

> Religion, insofar as it is definite, and has not as yet completed the circle of its determinateness—so far that is as it is finite religion, and exists as

finite—is historical religion, or a particular form of religion. Its principal moments, and also the manner in which they exist historically, being exhibited in the progress of religion from stage to stage, and in its development, there thus arises a series of forms of religion, or a history of religion.[14]

Thus, we now have for the first time a temporal succession of religious figures. Moreover, all of the previous forms are implicitly contained here in religion, and they all form a unitary whole which is represented by a single system of religious thought. This is what Hegel means when he says that they are moments which "have no existence in separation from one another." The various forms of consciousness are thus organically related and have their meaning only in their relation to the other moments.

The conceptual movement of "Religion" corresponds in its basics to the moments of "Consciousness," "Self-Consciousness," and "Reason," which we have already seen. This information at the beginning of the "Religion" chapter now helps us to complete our diagram, shown in figure 8.1. In the course of "Religion," Hegel is quite forthcoming about the structure of the chapter, and we can thus find evidence for these parallelisms in many places.

The "Religion" chapter consists of three sections—"Natural Religion," "Religion in the Form of Art," and "Revealed Religion"—which correspond generally to the three divisions in the later *Lectures on the Philosophy of Religion*. With respect to the parallelisms here in the *Phenomenology*, "Natural Religion" corresponds to "Consciousness," which can be seen from the emphasis on the object sphere and, most obviously, from a number of explicit references to this effect. "The first reality of Spirit," Hegel writes, "is the Notion of religion itself, or religion as *immediate*, and therefore Natural Religion. In this, Spirit knows itself as its object in a natural or immediate shape."[15] Here the divine exists in the sphere of objectivity. The shift to the for-itself moment and to "Self-Consciousness" comes with "Religion in the Form of Art." Hegel writes, "The second reality, however, is necessarily that in which Spirit knows itself in the shape of a *superseded* natural existence, or of the self. This, therefore, is the Religion of Art; for the shape raises itself to the form of the self through the creative activity of consciousness whereby this beholds in its object its act or the self."[16] Here the emphasis is no longer on the natural, objective entity as something given, but rather on self-consciousness's reshaping and reworking of it. "Revealed Religion" finally forms the apex of the triad and thus represents the in-and-for-itself moment. It therefore corresponds to the final third of the "Reason" and

Figure 8.1

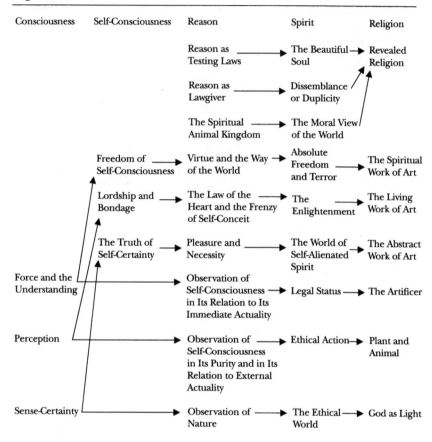

"Spirit" chapters, respectively, in which the dualisms and oppositions are ultimately overcome. Hegel tells us,

> Finally, the third reality overcomes the one-sidedness of the first two; the self is just as much an immediacy, as the immediacy is the self. If, in the first reality, Spirit in general is in the form of consciousness, and in the second, in that of self-consciousness, in the third it is in the form of the unity of both. It has the shape of being-in-and-for-itself; and when it is thus conceived as it is in and for itself, this is the Revealed Religion.[17]

In "Revealed Religion" the dualisms are overcome in the concept of revelation, since it is in revelation that man recognizes himself in God, and through this recognition man becomes reconciled with the world. This reconciliation comes about only in the revealed religion, i.e., in Christianity, according to which God is revealed to man in mundane form. By this action, God is no longer something purely transcendent and otherworldly, but rather he is a particular man living in this world. This account contains, on Hegel's view, a deep truth expressed in terms of a story. The truth of subject-object unity and individual self-awareness is expressed by the Christian account of God as revealed. Philosophical or scientific thinking understands this same truth in a different way, and this will constitute the final dialectical step to absolute knowing.

A. The Repetition of "Consciousness": Natural Religion (§§684–98)

General Introduction (§684)

In his introductory remarks Hegel confirms our thesis that the structure of the "Religion" chapter repeats the dialectical movements of "Consciousness," "Self-Consciousness," and "Reason." He notes clearly that religion, which is, as we have seen, Spirit having become aware of itself, contains within it the aspect of both consciousness and self-consciousness: "The Spirit that knows Spirit is consciousness of itself and is present to itself in objective form; it *is*; and is at the same time being that is *for itself. It is for itself,* it is the aspect of *self*-consciousness, and that too, in contrast to the aspect of its consciousness, or of the relating of itself to itself as *object.*"[18] What does it amount to here at the level of religion to say that the aspects of consciousness and self-consciousness are still present? For Hegel, the divine takes the form of both an object of consciousness and self-consciousness itself, i.e., it passes through the moments of in-itself and for-itself. Here in the first part of the triad of religion, "Natural Religion," Hegel examines different conceptions of god or the divine in the form of nature or objects generally. Thus, "Natural Religion" corresponds both as a whole and in its parts to the "Consciousness" chapter, which was concerned with the determination of the object sphere. The next section, "Religion in the Form of Art," represents the for-itself aspect of the divine and thus corresponds to the "Self-Consciousness" chapter.

In an interesting remark here, Hegel implies that at the level of the Notion there are no individual religions per se, but rather there is only one single religion that develops conceptually.[19] He expresses this when he writes, "The series of different religions which will come to view, just as much sets forth again only the different aspects of a *single* religion, and, moreover, of every single religion, and the ideas which seem to distinguish one actual religion from another occur in each one."[20] To this idea that all religions ultimately constitute a single religion there is an analogy in Hegel's account of history in the "Spirit" chapter. History can be viewed as distinct periods, each with its own Notion, but, for the speculative philosopher, world history as a whole constitutes an organic entity and a single Notion which develops in time. Moreover, according to this passage, the individual moments of universality, particularity, and individuality or of in-itself, for-itself, and in-and-for-itself, operate both at the level of individual religions, forming an internal dialectical movement, and at the level of the sequence of different religions, forming a larger Notion of which the individual religions are only component parts. It is in this way that Hegel can talk of natural religion as the consciousness of religion and of art religion as self-consciousness. With the structure of the "Religion" chapter and the organic conception of different religions clarified, Hegel proceeds to the first analysis of natural religion.

In "Natural Religion" Hegel examines in order Zoroastrianism, the religion of ancient Persia, Hinduism of both ancient and modern India, and the pantheistic religion of ancient Egypt. We should note that the field of Oriental studies was a nascent branch of learning in Hegel's time, and for this reason Hegel, like his European contemporaries was, generally speaking, ill-informed about Eastern cultures and religion. When judged by modern standards, his accounts of Eastern religion here in "Natural Religion" are doubtless gross oversimplifications, if not outright distortions. I forgo any detailed examination of the erroneous conceptions here, since this is not the purpose of the present study. Instead, I will attempt first to understand how Hegel orders these forms of religious consciousness into his system and then to sketch what role they are intended to play in the march to absolute knowing and complete subject-object determination.

I. God as Light: Zoroastrianism (§§685–88)

In this first form of natural religion, Hegel analyzes the religion of ancient Persia which is associated with the name of Zoroaster, and for which the *Zend-Avesta* is the canonical text. He characterizes the deity of this religion with the term *Lichtwesen*, or the being of light. The historical reference here is made clear in a passage from the corresponding analysis[21] in the

Lectures on the Philosophy of Religion, where we read, "This religion of light or of the immediate good is the religion of the ancient Parsis, founded by Zoroaster."[22] Due to its aspect of immediacy, this is the first religion in the historical succession of the forms of religious consciousness. Zoroastrianism is thus the first form of consciousness which represents the divine in the object sphere or in the sphere of consciousness: "*Zoroaster's* 'light' belongs to the world of consciousness—to Spirit as a relation to something distinct from itself."[23] Here religious consciousness conceives of itself as something separated from the divine and thus fails to recognize itself in it, as is the case in all the forms of "Natural Religion." Although Hegel's analysis in this section is rather terse, it is nevertheless quite rich and provocative when properly unpacked.[24] His *Lectures on the Philosophy of Religion, Lectures on the Philosophy of History* and *Lectures on Aesthetics* are a great aid to us in this regard, since in these lectures he analyzes Zoroastrianism in greater detail and in a much more comprehensible language than in the *Phenomenology.*

With respect to the parallelisms at the categorial level that we have been following up until now, Hegel unambiguously declares that this section, as we would expect, corresponds to "Sense-Certainty," the first section of the "Consciousness" chapter.[25] He says this explicitly when he writes,

> In the immediate, first diremption of self-knowing Absolute Spirit its "shape" has the determination which belongs to *immediate consciousness* or to *sense-*certainty. Spirit beholds itself in the form of *being,* though not of the non-spiritual being that is filled with the contingent determinations of sensation, the being that belongs to sense-certainty; on the contrary, it is being that is filled with Spirit.[26]

The category of pure being of "Sense-Certainty" takes on the form of the god of light here at the level of religious Spirit. Like pure being, god as light is the immediate, undifferentiated other. But now, in accordance with the higher level of conceptual knowledge here in "Religion," this Notion has a meaning that is somewhat different from that in the "Consciousness" chapter. Here pure being is the self-conscious subject of Spirit, which posits itself in the form of the divine. In "Natural Religion" religious consciousness posits itself in the form of objects, or, as Hegel says, it presents "itself objectively."[27] Naturally enough, the first form of self-conscious Spirit as object is the "*universal object*"[28] of pure light. As in "Sense-Certainty," it is the most abstract, general conception of objectivity possible.

The Notion: God as Light (§§685–86)

What does it mean to say that the Notion of this section is pure being understood at the level of religion, i.e., the divine conceived as an abstract, universal object? Specifically, what we find here is a conception of the divinity as amorphous and omnipresent—god as light. Hegel describes this as follows: "This being which is filled with the Notion of Spirit is, then, the *'shape'* of the *simple* relation of Spirit to itself, or the 'shape' of 'shapelessness.' In virtue of this determination, this 'shape' is the pure, all-embracing and all-pervading *essential light* of sunrise, which preserves itself in its formless substantiality."[29] The conception of the divine that is at work here is something universal, abstract, and immediate. It is the formless conception of the divine as pure light. Hegel says, the ancient Persians "attained to the consciousness, that absolute truth must have the form of universality—of unity. This universal, eternal, infinite essence is not recognized at first, as conditioned in any way; it is unlimited identity."[30] Here, although god is considered the omnipresent light, he is not just the particular light of the sun or the stars but the universal, abstract Notion of light which makes the world of objects possible in the first place. God, like light is everywhere, but is indeterminate, since he cannot be identified with any single form. Hegel writes, "But light is not a lama, a Brahmin, a mountain, a brute—this or that particular essence— but sensuous universality itself."[31] Thus, the divine for Zoroastrianism is essentially a universal term.

For this conception, pure light is conceived not just as a physical principle but also as a moral one, a symbol for the good in general: "In the Persian principle this unity is manifested as light, which in this case is not simply light as such, the most universal physical element, but at the same time also *spiritual* purity—the good."[32] The light or the good is necessarily opposed by its opposite—darkness or evil: "Its otherness is the equally negative, *darkness.*"[33] Just as nothingness is the opposite of being, so also darkness is the opposite or opposing principle of light. For Hegel, the principles of good and evil necessarily complement each other and cannot be seen in isolation: "But light directly involves an opposite, namely, darkness; just as evil is the antithesis of good. As man could not appreciate good, if evil were not; and as he can be really good only when he has become acquainted with the contrary, so the light does not exist without darkness."[34] In Zoroastrianism these two principles are represented by two deities: "Ormuzd is the Lord of the kingdom of light— of good; Ahriman that of darkness—of evil."[35] These two are united in the universal being. Thus, although Ormuzd is the divinity that is revered and worshiped, there is a negative principle opposing him.

God as light is conceived as the source of all life and creation. In the proliferation of light, he gives life to all living things, which are all testimony to his omnipotence. Thus, everything that exists is in some sense a manifestation of the universal power of light and of the divine: "The [moment of] difference which it gives itself does, it is true, proliferate unchecked in the substance of existence and shapes itself to the forms of nature."[36] Even though finite things, such as animals and stars, in a sense indicate the goodness and divinity of the god of light,[37] here the divine still remains over and above these manifestations: "We see in the Persian world a pure exalted unity, as the essence which leaves the special existences that inhere in it, free."[38] The good or universal light can be found in living things, since the god of light has given them life, but it cannot be reduced to them. Since the god of light creates nature, he stands over and above the natural order and is not continuous with it. Just as pure being is not any particular perceptual object but is in a sense all of them, so also here the omnipresent god is not any particular natural entity but is all of them at the same time.

The Experience of Consciousness (§687)

This conception of god remains abstract, and this proves to be its undoing. As pure light, god, like pure being, remains formless and indeterminate. The divine so understood is conceived only as an abstract unity, but he is never seen as a self or an individual, since ultimately he remains above nature: "The content developed by this pure *being*, or the activity of its perceiving, is, therefore, an essenceless by-play in this substance which merely *ascends*, without *descending* into its depths to become a subject and through the self to consolidate its distinct moments."[39] God remains universal and never condescends to enter the empirical world of particularity. Since god is never really a perceivable subject, he remains merely an empty individual on the other side of his various empirical manifestations in nature: "The determinations of this substance are only attributes which do not attain to self-subsistence, but remain merely names of the many-named One. This One is clothed with the manifold powers of existence and with the 'shapes' of reality as with an adornment that lacks a self."[40] God as pure light is a necessary condition for the natural order, but he remains abstract and thus formless and empty. Pure light needs to be determined further if it is to be a meaningful concept.[41]

Concluding Remarks (§688)

In order to establish itself, the universality of pure light must become something particular. Just as pure being proved to be indeterminate in

"Sense-Certainty" and needed to be made particular in the form of a thing in "Perception," so also here the pure being of god as light must be made into a particular entity in the sphere of perception in order to determine itself. Hegel writes, "this reeling, unconstrained life must determine itself as being-for-self and endow its vanishing 'shapes' with an enduring subsistence."[42] The believer, instead of projecting the divine as pure being, now tries to see it as a concrete object in the world, and this calls into being a new form of religious consciousness: "The *immediate being* in which it stands in antithesis to its consciousness is itself the *negative* power which dissolves its distinctions. It is thus in truth the self; and Spirit therefore passes on to know itself in the form of self."[43] Thus, we move to the form of religion that sees the divine in concrete objects of sense, such as plants and animals.

II. Plant and Animal: Hinduism (§§689–90)

The second religion that Hegel examines is the Hinduism of India, which sees the divine in any of a number of plants, animals, and finite sensible entities. Here the divine is no longer the abstract, indeterminate other as in "God as Light," but rather specific, determinate objects of nature, and for this reason Hegel refers to this religion as a "universal pantheism."[44] Although throughout his corpus, he is, generally speaking, fairly evenhanded in his treatment of non-Western cultures, Hegel does little to hide his disdain for what he perceives as the utter incoherence and irrationality of Hinduism. In his *Lectures on the Philosophy of Religion* and *Lectures on Aesthetics*, he refers to this form of religious consciousness disparagingly as the "Religion of Phantasy" since it is to his mind pure phantasy to imagine that plants and animals can be gods: "Here fancy makes everything into god."[45] In another passage, he comments that in the Hindu religion "differentiation and manifoldness are abandoned to the wildest, most outward forms of imagination."[46] We can thus imagine that Hegel is only too happy to assign Hinduism to one of the lowest, most rudimentary forms of religious consciousness.

Predictably enough, Hegel says directly that this second section of "Natural Religion" corresponds to the second section of the "Consciousness" chapter, i.e., "Perception": "Self-conscious Spirit that has withdrawn into itself from the shapeless essence, or has raised its immediacy to self in general, determines its unitary nature as a manifoldness of being-for-self, and is the religion of spiritual *perception*."[47] Here concrete objects of perception are considered to be the divine, and in this regard this section corresponds to "Perception." However, the conception of perception at work here differs from that which we examined in "Consciousness," since here we are concerned with "spiritual perception," i.e., the perception of the divine. Spirit posits itself as the divine in natural objects. This is clearly one of Hegel's least developed analyses, and thus we must try to fill in the details that he left out. Fortunately, this form of religion is treated in the *Lectures on the Philosophy of Religion*, the *Lectures on Aesthetics*, and the *Lectures on the Philosophy of History*.

The Notion: The Divine as Objects of Perception (§689)

In Hinduism the god Brahma is the one and the creator, and in this respect he is like the god of light of Zoroastrianism. Hegel describes this aspect of Brahma as follows: "One extreme in the Indian mind is the consciousness of the absolute as what in itself is purely universal, undifferentiated, and therefore completely indeterminate."[48] In this respect Brahma is simply an abstract unity, which can be neither thought nor perceived: "Since this extreme abstraction has no particular content and is not visualized as a concrete personality, it affords in no respect a material which intuition could shape in some way or other."[49] The abstract unity thus is empty of content and stands apart from all thought and perception. This represents the universal aspect of Brahma.

But there is another aspect of the divine in that Brahma does not remain universal and abstract, but instead spreads himself out and inhabits the plurality of sensuous things. This conception is thus the opposite of Zoroastrianism, which conceives of the divine exclusively as an abstract, omnipresent unity. The amorphous god of light is transformed here into concrete empirical objects of nature. Hegel explains that Brahma is a single deity who has a plurality of incarnations: "In this it falls apart into the numberless multiplicity of weaker and stronger, richer and poorer Spirits."[50] These deities all take on their own personalities, some being "stronger," others "richer," and yet others "poorer." Each possesses its own identity and characteristics and all become individual gods. In his lectures he describes the conceptual birth of the plurality of gods as follows: "Imposing natural objects, such as the Ganges, the sun, the Himalaya . . . become identified with Brahma himself. So too with love, deceit, theft, avarice, as well as the sensuous powers of nature in plants and animals. . . . All these are conceived of by imagination as free and independent, and thus there arises an infinite world of deities."[51] Here, contrary to the god of Zoroastrianism, god is not thought to be above nature, but rather is continuous with the natural realm: "The parrot, the cow, the ape, etc., are likewise incarnations of god, yet are not therefore elevated above their nature."[52] God is actually present in specific plants and animals which must be honored and worshiped accordingly.

This conception of the divine as essentially a unity which disseminates itself into a plurality corresponds straightforwardly to the Notion of "Perception." Just as in "Perception" the One constitutes the stabile unity behind the Also, i.e., the plurality of properties, so also here Brahma is the One or the unity who has a plurality of different sensible forms. Now religious consciousness sees the divine in a manifold of different plant and animal forms, which are available to perception: "for the principle of the Hindu religion is the manifestation of diversity [in 'avatars']. These then, fall outside that abstract unity of thought and, as that which deviates from it, constitute the variety found in the world of sense, the variety of intellectual conceptions in an unreflected sensuous form."[53] The emphasis on sense perception here also provides testimony for the parallelism with the "Perception" chapter. Hegel writes, "The Indian view of things is a universal pantheism, a pantheism, however, of imagination, not of thought. One substance pervades the whole of things, and all individualizations are directly vitalized and animated into particular powers."[54] Here the divine is grasped not with the faculty of abstraction or understanding but directly with the senses. The divine is everywhere in the objects of sense. Just as god as light represented the universal, so also here god in the form of particular plants and animals represents particularity. The divine exists in the plurality of natural forms of plants, animals and any other object of sense: "Everything, therefore—sun, moon, stars, the Ganges, the Indus, beasts, flowers—everything is a god to it."[55]

The Experience of Consciousness (§689)

On the one hand, Brahma in his universal aspect is only an empty One in the abstract unity of the divine. But the One alone, like the god of light, remains abstract and devoid of content. On the other hand, god in his particular aspect can be found in any number of sensible objects. But there is a chaotic, self-destructive plurality in this aspect of the divine. The fact that the divine is embodied in concrete plants and animals leads to animosity between the different forms. The various plants and animals appear as mutually independent, and each has its own personality and divinity. Just as in "Perception" the One was an abstract unity which could not bring together the various universal properties, so also here Brahma as abstract unity cannot unite the chaotic plurality of individual plants and animals. Thus, these individualities exist solely in their own independent life and movement. Hegel explains, "This pantheism which, to begin with, is the passive subsistence of these spiritual atoms develops into a hostile movement within itself."[56] The individual forms must negate one another in order to establish themselves as individuals, since an individual deity can only be what it is in contrast to other deities which it is not. Hegel writes,

> the ensoulment of this kingdom of Spirits bears this death within it owing to the determinateness and the negativity which encroach upon the innocent indifference of plant life. Through this negativity, the dispersion into the multiplicity of passive plant forms becomes a hostile movement in which the hatred which stems from being-for-self is aroused. The *actual* self-consciousness of this dispersed Spirit is a host of separate, antagonistic national Spirits who hate and fight each other to the death and become conscious of specific forms of animals as their essence.[57]

The empty One of Brahma cannot unite these competing entities, and the individual divinities simply develop into mutually negating rivalries and animosities. This ultimately proves to be the undoing of this Notion.

Hegel analyzes the conceptual contradiction here in terms of the fundamental inability to reconcile the idea of an abstract universal unity with the concrete plurality. Just as in "Perception" the One could not be brought into consistency with the manifold of properties, so also here Brahma, as an abstract unity, cannot be made consistent with the manifold of individual deities. Of the sublation of this Notion Hegel writes, "For, on the one hand, the purely invisible, the absolute as such . . . is grasped as the truly divine, while, on the other hand, individual things in concrete reality are also, in their sensuous existence, directly regarded by imagination as divine manifestations."[58] Thus, the Notion moves back and forth between universal and particular: "While a universal essence is wrongly transmuted into sensuous objectivity, the latter is also driven from its definite character into universality—a process whereby it loses its footing and is expanded to indefiniteness."[59] In the *Lectures on the Philosophy of Religion*, Hegel describes the sublation of this Notion in similar terms: "These shapes disappear again in the same manner in which they are begotten; fancy passes over from an ordinary external mode of existence to divinity, and this in like manner returns back again to that which was its starting-point."[60] Just as in "Perception," so also here we have the passing back and forth from plurality to singularity, from particularity to universality, without any stabilizing principle. There is a fundamental contradiction at the heart of the conception of the divine as Brahma, as both One and many, just as there was an incoherence in the Notion of the thing with properties: "This unity, however, comes to have an ambiguous meaning, inasmuch as Brahma is at one time the universal, the all, and at another a particularity as contrasted with particularity in general."[61]

Thus, just as the One ultimately collapses into a chaotic plurality of properties in "Perception," so also here we are left with a manifold of gods with no order or principle. For this reason Hegel writes, "The Hindu mythology is therefore only a wild extravagance of fancy, in which nothing has a settled form."[62] In another passage, he summarizes the chaotic Notion of Hinduism as follows: "As the Hindu Spirit is a state of dreaming and mental transiency—a self-oblivious dissolution—objects also dissolve for it into unreal images and indefinitude. This feature is absolutely characteristic; and this alone would furnish us with a clear idea of the Spirit of the Hindus, from which all that has been said might be deduced."[63] The sensible confusion in the colorful plurality of gods mirrors the conceptual confusion in the thinking of the religious consciousness of Hinduism.

Concluding Remarks (§690)

From this plurality of empirical gods, religious consciousness now must go beyond perception to find a principle capable of unifying the divine chaos. Just as previously consciousness had to appeal to a force behind the scenes to unify empirical appearances, so also here religious consciousness is now obliged to abstract from perception to the realm of thought: "Spirit's consciousness is thus now the movement which is above and beyond the immediate in-itself as it is above and beyond the abstract being-for-self."[64] Some stable principle of universality must be found to counter the flux of individual deities. This principle is provided by the artificer. Of the transition to the next section, Hegel writes,

> In this hatred, however, the determinateness of purely negative being-for-self consumes itself, and through this movement of the Notion Spirit enters into another shape. *Superseded being-for-self* is the *form of the object*, a form produced by the self, or rather is the produced self, the self-consuming self, i.e. the self that becomes a thing. The artificer therefore retains the upper hand over these mutually destructive animal spirits, and his action is not merely negative, but tranquil and positive.[65]

The mutual negation of natural entities is a purely negative movement of negative individualities lacking universality. The artificer or the builder, however, creates objects that represent the divine, and in this creative action invests the object with a sense of universality and thus stability, which was not present in the natural beings: "this consciousness is not only this being-for-self which supersedes its object, but it also produces its own idea, the being-for-self that is put forth in the form of an object."[66] The artificer negates the natural object in fashioning it, but unlike the pure negation of natural entities, it raises the object to a higher form in accordance with its idea. It is thus the abstract idea in the mind of the artificer which gives the object of perception its universal aspect. This constitutes the Notion of the third and final section of "Natural Religion."

III. The Artificer: Egypt (§§691–98)

The third form of "Natural Religion" is the religion of ancient Egypt, which represents the divine in the products of human creation, such as architectural monuments. The divine is still at least in part a natural entity, but now it must be brought to light in a structure or monument conceived and manufactured by a human subject. For Hegel, what is characteristic of the Egyptians with respect to their religion is their creative impulse to produce works of art which give outward expression to the divine, and it is for this reason that the Egyptian is, for Hegel, the artificer: "The impulse just described may be regarded as representing in general the cultus of the Egyptians, this endless impulse to work, to describe or represent outwardly what is as yet only inward, contained in idea, and for this reason has not become clear to the mind."[67] By shaping and forming objects of nature, the Egyptians represent an advance over the previous stages of natural religion, which see the divine in natural objects as such. Hegel, by contrasting the religion of Egypt with the previous forms of Eastern religion, makes clear the role of this form of religious consciousness: "In the Oriental Spirit there remains as a basis the massive substantiality of Spirit immersed in nature. To the Egyptian Spirit it has become impossible . . . to remain contented with *that*."[68] It is in Egypt that the conception of the divine for the first time begins to overcome its purely natural forms and to take on its true shape as a self-conscious human subject.[69] Although Egypt is still ultimately at the level of natural religion, in contrast to its predecessors, it raises the specter of the divine as a self-conscious subject without fully working out this conception. In the next section, the Greek religion will complete this movement from nature to Spirit and from object to subject.

At the level of the category, this third form of religion corresponds, naturally enough, to the third section of the "Consciousness" chapter, namely "Force and the Understanding," and operates with the categories, the inner and the outer, supersensible and appearance, ground and consequence, etc. Hegel makes this connection when he writes, "The first form, because it is immediate, is the abstract form of the understanding, and the work is not yet in its own self filled with Spirit."[70] The divine is no longer seized by the senses but rather, since it is thought to be hidden, with the faculty of the understanding. Here we find a split that corresponds to the appearance-reality dualism of "Force and the Understanding." One such dualism concerns the idea or plan of the artificer in contrast to its concrete realization. The artificer has an idea which he wishes to realize in the empirical sphere, but his plan is an idealized form which can only be imperfectly imitated with the medium of natural materials. Thus, there exist two spheres, one of the idea in the mind of the artificer or the formal cause, in Aristotelian terms, and one in the empirical sphere of appearance where the product has its reality. Another dualism has as its terms the inner sphere of the divine, or the spirits of the dead, and the outer sphere of artistic representation. But in the end these two forms of dualism amount to the same thing, since the inner sphere of the divine is simply self-consciousness's own positing of the divine, i.e., self-consciousness's own idea.

The Notion: The Construction of Monuments (§§691–95)

This Notion operates at the abstract level of the understanding in contrast to the concrete level of perception. Here religious consciousness conceives of the divine as something abstract and formal and then gives it shape by transforming natural materials in accordance with its idea. This Notion thus has an individual aspect in the natural materials that the artificer employs for his creation, and a universal aspect which is in the thought and plan of the artificer: "The division from which the artificer-spirit starts [is] the *in-itself* which becomes the material it fashions, and being-for-self which is the aspect of self-consciousness at work."[71] Given this split between matter and thought, the material becomes relatively unimportant. Indeed, the products of the artificer's labor are comprehensible only when compared to the abstract idea according to which they were shaped:

> The crystals of pyramids and obelisks, simple combinations of straight lines with plane surfaces and equal proportions of parts, in which the incommensurability of the round is destroyed, these are the works of this artificer of rigid form. On account of the merely *abstract* intelligibleness of the form, the significance of the work is not in the work itself, is not the spiritual self.[72]

The true meaning of the work is its universal aspect in thought. This universal aspect of the divine as portrayed in concrete works of architecture represents an improvement over the religion of plant and animal, which ended up with only a chaotic particularity of divinities in the sensible sphere. By reshaping the objects of nature according to a self-conscious plan, the artificer invests his work with a universal element, which transcends the realm of particularity and sense: "the artificer of the self-conscious form at the same time destroys the transitoriness inherent in the immediate existence of this life and brings its organic forms nearer to the more rigid and more universal forms of thought."[73] Thus, through the thought of the artificer the created objects take on a universal form, which was not present in the objects given in nature.

The dialectic of the inner and the outer from "Force and the Understanding" is present here in the creation of the artificer.[74] The created object has an outer appearance in the empirical sphere, but it is also supposed to have a divine inner aspect. The creative drive of the Egyptian artificer is to divulge the inner and to make it clear through art: "It has been the task, the deed of this people to produce these works . . . we see the Spirit laboring ceaselessly to render its idea visible to itself, to bring into clearness, into consciousness, what it inwardly is."[75] The works that Hegel has in mind here are above all grand-scale architectural structures and not simply any arbitrary work of art, as he indicates with his reference to "pyramids and obelisks."[76] These are architectural structures that are intended to house the dead spirits, and this function constitutes their essential relation to the divine: "The enormous works of the Egyptians which still remain to us are almost entirely those only which were destined for the dead."[77] The reference here to the monuments for the dead is made explicitly once again in Hegel's *Lectures on the Philosophy of History*, where he provides a number of concrete examples:

> Of these works I will mention no others than those devoted to the dead, and which especially attract our attention. These are, the enormous excavations in the hills along the Nile at Thebes, whose passages and chambers are entirely filled with mummies—subterranean abodes as large as the largest mining works of our time: next, the great field of the dead in the plain of Sais, with its walls and vaults: thirdly, those wonders of the world, the pyramids, whose destination, though stated long ago by Herodotus and Diodorus, has been only recently expressly confirmed—to the effect, viz., that these prodigious crystals, with their geometrical regularity, contain dead bodies: and lastly, that most astonishing work, the tombs of the kings, of which one has been opened by Belzoni in modern times.[78]

These monumental works are created for the divine spirits, and it is the Egyptian conception of the dead which is the key, for Hegel, for understanding the dialectical movement of the inner and the outer.[79]

The Egyptian doctrine of immortality makes clear the distinction between nature and Spirit, the mortal and the divine. The conception of an immortal soul represents a victory over pure nature: "this proposition that the soul is immortal, is intended to mean that it is something other than nature—that Spirit is inherently independent."[80] The Egyptians developed a cult of the dead and created monuments to house the departed spirits as a celebration of Spirit and its superiority to nature.

The opposition of the inner and the outer in Egyptian religion causes Hegel in his *Lectures on the Philosophy of Religion* to name this form of religious consciousness "The Religion of Mystery." The Egyptian religion always is veiled and maintains a hidden inner side.[81] For Hegel, this stands in sharp contrast to Greek religion and art, which forms the next stage of religious consciousness: "The Spirit of the Egyptian nation is, in fact, an enigma. In Greek works of art everything is clear, everything is evident; in Egyptian art a problem is everywhere presented; it is an external sign, by means of which something which has not been yet openly expressed is indicated."[82] While Egyptian art always tries to express something hidden or unseen, Greek art is transparent, since for Greek religion there are no inner mysteries, and there is nothing that is not accessible to all.

With the construction the artificer creates a "habitation" or "dwelling" for the divine spirits, and with the natural materials that he employs he provides the final proof of the sublation of the previous Notion, which saw the divine in particular plants and animals. Here plants and animals are used as means by the artificer for the creation of his monuments. At first "he employs plant-life . . . and reduces it to an outer aspect, to a mere ornament."[83] The plants are no longer divine, but rather are mere ornamental material with which to decorate the monument. They take on a universal aspect only in relation to the artificer, who brings these "organic forms nearer to the more rigid and more universal forms of thought"[84] in accordance with his architectural plan. Likewise, animal life, now purged of its divine element, is used only as a means, as hieroglyphic symbols: "the animal shape at the same time becomes superseded and the hieroglyph of another meaning, of a thought."[85] As Hegel says in his *Lectures on the Philosophy of History:* "The brute form is, on the other hand, turned into a symbol: it is also partly degraded to a mere hieroglyphical sign. I refer here to the innumerable figures on the Egyptian monuments, of sparrow-hawks or falcons, dung-beetles, scarabaei, etc."[86] Thus, the universal aspect of animal life is, as for plant life, found in the realm of thought. The outer aspect of the dwelling of the divine is adorned with forms of plant and animal life which have lost their divine significance. They are relegated to the mundane outer sphere, while the divine dwells within.

The Experience of Consciousness (§§695–98)

The dialectical relation of inner and outer ultimately proves to be the undoing of this Notion, since it implicitly gives evidence that the believer is separated from the divine. As we have seen, according to the dialectical relation of the inner and the outer, the monument created by the artificer must possess an inner aspect, which represents the divine: "Over against this outer shape of the self stands the other shape which proclaims its possession of an *inner being*. Nature, withdrawing into its essence, deposes its living, self-particularizing, self-entangling manifold existence to the level of an unessential husk, which is the *covering for the inner being.*"[87] Here religious consciousness abstracts from the natural material that it employed to give shape to the object and concentrates purely on its unseen internal aspect where the divine being is thought to be domiciled. But the fact that the dead spirits constitute the divine indicates implicitly that the gods are alien or separated from the believer. The spirits are gone and departed and no longer dwell in the human sphere, but rather in some mysterious beyond which must be represented by the artificer: "the works receive Spirit into them only as an alien, departed spirit that has forsaken its living saturation with reality and, being itself dead, takes up its abode in this lifeless crystal."[88] The outward appearance of the pyramid is a mere shell or husk for the divine being that dwells within. The inner is thought to be a self-conscious divinity, which the artificer is able to capture only imperfectly in his monuments. The work of the artificer is considered to be only an "unessential husk" with no meaning in itself. The outer is thus not a reflection of the inner at all; instead, the outer shell, which represents the side of the artificer, is merely something inessential. Since the inner and the outer remain unreconciled, there remains a separation or alienation of the divine from the creation of the artificer: "the inner being . . . is not immanently differentiated and is still separated from its outer existence."[89]

When this separation is recognized, the artificer sees in his works themselves the means for overcoming it. The inner and the outer moments must now be unified, and the artificer tries to unite the two spheres in constructing ambiguous forms which reflect both moments: "The artificer therefore unites the two by blending the natural and the self-conscious shape."[90] In other words, the artificer tries to represent the inner divine in its true self-conscious shape by ridding it of its natural elements and giving it the form of man: "the shape, too, is no longer solely and entirely used by the artificer, but is blended with the shape of thought, with a human form. But the work still lacks the shape and outer reality in which the self exists as self."[91] In his *Lectures on the Philosophy of History,* Hegel illustrates this by a provocative analysis of the Sphinx: "The Sphinx may be regarded as a symbol of the Egyptian Spirit. The human head looking out from the animal body, exhibits Spirit as it begins to emerge from the merely natural—to tear itself loose therefrom and already to look more freely around it; without, however, entirely freeing itself from the fetters nature had imposed."[92] For Hegel, the Sphinx is a perfect example of the inner divinity coming out of its animal embodiment, which is only an outward appearance, and coming forth in its true human form:

> we observe the conception liberating itself from the direct animal form, and the continued contemplation of it; and that which was only surmised and aimed at in that form, advancing to comprehensibility and conceivableness. The hidden meaning—the Spiritual—emerges as a human face from the brute. The multiform sphinxes, with lion's bodies and virgins' heads—or as male sphinxes (androsfugges) with beards—are evidence supporting the view that the meaning of the Spiritual is the problem which the Egyptians proposed to themselves.[93]

The Egyptian religion is filled with ambiguous images of this sort, e.g., the god Anubis, who is conceived as an entity having a human body and a dog's head.[94] The Egyptians tried to purge the divine or the inner of its natural aspect but were unable to do so completely, and thus ultimately the Egyptian religion remains a natural religion. The individual remains separated from the divine, and the divine has not yet gained the true form of self-conscious Spirit.

Concluding Remarks

We now arrive at what corresponds to the transition from "Consciousness" to "Self-Consciousness." Here at the level of religious Spirit, one self-consciousness confronts another when the artificer confronts his half-human, half-animal creations:

> In this work, there is an end of the instinctive effort which produced the work that, in contrast to self-consciousness, lacked consciousness; for in it, the activity of the artificer, which constitutes self-consciousness, comes face to face with an equally self-conscious, self-expressive inner being. In it he has worked himself up to the point where his consciousness is divided against it, where Spirit meets Spirit.[95]

Religious consciousness now takes a step toward seeing itself in the divine, first by realizing the divine in the products of its own labor, and second by recognizing its own human form in the divine. Self-consciousness must move beyond natural objects and represent the divine to itself in the form of a self-conscious subject: "the statue in human shape."[96] This realization marks the transition to the next section.

Just as in *Lectures on the Philosophy of History* the civilization of ancient Egypt appears immediately prior to the Greek world and constitutes a transition to it, so also here in the "Religion" chapter of the *Phenomenology* the religion of ancient Egypt is a transitional figure between natural religion and the Greek religion, which Hegel treats in the next section, entitled "Religion in the Form of Art." He says, "the Egyptian unity—combining contradictory elements—occupies a middle place."[97] For Hegel the hieroglyphics, like the half-human, half-animal artworks and monuments, represent an intermediary phase. Hieroglyphics are, on the one hand, not just pictures, since they represent something more— syllables—but, on the other hand, it is not yet writing per se, since it has not yet reached the form of individual letters. It is somewhere between pictures and a true alphabet: "Written language is still a hieroglyphic; and its basis is only the sensuous image, not the letter itself."[98] According to Hegel, the Greeks were the first to purge the conception of the divine of all its natural elements and to see the gods as anthropomorphic, self-conscious subjects. For Hegel, this indicates both the recognition of the unity of the divine with the human and a recognition of self-conscious Spirit in the divine other. The religion of ancient Egypt is an intermediary phase, insofar as it sees the divine in a partly natural and partly human form, the latter being the form of Spirit. The Egyptian religion was, for Hegel, caught in the contradiction between conceiving of the divine as both nature and self-conscious Spirit: "We thus see Egypt intellectually confined by a narrow, involved, close view of nature, but breaking through this; impelling it to self-contradiction, and proposing to itself the problem which that contradiction implies."[99] The Egyptians were caught up in natural religion, but at the same time attempted to free themselves from it. Hegel says that the "pervading principle" of the Egyptian Spirit "is found to be, that the two elements of reality—Spirit sunk in nature, and the impulse to liberate it—are here held together inharmoniously as contending elements."[100] The Greeks resolve this contradiction by eliminating the natural element altogether and presenting the gods in idealized human forms. The Sphinx sheds its pelt and tail; its paws are transformed into hands and feet; it stands upright and is metamorphized into the Greek sculpture of the god as self-conscious Spirit.

B. The Repetition of "Self-Consciousness": Religion in the Form of Art (§§699–747)

General Introduction (§§699–704)

We now move from the account of Eastern religion to the beginning of religious consciousness in the Western tradition. Hegel tells us that this section as a whole corresponds historically to the Greek world which, as we know from the "Spirit" chapter, he refers to as "the true Spirit." Here he makes this connection clear when he writes, "If we ask, which is the *actual* Spirit which has the consciousness of its absolute essence in the religion of art, we find that it is the *ethical* or the *true* Spirit."[101] Thus, in the three discussions in this section we will examine various aspects of the religion and culture of the ancient Greeks. Hegel's analysis here covers the Greeks' achievements in, among other things, the plastic arts, epic, and drama, and he explores other elements of Greek life that do not seem directly relevant for the account of religion that is the object of study here. According to Hegel's account, all of these forms of Greek art are ultimately manifestations of religion.[102] Hegel's intention by including Greek art in this context is to examine the way in which the divine is conceived and represented by the Greeks, and their artworks constitute an invaluable source of information in this regard. Thus, in this section he is not interested in art per se, but only in the way in which various art forms are used to represent the divine. In his *Lectures on the Philosophy of Religion* this discussion of Greek religion is referred to as "The Religion of Beauty," and, just as in the *Phenomenology*, it occupies an intermediary stage between Eastern religion and Christianity.

With the move to "Religion in the Form of Art," we now enter the realm of "Religion," which corresponds to "Self-Consciousness." Here religious Spirit posits the divine as another self-conscious subject and portrays it in various forms of art. Hegel writes, "Spirit has raised the shape in which it is present to its own consciousness into the form of consciousness itself and it produces such a shape for itself."[103] The representations of the divine are now wholly cleansed of their natural forms, which were still present in part in the Egyptian religious consciousness: "In this unity of self-conscious Spirit with itself, insofar as it is the shape and the object of its consciousness, its blendings with the unconscious shapes are purged of the immediate shapes of nature. These monsters in shape, word, and deed are dissolved into spiritual shape."[104] The artificer, as we have seen, was still bound up with nature and could not wholly free itself from it: "The Egyptian Spirit also was a similar laborer in matter, but the natural had not yet been subjected to the Spiritual. No advance was made beyond a struggle and contest with it; the natural still took an independent position, and formed one side of the image, as in the body of the Sphinx."[105] The Greek Spirit manages to purge the conception of the divine of its last vestiges of nature. Thus, we abandon the various conceptions of the divine as a natural object and turn to examine god in anthropomorphic terms as subject.

Although the Greek Spirit conceives of the divine in human form and has thus freed itself from nature to this extent, it is still nonetheless tied to nature to the degree to which it must use natural materials to represent the divine, for example, the marble of the sculpture. Hegel writes,

> The activity of Spirit does not yet possess in itself the material and organ of expression, but needs the excitement of nature and the matter which nature supplies: it is not free, self-determining Spirituality, but mere naturalness formed to Spirituality—Spiritual individuality. The Greek Spirit is the plastic artist, forming the stone into a work of art. In this formative process the stone does not remain mere stone—the form being only superinduced from without; but it is made an expression of the Spiritual, even contrary to its nature, and thus *trans*formed.[106]

Although Greek religion represents an improvement over natural religion, it has still not reached the highest form of religious consciousness, since it still requires the external impulse from nature. Only when Spirit can produce itself and determine itself such that it is wholly independent of nature do we reach the final stage of religion.

I. The Abstract Work of Art (§§705–19)

We now enter into the realm of the religious consciousness of ancient Greece, in which the individual comes to see itself in the divine, which is represented in the form of a self-conscious subject. Now, in "The Abstract Work of Art" self-consciousness no longer has natural entities for its object, but rather "Spirit brings itself forth as object."[107] Self-consciousness examines itself and conceives of the divine as a being like itself. In order to understand the Greeks' conception of the divine, Hegel examines various forms of Greek art in which the divine is manifested. For this reason, his account of religion here shades over into an account of aesthetics. The experience of consciousness will pass through three phases: (1) the work of art as a static object, i.e., a sculpture of the god; (2) the work of art in the medium of language, i.e., the hymn and the oracle; and (3) the synthesis of the two in the cult.

As we saw in our previous analyses, "Natural Religion" corresponded to the "Consciousness" chapter, and now, naturally enough, "Religion in the Form of Art" will correspond to "Self-Consciousness." Therefore, "The Abstract Work of Art" has as its analogue "The Truth of Self-Certainty," the first form of "Self-Consciousness," and it represents the transition from "Consciousness" to "Self-Consciousness" at the level of religious thinking. Now the god is no longer an object of nature but "has taken on consciousness."[108] In the history of religious consciousness that we have been surveying, this represents the first attempt to represent the divine in purely human form. Hegel confirms that this section corresponds to the transition to "Self-Consciousness" that we saw earlier in the dialectic when he writes at the beginning of this section that we now "move away from this immediate and objective mode towards self-consciousness."[109] Each of the figures in this section is thus an attempt to see the divine as a self-conscious subject.

The Notion: The Divine Manifestation in Natural Material (§705)

In this section Hegel sketches the general Notion only very briefly and in the vaguest of terms before moving on to discuss concrete instantiations of it in the experience of consciousness. This may be seen as evidence for the claim that the "Religion" chapter was written quickly and that Hegel did not have the opportunity to fill out some of his analyses in a way that he would have liked. Thus, we must do some reconstructive work to determine the nature of the Notion here. Hegel helps us in this regard by outlining the three moments in this section. He writes of the Greek sculpture that constitutes the first moment: "The first work of art, as immediate, is abstract and individual."[110] A word about the meaning of the term "abstract" in this context is in order, since Hegel's use of it here is somewhat at odds with current usage in the field of art. By "abstract art" Hegel means the idealized human forms that we find in Greek sculpture. These forms are abstract since one must abstract from the actual natural forms and their imperfections in order to arrive at them. Although in Greek sculpture the gods have human form, it is not a natural human form, but rather a perfected, idealized one. The second moment in the experience of consciousness introduces the element of language and thus moves from the sphere of the object with sculpture to the sphere of the subject: "As for itself, it has to move away from this immediate and objective mode towards self-consciousness."[111] Finally, these two moments are united in the cult: "self-consciousness . . . in the cult aims at getting rid of the distinction by which it distinguishes itself at first from its Spirit, and by so doing to produce a work of art which is in its own self animate."[112]

Given that these three moments collectively represent the Notion here, we must ask what all three of these moments have in common. What is the Notion that they collectively constitute? All three of these moments conceive of the divine as a human subject, at first as a sculpture, then in the form of a religious hymn in praise of a god, then in the spirit of objects of nature that are sacrificed in the cult. Although all of these conceptions are of anthropomorphic deities, these deities are manifested in the sphere of objects. The self-conscious god is in the object of the sculpture, the object of the hymn, and the sacrificial object of nature. Although the divine is conceived as a self-conscious subject, it is still represented in the form of an object. This is the general Notion here in "The Abstract Work of Art," which encompasses all three aspects or incarnations. This Notion can be made more clear by contrast to the Notion of the next section, "The Living Work of Art," according to which the divine subject is represented in an actual living subject. By contrast, we must explore here how religious consciousness represents the self-conscious god in the sphere of objects.

The Experience of Consciousness

The In-Itself Moment: The Sculpture of the God (§§706–9)

As we have already seen, the characteristic of Greek religion is that religious consciousness tries to see the divine in the form of a self-conscious human subject. Here the divine is self-consciously represented by the sculptor in the form of a statue that resembles a human being. No longer as in ancient Egypt are we concerned with "an instinctive fashioning of material,"[113] but rather now the artist is wholly aware of his actions and self-consciously attempts to represent the divine. The creation of the sculpture is considered a divinely inspired act with the *pathos* of the artist originating from the god: "The concrete existence of the pure Notion into which Spirit has fled from its body is an individual which Spirit selects to be the vessel of its sorrow. Spirit is present in this individual as his universal and as the power over him from which he suffers violence, as his *pathos*, by giving himself over to which his self-consciousness loses its freedom."[114] The god chooses specific individuals and makes artists out of them by inspiring them with the knowledge and skill to create. The inspired artist uses natural materials and, under the influence of the god, tries to shape them into forms of the divine: "This pure activity, conscious of its inalienable strength, wrestles with the shapeless essence. Becoming its master, it has made the *pathos* into its material and given itself its content, and this unity emerges as a work, universal Spirit individualized and set before us."[115] In the creative act, the sculptor is united with the divine from which he receives inspiration. A unity is also attained in the sculpture itself which, as a sculpture of a self-conscious divinity, has a universal element that is represented in natural materials in the concrete sphere of perception. This harmony stands at the center of the Notion that is treated in this section.

The god, portrayed in the form of a statue, is thus an object or an individual entity in the realm of immediacy. Hegel describes this as follows, "The first mode in which the artistic Spirit keeps its shape and its active consciousness farthest apart is the immediate mode, viz. the shape *is there* or is *immediately* present simply as a *thing*."[116] The artist creates a statue of the god, and thus gives the divine an immediate reality. The essence of the god is recognized in the idealized form of the statue. The perfection of the lines and figure of the statue of the god constitute an abstract form, i.e., abstracted from natural instantiations:

> the Notion strips off the traces of root, branches, and leaves still adhering to the forms and purifies the latter into shapes in which the crystal's straight lines and flat surfaces are raised into incommensurable ratios, so that the ensoulment of the organic is taken up into the abstract form of the understanding and . . . its essential nature—incommensurability—is preserved for the understanding.[117]

In contrast to the Notion of the artificer, according to which the god was domiciled in natural shapes, the divine here is purged of its natural forms and, now liberated, comes forth in its true human form: "The human form strips off the animal shape with which it was blended; the animal is for the god merely an accidental guise; it steps alongside its true shape and no longer has any worth on its own account."[118] The divine is no longer only half-human, like the Sphinx, but rather is wholly human in form. The mysterious god which for the artificer dwelled in the sphere of the inner is now seen in the light of day, accessible to all. This purging of the natural or individual element represents the sublation of nature and the appropriation of the object by self-consciousness: "Nature [is] transfigured by thought and united with self-conscious life. The form of the gods has, therefore, its nature-element within it as a transcended moment, as a dim memory."[119] This constitutes the ultimate sublation of natural religion.

Hegel interprets specific episodes of Greek mythology as symbolic of this overcoming of nature.[120] For Hegel, the revolution of the gods in which the Olympians displaced the earlier generation represents at the level of picture-thinking the sublation of the natural element and the movement from Oriental religious forms to Greek religion: "This degradation of nature is in the Greek mythology the turning point of the whole—expressed as the war of the gods, the overthrow of the Titans by the race of Zeus."[121] The earlier generation of gods, the Titans, represent the forces of nature or, more precisely, they are the forces of nature themselves: "Helios is not god of the sun . . . and Oceanos is not god of the sea in such a way that the god and that over which he rules are distinguished from each other; on the contrary these powers are natural powers."[122] The new generation, headed by Zeus, represents Spirit. Thus, when Zeus destroys Chronos and defeats the older generation, nature is overcome, and the world becomes invested with Spirit: "These ancient gods, first-born children of the union of light with darkness, heaven, earth, ocean, sun, the earth's blind typhonic fire, and so on, are supplanted by shapes which . . . are no longer creatures of nature, but lucid, ethical Spirits of self-conscious nations."[123]

The idealized statue of the god, however, does not express the true essence of the artist who creates it. The statue is a universal, idealized form which cannot reflect the individual idiosyncrasies of the individual artist. Thus, although the artist may have created a beautiful statue, he does not see himself as an individual reflected in it. Hegel describes this as follows: "What belongs to the substance, the artist gave entirely to his work, but to himself as a particular individuality he gave in his work no actual existence: he could impart perfection to his work only by emptying himself of his particularity, depersonalizing himself and rising to the abstraction of pure action."[124] The artistic work was performed by the particular sculptor with his hands and skill. But the true work is that which is inspired by the divine and in which the individuality of the particular artist plays no role. The artist must "declare the work of art to be in its own self absolutely inspired, and . . . forget himself as performer."[125] The recognition of the beauty of the sculpture by the general public is merely testimony to its divinely inspired nature and is in no way conceived as a reflection of the skill and discipline of the individual artist.[126] The work is considered only from the divine side and not from the human side. Since the artist is alienated from his project and realizes that "in his work . . . he did not produce a being *like himself*,"[127] he must now search for another medium more appropriate for expressing and portraying the divine.

The For-Itself Moment: The Hymn and the Oracle (§§710–13)

It is by introducing the element of speech that religious consciousness hopes to give a more adequate representation of the divine and to establish the unity of itself with it. Hegel describes this second moment as follows: "The work of art therefore demands another element of its existence, the god another mode of coming forth. . . . This higher element is language—an outer reality that is immediately self-conscious existence."[128] Language is the true characteristic of a self-conscious subject. Through the element of language the artist hopes to retain his individuality that was lost in the divinely inspired sculpture and to see himself reflected in the divine. In sculpture the divinity entered the material from the outside and was thus ultimately separated from it. Now with language this separation is overcome, and the divinity with his divine words does not need to enter into any foreign material: "The god, therefore, who has language for the element of his shape is the work of art that is in its own self inspired, that possesses immediately in its outer existence the pure activity which, when it existed as a thing, was in contrast to it. . . . [S]elf-consciousness, in the objectification of its essence, abides immediately with itself."[129] In language the self-conscious god is immediately present, since through language he can immediately reveal himself.

The element of language is introduced first into the religion of art via religious songs or hymns.[130] It is through the medium of the human voice that the divine is manifested: "Man has immediately in one of his organs, the voice, an element which admits and requires a more extensive purport than the mere sensuous present . . . it requires an import created by imagination and Spirit."[131] The element of language is, in contrast to the statue, something inward, and through religious hymns language brings the inward to expression in the external world. The divine comes to light in the singing of the religious songs of praise: "Abiding thus with itself in its essence, it is *pure thought*, or the devotion whose *inwardness* in the hymn has at the same time an *outer* existence. It retains within itself the individuality of self-consciousness."[132] Now in the singing of the hymn, the individual believer, like the sculptor, is inspired by the god. Thus, in the singing of the religious hymn, the individual, united with others in the community, is united with the divine: "Spirit, as this universal self-consciousness of all, has its pure inwardness, no less than the being-for-others and the being-for-self of the individuals, in a single unity."[133] Thus, it seems as if the introduction of this linguistic element into the Notion overcomes the limitation of the divine in the figure of the statue.

However, speech, as we learned in "Sense-Certainty," has no enduring existence. It is not like an object or a sculpture, which remains more or less stable through time. Indeed, the hymn is determined precisely by the contingent position of the individual sounds to one another in time. When the hymn is over, there no longer exists any sign of the divine. Hegel writes with respect to the hymn, "speech is a vanishing existence;

and whereas in the statue the liberated objectivity lacks an immediate self of its own, in speech, on the other hand, objectivity remains too much shut up within the self, falls short of attaining a lasting shape and is, like time, no longer immediately present in the very moment of its being present."[134] Just like the particular "Now" that never held fast but rather continually vanished into the universal "Now" or the universal stream of time, so also here the hymn passes as does the divinity and its unity with the individual.

The divine utterances of the oracle represent another form of the divine in the medium of language: "the gods, as themselves knowing and willing, declare their wisdom to men by way of natural phenomena."[135] The believer seeks to learn the divine will by consulting the oracle and other signs, such as the entrails of animals or the flight of birds,[136] in order that he might direct his actions in accordance with it: "the utterance peculiar to the god who is the Spirit of an ethical nation is the oracle, which knows its particular affairs and what is advantageous concerning them."[137] Through the utterances of the oracle, the divine will enters the empirical world and becomes known. The individuals can then gain a sort of unity with the divine by ordering their actions in accordance with the divine plan.

Despite consciousness' attempt to recognize its individuality in the utterance of the oracle and then unify its actions with the divine will, this form of religion also proves to be inadequate. The oracle collapses in the dialectic of universal and particular. The individual consults the oracle about particular undertakings in concrete contexts, but the divine can only utter universal truths. The universal truths, however, remain indeterminate in their generality and are of no use in directing concrete actions: "the universal Spirit . . . utters equally simple and universal statements about the divine being, the substantial content of which is sublime in its simple truth, but on account of this, universality at the same time appears trivial to the progressively developing self-consciousness."[138] Given that the utterances are universal and indeterminate, they must be given a particular meaning.[139] Thus, the individual must interpret the divine utterances, which are invariably indeterminate and ambiguous: "To the definite question, the god, as representing the divine in general, gives a general answer, for it is only what is general, and not the individual as such, that is included in the end aimed at by the gods. The general is, however, ambiguous, capable of a double meaning, for it comprises both sides."[140] The oracle reveals either universal platitudes, which are empty, or contingencies, which have no regularity and no law. Birds are considered to be messengers of divine will, and thus their flight, in itself a contingent event, must be made the subject of careful interpretation. By referring to the oracle, the individual must put aside his own judgment and assessment of the situation. He thus allows his action in the sphere of contingency to be dictated and directed by the contingent utterance of the oracle: "For the contingent is something that is not self-possessed and is alien, and therefore the ethical consciousness lets itself settle such matters too, as by a throw of the dice, in an unthinking and alien manner."[141] For Hegel, the Greeks have "not pressed on to the extreme of inwardness at which the subject draws the decision for his action purely from within himself."[142] The contingent events are alien to the self-conscious subject, who cannot find himself in them since they evince no regularity. Thus, speech in its particularity is sublated. We now need a way to unite the stability and enduring nature of the sculpture with the immediate utterance and divine speech found in the hymn. For Hegel, these two elements are united in the cult.

The In-and-For-Itself Moment: The Cult (§§714–19)

Finally, in the third moment the two previous elements are unified. The divine is portrayed not merely in the static form of a thing, or sculpture, or as a mere phenomenon of speech, but rather as both together. This synthesis takes place in the rites of the cult. Hegel introduces this third moment as follows: "The movement of the two sides constitutes the cult: a movement in which the divine shape *in motion* in the pure feeling element of self-consciousness, and the divine shape *at rest* in the element of thinghood, mutually surrender their distinctive characters, and the unity which is the Notion of their essence achieves an existence."[143] In the first moment, the divine entered the sculpture as an external other in which the subject could not find himself. In the second moment, the identity of the subject with the divine was only momentary and disappeared with the ending of the hymn. The divine and the human are finally united in the practice of the cult:[144] "In the cult, the self gives itself the consciousness of the divine being descending to it from its remoteness, and this divine being, which formerly was not actual but only an object over against it, through this act receives the actuality proper to self-consciousness."[145] On the one hand, the devotions of the sacred hymn raise the individual believer to the realm of the universal divinity: "The soul, because of its abstract character, is not consciousness which distinguishes its object from itself; it is thus only the night of its existence and the place prepared for its [outer] shape. The abstract cult therefore raises the self into being this pure divine element."[146] On the other hand, in the sculpture or statue, the divine is brought down into the realm of objects: "The divine being has in this the meaning of a free object."[147] Here in the cult both of these elements, the human and the divine, come together. Thus, in this parallel movement upward and downward, the previous moments are unified.

First, the universal divinity comes down to the realm of particularity, where it is embodied in the objects of nature. The god has already given "itself an [outer] existence and has made itself into an individual animal and into fruit."[148] The fruit on the tree and in the ground is thought to be the gift of the god. The divine dwells in the concrete objects of nature which are freely bestowed on man. Thus, when the believer sacrifices the individual objects of nature in accordance with the rites of the cult, he also sacrifices the divine in its natural element: "the divine being in its *immediacy* also perishes in this act. The animal sacrificed is the *symbol* of a god; the fruits consumed are the *living* Ceres and Bacchus themselves. In the former, die the powers of the upper law which has blood and actual life, in the latter, the powers of the lower law that possesses in bloodless form secret and cunning power."[149] The sacrifice makes sense only with the understanding that the divine exists not merely in the universal sphere but also in the particular sphere of natural objects. Thus, the universal enters the realm of particularity.

Second, the individual in the act of sacrifice ascends, so to speak, to the level of the gods. The divine is thought to dwell in the objects of nature in its inessential aspect.[150] Humans appropriate and make use of the objects which become their possessions. The individual believer by making a sacrifice of his property eliminates the particular and is united with the divine in the realm of the universal. Hegel describes this as follows:

> The act of the cult itself begins, therefore, with the pure *surrender* of a
> possession which the owner, apparently without any profit whatever to
> himself, pours away or lets rise up in smoke. In so doing, he renounces
> before the essence of his pure consciousness all possession and right of
> the property and enjoyment thereof, renounces [his] personality and the
> return of his act into himself; and he reflects the act into the universal, or
> into the divine being, rather than into himself.[151]

The individual eliminates the particularity of his natural object and of himself. There is thus in the gesture of sacrifice a movement of universality to particularity and particularity to universality. The individual is united with the divine.

The act of sacrifice and the rites of the cult ultimately prove inadequate in uniting the subject with the divine. By renouncing his individual possessions and offering them as a sacrifice to the gods, the individual does not attain the universality that he hopes to since the sacrifice is not wholly a sacrifice. Rather, the sacrificed animal is not simply discarded but rather is eaten and enjoyed in a feast: "the other act of sacrifice is merely the destruction of what cannot be used, and is really the preparation of the offering for a meal, the feast that cheats the act out of its negative significance."[152] There is thus no true sacrifice and no true renunciation at work here, but rather one is simply consuming and making use of natural products. The priest who sacrifices the animal plays the role of the local butcher, providing meat for the community. The unification with the divine self-consciousness cannot come about by the act of feigned renunciation. But despite this negative side of the sublation of the conception of the sacrifice, there is also a positive side from which a new unity of divine and human arises. Though the reconciliation does not come about through the renunciation of one's possessions, there is another aspect of the act of sacrifice which makes it possible.

Concluding Remarks

Just as at the end of "The Truth of Self-Certainty" consciousness finally came to see itself opposite another self-conscious subject, so also here self-consciousness in the enjoyment of the feast recognizes the divine in human form: "the divine being is transformed into *self-conscious* existence, and the self has consciousness of its unity with the divine being."[153] By consuming the fruit of the gods and the meat of the sacrificial animal, the individual becomes invested with the divine. The god enters the self-conscious subject by means of the objects of nature which the individual sacrifices. Thus, the god moves from the form of an object and takes on that of a subject: "This enjoyment is the negative power which puts an end both to the divine being and to the singleness."[154] Now the divine is seen in the person of the individual self-conscious subject. The act of sacrifice in the cult in which the god alone is honored is now transformed into the festival which is a celebration of man himself in the recognition of the divine in man. The celebration of the god is thus a celebration of man: "The dwellings and halls of the god are for the use of man, the treasures preserved therein are his own in case of need; the honor and glory enjoyed by the god in his adornment are the honor and glory of the nation."[155]

The divine as a simple, inanimate statue is now overcome. Now the gods are thought to be united with humans in a number of different ways. This ushers in the next Notion. One of the ways in which the divine is thought to be in the human being is as a source of power and strength with which to overcome the force of nature. Here the human body is itself thought to be possessed by the divine. Thus, we move from a static conception of the divine in the form of a statue to a Notion of god incarnated in actual living subjects. This is the content of the next section, "The Living Work of Art."

II. The Living Work of Art (§§720–26)

In this section Hegel continues his discussion of the Greek cult which he began in "The Abstract Work of Art." Now the god as self-conscious other finds a more satisfactory incarnation in a living human subject than in an inanimate statue. Since the statue proved to be an inadequate representation of the divine, here the living human body replaces the motionless marble as the medium in which the divine manifests itself, and thus the very person of the believer becomes the vessel of divine agency. In the experience of consciousness, the divine inhabits the body of the individual in two different contexts. At first the god is thought to possess his devotees unconsciously in their practice of the Bacchic rites, and then in the second moment the divine is thought to dwell in the person of the athlete who, in the cultivated perfection of his body, evinces the work of the divinity. The body of the athlete becomes a living work of art which, like the statue, is a mundane model of the divine.

As the second section in "Religion in the Form of Art," this discussion finds its categorial analogue in the "Lordship and Bondage" dialectic of the "Self-Consciousness" chapter. Thus, the discussion of recognition that was originally introduced there reappears once again. Regrettably, although the parallelism is clear enough given the indisputable evidence we have seen in previous discussions which allows us to locate the respective corresponding analyses, here Hegel does not provide us with much internal evidence to support this parallelism, and thus we are obliged to do a bit of reconstructive work in this regard by bringing out the implicit similarities in these two analyses. Here in "The Living Work of Art," the athlete enjoys the recognition of the other members of the community, who recognize the divine in him. He is granted honors and special privileges by his fellow citizens. His self-certainty is made universal and turned into truth by means of this recognition. In the various athletic contests individuals, each claiming to be invested with the divine, compete with one another. Each athlete attempts in this way to compel the others to recognize his divinity while obliging them to renounce their own claims to divine inspiration. Here the struggle for recognition takes place in the ethical sphere in the form of specific customs and actions, and is regulated by predetermined rules of the community. In this regard, the dialectical movement here, although parallel in form and category, is much more sophisticated than the "Lordship and Bondage" dialectic, which took place in, so to speak, a state of nature in abstraction from all ethical rules and customs.

The Notion: The Divine Manifestation in Self-Consciousness Itself (§§720–22)

Hegel outlines the Notion of this section by recapitulating the basic movement of the dialectic of the cult. As we saw in the previous discussion, the divine is thought to inhabit the objects of nature. Here a change comes about, and the object of the cult is transformed from the products of nature to the body of the believer himself. The believer eats the meat of the sacrificial animal and drinks the sacrificial wine:

> Coming down from its pure essential nature and becoming an objective force of nature and the expressions of that force, it is an outer existence for the "other," for the self by which it is consumed. The silent essence of self-less nature in its fruits attains to that stage where, self-prepared and digested, it offers itself to life that has a self-like nature. In its usefulness as food and drink it reaches its highest perfection; for in this it is the possibility of a higher existence and comes into contact with spiritual reality.[156]

Now in the sacrifice and consumption of these objects, the believer, who nourishes himself with these gifts of the gods, is unified with the divine. It is thus in the appropriation, consumption and enjoyment of the fruits of nature that the gods enter the very body of the believer which they grant strength and nourishment, and in this way, "Self-consciousness . . . comes forth from the cult satisfied in its essence, and the god enters into it as into its habitation."[157]

Through this metamorphosis from the objects of nature, the god comes out of the beyond and reveals himself in the body of the believer: "For the mystical is not concealment of a secret, or ignorance, but consists in the self knowing itself to be one with the divine being and that this, therefore, is revealed."[158] In the consummation of the fruits of nature and the objects of desire, the initiate in the cult can immediately feel his unity with the divine. Just as in "The Truth of Self-Certainty" consciousness had to destroy the object of its desire in order to confirm its own conception of itself, so also here religious consciousness must destroy the object of nature in order to confirm its sublime relation to the divinity: "as a thing that can be used, it [sc. divine being] not only has an existence that is seen, felt, smelled, tasted, but it is also an object of desire, and by being actually enjoyed becomes one with the self and thereby completely revealed to the self and manifest to it."[159] Thus, in the Greek religion, as in the Christian religion, god is revealed.

The concept of revelation (*Offenbarung*) is absolutely essential for Hegel's understanding of religion. As we have seen, the sweeping story that Hegel has been telling since the beginning of the "Spirit" chapter is an account of the coming to awareness of itself of Spirit. In the "Spirit" chapter itself we observed Spirit in its objective sphere in the conceptual movement of historical peoples and nations. Here in the "Religion" chapter we see the development of Spirit which posits itself as the divine, and this, for Hegel, is the story of Spirit in the subjective sphere. But, as we have seen in "Natural Religion," Spirit is not immediately aware of itself in the divine and does not immediately see itself in god. The divine is represented in natural forms, which are foreign to the self-conscious subject. Only gradually does the true form of god as a self-conscious subject come forth. This revelation of god in his true form is, according to Hegel, the key criterion for the level of sophistication of the truth of religious consciousness. In the Greek religion, the divine entities are conceived as self-conscious subjects, but they are still inadequately represented. Only in the Christian religion does God reveal himself as a fully human subject, and thus the Christian religion is, for Hegel, the "revealed religion." Since it is the religion in which Spirit finally becomes aware of itself, i.e., in which man recognizes himself in God, it is the highest form of religious consciousness. Here in "The Living Work of Art," we see the divine revealed in the person of human subjects, but this revelation is still inadequate and incomplete, as the experience of consciousness will teach us.

The Experience of Consciousness

The In-Itself Moment: The Bacchic Revelers (§§723–24)

The first form of "The Living Work of Art" concerns the initiates of the cult of Bacchus. As we have seen, the god enters into the body of the believer via the fruit and wine and other natural products which are conceived as gifts which the god provides. The divine "at first enters into the objective existence of the fruit, and then, surrendering itself to self-consciousness, in it attains to genuine reality—and now roams about as a crowd of frenzied females, the untamed revelry of nature in self-conscious form."[160] In the Bacchic revelries the god is thought to possess the bodies of the individual revelers. Like the statue of the divine from "The Abstract Work of Art," the body is that of a self-conscious human form, but here it is an animated living self and is thus a higher representation of the divine: "Man thus puts himself in the place of the statue as the shape that has been raised and fashioned for perfectly free *movement*, just as the statue is perfectly free *repose*."[161] This new representation of the divine has life and motion, both of which were absent in the unmoving statue.

Despite its improvements over the statue, this conception is nevertheless still inadequate, since the divine is revealed only partially and in its immediate existence as a natural object which it inhabits: "But what is disclosed to consciousness is still only absolute [i.e., abstract] Spirit, which is this simple essence, not Spirit as it is in its own self; in other words, it is only *immediate* Spirit, and the Spirit of nature."[162] What is not revealed is the divine in its universality. The divine possesses the bodies of the initiates, but in their revelries the initiates are utterly incoherent and seemingly driven by a maddening force. The god is clearly at work in the body of the individual revelers but not the god as a coherent, self-conscious subject. The essential self-conscious element of the divine is still missing in this incarnation. Although the believer thought he could attain the universality of the divine through the act of sacrifice, the divine, as self-consciousness, is not in the product of nature, and thus by consuming the objects of nature, the believer may become possessed by some aspect of the divine but not by the essential self-conscious aspect: "its self-conscious life is only the mystery of bread and wine, of Ceres and of Bacchus, not of the other, the strictly higher, gods whose individuality includes as an essential moment self-consciousness as such. Therefore, Spirit has not yet sacrificed itself as *self-conscious* Spirit to self-consciousness."[163] What is sacrificed is a physical, natural object, and this is not the essential self-conscious element of the god.

The For-Itself Moment: The Athlete (§§725–26)

The second moment tries to conceive of the divine in the cultivated body of the athlete. For the Greeks, the human body itself, as a product of nature, was an artistic medium to be shaped and formed. The body is to the athlete what the stone is to the sculptor or a canvas to the painter. In *Lectures on the Philosophy of History*, Hegel refers to this cultivation of the body as "The Subjective Work of Art": "This is the *subjective* beginning of Greek art—in which the human being elaborates his physical being, in free, beautiful movement and agile vigor, to a work of art."[164] The Greeks practiced, so to speak, a cult of the body, which took the form of organized athletic contests and festivals. The festival is the immediate occasion at which the divine reveals itself in the individual subject. During the festival, there is singing, dancing, games and contests, all of which evidence the divine in human form: "Man shows his spiritual and bodily ability and skill, his riches; he exhibits himself in all the glory of god, and thus enjoys the manifestation of god in the individual himself."[165] The athletes, like the sculptors, received the recognition of all and were honored among their people since they had achieved a kind of unity with the divine: "High honor was ascribed to the victors in battle; they were the most honored of the nation; on festive occasions they sat beside the Archons, and it even happened that in their lifetime they were revered as gods."[166] The body of the athlete becomes the object of divine agency and is regarded as living evidence of divine power. Through the cultivated body, the god is revealed in the individual: "He is an inspired and living work of art that matches strength with its beauty; and on him is bestowed, as a reward for his strength, the decoration with which the statue was honored, and the honor of being, in place of the god in stone, the highest bodily representation among his people of their essence."[167] Once again the inanimate stone becomes a living human body, and flesh and blood replace the sculpture as the medium for representing the divine. The honors are now bestowed not on the statue of the god but on the living human subject in which the god is present.

The cultivation and perfection of the body in the various forms of sport represents an overcoming of nature. First, cultivating the body, the athlete invests the simple material nature with a divine or spiritual element: "The spiritual interest of primary importance is, therefore, the development of the body to a perfect organ for the will."[168] The body becomes a means by which Spirit can attain and execute what it wants. The mastery over nature in the form of the athlete's mastery over his own body is an expression of freedom from natural existence: "in this exercise of his physical powers, man shows his freedom, viz. that he has transformed his body to an organ of Spirit."[169] Therefore, excelling in athletic contests is a demonstration of one's power of Spirit and freedom from nature. The hard training involved in the life of the athlete is proof that the athlete is not subject to nature but rather has overcome it, and this is, for Hegel, what is typical of the Greek world: "The exhilarating sense of personality, in contrast with sensuous subjection to nature, and the need, not of mere pleasure, but of the display of individual powers, in order thereby to gain special distinction and consequent enjoyment, constitute therefore the chief characteristic and principle occupation of the Greeks."[170]

Despite the fact that the divine appears in the body of the believer and thus takes on a living form, this is still an inadequate representation, since there is still lacking the inward aspect of the divine, namely, language. Just as in the cult a part of the god remains in the sphere of the divine and does not become incarnated in the natural world, so also here "still there yet remains for consciousness a 'beyond.' "[171] The divine can be observed in the living body of the athlete, but this living representation of the divine is still incomplete. There is no inward, divine aspect in the coherent speech of the athlete. Hegel writes, "The moment of subjectivity does not appear as infinite subjectivity, it is not Spirit as such which is contemplated in the objective forms."[172] The self-conscious Spirit, i.e., the divine as a self-conscious subject, is not revealed in the body of the athlete. Just as with the Bacchic revelers, so also here with the athlete it is precisely this self-conscious side which is still missing.

Concluding Remarks

Although there is no in-and-for-itself moment in this dialectical analysis, Hegel indicates that the two moments will come together in the Notion of the next section, "The Spiritual Work of Art." Now what is required is something that unites these two previous moments—the Bacchic revelries and the athlete's cultivation of the body—each of which alone is inadequate: "In the Bacchic enthusiasm it is the self that is beside itself, but in corporeal beauty it is spiritual essence. The stupor of consciousness and its wild stammering utterance in the former case must be taken up into the clear existence of the latter, and the non-spiritual clarity of the latter into the inwardness of the former."[173] On the one hand, the divine, yet incoherent, speech of the Bacchic revelers must be transformed into the coherent speech of a true self-conscious agent. On the other hand, the coherence and lucidity of the athlete must be invested with a divine element or "inwardness." The two sides are brought together in literature, which constitutes the subject of the next section. It is only in literature that speech displays "a lucid and universal content."[174] In the aspect of lucidity, the divine, as represented in literature, evinces a cogent self-conscious form, and in the aspect of universality, its divinity and spiritual depth.

Due to the introduction of universality, literature helps to overcome heretofore existing national rivalries. In literature "the content is universal, for in this festival which honors man there vanishes the one-sidedness of the statues which contain only a national Spirit, a specific character of the divine nature."[175] The statues of the divine invariably represent local divinities and are thus a celebration only of individual communities. Likewise, the athlete or "warrior is . . . the glory of his particular nation."[176] Now through the introduction of literature, the Greek Spirit moves beyond these local rivalries and arrives at a conception of mankind in general:

> In this kenosis, this externalization of itself, into complete corporeality, Spirit has laid aside the special influences and sympathies of nature which, as the Spirit of the nation, it contained shut up within it. Its nation is, therefore, no longer conscious in this Spirit of its particularity but rather of having laid this aside, and is conscious of the universality of its human existence.[177]

This movement from the particularity of individual communities to the universal conception of humanity is a watershed in the development of Spirit and will later prove to be important for Hegel's understanding of the Christian religion. Now we must examine "The Spiritual Work of Art," in which the divine entities are represented in their universality in the various literary forms of ancient Greece.

III. The Spiritual Work of Art (§§727–47)

In this third and final section of "Religion in the Form of Art," Hegel treats what he sees as the highest representation of the divine conceived by the Greek Spirit—the divine in the form of the literary arts. Here it is language in its various forms that is the medium in which the divine finds expression. Stories are told and enacted that portray the gods in anthropomorphic form and in constant interaction with human affairs. The portrayal of the divine in the medium of language constitutes a higher representation than the divine represented in the form of the plastic arts or in the body of the athlete. In the stories of literature and drama, the gods are conceived as living entities in contrast to the motionless statue in "The Abstract Work of Art." Moreover, the living representations are endowed with the gift of coherent speech in contrast to the Bacchic revelers in "The Living Work of Art." Here the gods resemble self-conscious human subjects more than ever before. Hegel calls this discussion "The Spiritual Work of Art," since for the first time the divine is portrayed in a medium that is pure Spirit and wholly devoid of nature. We no longer need marble or stone or even the body of the athlete to portray the divine, since now language alone is sufficient.

According to our scheme, this section corresponds to "Stoicism, Skepticism, and the Unhappy Consciousness," the third section of "Self-Consciousness." At the level of the category we are here concerned with ground and consequence, reality and appearance, etc. Evidence for this parallelism is abundant throughout this section; indeed, Hegel often speaks here of dualisms of this kind, referring for instance to the "inner essential world and the world of action"[178] or the "two worlds,"[179] i.e., the divine and the human. Just as the two-world split was what characterized "Stoicism, Skepticism, and the Unhappy Consciousness," so also here there is a split between the realm of the gods along with fate and the realm of humans. Hegel explicitly draws the parallelism between the unhappy consciousness and comedy, each of which represents the third moment in the respective sections: "We see that this unhappy consciousness constitutes the counterpart and the completion of the comic consciousness."[180] "The Spiritual Work of Art" contains, as we have come to expect, three different stages. Hegel begins with an account of Homeric epic, which establishes the various gods in a unified religious system for the first time. In the second moment, he treats the tragedy of Sophocles[181] and Aeschylus, and finally with the third moment he turns to the comedy of Aristophanes[182] which is, according to this outline, the highest representation of the divine to which the Greeks ever attained. Generally speaking, this scheme corresponds to the historical development of these three literary genres in the Greek world.

The Notion: The Divine Portrayed in the Language of Literature and Drama (§§727–28)

Anyone who has ever read Homer or the Greek tragedians has some feel for the Greek conception of the gods. They are portrayed as being very much like humans in virtually all respects except for the fact that they possess special powers and are immortal. The vivid literary representations of the divine constitute the general Notion at this stage. Hegel begins his discussion by indicating the crucial role of language and stories in the creation of Greek religion. Although each Greek *polis* had its own patron god and conceived of certain divinities as particularly favorable to it, all of the gods were united in the pantheon, which gave the Greek world a sense of community at the ethical level which it in no way possessed politically. The pantheon represented a sort of divine community in which the gods lived and interacted. According to Hegel, it is through language in the various literary forms, such as oral epic poetry and performed drama, that the gods are first brought together in this community and find their most vivid expression. As he indicated at the end of the previous section, language joins the different national elements into a universality of mankind: "The national Spirits which become conscious of their essence in the shape of a particular animal coalesce into a single Spirit. Thus it is that separate beautiful national Spirits unite into a single pantheon, the element and habitation of which is language."[183] Hegel describes here how this conception of a pantheon came about and how the individual gods originally came together.[184] On his view, the individual Greek nations or "Spirits" were originally brought together for a common purpose: "The pure intuition of itself as *universal humanity* has, in the actuality of the national Spirit, this form: the national Spirit combines with the others with which it constitutes through nature a single nation, in a common undertaking, and for this common task forms a collective nation and therewith a collective heaven."[185] The common undertaking at the mythological level was the Trojan War, which brought the Greek states together into an alliance against a common enemy. The union of the Greek expedition to Troy brings together the various gods into a single religious system, unifying them in a pantheon. In this way the individual nationalities are in a sense sublated. The war also provides material for filling out the personalities of the individual divinities and for clarifying their relation to man.

In the political order there is a parallelism between the gods and the chieftains of the Greek expedition to Troy. Agamemnon is the leader of the Greek expedition, but the other heroes are not genuinely subordinate to him. He is merely the first among equals, so to speak, and his powers are limited: "he is obliged to arrange everything to the satisfaction of the others."[186] This arrangement mirrors at the human level the order of things in the divine sphere: "A perfect resemblance to these relations is also presented in the Greek pantheon. Zeus is the father of the gods, but each one of them has his own will."[187] Just as Agamemnon must on occasion placate and indulge his fellow warriors, so also Zeus is obliged to make concessions to his fellow gods, and his power can by no means be conceived as infinite. The model for the conception of the gods is thus taken from human life.

The pantheon stands over and above the human world, but there is interaction between the two spheres, since the gods constantly attempt to shape and direct the course of human actions. In this interaction the gods display any number of human characteristics. In a sense, the gods are simply universal beings or copies of humans, which self-consciousness projects into a beyond: "By themselves, they are the universal substances of what the *self-conscious* essence *in itself* is and does."[188] However, self-consciousness is not yet aware of this as a projection and does not ultimately see the unity of itself with the divine: "it is the return of the divine being into self-consciousness that already contains the reason why self-consciousness forms the center for those divine powers and conceals their unity, to begin with, under the form of a friendly, external connection of the two worlds."[189] The profoundly human aspect of the divine is overlooked, and self-consciousness sees itself as alienated from the gods who inhabit a different sphere. The course of the dialectical movement in this section will bring self-consciousness to see its unity with the divine, but in order to reach this end it must work through various literary portrayals of the divine in which there is always an alienation between the human and the divine spheres. The first of these literary forms is epic poetry.

The Experience of Consciousness

The In-Itself Moment: Epic (§§729–32)

In epic the gods are represented in picture-thinking, as Hegel says, i.e., in stories that are orally transmitted by a bard. The divine in the form of the Muse inspires the bard by giving him the gift of memory, which enables him to sing his song. With this inspiration, the bard, like the sculptor, is unified with the divine and accordingly honored among men. The categories of universality and particularity appear once again in this constellation. The gods in the beyond represent the universals, while the individual bard is the particular. These two terms are united in the heroes, which constitute the focal point of the bard's song. Hegel describes this relation in terms of a syllogism: "What, however, is in fact present is the syllogism in which the extreme of universality, the world of the gods, is linked with individuality, with the minstrel, through the middle term of particularity. The middle term is the nation in its heroes."[190] The Homeric heroes are on the one hand human and thus particular, but at the same time they are universals, since they are portrayed in the universal sphere of language, or, as Hegel says, they are "presented only in idea"[191] and have no concrete form like, for example, a statue. In epic it is thus through the bard that humans have contact with the divine.

This first portrayal of the divine proves to be internally contradictory, due to the conflicting aspects of universality and particularity found not in relation to the bard or the heroes but rather within the Notion of the divine itself. The gods, although originally universal, unchanging, and eternal entities, enter into human action and thus become particular, like humans: "They are the eternal, beautiful individuals who, serene in their own existence, are exempt from transitoriness and the influence of alien powers. But they are at the same time *specific* elements, *particular* gods, which therefore stand in relation to others."[192] This transition from the immobile and eternal beyond to the world of action and from the divine to the human sphere causes a conflict between the two aspects of the gods. Hegel describes this elsewhere as follows:

> Yet neither, in the true ideal, may this determinacy terminate in a sharp restriction to *one-sidedness* of character but must equally appear as drawn

back again into the universality of the divine. In this way, since each god bears in himself the determinate attribute of being a divine and therewith universal individual, he is partly a determinate character and partly all in all, and he hovers in the very middle between pure universality and equally abstract particularity.[193]

As universal, the gods remain indeterminate, but they maintain their otherworldly majesty and superiority over mortals. But when they enter into the sphere of human action and become particular personalities, they become all too human:

These separate relationships into which the gods enter as individual agents retain an aspect of contingency which obscures the substantiality of the divine, however much that may remain also as the dominant basis, and lures the gods into the clashes and battles of the finite world and its restrictions. Through this finitude immanent in the gods themselves they become involved in a contradiction between their grandeur and dignity and the beauty of their existent embodiment, and this too brings them down into the field of caprice and contingency.[194]

As Plato observed, the childish behavior of the gods with their petty deceptions and tricks sharply contrasts with the seriousness and sublimity normally associated with the divine. In their interaction in human affairs the gods can be tricked, disappointed, and even injured, none of which is consonant with their eternal divine status. The universal immortal aspect of the gods stands in direct opposition to and contradiction with this particular finite aspect.

Since the gods move further and further away from their divine aspect and resemble more and more human beings, there opens up another divine principle above them. Ultimately, the gods, having become particulars, must yield to the universal principle of fate or necessity: "the universal self . . . hovers over them and over this whole world of picture-thinking to which the entire content belongs, as the irrational void of necessity."[195] The impersonal principle of divine necessity is ushered in precisely because the gods, by taking up human characteristics, begin to lose their divine status: "Since the whole range of spiritual and moral qualities was appropriated by the gods, the unity, which stood above them all, necessarily remained abstract; it was therefore formless and unmeaning fact—necessity, whose oppressive character arises from the absence of the Spiritual in it."[196] The universal force of fate and the strength of necessity are acknowledged by the gods themselves, in that they recognize a power higher than themselves. They see it as "a mere happening which they must face as beings without a self and sorrowfully."[197] For Hegel, portrayals of the divine as sad and mourning an unhappy fate are evidence of this acknowledgment. Fate is the impersonal alien concept of necessity itself, which becomes the new principle that is operative in the next literary form—tragedy.

The For-Itself Moment: Tragedy (§§733–43)

Greek tragedy constitutes the second moment of the representation of the divine in the medium of language.[198] This representation is "higher"[199] than epic since, instead of a simple narrative told by a single bard, now we have living actors who play the various characters and act out the events: "these characters *exist* as actual human beings who impersonate the heroes and portray them, not in the form of a narrative, but in the actual speech of the actors themselves."[200] Now the heroes are not abstract universal beings who dwell only in the sphere of language and in the imagination of the auditors, but instead are concrete, empirical individuals on the stage. The actor replaces the bard, and his living representation of the divine is more real than that of his predecessor and is more like Spirit or a true human being.

In tragedy the chorus replaces the general population in epic, i.e., those who stand under the rule of the individual chieftains without enjoying any political power of their own. Hegel discusses this transition in *Lectures on the Philosophy of History:*

> The royal houses perished, partly as the consequence of particular atrocities, partly through gradual extinction. There was no strictly moral bond connecting them with the tribes which they governed. The same relative position is occupied by the people and the royal houses in Greek tragedy also. The people is the chorus—passive, deedless: the heroes perform the deeds, and incur the consequent responsibility. There is nothing in common between them.[201]

The chorus in this subordinate role is thus limited to hollow utterances of pity or general platitudes about fate. Like the common people, the chorus is simply passive, lamenting the fate of others while risking no action itself: "in the powerlessness of this chorus the commonality has its representative, because the common people themselves constitute merely the positive and passive material of the individuality of the government confronting it."[202]

As Hegel reminds us,[203] we have already seen the essential conflict in the Greek world in the clash of family and state rights that was discussed in

"The Ethical World" and "Ethical Action" in the analysis of *Antigone*. Now we are concerned with the contradiction in the conception of the divine as displayed in Greek tragedy. Just as in "Ethical Action," so also here the tragic hero sets the dialectic into motion by his deed. At work here is the dialectical movement of knowledge and ignorance into which the tragic heroes invariably fall. The knowledge of the hero is always one-sided and based on his own essential character as a hero: "He takes his purpose from his character and knows it as an ethical essentiality; but on account of the determinateness of his character he knows only the *one* power of substance, the other remaining for him concealed."[204] It is the other side, the one which remains hidden from view, which brings the tragic conflict to a head when it asserts its right. In the hero's action and its results, he sees that his purpose and the principle for which his character stands are one-sided and partial: "Consciousness disclosed this antithesis through action; acting in accordance with the knowledge revealed, it finds out that that knowledge is deceptive; and being committed as regards the content of that knowledge to one of the attributes of substance, it violated the other and so gave it the right as against itself."[205] Thus, the tragic conflict is not between a virtuous hero battling the forces of injustice, but rather between two principles which are legitimate and which both claim their right: "The truth, however, of the opposing powers of the content [of the knowledge] and for consciousness is the result that both are equally right, and therefore in their antithesis, which is brought about by action, are equally wrong."[206]

The two-world split that began in "Force and the Understanding" and which is typical of the third analysis of each discussion is present here in the form of the known and the hidden side of the conflict, which form the two principles in this dialectical movement. These are represented in picture-thinking as "the revelatory god" Apollo and "the Furies who keep themselves concealed."[207] Together these two principles constitute the entirety of this sphere. Of the visible side of the dichotomy, Hegel writes, "The one is the aspect of light, the god of the oracle who, in accordance with its natural moment, has sprung from the all-illuminating sun, knows all and reveals all—Phoebus and Zeus who is his father."[208] This side, the visible truth, is, however, necessarily misleading and deceptive, since it is only one side of the whole. For this reason, this aspect is simultaneously the negative aspect represented by the Furies:

> The action itself is this inversion of the *known* into its opposite, into *being*, is the changing-round of the rightness based on character and knowing into the rightness of the very opposite with which the former is bound up

in the essential nature of the substance—converts it into the Furies who embody the other power and character aroused into hostility.[209]

The known and the unknown, the visible and the invisible, are thus dialectically related and constitute a single concept.

This representation of the divine ultimately proves to be inadequate, due to the tension caused by the fact that the divine is responsible for both knowledge and ignorance, for what lies open and for what remains hidden. In epic the gods were compelled to recognize fate as a power that stood above them, and now here in tragedy, they gradually melt away into the impersonal concept of fate. As we have just seen, the dialectical movement of knowing and ignorance represented by Apollo and the Furies was what led to the tragic downfall of the hero who only knows or recognizes partial truths without seeing the whole. These two principles are simply two sides of the same concept. Knowledge in its incompleteness is ignorance. This is represented in picture-thinking by the belief that Zeus stands for both Apollo and the Furies. Zeus is on the one hand "the father of the *particular* that is taking shape in the knowing," and is also "the Zeus of the *universal*, of the inner being dwelling in concealment."[210] Given that these concepts stand in opposition to one another and lead to the tragic fall of the hero, they are conceived impersonally as necessity or fate, which is once again associated with Zeus: "But self-consciousness, the simple *certainty* of self, is in fact the negative power, the unity of Zeus, of *substantial* being and of *abstract* necessity."[211] Thus, instead of the gods bending to a higher necessity as in epic, here Zeus and necessity coalesce into one. But since necessity is seen as something alien, the individual is alienated from both Zeus and the divine sphere as a whole. Despite the anthropomorphic representation of the divine, the individual sees the blind force of fate and thus Zeus as something alien and terrifying: "Necessity has, in contrast to self-consciousness, the characteristic of being the negative power of all the shapes that appear, a power in which they do not recognize themselves but, on the contrary, perish."[212] The Notion of the divine ceases to be a self-conscious subject and is transformed into the impersonal, unconscious force of fate, which is indifferent to the passions and sufferings of individuals. The individual is still alienated from the world and from god, and "the true union, that of the self, fate, and substance, is not yet present."[213] This contradiction in the Notion of the divine spills over into a contradiction in the person of the actor himself. In the role that he is playing, the actor stands apart from the chorus and the public and is united with the divine which is bound up in his actions. Yet, as an actual person, the actor, like the chorus and the public, is separated and alienated from the divine and fate. There is thus a contradiction between the actor himself and the role he is playing, and in the end tragic acting becomes "a hypocrisy."[214]

The In-and-For-Itself Moment: Comedy (§§744–47)

While tragedy is still caught up in the dualism of the hero on the stage and the actor who represents him in the performance, this inconsistency is overcome in comedy.[215] In tragedy, the actor, while on the stage, is not who he truly is: "The hero who appears before the onlookers splits up into his mask and the actor, into the person in the play and the actual self."[216] In comedy by contrast the individual can, by means of jokes and ironic self-reference, step out of the particular role he is playing and come forth as the individual who he really is. As a part of the humor, he is able to strip off his mask and reveal that he is the same as the spectators: "The self, appearing here in its significance as something actual, plays with the mask which it once put on in order to act its part; but it as quickly breaks out again from this illusory character and stands forth in its own nakedness and ordinariness, which it shows to be not distinct from the genuine self, the actor, or from the spectator."[217] The actor portraying a hero or a god, as a part of the humor, shows that he is in fact an ordinary human being. Thus, even the gods are brought down to earth and made the subject of satirical criticism, and the contradiction between their divine sublimity and their childish comportment is consciously brought to the fore.

Comedy demonstrates a new and higher understanding of the terms "nature" and "Spirit."[218] With regard to nature, the irony and self-detachment in comedy indicates a detachment from nature itself. Hegel writes, "As regards the natural element, actual self-consciousness shows . . . that it is . . . the truth about the essential independence of nature . . . and in comedy, it is conscious of the irony of this meaning generally."[219] Only in comedy does the Greek consciousness recognize the irony of "feasting on its sacrificial offering"[220] that we saw in the cult. This irony displays a self-conscious detachment and independence from nature. Thus, in comedy, self-consciousness overcomes its fear of the divine fate and nature, and is no longer alienated from it. With respect to the realm of Spirit, comedy criticizes the state and its institutions by means of constant contrast between the state's universal pretensions and its particular finite existence. The state "is constrained and befooled through the particularity of its actual existence, and exhibits the ludicrous contrast between its own opinion of itself and its immediate existence, between its necessity and contingency, its universality and its commonness."[221] The civic institutions and customs are subjected to critical scrutiny with a humorous result. In this ironic view toward nature and this critical view toward Spirit, self-consciousness reduces everything to laughter and sets itself up as the ultimate judge: "In comedy there comes before our contemplation, in the laughter in which the characters dissolve everything, including themselves, the victory of their own subjective personality which nevertheless persists self-assured."[222] Just as for the skeptical consciousness earlier, so also here in comedy everything is negated when it becomes the object of satire and criticism, and in this way "the comic subjective personality has become the overlord of whatever appears in the real world."[223]

It is, according to Hegel, the Spirit of "rational thinking"[224] of Socrates and the sophists which makes this sort of criticism possible. Socratic rationalism posits abstract ideas of the good and justice and demands that finite human institutions justify themselves in terms of this lofty standard. There now arises a new sphere of the divine—the Platonic ideas—in which the gods of picture-thinking lose their individuality and dissolve: "With the vanishing of the contingent character and superficial individuality which imagination lent to the divine beings, all that is left to them as regards their *natural* aspect is the bareness of their immediate existence; they are clouds, an evanescent mist."[225] The gods thus lose their colorful personalities and collapse into the world of abstract thought. Such ideas, however, are empty and devoid of any empirical content and collapse into the dialectical sophistry which, in the words of Plato, "make the weaker argument the stronger." In the midst of this sophistry and relativism, the individual ultimately becomes the true standard in accordance with the sophists' maxim: "man is the measure of all things." Thus, the divine and the dreaded forces of fate are replaced by the rational self-conscious human subject: "The *individual self* is the negative power through which and in which the gods, as also their moments, viz. existent nature and the thoughts of their specific characters, vanish. . . . [T]he individual self is not the emptiness of this disappearance but, on the contrary, preserves itself in this very nothingness, abides with itself and is the sole actuality."[226] Personal conviction and individuality take on a meaning heretofore unknown and prove to be destructive. What originally began as a new representation of the divine in the form of comedy has now grown out of control and now turns on itself. Thus, the very principle of critical rationality that is necessary for comedy proves also to be its destruction. In his *Lectures on the Philosophy of History*, Hegel attributes the collapse of the Greek world to this principle which he calls "subjective freedom."[227] He traces the origin of subjective freedom back to the sophists:

> It was the sophists . . . who first introduced subjective reflection, and the new doctrine that each man should act according to his own conviction. . . .

> Instead of holding by the existing state of things, *internal* conviction is
> relied upon; and thus begins a subjective independent freedom, in which
> the individual finds himself in a position to bring everything to the test of
> his own conscience, even in defiance of the existing constitution.[228]

Personal opinion is now set up in the place of absolute truth. It should be
noted here that Hegel's analysis strongly resembles that of Nietzsche in
the latter's *Birth of Tragedy*. There Nietzsche ascribes the collapse of Greek
tragedy to Socratic rationality, which unceasingly requires reasons and
explanations for customs and traditions. Similarly, for Hegel, the critical
rationality common to comedy, Socrates, and the sophists ultimately
destroys the Greek religion.[229]

The arrival at this principle of subjective freedom marks a revolutionary change in the conception of the divine. Now a self-conscious
subject with private convictions replaces the gods. This is superior to the
previous forms of "Religion in the Form of Art":

> Through the fact that it is the individual consciousness in the certainty of
> itself that exhibits itself as this absolute power, this latter has lost the form
> of something *presented to consciousness*, something altogether *separate* from
> *consciousness* and alien to it, as were the statue, and also the living beautiful
> corporeality, or the content of the epic and the powers and persons of
> tragedy.[230]

Now the dualism and alienation are overcome, and each self-consciousness is truly united with the divine with the realization that its own
conviction is the manifestation of the divine. God is not presented to
the subject as something foreign in a form of art but rather is in each
self-conscious agent.

Concluding Remarks

Hegel now moves to his final section and the highest form of religious
consciousness—Christianity. The Greek religion reached an advanced
stage since it, like Christianity, saw god as revealed or manifested in
human form: "But in referring to this common element of the Greek and
the Christian religions, it must be said of both, that if a manifestation of
God is to be supposed at all, his natural form must be that of Spirit, which
for sensuous conception is essentially the human; for no other form can
lay claim to spirituality."[231] But the Christian religion goes one step further
and does not stop at the manifestation of the divine in human form, and
for this reason it represents a higher stage of religious consciousness:
"The real defect of the Greek religion, as compared with the Christian,

is, therefore, that in the former the *manifestation* constitutes the highest mode in which the divine being is conceived to exist—the sum and substance of divinity; while in the Christian religion the manifestation is regarded only as a *temporary phase* of the divine."[232] Christ reveals himself in the world, but this is only one aspect of the divinity. For Hegel, the Greek religion stops here, while Christianity brings the dialectical movement of religion to its logical conclusion. This constitutes the subject of the next section, "Revealed Religion."

C. Revealed Religion: Christianity (§§748–87)

General Introduction (§§748–53)

With "Revealed Religion" we finally reach the end of the dialectical movement of the "Religion" chapter, and, as we shall see, it represents a very appropriate completion to the entire discussion of religious consciousness. The revealed religion of Christianity provides Hegel with a symbolic way of portraying both the structure and content of the speculative and dialectical Concept. The Christian Trinity represents a template which captures the dialectical movement of the *Phenomenology*—the internal development of the self-knowledge of Spirit. In my analysis of this section, I will have occasion to allude to Hegel's early works from the so-called *Early Theological Writings*, in particular, "The Spirit of Christianity and Its Fate." In some respects, the association of the early writings with the "Revealed Religion" section is awkward, since the former deal primarily with discussions in the *Phenomenology* which precede the "Religion" chapter (such as the criticisms of Kantian morality) and with lengthy treatments of the historical development of Christianity as a religion of "positivity," while the "Religion" chapter is Hegel's way of depicting the significance of the movement of the entire *Phenomenology* from the standpoint of Spirit as Spirit. Nevertheless, Hegel's treatment of the movement from Judaism to Christianity and his analysis of the significance of the incarnation, teaching, and resurrection of Christ in his early works provide supplemental material which will help us explicate his interpretation of the meaning of Christianity as discussed in the "Revealed Religion" section of the *Phenomenology*.

As the third section in the "Religion" chapter, the "Revealed Religion" corresponds to "Individuality Which Takes Itself to Be Real In and For Itself" from "Reason," and "Spirit That Is Certain of Itself" from "Spirit." Each of these represents the in-and-for-itself moment of its respective chapter. At first glance, there appears to be an asymmetry here, in that "Revealed Religion" contains only a single analysis, while the two aforementioned sections which run parallel to it are divided into three subsections. This asymmetry, however, disappears when we examine the actual content of the "Revealed Religion" section more closely, and discover that it too is divided into three sections, which Hegel did not bother to separate or set off with individual headings. Nonetheless, it is fairly straightforward and uncontroversial that he treats Christianity in three different phases, just as he divided the different aspects of the Greek religion into three separate subsections. In a number of places, Hegel tells us directly that the movement of "Revealed Religion" contains three stages: "There are thus three distinct moments: essence, being-for-self which is the otherness of essence and for which essence is, and being-for-self, or the knowledge of itself *in the 'other.'* "[233] He describes the content of the three moments no less obliquely in another passage as follows: "Spirit is the content of its consciousness at first in the form of *pure substance*, or is the content of its pure consciousness. This element of thought is the movement of descending into existence or into individuality. . . . The third moment is the return from picture-thinking and otherness, or the element of self-consciousness itself."[234] Although Hegel's description of the three moments is rather abstract, he is in fact referring to familiar events in the Christian religion. The first moment, referred to as "essence," "pure substance," or "thought," is the abstract conception of God in the beyond. Hegel says, "Spirit is at first conceived of as substance in the element of pure thought; it is immediately simple and self-identical, eternal essence."[235] This substance in the element of pure thought is nothing other than the God of the Jews, Yahweh. With the second moment, the abstract God becomes particular or becomes other to himself. Hegel clearly refers here to the incarnation of God in man in the person of Christ. Finally, with the death of Christ, the Son returns to the Father, and his spirit lives on in the universal self-consciousness of the religious community. This basic scheme corresponds to the structure of Hegel's treatment of the revealed religion in both the *Encyclopaedia* and *Lectures on the Philosophy of Religion*. The three aspects of the Christian Trinity form the three moments here and thus can unproblematically be seen as corresponding to the three moments of "Individuality Which Takes Itself to Be Real In and For Itself" from "Reason," and "Spirit That Is Certain of Itself" from "Spirit."

The speculative or dialectical structure within the "Revealed Religion" section is really a dialectical template for the entire *Phenomenology*. The movement begins with the in-itself or objective aspect, then moves to the moment of being-for-itself, which is the otherness of essence or the subjective aspect, and finally culminates in the being-in-and-for-itself moment. The revealed religion is supposed to represent the unity of, on the one hand, consciousness, which was represented by natural religion, and, on the other hand, self-consciousness, which was represented by art religion. The religious shape of Christianity, which portrays that unity in picture-thoughts, thus represents the content of Spirit as Spirit. In the Trinity, Christianity contains the categorial movement of consciousness that we have been following. At first God is pure, undifferentiated being, the "This" of "Sense-Certainty," and then in the person of Christ he becomes "the thing of *perception*" and finally in the Spirit of the religious community "the *universal* of the understanding."[236] With respect to the internal structure of the "Religion" chapter, we can thus represent Hegel's account of revealed religion here in relation to the religious forms of natural religion and the religion of art. (See figure 8.2.)

The dialectical analysis of religion that we have examined so far consisted in two different movements, proceeding in opposite directions. In "Natural Religion" the self-conscious believer posits the divine in the form of an object of nature. This object is then the substance which in the course of the development of religious forms gradually comes to take on human form, which it reaches in the Greek religion: "substance alienates itself from itself and becomes self-consciousness."[237] In "Religion in the Form of Art," on the other hand, the movement was in the opposite direction: "self-consciousness alienates itself from itself and gives itself the nature of a thing, or makes itself a universal self."[238] The Greek religion began with a conception of the divine as individual self-conscious subjects, and the course of the dialectical analysis led us to comedy and the rationalistic criticism of the sophists, which ultimately posited the

Figure 8.2

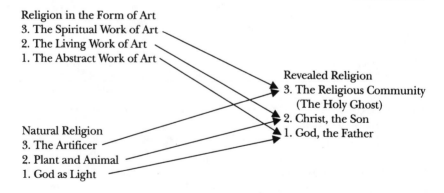

Religion in the Form of Art
3. The Spiritual Work of Art
2. The Living Work of Art
1. The Abstract Work of Art

Revealed Religion
3. The Religious Community (The Holy Ghost)
2. Christ, the Son
1. God, the Father

Natural Religion
3. The Artificer
2. Plant and Animal
1. God as Light

human subject as absolute substance in the place of the divine. These two moments of in-itself and for-itself are contained in Christianity. In the three persons of the Trinity, the Christian God evinces the same movement we have just seen. At first, God, the Father, is conceived as a universal substance as in the figures of "Natural Religion." Then this substance externalizes itself and becomes an individual self-conscious subject in the person of Christ. Thus, God, the Son, represents the for-itself moment of revealed religion, corresponding to "Religion in the Form of Art." But the self-conscious subject dies and becomes substance again in the form of the Spirit of the community or the Holy Ghost, which represents the apex of the triad, the in-and-for-itself moment. Thus, in this movement Christianity contains the earlier religious forms within itself and sublates them, bringing them to a higher conceptual level.

Concentrating on the transition from the previous section, Hegel begins his discussion of the revealed religion by attempting to fix its place in terms of the argument of the entire book up until this point. In his introductory comments, he provides us with further evidence for the systematic structure of the work that we have been reconstructing. As we saw in the previous section, "The Spiritual Work of Art," the dialectical movement which ended with comedy and sophistic criticism corresponded to the similar movement in "Stoicism, Skepticism, and the Unhappy Consciousness" from the "Self-Consciousness" chapter.[239] Just as skeptical self-consciousness led to a universal nihilism in "Self-Consciousness," so also here in "Religion" the same result is reached by the social criticism of comedy and sophistic rationality in the Greek world. The result is a complete alienation and a loss of belief in the divine: "Trust in the eternal laws of the gods has vanished, and the oracles, which pronounced on particular questions, are dumb. The statues are now only stones from which the living soul has flown, just as the hymns are words from which belief has gone."[240] Critical rationality has destroyed the Greeks' immediate relation to the ethical life of their culture, an important part of which is religious belief. In the face of critical analysis, the myths and divine representations appear wholly implausible and fall into discredit. With this, an entire religious worldview collapses: "It is the consciousness of . . . the loss of substance as well as of the self, it is the grief which expresses itself in the hard saying that 'God is dead.' "[241] Just as in his analysis of Greek drama, so also in this formulation Hegel anticipates one of Nietzsche's best known discussions.[242] As we saw at the end of the previous section, in place of the lost belief and the dead gods, self-consciousness now sets itself up and declares itself to be absolute being. Hegel expresses this with the simple phrase: "The self is absolute being."[243] Formerly, absolute being was represented by the Greek gods, but now that belief in them has proven implausible, the individual self steps forth to fill the vacant place left behind and thus becomes the new absolute being. The result of the Greeks' critical rationality is thus twofold: (1) nihilism and skepticism regarding the gods, and (2) the new conception of the individual self-conscious subject as absolute being.

It is in this milieu that the revealed religion comes about.[244] Now in revealed religion the two moments of subject and object will come together. Just as "Consciousness" and "Self-Consciousness" are joined in "Reason," so also "Natural Religion" and "Religion in the Form of Art" come together in "Revealed Religion." This is the reason why Hegel spends so much time comparing the constellation of figures discussed here with the transition from the unhappy consciousness to "Reason." He now begins his analysis of the birth of the Notion of the revealed religion itself, which he introduces by saying, "All the conditions for its production are to hand, and this totality of its conditions constitutes its coming-to-be, its Notion."[245]

The Notion: Revelation (§§754–71)

What characterizes the revealed religion in contrast to the preceding forms of religious consciousness is the fact that the divine manifests or "reveals" itself to the believer in the form of an actual living self-conscious subject. This revelation takes the form of an immediate sensuous being, and this is the point where Christianity has its beginning: "That Absolute Spirit has given itself *implicitly* the shape of self-consciousness, and therefore has also given it for its *consciousness*—this now appears as the *belief of the world* that Spirit is *immediately present* as a self-conscious being, i.e. as an *actual man*, that the believer is immediately certain of Spirit, *sees*, *feels*, and *hears* this divinity."[246] Here God is an actual immediate entity, as in "Natural Religion," but at the same time is a self-conscious subject as in "Religion in the Form of Art." It is thus the dual aspect of Christ which unifies the two previous religious movements. Hegel tells us directly that the incarnation of Christ is what typifies this religious form: "This incarnation of the divine being, or the fact that it essentially and directly has the shape of self-consciousness, is the simple content of the absolute religion."[247] The key to revealed religion is that the divine is no longer hidden or only partially revealed, as was the case in the previous forms of religious consciousness, but rather makes itself known to man as it truly is: "In the Christian religion God has revealed himself—that is, he has given us to understand what he is; so that he is no longer a concealed or secret existence."[248]

This revelation makes reconciliation possible, and the various dualisms characterized by the accustomed forms of alienation from the divine are overcome. Now the self-conscious subject can truly recognize himself in the divine, since it too has the form of a self-conscious subject: "Spirit is known as self-consciousness and to this self-consciousness it is immediately revealed, for Spirit is this self-consciousness itself. The divine nature is the same as the human, and it is this unity that is beheld."[249] In the previous forms of religious consciousness there was ultimately always a separation of the individual from the god, since the divine was always conceived as something in some respect different from a human subject. But now Christianity overcomes this difference with the person of Christ, a god in the form of man. For Hegel, Christianity represents the highest form of religious consciousness, since only here is the individual united with absolute being in this manner: "The hopes and expectations of the world up till now had pressed forward solely to this revelation, to behold what absolute being is, and in it to find itself."[250]

Although the Notion of revelation is what characterizes the Christian religion for Hegel, this Notion must now unfold itself conceptually,[251] and this is of course what happens in the experience of consciousness. Thus, the Notion here constitutes a process in which the concept of God is continually metamorphized into new forms as it moves to ever higher conceptual levels. The actual discussion of the dialectical movement of consciousness at this stage begins when Hegel tells us, "This content is to be considered as it exists in its consciousness."[252] With this statement, Hegel signals that the discussion of the Notion per se is now complete, and we are about the embark on another phenomenological movement, which will examine this Notion of the Christian religion in the experience of consciousness.

The Experience of Consciousness

The In-Itself Moment: God as Pure Essence (§§772–77)

At this first stage, consciousness posits an abstract God in thought, an act to which Hegel refers with the term "othering." In other words, consciousness divides itself by positing another substantial consciousness in the beyond: "The element of pure thought, because it is an abstract element, is itself rather the 'other' of its simple, unitary nature, and therefore passes over into the element proper to picture-thinking—the element in which the moments of the pure Notion obtain a *substantial* existence relatively to one another."[253] At first it is merely the faculty of abstraction at work, which allows the individual to see itself from the perspective of an omniscient other, but then religious consciousness by means of picture-thinking reifies this other as an actual "*substantial* existence," which stands in relation to itself. This account squares with Hegel's treatment of revealed religion in the *Encyclopaedia of the Philosophical Sciences*. There he outlines the three moments of "Revealed Religion" very clearly in terms of the fundamental ontological categories of universality (*Allgemeinheit*), particularity (*Besonderheit*), and their unity in individuality (*Einzelheit*). He characterizes this first stage of universality as follows: "Under the 'moment' of *Universality*—the sphere of pure thought or the abstract medium of essence—it is therefore the Absolute Spirit, which is at first the presupposed principle, not, however, staying aloof and inert, but (as underlying and essential power under the reflective category of causality) creator of heaven and earth."[254] Since God is a projection of the self-conscious subject and not an actual sensible entity, he dwells in "the sphere of pure thought" and is a universal. God as universality is thus the immobile God of the beyond, and it is here that the dialectic of the revealed religion begins.

God as abstract universality represents Yahweh, the God of Judaism. In his early essays, Hegel portrays the Spirit of Judaism as the fate of servitude and harsh alienation. The relationship between man and Yahweh is a relationship of a submissive, wholly dependent man to a jealous God who exists completely outside of, and thus independent from, human experience. There is thus an irreconcilable difference between the human and the divine, since man is seen as a passive, dependent, and finite being, while Yahweh is the autonomous, independent, and infinite being with whom supplication and surrender are man's only possible relations. The significance of Abraham's experience (and that of Judaism in general) is that what is universal and objective, i.e., God, is conceived as a subject, and this connection between objectivity and subjectivity is the first step in consciousness's eventual realization that the objective natural order is spiritual in reality and that when man beholds the divine he recognizes himself in this "other."

Hegel explores the question about what is behind the Spirit of Judaism that leads its believers to become passive slaves, incapable of autonomy, and forever dwelling in an alienated relationship to the capricious master Yahweh. Hegel sees Abraham's alienation of himself from his communal life in Mesopotamia as a Spirit of independence and a "self-maintenance in strict opposition to everything."[255] Hegel claims that since Abraham faced an infinite world opposing him, mastery of the external world became the only strategy by which he could assert his independence. Because Abraham was not able actually to master the world, he created an ideal or a master in thought which was able to do so. This being is projected out into a beyond in order that it might control what happens in the world; indeed, God cannot be part of the natural order or continuous with it if he is going to control or master it, since to be a part of nature is to be determined by natural processes. Now, in "Revealed Religion" we see how consciousness lives under its conception of an eternal substance, which exists beyond the realm of consciousness; in other words, Hegel provides us with a phenomenology of Judaic consciousness. For the Judaic consciousness, God is the pure, objective substance, which is beyond nature and thus is contraposed to it; this represents the departure from this world into a beyond of thought. Even though God is a subject for the Jews, he is a non-natural, nontemporal self outside of the human realm, whereas the God of Christianity appears in the form of a natural being in time.

As we have learned from previous dialectical movements, for any substance to be what it is, it must distinguish itself from another, i.e., there must be a moment of difference. In order for the abstract God to become real, he too needs opposition or otherness. Thus, God must create an opposing term and thus become an other to himself. Hegel writes, "Spirit is the knowledge of oneself in the externalization of oneself; the being that is the movement of retaining its self-identity in its otherness."[256] Thus, the first act of the abstract God posited by consciousness is that of creation. God creates the world and with it an opposition to himself. As Hegel explains, the mythological story of creation is religious consciousness's understanding in terms of picture-thinking of the conceptual movement from the abstract God to a determinate God in relation to particularity: "This 'creating' is picture-thinking's word for the Notion itself in its absolute movement."[257] The creation of the world is a creation of particularity, which stands opposed to the universal God: "Spirit, in the determination of being-for-another, is the inert subsistence of the moments formerly enclosed within pure thought, is therefore the dissolution of their simple universality and the parting asunder of them into their own particularity."[258] It is thought that this particularity will determine the divine in that it represents the opposite pole of God's universality.

But this initial opposition of God and the world is inadequate. Since God is conceived essentially as a self-conscious subject, he cannot be opposed to and contrasted with a mere thing, but instead he must find another self-conscious subject as a contrasting term: "Absolute Spirit is the *content*, and is thus in the shape of its *truth*. But its truth is to be not merely the substance or the *in-itself* . . . not merely to step forth out of this inwardness into the objectivity of picture-thinking, but to become an actual self, to reflect itself into itself and to be subject."[259] God must create that which can embody his own identity, that is, the self-opposed other which at the same time is not an other but is his own self. Thus, God must create man as a second more satisfactory term of opposition. This transition is conceived by picture-thinking in terms of the myth of the Fall of man. At first, man is one with nature and "is not yet Spirit *for itself*" or "does not *exist as* Spirit."[260] Here, since man prior to the Fall is continuous with nature and thus more like an animal than a human being, he cannot represent a true self-conscious subject opposed to the divine. Thus, man must become self-conscious if the divine is to be determined in terms of him. This movement from nature to Spirit, from consciousness to self-consciousness, takes place with the knowledge of good and evil. With this knowledge man attains the level of thought and becomes like God. Thus, the dualism of good and evil comes into being simultaneously with self-consciousness itself. Now the world is inhabited not just by objects of nature but also by self-conscious subjects.

Finally, God in the beyond is opposed to individual self-conscious subjects. But these finite, insignificant subjects are still inadequate as true contrasting terms by which God could be determined. What is needed is a subject that is divine and essential like God himself. Picture-thinking understands this ontological truth as absolute substance externalizing itself in the form of Christ: "That which in the pure thought of Spirit is in general merely hinted at as the *othering* of the divine being, here comes nearer to its realization for picture-thinking: this realization consists for picture-thinking in the self-abasement of the divine being who renounces his abstract and non-actual nature."[261] God cannot remain an abstract, universal in the beyond. The necessity of conceptual thought demands that he externalize and particularize himself and enter into the realm of actuality. The absolute, abstract thought or "the word" becomes the negative or self-opposed other of itself, i.e., nature or "the flesh." Thus, Christ comes into existence in the sphere of the actual, and this marks the move to the second moment.

The For-Itself Moment: God as Otherness of Essence (§§777–79)

God now abandons his universality and enters the realm of particularity as a concrete individual. Hegel claims that since Spirit is at first understood as substance in the element of thought and since this substance is an abstraction, it (Yahweh or God as thought) "is, in fact, the negative in its own self and, moreover, the negativity of thought or negativity as it is in itself in essence; i.e. simple essence is absolute *difference* from itself, or its pure othering of itself."[262] By the fact that the God of Christianity (before κένωσις) is abstract, this pure thought is itself the "other" of its simple, unitary nature, and thus it passes into the element of picture-thinking in which the moments of this pure thought obtain a "substantial existence" or become natural. As we have seen, something abstract and simple requires the contrast of substantiality and plurality which is found in the empirical realm of nature, "the self-opposed or 'other' of itself."[263] In order for God to be God or to have an identity as something determinate, he must become other to himself since, as we have seen for Hegel, identity requires a self-opposed difference. This difference or "other" is Christ in the form of a natural being (in contrast to the form of thought). Objective substance becomes subjective self-consciousness, and this is represented in picture-thinking as the word becoming flesh or thought becoming nature. As Hegel says, the "*actuality* or self-consciousness [sc. Christ], and the *in-itself* as substance [sc. God], are its two moments through whose reciprocal externalization, each becoming the other, Spirit comes into existence as this their unity."[264] The deep significance of the incarnation is that the divine being is revealed, i.e., is made known in becoming a self-conscious being. God, as divine substance, is thus not an alien entity which is essentially different from man or which confronts man as an "other."

The immediate, sensuous presence of Christ has two meanings. Christ's existence not only has the meaning "of a self-consciousness that immediately *is*, but also of the supreme being as an absolute essence in pure thought, or absolute being."[265] The synthesis of thought and immediate existence in the person of Christ in a sense represents the culmination of the Notion: the unity of being and essence, existence and thought, universality and particularity. The unity of being and thought is self-consciousness in the person of Christ, and God therefore is "*revealed as he is*."[266] Christ is both the particular and finite (an immediate, existing natural creature) and the universal and infinite (the universal God). Hegel summarizes the significance of the figure of Christ thus: "Spirit is known as self-consciousness and to this self-consciousness it is immediately revealed, for Spirit is this self-consciousness itself. The divine nature is the same as the human, and it is this unity that is beheld."[267]

Religious consciousness portrays the mission of Christ in picture-thinking in terms of the struggle of good and evil. God is separated from the mundane sphere of nature which man inhabits, and the sphere in which he dwells is that of good, while the world along with man is evil: "Picture-thinking takes the other aspect, evil, to be a happening alien to the divine being."[268] Since all that is essential and holy lies entirely outside the mundane sphere,[269] there is nothing in Judaic laws of service and in the objects of religious devotion, such as the tabernacle and temple, which is essential or sacred. There is thus nothing in man or in the world that is intrinsically good or holy. Christ's mission is to purge the world of evil and thus to effect the reconciliation of God with the world and with man. In order to destroy evil, Christ must become a part of the world and combat evil at its source. His self-sacrifice represents the conquest over evil; in the death of Christ, evil and the sins of man die as well: "For the true consciousness of Spirit the finitude of man is slain in the death of Christ. This death of the natural gets in this way a universal signification, the finite, evil, in fact, is destroyed."[270] Now the world and God are not essentially different or alienated from one another. The overcoming of the natural order and the evil of the world with the death of Christ brings about the reconciliation of God with the world: "The world is thus reconciled, and through this death the world is implicitly freed from its evil."[271]

But despite this overcoming of old oppositions, with the incarnation of Christ a dualism in the conception of the divinity is created. The divine is both the abstract universal God in the beyond and the concrete particular man: "the self of Spirit and its simple thought are the two moments whose absolute unity is Spirit itself."[272] There is a clear contradiction in this Notion, which conceives of the divine at once as a universal and at the same time as a particular. Moreover, this Notion divides the world of thought from the world of sense. The tension in this second moment of revealed religion is characterized in the *Encyclopaedia of the Philosophical Sciences* as follows: "The eternal 'moment' of mediation— of the only Son—divides itself to become the antithesis of two separate worlds."[273] Religious consciousness tries to resolve this dilemma by putting emphasis on the one term or the other, claiming at once that God the Father, as source and creator of all, is the true God and Christ merely an accidental appearance, and at the same time that Christ with his unique message and mission is the true aspect of the divine, since he opens the way to reconciliation and salvation: "In one of them, the divine being counts as essence, while natural existence and the self count as the unessential aspect which is to be superseded. In the other, on the contrary, being-for-self counts as the essential and the simple, divine being as unessential."[274] This shuffling back and forth is obviously inadequate, and a more satisfactory resolution must be found.

Ultimately, this dualism can only be resolved by the death of Christ. In death Christ, the Son, returns to the Father, and the two aspects of the divine are reunited. But this unity of the divine is not the same as it was before in the first moment, but rather it has been raised to a higher level. Now the universal is united with the particular and sensible, and the divine becomes the Spirit of the community:

> its otherness, or its sensuous presence, is taken back again by the second othering and posited as superseded, as *universal*. The [absolute] essence

has thereby come to be its own self in its sensuous presence; the immediate existence of actuality has ceased to be something alien and external for the absolute essence, since that existence is superseded, is universal. This death is, therefore, its resurrection as Spirit.[275]

From the death of Christ arises the Spirit of the community, which unites the two previous aspects of the divine. Particularity is retained in that we are concerned with a concrete, empirical religious community, but universality is also present in the general belief shared by the various individuals.

The In-and-For-Itself Moment: Universal Self-Consciousness (§§780–87)

The third moment of revealed religion brings together the categories of universality and particularity: "Spirit is thus posited in the third element in *universal self-consciousness;* it is its *community*."[276] Now both the universal moment of God in the beyond and the particular moment of Christ in the empirical sphere are overcome, and we enter the sphere of the universal self-consciousness, which is Hegel's way of referring to the community. The resurrection of Christ represents self-consciousness becoming substance in the sense that the death of the particular self-conscious individual establishes the ethical substance or universal self of a religious community. The creation of the universal self-consciousness in the religious community as a result of the death of Christ is simply a making explicit of the person of Christ himself: "The movement of the community as self-consciousness that has distinguished itself from its picture-thought is to make explicit what has been implicitly established. The dead divine man or human God is *in himself* the universal self-consciousness."[277] In the *Encyclopaedia*, Hegel writes, "Under the 'moment' of *individuality* [*Einzelheit*] as such—of subjectivity and the Notion itself, in which the contrast of universal and particular has sunk to its identical ground, the place of presupposition (1) is taken by the *universal* substance, as actualized out of its abstraction into an *individual* self-consciousness."[278] Insofar as Christ is divine, he is universal, and insofar as he is man, he is self-conscious. Both of these aspects are present in a higher form in the religious community. The death of Christ thus pictorially represents an important philosophical truth for Hegel: the reconciliation of all the dualisms which have plagued philosophy and theology, namely, the relationship between thought and being, infinite and finite, universal and particular, object and subject and, not least of all, man and God. The revealed religion of Christianity captures this fundamental human need for reconciliation: "The need to unite subject with object, to unite feeling, and feeling's demand for objects, with the intellect, to unite them in something beautiful, in a god, by means of fancy, is the supreme need of the human spirit and the urge to religion."[279] Christ unites feeling (associated with man) with thought (associated with the divine), and this Christian Notion is the picture-thinking which represents for man the fulfillment (πλήρωμα) of this deepest need, the need to reconcile the above oppositions of human life.

The internalization of the Spirit of Christ in each man who participates in the religious community is symbolically represented by the religious idea of resurrection. This internalization of the Spirit or subjectivity of Christ is made possible when the particular, sensuous man Jesus dies a physical death. The profound significance of the resurrection of Christ has three aspects: (1) only the death of the actual person of Christ in his natural existence can remove his sensuous particularity; (2) the death of the particular man-God is the birth of the universal life of the religious community characterized by universal love; and (3) self-consciousness becomes substance, thereby completing the dialectical movement—the movement which began with substance becoming self-consciousness in the incarnation.

With respect to the first aspect, the significance of the death of Christ and the fact that his body disappears is that death robs the intellect of the temptation to venerate the physical figure of Christ. The true meaning of his death is spiritual and universal and thus cannot be attached to a particular thing or relic. Thus, any attempt to worship Christ by concentrating on external artifacts, such as his shroud, sandals, the cross, etc., is merely a misconception of the fundamental significance of Christ's teaching, for the incarnation and death signify the life of his spirit or his subjectivity in man: "The death of the mediator as grasped by the self is the supersession of his objective essence or his particular being-for-self."[280] The significance of the particular sensible person of Christ therefore is sublated by understanding the true significance of his death: "This self-consciousness therefore does not actually *die*, as the particular self-consciousness is pictured as being actually dead, but its particularity dies away in its universality, i.e. in its knowledge, which is essential being reconciling itself with itself."[281] The death of the physical person of Christ "represents the transition from what is outward, from outward manifestation to what is inward."[282] For this reason it belongs to the Notion that the individuality of Christ is "removed from the sphere of the senses" and "must disappear and mount into the region of idea or mental representation."[283] Hegel makes a similar point in connection with the reading of the gospel which captures the upshot of his interpretation of the significance of the actual death of Christ. He says that the true inner meaning of Christ's teachings would be better captured if the written word could be read away, since "if by being understood it vanished as a thing,"[284] there would be no object (i.e., no actual gospel) to venerate, and only the spirit of Christ's teaching would live in us (and not the fact that the natural object Christ, as a man-God, taught it). Hegel illuminates this same point with the example of the ritual of the Eucharist: "just as in the enjoyment of bread and wine not only is a feeling for these mystical objects aroused, not only is the spirit made alive, but the objects vanish as objects. Thus, the action seems purer, more appropriate to its end, in so far as it affords spirit only, feeling only, and robs the intellect of its own, i.e., destroys the matter, the soulless."[285] The meaning of the Eucharist does not lie in the physical object of the bread, but rather in its inner significance. This is confirmed in the ritual itself by the fact that the physical object is consumed. Likewise, the physical person of Christ must die in order that he might take on a universal, inner meaning that transcends the particular historical entity.

We now move to the second aspect of the significance of the resurrection, which involves the ushering in of the universal life of the religious community. With regard to this second point, Hegel says, "The transcended immediate presence of the self-conscious essence has the form of universal self-consciousness. This Notion of the transcended individual self that is absolute being immediately expresses, therefore, the establishing of a community."[286] Thus, the death of Christ is not merely a natural death of a particular individual, but rather it is an event that has universal significance, in that it creates the conditions for the establishment of a spiritual community:

> The *death* of the divine man, *as death*, is *abstract* negativity, the immediate result of the movement which ends only in *natural* universality. Death loses this natural meaning in spiritual self-consciousness, i.e. it comes to be its just stated Notion; death becomes transfigured from its immediate meaning, viz. the non-being of this *particular* individual, into the *universality* of the Spirit who dwells in his community, dies in it every day, and is daily resurrected.[287]

The chief characteristic of the community that is the result of Christ's death is universal love.[288] In his *Early Theological Writings*, Hegel gives a much fuller account of the life of such a community, for he explicates what is involved in such a religious, communal life in light of his lengthy discourse on the nature of Christ's teaching. In "The Spirit of Christianity," Hegel spells out what is implied in his point about the "loving recognition" between the Father and the Son in Christianity. In the *Phenomenology*, Hegel says that there is "a *loving* recognition in which the two sides, as regards their essence, do not stand in an antithetical relation to each other."[289] This represents the loving recognition in the Church between man and God, between man and other men (the universal self of the religious community as symbolized by the life and death of Christ). The main point that Hegel emphasizes here is that love in the Christian community is characterized not by love of any particular person or object but rather of the universal: "The love of the Spiritual community . . . is directly mediated by the worthlessness of all particularity."[290] The object of Christian love is not the particular person of Christ or anyone else but rather the universal Spirit of Christ in man: "Thus this love is Spirit as such, the Holy Spirit. It is in them, and they are and constitute the universal Christian Church."[291] The Christian community is thus a universal substance animated by the Spirit of Christ and universal love.

With regard to the final meaning of the resurrection, the movement from self-consciousness to the ethical substance of the community completes the required othering on the side of self-consciousness. At first pure substance externalized itself in the incarnation and became a self-conscious subject in the person of Christ. Now, with the death of Christ, the self-consciousness becomes substance again in the community, but the substance is higher than the original substance from which the dialectic started. It is spiritual substance which contains the collective self-consciousness of the believers. This again represents a reconciliation between substance and subject, God and man. This is the third moment, which Hegel terms "the knowledge of itself *in the 'other.'* "[292] The fact that the dualism between God and man is overcome means two different things. First, God, as an absolute other in the beyond, no longer exists per se. Hegel expresses this as follows:

> The death of this picture-thought contains, therefore, at the same time the death of the *abstraction of the divine being* which is not posited as self. That death is the painful feeling of the unhappy consciousness that *God himself is dead.* This hard saying is the expression of the innermost simple self-knowledge, the return of consciousness into the depths of the night in which "I = I," a night which no longer distinguishes or knows anything outside of it.[293]

The concept of an abstract God apart from the world is dead as a result of this dialectical movement. Second, not only is the purely transcendent God overcome, but the religious community sees the divine in itself, and thus it finally sees itself as Spirit: "In this way, therefore, Spirit, is *self-knowing* Spirit; it knows *itself.*"[294] This self-knowledge of Spirit was the original goal of the entire movement of the *Phenomenology*. The abstract God in the beyond is metamorphized into the ethical Spirit of the religious community, and this is the final result of the incarnation and death of Christ.

In the *Phenomenology*, Hegel claims that the mode in which religious consciousness within the community becomes aware of itself is through the form of picture-thinking. Absolute being has appeared or has been revealed as Spirit, and this revelation is itself immediate in the actual presence of Christ, but religious consciousness' picture-thinking is unable to comprehend that this pure immediacy "is equally pure mediation or thought."[295] In other words, Spirit's self-consciousness has not advanced to its Notion or to the philosophical understanding of the fact that Christ in his death represents a universal self, "the Self that in its immediate actuality is at the same time a superseded self, viz. thought, universality, without losing its actuality in this universality."[296] The witness of the historical Christ must abstract from the immediate particularity of the person of Christ and comprehend him and his mission in its universal inner significance. Without this ability to abstract, religious consciousness remains fixated on the particular figure of the historical man and fails to recognize his full historical and religious significance. As Hegel says, "a consciousness that sensuously sees and hears Him is itself a merely immediate consciousness, which has not overcome the disparity of objectivity, has not taken it back into pure thought: it knows this objective individual, but not itself, as Spirit."[297] Hegel's claim is that after the death of Christ and of his particularity, the religious consciousness is not able to recognize itself in the "other" of Christ, since he is no longer immediately present, and thus a division between the divine and human still remains for the Christian consciousness.

Hegel's position is that the Christian religion ultimately produces an incomplete mediation because of its limited mode of understanding the meaning of the incarnation and resurrection of Christ. Hegel claims that religious consciousness conceives of the universality of Christ as a *"remoteness in time and space."*[298] Christ, the man-God, dies, and the religious consciousness is unable to think of Christ's significance for itself without a sensuous element. Due to the very nature of picture-thinking—that its form of representation must include a sensuous element—the true universal meaning of Christ cannot be understood apart from his sensuous actuality, and thus there is fated to be an inseparable mixture between the universality of Christ's message and the sensuous person of Christ, qua natural being, who must die and thus depart from the scene into the beyond once again. As Hegel says, "spiritual being is still burdened with an unreconciled split into a here and a beyond."[299] Christ has been revealed to man as God, and thus God has become the same as man, since God assumes the form of self-consciousness. But since the mode of picture-thinking by necessity incorporates a sensuous (objective) element, the moral reality of his teaching or the profound significance of his mission cannot be separated from the actual person of Christ himself. When Christ dies, a gap is then created again, since man is separated from God. Christ becomes a figure lost in the shadows of the past, and salvation is projected into the haze of the future. Because Christ is "other" than man, religious consciousness "does not recognize itself in this thought of Spirit, does not recognize the nature of pure self-consciousness."[300] Religious consciousness is therefore always confronted by the individual personality of Christ, by something objective, and thus there can only be a reestablishment of a dualism or gap, and hence the unhappy consciousness in a sense reappears.

Religious consciousness, since it dwells in the realm of picture-thinking, is always confronted by a particular and not a universal. The deepest urge for a satisfying religious life "was thus turned into an endless, unquenchable, and unappeased longing. . . . The longing remains unsatisfied because . . . it is always confronted by the individual, by something objective."[301] This is the final restless place of the religious consciousness in Hegel's "Revealed Religion" section. The universal self of the community, the final reconciliation of all of the troubling dualisms for man, can ultimately never overcome the particular man-God, and thus it must remain unhappy and alienated. Only an external element in belief is retained "as something therefore that is dead and cannot be known; but the *inner* element in faith has vanished, because this would be the Notion that knows itself as Notion."[302]

Concluding Remarks

Hegel claims that "Religion" has the same content as philosophical knowing, i.e., absolute knowing, but that it understands it in a different way, namely, metaphorically.[303] He says that, at the stage of the "Religion" chapter, "Spirit itself as a whole, and the self-differentiated moments within it, fall within the sphere of picture-thinking and in the form of objectivity. The *content* of this picture-thinking is Absolute Spirit."[304] He expresses this more straightforwardly in the *Encyclopaedia Logic:* "The objects of philosophy, it is true, are upon the whole the same as those of religion."[305] Finally, in the *Philosophy of Right*, he writes, "The content of religion is absolute truth, and consequently the religious is the most sublime of all dispositions."[306] What all of these passages tell us is that, for Hegel, the content that the dialectic has reached in "Religion" is the same as "Absolute Knowing."[307] Thus, by the time we reach the end of "Religion," the content of our account of the self-determination of truth is complete and exhaustive. This would mean that in a sense the story of the determination of subject and object ends with the "Religion" chapter, since a complete account has been given.[308] The point of this account was to show the ultimate unity of all the various factors, at first thought to be unrelated, in the overall truth process. We thus see the grand unity and interconnectedness of the subject with the object, of the subject with the community, of the community with other historically related communities, of conceptions of the divine with religious Spirit, in short of everything with everything else in the broadest sense. In other words, the dialectic has shown us the totality of the interconnectedness of all forms of subject and object in the course of our attempt to give a complete account of the subject-object Notion. The dialectic has thus demonstrated the truth of a certain sort of epistemic monism, according to which everything is necessarily related to the whole, and the whole thus corresponds to the ultimate account of the Notion. This represents the actual content that the dialectic has produced.

The question is now how to interpret this account of the monistic unity of the world. For Hegel, there are two possibilities: the religious interpretation and the philosophical interpretation. As we have seen, the religious interpretation understands this monistic truth with stories, symbols, and metaphors or, as Hegel says, in terms of picture-thinking. In the figure of the Christian Trinity, the religious interpretation personifies the great monistic unity of the universe. For the religious consciousness, these most abstract truths must thus be seen through the veil of simplified concrete examples drawn from normal human experience. God's othering of himself into the world and the reintegration of this other within itself in the knowledge of this incarnation (the knowledge of the religious community in the Holy Spirit) is not grasped as a necessary movement of the Notion but instead as a religious mystery. Therefore, religious consciousness is not yet adequate or complete knowing:

> This form is not yet Spirit's self-consciousness that has advanced to its Notion *qua* Notion: the mediation is still incomplete. This combination of being and thought is, therefore, defective in that . . . the *content* is the true content, but all its moments, when placed in the medium of picture-thinking, have the character of being uncomprehended [in terms of the Notion], of appearing as completely independent sides which are externally connected with each other.[309]

It is only Hegel's speculative understanding of what Christianity represents in picture-thought as the movement of the Trinity which can account for the necessity of such a movement, for the understanding of the Notion is the understanding of the "logical necessity" of the unfolding of the Notion. What is lacking in the picture-thinking of Christianity is not the content of the Notion but the form, and part of this form is the fact of the logically necessary structure of the Notion. The philosophical consciousness, on the other hand, sees these truths for what they are and is able to extricate them from their metaphorical form. Thus, although the monistic content of both interpretations is the same, the difference exists in how that content is understood:

> So far as Spirit in religion *pictures* itself to itself, it is indeed consciousness, and the reality enclosed within religion is the shape and the guise of its picture-thinking. But, in this picture-thinking, reality does not receive its perfect due, viz. to be not merely a guise but an independent free existence; and conversely, because it lacks perfection within itself it is a *specific* shape which does not attain to what it ought to show forth, viz. Spirit that is conscious of itself.[310]

Ultimately Hegel, like Plato, wants to purge religion of its conception of the divine in terms of picture-thinking. Only when self-conscious Spirit grasps itself as Notion in absolute knowing is the experience of consciousness at an end.

9

Absolute Knowing

The ultimate chapter of the *Phenomenology* is one of the most per-plexing in the entire Hegelian corpus. With its enchanting and tantalizing title, it has been the source of a number of disputes in the history of Hegel studies. Does Hegel mean by "absolute knowing" that we can obtain an exhaustive knowledge of everything? Does he mean, as he seems to say in his Berlin *Lectures on the Philosophy of History,* that history really comes to an end?[1] Does the claim about absolute knowing imply that there is some ultimate piece of wisdom which constitutes something like the secret of the universe? Is he claiming, as Nietzsche sarcastically implied, that with his philosophy he actually reached the endpoint of history[2] or that he discovered absolute knowledge, while this knowledge had escaped other philosophers prior to him? To respond individually to every misinterpretation and caricature of this disputed concept would prove to be too tedious and would not serve the goals of the work at hand. I wish, instead, simply to indicate the broad lines of interpretation on this issue and to situate my thesis within this larger picture.

In the history of Hegel research, the so-called "metaphysical inter-pretation" of absolute knowing has been the most widespread. According to the religious version of this view, Absolute Spirit represents God, who stands over and above all finite human perspectives and ways of knowing. Only God or "the self-conscious absolute thinking being"[3] can gain a panoptic view of the universe in all its aspects. Such a view would, of course, be absolute knowing, since it would be exhaustive of all finite kinds of knowing. This interpretation, however, loses its plausibility im-mediately when we recall Hegel's constant criticisms, for example, in "Force and the Understanding" and the "Unhappy Consciousness" of any theory or Notion which posits something transcendent and beyond human reality and experience.[4] Moreover, it implies that there is a sphere of knowledge, namely divine knowledge, which remains forever inaccessible to human comprehension, but we need only recall Hegel's negative assessment of the Kantian thing-in-itself to realize that it is precisely this kind of view that he wants to criticize. Thus, this clearly cannot be what he means by "absolute knowing" here.

According to the secular metaphysical readings of Taylor[5] or McTaggart,[6] Absolute Spirit is not God but rather a real metaphysical entity, which is expressed in nature and in history, and which comes to know itself in time. This interpretation is likewise implausible given Hegel's consistently negative statements about pre-Kantian metaphysics in contrast to his positive reception of Kant's transcendental philosophy. It would be extremely unlikely that Hegel would revert to a precritical position with an extravagant metaphysical notion of Absolute Spirit given his clearly stated intention to construct a philosophical system which builds on the various forms of transcendental philosophy in the work of Kant, Fichte, and Schelling. In accordance with the thesis I have been developing throughout this book, I propose to interpret this concept of absolute knowing above all as an epistemological claim. It thus forms, I will argue, the final part of Hegel's transcendental argument in the *Phenomenology*.

Hegel's Review (§§789–96)

Hegel begins this final chapter with a review of the various forms of consciousness that the work has explored. His summary here of the previous dialectical movements emphasizes in each case how the various Notions of an object ultimately proved to be linked to the categories of thought of the subject. Thus, the object, which was in each case thought to be independent of consciousness, in fact proves to be ideal in this sense. Characterizing the moments of the "Consciousness" chapter, Hegel writes, "Thus the object is in part *immediate* being or, in general, a thing—corresponding to immediate consciousness; in part, an othering of itself, its relationship or *being-for-an-other*, and *being-for-itself*, i.e. determinateness—corresponding to perception; and in part *essence*, or in the form of a universal—corresponding to the understanding."[7] Here "immediate consciousness" clearly refers to the "Sense-Certainty" chapter, which has as its object "*immediate* being." In "Perception" the object of consciousness was brought into relation with other objects and thus was determined by a relation of identity and difference, i.e., a self-relation and a relation to another object. Finally, in "Force and the Understanding" the object was determined as a universal force behind the world of phenomena, which constituted the hidden truth or essence of the empirical experience. In this passage, Hegel underscores the fact that a Notion that gives an account solely of the object sphere is always partial or incomplete. He says the object is "in part *immediate* being," but this is not the whole story. This account must be continued in "Self-Consciousness," where the same categories are repeated, and the self-conscious subject comes to see itself as determining objectivity. We work through the same set of categories that we saw in "Consciousness," but this time in the sphere of the self-conscious subject.

The "Reason" chapter encompasses the same fundamental movement of the first two chapters. At first, in "Observing Reason," truth was thought to be found in the object sphere of scientific inquiry: "in regard to the object so far as it is an immediacy, i.e. is an *indifferent being*, we saw Observing Reason *seeking* and *finding* itself in this indifferent thing, i.e. we saw it equally conscious of its action being external to it, as it was conscious of the object only as an immediate object."[8] Observing Reason tried to reduce everything, including the self-conscious subject, to the status of an object. Hegel writes, "And we saw Observing Reason at its peak express its specific character in the infinite judgment that the *being of the 'I' is a thing*, and, moreover, a sensuous immediate thing."[9] But, as we learned in that section, the scientific models such as, for instance, the categorization of the natural sphere, are in fact products of human thought, and thus the object considered on such a model is to this extent ideal. The result of this conclusion is that the subject is the key term in the determination of truth-claims, and this is worked out "in the two other moments,"[10] i.e., in "The Actualization of Rational Self-Consciousness through Its Own Activity" and "Individuality Which Takes Itself to Be Real In and For Itself."

In the "Spirit" chapter it is with the historical movement of the Enlightenment that the new collective subject, historical Spirit, first reaches the conclusion that objectivity is in fact necessarily bound up with itself, qua subject.[11] It is with the Enlightenment's concept of utility that objects are ultimately defined essentially in their relation to human interests: "Things are simply *useful* and to be considered only from the standpoint of utility. The *cultivated* self-consciousness which has traversed the world of self-alienated Spirit has, through its self-alienation, produced the thing as its own self."[12] This conclusion that the self is the essential is explored further in the third part of "Spirit," namely "Spirit That Is Certain of Itself. Morality": "However, at this stage, knowledge of the thing is still not complete; it must be known not only from the standpoint of the immediacy of being and of determinateness, but also as *essence* or *inner being*, as self. This occurs in *moral self-consciousness*."[13] Ultimately, reconciliation is reached in the realm of Spirit with the concept of conscience: "Finally, as conscience, it is no longer this continual alternation of existence being placed in the self, and *vice versa*; it knows that its *existence* as such is this pure certainty of itself."[14] Here Spirit sees the conscience of the individual as the absolute criterion for truth, thus fixing truth on the side of the subject at the expense of the object sphere. It is the beautiful soul that brings the previous moments together.[15] The beautiful soul, however, proves to be pure subjectivity empty of content, and consciousness then turns to seek this content in the divine, "an essential being which is *this* knowledge, *this* pure self-conscious being which is, therefore, at the same time a genuine *object*, for the Notion is the self that is for itself."[16] This ushers in the "Religion" chapter, which in its first section conceives of the divine as an object.

The movement of "Religion" follows the same pattern as the previous dialectical movement. In "Natural Religion" the divine is conceived as an object of nature, but in the course of the dialectic, religious consciousness comes to realize that conceptions of this kind are incomplete and inconsistent. Gradually, the Notions of the divine lose their object form and take on the shape of self-conscious subjects as in the religion of ancient Greece. Christianity represents the apex of this movement, since it conceives of the divine in the form of a particular self-conscious subject and then goes beyond this conception: Christ dies, but his Spirit lives on in the Christian community. As Hegel says, Spirit becomes aware of itself: "Through this movement of action, Spirit has come on the scene as a pure universality of knowing, which is self-consciousness, as self-consciousness that is the simple unity of knowing."[17] This then leads us up to absolute knowledge.

Hegel's summary of the previous forms of consciousness is not merely a review for its own sake,[18] but rather it is intended to bring out certain features of the dialectical movement that will help to make clear the difficult concept of absolute knowledge. Thus, it is after this brief overview of the previous sections that Hegel begins to respond to the question of the nature of the notion of absolute knowing itself. With this review he above all tries to indicate how every independent conception of objectivity ultimately proved to be dependent on the self-conscious subject. This is the key claim for grounding the idealist thesis of the book as a whole. Hegel explores the different aspects of this insight here in the final pages.

The Notion of Absolute Knowing (§§797–808)

The Panoptic View (§§797–98)

The first point that Hegel wants to make with this review is that absolute knowing is the Notion that encompasses all of the previous Notions. In a number of different places, he tells us in a fairly straightforward fashion that absolute knowing is merely the understanding of all of the previous modes of knowing taken together in their systematic context. For instance, he writes, "The realm of Spirits which is formed in this way in the outer world constitutes a succession in time in which one Spirit relieved another of its charge and each took over the empire of the world from its predecessor. Their goal is the revelation of the depth of Spirit, and this is *the Absolute Notion*."[19] Thus, the Absolute Notion is the Notion that contains all other Notions within itself and sees these previous Notions in their systematic interconnection. It is thus the complete or exhaustive Notion. With this explanation, Hegel makes clear that absolute knowing is not the knowledge of any particular fact or ultimate piece of wisdom, but rather is merely the grasping of the various forms of thought as a whole.

This account of absolute knowing squares with our transcendental reading of the argument of the *Phenomenology* as a whole. Every partial view or Notion implies a more complete one, and the organic aggregate of these would be represented by a panoptic one, which encompasses them all. Hegel writes, "This last shape of Spirit—the Spirit which at the same time gives its complete and true content the form of the Self and thereby realizes its Notion as remaining in its Notion in this realization—this is absolute knowing."[20] Here absolute knowing is characterized as complete with respect to its content. This was the goal of the transcendental argument, i.e., to unpack all of the necessary conditions for truth. The dialectical process that we have been following so far has examined various Notions or truth-claims, all of which proved to be one-sided or incomplete in character. Each of these views implied other conditions for knowing, which they themselves did not and could not account for. For Hegel, there must be a point at which all of the transcendental conditions for knowing are unpacked. This point is then absolute knowing. This means that the dialectic is teleological since it naturally aims at and tends toward a complete account.

Here we find at the end of the *Phenomenology* a powerful statement of Hegel's holism and his conception of philosophy as a system. Every individual truth-claim must be understood in a larger systematic context. Only with this panoptic overview of the complex network of interrelations of truth-claims, individuals, institutions, historical events, and religious conceptions are we able to come to understand the true nature of such claims and give a complete account of objectivity. The piecemeal interpretations of the *Phenomenology* utterly fail to do justice to this crucial aspect of Hegel's philosophical intentions. Thus, we cannot adequately interpret the difficult and pivotal concept of absolute knowing without an understanding of Hegel's systematic pretensions.

Substance as Subject (§§799–804)

From the claim that absolute knowing is the understanding of the movement of consciousness in its totality, Hegel proceeds to the claim that only with this panoptic view is true understanding of the essential *spiritual* or *ideal* nature of world history possible. Each of the various forms of consciousness that we have traced throughout the course of the book, beginning with an understanding of the object as an external other in "Consciousness," and then as something to be negated in "Self-Consciousness," and then as a reflection of consciousness itself, posited a Notion of the object that was independent of the self-conscious subject. The goal of the dialectical movement was to explore each of these and expose the contradictions involved in thinking the object independently of the subject. The dialectical movement in this way gradually purged the various object Notions of their independent and purely objective status: "At first, therefore, only the *abstract moments* of substance belong to *self*-consciousness; but since these, as pure movements, spontaneously impel themselves onward, self-consciousness enriches itself till it has wrested from consciousness the entire substance and has absorbed into itself the entire structure of the essentialities of substance."[21] The result of this purging of the object sphere of its independent status is to see it as necessarily connected with the subject. Now the object understood in all of its spheres—as object of nature, as object of history, as object of religion—is seen to be posited by the subject. We recall how Schelling wanted to start with nature or the object sphere and to derive pure thought. This is also the procedure of self-consciousness in the *Phenomenology* and is in part the point of Hegel's review.

Now that the dialectical movement is complete and consciousness looks back on all of its previous forms, it realizes that nothing remains of the Notions that conceived of an independent object, but rather the various objects have all proven to be ideal. Hegel writes,

> Equally, consciousness must have related itself to the object in accordance with the totality of the latter's determinations and have thus grasped it from the standpoint of each of them. This totality of its determinations

establishes the object as an *implicitly* spiritual being, and it does truly become a spiritual being for consciousness when each of its individual determinations is grasped as a determination of the self, or through the spiritual relationship to them that was just mentioned.[22]

Only when consciousness sees the entirety of the forms of objectivity does it grasp its "spiritual being." By this Hegel means that only when consciousness looks back on the various subject-object Notions that it has traversed does it realize that these Notions are ultimately the result of the process of Spirit, i.e., of the complex social, historical, and conceptual determination of truth. It realizes that the object sphere is not independent and autonomous but instead is necessarily connected with the subject and the forms of thought.

At this point, self-consciousness recognizes this movement of thought for what it is, namely, its own self-movement: "Truth is not only *in itself* completely identical with certainty, but it also has the shape of self-certainty, or it is in its existence in the form of self-knowledge."[23] Thus, absolute knowing is the self-knowing of Spirit. The movement of the dialectic of the *Phenomenology* can then be described as "the process in which Spirit *becomes* what it is *in itself;* and it is only as this process of reflecting itself into itself that it is in itself truly Spirit."[24] This insight is what Hegel means by his famous statement from the Preface to the *Phenomenology* in which he emphasizes the importance of "grasping and expressing the true, not only as *substance*, but equally as *subject*."[25] Here Hegel refers back to this passage now that the dialectic is complete: "For this Notion is, as we see, the knowledge of the self's act within itself as all essentiality and all existence, the knowledge of this subject as substance and of the substance as this knowledge of its act."[26] Now we can see this same passage in light of the completed dialectical movement. Grasping truth as subject means grasping the whole of world history, not in its inessential or accidental aspects, but rather in its necessary thought-forms. Likewise, it means seeing the divine as a projection of the self-conscious subject itself. To do so is to reduce world history to thought or to subject. This is brought to consciousness by the movement of religious Spirit, which sees itself in the divine in the revealed religion of Christianity. Finally, in absolute knowing "this identity is complete and immediate oneness with self, or *this subject* is just as much *substance*."[27]

Science and Conceptual Knowing (§§805–8)

The understanding of world history and of the divine according to their conceptual movement differs from the level of thinking that we saw in

"Spirit" and "Religion," respectively. As we have seen in the previous chapter, Hegel mentions in several places that religion has already in some sense attained the panoptic view of world Spirit, and thus expresses the same content as absolute knowing but in a different way. In this final chapter, Hegel once again distinguishes absolute knowing from the level of knowing obtained in "Revealed Religion." He writes,

> The Spirit of the revealed religion has not yet surmounted its consciousness as such, or what is the same, its actual self-consciousness is not the object of its consciousness; Spirit itself as a whole, and the self-differentiated moments within it, fall within the sphere of picture-thinking and in the form of objectivity. The *content* of this picture-thinking is Absolute Spirit; and all that now remains to be done is to supersede this mere form.[28]

Religion, for Hegel, already contains absolute knowing, but, as we have seen, it represents this knowledge to itself in terms of myths and stories, i.e., in terms of picture-thinking. The content, however, is the same as absolute knowing, although it is understood differently. Religious consciousness understands truth in terms of pictures, whereas absolute knowing grasps philosophical truth conceptually or according to the necessary systematic development of the Notion. Hegel thus indicates that absolute knowing is knowing according to the Notion: "it [absolute knowing] is Spirit that knows itself in the shape of Spirit, or a *comprehensive knowing* [in terms of the Notion]."[29] The question is now what it means to know something according to the Notion.

First, knowledge according to the Notion involves seeing the dialectical movement in terms of the categories themselves—i.e., universality, particularity, and individuality—and not filtered through the medium of an image, a symbol, or a story. When we recognize the dialectical movement in the various spheres as a necessary categorial movement, then we have reached absolute knowing. Knowledge according to the Notion is thus nontemporal, in contrast to the individual historical moments of Spirit. The Greek Spirit or the Roman Spirit are essentially bound to their temporal forms and are thus limited. The Absolute Notion, by contrast, is a conceptual movement that transcends time: "Spirit necessarily appears in time, and it appears in time just so long as it has not *grasped* its pure Notion, i.e. has not annulled time."[30] Now, at the end of the dialectic, consciousness "sets aside its time-form."[31] Absolute knowing is an understanding not of any particular historical development, but of the necessary categorial movement hidden in history and religion, which is timeless.

Second, conceptual knowing, i.e., knowing according to the Notion, involves seeing the forms of consciousness and forms of historical Spirit in their unitary movement. Self-consciousness previously grasped isolated, individual Notions, but the key move here is that for the first time it grasps world history conceptually and recognizes the unified patterns of world history as patterns of its own thought. In other words, consciousness ceases to see each Notion individually in its particular phenomenological form, but instead comes to see the unitary nature of all of these forms. It sees that all of the forms of consciousness display the same categorial movement and are thus systematically related to one another. This, as we have seen, is the Absolute Notion. Now the individual Notions are not seen individually, but are taken in "their organic self-grounded movement."[32] Here we see once again the importance of a systematic analysis of the *Phenomenology*. In other words, it is not the individual discussions or analyses which are important, but rather their relation to one another in the systematic whole.

Hegel underscores the necessity of a systematic understanding of the various Notions in order to gain the key insight of philosophical or conceptual knowing. Only when the process is at an end and is grasped in its systematic context can Spirit see itself as substance. He writes, "Only when the objective presentation is complete is it at the same time the reflection of substance or the process in which substance becomes self. Consequently, until Spirit has completed itself *in itself*, until it has completed itself as World-Spirit, it cannot reach its consummation as *self-conscious* Spirit."[33] This Hegel repeats when he writes, "As Spirit that knows what it is, it does not exist before, and nowhere at all, till after the completion of its work of compelling its imperfect 'shape' to procure for its consciousness the 'shape' of its essence, and in this way to equate its *self-consciousness* with its *consciousness*."[34] What Hegel says here squares with his famous allusion to the owl of Minerva[35] in the Preface to the *Philosophy of Right*, where he indicates that the historical movement can only be understood philosophically after that movement is complete.[36] In other words, philosophy, despite Hegel's claims to the necessity of its subject matter, has no predictive power. It cannot tell us what will happen ahead of time; instead, it can only analyze what has happened after the fact. This does not mean that history is actually at an end, but merely that we can only understand and interpret philosophically those events which have already taken place. The subject matter of philosophy is necessarily a completed movement.

Now, with absolute knowing, we have finally reached the level of science, which was the original goal of the phenomenological odyssey. Hegel makes this clear when he writes, "Spirit, *manifesting* or *appearing* in consciousness in this element, or what is the same thing, produced in it by consciousness, *is science*."[37] Science is thus synonymous with absolute knowing or knowing the Notion, qua Notion. Moreover, science implies that there is no longer any separation between the spheres of subject and object. With the unity of the subject and substance, we have overcome the various dualisms that separated the two: "In this knowing, then, Spirit has concluded the movement in which it has shaped itself, insofar as this shaping was burdened with the difference of consciousness [i.e. of the latter from its object], a difference now overcome."[38] It is at this point that science is reached. Hegel confirms this when he discusses the role of history for absolute knowing and science:

> The *goal*, absolute knowing, or Spirit that knows itself as Spirit, has for its path the recollection of the Spirits as they are in themselves and as they accomplish the organization of their realm. Their preservation, regarded from the side of their free existence appearing in the form of contingency, is history; but regarded from the side of their [philosophically] comprehended organization, it is the Science of Knowing in the sphere of appearance.[39]

As we know from the Introduction, the *Phenomenology* is the science of appearances, i.e., a λόγος of the phenomena. It is the "philosophically comprehended organization" of the forms of consciousness which renders this study a science, but this is only from the perspective of absolute knowing and is not valid for the individual Notions leading up to it, which along the way are seen only in separation and isolation from one another. Until natural consciousness is able to see this panoptic picture, it has not yet reached the level of science. These two perspectives explain Hegel's seemingly ambiguous statements in the Introduction about the status of the *Phenomenology* as a science. Seen from the final perspective of absolute knowing, it is a science, since it has philosophical knowing, but seen from the perspective of any of the Notions prior to absolute knowing, it is only the road to science and not a science as such.

Transcendental Idealism and Absolute Idealism

This analysis affords us another opportunity to contrast Hegel's idealism with Kant's. As we saw earlier, for Kant, the a priori elements in human cognition were applied to the sphere of appearances, i.e., to concrete individual objects or, more precisely, representations of objects. There was no claim to any a priori elements in history or in social relations. These matters remained outside the realm of transcendental philosophy. Transcendental idealism on this account is limited to the objects of possible experience. These are ideal in the sense that they are constituted by a priori human categories. But these categories do not apply to things-in-themselves. In the *Encyclopaedia Logic*, Hegel contrasts his conception of idealism with this Kantian notion:

> The things of which we have direct consciousness are mere phenomena, not for us only, but in their own nature; and the true and proper case of these things, finite as they are, is to have their existence founded not in themselves but in the universal divine Idea. This view of things, it is true, is as idealist as Kant's; but in contradistinction to the subjective idealism of the critical philosophy should be termed absolute idealism.[40]

Hegel extends this transcendental idealism to all spheres of human activity: history, culture, religion. All of these realms display a priori elements of human thought, and as such they are all to this extent ideal. Thus, Hegel's idealism is not limited to any specific or subjective forms of thought which contrast to a reality in itself; instead, it is all-encompassing or *absolute* idealism. It makes no distinction between appearance and something else. Everything is what it is only in accordance with a certain Notion, and every Notion evinces universal categories of thought—universality, particularity, and individuality. The *Phenomenology* has now completed a deduction of these categories by demonstrating their presence in all human thought forms. Now, in absolute knowing, the content of the dialectic has been purged of everything empirical, and we are left with the categories as categories. Hegel's idealism thus takes in all aspects of human reality and demonstrates how they are all necessarily bound together. Only in this way is a deduction of the subject-object Notion complete. For Hegel, Kant's transcendental philosophy remains incomplete, since it did not go far enough in the unpacking of the necessary conditions of understanding. In this sense, Hegel sees himself as pushing Kantian philosophy further and completing the system of transcendental philosophy that Kant began.

As we saw earlier in our comparative analysis of Kant and Hegel, the disputed notion of absolute knowing is meant specifically as a criticism of Kant's agnosticism with respect to the Absolute. For Kant, since knowledge is always limited to our representations, we can never have access to things as they are in themselves. For Hegel, as we have seen, this is problematic, since the very idea of a thing-in-itself is produced by a certain Notion or epistemological framework, and as such we always stand in a relation to it, qua object, and it is not something beyond our experience. For Hegel, we can indeed know the truth about objects, and we need only look to our experience to know it. Absolute knowing is the truth of the subject-object Notion, not in the sense that it is some absolute, divine truth beyond our human experience; rather, it is precisely the truth of our experience itself. It is, in fact, the totality of the human experience understood at the conceptual level in its systematic context.

Hegel's Doctrine of Reconciliation

Given that conceptual knowing allows us to see subject as substance and to see self-consciousness in world history, a *rapprochement* is effected between the subject and the world. As we have seen, conceptual knowing represents, for Hegel, the highest kind of knowledge, because only here does the subject see itself in the object sphere writ large, but it is also the key for Hegel's doctrine of reconciliation (*Versöhnung*), to which we now turn. This reconciliation is, for Hegel, one of the highest tasks of philosophy and fulfills the most basic of human needs. The world appears to us at first glance as something alien or evil. Common sense sees in it only injustice and confusion. Hegel takes himself to have demonstrated in the "Spirit" chapter that the movement of history is not haphazard or random, despite its often chaotic appearance. Instead, its movements can be comprehended in terms of certain general Notions or worldviews, which are ultimately posited by the subject. Likewise, the development of religious consciousness follows a certain conceptual movement. The key insight of absolute knowing is that these Notions of the divine and of historical movements are in fact not something "out there" in the world. Instead, the Notions are a product of thought, and as such they are a part of the human subject. When *self*-consciousness realizes this, it sees itself in history when it sees the Notion in history and its movement. Likewise, it sees itself in the divine, as we saw in "Revealed Religion."

Self-consciousness thus becomes reconciled with the external order, and the world and its historical events no longer appear as something other or alien. In *Lectures on the Philosophy of History*, Hegel refers to his philosophy as a theodicy in this regard: "Our mode of treating the subject is, in this aspect, a theodicy—a justification of the ways of God . . . so that the ill that is found in the world may be comprehended, and the thinking Spirit reconciled with the fact of the existence of evil."[41] It is philosophy which teaches us that when we perceive something as alien or other, we are operating with only a partial view and that, in fact, there is a deeper truth to the matter. In the Preface to the *Philosophy of Right*, Hegel describes this as follows: "To recognize reason as the rose in the cross of the present and thereby to enjoy the present, this is the rational insight which reconciles us to the actual, the reconciliation which philosophy affords to those in whom there has once arisen an inner voice bidding them to comprehend."[42] In this passage Hegel portrays his doctrine of reconciliation with a Christian image. Although it may appear that the world is evil, since its wicked inhabitants crucified the God-man who preached love and forgiveness, nonetheless in this most wicked of all events in human history, in the cross, there is a rose, i.e., a positive aspect; specifically, without Christ and his crucifixion, mankind would still be lost, and there would be no reconciliation. According to this paradoxical doctrine, only through the sacrifice of Christ can mankind be saved from its sins and reconciled with God. Thus, this event, the crucifixion has, despite everything else, a positive symbolic meaning which only abstract philosophical reason can grasp. Only philosophical knowing, which sees the whole picture in its conceptual interrelations, can recognize the rose in the cross, i.e., the good in the evil. With this philosophical knowing, all alienation and all otherness encountered in the world are overcome. The lofty goal of Hegel's philosophy is to help us overcome this alienation in all its forms, and it is this task that the *Phenomenology* has performed.

The Unity of the *Phenomenology of Spirit*

Is there anything philosophically interesting that this interpretation of the architectonic of the *Phenomenology* as a whole brings with it, or are the parallelisms we have been following of interest only to the despairing Hegel philologist trying to patch together the Hegelian system for its own sake? The philosophically provocative point that these parallelisms implicitly indicate is that the conceptual logic that governs the development of the object-Notion and the subject-Notion is the same logic that governs world-historical forces. In other words, the moments of in-itself, for-itself, and in-and-for-itself and the dialectic of universal, particular, and individual are not categories which apply only to a particular limited subject matter; instead, they are universal categories which govern all human thought, and which can be found in any and every field of human inquiry. Precisely this point is overlooked when we analyze individual arguments of Hegel's philosophy in abstraction from their systematic context.

With this interpretation, I have tried to demonstrate the futility of attempting to understand the *Phenomenology* in an episodic manner.

This interpretive approach can understand (1) neither the conceptual movement of the individual sections, nor (2) the notion of absolute knowing which is, of course, the upshot of the entire work. (1) To understand the Notions in the individual sections of the *Phenomenology*, one must first locate the relevant category, and then try to see how the subject matter of the individual section is interpreted in terms of this category. If we analyze a given section on its own and in isolation, then we cannot see the categorial structure that Hegel intends for it to contain. Moreover, we cannot see how the section in question stands in relation to the other sections and the argument of the work as a whole. (2) As we have just seen, the concept of absolute knowing is precisely the grasping of all the individual Notions in their systematic context. Thus, this very concept presupposes a systematic understanding of the text. For this reason, any episodic interpretive approach to the *Phenomenology* would not be able to make sense of the notion of absolute knowing and thus the very point of the work as a whole. Given this, as interpreters, we are obliged first and foremost to seek the systematic structure of the text, difficult though that may be at times.

In this reconstruction, we have seen evidence that, indeed, Hegel may have hurried some parts of the *Phenomenology* during the composition of the text. We do not find everywhere the careful three-step process that we would expect. In sections such as "Legal Status" or in some of the analyses in "Religion," it is clear that Hegel's account is somewhat incomplete and must be supplemented with fuller discussions of the same themes from other texts. Nonetheless there is still a recognizable systematic unity in the text as it stands, and it is this that I have tried to sketch. In a letter to Schelling, Hegel laments that he was unable to make all of the systematic points of the text explicit: "Working into the detail has, I feel, damaged the overview of the whole. This whole, however, is itself by nature such an interlacing of cross-references back and forth that even were it set in better relief, it would still cost me much time before it would stand out more clearly and in more finished form."[43] The present interpretation should suffice to show that Hegel in fact had a systematic structure in mind when he wrote the book, as he indicates in this letter. With careful analysis we can set this structure "in better relief," as Hegel intended. One can always dispute the question concerning to what degree he adhered to this structure in any given analysis, but it would be absurd at this point to claim that such a structure simply does not exist. Moreover, we need not even find Hegel's structure here philosophically compelling in order to use it to understand the individual analyses which he gives. But, on the other hand, the risk that we run by ignoring his systematic pretensions entirely is not understanding him at all.

Notes

Introduction

1. Cf. *PhS*, § 26; *PhG*, 23.

2. Walter Kaufmann, *Hegel: A Reinterpretation* (Notre Dame: University of Notre Dame Press, 1978), 133.

3. Outstanding recent examples of this line of interpretation are M. J. Inwood, *Hegel* (London: Routledge and Kegan Paul, 1983); Charles Taylor, *Hegel* (Cambridge: Cambridge University Press, 1975).

4. Outstanding recent examples of this line of interpretation are Robert Pippin, *Hegel's Idealism: The Satisfactions of Self-Consciousness* (Cambridge: Cambridge University Press, 1989); Klaus Hartmann, "Hegel: A Non-Metaphysical View," in *Hegel: A Collection of Critical Essays*, ed. Alasdair MacIntyre (Notre Dame: University of Notre Dame Press, 1976), 101–24; Klaus Hartmann, "On Taking the Transcendental Turn," *Review of Metaphysics* 20 (1966), 223–49; Robert R. Williams, "Hegel and Transcendental Philosophy," *Journal of Philosophy* 82 (1985), 595–606; Ulrich Claesges, *Darstellung des erscheinenden Wissens. Hegel-Studien*, Beiheft 21 (Bonn: Bouvier, 1981), cf. especially 13–24. H. S. Harris calls the *Phenomenology* "Hegel's great 'transcendental argument,'" *Hegel's Development: Night Thoughts (Jena 1801–6)* (Oxford: Clarendon Press, 1983), 343. John Burbidge writes, "The *Phenomenology* is not primarily a philosophy of history. Despite its analysis of developmental stages, it more closely approximates traditional epistemology. For it seeks to outline the universal conditions necessary for any knowledge whatsoever." Burbidge, "'Unhappy Consciousness' in Hegel—an Analysis of Medieval Catholicism?" *Mosaic* 11 (1978), 80.

5. For a more detailed account of all this, see chapter 3 below, in which I discuss Hegel's relation to Kant.

6. The question of whether or not the entirety of Hegel's philosophy can be viewed as transcendental I wish to leave open. My main thesis is that the *Phenomenology* is essentially a transcendental argument. Cf. Pippin, *Hegel's Idealism;* Ludwig Siep, "Hegel's Idea of a Conceptual Scheme," *Inquiry* 34 (1991), 71ff; Klaus Hartmann, "On Taking the Transcendental Turn," *Review of Metaphysics* 78 (1966), 223–49.

Chapter 1

1. In *Dokumente zu Hegels Entwicklung*, ed. Johannes Hoffmeister (Stuttgart: Frommann, 1936). For an account in English of the contents of this address, see Shlomo Avineri, *Hegel's Theory of the Modern State* (Cambridge: Cambridge University Press, 1972), chapter 1.

2. Cf. Mechthild Lemcke and Christo Hackenesch, eds., *Hegel in Tübingen* (Tübingen: Konkursbuchverlag, 1984), 24: "In other aspects as well the seminary gave the impression of a cloister: its statutes, though reformed in a half-hearted manner in 1752, provided for a strict, truly monk-like system of regulation. When one looks at the daily schedule of the students, what is particularly striking is the unflagging supervision and patronizing regimentation." Cf. also Ludwig Sehring, *Hegel: Sein Leben und sein Wirken* (Berlin: Hermann Seemann Nachfolger), 11: "Indeed Hegel had to accept the strict outward discipline at the seminary, yet the cloister-like atmosphere and the seclusion which surrounded him there seemed not to bother him very much."

3. Cf. H. S. Harris, "Hegel and the French Revolution," *Clio* 7 (1977), 6ff.

4. These writings are available in English as *Early Theological Writings*, trans. T. M. Knox (Philadelphia: University of Pennsylvania Press, 1971). For an account of these writings see Avineri, *Hegel's Theory of the Modern State*, chapter 2.

5. This essay is available in English in *Hegel's Political Writings*, trans. T. M. Knox, with an introductory essay by Z. A. Pelcynski (Oxford: Clarendon, 1964). For an account of this essay see Avineri, *Hegel's Theory of the Modern State*, chapter 3.

6. This essay is available in English as *Difference between the Systems of Fichte and Schelling*, trans. H. S. Harris and W. Cerf (Albany: SUNY Press, 1977).

7. G. W. F. Hegel, *"Philosophical Dissertation on the Orbits of the Planets* (1801). Preceded by the 12 Theses defended on August 27, 1801," trans. Pierre Adler, *Graduate Faculty Philosophy Journal* 12 (1987), 269–309. A useful Latin edition of this text along with a German translation can be found in the following bilingual edition: *Dissertatio Philosophica de Orbitis Planetarum/Philosophische Erörterung über die Planetbahnen*, ed. Wolfgang Neuser (Weinhem: Acta Humaniora, 1986).

8. These works are as follows in German: *Jenaer Systementwürfe I–III, GW*, vols. 6–8. The English translations are as follows: G. W. F. Hegel, *The Jena System, 1804–5: Logic and Metaphysics*, translation edited by John W. Burbidge and George di Giovanni (Montreal: McGill-Queen's University Press, 1986); *The Jena Lectures on the Philosophy of Spirit (1805–6)*, in *Hegel and the Human Spirit*, trans. Leo Rauch (Detroit: Wayne State University Press, 1983); *First Philosophy of Spirit* in G. W. F. Hegel, *System of Ethical Life and First Philosophy of Spirit*, ed., trans. H. S. Harris and T. M. Knox (Albany: SUNY Press, 1979).

9. "*Logicam et Metaphysicam s. philosophiam speculativam praemissa Phaenomenologia mentis ex libri sui:* System der Wissenschaft, *proxime proditura parte prima*." Quoted from Heinz Kimmerle, "Dokumente zu Hegels Jenaer Dozententätigkeit (1801-7)," *Hegel-Studien* 4 (1967), 55–56.

10. For a more detailed discussion of the circumstances see Walter Kaufmann, *Hegel: A Reinterpretation* (Notre Dame: University of Notre Dame Press, 1978), 90.

11. Cf. Hegel to Schelling [95], Bamberg, 1 May 1807. Letters, 80; *Briefe* I, 159–62: "I actually completed the draft in its entirety in the middle of the night before the Battle of Jena."

12. Cf. Letters to Niethammer [77], [78], [79]; *Briefe* I, 125–27.

13. Hegel to Niethammer [74], 13 October 1806. *Letters*, 114; *Briefe* I, 119–22.

14. For an account of the problematic dating of this text, see Kaufmann, *Hegel*, 177–78.

15. Cf. Shlomo Avineri, "Hegel and Nationalism," in *Hegel's Political Philosophy*, ed. Walter Kaufmann (New York: Atherton Press, 1970), 109ff.

16. Cf. William Wallace, "Biographical Notice," in *Hegel's Logic*, trans. William Wallace (Oxford: Oxford University Press, 1975), xxxi: "The *Encyclopaedia* is the only complete, matured, and authentic statement of Hegel's philosophical system." Cf. also Christian Topp, *Philosophie als Wissenschaft* (Berlin: de Gruyter, 1982), xxxvii.

17. For a discussion of the dating of the *Philosophy of Right*, see Adriaan Peperzak, *Philosophy and Politics: A Commentary on the Preface to Hegel's "Philosophy of Right"* (Dordrecht: Nijhoff, 1987), 1ff.

18. The standard English translation is *The Philosophy of History*, trans. J. Sibree (New York: Willey Book Co., 1944; Dover, 1956; Prometheus Books, 1990).

19. The standard English translation is *Hegel's Aesthetics*, 2 vols., trans. T. M. Knox (Oxford: Clarendon, 1975). Cf. also the earlier translation: *The Philosophy of Fine Art*, 4 vols., trans. Franceis Plumptre Beresford Osmaston (London: G. Bell and Sons, Ltd., 1920). Also available is *Introductory Lectures on Aesthetics*, trans. Bernard Bosanquet, ed. Michael Inwood (Hamondsworth: Penguin, 1993).

20. The standard English translation is *Lectures on the Philosophy of Religion*, 3 vols., trans. Ebenezer Brown Speirs and J. Burdon Sanderson (London: K. Paul, Trench, Trübner and Co., 1895; reprint, London: Routledge and Kegan Paul, 1967). Also available, *Lectures on the Philosophy of Religion*, ed. Peter C. Hodgson, trans. R. F. Brown, P. C. Hodgson, and J. M. Stewart, with the assistance of H. S. Harris (Berkeley: University of California Press, 1988).

21. The standard English translation is *Lectures on the History of Philosophy*, 3 vols., trans. E. S. Haldane and Frances H. Simson (London: Routledge and Kegan Paul; New York: The Humanities Press, 1894–96).

22. Cf. Wolfgang Bonsiepen, "Erste zeitgenössische Rezensionen der *Phänomenologie des Geistes*," *Hegel-Studien* 14 (1979), 9–38; Eric von der Luft, "An Early Interpretation of Hegel's *Phenomenology of Spirit*," *Hegel-Studien* 24 (1989), 183–94.

23. This famous dictum of Hegel's appears in the following places: *PR*, Preface, 10; *RP*, 33; *EL*, § 6; *Enz.*, 32. Cf. Emil L. Fackenheim, "On the Actuality of the Rational and the Rationality of the Actual," *Review of Metaphysics* 89 (1969), 690–98; M. W. Jackson, "Hegel, the Real and the Rational," *International Studies in Philosophy* 19 (1987), 11–19; Yirmiahu Yovel, "Hegel's Dictum That the Rational Is Actual and the Actual Is Rational," in *Konzepte der Dialektik*, ed. Werner Becker and

Wilhelm K. Essler (Frankfurt: Klostermann, 1981), 111–27; Peperzak, *Philosophy and Politics*, 92–103.

24. Cf. Hoffmeister's discussion of K. F. Bachmann's impression of Hegel, in "Einleitung des Herausgebers," in *Georg Wilhelm Friedrich Hegel, Sämtliche Werke*, vol. 11: *Phänomenologie des Geistes* (Leipzig: Meiner, 1937), xxxixff. Cf. Bonsiepen, "Erste zeitgenössische Rezensionen der *Phänomenologie des Geistes*," 9–38. Cf. John Findlay, *Hegel: A Re-Examination* (London: Allen and Unwin, 1958), 359: "He [sc. Hegel] is without doubt, the Aristotle of our post-Renaissance world, our synoptic thinker without peer." Cf. James Hutchison Stirling, *The Secret of Hegel: Being the Hegelian System in Origin, Principle, Form and Matter* (London: Longman, Green and Longman, Roberts and Green, 1865).

25. Cf. Schopenhauer's criticisms in *On the Basis of Morality*, trans. E. F. J. Payne (Indianapolis: Bobbs-Merrill, Library of the Liberal Arts, 1965); and his "Preface to the Second Edition," in *The Fourfold Root of the Principle of Sufficient Reason*, trans. E. F. J. Payne (La Salle: Open Court, 1974). Cf. Michael Kelly, *Hegel's Charlatanism Exposed* (London: George Allen, 1911).

26. T. M. Knox, "Hegel and Prussianism," *Philosophy* 15 (1940), 51–63; Hans-Christian Lucas and Udo Rameil, "Furcht vor der Zensur?" *Hegel-Studien* 15 (1980), 63–93; Hans-Christian Lucas, "Philosophie und Wirklichkeit: Einige Bemerkungen wider die Legende von Hegel als preußischem Staatsphilosophen," *Zeitschrift für Didaktik der Philosophie* 9 (1987), 154–61; E. F. Carritt, "Hegel and Prussianism," *Philosophy* 15 (1940), 315–17; Sidney Hook, "Hegel and His Apologists" and "Hegel Rehabilitated," in *Hegel's Political Philosophy*, 87–105; Avineri, "Hegel and Nationalism," 109–36.

27. The classic example of this is of course Popper's account in *The Open Society and Its Enemies* (London: Routledge and Kegan Paul, 1952). Cf. also Gilbert Ryle, "Critical Notice," *Mind* 56 (1947), 170; Bertrand Russell, *Unpopular Essays* (London: Allen and Unwin, Ltd., 1950), 22; Jacques Maritain, *La philosophie morale* (Paris: Gallimard, 1960), 159. For a debunking of this myth, see Walter A. Kaufmann's "The Hegel Myth and Its Method," *Philosophical Review* 60 (1951), 459–86.

28. Cf. Gustav E. Müller, "Some Hegel Legends," in his *Hegel: The Man, His Vision and Work* (New York: Pageant Press, 1968). Originally, *Hegel: Denkgeschichte eines Lebendigen* (Bern: Francke, 1959). Cf. also Wilhelm Seeberger, "Vorurteile gegen Hegel," in his *Hegel oder die Entwicklung des Geistes zur Freiheit* (Stuttgart: Ernst Klett, 1961), 42ff. Cf. also John Findlay, *The Philosophy of Hegel: An Introduction and Re-Examination* (New York: Collier, 1962), 15ff.

29. Benedetto Croce, *What Is Living and What Is Dead in the Philosophy of Hegel*, trans. Douglas Ainslie (London: Macmillan and Co.; reprint, New York: Russell and Russell, 1969), 217.

30. Cf. Maurice Merleau-Ponty: "All the great philosophical ideas of the past century—the philosophies of Marx and Nietzsche, phenomenology, German existentialism, and psychoanalysis—had their beginnings in Hegel." "Hegel's Existentialism," in *Sense and Nonsense*, trans. Hubert L. Dreyfus and Patricia

Allen Dreyfus (Evanston: Northwestern University Press, 1964), 63–70. Originally, "L'existentialisme chez Hegel," *Les Temps Modernes* 2 (1945).

31. Cf. Merleau-Ponty, "Hegel's Existentialism." See also Sonia Kruks, "Merleau-Ponty, Hegel and the Dialectic," *Journal of the British Society for Phenomenology* 7 (1976), 96–110; Joseph C. Flay, "Hegel and Merleau-Ponty: Radical Essentialism," in *Ontology and Alterity in Merleau-Ponty*, ed. Galen A. Johnson and Michael B. Smith (Evanston: Northwestern University Press, 1990), 142–57; Jean Hyppolite, "La *Phénoménologie* de Hegel et la pensée française contemporaine," in his *Figures de la pensée philosophique: Écrits (1931–68)*, vol. 1 (Paris: Presses Universitaires de France, 1971), 231–41; Jon Stewart, "Hegel and the Myth of Reason," *Owl of Minerva* 26 (1995), 187–200.

32. Cf. Quentin Lauer, *A Reading of Hegel's Phenomenology of Spirit* (New York: Fordham University Press, 1976), 2–3. Cf. also his "Phenomenology: Hegel and Husserl," in *Beyond Epistemology: New Studies in the Philosophy of Hegel*, ed. Frederick G. Weiss (The Hague: Nijhoff, 1974), 174–96; Alphonse de Waelhens, "Phénoménologie husserlienne et phénoménologie hégélienne," *Revue philosophique de Louvain* 52 (1954), 234–49; Frank M. Kirkland, "Husserl and Hegel: A Historical and Religious Encounter," *Journal of the British Society of Phenomenology* 16 (1985), 70–87; Ernst Wolfgang Orth, "Husserl und Hegel: Ein Beitrag zum Problem des Verhältnisses historischer und systematischer Forschung in der Philosophie," in *Die Welt des Menschen—Die Welt der Philosophie: Festschrift für Jan Patocka*, ed. Walter Biemel (The Hague: Nijhoff, 1976), 213–50; Leo Rauch, "Hegel's *Phenomenology of Spirit* as a Phenomenological Project," *Thought* 56 (1981), 328–41.

33. Cf. Jon Stewart, "Berührungspunkte in der Religionsphilosophie Hegels und Schopenhauers," *Prima Philosophia* 6 (1993), 3–8.

34. *PhS*, § 785; *PhG* 419. Cf. Roger Garaudy, *Dieu est mort: Étude sur Hegel* (Paris: Presses Universitaires de France, 1962); Christian Link, *Hegels Wort "Gott selbst ist tot"* (Zürich: Theologischer Verlag, 1974); Dorothee Sölle, *Stellvertretung: Ein Kapitel Theologie nach dem Tode Gottes* (Stuttgart: Kreuz-Verlag, 1965).

35. Alexandre Kojève, *Introduction à la lecture de Hegel* (Paris: Gallimard, 1947). Translated as *An Introduction to the Reading of Hegel*, ed. Alan Bloom, trans. J. H. Nichols (Ithaca: Cornell University Press, 1969). Cf. Patrick Riley, "Introduction to the Reading of Alexandre Kojève," *Political Theory* 9 (1981), 5–48; Dennis Goldford, "Kojève's Reading of Hegel," *International Philosophical Quarterly* 22 (1982), 275–93; Michael S. Roth, "A Problem of Recognition: Alexandre Kojève and the End of History," *History and Theory* 24 (1985), 293–306; Gaston Fessard, "Deux interprètes de la *Phénoménologie* de Hegel: Jean Hyppolite et Alexandre Kojève," *Études* 255 (1947), 368–73; Jean Wahl, "A propos de l'introduction à la *Phénoménologie* de Hegel par A. Kojève," *Deucalion* 5 (1955), 77–99.

36. I discuss the issue of Hegel's position with respect to reason at some length in "Hegel and the Myth of Reason," 187–200.

37. Cf. Tom Rockmore, "Modernity and Reason: Habermas and Hegel," *Man and World* 22 (1989), 233–46.

38. See Thomas Kesselring, *Entwicklung und Widerspruch: Ein Vergleich zwischen Piagets genetischer Erkenntnistheorie und Hegels Dialektik* (Frankfurt: Suhrkamp, 1981).

39. In the *Philosophy of Right,* Hegel discusses the way in which the rational is found in the world by the philosopher:

> For since rationality . . . enters upon external existence simultaneously
> with its actualization, it emerges with an infinite wealth of forms, shapes
> and appearances. Around its heart it throws a motley covering with which
> consciousness is at home to begin with, a covering which the concept has
> first to penetrate before it can find the inward pulse and feel it still beating
> in the outward appearances. But the infinite variety of circumstance which is
> developed in this externally by the light of the essence glinting in it—this endless
> material and its organization—this is not the subject matter of philosophy. . . .
> To comprehend what is, this is the task of philosophy, because what is, is reason.
> (*PR,* 10–11; *RP,* 4–35)

40. See for instance Michael H. Mitias, "Hegelian Impact on Dewey's Concept of Moral Obligation," *Indian Philosophical Quarterly* 8 (1980–81), 121–36; R. J. Wilson, "Dewey's Hegelianism," *History of Education Quarterly* 15 (1975), 87–92.

41. See David Watson, "The Neo-Hegelian Tradition in America," *Journal of American Studies* 14 (1980), 219–34; William H. Goetzmann, ed., *The American Hegelians: An Intellectual Episode in the History of Western America* (New York: Knopf, 1973).

42. Josiah Royce, *Lectures on Modern Idealism* (New Haven: Yale University Press, 1919; reprint, 1964); *The Spirit of Modern Philosophy: An Essay in the Form of Lectures* (Boston: Houghton, Mifflin and Co., 1892), 190–227.

43. Cf. Gustav E. Müller, "Hegel in Amerika," *Zeitschrift für Deutsche Kulturphilosophie* 5 (1939), 269; Burleigh Taylor Wilkins, "James, Dewey, and Hegelian Idealism," *Journal of the History of Ideas* 17 (1956), 332–46.

44. Cf. Robert C. Solomon, "Truth and Self-Satisfaction," *Review of Metaphysics* 28 (1975), 701ff.

45. Cf. Theodore Kisiel, "Hegel and Hermeneutics," in *Beyond Epistemology: New Studies in the Philosophy of Hegel,* ed. Frederick G. Weiss (The Hague: Nijhoff, 1974), 197–220; Garbis Kortian, "Die Auflösung von Hegels Phänomenologie in Hermeneutik: Zum Wahrheitsanspruch eines spekulativen Erfahrungsbegriffes," in *Die Krise der Phänomenologie und die Pragmatik des Wissenschaftsfortschritts,* ed. Michael Benedikt and Rudolf Burger (Vienna: Edition S, Verlag der Österreichischen Staatsdruckeri, 1986), 53–64.

46. Cf. Peter Hylton, *Russell, Idealism and the Emergence of Analytic Philosophy* (Oxford: Clarendon Press, 1992).

47. Cf. Richard Rorty, "Philosophy in America Today," in his *Consequences of Pragmatism* (Minneapolis: University of Minnesota Press, 1982), 211–30.

48. Cf. Merleau-Ponty: "interpreting Hegel means taking a stand on all the philosophical, political, and religious problems of our century" ("Hegel's Existentialism," 64).

Chapter 2

1. Immanuel Kant, *Critique of Pure Reason*, trans. N. Kemp Smith (New York: St. Martin's Press, 1929), Bxxxv.

2. Ibid., A76, B102ff.

3. Cf. Robert C. Solomon, "Truth and Self-Satisfaction," *Review of Metaphysics* 28 (1975), 700ff.

4. *PhS*, § 75; *PhG*, 54.

5. *PhS*, § 75; *PhG*, 54.

6. *SL*, 45–46; *WL*, 29–30.

7. Cf. *EL*, § 42, Remark; *Werke*, vol. 8, 119: "Still, though the categories, such as unity, or cause and effect, are strictly the property of thought, it by no means follows that they must be ours merely and not also characteristics of objects. Kant, however, confines them to the subject-mind, and his philosophy may be styled subjective idealism: for he holds that both the form and the matter of knowledge are supplied by the ego—or knowing subject—the form by our intellectual, the matter by our sentient ego." Cf. also *SL*, 45; *WL*, 29: "[on Kant's view] self-conscious determining, moreover, belongs only to thinking."

8. Cf. *PhS*, § 72; *PhG*, 49: "the individual must all the more forget himself, as the nature of science implies and requires."

9. Cf. *EL*, § 12; *Enz.*, 39.

10. For an interesting comparison of Kant's and Hegel's accounts of the subject, see W. H. Werkmeister, "Hegel's *Phenomenology of Mind* as a Development of Kant's Basic Ontology," in *Hegel and the Philosophy of Religion: The Wofford Symposium*, ed. Darrel E. Christenson (The Hague: Nijhoff, 1970), 93–110; James Griffiss, "The Kantian Background of Hegel's Logic," *New Scholasticism* 43 (1969), 512ff.

11. Cf. Kant, *Critique of Pure Reason*, A106ff, B131ff.

12. Cf. Ibid., B131–32, to which Hegel here refers.

13. *EL*, § 20; *Enz.*, 47.

14. *EL*, § 20; *Enz.*, 48.

15. E.g., Henry Allison, *Kant's Transcendental Idealism: An Interpretation and Defense* (New Haven: Yale University Press, 1983).

16. Most notably, Robert Pippin, *Hegel's Idealism: The Satisfactions of Self-Consciousness* (Cambridge: Cambridge University Press, 1989).

17. See Hugh A. Reyburn, *The Ethical Theory of Hegel: A Study of the "Philosophy of Right"* (Oxford: Clarendon Press, 1921), 159ff.

18. *PR*, § 32, Remark; *RP*, 82 (my italics).

19. *EL*, § 25; *Enz.*, 50 (my italics).

20. I would not wish to claim that Hegel was wholly original in this innovation, since clearly Fichte and Schelling provided important advances in this direction. For a clear statement of this development, see Werner Marx's *Hegel's "Phenomenology of Spirit," Its Point and Purpose: A Commentary on the Preface and Introduction*, trans. Peter Heath (New York: Harper and Row, 1975). Originally, *Hegel's Phänomenologie des Geistes: Die Bestimmung ihrer Idee in "Vorrede" und "Einleitung"* (Frankfurt: Klostermann, 1971), 14ff.

21. See Robert R. Williams, "Hegel and Transcendental Philosophy," *Journal of Philosophy* 82 (1985), 601.

22. Following Miller, I have made a practice of capitalizing the word "Notion" (*Begriff*) when it is used in this technical Hegelian sense in order to distinguish it from "concept" in its ordinary usage or in the Kantian sense of category.

23. Cf. Maurice Merleau-Ponty, "Hegel's Existentialism," in *Sense and Nonsense*, trans. Hubert L. Dreyfus and Patricia Allen Dreyfus (Evanston: Northwestern University Press, 1964), 65:

> The question is no longer limited, as it was in the *Critique de la raison pure théorique* [i.e., Kant's *Critique of Pure Reason*], to discovering what conditions make scientific experience possible but is one of knowing in a general way how moral, aesthetic, and religious experiences are possible, of describing man's fundamental situation in the face of the world and other men, and of understanding religions, ethics, works of art, economic and legal systems as just so many ways for man to flee or to confront the difficulties of his condition. Experience here no longer simply means our entirely contemplative contact with the sensible world as it did in Kant.

24. Cf. *Propaedeutic*, §§ 2–3; *Werke*, vol. 4, 111–12.

25. See Rudolf Haym, *Hegel und seine Zeit: Vorlesungen über Entstehung und Entwicklung, Wesen und Werth der hegel'schen Philosophie* (Berlin: Verlag von Rudolf Gaertner, 1857; reprint, Hildesheim: Olms, 1962), 235ff. Haym argues that the *Phenomenology* is a combination of transcendental and historical argumentation.

26. *PR*, § 3, Addition; *RP*, 42ff.

27. Cf. the Introduction to Hegel's *EL*, §§ 13–14; *Enz.*, 40–41.

28. *Phil. of Hist*, 1ff.; *VPG*, 33ff.

29. In my view, Kaufmann is mistaken on this point to attribute to Hegel a sociological theory: "The widespread acceptance of a point of view is determined [sc. for Hegel] sociologically." Walter Kaufmann, *Hegel: A Reinterpretation* (Notre Dame: University of Notre Dame Press, 1978), 138.

30. Cited from Heinz Kimmerle, "Dokumente zu Hegels Jenaer Dozententätigkeit (1801–7)," *Hegel-Studien* 4 (1967), 71.

31. Cf. Pöggeler's treatment of the role of history. Otto Pöggeler, "Die Komposition der *Phänomenologie des Geistes*," in *Materialien zu Hegels Phänomenologie des Geistes*, ed. Hans Friedrich Fulda and Dieter Henrich (Frankfurt: Suhrkamp, 1973), 335ff. Cf. also Hoffmeister's discussion of the role of history in the *Phenomenology*. Johannes Hoffmeister, "Einleiting des Herausgebers," in *Georg Wilhelm Friedrich Hegel, Sämtliche Werke, Kritische Ausgabe*, vol. 11: *Phänomenologie des Geistes* (Leipzig: Felix Meiner, 1937), xviiff. Cf. also Hans Friedrich Fulda, *Das Problem einer Einleitung in Hegels Wissenschaft der Logik* (Frankfurt: Klostermann, 1965), 217ff., 251ff.

32. Cf. Henry Allison, "Kant's Concept of the Transcendental Object," *Kant-Studien* 59 (1968), 165–86; Allison, "The Non-Spatiality of Things-in-Themselves for Kant," *Journal of the History of Philosophy* 14 (1976), 313–21; Merold Westphal, "In Defense of the Thing-in-Itself," *Kant-Studien* 59 (1968), 135–41.

33. Fichte, *The Science of Knowledge,* ed., trans., Peter Heath and John Lachs (Cambridge: Cambridge University Press, 1982), 10.

34. *EL,* § 44; *Enz.,* 60.

35. *PhS,* § 84; *PhG,* 59.

36. For this comparison, see John McCumber, "Scientific Progress and Hegel's *Phenomenology of Spirit,*" *Idealistic Studies* 13 (1983), 1–10.

37. *PhS,* § 84; *PhG,* 59.

38. René Descartes, *Meditations on First Philosophy with Selections from the Objections and Replies,* trans. John Cottingham (Cambridge: Cambridge University Press, 1986), 27; *Oeuvres de Descartes,* vol. 7, ed. Charles Adam and Paul Tannery (Paris: Cerf, 1891–1913; reprint, Paris: J. Vrin, 1957ff.), 39.

39. *PhS,* § 84; *PhG,* 59.

40. *PhS,* § 84; *PhG,* 59.

41. For the word "phenomenology," see Hoffmeister, "Einleiting des Herausgebers," vii; Kaufmann, *Hegel: A Reinterpretation,* 148ff; Kaufmann, "Hegel's Conception of Phenomenology," in *Phenomenology and Philosophical Understanding,* ed. Edo Pivcevic (Cambridge: Cambridge University Press, 1975), 211–30; Theodore Haering, "Entstehungsgeschichte der *Phänomenologie des Geistes,*" in *Verhandlungen des III. Internationalen Hegel Kongresses 1933,* ed. B. Wigersma (Haarlem: N/VH.D. Tjeenk Willink and Zn. and Tübingen: J. C. B. Mohr, 1934), 137–38.

42. *SL,* 54; *WL,* 38.

43. Cf. Findlay, who sees this insistence on necessity and the lack of possible alternatives as Hegel's gravest error: "Here we may merely maintain that Hegel's main mistake both in what he *says* about his dialectic and in what he tries to do with it, lies in his assumption that it has *a kind of deductive necessity,* different from, but akin to, that of a mathematical system, whereby we shall find ourselves forced along a *single* line of reasoning, culminating in 'the Idea,' and then leading back to our point of origin." John Findlay, *The Philosophy of Hegel: An Introduction and Re-Examination* (New York: Collier Books, 1962), 78. Cf. also Mark B. Okrent, "Consciousness and Objective Spirit in Hegel's *Phenomenology,*" *Journal of the History of Philosophy* 18 (1980), 46ff.

Chapter 3

1. *EL,* § 1; *Enz.,* 27; cf. *EL,* § 25; *Enz.,* 50. Cf. Quentin Lauer, "Hegel on the Identity of Content in Religion and Philosophy," in *Hegel and the Philosophy of Religion,* ed. Darrel E. Christensen (The Hague: Nijhoff, 1970), 261–78.

2. For a useful discussion of this issue, see Robert C. Solomon, *In the Spirit of Hegel* (Oxford: Oxford University Press, 1983), 172ff.

3. Cf. Rorty's discussion of the term "science" in "Nineteenth-Century Idealism and Twentieth-Century Textualism," in his *Consequences of Pragmatism* (Minneapolis: University of Minnesota Press, 1982), 147: "Hegel invented a literary genre which lacked any trace of argumentation, but which obsessively captioned itself *System der Wissenschaft* or *Wissenschaft der Logik,* or *Enzyklopädie der philosophischen Wissenschaften.*" For a discussion of philosophy as "the science" vis-à-vis the other sciences, see Friedrich Kaulbach, "Hegels Stellung zu den

Einzelwissenschaften," in *Weltaspekte der Philosophie,* ed. Werner Beierwaltes and Weibke Schrader (Amsterdam: Editions Rodopi, 1972), 181–206.

4. *PhS,* § 70; *PhG,* 48.

5. Friedrich Schelling, *System of Transcendental Idealism,* trans. Peter Heath, with an Introduction by Michael Vater (Charlottesville: University Press of Virginia, 1978), 10.

6. *PhS,* § 26; *PhG,* 23.

7. *EL,* § 45, Remark; *Werke,* vol. 8, 123.

8. *SL,* 49; *WL,* 33.

9. *PhS,* § 71; *PhG* 48.

10. Haym suggests that Hegel saw the need for this preliminary justification primarily for the practical reason of persuading his students in the classroom. Rudolf Haym, *Hegel und seine Zeit: Vorlesungen über Entstehung und Entwicklung, Wesen und Werth der hegel'schen Philosophie* (Berlin: Rudolf Gaertner, 1857; reprint, Hildesheim: Olms, 1962), 232.

11. *PhS,* § 71; *PhG,* 49.

12. *EL,* § 1; *Enz.,* 27.

13. *PhS,* § 13; *PhG,* 15–16.

14. Cf. John Sallis, "Hegel's Concept of Presentation: Its Determination in the Preface to the *Phenomenology of Spirit,*" *Hegel-Studien* 12 (1977), 129–56.

15. *PhS,* § 26; *PhG,* 23.

16. *PhS,* § 89; *PhG,* 61–62.

17. *PhS,* § 27; *PhG,* 24.

18. *SL,* 49; *WL,* 33.

19. Cf. Robert Pippin, *Hegel's Idealism: The Satisfactions of Self-Consciousness* (Cambridge: Cambridge University Press, 1989), 94–99.

20. *PhS,* § 76; *PhG,* 55.

21. *PhS,* § 76; *PhG,* 55.

22. *SL,* 48–49; *WL,* 32. Cf. also the passage from the *Encyclopaedia Logic,* § 25 cited in the previous chapter. Cf. *PR,* § 2, Addition; *RP,* 40: "The truth is that in philosophical knowledge the necessity of a concept is the principal thing; and the process of its production as a result is its proof and deduction."

23. *PhS,* § 113; *PhG,* 72. Cf. also *PhS,* § 59; *PhG,* 42. Cf. also Hegel's discussion in the *Science of Logic* of the word *"aufheben,"* which he feels embodies the essence of the dialectic: " *'To sublate'* has a twofold meaning in the language: on the one hand it means to preserve, to maintain, and equally it also means to cause to cease, to put an end to" (*SL,* 106ff.; *WL,* 94ff).

24. Cf. B. C. Birchall, "Hegel's Notion of *Aufheben,*" *Inquiry* 24 (1981), 75–103.

25. See Howard Kainz's discussion, "Some Problems with the English Translations of Hegel's *Phänomenologie des Geistes,*" *Hegel-Studien* 21 (1986), 177.

26. *PhS,* § 59; *PhG,* 42.

27. Cf. Hans-Georg Gadamer, "Hegel and the Dialectic of the Ancient Philosophers," in his *Hegel's Dialectic,* trans. P. C. Smith (New Haven: Yale Uni-

versity Press, 1976); Charles Griswold, "Reflections on 'Dialectic' in Plato and Hegel," *International Philosophical Quarterly* 22 (1982), 115–30.

28. Cf. *Hist. of Phil.* I, 406; *VPG* II, 71.

29. *SL*, 55–56; *WL*, 40.

30. *PR*, § 31, Remark; *RP*, 81.

31. *PhS*, § 79; *PhG*, 57.

32. *PR*, § 31, Remark; *RP*, 81.

33. See Franz Ungler, "Die Bedeutung der bestimmten Negation in Hegels *Wissenschaft der Logik*," *Wiener Jahrbuch für Philosophie* 8 (1975), 154–94. For an expanded account of this discussion, see my "Hegel's Doctrine of Determinate Negation: An Example from 'Sense-Certainty' and 'Perception,' " *Idealistic Studies* 26 (1996), 57–75.

34. *PhS*, § 59; *PhG*, 42.

35. *PhS*, § 79; *PhG*, 57.

36. *EL*, § 82; *Enz.*, 92.

37. *SL*, 54; *WL*, 38.

38. *Dissertatio*, 76; *Phil. Diss.*, 276.

39. *PR*, § 32, Addition; *RP*, 83.

40. For the moment I leave aside Hegel's short early work *Difference between the Systems of Fichte and Schelling*, trans. H. S. Harris and W. Cerf (Albany: SUNY Press, 1977).

41. *PR*, Preface 1; *RP*, 19.

42. *PhS*, § 81; *PhG*, 58.

43. *PhS*, § 81; *PhG*, 58.

44. Cf. Heribert Boeder, "Das natürliche Bewußtsein," *Hegel-Studien* 12 (1977), 157–78. Cf. Gerhard Krüger, "Die dialektische Erfahrung des natürlichen Bewußtseins bei Hegel," in *Hermeneutik und Dialektik*, ed. Rüdiger Bubner, Conrad Cramer, and Reiner Wiehl (Tübingen: Mohr, 1970), 285–303.

45. This third-person perspective comes out in a number of different passsages. Cf. *PR*, § 32, Addition; *RP*, 83: "This is not our procedure; we only wish to look on at the way in which the concept determines itself and to restrain ourselves from adding thereto anything of our thoughts and opinions." Cf. *PhS*, § 85; *PhG*, 59: "But not only is a contribution by us superfluous, since Notion and object, the criterion and what is to be tested, are present in consciousness itself, but we are also spared the trouble of comparing the two and really *testing* them, so that, since what consciousness examines is its own self, all that is left for us to do is simply look on."

46. For this term, see Joseph Gauvin, "Für uns dans la *Phénoménologie de l'esprit*," *Archives de Philosophie* 33 (1970), 829–54; Kenley Dove, "Hegel's Phenomenological Method," *Review of Metaphysics* 23 (1969–70), 627ff.; Joseph C. Flay, "The History of Philosophy and the *Phenomenology of Spirit*," in *Hegel and the History of Philosophy: Proceedings of the 1972 Hegel Society of America Conference*, ed. Joseph O'Malley, Keith W. Algozin, and Frederick G. Weiss (The Hague: Nijhoff, 1974), 54ff. Loewenberg refers to the distinction between the philosophical observer and natural consciousness as the distinction between the "comic" and the "histrionic."

480

NOTES TO PAGES 46-50

Jacob Loewenberg, "The Comedy of Immediacy in Hegel's *Phenomenology* (II)," *Mind* 44 (1935), 21.

47. *PhS,* § 28; *PhG,* 24.

48. Cf. *PhS,* § 78; *PhG,* 56.

49. *PhS,* § 31; *PhG,* 26–27.

50. See Loewenberg, who associates knowledge of natural consciousness with the German term *"Erscheinung,"* which has the following three senses: "(1) that which appears or (2) that which is self-evident or (3) that which is specious." Jacob Loewenberg, "The Exoteric Approach to Hegel's *Phenomenology* (I)," *Mind* 43 (1934), 434.

51. Cf. Graeser's discussion of the term "natural" in this context. Andreas Graeser, *Einleitung zur "Phänomenologie des Geistes." Kommentar* (Stuttgart: Reclam, 1988), 25–26. Cf. Hegel's discussion of "natural existence" and "natural will" in *Phil. of Hist.,* 25; *VPG,* 54.

52. Schelling, *System of Transcendental Idealism,* 10 (translation slightly modified).

53. Ibid. (translation slightly modified).

54. See Pippin, *Hegel's Idealism,* 36–38.

55. Cf. Graeser, who also supports this view. Graeser, *Einleitung zur "Phänomenologie des Geistes,"* 28. Cf. John Findlay, *The Philosophy of Hegel: An Introduction and Re-Examination* (New York: Collier Books, 1962), 21: "For the purpose of Hegel is to explore notions from a particular angle, to see them as embodying half-formed *tendencies.*"

56. *PhS,* § 82; *PhG,* 58.

57. *PhS,* § 84; *PhG,* 59.

58. *PhS,* § 84; *PhG,* 59 (my italics).

59. *PhS,* § 17; *PhG,* 18. Cf. Henrich's analysis of this famous line. Dieter Henrich, *Hegel im Kontext* (Frankfurt: Suhrkamp, 1981), 95ff. Cf. *PR,* § 152; *RP,* 234–35: "Subjectivity is itself the absolute form and existent actuality of the substantial order, and the distinction between subject on the one hand and substance on the other, as the object, end, and controlling power of the subject, is the same as, and has vanished directly along with, the distinction between them in form."

60. *PhS,* § 73; *PhG,* 53.

61. Solomon and Krahl attribute these metaphors to Kant, while Findlay attributes them to Locke. See Robert C. Solomon, *In the Spirit of Hegel* (Oxford: Oxford University Press, 1983), 295ff; Hans-Jürgen Krahl, *Erfahrung des Bewußtseins: Kommentare zu Hegels Einleitung der "Phänomenologie des Geistes" und Exkurse zur materialistischen Erkenntnistheorie* (Frankfurt: Materialis Verlag, 1979), 12ff.; Findlay, *The Philosophy of Hegel,* 86. Cf. also Graeser's discussions in *Einleitung zur "Phänomenologie des Geistes,"* 29ff.

62. *EL,* § 43; *Enz.,* 59 (my italics).

63. Cf. *EL,* § 10; *Enz.,* 36: "We ought, says Kant, to become acquainted with the *instrument,* before we undertake the work for which it is to be employed" (my italics).

64. *PhS,* § 73; *PhG,* 53.
65. *PhS,* § 73; *PhG,* 54.
66. *PhS,* § 74; *PhG,* 54.
67. *PhS,* § 85; *PhG,* 59.
68. *PhS,* § 85; *PhG,* 60.
69. *PhS,* § 85; *PhG,* 60.
70. Cf. *PhS,* § 85; *PhG,* 60: "in the alteration of the knowledge, the object itself alters for it too."

Chapter 4

1. *PhS,* § 112; *PhG,* 71.
2. *PhS,* § 91; *PhG,* 63.
3. *PhS,* § 91; *PhG,* 63.
4. *PhS,* § 91; *PhG,* 63.
5. *PhS,* § 90; *PhG,* 63.
6. *PhS,* § 91; *PhG,* 63.
7. *PhS,* § 91; *PhG,* 63.
8. Cf. Gilbert Plumer, "Hegel on Singular Demonstrative Reference," *Southwestern Journal of Philosophy* 11 (1980), 71–94; David Lamb, "Hegel and Wittgenstein on Language and Sense-Certainty," *Clio* 7 (1978), 285–301.
9. *SL,* 44; *WL,* 28.
10. *PhS,* § 93; *PhG,* 64.
11. *SL,* 44; *WL,* 28.
12. *SL,* 44; *WL,* 28.
13. *PhS,* § 94; *PhG,* 64.
14. *PhS,* § 95; *PhG,* 64. Cf. *Propaedeutic,* § 11; *Werke,* vol. 4, 113–14.
15. *Phil. of Mind,* § 418; *Enz.,* 318.
16. *PhS,* § 95; *PhG,* 64.
17. *EL,* § 42, Remark; *Werke,* vol. 8, 117.
18. *PhS,* § 98; *PhG,* 65.
19. *EL,* § 38; *Werke,* vol. 8, 109. Cf. *EL,* § 20: *Werke,* vol. 8, 72: "The real distinction between sense and thought lies in this—that the essential feature of the sensible is individuality."
20. *EL,* § 20; *Enz.,* 47.
21. *PhS,* § 100; *PhG,* 66.
22. *PhS,* § 100; *PhG,* 66. The German is as follows: "*Ihre Wahrheit ist in dem Gegenstande als* meinem *Gegenstande oder im* Meinen; *er ist, weil Ich von ihm weiß.*" In this passage, Hegel plays on the possessive pronoun "my" or "mine" (*mein*) and the verb "to mean" or "to intend" (*meinen*), which he uses in the sense of meaning or intending a particular object whose particularity is not able to be captured linguistically due to the universality of language. Cf. *PhS,* § 117; *PhG,* 75.
23. *PhS,* § 101; *PhG,* 66.
24. *PhS,* § 100; *PhG,* 66.
25. *PhS,* § 102; *PhG,* 66.

26. *EL*, § 20; *Enz.*, 47. Cf. *EL*, § 24, Remark; *Werke*, vol. 8, 83: "Every man is a whole world of conceptions that lie buried in the night of the 'ego.' It follows that the 'ego' is the universal in which we leave aside all that is particular, and in which at the same time all particulars have a latent existence." Cf. also *PR*, § 4, Addition; *RP*, 51: "The ego is thought and so the universal. When I say 'I,' I *eo ipso* abandon all my characteristics, my disposition, natural endowment, knowledge, and age. The ego is quite empty, a mere point, simple, yet active in this simplicity."

27. Cf. *Phil. of Mind*, § 381, Remark; *Werke*, vol. 10, 21.

28. *EL*, § 24, Remark; *Werke*, vol. 8, 82–83.

29. *PhS*, § 103; *PhG*, 66–67.

30. *PhS*, § 104; *PhG*, 67.

31. *PhS*, § 105; *PhG*, 67.

32. *PhS*, § 106; *PhG*, 67. In this passage, Hegel is playing on words again. In German the past participle of the verb *sein*, "to be" is *gewesen*, which is etymologically related to the word *Wesen* or "essence." Thus, something which has been or no longer is has, so to speak, no essence.

33. *PhS*, § 108; *PhG*, 68. Cf. *SL*, 441; *WL* I, 548.

34. *Jena System*, 1804–5, 151; *JSE* II, 144.

35. *PhS*, § 109; *PhG*, 69.

36. *PhS*, § 110; *PhG*, 70.

37. Cf. Daniel J. Cook, "Sprache und Bewußtsein in Hegels *Phänomenologie des Geistes*," *Hegel-Jahrbuch* (1970), 121.

38. *PhS*, § 109; *PhG*, 69.

39. *PhS*, § 109; *PhG*, 69.

40. *PhS*, § 171; *PhG*, 106.

41. For the concept of mediation in this section, see Jacob Loewenberg, "The Comedy of Immediacy in Hegel's *Phenomenology* (II)," *Mind* 44 (1935), 21–38; Paul S. Miklowitz, "The Ontological Status of Style in Hegel's *Phenomenology*," *Idealistic Studies* 13 (1983), 61–73.

42. *PhS*, § 112; *PhG*, 71.

43. *PhS*, § 116; *PhG*, 74.

44. *PhS*, § 111; *PhG*, 71.

45. *PhS*, § 116; *PhG*, 73.

46. Cf. *Propaedeutic.* §§ 13–14; *Werke*, vol. 4, 114–15. Cf. *EL*, §§ 124–25; *Enz.*, 118.

47. *PhS*, § 113; *PhG*, 72.

48. *PhS*, § 112; *PhG*, 71.

49. *PhS*, § 113; *PhG*, 72.

50. Cf. Cook, "Sprache und Bewußtsein in Hegels *Phänomenologie des Geistes*," 122–23.

51. *PhS*, § 113; *PhG*, 72 (translation slightly modified).

52. Beginning at *PhS*, § 115; *PhG*, 73.

53. Cf. Wim van Dooren, "Der Begriff der Materie in Hegels *Phänomenologie des Geistes*," *Hegel-Jahrbuch* (1976), 84–89; Lucio Colletti, "Hegel und die Dialektik

der Materie," *Neue Hefte für Philosophie* 10 (1976), 1–19. Hegel takes up this concept again at *PhS*, § 251; *PhG*, 144. See also *EL*, § 126; *Enz.*, 119.

54. *PhS*, § 114; *PhG*, 73.
55. *PhS*, § 120; *PhG*, 76.
56. *PhS*, § 115; *PhG*, 73
57. *PhS*, § 115; *PhG*, 73.
58. *PhS*, § 117; *PhG*, 74.
59. *PhS*, § 94; *PhG*, 64.
60. *PhS*, § 117; *PhG*, 74.
61. *PhS*, § 117; *PhG*, 74.
62. *PhS*, § 116; *PhG*, 74.
63. *PhS*, § 117; *PhG*, 74.
64. *PhS*, § 117; *PhG*, 74.
65. *PhS*, § 117; *PhG*, 74.
66. *PhS*, § 117; *PhG*, 74.
67. *PhS*, § 117; *PhG*, 74.
68. *PhS*, § 117; *PhG*, 74.
69. *PhS*, § 117; *PhG*, 74.
70. *PhS*, § 117; *PhG*, 74.
71. *PhS*, § 117; *PhG*, 74–75.
72. *PhS*, § 118; *PhG*, 75.
73. *PhS*, § 118; *PhG*, 75.
74. *PhS*, § 100; *PhG*, 66.
75. *PhS*, § 118; *PhG*, 75.
76. *PhS*, § 119; *PhG*, 75.
77. *PhS*, § 119; *PhG*, 75.
78. *PhS*, § 119; *PhG*, 75–76.
79. *PhS*, § 101; *PhG*, 66.
80. *PhS*, § 120; *PhG*, 76.
81. *PhS*, § 120; *PhG*, 76.
82. *PhS*, § 121; *PhG*, 76.
83. *PhS*, § 121; *PhG*, 76. Cf. *SL*, 420, 423; *WL* I, 520, 524.
84. *PhS*, § 122; *PhG*, 77.
85. *PhS*, § 122; *PhG*, 77.
86. *PhS*, § 123; *PhG*, 77.
87. *PhS*, § 123; *PhG*, 77.
88. *PhS*, § 103; *PhG*, 67.
89. *PhS*, § 125; *PhG*, 78.
90. *PhS*, § 130; *PhG*, 80.
91. *PhS*, § 132; *PhG*, 82.
92. *EL*, § 21, Remark; *Werke*, vol. 8, 78.
93. *PhS*, § 141; *PhG*, 87.
94. Cf. *Propaedeutic*, §§ 18–19; *Werke*, vol. 4, 115–16.
95. Immanuel Kant, *Critique of Pure Reason*, trans. N. Kemp Smith (New York: St. Martin's Press, 1929), Bxxvi.

96. *PhS,* § 132; *PhG,* 82.
97. *PhS,* § 132; *PhG,* 82.
98. *PhS,* § 135; *PhG,* 83.
99. *PhS,* § 135; *PhG,* 83.
100. *PhS,* § 135; *PhG,* 83.
101. *PhS,* § 136; *PhG,* 85.
102. *PhS,* § 136; *PhG,* 83.
103. *PhS,* § 136; *PhG,* 83–84.
104. *PhS,* § 136; *PhG,* 84.
105. *PhS,* § 136; *PhG,* 84.
106. *PhS,* § 136; *PhG,* 84.
107. *PhS,* § 136; *PhG,* 84.
108. *PhS,* § 136; *PhG,* 84.
109. *PhS,* § 137; *PhG,* 85.
110. *PhS,* § 136; *PhG,* 84.
111. *PhS,* § 137; *PhG,* 85.
112. *PhS,* § 136; *PhG,* 84–85.
113. *PhS,* § 137; *PhG,* 85.
114. *PhS,* § 138; *PhG,* 85.
115. *PhS,* § 139; *PhG,* 86.
116. Cf. Fichte's "Second Introduction," in *The Science of Knowledge,* ed., trans., Peter Heath and John Lachs (Cambridge: Cambridge University Press, 1982), 55: "This thought of a thing-in-itself is grounded upon sensation, and sensation they again wish to have grounded upon the thought of a thing-in-itself."
117. *PhS,* § 144; *PhG,* 89.
118. *PhS,* § 146; *PhG,* 89.
119. *PhS,* § 146; *PhG,* 89.
120. *PhS,* § 147; *PhG,* 90.
121. *PhS,* § 147; *PhG,* 90.
122. Cf. *PhS,* § 148; *PhG,* 91: "It is the *law of force.*"
123. *EL,* § 21, Remark; *Werke,* vol. 8, 77.
124. *EL,* § 21, Remark; *Werke,* vol. 8, 77.
125. *PhS,* § 149; *PhG,* 91.
126. *PhS,* § 150; *PhG,* 91.
127. *PhS,* § 150; *PhG,* 92.
128. *PhS,* § 150; *PhG,* 92.
129. *PhS,* § 150; *PhG,* 92.
130. *PhS,* § 150; *PhG,* 92.
131. *PhS,* § 150; *PhG,* 91–92.
132. *PhS,* § 150; *PhG,* 92.
133. *PhS,* § 150; *PhG,* 92.
134. *PhS,* § 150; *PhG,* 92.
135. *PhS,* § 154; *PhG,* 95.
136. *PhS,* § 154; *PhG,* 95.
137. *PhS,* § 154; *PhG,* 95.

138. *PhS*, § 154; *PhG*, 95.
139. *PhS*, § 155; *PhG*, 95.
140. *PhS*, §§ 156–65; *PhG*, 96–102.
141. Alexandre Kojève, *An Introduction to the Reading of Hegel*, ed. Alan Bloom, trans. J. H. Nichols (Ithaca: Cornell University Press, 1969); Charles Taylor, *Hegel* (Cambridge: Cambridge University Press, 1975).
142. John Findlay, *Hegel: A Re-Examination* (London: Allen and Unwin, 1958), 92.
143. W. H. Bossart, "Hegel on the Inverted World," *Philosophical Forum* 8 (1982), 326–41; Hans-Georg Gadamer, "Hegel's 'Inverted World,' " in his *Hegel's Dialectic: Five Hermeneutical Studies*, trans. C. Smith (New Haven: Yale University Press, 1976), 35–53; Robert Zimmerman, "Hegel's 'Inverted World' Revisited," *Philosophical Forum* 8 (1982), 342–70; Joseph Flay, "Hegel's 'Inverted World,' " *Review of Metaphysics* 8 (1970), 662–78.
144. Jean Hyppolite, *Genesis and Structure of Hegel's "Phenomenology of Spirit,"* trans. S. Cherniak and J. Heckman (Evanston: Northwestern University Press, 1974).
145. Gadamer, "Hegel's 'Inverted World,' " 35–53.
146. Joseph Flay, *Hegel's Quest for Certainty* (Albany: SUNY Press, 1984).
147. *PhS*, § 154; *PhG*, 95.
148. *PhS*, § 156; *PhG*, 96.
149. *PhS*, § 157; *PhG*, 96.
150. *PhS*, § 157; *PhG*, 96.
151. *PhS*, § 157; *PhG*, 96–97.
152. *PhS*, § 158; *PhG*, 97.
153. *PhS*, § 158; *PhG*, 97.
154. *Phil. of Mind*, § 423; *Werke*, vol. 10, 212.
155. *PhS*, § 160; *PhG*, 98–99.
156. *PhS*, § 163; *PhG*, 100–1.
157. *PhS*, § 163; *PhG*, 100–1.
158. *PhS*, § 163; *PhG*, 101.
159. *PhS*, § 164; *PhG*, 101.
160. *PhS*, § 165; *PhG*, 102.
161. *PhS*, § 165; *PhG*, 102.
162. *PhS*, § 164; *PhG*, 102.
163. *PhS*, § 165; *PhG*, 102.

Chapter 5

1. See Pöggeler for an account of the importance of this chapter. Otto Pöggeler, "Hegels Phänomenologie des Selbstbewußtseins," in his *Hegels Idee einer Phänomenologie des Geistes* (Freiburg: Karl Alber, 1973), 231–98.
2. Alexandre Kojève, *Introduction à la lecture de Hegel* (Paris: Gallimard, 1947). Translated as *An Introduction to the Reading of Hegel*, ed. Alan Bloom, trans. J. H. Nichols (Ithaca: Cornell University Press, 1969).

3. *PhS*, § 177; *PhG*, 108–9.

4. Robert Pippin, *Hegel's Idealism: The Satisfactions of Self-Consciousness* (Cambridge: Cambridge University Press, 1989), 138.

5. Cf. *PhS*, § 167; *PhG*, 104: "Thus it seems that only the principal moment itself has been lost, viz. the *simple self-subsistent existence* for consciousness" (cited below).

6. E.g., Ivan Soll, *An Introduction to Hegel's Metaphysics* (Chicago: University of Chicago Press, 1969), 10.

7. E.g., Jean Hyppolite, *The Genesis and Structure of Hegel's "Phenomenology of Spirit,"* trans. S. Chernick and J. Heckman (Evanston: Northwestern University Press, 1974), 146ff.

8. *Propaedeutic*, § 24; *Werke*, vol. 4, 117.

9. *PhS*, § 208; *PhG*, 122. Hegel uses the same language to refer to God in the *Philosophy of Right*. See *PR*, § 270, Remark; *RP*, 350: "It is for this reason that in religion there lies the place where man is always assured of finding a consciousness of the unchangeable, of the highest freedom and satisfaction, even within all the mutability of the world and despite the frustrations of his aims and the loss of his interests and possessions."

10. Eliot Jurist, "Hegel's Concept of Recognition," *Owl of Minerva* 19 (1987), 8.

11. *PhS*, § 166; *PhG*, 103.

12. *Phil. of Spirit, 1805–6*, 95; *JSE* III, 196. See also *Phil. of Spirit, 1805–6*, 97; *JSE* III, 199: "The understanding is reason, and its object is the I itself." See also *Phil. of Spirit, 1805–6*, 98; *JSE* III, 200–201: "In this light, intelligence has no other object for its content, but having grasped *itself* in its own object."

13. *PhS*, § 167; *PhG*, 103.

14. *PR* § 6, Remark; *RP*, 57.

15. *PhS*, § 166; *PhG*, 103.

16. *PhS*, § 166; *PhG*, 103.

17. *PhS*, § 167; *PhG*, 104.

18. *PhS*, § 167; *PhG*, 103.

19. *PhS*, § 167; *PhG*, 104; also cf. *Phil. of Spirit, 1805–6*, 93; *JSE* III, 194.

20. Cf. Marcuse's insightful analysis of this concept. Herbert Marcuse, "Leben als Seinsbegriff in der *Phänomenologie*," in his *Hegels Ontologie und die Theorie der Geschichtlichkeit* (Frankfurt: Klostermann, 1968), 257ff. Cf. Werner Marx's "Das Selbstbewußtsein als 'Leben,' " in his *Das Selbstbewußtsein in Hegels Phänomenologie des Geistes* (Frankfurt: Klostermann, 1986), 35–53.

21. *PhS*, § 166; *PhG*, 103.

22. *EL*, § 24, Remark; *Werke*, vol. 8, 83.

23. *PhS*, § 166; *PhG*, 103.

24. *PhS*, § 167; *PhG*, 103–4.

25. *PhS*, § 167; *PhG*, 104.

26. *PhS*, § 167; *PhG*, 104.

27. *PR*, § 25; *RP*, 75–76.

28. Cf. Fichte, *The Science of Knowledge*, ed., trans., Peter Heath and John

Lachs (Cambridge: Cambridge University Press, 1982), 95–96: "Thus the self asserts, by means of X, that *A exists absolutely for the judging self, and that simply in virtue of its being posited in the self as such*; which is to say, it is asserted that within the self—whether it be specifically positing, or judging, or whatever it may be—there is something that is permanently uniform, forever one and the same; and hence the X that is absolutely posited can also be expressed as I = I; I am I."

29. *PhS*, § 172; *PhG*, 107.

30. *PhS*, § 169; *PhG*, 105.

31. *PhS*, § 167; *PhG*, 104. Cf. *Phil. of Spirit, 1805–6*, 10; *JSE* III, 203–4. Also cf. *Propaedeutic*, §§ 25–28; *Werke*, vol. 4, 117–19.

32. Cf. Frederick Neuhauser, "Deducing Desire and Recognition in the *Phenomenology of Spirit*," *Journal of the History of Philosophy* 24 (1986), 243–62; Leo Rauch, "Desire: An Elemental Passion in Hegel's *Phenomenology*," *Analecta Husserliana* 28 (1990), 195ff.

33. Peter Preuss, "Selfhood and the Battle: the Second Beginning of the *Phenomenology*," in *Method and Speculation in Hegel's Phenomenology*, ed. Merold Westphal (Atlantic Highlands: Humanities Press, 1982), 75.

34. *PhS*, § 168; *PhG*, 105

35. *PR*, § 11; *RP*, 63.

36. *PhS*, § 168; *PhG*, 105.

37. *Phil. of Spirit, 1805–6*, 97; *JSE* III, 199.

38. *PhS*, § 168; *PhG*, 105.

39. For a useful account of Hegel's uses of this term, see Joseph Flay, *Hegel's Quest for Certainty* (Albany: SUNY Press, 1984), 82–83. Cf. also Neuhauser, "Deducing Desire and Recognition in the *Phenomenology of Spirit*," 246ff.

40. *PhS*, § 168; *PhG*, 104.

41. *PR*, § 70; *RP*, 128.

42. I am not the first to interpret Hegel's notion of life as a logical category. Cf. Düsing, who supports this view. Klaus Düsing, *Das Problem der Subjektivität in Hegels Logik. Hegel-Studien*, Beiheft 15 (Bonn: Bouvier, 1976), 157.

43. *PhS*, § 186; *PhG*, 111.

44. *PhS*, § 171; *PhG*, 106.

45. *PhS*, § 169; *PhG*, 105.

46. *PhS*, § 171; *PhG*, 106.

47. *PhS*, § 171; *PhG*, 106.

48. *PhS*, § 109; *PhG*, 69.

49. *PhS*, § 169; *PhG*, 105.

50. *PhS*, § 171; *PhG*, 106.

51. *PhS*, § 172; *PhG*, 107.

52. *PhS*, § 172; *PhG*, 107.

53. *PhS*, § 173; *PhG*, 107.

54. *PhS*, § 176; *PhG*, 108.

55. *PhS*, § 176; *PhG*, 108.

56. *PR*, § 52, Remark; *RP*, 105.

57. *PhS*, § 171; *PhG*, 106.

58. *First Phil. of Spirit*, 214; *JSE* I, 275.

59. *Jena System, 1804–5*, 167; *JSE* II, 159. Also cf. *Jena System, 1804–5*, 170; *JSE* II, 163: "For this determinacy, here under consideration, is already in itself the negatively posited of the species itself, or of absolute essence as something existing." Also cf. *First Phil. of Spirit*, 212–13; *JSE* I, 273–74.

60. *PhS*, § 171; *PhG*, 106.

61. *Jena System, 1804–5*, 169; *JSE* II, 162.

62. *PhS*, § 174; *PhG*, 107.

63. *First Phil. of Spirit*, 212; *JSE*, I, 273.

64. *First Phil. of Spirit*, 212; *JSE* I, 274.

65. *PhS*, § 175; *PhG*, 107.

66. *PhS*, § 175; *PhG*, 107.

67. *Phil. of Spirit, 1805–6*, 96; *JSE* III, 197.

68. *Jena System, 1804–5*, 167; *JSE* II, 160.

69. *Phil. of Spirit, 1805–6*, 100; *JSE* III, 203.

70. *PhS*, § 176; *PhG*, 108.

71. *PhS*, § 175; *PhG*, 108.

72. *PR*, §§ 5ff.; *RP*, 54ff.

73. *PhS*, § 175; *PhG*, 108.

74. *PhS*, § 178; *PhG*, 109.

75. *PhS*, § 177; *PhG*, 108.

76. *PhS*, § 177; *PhG*, 108.

77. Cf. Shlomo Avineri, *Hegel's Theory of the Modern State* (Cambridge: Cambridge University Press, 1972), 22ff.

78. Cf. John Findlay, *Hegel: A Re-Examination* (London: Allen and Unwin, 1958), 93: "Hegel becomes much more lucid and illuminating when he has to deal with such concrete and congenial notions as mastership and slavery, Stoicism, Skepticism, and the 'unhappy' religious consciousness."

79. Robert C. Solomon, *In the Spirit of Hegel* (Oxford: Oxford University Press, 1983), 428. Cf. also Preuss, "Selfhood and the Battle," 76.

80. Charles Taylor, *Hegel* (Cambridge: Cambridge University Press, 1975); Kojève, *Introduction à la lecture de Hegel.*

81. Jurist, "Hegel's Concept of Recognition," 5–22; Ludwig Siep, *Anerkennung als Prinzip der praktischen Philosophie* (Freiburg: Alber, 1979); H. S. Harris, "The Concept of Recognition in Hegel's Jena Manuscripts," *Hegel in Jena*, ed. Dieter Henrich and Klaus Düsing (*Hegel-Studien*, Beiheft 20 [Bonn: Bouvier, 1980], 229–48); George Armstrong Kelly, "Notes on Hegel's Lordship and Bondage," *Review of Metaphysics* 19 (1965), 780–802; also in *Hegel: A Collection of Critical Essays*, ed. Alasdair MacIntyre (Notre Dame: University of Notre Dame Press, 1976).

82. *PhS*, § 178; *PhG*, 109.

83. *PhS*, § 178; *PhG*, 109.

84. *First Phil. of Spirit*, 214; *JSE* I, 275.

85. *PhS*, § 185; *PhG*, 110.

86. *First Phil. of Spirit*, 236; *JSE* I, 307.

87. *First Phil. of Spirit*, 237; *JSE* I, 308.

88. *PhS,* § 187; *PhG,* 111–12.
89. *PhS,* § 182; *PhG,* 110. Cf. also *PhS,* § 183; *PhG,* 110.
90. *PhS,* § 184; *PhG,* 110.
91. *PhS,* § 185; *PhG,* 110.
92. *PhS,* § 186; *PhG,* 110–11.
93. *PhS,* § 186; *PhG,* 111.
94. *First Phil. of Spirit,* 238; *JSE* I, 309.
95. *First Phil. of Spirit,* 214–15; *JSE* I, 276.
96. *PhS,* § 187; *PhG,* 111.
97. *First Phil. of Spirit,* 227–28; *JSE* I, 296.
98. *PhS,* § 187; *PhG,* 111.
99. *PhS,* § 187; *PhG,* 111. Cf. *PR,* § 57, Remark; *RP,* 112: "The dialectic of the concept and of the purely immediate consciousness of freedom brings about at that point the fight for recognition and the relationship of master and slave."
100. *PhS,* § 188; *PhG,* 112.
101. *PhS,* § 189; *PhG,* 112.
102. *First Phil. of Spirit,* 240; *JSE* I, 311.
103. *PhS,* § 189; *PhG,* 112.
104. *First Phil. of Spirit,* 241; *JSE* I, 313.
105. *PhS,* § 191; *PhG,* 113.
106. *PhS,* § 190; *PhG,* 112.
107. *PhS,* § 190; *PhG,* 113.
108. *PhS,* § 190; *PhG,* 113.
109. *PhS,* § 192; *PhG,* 114.
110. *First Phil. of Spirit,* 237; *JSE* I, 308.
111. *PhS,* § 191; *PhG,* 113.
112. *PhS,* § 193; *PhG,* 114.
113. *PhS,* § 194; *PhG,* 114.
114. *PhS,* § 195; *PhG,* 114. See Psalms 111:10: "The fear of the Lord is the beginning of wisdom; / a good understanding have all those who practice it. / His praise endures forever." *The Holy Bible,* Revised Standard Version translation.
115. *PhS,* § 195; *PhG,* 114.
116. *PhS,* § 195; *PhG,* 114–15.
117. *First Phil. of Spirit,* 230; *JSE* I, 300.
118. *PhS,* § 195; *PhG,* 115.
119. Cf. *First Phil. of Spirit,* 247; *JSE* I, 322.
120. *PhS,* § 195; *PhG,* 115.
121. *PhS,* § 196; *PhG,* 115.
122. *PhS,* § 196; *PhG,* 115.
123. Cf. the classic study by Jean Wahl, *Le Malheur de la conscience dans la philosophie de Hegel* (Paris: Presses Universitaires de France, 1951).
124. I have argued for this parallelism in "Die Rolle des unglücklichen Bewußtseins in Hegels *Phänomenologie des Geistes,*" *Deutsche Zeitschrift für Philosophie* 39 (1991), 12–21.
125. Solomon, *In the Spirit of Hegel,* 459.

126. *PhS*, § 198; *PhG*, 117.
127. *PhS*, § 197; *PhG*, 116.
128. *PhS*, § 197; *PhG*, 116.
129. *PhS*, § 197; *PhG*, 116.
130. *PhS*, § 197; *PhG*, 116.
131. *PhS*, § 197; *PhG*, 116.
132. *PhS*, § 197; *PhG*, 116.
133. *PhS*, § 197; *PhG*, 117.
134. *PhS*, § 199; *PhG*, 117.
135. I capitalize "Stoicism" and "Skepticism" here when referring to the moments of the Hegelian dialectic in contrast to the actual historical movements or the everyday usage, for both of which the lower case is used.
136. *PhS*, § 198; *PhG*, 117.
137. *PhS*, § 200; *PhG*, 118.
138. *PhS*, § 199; *PhG*, 117.
139. *PhS*, § 200; *PhG*, 118.
140. *PhS*, § 200; *PhG*, 118.
141. *PR*, § 48, Remark; *RP*, 102. Cf. *PR*, § 5; *RP*, 54, and the corresponding section in the student lecture notes edited by Henrich where the reference to stoicism is made explicit. Dieter Henrich, *Hegel: Philosophie des Rechts. Die Vorlesung von 1819/20 in einer Nachschrift* (Frankfurt: Suhrkamp, 1983), 59.
142. *PR*, § 48, Remark; *RP*, 102.
143. *PhS*, § 200; *PhG*, 118.
144. *PhS*, § 200; *PhG*, 118.
145. *PhS*, § 201; *PhG*, 118.
146. *PhS*, § 202; *PhG*, 119.
147. *PhS*, § 202; *PhG*, 119.
148. *PhS*, § 202; *PhG*, 119.
149. *PhS*, § 205; *PhG*, 120.
150. *PhS*, § 205; *PhG*, 120.
151. *PhS*, § 204; *PhG*, 120.
152. *PhS*, § 205; *PhG*, 120.
153. *PhS*, § 205; *PhG*, 121.
154. *PhS*, § 206; *PhG*, 121.
155. Hegel uses the same language to refer to God in the *Philosophy of Right*. See *PR*, § 270, Remark; *RP*, 350: "It is for this reason that in religion there lies the place where man is always assured of finding a consciousness of the unchangeable, of the highest freedom and satisfaction, even within all the mutability of the world and despite the frustrations of his aims and the loss of his interests and possessions."
156. *PhS*, § 208; *PhG*, 122.
157. *PhS*, § 216; *PhG*, 125.
158. *PhS*, § 216; *PhG*, 125.
159. *PhS*, § 146; *PhG*, 89.
160. *PhS*, § 217; *PhG*, 126.

161. *PhS*, § 214; *PhG*, 124.
162. Although he interprets it somewhat differently than I, Bonsiepen also points out this parallelism between the "Unhappy Consciousness" and "Force and the Understanding": "The opposition between the sensible and the supersensible world, between the here and the beyond in the 'Force and the Understanding' Chapter corresponds to the relation between the individual and the unchangeable." Wolfgang Bonsiepen, *Der Begriff der Negativität in den Jenaer Schriften Hegels. Hegel-Studien*, Beiheft 16 (Bonn: Bouvier, 1977), 160.
163. *PhS*, § 217; *PhG*, 125.
164. *PhS*, § 217; *PhG*, 125.
165. *PhS*, § 217; *PhG*, 126.
166. *PhS*, § 217; *PhG*, 126: "Where that 'other' is sought, it cannot be found, for it is supposed to be just a *beyond*, something that can *not* be found" (cited above).
167. *PhS*, § 218; *PhG*, 126.
168. *PhS*, § 221; *PhG*, 128.
169. *PhS*, § 222; *PhG*, 128.
170. *PhS*, § 222; *PhG*, 128.
171. *PhS*, § 222; *PhG*, 128.
172. *PhS*, § 227; *PhG*, 129–30.
173. *PhS*, § 228; *PhG*, 130.
174. *PhS*, § 228; *PhG*, 130.
175. *PhS*, § 231; *PhG*, 132.
176. *PhS*, § 230; *PhG*, 131.
177. *PhS*, § 230; *PhG*, 131.
178. *PhS*, § 230; *PhG*, 131.
179. *PhS*, § 230; *PhG*, 131.

Chapter 6

1. Particularly problematic are the cursory treatments of the "Reason" chapter in John Findlay, *Hegel: A Re-Examination* (London: Allen and Unwin, 1958), 101–13; Pierre-Jean Labarrière, *Structures et mouvement dialectique dans la "Phénoménologie de l'esprit" de Hegel* (Paris: Aubier 1968), 95–108; and Charles Taylor, *Hegel* (Cambridge: Cambridge University Press, 1975), 161–70.
2. See, for instance, Robert C. Solomon, *In the Spirit of Hegel* (Oxford: Oxford University Press, 1983), 213–14; Quentin Lauer, *A Reading of Hegel's "Phenomenology of Spirit"* (New York: Fordham University Press, 1982), 125ff; Labarrière, *Structures et mouvement dialectique*, 26.
3. Walter Kaufmann, "Hegel's Conception of Phenomenology," in *Phenomenology and Philosophical Understanding*, ed. Edo Pivcevic (Cambridge: Cambridge University Press, 1975), 219.
4. Hyppolite reads this transition, in my view in error, as a truly historical one: "More than either the *Propaedeutic* or the phenomenological section of the *Encyclopaedia*, the 1807 *Phenomenology* is really a concrete history of human

consciousness. . . . Hegel envisages the transition from unhappy consciousness to Reason as the transition from the medieval church to the Renaissance and modern times." Jean Hyppolite, *Genesis and Structure of Hegel's "Phenomenology of Spirit,"* trans. Samuel Cherniak and John Heckman (Evanston: Northwestern University Press, 1974), 222–23. If we interpret his transition as the actual historical moment of transition from the Middle Ages to the Renaissance and modern world, then we have no way to explain what Hegel is doing in the "Spirit" chapter when he reverts to analyses of the Greek and Roman worlds, which on Hyppolite's reading ought to come before this transition from "Self-Consciousness" to "Reason."

5. *PhS,* § 231; *PhG,* 132.

6. Cf. *PR,* § 41; *RP,* 94–95.

7. *PhS,* § 231; *PhG,* 132.

8. *PhS,* § 232; *PhG,* 132.

9. Cf. Findlay, *Hegel;* 101–2; Lauer, *A Reading of Hegel's "Phenomenology of Spirit,"* 127–31; Hyppolite, *Genesis and Structure,* 225ff; Eugen Fink, *Hegel: Phänomenologische Interpretationen der "Phänomenologie des Geistes"* (Frankfurt: Klostermann, 1977), 214ff.

10. Cf. *PhS,* § 233; *PhG,* 133: "I am I."

11. See Joseph C. Flay, "The History of Philosophy and the *Phenomenology of Spirit,"* in *Hegel and the History of Philosophy: Proceedings of the 1972 Hegel Society of America Conference,* ed. Joseph O'Malley, Keith W. Algozin, Frederic G. Weiss (The Hague: Nijhoff, 1974), 52ff.

12. *PhS,* § 233; *PhG,* 133.

13. *PhS,* § 234; *PhG,* 134.

14. *PhS,* § 238; *PhG,* 136.

15. Cf. Findlay, *Hegel;* 102: "In the treatment of observation which follows Hegel retraces at a higher level some of the ground covered in his previous study of sense-certainty, perception and scientific understanding." See also Taylor, *Hegel,* 162.

16. *PhS,* § 344; *PhG,* 191.

17. As Lamb's discussion points out: David Lamb, "Observation of Organic Nature (A)," in his *Hegel—From Foundation to System* (The Hague: Nijhoff, 1980), 111.

18. Solomon, *In the Spirit of Hegel,* 401.

19. *PhS,* § 240; *PhG,* 137; See also *PhS,* § 344; *PhG,* 191: "The category which is the *immediate* unity of *being* and *self* [*Einheit des Seins und des Seinen*] must pass through both forms."

20. *PhS,* § 240; *PhG,* 137.

21. *PhS,* § 243; *PhG,* 138.

22. *PhS,* § 240; *PhG,* 137.

23. *PhS,* § 235; *PhG,* 134.

24. *PhS,* § 234; *PhG,* 134.

25. *PhS,* § 243; *PhG,* 138.

26. *PhS,* § 243; *PhG,* 138.

27. Cf. Lamb, who notes this parallelism in "Observation of Organic Nature (A)," 126.

28. *PhS*, § 242; *PhG*, 138.

29. *PhS*, § 242; *PhG*, 138.

30. *PhS*, § 242; *PhG*, 138.

31. *PhS*, § 347; *PhG*, 193.

32. Friedrich Schelling, *System of Transcendental Idealism*, trans. Peter Heath, with an Introduction by Michael Vater (Charlottesville: University Press of Virginia, 1978), 6.

33. *PhS*, § 245; *PhG*, 139.

34. *PhS*, § 246; *PhG*, 140.

35. Cf. *PhS*, § 245; *PhG*, 139.

36. *PhS*, § 246; *PhG*, 140.

37. *PhS*, § 246; *PhG*, 140.

38. *PhS*, § 247; *PhG*, 141.

39. *PhS*, § 247; *PhG*, 141.

40. *PhS*, § 248; *PhG*, 142.

41. *PhS*, § 249; *PhG*, 142.

42. *PhS*, § 250; *PhG*, 143.

43. See David Hume, "Of the Idea of Necessary Connection" and "Of Liberty and Necessity," in his *Enquiry concerning Human Understanding*; and Book I, Part 3, "Of Knowledge and Probability," and Book II, Part 3, "Of Liberty and Necessity," in his *Treatise on Human Nature*.

44. *PhS*, § 250; *PhG*, 143.

45. *PhS*, § 250; *PhG*, 143.

46. *PhS*, § 251; *PhG*, 143.

47. *PhS*, § 251; *PhG*, 144.

48. *PhS*, § 251; *PhG*, 144.

49. *PhS*, § 251; *PhG*, 144.

50. *PhS*, § 252; *PhG*, 144.

51. *PhS*, § 253; *PhG*, 144.

52. *PhS*, § 254; *PhG*, 145.

53. *PhS*, § 253; *PhG*, 144–45.

54. *PhS*, § 254; *PhG*, 145.

55. *PhS*, § 255; *PhG*, 145.

56. *PhS*, § 255; *PhG*, 146.

57. Cf. Lamb, "Observation of Organic Nature (A)," 130.

58. See *PhS*, § 256; *PhG*, 146.

59. For *Selbstzweck*, see *Phil. of Nature*, § 360; *Enz.*, 273.

60. Cf. Karl Christian Eberhard Schmid's *Versuch einer Moralphilosophie* (1790), and Baumgarten's *Metaphysica* (1739).

61. *PhS*, § 258; *PhG*, 147.

62. *PhS*, § 259; *PhG*, 148.

63. *PhS*, § 261; *PhG*, 149.

64. *PhS*, § 262; *PhG*, 149.

65. Cf. Lamb, "Observation of Organic Nature (B)," 137ff.

66. Ibid., 142.

67. *PhS*, § 264; *PhG*, 150.

68. Cf. *Hist. of Phil.* III, 514; *VPG* III, 648–49.

69. Most of the commentaries on the *Phenomenology*, including Hyppolite (*Genesis and Structure*, 249–50), seem entirely to miss this reference. Cf. *Phil. of Nature*, § 353; *Enz.*, 267–68. *PR*, § 271, Addition; *RP*, 366–67. *PR*, § 263, Addition; *RP*, 342–43.

70. Cf. Erich Mende, "Die Entwicklungsgeschichte der Faktoren Irritabilität und Sensibilität in deren Einfluß auf Schellings 'Prinzip' als Ursache des Lebens," *Philosophia Naturalis* 17 (1978), 327–48.

71. Jochen Kirchhoff, *Friedrich Wilhelm Joseph von Schelling* (Reinbek bei Hamburg: Rowohlt, 1982), 27.

72. *PhS*, § 267; *PhG*, 151.

73. *PhS*, § 268; *PhG*, 151.

74. *PhS*, § 268; *PhG*, 151.

75. *PhS*, § 269; *PhG*, 151.

76. *PhS*, § 270; *PhG*, 151.

77. *PhS*, § 270; *PhG*, 151.

78. *PhS*, § 271; *PhG*, 152–53.

79. *PhS*, § 271; *PhG*, 153.

80. *PhS*, § 273; *PhG*, 154.

81. *PhS*, § 275; *PhG*, 154.

82. *PhS*, § 276; *PhG*, 155.

83. *PhS*, § 276; *PhG*, 155.

84. *PhS*, § 278; *PhG*, 156.

85. Hegel discusses these differences beginning at *PhS*, § 279; *PhG*, 156.

86. *PhS*, § 279; *PhG*, 156.

87. *PhS*, § 280; *PhG*, 157.

88. *PhS*, § 282; *PhG*, 157.

89. *PhS*, § 282; *PhG*, 158. For an analysis of this passage, see Wolfgang Bonsiepen, "Zu Hegels Auseinandersetzung mit Schellings Naturphilosophie in der *Phänomenologie des Geistes*," in *Schelling: Seine Bedeutung für eine Philosophie der Natur und der Geschichte*, ed. Ludwig Hasler (Stuttgart: Frommann-Holzboog, 1981), 167–72.

90. *PhS*, § 283; *PhG*, 158–59.

91. *PhS*, § 284; *PhG*, 159.

92. *PhS*, § 285; *PhG*, 159.

93. *PhS*, § 285; *PhG*, 159.

94. *PhS*, § 285; *PhG*, 160.

95. *PhS*, § 287; *PhG*, 160.

96. Cf. *PhS*, § 291; *PhG*, 163.

97. *PhS*, § 287; *PhG*, 160.

98. Cf. *PhS*, § 291; *PhG*, 163.

99. *PhS*, § 287; *PhG*, 160.

100. *PhS*, § 288; *PhG*, 160. Cf. *Phil. of Nature*, § 293; *Enz.*, 226.

101. *PhS*, § 288; *PhG*, 160.

102. *PhS*, § 290; *PhG*, 162.

103. Cf. *Phil. of Nature*, § 293; *Enz.*, 227ff.

104. *PhS*, § 289; *PhG*, 161.

105. *PhS*, § 289; *PhG*, 161.

106. *PhS*, § 290; *PhG*, 162.

107. Cf. *Phil. of Nature*, §§ 370ff.; *Enz.*, 278ff.

108. *PhS*, § 293; *PhG*, 164.

109. *PhS*, § 292; *PhG*, 164.

110. *PhS*, § 292; *PhG*, 164.

111. See *JSE* I, 31ff.

112. *PhS*, § 294; *PhG*, 165.

113. *PhS*, § 295; *PhG*, 165.

114. See Hans Querner, "Die Stufenfolge der Organismen in Hegels Philosophie der Natur," *Stuttgarter Hegel-Tage 1970*, ed. Hans-Georg Gadamer. *Hegel-Studien*, Beiheft 11 (Bonn: Bouvier, 1983), 162–63.

115. Cf. Lamb, "Observation of Organic Nature (B)," 159.

116. *PhS*, § 295; *PhG*, 165–66.

117. *PhS*, § 297; *PhG*, 166.

118. *PhS*, § 297; *PhG*, 166.

119. *PhS*, § 295; *PhG*, 166.

120. See Ulrich Sonnemann, "Hegel und Freud: Die Kritik der *Phänomenologie* am Begriff der psychologischen Notwendigkeit und ihre anthropologischen Konsequenzen," *Psyche* 24 (1970), 208–18.

121. *PhS*, §§ 240–43; *PhG*, 137–38.

122. *PhS*, § 298; *PhG*, 167.

123. *PhS*, § 298; *PhG*, 167.

124. *PhS*, § 298; *PhG*, 167.

125. *PhS*, § 243; *PhG*, 138.

126. *PhS*, § 299; *PhG*, 167.

127. *PhS*, § 75; *PhG*, 54.

128. *PhS*, § 300; *PhG*, 168.

129. *PhS*, § 300; *PhG*, 168.

130. *PhS*, § 300; *PhG*, 168.

131. *PhS*, § 300; *PhG*, 168.

132. *PhS*, § 303; *PhG*, 169.

133. *PhS*, § 301; *PhG*, 168.

134. *PhS*, § 301; *PhG*, 168.

135. *PhS*, § 301; *PhG*, 168.

136. *PhS*, § 302; *PhG*, 169

137. *PhS*, § 305; *PhG*, 169–70.

138. *PhS*, § 307; *PhG*, 170–71.

139. *PhS*, § 306; *PhG*, 170.

140. *PhS*, § 307; *PhG*, 171.

141. Alasdair MacIntyre, "Hegel on Faces and Skulls," in *Hegel: A Collection of Critical Essays,* ed. Alasdair MacIntyre (Notre Dame: University of Notre Dame Press, 1976), 219–36.

142. *PhS,* § 309; *PhG,* 171.

143. *PhS,* § 310; *PhG,* 171–72.

144. *PhS,* § 311; *PhG,* 172.

145. *PhS,* § 136; *PhG,* 84.

146. *PhS,* § 243; *PhG,* 138.

147. Cf. *PhS,* § 328; *PhG,* 182: "What has been determined here in the first instance is only that just as the brain is the living head, the skull is the *caput mortuum* [sc. the dead head]."

148. *PhS,* § 311; *PhG,* 172.

149. *PhS,* § 312; *PhG,* 173.

150. *PhS,* § 312; *PhG,* 173.

151. *PhS,* § 312; *PhG,* 173.

152. *PhS,* § 314; *PhG,* 174. Cf. *PhS,* § 315; *PhG,* 174.

153. *PhS,* § 317; *PhG,* 175.

154. *PhS,* § 319; *PhG,* 177.

155. *PhS,* § 319; *PhG,* 177.

156. *PhS,* § 318; *PhG,* 176.

157. *PhS,* § 318; *PhG,* 176.

158. *PhS,* § 318; *PhG,* 176.

159. *PhS,* § 318; *PhG,* 176.

160. *PhS,* § 321; *PhG,* 178.

161. *PhS,* § 321; *PhG,* 178.

162. *PhS,* § 322; *PhG,* 178.

163. *PhS,* § 322; *PhG,* 179.

164. *PhS,* § 323; *PhG,* 179–80.

165. *PhS,* § 323; *PhG,* 179.

166. *PhS,* § 323; *PhG,* 179–80.

167. *PhS,* § 324; *PhG,* 180.

168. *PhS,* § 325; *PhG,* 180.

169. *PhS,* § 329; *PhG,* 182.

170. *PhS,* § 329; *PhG,* 182–83.

171. Cf. *Aesthetics* II, 716; *Aesthetik* II, 375.

172. *PhS,* § 331; *PhG,* 184.

173. *PhS,* § 334; *PhG,* 184–85.

174. *PhS,* § 335; *PhG,* 185–86.

175. *PhS,* § 336; *PhG,* 186.

176. *PhS,* § 337; *PhG,* 187.

177. *PhS,* § 339; *PhG,* 188.

178. *PhS,* § 343; *PhG,* 190.

179. I.e., first result, § 344; *PhG,* 190–91; second result, § 345; *PhG,* 191.

180. *PhS,* § 344; *PhG,* 190–91.

181. *PhS,* § 344; *PhG,* 191.

182. See *Phil. of Nature*, § 365, Addition, 404; *Werke*, vol. 9, 492.

183. *PhS*, § 346; *PhG*, 192.

184. Cf. Otto Pöggeler, *Hegel und die Romantik* (Bonn: Rheinische Friedrich Wilhelms-Universität, 1956).

185. *PhS*, § 347; *PhG*, 193.

186. *PhS*, § 347; *PhG*, 193.

187. *PhS*, § 347; *PhG*, 193.

188. *PhS*, § 347; *PhG*, 193.

189. Esp. *PhS*, § 348; *PhG*, 193.

190. *PhS*, § 348; *PhG*, 193.

191. *PhS*, § 348; *PhG*, 193.

192. *PhS*, § 349; *PhG*, 194.

193. Hegel does of course use the term "Spirit" earlier; however, here we find it for the first time in its systematic context with its definition and corresponding discussion. For accounts of this term, see Allen Wood, *Hegel's Ethical Thought* (Cambridge: Cambridge University Press, 1990), 195; Theodor Litt, "Hegels Begriff des 'Geistes' und das Problem der Tradition," *Studium Generale* 4 (1951), 311–21; Robert Solomon, "Hegel's Concept of *Geist*," in *Hegel: A Collection of Critical Essays*, ed. Alasdair MacIntyre, 151–88; Wilhelm Seeberger, *Der Begriff des Geistes im System Hegels* (Stuttgart: Ernst Klett, 1961).

194. *PhS*, § 347; *PhG*, 193.

195. *PhS*, § 349; *PhG*, 194.

196. *PR*, § 264; *RP*, 343.

197. *PhS*, § 349; *PhG*, 194.

198. See Ludwig Siep, *Anerkennung als Prinzip der praktischen Philosophie: Untersuchung zu Hegels Jenaer Philosophie des Geistes* (Freiburg: Verlag Karl Alber, 1979).

199. By an apparently unspoken agreement, most scholars, following the standard translations of Knox and Miller, use the expression "ethical life" for *Sittlichkeit.*

200. *PR*, § 151; *RP*, 233.

201. See Alfred Elsigan, "Zum Begriff der Moralität in Hegels Rechtsphilosophie," *Weiner Jahrbuch für Philosophie* 5 (1972), 188.

202. *PR*, § 33, Remark; *RP*, 85.

203. *PhS*, § 349; *PhG*, 194.

204. *PhS*, § 350; *PhG*, 194.

205. *PhS*, § 351; *PhG*, 195.

206. *PhS* § 350; *PhG*, 194.

207. *PhS*, §§ 350–55; *PhG*, 194–96.

208. *PhS*, § 356; *PhG*, 196.

209. *PhS*, § 357; *PhG*, 197.

210. *PhS*, § 357; *PhG*, 197.

211. *PhS*, § 360; *PhG*, 198.

212. *PhS* §§ 356–58; *PhG*, 196–97.

213. *PhS*, § 356; *PhG*, 196.

214. *PhS*, § 357; *PhG*, 197.

215. *PhS*, § 358; *PhG*, 197.

216. *PhS*, § 359; *PhG*, 197–98. This passage corresponds to *PhS*, § 243; *PhG*, 138 in "Observing Reason."

217. *PhS*, § 359; *PhG*, 197.

218. *PhS*, § 359; *PhG*, 198.

219. *PhS*, § 359; *PhG*, 198.

220. *PhS*, § 359; *PhG*, 198.

221. *PhS*, § 359; *PhG*, 198.

222. *PhS*, § 363; *PhG*, 200.

223. *PhS*, § 362; *PhG*, 199.

224. *PhS*, § 361; *PhG*, 199.

225. Cf. Joseph Gauvin, "Plaisir et nécessité," *Archives de Philosophie* 28 (1965), 483–509. Also in *Beiträge zur Deutung der "Phänomenologie des Geistes,"* ed. Hans-Georg Gadamer, *Hegel-Studien*, Beiheft 3 (Bonn: Bouvier, 1966), 158ff; Klaus Kähler and Werner Marx, *Die Vernunft in Hegels "Phänomenologie des Geistes"* (Frankfurt: Klostermann, 1992), 162; Josiah Royce, *Lectures on Modern Idealism* (New Haven: Yale University Press, 1919; reprint 1964), 190ff; Kuno Fischer, *Hegels Leben, Werke und Lehre* (Heidelberg: Winters, 1901), 355ff; Hyppolite, *Genesis and Structure*, 281.

226. *PhS*, § 360; *PhG*, 199. Hegel cites this same passage in the Preface to the *Philosophy of Right*, 6; *RP*, 28.

227. *PhS*, § 808; *PhG*, 434.

228. Kaufmann, *Hegel*, 123.

229. *PhS*, § 360; *PhG*, 198.

230. *PhS*, § 363; *PhG*, 200.

231. *PhS*, § 360; *PhG*, 198.

232. *PhS*, § 360; *PhG*, 198.

233. *PhS*, § 360; *PhG*, 198.

234. Solomon, *In the Spirit of Hegel*, 498ff; Ferruccio Andolfi, "Die Gestalten des Individualismus in der *Phänomenologie des Geistes*," *Hegel-Jahrbuch* (1991), 214ff.

235. *PhS*, § 362; *PhG*, 199.

236. *PhS*, § 362; *PhG*, 199.

237. *PhS*, § 362; *PhG*, 199.

238. I.e., in *PhS*, § 363; *PhG*, 199.

239. *PhS*, § 363; *PhG*, 199–200.

240. *PhS*, § 363; *PhG*, 200.

241. Cf. *PR*, § 190, § 194; *RP*, 272–73, 274–75.

242. *PhS*, § 366; *PhG*, 201.

243. *PhS*, § 364; *PhG*, 200–1.

244. *PhS*, § 365; *PhG*, 201.

245. Cf. Knox's n. 21 in *PR*, 339.

246. *PR*, § 126, Remark; *RP*, 184.

247. *PR*, § 126, Remark; *RP*, 185.

248. *PhS*, § 367; *PhG*, 202.

249. *PhS*, § 367; *PhG*, 202.
250. *PhS*, § 367; *PhG*, 202.
251. *PhS*, § 370; *PhG*, 203.
252. *PhS*, § 368; *PhG*, 202.
253. *PhS*, § 368; *PhG*, 202.
254. *PhS*, § 369; *PhG*, 202.
255. *PhS*, § 369; *PhG*, 202.
256. *PhS*, § 369; *PhG*, 202.
257. *PhS*, § 370; *PhG*, 202.
258. *PhS*, § 370; *PhG*, 202–3.
259. *PhS*, § 371; *PhG*, 203.
260. *PhS*, § 372; *PhG*, 203.
261. *PhS*, § 372; *PhG*, 203.
262. *PhS*, § 372; *PhG*, 204.
263. *PhS*, § 373; *PhG*, 204.
264. *PhS*, § 373; *PhG*, 204.
265. *PhS*, § 375; *PhG*, 205.
266. *PhS*, § 376; *PhG*, 205.
267. *PhS*, § 377; *PhG*, 206.
268. *PhS*, § 377; *PhG*, 206.
269. *PhS*, § 376; *PhG*, 206.
270. *PhS*, § 374; *PhG*, 204–5.
271. *PR*, § 140, Remark; *RP*, 215.
272. *PhS*, § 376; *PhG*, 206.
273. *PhS*, § 378; *PhG*, 206–7.
274. *PhS*, § 379; *PhG*, 207.
275. Cf. *PhS*, § 382; *PhG*, 208: "The general *content* of the actual 'way of the world' we already know; looked at more closely, it is again nothing else but the two preceding movements of self-consciousness."
276. *PhS*, § 374; *PhG*, 204. *PhS*, § 367; *PhG*, 202.
277. *PhS*, § 389; *PhG*, 212.
278. *PhS*, § 381; *PhG*, 208.
279. *PhS*, § 384; *PhG*, 209.
280. *PhS*, § 381; *PhG*, 208.
281. *PhS*, § 381; *PhG*, 208.
282. *PhS*, § 382; *PhG*, 208.
283. *PhS*, § 382; *PhG*, 209.
284. *PhS*, § 381; *PhG*, 208.
285. *PhS*, § 383; *PhG*, 209.
286. *PhS*, § 381; *PhG*, 208.
287. *PhS*, § 390; *PhG*, 212.
288. Cf. *PhS*, § 200; *PhG*, 118.
289. *PhS*, § 384; *PhG*, 209–10.
290. *PhS*, § 385; *PhG*, 210.
291. *PhS*, § 389; *PhG*, 212.

292. *PhS*, § 386; *PhG*, 211.
293. *PhS*, § 389; *PhG*, 212.
294. *PhS*, § 390; *PhG*, 212.
295. *PhS*, § 390; *PhG*, 212.
296. *PhS*, § 390; *PhG*, 212–13.
297. *PhS*, § 391; *PhG*, 213.
298. *PhS*, § 392; *PhG*, 213.
299. *PR*, § 199; *RP*, 278.
300. *PR*, § 199; *RP*, 278.
301. Cf. The classic example of this is of course Popper's account in *The Open Society and Its Enemies* (London: Routledge and Kegan Paul, 1952). Cf. Grégoire's discussion. Franz Grégoire, "L'État hégélien est-t-il totalitaire?" *Revue Philosophique de Louvain* 60 (1962), 244–53.
302. *PhS*, § 394; *PhG*, 214.
303. *PhS*, § 394; *PhG*, 214.
304. *PhS*, § 396; *PhG*, 215.
305. *PhS*, § 395; *PhG*, 215.
306. Cf. *PhS*, § 410; *PhG*, 223.
307. For an interesting interpretation of this section specifically, see Gary Shapiro, "Notes on the Animal Kingdom of the Spirit," *Clio* 8 (1979), 323–38.
308. *PhS*, § 410; *PhG*, 223.
309. *PhS*, § 411; *PhG*, 224.
310. *PhS*, § 419; *PhG*, 228.
311. *PhS*, § 405; *PhG*, 220.
312. *PhS*, §§ 397–99; *PhG*, 216–17.
313. *PhS*, § 397; *PhG*, 216
314. *PhS*, §§ 400–402; *PhG*, 217–19.
315. *PhS*, § 398; *PhG*, 216.
316. *PhS*, § 398; *PhG*, 216.
317. *PhS*, § 401; *PhG*, 218.
318. This analysis can be seen as an important source for Hegel's theory of action, although it is overlooked in the standard treatments of this issue: Josef Derbolav, "Hegels Theorie der Handlung," in *Materialien zu Hegels Rechtsphilosophie*, vol. 2, ed. Manfred Riedel (Frankfurt: Suhrkamp, 1975), 201–16; Miguel Giusti, "Bemerkungen zu Hegels Begriff der Handlung," *Hegel-Studien* 22 (1987), 51–71; Charles Taylor, "Hegel and the Philosophy of Action," in *Hegel's Philosophy of Action*, ed. Lawrence S. Stepelevich and David Lamb (Atlantic Highlands: Humanities Press, 1983), 1–18; G. Planty-Bonjour, "Hegel's Concept of Action as Unity of Poiesis and Praxis," in *Hegel's Philosophy of Action*, 19–29.
319. *PhS*, § 400; *PhG*, 217.
320. *PhS*, § 400; *PhG*, 217.
321. *PhS*, § 401; *PhG*, 218.
322. *PhS*, § 400; *PhG*, 217.
323. *PhS*, § 402; *PhG*, 219.
324. *PhS*, § 403; *PhG*, 220.

325. *PhS*, § 404; *PhG*, 220.
326. *PhS*, § 405; *PhG*, 220.
327. *PhS*, § 405; *PhG*, 220.
328. *PhS*, § 405; *PhG*, 220.
329. *PhS*, § 406; *PhG*, 221.
330. *PhS*, § 407; *PhG*, 222.
331. *PhS*, § 407; *PhG*, 222.
332. *PhS*, § 407; *PhG*, 222.
333. *PhS*, § 409; *PhG*, 223.
334. *PhS*, § 411; *PhG*, 224.
335. *PhS*, § 413; *PhG*, 224–25.
336. *PhS*, § 414; *PhG*, 225.
337. *PhS*, § 417; *PhG*, 226.
338. *PhS*, § 417; *PhG*, 226.
339. *PhS*, § 415; *PhG*, 225.
340. *PhS*, § 418; *PhG*, 227.
341. *PhS*, § 418; *PhG*, 227.
342. *PhS*, § 418; *PhG*, 227.
343. *PhS*, § 418; *PhG*, 227.
344. *PhS*, § 418; *PhG*, 228.
345. *PhS*, § 418; *PhG*, 227.
346. *PhS*, § 405; *PhG*, 220.
347. Shapiro makes this same connection with "Sense-Certainty": "Just as the sheer *meinen* of sense-certainty . . . collapses into the most abstract and universal language, so *my* work, the more rigidly I insist that it is mine, turns out to be one more minor variation on the texts, commentaries, thematics, and traditions of one school of thought or another." Shapiro,"Notes on the Animal Kingdom of the Spirit," 324.
348. *PhS*, § 419; *PhG*, 228.
349. *PhS*, § 419; *PhG*, 228.
350. *PhS*, § 420; *PhG*, 228.
351. *PhS*, § 420; *PhG*, 228.
352. *PhS*, § 419; *PhG*, 228.
353. *PhS*, § 420; *PhG*, 228.
354. *PhS*, § 420; *PhG*, 229.
355. *PhS*, § 420; *PhG*, 229.
356. John Findlay, "Analysis of the Text," in *Hegel's Phenomenology of Spirit*, trans. A. V. Miller (Oxford: Oxford University Press, 1977), 548.
357. *PhS*, § 420; *PhG*, 229.
358. *PhS*, § 421; *PhG*, 229.
359. *PhS*, § 422; *PhG*, 229.
360. *PhS*, § 423; *PhG*, 229.
361. *PhS*, § 424; *PhG*, 229–30.
362. *PhS*, § 425; *PhG*, 230–31.
363. *PhS*, § 424; *PhG*, 230.

364. *PhS*, § 424; *PhG*, 230.
365. *PhS*, § 425; *PhG*, 231.
366. *PhS*, § 425; *PhG*, 231.
367. *PhS*, § 420; *PhG*, 228.
368. *PhS*, § 427; *PhG*, 231.
369. *PhS*, § 428; *PhG*, 232.
370. *PR*, § 135; *RP*, 194.
371. *PR*, § 135, Remark; *RP*, 194.
372. *PhS*, § 430; *PhG*, 233.
373. *PhS*, § 429; *PhG*, 232–33.
374. *PhS*, § 430; *PhG*, 233.
375. *PhS*, § 430; *PhG*, 233.
376. *PR*, § 135, Remark; *RP*, 194.
377. *PR*, § 135, Remark; *RP*, 194.
378. *PhS*, § 430; *PhG*, 233.
379. *PhS*, § 431; *PhG*, 233.
380. *PhS*, § 431; *PhG*, 234.
381. *PhS*, § 431; *PhG*, 234.
382. *PhS*, § 432; *PhG*, 234.
383. *PhS*, § 435; *PhG*, 235.
384. *PhS*, § 436; *PhG*, 235.
385. *PhS*, § 436; *PhG*, 235.

Chapter 7

1. See Theodore Haering, "Entstehungsgeschichte der *Phänomenologie des Geistes*," in *Verhandlungen des III. Internationalen Hegel Kongresses 1933*, ed. B. Wigersma (Haarlem: N/VH.D. Tjeenk Willink and Zn.; and Tübingen: J. C. B. Mohr, 1934), 118–36; Theodore Haering, *Hegel sein Wollen und sein Werk II* (Leipzig: Teubner, 1929), 479ff; Otto Pöggeler, "Die Komposition der *Phänomenologie des Geistes*," in *Hegel-Tage Royaumont 1964: Beiträge zur "Phänomenologie des Geistes,"* ed. Hans-Georg Gadamer—*Hegel-Studien*, Beiheft 3 (Bonn: Bouvier, 1966), 27–74 (reprinted in *Materialien zu Hegels "Phänomenologie des Geistes,"* ed. Hans Friedrich Fulda and Dieter Henrich [Frankfurt: Suhrkamp, 1973], 329–90).
2. *PhS*, § 438; *PhG*, 238.
3. *PhS*, § 438; *PhG*, 238.
4. *PhS*, § 438; *PhG*, 238.
5. *PhS*, § 438; *PhG*, 238.
6. *PhS*, § 440; *PhG*, 239.
7. Cf. Jean Hyppolite, *Genesis and Structure of Hegel's "Phenomenology of Spirit,"* trans. S. Cherniak and J. Heckman (Evanston: Northwestern University Press, 1974), 64.
8. Cf. *Hist. of Phil.* III, 547; *VGP* III, 686: "These notions are the simplest revelation of the World Spirit: in their more concrete form they are history." Cf.

Labarrière's account. Pierre-Jean Labarrière, *Structures et mouvement dialectique dans la "Phénoménologie de l'esprit de Hegel"* (Paris: Aubier, 1968), 221–31.
9. *PhS*, § 803; *PhG*, 430.
10. *PR*, § 273, Remark; *RP*, 371.
11. *PhS*, § 679; *PhG* 365.
12. *PhS*, § 441; *PhG*, 240.
13. *PhS*, § 679; *PhG*, 365.
14. *PhS*, § 437; *PhG*, 236.
15. *PhS*, § 440; *PhG*, 239.
16. *PhS*, § 440; *PhG*, 239.
17. *PhS*, § 596; *PhG*, 323.
18. *PhS*, § 440; *PhG*, 239.
19. *Phil. of Hist.*, 116; *VPG*, 163–64.
20. *Phil. of Hist.*, 223; *VPG*, 295.
21. *Phil. of Hist.*, 116; *VPG*, 163.
22. *PhS*, § 446; *PhG*, 241.
23. *PhS*, § 446; *PhG*, 241.
24. *PhS*, § 444; *PhG*, 240.
25. *PhS*, § 444; *PhG*, 240.
26. *PhS*, § 446; *PhG*, 241.
27. *PhS*, § 441; *PhG*, 240.
28. Cf. *PhS*, § 461; *PhG*, 249.
29. *Phil. of Hist.*, 253; *VPG*, 330.
30. *PhS*, § 447; *PhG*, 242.
31. *PhS*, § 445; *PhG*, 241.
32. *PhS*, § 448; *PhG*, 242.
33. *PhS*, § 453; *PhG*, 245.
34. *PhS*, § 450; *PhG*, 242.
35. *PhS*, § 457; *PhG*, 247.
36. Cf. Patricia Jagentowicz Mills, "Hegel's Antigone," *Owl of Minerva* 17 (1986), 131–52.
37. *PhS*, § 465; *PhG*, 252.
38. *PR*, § 166; *RP*, 246.
39. *PR*, § 166; *RP*, 246.
40. *PhS*, § 452; *PhG*, 244.
41. *PhS*, § 453; *PhG*, 245.
42. *PhS*, § 456; *PhG*, 246–47.
43. *PhS*, § 457; *PhG*, 242.
44. *PhS*, § 457; *PhG*, 242.
45. *Phil. of Hist.*, 239; *VPG*, 315.
46. *PhS*, § 460; *PhG*, 249.
47. *PhS*, § 460; *PhG*, 248.
48. *PhS*, § 466; *PhG*, 252.
49. *PhS*, § 466; *PhG*, 252.
50. He speaks of tragedy in the same way in a footnote to the *Philosophy of*

Right: "The *tragic* destruction of figures whose ethical life is on the highest plane can interest and elevate us and reconcile us to its occurrence only in so far as they come on the scene in opposition to one another together with equally justified but different ethical powers which have come into collision through misfortune, because the result is that then these figures acquire guilt through their opposition to an ethical law" (*PR*, § 140, n. *RP*, 218).

51. *PhS*, § 464; *PhG*, 251.

52. *Antigone*, 206–7. All quotations from Sophocles' *Antigone* are taken from *The Complete Greek Tragedies*, ed. David Grene and Richard Lattimore (Chicago: University of Chicago Press, 1954). (Hereafter simply *Antigone*.) The references are to line numbers.

53. *Antigone*, 209–10.

54. *Antigone*, 519.

55. *Antigone*, 450–57. Cf. *Hist. of Phil.* I, 386; *VGP* II, 45.

56. *PhS*, § 468; *PhG*, 253.

57. *PhS*, § 465; *PhG*, 251.

58. *Antigone*, 672–76.

59. *PhS*, § 473; *PhG*, 257.

60. *Antigone*, 902–4.

61. *PhS*, § 474; *PhG*, 258.

62. Cf. *Hist. of Phil.* I, 446–47; *VGP* II, 120.

63. *PhS*, § 472; *PhG*, 256.

64. *Antigone*, 877.

65. *PhS*, § 468; *PhG*, 254.

66. *Antigone*, 1319–21.

67. *Antigone*, 855.

68. *PhS*, § 476; *PhG*, 260.

69. *PhS*, § 476; *PhG*, 260.

70. *Phil. of Hist.*, 19; *VPG*, 46. Cf. *PR*, § 342; *RP*, 447: "World history is the necessary development, out of the concept of mind's freedom alone, of the moments of reason and so of the self-consciousness and freedom of mind." Cf. Reinhart Klemens Maurer, "Teleologische Aspekte der Hegelschen Philosophie," in his *Hegel und das Ende der Geschichte* (Freiburg: Karl Alber, 1980), 192.

71. Cf. *EL*, § 24, Addition; *Werke*, vol. 8, 68–69. Cf. also *Phil. of Hist.*, 321ff.; *VPG*, 412ff.

72. Cf. *PhS*, §§ 479–80, 483; *PhG*, 261–64. Cf. also *Phil. of Hist.*, 318; *VPG*, 408. For the connection between the "Unhappy Consciousness" and "Legal Status," see John Burbidge, "Unhappy Consciousness in Hegel—an Analysis of Medieval Catholicism?" *Mosaic* 11 (1978), 72.

73. *PhS*, § 479; *PhG*, 261.

74. *PhS*, § 480; *PhG*, 261–62.

75. *PhS*, § 483; *PhG*, 263–64.

76. *PhS*, § 480; *PhG*, 261.

77. *Phil. of Hist.*, 290; *VPG*, 375.

78. *Phil. of Hist.*, 295; *VPG*, 381.

79. *PhS*, § 476; *PhG*, 260. Cf. *Phil. of Hist.*, 317; *VPG*, 407.

80. *PhS*, § 477; *PhG*, 260.

81. *PhS*, § 477; *PhG*, 260.

82. *Phil. of Hist.*, 317; *VPG*, 407–8.

83. Cf. *PR*, § 36; *RP*, 90–91: "Personality essentially involves the capacity for rights and constitutes the concept and the basis (itself abstract) of the system of abstract and therefore formal right."

84. Cf. *Phil. of Hist.*, 281, 288; *VPG*, 365, 273.

85. *PhS*, § 480; *PhG*, 262.

86. *Phil. of Hist.*, 316–17; *VPG*, 407.

87. *Phil. of Hist.*, 279; *VPG*, 362.

88. *PhS*, § 480; *PhG*, 262.

89. Cf. *PhS*, § 480; *PhG*, 262: Property "consists in its being *mine* in the sense of the category, as something whose validity is *recognized* and *actual*."

90. *PhS*, § 481; *PhG*, 263.

91. *Phil. of Hist.*, 315; *VPG*, 405–6.

92. *PhS*, § 482; *PhG*, 263.

93. *PhS*, § 483; *PhG*, 263–64.

94. *Phil. of Hist.*, 320; *VPG*, 411.

95. Cf. *Phil. of Hist.*, 307; *VPG*, 396.

96. *Phil. of Hist.*, 320; *VPG*, 411.

97. *Phil. of Hist.*, 316; *VPG*, 406.

98. *PhS*, § 437; *PhG*, 236. Cf. *PR*, § 144, Addition; *RP*, 227. *PR*, § 166, Remark; *RP*, 246.

99. Cf. Robert C. Solomon, *In the Spirit of Hegel* (Oxford: Oxford University Press, 1983), 554; John Findlay, *Hegel: A Re-Examination* (London: Allen and Unwin, 1958), 118.

100. This view is shared by Lauener. Cf. Henri Lauener, "Die Sprache der Zerrissenheit als Dasein des sich entfremdeten Geistes bei Hegel," *Studia philosophica* 24 (1964), 168.

101. *Phil. of Hist.*, 427; *VPG*, 536.

102. *PhS*, § 508; *PhG*, 276.

103. *PhS*, § 177; *PhG*, 108

104. *PhS*, § 517; *PhG*, 280.

105. *Phil. of Hist.*, 429–30; *VPG*, 539.

106. *PhS*, § 489; *PhG*, 267.

107. *PhS*, § 490; *PhG*, 268.

108. *PhS*, § 492; *PhG*, 269.

109. *PhS*, § 491; *PhG*, 269.

110. *PhS*, § 492; *PhG*, 269.

111. *PhS*, § 493; *PhG*, 269.

112. *PhS*, § 493; *PhG*, 269–70.

113. *PhS*, § 493; *PhG*, 270.

114. *PhS*, § 494; *PhG*, 270.

115. *PhS*, § 494; *PhG*, 270.

116. *PhS,* § 494; *PhG,* 270.
117. *PhS,* § 494; *PhG,* 270.
118. *PhS,* § 497; *PhG,* 272.
119. *PhS,* § 497; *PhG,* 272.
120. *PhS,* § 497; *PhG,* 272.
121. *PhS,* § 498; *PhG,* 272.
122. *PhS,* § 498; *PhG,* 272.
123. *PhS,* § 499; *PhG,* 272.
124. *PhS,* § 500; *PhG,* 273.
125. *PhS,* § 503; *PhG,* 274.
126. *PhS,* § 503; *PhG,* 274.
127. *PhS,* § 501; *PhG,* 273.
128. *Phil. of Hist.,* 370; *VPG,* 471.
129. *PhS,* § 501; *PhG,* 273.
130. *PhS,* § 505; *PhG,* 275.
131. *Phil. of Hist.,* 369; *VPG,* 469–70.
132. *Phil. of Hist.,* 370; *VPG,* 472.
133. *PhS,* § 505; *PhG,* 275.
134. *PhS,* § 511; *PhG,* 277–78.
135. *PhS,* § 513; *PhG,* 279.
136. *PhS,* § 513; *PhG,* 279.
137. *PhS,* § 517; *PhG,* 280.
138. *PhS,* § 518; *PhG,* 281.
139. *PhS,* § 517; *PhG,* 280.
140. *PhS,* § 519; *PhG,* 281.
141. *Phil. of Hist.,* 438; *VPG,* 548.
142. *PhS,* § 521; *PhG,* 283.
143. *PhS,* § 526; *PhG,* 286.
144. *PhS,* § 529; *PhG,* 288.
145. *PhS,* § 527; *PhG,* 287.
146. *PhS,* § 536; *PhG,* 291.
147. *PhS,* § 525; *PhG,* 285.
148. *PhS,* § 529; *PhG,* 289.
149. *PhS,* § 529; *PhG,* 288.
150. *PhS,* § 537; *PhG,* 292.
151. *PhS,* § 527; *PhG,* 289.
152. *PhS,* § 529; *PhG,* 288.
153. *PhS,* § 529; *PhG,* 288.
154. *PhS,* § 527; *PhG,* 286.
155. Cf. Howard P. Kainz, "Some Problems with English Translations of Hegel's *Phänomenologie des Geistes," Hegel-Studien* 21 (1986), 177.
156. *PhS,* § 530; *PhG,* 289.
157. *PhS,* § 532; *PhG,* 289–90.
158. *PhS,* § 533; *PhG,* 290.
159. *PhS,* § 533; *PhG,* 290.

160. *PhS,* § 534; *PhG,* 290.
161. *PhS,* § 534; *PhG,* 290.
162. *PhS,* § 534; *PhG,* 290.
163. *PhS,* § 534; *PhG,* 290.
164. *PhS,* § 535; *PhG,* 290–91.
165. *PhS,* § 537; *PhG,* 291.
166. *PhS,* § 536; *PhG,* 291.
167. *PhS,* § 537; *PhG,* 291–92.
168. *PhS,* § 537; *PhG,* 292.
169. Cf. *Phil. of Hist.,* 439; *VPG,* 549–50.
170. *PhS,* § 546; *PhG,* 296.
171. *PhS,* § 549; *PhG,* 298.
172. *PhS,* § 540; *PhG,* 293.
173. *PhS,* § 539; *PhG,* 292.
174. *PhS,* § 548; *PhG,* 296.
175. *PhS,* § 541; *PhG,* 293.
176. *PhS,* § 540; *PhG,* 293.
177. *Phil. of Hist.,* 441; *VPG,* 551–52.
178. *PhS,* § 541; *PhG,* 293.
179. *PhS,* § 542; *PhG,* 294
180. *PhS,* § 542; *PhG,* 294.
181. *PhS,* § 543; *PhG,* 294.
182. Cf. Jon Stewart, "Hegel and the Myth of Reason," *Owl of Minerva* 26 (1995), 187–200.
183. *PhS,* § 545; *PhG,* 295.
184. *PhS,* § 545; *PhG,* 295.
185. *PhS,* § 551; *PhG,* 299.
186. *PhS,* § 551; *PhG,* 299.
187. *PhS,* § 552; *PhG,* 299.
188. *PhS,* § 552; *PhG,* 299.
189. *PhS,* § 552; *PhG,* 300. Cf. *Phil. of Hist.,* 440; *VPG,* 550: "The assertion was even ventured on, and that by Catholics no less than by Protestants, that the external [and material], with which the Church insisted upon associating superhuman virtue, was external and material, and nothing more—that the host was simply *dough,* the relics of the saints mere *bones.*"
190. *PhS,* § 553; *PhG,* 300.
191. *PhS,* § 554; *PhG,* 301.
192. *PhS,* § 554; *PhG,* 301.
193. *PhS,* § 555; *PhG,* 301.
194. *PhS,* § 556; *PhG,* 302.
195. *PhS,* § 556; *PhG,* 302.
196. *PhS,* § 557; *PhG,* 302.
197. *PhS,* § 557; *PhG,* 303.
198. *PhS,* § 557; *PhG,* 303.
199. *PhS,* § 558; *PhG,* 303.

200. *PhS,* § 558; *PhG,* 303.
201. *PhS,* § 559; *PhG,* 304.
202. *PhS,* § 559; *PhG,* 304.
203. *PhS,* § 561; *PhG,* 305.
204. *PhS,* § 563; *PhG,* 306.
205. *PhS,* § 566; *PhG,* 307.
206. *PhS,* § 567; *PhG,* 308.
207. *PhS,* § 568; *PhG,* 308.
208. *PhS,* § 569; *PhG,* 309.
209. *PhS,* § 570; *PhG,* 309.
210. *PhS,* § 572; *PhG,* 310.
211. *PhS,* § 573; *PhG,* 310.
212. *PhS,* § 545; *PhG,* 296.
213. *PhS,* § 574; *PhG,* 311.
214. *PhS,* § 574; *PhG,* 311.
215. *PhS,* § 574; *PhG,* 311.
216. *PhS,* § 574; *PhG,* 311–12.
217. *PhS,* § 576; *PhG,* 312.
218. *PhS,* § 578; *PhG,* 312.
219. *PhS,* § 576; *PhG,* 312.
220. *PhS,* § 576; *PhG,* 312.
221. *PhS,* § 577; *PhG,* 312.
222. *PhS,* § 577; *PhG,* 312.
223. *PhS,* § 578; *PhG,* 313.
224. *PhS,* § 578; *PhG,* 313.
225. *PhS,* § 578; *PhG,* 313.
226. *PhS,* § 579; *PhG,* 313.
227. *PhS,* § 580; *PhG,* 314.
228. *PhS,* § 580; *PhG,* 314.
229. *PhS,* § 580; *PhG,* 314.
230. *PhS,* § 581; *PhG,* 315.
231. *PhS,* § 581; *PhG,* 315.
232. *PhS,* § 581; *PhG,* 315.
233. *Phil. of Hist.,* 447; *VPG,* 557.
234. *PhS,* § 580; *PhG,* 315.
235. E.g. Jürgen Habermas, "Hegel's Critique of the French Revolution," in his *Theory and Practice,* trans. J. Viertel (Boston: Beacon Press, 1973), 121–41; Joachim Ritter, *Hegel und die französische Revolution* (Frankfurt: Suhrkamp, 1965).
236. Cf. Solomon, *In the Spirit of Hegel,* 561.
237. *Phil. of Hist.,* 444; *VPG,* 554.
238. *PhS,* § 582; *PhG,* 316.
239. *PhS,* § 583; *PhG,* 317.
240. *PhS,* § 583; *PhG,* 316–17.
241. Cf. *Phil. of Hist.,* 445–46; *VPG,* 556:

An *intellectual principle* was thus discovered to serve as a basis for the state—one which does not, like previous principles, belong to the sphere of opinion, such as the social impulse, the desire of security for property, etc. nor owe its origin to the religious sentiment, as does that of the divine appointment of the governing power—but the principle of certainty, which is identity with my self-consciousness, stopping short however of that of truth, which needs to be distinguished from it. This is a vast discovery in regard to the profoundest depths of being and freedom. The consciousness of the spiritual is now the essential basis of the political fabric, and *philosophy* has thereby become dominant.

242. *PhS,* § 584; *PhG,* 317.

243. *PhS,* § 582; *PhG,* 316.

244. Cf. *PR,* § 258; *RP,* 331. Cf. *Rousseau, die Revolution und der junge Hegel,* ed. Hans Friedrich Fulda and Rolf-Peter Horstmann (Stuttgart: Klett-Cotta, 1991).

245. *PhS,* § 584; *PhG,* 317.

246. Cf. *PR,* § 258, Remark; *RP,* 331:

When these abstract conclusions came into power, they afforded for the first time in human history the prodigious spectacle of the overthrow of the constitution of a great actual state and its complete reconstruction *ab initio* on the basis of pure thought alone, after the destruction of all existing and given material. The will of its re-founders was to give it what they alleged was a purely rational basis, but it was only abstractions that were being used; the Idea was lacking; and the experiment ended in the maximum of frightfulness and terror.

247. *PhS,* § 585; *PhG,* 318.

248. *PhS,* § 585; *PhG,* 318.

249. Cf. *PhS,* § 586; *PhG,* 318: "The antithesis consists, therefore, solely in the difference between the *individual* and the *universal* consciousness; but the individual consciousness itself is directly in its own eyes that which had only the *semblance* of an antithesis; it is universal consciousness and will."

250. *PhS,* § 587; *PhG,* 318.

251. *PhS,* § 587; *PhG,* 318.

252. *PhS,* § 588; *PhG,* 318.

253. *PhS,* § 589; *PhG,* 319.

254. *PhS,* § 588; *PhG,* 318.

255. *PhS,* § 588; *PhG,* 319.

256. *PhS,* § 588; *PhG,* 319.

257. *PhS,* § 589; *PhG,* 319.

258. *PhS,* § 590; *PhG,* 320.

259. *PhS,* § 590; *PhG,* 320.

260. *PhS,* § 590; *PhG,* 320.

261. *PhS,* § 591; *PhG,* 320.

262. *PhS,* § 591; *PhG,* 320.

263. *PhS,* § 591; *PhG,* 320.

264. *PR,* § 5, Addition; *RP,* 56.

265. *PhS,* § 592; *PhG,* 320.

266. *PhS,* § 594; *PhG,* 322.

267. *PhS*, § 594; *PhG*, 322–23.

268. *Phil. of Hist.*, 443; *VPG*, 554.

269. *PhS*, § 598; *PhG*, 324.

270. *PhS*, § 596; *PhG*, 323.

271. *Phil. of Hist.*, 443; *VPG*, 553.

272. Cf. Moltke S. Gram, "Moral and Literary Ideals in Hegel's Critique of 'The Moral View of the World,'" *Clio* 7 (1978), 375–402.

273. *PhS*, § 602; *PhG*, 326.

274. *PhS*, § 599; *PhG*, 324.

275. *PR*, § 131; *RP*, 188.

276. *PR*, § 133; *RP*, 192.

277. *PhS*, § 599; *PhG*, 325. Cf. *PR*, § 135; *RP*, 193: "Duty itself in the moral self-consciousness is the essence or the universality of that consciousness, the way in which it is inwardly related to itself alone."

278. *PhS*, § 600; *PhG*, 325.

279. *PhS*, § 601; *PhG*, 325: Moral consciousness "learns from experience that nature is not concerned with giving the moral consciousness a sense of unity of its reality with that of nature, and hence that nature perhaps may let it become happy, or perhaps may not."

280. *PhS*, § 602; *PhG*, 326.

281. Immanuel Kant, *Critique of Practical Reason*, trans. Lewis White Beck (Indianapolis: Bobbs-Merrill, 1956), 123. Cf. Kant, *Critique of Judgment*, trans. Werner Pluhar (Indianapolis: Hackett, 1987), § 86.

282. *PhS*, § 602; *PhG*, 326.

283. *PhS*, § 602; *PhG*, 326.

284. *EL*, § 60; *Enz.*, 73.

285. *PhS*, § 603; *PhG*, 327.

286. Cf. *PR*, § 139, Remark; *RP*, 201:

> But since the will here makes into a determinant of its content both these impulses in this contingent character which they possess as natural, and also, therefore, the form which it has at this point, the form of particularity itself, it follows that it is set in opposition to the universal as inner objectivity, to the good, which comes on the scene as the opposite extreme to immediate objectivity, the natural pure and simple, as soon as the will is reflected into itself and consciousness is a *knowing* consciousness. It is in this opposition that this inwardness of the will is evil.

287. *PhS*, § 603; *PhG*, 327. Cf. Hegel's discussion of the conflict between reason and inclination in *ETW*, 211ff.; *TJ*, 266ff.

288. *PhS*, § 603; *PhG*, 327.

289. *PhS*, § 603; *PhG*, 327.

290. Kant, *Critique of Practical Reason*, 126–27. Cf. *PhS*, § 603; *PhG*, 327: "Consciousness has, therefore, itself to bring about this harmony and continually to be making progress in morality. But the consummation of this progress has to be projected into a future infinitely remote."

291. *PhS*, § 603; *PhG*, 328.

292. *EL*, § 60; *Enz.*, 73.

293. *PhS*, § 603; *PhG*. 327–28.

294. Cf. *PhS*, § 603; *PhG*, 328: "the contradiction of a task which is to remain a task and yet ought to be fulfilled, and the contradiction of a morality which is no longer to be [a moral] *consciousness*, i.e. not actual."

295. *PhS*, § 604; *PhG*, 328.

296. *PhS*, § 604; *PhG*, 328.

297. *PhS*, § 605; *PhG*, 328. Cf. *PR*, § 119; *RP*, 177: "An action as an external event is a complex of connected parts which may be regarded as divided into units *ad infinitum*, and the action may be treated as having touched in the first instance only one of these units."

298. *PhS*, § 605; *PhG*, 328.

299. *PhS*, § 605; *PhG*, 328.

300. *PhS*, § 605; *PhG*, 328–29.

301. *PhS*, § 605; *PhG*, 328.

302. *PhS*, § 606; *PhG*, 329.

303. *EL*, § 59; *Enz.*, 72. Cf. Kant, *Critique of Practical Reason*, 119: "it is not impossible that the morality of intention should have a necessary relation as a cause to happiness as an effect in the sensuous world; but this relation is indirect, mediated by an intelligible author of nature."

304. *PhS*, § 606; *PhG*, 329.

305. *PhS*, § 606; *PhG*, 329.

306. *PhS*, § 607; *PhG*, 329.

307. *PhS*, § 608; *PhG*, 330.

308. *PhS*, § 609; *PhG*, 330.

309. *PhS*, § 610; *PhG*, 330.

310. *PhS*, § 611; *PhG*, 331: "Because both are equally present in it, i.e. the *freedom* of [mere] *being*, and the inclusion of this being within consciousness, its object becomes one that has *being*, but at the same time exists only in *thought*; in the last stage of the moral view of the world, the content is explicitly such that its *being* is given to it by *thought*, and this conjunction of being and thought is pronounced to be what in fact it is—*imagining*."

311. *PhS*, § 631; *PhG*, 340.

312. *EL*, § 54; *Enz.*, 70.

313. *PhS*, § 630; *PhG*, 339.

314. *PhS*, § 617; *PhG*, 333.

315. *PhS*, § 616; *PhG*, 332.

316. *PhS*, § 618; *PhG*, 333.

317. *PhS*, § 618; *PhG*, 333.

318. *PhS*, § 618; *PhG*, 333.

319. *PhS*, § 618; *PhG*, 333.

320. *PhS*, § 618; *PhG*, 333.

321. *PhS*, § 619; *PhG*, 334.

322. *PhS*, § 620; *PhG*, 334.

323. *PhS*, § 620; *PhG*, 334.

324. *PhS*, § 620; *PhG*, 334.
325. *PhS*, § 621; *PhG*, 335.
326. *PhS*, § 621; *PhG*, 334–35.
327. *PhS*, § 622; *PhG*, 335.
328. *PhS*, § 622; *PhG*, 335.
329. *PhS*, § 622; *PhG*, 335.
330. *PhS*, § 622; *PhG*, 335.
331. *PhS*, § 622; *PhG*, 335.
332. *PhS*, § 622; *PhG*, 335–36.
333. *PhS*, § 622; *PhG*, 336.
334. *PhS*, § 623; *PhG*, 336.
335. *PhS*, § 623; *PhG*, 336.
336. *PhS*, § 625; *PhG*, 337.
337. *PhS*, § 626; *PhG*, 337.
338. *PhS*, § 626; *PhG*, 337–38.
339. *PhS*, § 627; *PhG*, 338.
340. *PhS*, § 627; *PhG*, 338.
341. *PhS*, § 628; *PhG*, 338.
342. *PhS*, § 628; *PhG*, 338.
343. *PhS*, § 628; *PhG*, 338.
344. *PhS*, § 630; *PhG*, 339.
345. *PhS*, § 630; *PhG*, 339.
346. *PhS*, § 631; *PhG*, 340.
347. *PR*, § 140, Remark; *RP*, 220.
348. *Aesthetics* I, 241–42; *Aesthetik* I, 326.
349. Cf. *PhS*, § 660; *PhG*, 355–56.
350. *PhS*, § 634; *PhG*, 342.
351. *PhS*, § 644; *PhG*, 347.
352. *PhS*, § 632; *PhG*, 341.
353. *PhS*, § 632; *PhG*, 341.
354. *PhS*, § 639; *PhG*, 344.
355. *PhS*, § 633; *PhG*, 341.
356. *PhS*, § 637; *PhG*, 343.
357. *PhS*, § 635; *PhG*, 342.
358. *PhS*, § 635; *PhG*, 342.
359. *PhS*, § 640; *PhG*, 345.
360. *PhS*, § 642; *PhG*, 346.
361. *PhS*, § 642; *PhG*, 346.
362. *PhS*, § 642; *PhG*, 346.
363. *PhS*, § 643; *PhG*, 346.
364. *PhS*, § 643; *PhG*, 346.
365. *PhS*, § 643; *PhG*, 346–47.
366. *PhS*, § 643; *PhG*, 347.
367. *PhS*, § 644; *PhG*, 348.
368. *PhS*, § 645; *PhG*, 349.
369. *PhS*, § 646; *PhG*, 349.

370. *PhS*, § 648; *PhG*, 350.

371. *PhS*, § 648; *PhG*, 350. Cf. *PhS*, § 649; *PhG*, 350: "Others, therefore, do not know whether this conscience is morally good or evil."

372. *PhS*, § 648; *PhG*, 350.

373. *PhS*, § 651; *PhG*, 351.

374. *PhS*, § 653; *PhG*, 351.

375. *PhS*, § 654; *PhG*, 352. Cf. *PhS*, § 656; *PhG*, 353: "the declaration of conscience affirms the certainty of itself to be pure self, and thereby to be a universal self."

376. *PhS*, § 658; *PhG*, 354.

377. *PhS*, § 648; *PhG*, 350.

378. *PhS*, § 658; *PhG*, 354.

379. *PR*, § 13, Addition; *RP*, 65–66.

380. *PhS*, § 657; *PhG*, 354.

381. *PhS*, § 659; *PhG*, 355.

382. *PhS*, § 659; *PhG*, 355.

383. *PhS*, § 659; *PhG*, 355.

384. *PhS*, § 660; *PhG*, 356.

385. *PhS*, § 660; *PhG*, 356. Cf. *PR*, § 140; *RP*, 204. Cf. *Hist. of Phil.* I, 401; *VGP* II, 63. *Hist. of Phil.* I, 420; *VGP* II, 94. *Hist. of Phil.* I, pp. 442–43; *VGP* II, pp. 115–16.

386. *PhS*, § 662; *PhG*, 356.

387. *PhS*, § 663; *PhG*, 357.

388. *PhS*, § 664; *PhG*, 357.

389. *PhS*, § 668; *PhG*, 360. Cf. *Aesthetics* I, 242; *Aesthetik* I, 326–27:

> Inability to endure pedantry and rudeness, trifling circumstances and blunders which a greater and stronger character overlooks and by which he is uninjured, is beyond all imagination, and it is just the most trifling matter which brings such a beautiful heart to the depths of despair. Then, therefore, mournfulness, worry, grief, bad temper, sickness, melancholy, and misery have no end. Thence there springs a torture of reflections on self and others, a convulsiveness and even a harshness and cruelty of soul, in which at the last the whole miserableness and weakness of the inner life of this beautiful soul is exposed.

390. *PR*, § 140, Remark; *RP*, 219–20 (translation slightly modified).

391. *PhS*, § 667; *PhG*, 359.

392. *PhS*, § 669; *PhG*, 361.

393. *PhS*, § 669; *PhG*, 361.

394. *PhS*, § 670; *PhG*, 361.

395. *PhS*, § 671; *PhG*, 362.

396. *PhS*, § 671; *PhG*, 362.

Chapter 8

1. Cf. Robert C. Solomon, *In the Spirit of Hegel* (Oxford: Oxford University Press, 1983), 599ff.

2. Cf. Hegel's review: *PhS*, §§ 672–76; *PhG*, 363–64.

3. Cf. *PhS*, § 673; *PhG*, 363.

4. Cf. *PhS*, §§ 674–76; *PhG*, 363–64.

5. *PhS*, § 672; *PhG*, 363.

6. Cf. *PhS*, § 677; *PhG*, 364. *PhS*, § 678; *PhG*, 365. *PhS*, § 682; *PhG*, 368.

7. *PhS*, § 677; *PhG*, 364.

8. *Phil. of Hist.*, 335; *VPG*, 429.

9. *Phil. of Hist.*, 335; *VPG*, 429.

10. *PhS*, § 680; *PhG*, 366.

11. *PhS*, § 679; *PhG*, 365.

12. *PhS*, § 680; *PhG*, 366.

13. *PhS*, § 679; *PhG*, 365.

14. *Phil. of Religion* I, 76; *VPR* I, 92.

15. *PhS*, § 683; *PhG*, 368.

16. *PhS*, § 683; *PhG*, 368.

17. *PhS*, § 683; *PhG*, 368.

18. *PhS*, § 684; *PhG*, 369.

19. Cf. Jean-Louis Vieillard-Baron, "La 'religion de la nature': Étude de quelques pagés de la *Phénoménologie de l'esprit* de Hegel," *Revue de Métaphysique et de morale* 76 (1971), 325–27.

20. *PhS*, § 684; *PhG*, 369.

21. *Phil. of Religion* II, 70–82; *VPR* I, 424–34.

22. *Phil. of Religion* II, 77; *VPR* I, 429. Cf. *Phil. of Hist.*, 177; *VPG*, 239: "The chief point—that which especially concerns us here—is the *doctrine* of Zoroaster." Cf. *Aesthetics* I, 325; *Aesthetik* I, 435.

23. *Phil. of Hist.*, 173; *VPG*, 234.

24. Cf. the rich analysis of Vieillard-Baron, "La 'religion de la nature,'" 323–43.

25. Cf. John Burbidge, "Unhappy Consciousness in Hegel—an Analysis of Medieval Catholicism?" *Mosaic* 11 (1978), 70.

26. *PhS*, § 686; *PhG*, 371.

27. *PhS*, § 685; *PhG*, 370.

28. *PhS*, § 685; *PhG*, 371.

29. *PhS*, § 686; *PhG*, 371.

30. *Phil. of Hist.*, 178; *VPG*, 239.

31. *Phil. of Hist.*, 178; *VPG*, 239. Cf. *Phil. of Hist.*, 179; *VPG*, 241: "Ormuzd is present in all light; but he is not the sun or the moon itself."

32. *Phil. of Hist.*, 175; *VPG*, 235. Cf. *Aesthetics* I, 325; *Aesthetik* I, 436.

33. *PhS*, § 686; *PhG*, 371. Cf. *Phil. of Religion* II, 75; *VPR* I, 427. Cf. *Phil. of Hist.*, 174; *VPG*, 234. Cf. *Aesthetics* I, 325; *Aesthetik* I, 436

34. *Phil. of Hist.*, 178; *VPG*, 240. In his *Lectures on Aesthetics*, he writes, Ormuzd "is only the universal in all particular existents in which the light, and therefore the divine and the pure, is actual" (*Aesthetics* I, 325; *Aesthetik* I, 436).

35. *Phil. of Hist.*, 178; *VPG*, 240. Cf. *Aesthetics* I, 325; *Aesthetik* I, 436.

36. *PhS*, § 686; *PhG*, 371.

37. *Phil. of Religion* II, 80; *VPR* I, 432. Cf. *Aesthetics* I, 325, 327; *Aesthetik* I, 435, 437.

38. *Phil. of Hist.*, 173; *VPG*, 234.

39. *PhS*, § 687; *PhG*, 371.

40. *PhS*, § 687; *PhG*, 371.

41. In his *Lectures on the Philosophy of History*, Hegel describes the sublation of the Notion of Zoroastrianism in somewhat different terms: "The deficiency in the Persian principle is only that the unity of the antithesis is not completely recognized; for in that indefinite conception of the uncreated all, whence Ormuzd and Ahriman proceeded, the unity is only the absolutely *primal* existence, and does not reduce the contradictory elements to harmony itself" (*Phil. of Hist.*, 179; *VPG*, 240). Apparently, for Hegel, the elements do not interact in a dialectical fashion, mutually shaping and conditioning each other, but instead Ormuzd or the principle of good is simply thought to win out in the end. The principle of evil is simply excluded without any genuine dialectical sublation. Thus, the dialectical movement does not advance but simply remains at the level of indeterminate universality.

42. *PhS*, § 688; *PhG*, 371.

43. *PhS*, § 688; *PhG*, 371.

44. *Phil. of Hist.*, 141; *VPG*, 193.

45. *Phil. of Religion* II, 45; *VPR* I, 397.

46. *Phil. of Religion* II, 2; *VPR* I, 356. Cf. *Aesthetics* I, 334–35; *Aesthetik* I, 449.

47. *PhS*, § 689; *PhG*, 372.

48. *Aesthetics* I, 335; *Aesthetik* I, 449. Cf. also *Phil. of Religion* II, 11; *VPR* I, 364: "This simple substance, which the Hindus call Brahma, is regarded as the universal, the self-existing power."

49. *Aesthetics* I, 335; *Aesthetik* I, 449.

50. *PhS*, § 689; *PhG*, 372.

51. *Phil. of Religion* II, 24–25; *VPR* I, 377.

52. *Phil. of Hist.*, 141; *VPG*, 194.

53. *Phil. of Hist.*, 156; *VPG*, 213.

54. *Phil. of Hist.*, 141; *VPG*, 193–94.

55. *Phil. of Hist.*, 141; *VPG*, 194. Cf. *Phil. of Hist.*, 156; *VPG*, 213: "The other deities are therefore things of sense: mountains, streams, beasts, the sun, the moon, the Ganges." Cf. also *Phil. of Hist.*, 157; *VPG*, 214: "Every bird, every monkey is a present god, an absolutely universal existence."

56. *PhS*, § 689; *PhG*, 372.

57. *PhS*, § 689; *PhG*, 372.

58. *Aesthetics* I, 337–38; *Aesthetik* I, 451.

59. *Phil. of Hist.*, 157; *VPG*, 215.

60. *Phil. of Religion* II, 25; *VPR* I, 378.

61. *Phil. of Religion* II, 26; *VPR* I, 379.

62. *Phil. of Hist.*, 155; *VPG*, 212.

63. *Phil. of Hist.*, 162; *VPG*, 221. Cf. *Phil. of Religion* II, 24; *VPR* I, 377: "Thus the development issues only in a wild whirl of delirium."

64. *PhS*, § 690; *PhG*, 372–73.
65. *PhS*, § 690; *PhG*, 372.
66. *PhS*, § 690; *PhG*, 373.
67. *Phil. of Religion* II, 109; *VPR* I, 459. Cf. *Aesthetics* I, 354; *Aesthetik* I, 472–73.
68. *Phil. of Hist.*, 220; *VPG*, 291.
69. *Phil. of Hist.*, 220; *VPG*, 292: "The solution and liberation of that Oriental Spirit, which in Egypt had advanced so far as to propose the problem, is certainly this: that the inner being of nature is thought, which has its existence only in the human consciousness."
70. *PhS*, § 692; *PhG*, 373.
71. *PhS*, § 693; *PhG*, 373.
72. *PhS*, § 692; *PhG*, 373.
73. *PhS*, § 694; *PhG*, 374.
74. *Aesthetics* I, 348–49, 354–55; *Aesthetik* I, 465–66, 473.
75. *Phil. of Religion* II, 109; *VPR* I, 459–60. Cf. also *Phil. of Religion* II, 108–9, 121; *VPR* I, 458–59, 471.
76. *PhS*, § 692; *PhG*, 373. Cf. *Aesthetics* I, 354ff.; *Aesthetik* I, 473ff. Cf. *Aesthetics* II, 642ff., 651ff.; *Aesthetik* II, 281ff., 293ff.
77. *Phil. of Religion* II, 110; *VPR* I, 460. Cf. *Aesthetics* II, 650ff.; *Aesthetik* II, 290ff.
78. *Phil. of Hist.*, 215; *VPG*, 285.
79. *Aesthetics* I, 348–49; *Aesthetik* I, 465–66.
80. *Phil. of Hist.*, 215; *VPG*, 285. Cf. *Phil. of Religion* II, 101–2; *VPR* I, 452.
81. Cf. *Phil. of Religion* II, 122; *VPR* I, 472.
82. *Phil. of Religion* II, 114; *VPR* I, 464. Cf. *Phil. of Religion* II, 257–58; *VPR* II, 127: "In this religion [the Greek religion] there is nothing incomprehensible, nothing which cannot be understood; there is no kind of content in the god which is not known to man, or which he does not find and know in himself."
83. *PhS*, § 694; *PhG*, 374.
84. *PhS*, § 694; *PhG*, 374.
85. *PhS*, § 695; *PhG*, 374.
86. *Phil. of Hist.*, 213; *VPG*, 282.
87. *PhS*, § 696; *PhG*, 375.
88. *PhS*, § 692; *PhG*, 373.
89. *PhS*, § 697; *PhG*, 375.
90. *PhS*, § 697; *PhG*, 375.
91. *PhS*, § 695; *PhG*, 374.
92. *Phil. of Hist.*, 199; *VPG*, 265 (translation slightly modified). Cf. *Aesthetics* I, 360–61; *Aesthetik* I, 480–81.
93. *Phil. of Hist.*, 213; *VPG*, 282–83. Cf. also *Phil. of Religion* II, 119; *VPR* I, 469. Cf. *Aesthetics* II, 643–44; *Aesthetik* II, 282–83.
94. *Aesthetics* I, 357; *Aesthetik* I, 475–76.
95. *PhS* § 698; *PhG*, 375.
96. *PhS*, § 697; *PhG*, 375.
97. *Phil. of Hist.*, 218; *VPG*, 289. Cf. also *Phil. of Religion* II, 87–88; *VPR* I,

439: "Here we have reached the ultimate determination of natural religion in this sphere, and in fact the stage which constitutes the transition to the religion of free subjectivity."

98. *Phil. of Hist.*, 199; *VPG*, 265. Cf. *Aesthetics* I, 357; *Aesthetik* I, 476.

99. *Phil. of Hist.*, 214; *VPG*, 283. Cf *Phil. of Hist.*, 208; *VPG*, 276: In Egyptian religion, "natural and spiritual powers are regarded as most intimately united . . . but in such a way, that the extremes of the antithesis were united in the harshest contrast."

100. *Phil. of Hist.*, 218; *VPG*, 289.

101. *PhS*, § 700; *PhG*, 376.

102. Cf. Solomon, *In the Spirit of Hegel*, 605ff.

103. *PhS*, § 699; *PhG*, 376. Cf. *Aesthetics* I, 477ff.; *Aesthetik* II, 9ff.

104. *PhS*, § 698; *PhG*, 375.

105. *Phil. of Hist.*, 239; *VPG*, 314–15.

106. *Phil. of Hist.*, 238–39; *VPG*, 314.

107. *PhS*, § 703; *PhG*, 377.

108. *PhS*, § 712; *PhG*, 381.

109. *PhS*, § 705; *PhG*, 378.

110. *PhS*, § 705; *PhG*, 378.

111. *PhS*, § 705; *PhG*, 378.

112. *PhS*, § 705; *PhG*, 378.

113. *PhS*, § 702; *PhG*, 377.

114. *PhS*, § 704; *PhG*, 378.

115. *PhS*, § 704; *PhG*, 378.

116. *PhS*, § 706; *PhG*, 378.

117. *PhS*, § 706; *PhG*, 378.

118. *PhS*, § 707; *PhG*, 378–79.

119. *PhS*, § 707; *PhG*, 379.

120. *Phil. of Religion* II, 229–39; *VPR* II, 99–109. Cf. *Aesthetics* I, 458–59, 465–68; *Aesthetik* II, 44ff., 53–56.

121. *Phil. of Hist.*, 244; *VPG*, 320.

122. *Phil. of Religion* II, 231; *VPR* II, 101. Cf. *Phil. of Hist.*, 245; *VPG*, 320–21.

123. *PhS*, § 707; *PhG*, 379.

124. *PhS*, § 708; *PhG*, 379.

125. *PhS*, § 708; *PhG*, 380.

126. In his *Lectures on the Philosophy of Religion*, Hegel describes this as follows: "If the work of art is the self-revelation of God and the revelation of the productivity of man as the positing of this revelation by the abrogation of his particular knowledge and will, on the other hand, the work of art equally involves the fact that God and man are no longer beings alien to one another, but have been taken up into a higher unity" (*Phil. of Religion* II, 256; *VPR* II, 126).

127. *PhS*, § 709; *PhG*, 380.

128. *PhS*, § 710; *PhG*, 380.

129. *PhS*, § 710; *PhG*, 380.

130. According to Hegel, for the Greeks the hymn's "essential and absolute purport is *religious*" (*Phil. of Hist.*, 244; *VPG*, 319).

131. *Phil. of Hist.*, 243; *VPG*, 319.

132. *PhS*, § 710; *PhG*, 380.

133. *PhS*, § 710; *PhG*, 381.

134. *PhS*, § 713; *PhG*, 382.

135. *Aesthetics* I, 457; *Aesthetik* II, 42. Cf. *Phil. of Hist.*, 254; *VPG*, 331–32.

136. *Phil. of Religion* II, 277; *VPR* II, 146.

137. *PhS*, § 712; *PhG*, 381.

138. *PhS*, § 711; *PhG*, 381. Cf. *Aesthetics* I, 457–58; *Aesthetik* II, 43.

139. Cf. *Aesthetics* I, 457; *Aesthetik* II, 42: "In this obscurity of form the spiritual content is itself dark and therefore needs clarification and explanation."

140. *Phil. of Religion* II, 278; *VPR* II, 147.

141. *PhS*, § 712; *PhG*, 382.

142. *Aesthetics* I, 458; *Aesthetik* II, 43.

143. *PhS*, § 714; *PhG*, 382.

144. Cf. *Phil. of Religion* II, 267; *VPR* II, 136.

145. *PhS*, § 714; *PhG*, 382.

146. *PhS*, § 715; *PhG*, 383.

147. *PhS*, § 716; *PhG*, 383.

148. *PhS*, § 718; *PhG*, 384.

149. *PhS*, § 718; *PhG*, 384.

150. Cf. *Phil. of Religion* II, 267–68; *VPR* II, 136–37.

151. *PhS*, § 718; *PhG*, 383–84.

152. *PhS*, § 718; *PhG*, 384. Cf. *Phil. of Religion* II, 237, 268–69; *VPR* II, 107, 137.

153. *PhS*, § 718; *PhG*, 384.

154. *PhS*, § 718; *PhG*, 384.

155. *PhS*, § 719; *PhG*, 385.

156. *PhS*, § 721; *PhG*, 386.

157. *PhS*, § 721; *PhG*, 386.

158. *PhS*, § 722; *PhG*, 386.

159. *PhS*, § 722; *PhG*, 386.

160. *PhS*, § 723; *PhG*, 387.

161. *PhS*, § 725; *PhG*, 387.

162. *PhS*, § 724; *PhG*, 387.

163. *PhS*, § 724; *PhG*, 387.

164. *Phil. of Hist.*, 242; *VPG*, 317.

165. *Phil. of Religion* II, 273; *VPR* II, 141.

166. *Phil. of Religion* II, 273; *VPR* II, 142.

167. *PhS*, § 725; *PhG*, 388.

168. *Phil. of Hist.*, 241; *VPG*, 317.

169. *Phil. of Hist.*, 243; *VPG*, 318–19.

170. *Phil. of Hist.*, 242; *VPG*, 317.

171. *Phil. of Religion* II, 274; *VPR* II, 142.

172. *Phil. of Religion* II, 274; *VPR* II, 143.
173. *PhS*, § 726; *PhG*, 388.
174. *PhS*, § 726; *PhG*, 388.
175. *PhS*, § 726; *PhG*, 388.
176. *PhS*, § 726; *PhG*, 388.
177. *PhS*, § 726; *PhG*, 388.
178. *PhS*, § 733; *PhG*, 392.
179. *PhS*, § 728; *PhG*, 389.
180. *PhS*, § 752; *PhG*, 401.
181. Cf. *Phil. of Religion* II, 264; *VPR* II, 133.
182. Cf. *Aesthetics* II, 1201; *Aesthetik* III, 536.
183. *PhS*, § 727; *PhG*, 388–89.
184. Cf. *Phil. of Religion* II, 227–28; *VPR* II, 98.
185. *PhS*, § 727; *PhG*, 389. Cf. *Phil. of Hist.*, 225–26; *VPG*, 298.
186. *Phil. of Hist.*, 230; *VPG*, 303–4.
187. *Phil. of Hist.*, 230; *VPG*, 304.
188. *PhS*, § 728; *PhG*, 389.
189. *PhS*, § 728; *PhG*, 389.
190. *PhS*, § 729; *PhG*, 390.
191. *PhS*, § 729; *PhG*, 390.
192. *PhS*, § 731; *PhG*, 391. Cf. also *Phil. of Hist.*, 246; *VPG*, 322: "It must be further observed, that the Greek gods are to be regarded as individualities—not abstractions, like 'knowledge,' 'unity,' 'time,' 'heaven,' 'necessity.' . . . The gods are personalities, concrete individualities."
193. *Aesthetics* I, 482; *Aesthetik* II, 74.
194. *Aesthetics* I, 502–3; *Aesthetik* II, 101.
195. *PhS*, § 731; *PhG*, 391. Cf. *Phil. of Religion* II, 239ff.; *VPR* II, 109ff.
196. *Phil. of Hist.*, 246; *VPG*, 322–23.
197. *PhS*, § 731; *PhG*, 391.
198. Cf. *Aesthetics* II, 1193ff.; *Aesthetik* III, 526–33.
199. *PhS*, § 733; *PhG*, 392.
200. *PhS*, § 733; *PhG*, 392.
201. *Phil. of Hist.*, 231; *VPG*, 305.
202. *PhS*, § 734; *PhG*, 393.
203. *PhS*, § 736; *PhG*, 393–94.
204. *PhS*, § 737; *PhG*, 394.
205. *PhS*, § 740; *PhG*, 395.
206. *PhS*, § 740; *PhG*, 396. Cf. *Phil. of Religion* II, 264–65; *VPR* II, 133–34.
207. *PhS*, § 739; *PhG*, 395.
208. *PhS*, § 737; *PhG*, 394.
209. *PhS*, § 738; *PhG*, 395.
210. *PhS*, § 741; *PhG*, 396.
211. *PhS*, § 742; *PhG*, 397.
212. *PhS*, § 742; *PhG*, 397.
213. *PhS*, § 742; *PhG*, 397.

214. *PhS*, § 742; *PhG*, 397.

215. Cf. *Aesthetics* II, 1199ff.; *Aesthetik* III, 533ff.

216. *PhS*, § 742; *PhG*, 397.

217. *PhS*, § 744; *PhG*, 398. Cf. *PhS*, § 745; *PhG*, 398: "The divine substance unites within itself the meaning of natural and ethical essentiality."

218. *PhS*, § 745; *PhG*, 398.

219. *PhS*, § 745; *PhG*, 398.

220. *PhS*, § 745; *PhG*, 398.

221. *PhS*, § 745; *PhG*, 398. Cf. *Aesthetics* II, 1201; *Aesthetik* III, 536.

222. *Aesthetics* II, 1199; *Aesthetik* III, 533.

223. *Aesthetics* II, 1202; *Aesthetik* III, 537.

224. *PhS*, § 745; *PhG*, 398.

225. *PhS*, § 746; *PhG*, 398–99.

226. *PhS*, § 747; *PhG*, 399.

227. *Phil. of Hist.*, 252; *VPG*, 330: "That very subjective freedom which constitutes the principle and determines the peculiar form of freedom in *our* world . . . could not manifest itself in Greece otherwise than as a *destructive* element."

228. *Phil. of Hist.*, 253; *VPG*, 330–31.

229. Cf. *Hist. of Phil.* I, 407; *VGP* II, 71.

230. *PhS*, § 747; *PhG*, 399.

231. *Phil. of Hist.*, 249; *VPG*, 325–26.

232. *Phil. of Hist.*, 249; *VPG*, 326.

233. *PhS*, § 770; *PhG*, 410. Cf. *Phil. of Religion* III, 2; *VPR* II, 219: "The three forms indicated are: eternal being in and with itself, the form of universality; the form of manifestation or appearance, that of particularization, being for another; the form of the return from appearance into itself, absolute singleness or individuality."

234. *PhS*, § 767; *PhG*, 409.

235. *PhS*, § 769; *PhG*, 410.

236. *PhS*, § 762; *PhG*, 407.

237. *PhS*, § 755; *PhG*, 403.

238. *PhS*, § 755; *PhG*, 403.

239. Cf. *PhS*, § 752; *PhG*, 401 (cited above): "We see that this unhappy consciousness constitutes the counterpart and the completion of the comic consciousness."

240. *PhS*, § 753; *PhG*, 402.

241. *PhS*, § 752; *PhG*, 401. Cf. *PhS*, § 785; *PhG*, 419.

242. Cf. Roger Garaudy, *Dieu est mort: Étude sur Hegel* (Paris: Presses Universitaires de France, 1962); Christian Link, *Hegels Wort "Gott selbst ist tot"* (Zürich: Theologischer Verlag, 1974).

243. *PhS*, § 748; *PhG*, 400.

244. Cf. *PhS*, § 754; *PhG*, 403: "These forms . . . the destructive ferocity of the freed elements of the content, as also the person as *thought* in Stoicism, and the unstable restlessness of the skeptical consciousness, constitute the periphery

of shapes which stands impatiently expectant round the birthplace of Spirit as it becomes self-consciousness."

245. *PhS*, § 754; *PhG*, 402.

246. *PhS*, § 758; *PhG*, 404.

247. *PhS*, § 759; *PhG*, 405.

248. *Phil. of Hist.*, 15; *VPG*, 41. Cf. *PhS*, § 769; *PhG*, 405: "In this religion the divine being is *revealed*. Its being revealed obviously consists in this, that what it is, is known. But it is known precisely in its being known as Spirit, as a being that is essentially a *self-conscious being*." Cf. *PhS*, § 761; *PhG*, 406–7: "Here, therefore, God is *revealed as he is*; he is immediately present as he is *in himself*, i.e. he is immediately *present* as Spirit."

249. *PhS*, § 759; *PhG*, 406.

250. *PhS*, § 761; *PhG*, 407.

251. Cf. *PhS*, § 762; *PhG*, 407: "This Notion of Spirit that knows itself as Spirit is itself the immediate Notion and is not yet developed."

252. *PhS*, § 766; *PhG*, 408.

253. *PhS*, § 773; *PhG*, 411.

254. *Phil. of Mind*, § 567; *Enz.*, 402.

255. *ETW*, 186; *TJ*, 246.

256. *PhS*, § 759; *PhG*, 405.

257. *PhS*, § 774; *PhG*, 412.

258. *PhS*, § 774; *PhG*, 412.

259. *PhS*, § 766; *PhG*, 408.

260. *PhS*, § 775; *PhG*, 412.

261. *PhS*, § 777; *PhG*, 414.

262. *PhS*, § 769; *PhG*, 410.

263. *PhS*, § 774; *PhG*, 412.

264. *PhS*, § 755; *PhG*, 403.

265. *PhS*, § 761; *PhG*, 406.

266. *PhS*, § 761; *PhG*, 406–7.

267. *PhS*, § 759; *PhG*, 406.

268. *PhS*, § 777; *PhG*, 414.

269. Cf. *ETW*, 193; *TJ*, 252: "The holy was always outside them, unseen and unfelt."

270. *Phil. of Religion* III, 96; *VPR* II, 305.

271. *Phil. of Religion* III, 96; *VPR* II, 305. Cf. *Phil. of Religion* III, 96; *VPR* II, 304: "God has through death reconciled the world, and reconciled it eternally with himself." Cf. also *Phil. of Hist.*, 323; *VPG*, 415.

272. *PhS*, § 778; *PhG*, 414.

273. *Phil. of Mind*, § 568; *Enz.*, 402.

274. *PhS*, § 778; *PhG*, 414.

275. *PhS*, § 779; *PhG*, 415

276. *PhS*, § 781; *PhG*, 417.

277. *PhS*, § 781; *PhG*, 417.

278. *Phil. of Mind*, § 569; *Enz.*, 402.

279. *ETW*, 289; *TJ*, 332.

280. *PhS*, § 785; *PhG*, 418. Cf. *Phil. of Religion* III, 103–4; *VPR* II, 311–12: "It follows from this that it is not merely the corporeal form and the body of Christ which is able to satisfy the sensuous need, but rather the sensuous aspect of his bodily presence in general, the cross, the places in which he moved about, and so on. To this, relics, etc., come to be added. There is no lack of such mediate means of satisfying the craving felt."

281. *PhS*, § 785; *PhG*, 418–19.

282. *Phil. of Religion* III, 104; *VPR*, II, 312.

283. *Phil. of Religion* III, 102–3; *VPR* II, 311.

284. *ETW*, 251; *TJ*, 299.

285. *ETW*, 251; *TJ*, 300.

286. *PhS*, § 780; *PhG*, 415.

287. *PhS*, § 784; *PhG*, 418.

288. Cf. *Phil. of Religion* III, 106; *VPR* II, 314.

289. *PhS*, § 772; *PhG*, 411.

290. *Phil. of Religion* III, 106; *VPR* II, 314.

291. *Phil. of Religion* III, 107; *VPR* II, 315.

292. *PhS*, § 770; *PhG*, 410.

293. *PhS*, § 785; *PhG*, 419. Cf. *Phil. of Religion* III, 91, 98; *VPR* II, 300, 306.

294. *PhS*, § 786; *PhG*, 419.

295. *PhS*, § 762; *PhG*, 407.

296. *PhS*, § 762; *PhG*, 407.

297. *PhS*, § 763; *PhG*, 408.

298. *PhS*, § 764; *PhG*, 408.

299. *PhS*, § 765; *PhG*, 408.

300. *PhS*, § 771; *PhG*, 411.

301. *ETW*, 300–1; *TJ*, 341.

302. *PhS*, § 771; *PhG*, 411.

303. For Hegel's most complete account, see "The Position of the Philosophy of Religion Relatively to Philosophy and Religion," *Phil. of Religion* I, 18–35; *VPR* I, 24–52. Cf. Quentin Lauer, "Hegel on the Identity of Content in Religion and Philosophy," in *Hegel and the Philosophy of Religion*, ed. Darrel E. Christensen (The Hague: Nijhoff, 1970), 261–78; Walter Kaufmann, *Hegel: A Reinterpretation* (Notre Dame: University of Notre Dame Press, 1978), 272–73.

304. *PhS*, § 788; *PhG*, 422.

305. *EL*, § 1; *Enz.*, 27.

306. *PR*, § 270, Remark; *RP*, 349. Cf. *Encyclopaedia Logic*, § 45, Remark; *Werke*, vol. 8, 123: "Absolute idealism . . . is by no means merely restricted to philosophy. It lies at the root of all religion; for religion too believes the actual world we see, the sum total of existence, to be created and governed by God."

307. Cf. *PhS*, § 802; *PhG*, 430: "The content of religion proclaims earlier in time than does science, what *Spirit is*, but only science is its true knowledge of itself."

308. This interpretation is confirmed by Hegel's announcement of the

publication of the *Phenomenology*, in which he clearly separates "Religion" from the other forms of consciousness and associates it with truth and science: "The *Phenomenology* contains within itself the various forms of Spirit as stations along the road by which it becomes pure knowing or Absolute Spirit. . . . The ultimate truth is found at first in religion and then in science as the result of the whole.*"* Cited from Hoffmeister's Introduction in his edition of the *Phänomenologie des Geistes* (Hamburg: Meiner, 1952), xxxviii.

309. *PhS*, § 765; *PhG*, 408. Cf. also *PhS*, § 771; *PhG*, 410–11. *PhS*, § 787; *PhG*, 420–21.

310. *PhS*, § 678; *PhG*, 365.

Chapter 9

1. Cf. *Phil. of Hist.*, 103; *VPG*, 150: "The history of the world travels from East to West, for Europe is absolutely the end of history." See Reinhart Klemens Maurer, "Teleologische Aspekte der Hegelschen Philosophie," in his *Hegel und das Ende der Geschichte* (Freiburg: Karl Alber, 1980), 173–208; Joseph L. Esposito, "Hegel, Absolute Knowledge, and the End of History," *Clio* 12 (1983), 355–65.

2. Cf. Nietzsche, *Untimely Mediations* II, "On the Uses and Disadvantages of History for Life," trans. R. J. Hollingdale (Cambridge: Cambridge University Press, 1983), § 8, p. 104: "For Hegel the climax and terminus of the world-process coincided with his own existence in Berlin."

3. William Torrey Harris, *Hegel's Logic: A Book on the Genesis of the Categories of the Mind—a Critical Exposition* (Chicago: Griggs, 1890), 120.

4. See Lisabeth During, "Hegel's Critique of Transcendence," *Man and World* 21 (1988), 287–305.

5. Charles Taylor, *Hegel* (Cambridge: Cambridge University Press, 1975).

6. J. M. E. McTaggart, *Studies in the Hegelian Dialectic* (Cambridge: Cambridge University Press, 1896); *Studies in Hegelian Cosmology* (Cambridge: Cambridge University Press, 1901); *A Commentary on Hegel's Logic* (Cambridge: Cambridge University Press, 1910); *The Nature of Existence* (Cambridge: Cambridge University Press, vol. 1, 1921; vol. 2, 1927).

7. *PhS*, § 789; *PhG*, 422–23.

8. *PhS*, § 790; *PhG*, 423.

9. *PhS*, § 790; *PhG*, 423.

10. *PhS*, § 790; *PhG*, 423.

11. *PhS*, § 791; *PhG*, 423: "This moment manifested itself for consciousness in pure insight and enlightenment."

12. *PhS*, § 791; *PhG*, 423–24.

13. *PhS*, § 792; *PhG*, 424.

14. *PhS*, § 792; *PhG*, 424.

15. *PhS*, § 795; *PhG*, 425–26: "The 'beautiful soul' is its own knowledge of itself in its pure, transparent unity—the self-consciousness that knows this pure knowledge of *pure inwardness* as Spirit."

16. *PhS*, § 795; *PhG*, 426.

17. *PhS*, § 796; *PhG*, 427.

18. Solomon implies just this: Robert C. Solomon, *In the Spirit of Hegel* (Oxford: Oxford University Press, 1983), 635.

19. *PhS*, § 808; *PhG*, 433.

20. *PhS*, § 798; *PhG*, 427. Cf. *PhS*, § 797; *PhG*, 427: "Our *own* act here has been simply to *gather together* the separate moments, each of which in principle exhibits the life of Spirit in its entirety, and also to stick to the Notion in the form of the Notion." Cf. *Hist. of Phil.* III, 551; *VGP* III, 689: "To know opposition in unity, and unity in opposition—this is absolute knowledge, and science is the knowledge of this unity in its whole development by means of itself."

21. *PhS*, § 801; *PhG*, 428–29.

22. *PhS*, § 788; *PhG*, 422.

23. *PhS*, § 798; *PhG*, 427. Cf. *PR*, § 352; *RP*, 451: "The concrete Ideas, the minds of the nations, have their truth and their destiny in the concrete Idea which is absolute universality, i.e. in the world mind. . . . As mind, it is nothing but its active movement towards absolute knowledge of itself and therefore towards freeing its consciousness from the form of natural immediacy and so coming to itself."

24. *PhS*, § 802; *PhG*, 429.

25. *PhS*, § 17; *PhG*, 18.

26. *PhS*, § 797; *PhG*, 427.

27. *PhS*, § 803; *PhG*, 430–31.

28. *PhS*, § 788; *PhG*, 422.

29. *PhS*, § 798; *PhG*, 427.

30. *PhS*, § 801; *PhG*, 429.

31. *PhS*, § 801; *PhG*, 429.

32. *PhS*, § 805; *PhG*, 432.

33. *PhS*, § 802; *PhG*, 429–30.

34. *PhS*, § 800; *PhG*, 428.

35. See Adriaan Peperzak, *Philosophy and Politics: A Commentary on the Preface to Hegel's "Philosophy of Right"* (Dordrecht: Nijhoff, 1987), 115ff; Eugène Fleischmann, *La philosophie politique de Hegel sous forme d'un commentaire des fondaments de la philosophie du droit* (Paris: Librairie Plon, 1964), 8–9.

36. *PR*, Preface 12–13; *RP*, 36–37:

As the thought of the world, it [philosophy] appears only when actuality is already there cut and dried after its process of formation has been completed. The teaching of the concept, which is also history's inescapable lesson, is that it is only when actuality is mature that the ideal first appears over against the real and that the ideal apprehends this same real world in its substance and builds it up for itself into the shape of an intellectual realm. When philosophy paints its grey in grey, then has a shape of life grown old. By philosophy's grey in grey it cannot be rejuvenated but only understood. The owl of Minerva spreads its wings only with the falling of the dusk.

37. *PhS*, § 789; *PhG*, 428.

38. *PhS*, § 805; *PhG*, 431–32. Cf. also *PhS*, § 805; *PhG*, 432: "Spirit, therefore, having won the Notion, displays its existence and movement in this ether of its life and is *Science.*"

39. *PhS*, § 808; *PhG*, 433–34.

40. *EL*, § 45, Remark; *Werke*, vol. 8, 122–23.

41. *Phil. of Hist.*, 15; *VPG*, 42. Cf. *Phil. of Hist.*, 457; *VPG*, 569: "That the history of the world, with all the changing scenes which its annals present, is this process of development and the realization of Spirit—this is the true theodicy, the justification of God in history. Only *this* insight can reconcile Spirit with the history of the world."

42. *PR*, Preface 12; *RP*, 35. See Peperzak, 105ff.

43. Hegel to Schelling [95], Bamberg, 1 May 1807. *Letters*, 80; *Briefe* I, 159–62.

Bibliography

The following bibliography was assembled largely with the help of the following works: Kurt Steinhauer, *Hegel Bibliography: Background Material on the International Reception of Hegel within the Context of the History of Philosophy* (New York, London, Paris: Saur, 1980); *Répertoire bibliographique de la Philosophie* (Louvain-la-Neuve: Éditions de l'Institut Supérieur de Philosophie, 1946–91); Pierre-Jean Labarrière, Gwendoline Jarczyk, and Jean-Louis Schlegel, "Bulletin de littérature hégélienne," *Archives de Philosophie* 44 (1981), 277–330.

General Works and Commentaries on Hegel's Philosophy as a Whole

Aboulafia, Mitchell. *The Self-Winding Circle: A Study of Hegel's System.* St. Louis: Warren H. Green, 1982.

Bloch, Ernst. *Subjekt-Objekt: Erläuterungen zu Hegel.* Berlin: Aufbau-Verlag, 1952; Frankfurt: Suhrkamp, 1962.

Butler, Clark. *G.W.F. Hegel.* Boston: Twayne Publishers, 1977.

Caird, Edward. *Hegel.* Edinburgh and London: W. Blackwood and Sons, 1903.

Daniel, Claus. *Hegel Verstehen: Eine Einführung in sein Denken.* Frankfurt and New York: Campus, 1983.

Findlay, John. *Hegel: A Re-Examination.* London: Allen and Unwin, 1958.

Fischer, Kuno. *Hegels Leben, Werke und Lehre.* Heidelberg: Winters, 1901.

Haering. Theodor. *Hegel, sein Wollen und sein Werk.* 2 vols. Leipzig and Berlin: Teubner, 1929, 1938.

Harris, Errol E. *The Spirit of Hegel.* Atlantic Highlands: Humanities Press, 1993.

Haym, Rudolf. *Hegel und seine Zeit: Vorlesungen über Entstehung und Entwicklung, Wesen und Werth der hegel'schen Philosophie.* Berlin: Rudolf Gaertner, 1857; reprint, Hildesheim: Olms, 1962.

Houlgate, Stephen. *Freedom, Truth, and History: An Introduction to Hegel's Philosophy.* London: Routledge, 1991.

Inwood, Michael J. *Hegel.* London: Routledge and Kegan Paul, 1983.

Kainz, Howard P. *Paradox, Dialectic, and System: A Contemporary Reconstruction of the Hegelian Problematic.* University Park: Pennsylvania State University Press, 1988.

Kaufmann, Walter. *Hegel: A Reinterpretation.* Notre Dame: University of Notre Dame Press, 1978.

Lakebrink, Bernhard. *Studien zur Metaphysik Hegels.* Freiburg im Breisgau: Rombach and Co., 1969.

Litt, Theodor. *Hegel.* Heidelberg: Quelle und Meyer, 1953.

Longuenesse, Béatrice. *Hegel et la critique de la métaphysique.* Paris: Vrin, 1981.

Marcuse, Herbert. *Reason and Revolution: Hegel and the Rise of Social Theory.* New York: Beacon Press, 1960.

Moog, Willy. *Hegel und die Hegelsche Schule.* Munich: Ernst Reinhardt, 1930.

Moran, Philip. *Hegel and the Fundamental Problems of Philosophy.* Amsterdam: B. R. Grüner Publishing Co., 1988.

Mure, G. R. G. *An Introduction to Hegel.* Oxford: Clarendon Press, 1948.

———. *The Philosophy of Hegel.* Oxford: Oxford University Press, 1965; Bristol: Thoemmes Press, 1993.

Pippin, Robert. *Hegel's Idealism: The Satisfactions of Self-Consciousness.* Cambridge: Cambridge University Press, 1989.

Plant, Raymond. *Hegel: An Introduction.* Oxford: Basil Blackwell, 1983.

Puntel, L. Bruno. *Darstellung, Methode und Struktur: Untersuchung zur Einheit der systematischen Philosophie G.W. F. Hegels.* Bonn: Bouvier, 1973.

Rockmore, Tom. *Before and After Hegel: A Historical Introduction to Hegel's Thought.* Berkeley: University of California Press, 1993.

Rosen, Stanley. *G.W. F. Hegel: An Introduction to the Science of Wisdom.* New Haven: Yale University Press, 1974.

Seeberger, Wilhelm. *Hegel oder die Entwicklung des Geistes zur Freiheit.* Stuttgart: Ernst Klett Verlag, 1961.

Singer, Peter. *Hegel.* Oxford: Oxford University Press, 1983.

Soll, Ivan. *An Introduction to Hegel's Metaphysics.* Chicago: University of Chicago Press, 1969.

Stirling, James Hutchison. *The Secret of Hegel: Being the Hegelian System in Origin, Principle, Form and Matter.* London: Longman, Roberts and Green, 1865.

Taylor, Charles. *Hegel.* Cambridge: Cambridge University Press, 1975.

Topp, Christian. *Philosophie als Wissenschaft.* Berlin: de Gruyter, 1982.

White, Allen. *Absolute Knowledge: Hegel and the Problem of Metaphysics.* Athens: Ohio University Press, 1983.

Commentaries on the Whole or Parts of the *Phenomenology*

Beaufort, Jan. *Die drei Schlüsse: Untersuchungen zur Stellung der Phänomenologie in Hegels System der Wissenschaft.* Würzburg: Königshausen und Neumann, 1983.

Becker, Werner. *Hegels "Phänomenologie des Geistes": Eine Interpretation.* Stuttgart: Kohlhammer, 1971.

Boey, Conrad. *L'Esprit devenu étranger à soi-même: Une Monographie consacrée à la figur du même nom dans 'La Phénoménologie de l'esprit' de G.W. F. Hegel.* Paris: Desclée de Brower, 1968.

Claesges, Ulrich. *Darstellung des erscheinenden Wissens: Systematische Einleitung in Hegels "Phänomenologie des Geistes."* Bonn: Bouvier, 1974.

Dudeck, Caroline U. *Hegel's "Phenomenology of Mind": Analysis and Commentary*. Lanham: University Press of America, 1982.

Findlay, John. "Analysis of the Text." In *Hegel's Phenomenology of Spirit*. Translated by A.V. Miller. Oxford: Oxford University Press, 1977. 479–592.

Fink, Eugen. *Hegel: Phänomenologische Interpretationen der "Phänomenologie des Geistes."* Frankfurt: Klostermann, 1977.

Flay, Joseph. *Hegel's Quest for Certainty*. Albany: SUNY Press, 1984.

Forster, Michael N. *Hegel's Idea of a Phenomenology of Spirit*. Chicago: University of Chicago Press, 1998.

Graeser, Andreas. *Einleitung zur "Phänomenologie des Geistes": Kommentar*. Stuttgart: Reclam, 1988.

Hansen, Frank-Peter. *G.W.F. Hegel: "Phänomenologie des Geistes."* Paderborn: Schöningh, 1994.

Harris, H. S. *Hegel's Ladder*. Vol. 1: *The Pilgrimage of Reason*. Vol. 2: *The Odyssey of Spirit*. Indianapolis: Hackett, 1997.

Heidegger, Martin. *Hegel's "Phenomenology of Spirit."* Translated by Parvis Emadt and Kenneth May. Bloomington: Indiana University Press, 1988.

Heinrichs, Johannes. *Die Logik der "Phänomenologie des Geistes."* Bonn: Bouvier, 1974.

Hessing, J. *Das Selbstbewußtwerden des Geistes*. Stuttgart: Frommann, 1936.

Hyppolite, Jean. *Genèse et structure de la "Phénoménologie de l'esprit" de Hegel*. Paris: Aubier, 1946. *Genesis and Structure of Hegel's "Phenomenology of Spirit."* Translated by Samuel Cherniak and John Heckman. Evanston: Northwestern University Press, 1974.

Jamros, Daniel P. *The Human Shape of God: Religion in Hegel's "Phenomenology of Spirit."* New York: Paragon House, 1994.

Kähler, Klaus, and Werner Marx. *Die Vernunft in Hegels "Phänomenologie des Geistes."* Frankfurt: Klostermann, 1992.

Kainz, Howard P. *Hegel's Phenomenology, Part 1: Analysis and Commentary*. Alabama: University of Alabama Press, 1976; Athens: Ohio University Press, 1988. *Part 2: The Evolution of Ethical and Religious Consciousness to the Absolute Standpoint*. Athens: Ohio University Press, 1983.

Kamm, Peter. *Hegels Vorrede zur "Phänomenologie des Geistes."* Garus: Tschudi, 1939.

Kettner, Matthias. *Hegels Sinnliche Gewißheit*. Frankfurt: Campus, 1990.

Kimmerle, Gerd. *Sein und Selbst: Untersuchung zur kategorialen Einheit von Vernunft und Geist in Hegels "Phänomenologie des Geistes."* Bonn: Bouvier, 1978.

Kojève, Alexandre, *Introduction à la lecture de Hegel*. Paris: Gallimard, 1947. *An Introduction to the Reading of Hegel*. Edited by Alan Bloom, translated by J. H. Nichols. Ithaca: Cornell University Press, 1969.

Krahl, Hans-Jürgen. *Erfahrung des Bewußtseins: Kommentare zu Hegels Einleitung der "Phänomenologie des Geistes" und Exkurse zur materialistischen Erkenntnistheorie*. Frankfurt: Materialis Verlag, 1979.

Labarrière, Pierre-Jean. *Structures et mouvement dialectique dans la "Phénoménologie de l'esprit" de Hegel*. Paris: Aubier, 1968.

Labarrière, Pierre-Jean, and Gwendoline Jarczyk. *Hegel: Les premiers combats de la reconnaissance, maîtrise et servitude dans la Phénoménologie de Hegel.* Paris: Aubier, 1987.

———. *Le malheur de la conscience ou l'accès à la raison. Liberté de l'autoconscience: stoïcisme, scepticisme et la conscience malheureuse. Texte et commentaire.* Paris: Aubier, 1989.

Lamb, David. *Hegel: From Foundation to System.* The Hague: Nijhoff, 1980.

Lauer, Quentin. *A Reading of Hegel's "Phenomenology of Spirit."* New York: Fordham University Press, 1982.

Liebrucks, Bruno. *Sprache und Bewußtsein.* Vol. 5: *Die zweite Revolution der Denkungsart. Hegel: "Phänomenologie des Geistes."* Frankfurt: Akademische Verlagsgesellschaft, 1970.

Loewenberg, Jacob. *Hegel's Phenomenology: Dialogues on the Life of the Mind.* La Salle: Open Court, 1965.

Marx, Werner. *Hegels "Phänomenologie des Geistes:" Die Bestimmung ihrer Idee in Vorrede und Einleitung.* Frankfurt: Klostermann, 1981. *Hegel's "Phenomenology of Spirit," Its Point and Purpose: A Commentary on the Preface and Introduction.* Translated by Peter Heath. New York: Harper and Row, 1975.

———. *Das Selbstbewußtsein in Hegels "Phänomenologie des Geistes."* Frankfurt: Klostermann, 1986.

Naeher, Jürgen. *Einführung in die idealistische Dialektik Hegels.* Opladen: Leske Verlag and Budrich GmbH, 1981.

Navickas, Joseph L. *Consciousness and Reality: Hegel's Philosophy of Subjectivity.* The Hague: Nijhoff, 1976.

Negele, Manfred. *Grade der Freiheit: Versuch einer Interpretation von G.W. F. Hegels "Phänomenologie des Geistes."* Würzburg: Königshausen and Neumann, 1991.

Nink, Caspar. *Kommentar zu den grundlegenden Abschnitten von Hegels "Phänomenologie des Geistes."* Regensburg: Josef Habbel, 1931.

Norman, Richard. *Hegel's Phenomenology: A Philosophical Introduction.* New York: St. Martin's Press, 1976; Sussex: Harvester Press, 1981.

Parry, David M. *Hegel's Phenomenology of the "We."* New York: Peter Lang, 1988.

Pinkard, Terry. *Hegel's Phenomenology: The Sociality of Reason.* Cambridge: Cambridge University Press, 1994.

Purpus, Wilhelm. *Zur Dialektik des Bewußtseins nach Hegel.* Berlin: Trowitzsch, 1908.

Rockmore, Tom. *Cognition: An Introduction to Hegel's Phenomenology of Spirit.* Berkeley: University of California Press, 1997.

Russon, John. *The Self and Its Body in Hegel's Phenomenology of Spirit.* Toronto: University of Toronto Press, 1997.

Scheier, Claus-Artur. *Analytischer Kommentar zu Hegels "Phänomenologie des Geistes." Die Architektonik des erscheinenden Wissens.* Freiburg: Karl Alber, 1980.

Shklar, Judith. *Hegel's Phenomenology.* Cambridge: Cambridge University Press, 1971.

Solomon, Robert C. *In the Spirit of Hegel.* Oxford: Oxford University Press, 1983.

Verene, Donald P. *Hegel's Recollection: A Study of Images in the "Phenomenology of Spirit."* Albany: SUNY Press, 1985.

Welker, Michael. *Das Verfahren von Hegels "Phänomenologie des Geistes" und die*

Funktion des Abschnitts: "Die offenbare Religion." Heidelberg: Ruprecht-Karls-Universität, 1978.

Well, Karlheinz. *Die schöne Seele und ihre sittliche Wirklichkeit.* Frankfurt: Peter Lang, 1986.

Westphal, Kenneth. *Hegel's Epistemological Realism: A Study of the Aim and Method of Hegel's "Phenomenology of Spirit."* Leuven: Kluwer Academic Publishers, 1989.

Westphal, Merold. *History and Truth in Hegel's Phenomenology.* Atlantic Highlands: Humanities Press, 1979.

Special Themes in the *Phenomenology*

Boey, Conrad. *L'aliénation dans la "Phénoménologie de l'esprit" de G.W. F. Hegel.* Paris: Desclée, De Brouwer, 1970.

Busse, Martin. *Hegels "Phänomenologie des Geistes" und der Staat.* Berlin: Junker and Dünnhaupt, 1931.

Fulda, Hans Friedrich. *Das Problem einer Einleitung in Hegels "Wissenschaft der Logik."* Frankfurt: Klostermann, 1965.

Gretic, Goran. *Das Problem des absoluten Wissens in Hegels "Phänomenologie des Geistes."* Zagreb: Universitäts-Verlag Liber, 1975.

Jung, Erich. *Entzweiung und Versöhnung in Hegels "Phänomenologie des Geistes."* Leipzig: Felix Meiner, 1940.

Lim, Sok-Zin. *Der Begriff der Arbeit bei Hegel: Versuch einer Interpretation der "Phänomenologie des Geistes."* Bonn: Bouvier, 1966.

Maurer, Reinhard Klemens. *Hegel und das Ende der Geschichte: Interpretationen zur "Phänomenologie des Geistes."* Stuttgart: Kohlhammer, 1965.

Ottmann, Horst Henning. *Das Scheitern einer Einleitung in Hegels Philosophie: Eine Analyse der "Phänomenologie des Geistes."* Munich: Verlag Anton Pustet, 1973.

Pöggeler, Otto. *Hegels Idee einer Phänomenologie des Geistes.* Freiburg: Karl Alber, 1973.

Robinson, Jonathan. *Duty and Hypocrisy in Hegel's "Phenomenology of Mind": An Essay in the Real and the Ideal.* Toronto: University of Toronto Press, 1977.

Shklar, Judith N. *Freedom and Independence: A Study of the Political Ideas in Hegel's "Phenomenology of Mind."* Cambridge: Cambridge University Press, 1976.

Smith, Henry B. *The Transition from Bewußtsein to Selbstbewußtsein.* Philadelphia: University of Pennsylvania Press, 1947.

Stiehler, Gottfried. *Die Dialektik in Hegels "Phänomenologie des Geistes."* Berlin: Akademie-Verlag, 1964.

Wahl, Jean. *Le Malheur de la conscience dans la philosophie de Hegel.* Paris: Presses Universitaires de France, 1951.

Collections on the *Phenomenology*

Browning, Gary K., ed. *Hegel's Phenomenology of Spirit: A Reappraisal.* Utrecht: Kluwer Academic Publishers, 1997.

Bulletin of the Hegel Society of Great Britain. Special issue: *Hegel's "Phenomenology of Spirit."* Vol. 29. (Spring/Summer 1994).

Fulda, Hans Friedrich, and Dieter Henrich, eds. *Materialien zu Hegels "Phänomenologie des Geistes."* Frankfurt: Suhrkamp, 1973.

Gadamer, Hans-Georg, ed. *Hegel-Tage Royaumont 1964: Beiträge zur Deutung der "Phänomenologie des Geistes."* Hegel-Studien, Beiheft 3. Bonn: Bouvier, 1966.

Stewart, Jon, ed. *The "Phenomenology of Spirit" Reader: A Collection of Critical and Interpretive Essays.* Albany: SUNY Press, 1998.

Westphal, Merold, ed. *Method and Speculation in Hegel's Phenomenology.* New Jersey: Humanities Press, 1982.

Hegel Journals

Annalen der Internationalen Gesellschaft für Dialektische Philosophie. Societas Hegeliana.

Bulletin of the Hegel Society of Great Britain.

Hegel-Jahrbuch.

Hegel-Studien.

Journal of Speculative Philosophy (St. Louis, 1867–93).

Jahrbuch für Hegelforschung.

The Owl of Minerva.

Hegel's Life

Althaus, Horst. *Hegel und die heroischen Jahre der Philosophie.* Munich: Hanser, 1992.

Beyer, Wilhelm R. *Zwischen Phänomenologie und Logik: Hegel als Redakteur der Bamberger Zeitung.* Frankfurt: G. Schulte-Bulmke, 1955.

Biedermann, Georg. *Georg Wilhelm Friedrich Hegel.* Cologne: Paul-Rugenstein, 1981.

Bondeli, Martin. *Hegel in Bern.* Hegel-Studien, Beiheft 33. Bonn: Bouvier, 1990.

Châtelet, François. *Hegel.* Paris: Éditions du Seuil, 1969.

D'Hondt, Jacques. *Hegel in His Time.* Translated by John Burbidge. New York: Broadview Press, 1988.

Fischer, Kuno. *Hegels Leben, Werke und Lehre.* Heidelberg: Winters, 1901.

Göschel, Karl Friedrich. *Hegel und seine Zeit.* Reprint of the 1832 edition. Frankfurt: Minerva, 1984.

Gulyga, Arseni. *Georg Wilhelm Friedrich Hegel.* Leipzig: Philipp Reclam, 1980.

Haering, Theodore. *Hegel: sein Wollen und sein Werk.* 2 vols. Leipzig and Berlin: Teubner, 1929, 1938.

Haym, Rudolf. *Hegel und seine Zeit: Vorlesungen über Entstehung und Entwicklung, Wesen und Werth der hegel'schen Philosophie.* Berlin: Rudolf Gaertner, 1857; reprint, Hildesheim: Olms, 1962.

Hosfeld, Rolf. *Georg Wilhelm Friedrich Hegel.* Berlin: Stapp, 1988.

Lemcke, Mechthild and Christa Hackenesch, ed. *Hegel in Tübingen.* Tübingen: Konkursbuchverlag, 1984.

Müller, Gustav E. *Hegel: The Man, His Vision and Work.* New York: Pageant Press, 1968. Originally, *Hegel Denkgeschichte eines Lebendigen.* Bern: Francke, 1959.

Nicolin, Friedhelm. *Hegel 1770–1970: Leben, Werk, Wirkung.* Eine Ausstellung des Archivs der Stadt Stuttgart. Stuttgart: Ernst Klett, 1970.

———. *Von Stuttgart nach Berlin: Die Lebensstationen Hegels. Marbacher Magazin,* 56. Marbach am Neckar: Deutsche Schillergesellschaft, 1991.

———. *Zur Situation der biographischen Hegel-Forschung.* Stuttgart: Ernst Klett, 1975.

Nicolin, Günter, ed. *Hegel in Berichten seiner Zeitgenossen.* Hamburg: Meiner, 1970.

Pöggeler, Otto, ed. *Hegel in Berlin.* Berlin: Staatsbibliothek Preußischer Kulturbesitz, 1981.

Rosenkranz, Karl. *Georg Wilhelm Friedrich Hegels Leben.* Berlin, 1844; reprint, Darmstadt: Wissenschaftliche Buchgesellschaft, 1963.

Sehring, Ludwig. *Hegel: Sein Leben und sein Wirken.* Berlin: Hermann Seeman Nachfolger Verlagsgesellschaft, 1904.

Widmann, Franz. *Hegel: An Illustrated Biography.* Translated by Joachim Neugroschel. New York: Pegasus, 1968. Originally, *Georg Wilhelm Friedrich Hegel in Selbstzeugnissen und Bilddokumenten.* Reinbek bei Hamburg: Rowohlt, 1965.

Hegel's Influence

Bernstein, Richard. "Why Hegel Now?" *Review of Metaphysics* 31 (1977), 29–60.

Bonsiepen, Wolfgang. "Erste zeitgenössische Rezensionen der *Phänomenologie des Geistes.*" *Hegel-Studien* 14 (1979), 9–38.

Brazill, William J. "Hegel in America." *Reports on Philosophy* 9 (1985), 83–92.

———. *The Young Hegelians.* New Haven: Yale University Press, 1970.

Crites, Stephen D. "Hegelianism." In the *Encyclopedia of Philosophy.* Vol. 3. Edited by Paul Edwards. New York: Macmillan Co. and the Free Press, 1967. 450–59.

Croce, Benedetto. *What Is Living and What Is Dead in the Philosophy of Hegel.* Translated by Douglas Ainslie. London: Macmillan and Co., 1915; reprint, New York: Russell and Russell, 1969.

Cullen, Bernard, ed. *Hegel Today.* Aldershot: Gower Publishing Company, 1988.

D'Hondt, Jacques. *Hegel et hégélianisme.* Paris, 1982.

Easton, Loyd. "Hegelianism in Ninteenth-Century Ohio." *Journal of the History of Ideas* 23 (1962), 355–78.

Erdmann, Johann E. *A History of Philosophy.* Vol. 3: *German Philosophy since Hegel.* Translated by W. S. Hough. London: S. Sonnenschein, 1890.

Findlay, John. "The Contemporary Relevance of Hegel." In *Hegel: A Collection of Critical Essays.* Edited by Alasdair MacIntyre. Notre Dame: University of Notre Dame Press, 1976. 1–20.

Gadamer, Hans-Georg, and Jürgen Habermas, eds. *Das Erbe Hegels.* Frankfurt: Suhrkamp, 1979.

Goetzmann, William H., ed. *The American Hegelians: An Intellectual Episode in the History of Western America.* New York: Knopf, 1973.

Haldar, Hiralal. *Neohegelianism.* New York: Garland, 1984.

Heede, Reinhard and Joachim Ritter. *Hegel-Bilanz: Zur Aktualität und Inaktualität der Philosophie Hegels.* Frankfurt: Klostermann, 1973.

Heidtmann, Bernhard, ed. *Hegel—Perspektiven seiner Philosophie heute.* Cologne: Pahl-Rugenstein, 1981.

Hyppolite, Jean. "La *Phénoménologie* de Hegel et la pensée française contemporaine." In his *Figures de la pensée philosophique: Écrits (1931–68).* Vol. 1. Paris: Presses Universitaires de France, 1971. 231–41.

Jakobson, Roman, et al., eds. *Das Erbe Hegels II.* Frankfurt: Suhrkamp, 1984.

Kaltenbrunner, G. K., ed. *Hegel und die Folgen.* Freiburg i.B.: Verlag Rombach, 1970.

Kroner, Richard. "Hegel Heute." *Hegel-Studien* 1 (1961), 135–54.

Labarrière, Pierre-Jean. "Hegel 150 ans après." *Archives de Philosophie* 44 (1981), 177–88.

Lasson, Georg. *Was heißt Hegelianismus?* Berlin: Reuther and Reichard, 1916.

Levy, Heinrich. *Die Hegel-Renaissance in der deutschen Philosophie.* Charlottenburg: Pan-Verlag, 1927.

Löwith, Karl, ed. *Die Hegelsche Linke.* Stuttgart: Frommann, 1962.

Lübbe, Hermann, ed. *Die Hegelsche Rechte.* Stuttgart: Frommann, 1962.

MacKintosh, Robert. *Hegel and Hegelianism.* New York: Charles Scribner's Sons, 1903.

Moog, Willy. *Hegel und die Hegelsche Schule.* Munich: Ernst Reinhardt, 1930.

Müller, Gustav E. "Hegel in Amerika." *Zeitschrift für Deutsche Kulturphilosophie* 5 (1939), 255–70.

Negt, O., ed. *Aktualität und Folgen der Philosophie Hegels.* Frankfurt: Suhrkamp, 1970.

Puntel, Bruno. "Hegel heute: Zur *Phänomenologie des Geistes.*" *Philosophisches Jahrbuch* 80 (1973), 133–60.

Régnier, M. "Hegel in France." *Bulletin of the Hegel Society of Great Britain* 8 (1983), 10–20.

Serreau, René. *Hegel et hégélianisme.* Paris: Presses Universitaires de France, 1963.

Simeunivic, Vojin. "Die Aktualität von Hegels *Phänomenologie des Geistes.*" *Praxis* 7 (1971), 73–83.

Smith, John E. "Hegel in St. Louis." In *Hegel's Social and Political Thought.* Edited by Donald Phillip Verene. Atlantic Highlands: Humanities Press, 1980. 215–25.

Taylor, Charles. "Hegel Today." In his *Hegel.* Cambridge: Cambridge University Press, 1975. 537–71.

Toews, John Edward. *Hegelianism: The Path toward Dialectical Humanism, 1805–41.* Cambridge: Cambridge University Press, 1980.

Watson, David. "Hegelianism in the United States." *Bulletin of the Hegel Society of Great Britain* 6 (1982), 18–28.

———. "The Neo-Hegelian Tradition in America." *Journal of American Studies* 14 (1980), 219–34.

The Kant-Hegel Relation

Alexander, J. Davidson. "Kant, Hegel and the Problem of Grounds." *Kant-Studien* 70 (1979), 451–70.

Ameriks, Karl. "Hegel's Critique of Kant's Theoretical Philosophy." *Philosophy and Phenomenological Research* 46 (1985), 1–35.

Burkhardt, Bernd. *Hegels Kritik an Kants theoretischer Philosophie dargestellt und beurteilt an den Themen der metaphysica specialis.* Munich: Profil, 1989.

Düsing, Klaus. "Constitution and Structure of Self-Identity: Kant's Theory of Apperception and Hegel's Criticism." *Midwest Studies in Philosophy* 8 (1983), 409–31.

———. "Die Rezeption der Kantischen Postulatenlehre in den frühen philosophischen Entwürfen Schellings und Hegels." In *Das älteste Systemprogramm: Studien zur Frühgeschichte des deutschen Idealismus.* Edited by Rüdiger Bubner. *Hegel-Studien,* Beiheft 9. Bonn: Bouvier, 1973. 53–90.

Fleischmann, Eugène J. "Hegels Umstaltung der Kantischen Logik." *Hegel-Studien* 3 (1965), 181–207.

Görland, Ingtraud. *Die Kantkritik des jungen Hegel.* Frankfurt: Klostermann, 1966.

Griffiss, James. "The Kantian Background of Hegel's Logic." *New Scholasticism* 43 (1969), 509–29.

Guéroult, Martial. "Le jugement de Hegel sur l'antithétique de la raison pure." *Revue de Métaphysique et de Morale* 38 (1931), 413–39.

Hartmann, Klaus. "On Taking the Transcendental Turn." *Review of Metaphysics* 20 (1966), 223–49.

Henrich, Dieter. "Kant und Hegel: Versuch einer Vereinigung ihrer Grundgedanken." In his *Selbstverhältnisse: Gedanken und Auslegungen zu den Grundlagen der klassischen deutschen Philosophie.* Stuttgart: Klett-Cotta, 1982. 173–208.

———, ed. *Kant oder Hegel? Über Formen der Begründung in der Philosophie. Stuttgarter Hegel-Kongress 1981.* Stuttgart: Klett-Cotta, 1983.

Hyppolite, Jean. "La critique hégélienne de la réflexion kantienne." In his *Figures de la pensée philosophique: Écrits (1931–68).* Vol. 1. Paris: Presses Universitaires de France, 1971. 175–95.

Kirscher, Gilbert. "Hegel et Jacobi Critiques de Kant." *Archives de Philosophie* 33 (1970), 801–28.

Klein, Hans-Dieter. "Kants Postulatenlehre und Hegels Philosophie des Geistes." In *Geschichte und System: Festschrift für Erich Heintel zum 60. Geburtstag.* Edited by Hans-Dieter Klein and Erhard Oeser. Vienna: Oldenbourg, 1972. 253–78.

Lauer, Quentin. "Hegel's Critique of Kant's Theology." In *God Knowable and Unknowable.* Edited by Robert J. Roth. New York: Fordham University Press, 1973. 85–105.

Maier, Josef. *On Hegel's Critique of Kant.* New York: Columbia University Press, 1939.

Marck, Siegfried. *Kant und Hegel: Eine Gegenüberstellung ihrer Grundbegriffe.* Tübingen: Mohr, 1917.

Philonenko, Alexis. "Hegel critique de Kant." *Bulletin de la Société Française de Philosophie* 63 (1969), 29–70.

Pippin, Robert B. "Kantian and Hegelian Idealism." In his *Hegel's Idealism: The Satisfactions of Self-Consciousness.* Cambridge: Cambridge University Press, 1989. 16–41.

Priest, Stephen, ed. *Hegel's Critique of Kant.* Oxford: Clarendon Press, 1987.

Pringle-Pattison, Andrew Seth. *The Development from Kant to Hegel.* London: Williams and Norgate, 1882.

Smith, John C. "Hegel's Critique of Kant." *Review of Metaphysics* 36 (1973), 438–60.

Soll, Ivan. *An Introduction to Hegel's Metaphysics.* Chicago: University of Chicago Press, 1969.

Stanguennec, André. *Hegel critique de Kant.* Paris: Presses Universitaires de France, 1985.

Stern, Robert. *Hegel, Kant, and the Structure of the Object.* New York: Routledge, 1990.

Werkmeister, William Henry. "Hegel's *Phenomenology of Mind* as a Development of Kant's Basic Ontology." In *Hegel and the Philosophy of Religion: The Wofford Symposium.* Edited by Darrel E. Christenson. The Hague: Nijhoff, 1970. 93–110.

Werner, Hans-Joachim. "Spekulative und transzendentale Dialektik: Zur Entwicklung des dialektischen Denkens im Deutschen Idealismus (Kant-Hegel)." *Philosophisches Jahrbuch* 81 (1974), 77–87.

Individual Chapters of the *Phenomenology*

Preface

Adelman, Howard. "Hegel's *Phenomenology*: Facing the Preface." *Idealistic Studies* 14 (1984), 159–70.

De la Iglesia Duarte, José-Ignacio. "Commentario al prólogo de la *Fenomenología de espíritu.*" *Crisis* 18 (1971), 194–200.

Finacchiaro, Maurice A. "Dialectic and Argument in Philosophy: A Case Study of Hegel's Phenomenological Preface." *Argumentation* 2 (1988), 175–90.

Flay, Joseph C. "Rupture, Closure, and Dialectic." *Bulletin of the Hegel Society of Great Britain* 29 (1994), 23–37.

Harris, H. S. "The Cows in the Dark Night." *Dialogue* (Canada) 26 (1987), 627–43.

Hyppolite, Jean. "Essai d'interprétation de la préface de la *Phénoménologie.*" In his *Figures de la pensée philosophique: Écrits (1931–68).* Vol. 1. Paris: Presses Universitaires de France, 1971. 275–308.

———. "Note sur la préface de la *Phénoménologie de l'esprit* et le thème: l'absolu est sujet." *Hegel-Tage Urbino 1965.* Edited by Hans-Georg Gadamer. *Hegel-Studien,* Beiheft 4. Bonn: Bouvier, 1969. 75–80.

———. "Structure du langage philosophique d'après la préface de la *Phénoménologie de l'esprit.*" In his *Figures de la pensée philosophique: Écrits (1931–68).* Vol. 1. Paris: Presses Universitaires de France, 1971. 340–52.

Jähing, Dieter. "Die Beseitigung der Geschichte durch 'Bildung' und 'Erinnerung.' " *Praxis* 7 (1971), 63–72.

Jamme, Christoph. "Platon, Hegel und der Mythos zu den Hintergründen eines Diktums aus der Vorrede zur *Phänomenologie des Geistes.*" *Hegel-Studien* 15 (1980), 151–69.

Kainz, Howard. "Hegel's Characterization of Truth in the Preface to His *Phenomenology.*" *Philosophy Today* 13 (1969–70), 206–13.

Kamm, Peter. *Hegels Vorrede zur "Phänomenologie des Geistes."* Garus: Tschudi, 1939.

Kaufmann, Walter. "The Preface to the *Phenomenology.*" In his *Hegel: Texts and Commentary.* Vol. 2. Garden City: Anchor, 1966. 6–110.

Liebrucks, Bruno. "Reflexionen über den Satz Hegels 'Das Wahre ist das Ganze.' " *Zeugnisse* (Frankfurt) (1963), 74–114.

Marx, Werner. *Hegel's "Phenomenology of Spirit," Its Point and Purpose: A Commentary on the Preface and Introduction.* Translated by Peter Heath. New York: Harper and Row, 1975. Originally, *Hegels "Phänomenologie des Geistes": Die Bestimmung ihrer Idee in "Vorrede" und "Einleitung."* Frankfurt: Klostermann, 1971.

Metzke, Erwin. "Vorrede zur *Phänomenologie des Geistes.*" In his *Hegels Vorreden mit Kommentar zur Einführung in seine Philosophie.* Heidelberg: F. H. Kerle, 1949. 137–208.

Philonenko, Alexis. *Lecture de la Phénoménologie de Hegel: Préface—Introduction.* Paris: Librarie Philosophique Joseph Vrin, 1993.

Rauch, Leo. "Hegel's *Phenomenology of Spirit* as a Phenomenological Project." *Thought* 56 (1981), 328–41.

Sallis, John. "Hegel's Concept of Presentation: Its Determination in the Preface to the *Phenomenology of Spirit.*" *Hegel-Studien* 12 (1977), 129–56.

Schacht, Richard. "A Commentary on the Preface to Hegel's *Phenomenology of Spirit.*" *Philosophical Studies* 23 (1972), 1–31.

Schmitz, Kenneth L. "Substance Is Not Enough: Hegel's Slogan: From Substance to Subject." *Proceedings of the Catholic Philosophers' Association* 61 (1987), 52–68.

Schulte, Günter. "Über die Weltlichkeit des Bewußtseins bei Hegel." *Kant-Studien* 64 (1973), 450–65.

Solomon, Robert C. "Approaching Hegel's *Phenomenology.*" *Philosophy Today* 13 (1969), 115–25.

———. "A Small Problem in Hegel's *Phenomenology.*" *Journal of the History of Philosophy* 13 (1975), 399–400.

Introduction

Bahti, Timothy. "The Indifferent Reader: The Performance of Hegel's Introduction to the *Phenomenology.*" *Diacritics* 11 (1981), 68–87.

Boeder, Heribert. "Das natürliche Bewußtsein." *Hegel-Studien* 12 (1977), 157–78.

Cramer, Konrad. "Bemerkungen zu Hegels Begriff vom Bewußtsein in der Einleitung zur Hegels *Phänomenologie des Geistes.*" In *Seminar: Dialektik in der*

Philosophie Hegels. Edited by Rolf-Peter Horstmann. Frankfurt: Suhrkamp, 1978. 360–97.

Dove, Kenley. "Hegel's Phenomenological Method." *Review of Metaphysics* 23 (1969–70), 641–61.

Fink, Eugen. "Hegels Problemformel 'Prüfung der Realität des Erkennens' in der *Phänomenologie des Geistes.*" *Praxis* 7 (1971), 39–47.

Graeser, Andreas. *Einleitung zur Phänomenologie des Geistes: Kommentar.* Stuttgart: Reclam, 1988.

Heidegger, Martin. *Hegel's Concept of Experience.* New York: Harper and Row, 1970.

Jähing, Dieter. "Die Beseitigung der Geschichte durch 'Bildung' und 'Erinnerung.'" *Praxis* 7 (1971), 63–72.

Krahl, Hans-Jürgen. *Erfahrung des Bewußtseins: Kommentare zu Hegels Einleitung der "Phänomenologie des Geistes" und Exkurse zur materialistischen Erkenntnistheorie.* Frankfurt: Materialis, 1979.

Krüger, Gerhard. "Die dialektische Erfahrung des natürlichen Bewußtseins bei Hegel." In *Hermeneutik und Dialektik.* Edited by Rüdiger Bubner, Konrad Cramer, and Reiner Wiehl. Tübingen: Mohr, 1970. 285–303.

Loewenberg, Jacob. "The Exoteric Approach to Hegel's *Phenomenology* (I)," *Mind* 43 (1934), 424–45.

Löwith, Karl. "Nachwort zu Hegels Einleitung in die *Phänomenologie des Geistes.*" In his *Aufsätze und Vorträge 1930–80.* Stuttgart: Kohlhammer, 1971. 204–10.

Marx, Werner. *Hegel's "Phenomenology of Spirit," Its Point and Purpose: A Commentary on the Preface and Introduction.* Translated by Peter Heath. New York: Harper and Row, 1975. Originally, *Hegels Phänomenologie des Geistes: Die Bestimmung ihrer Idee in "Vorrede" und "Einleitung."* Frankfurt: Klostermann, 1971.

Philonenko, Alexis. *Lecture de la Phénoménologie de Hegel: Préface—Introduction.* Paris: Librarie Philosophique Joseph Vrin, 1993.

Rauch, Leo. "Hegel's *Phenomenology of Spirit* as a Phenomenological Project." *Thought* 56 (1981), 328–41.

Schulte, Günter. "Über die Weltlichkeit des Bewußtseins bei Hegel," *Kant-Studien* 64 (1973), 450–65.

Van Riet, Georges. "Y-a-t-il un chemin vers la vérite? À propos de l'introduction à la *Phénoménologie de l'esprit* de Hegel." *Revue philosophique de Louvain* 62 (1964), 466–76.

Westphal, Kenneth, R. "Hegel's Solution of the Dilemma of the Criterion." *History of Philosophy Quarterly* 5 (1988), 173–88.

Consciousness

"Consciousness" in General

Becker, Werner. *Hegels Begriff der Dialektik und das Prinzip des Idealismus.* Stuttgart: Kohlhammer, 1969.

Breton, Stanislas. "La dialectique de la conscience dans la *Phénoménologie de l'esprit* de Hegel." *Euntes docete* 6 (1956), 323–60.

Cook, Daniel J. "Sprache und Bewußtsein in Hegels *Phänomenologie des Geistes*." *Hegel-Jahrbuch* (1970), 117–24.

De Nys, Martin J. "The Motion of the Universal: Hegel's Phenomenology of Consciousness." *Modern Schoolman* 56 (1978–79), 301–20.

Hossfeld, Paul. "Zur Auslegung der *Phänomenologie des Geistes* von Hegel." *Philosophisches Jahrbuch* 65 (1957), 232–44.

Nink, Caspar. *Kommentar zu den grundlegenden Abschnitten von Hegels "Phänomenologie des Geistes."* Regensburg: Habbel, 1948.

Purpus, Wilhelm. *Zur Dialektik des Bewußtseins nach Hegel.* Berlin: Trowitzsch, 1908.

Sobotka, Milan. "Die Auffassung des Gegenstandes in Hegels *Phänomenologie des Geistes*." *Wiener Jahrbuch für Philosophie* 8 (1975), 133–53.

Taylor, Charles. "The Opening Arguments of the *Phenomenology*." In *Hegel: A Collection of Critical Essays*. Edited by Alasdair MacIntyre. Notre Dame: University of Notre Dame Press, 1976. 151–87.

Sense-Certainty

De Nys, Martin. "Sense-Certainty and Universality: Hegel's Entrance into the *Phenomenology*." *International Philosophical Quarterly* 18 (1978), 445–65.

Donato, Eugenio. "Here, Now Always, Already." *Diacritics* 6 (1976), 24–29.

Dulckeit, Katharina. "Can Hegel Refer to Particulars?" *Owl of Minerva* 17 (1986), 181–94.

Düsing, Klaus. "Die Bedeutung des antiken Skeptizismus für Hegels Kritik der sinnlichen Gewißheit." *Hegel-Studien* 8 (1973), 119–30.

Eley, Lothar. "Sinnliche Gewißheit, Sprache und Gesellschaft." *Sprache im Technischen Zeitalter* 43 (1972), 205–14.

Graeser, Andreas. "Hegels Kritik der sinnlichen Gewißheit und Platons Kritik der Sinneswahrnehmung im *Theaitet*." *Revue de Philosophie Ancienne* 3 (1985), 39–57.

———. "Zu Hegels Portrait der sinnlichen Gewißheit." *Freiburger Zeitschrift für Philosophie und Theologie* 34 (1987), 437–53.

Kettner, Matthias. *Hegels Sinnliche Gewißheit.* Frankfurt: Campus, 1990.

Lamb, David. "Hegel and Wittgenstein on Language and Sense-Certainty." *Clio* 7 (1978), 285–301.

Loewenberg, Jacob. "The Comedy of Immediacy in Hegel's *Phenomenology* (II)." *Mind* 44 (1935), 21–38.

Marsh, James L. "The Play of Difference/Différance in Hegel and Derrida." *The Owl of Minerva* 21 (1990), 145–53.

Miklowitz, Paul S. "The Ontological Status of Style in Hegel's *Phenomenology*." *Idealistic Studies* 13 (1983), 61–73.

Naeher, Jürgen. *Einführung in die idealistische Dialektik Hegels.* Opladen: Leske Verlag and Budrich GmbH, 1981.

Plumer, Gilbert. "Hegel on Singular Demonstrative Reference." *Southwestern Journal of Philosophy* 11 (1980), 71–94.

Purpus, Wilhelm. *Die Dialektik der sinnlichen Gewißheit bei Hegel.* Nürnberg: Sebald, 1905.

Schulte, Günter. "Über die Weltlichkeit des Bewußtseins bei Hegel." *Kant-Studien* 64 (1973), 450–65.

Soll, Ivan. "Das Besondere und das Allgemeine in der sinnlichen Gewißheit bei Hegel." *Hegel-Jahrbuch* (1976), 283–87.

Verene, Donald Phillip. "*Das Meinen,* 'Meaning.' " In his *Hegel's Recollection: A Study of Images in the "Phenomenology of Spirit."* Albany: SUNY Press, 1985. 27–38.

Verneaux, R. "De la dialectique du sensible selon Hegel." *Sapienza* 21 (1968), 421–38.

Warminski, Andrzej. "Reading for Example 'Sense Certainty' in Hegel's *Phenomenology of Spirit.*" *Diacritics* 11 (1981), 83–96.

Wiehl, Reiner. "Über den Sinn der sinnlichen Gewißheit in Hegels *Phänomenologie des Geistes.*" *Hegel-Tage Royaumont 1964: Beiträge zur Deutung der "Phänomenologie des Geistes."* Edited by Hans-Georg Gadamer. *Hegel-Studien,* Beiheft 3. Bonn: Bouvier, 1966. 103–34.

Wieland, Wolfgang. "Hegels Dialektik der sinnlichen Gewißheit." In *Orbis Scriptus: Dmitrij Tschizewskij zum 70. Geburtstag.* Edited by Dietrich Gerhardt, Wiktor Weintraub, and Hans-Jürgen zum Winkel. Munich: Wilhelm Fink, 1966. 933–41. Reprinted in *Materialien zu Hegels "Phänomenologie des Geistes."* Edited by Hans Friedrich Fulda and Dieter Henrich. Frankfurt: Suhrkamp, 1973. 67–82.

Perception

Purpus, Wilhelm. *Die Dialektik der Wahrnehmung bei Hegel: Ein Beitrag zur Würdigung der "Phänomenologie des Geistes."* Part 1. Schweinfurt: Fr. J. Reichardts Buchdruckerei, 1908.

Vaught, Carl G. "Subject, Object, and Representation: A Critique of Hegel's Dialectic of Perception." *International Philosophical Quarterly* 26 (1986), 117–29.

Westphal, Merold. "Hegels Phänomenologie der Wahrnehmung." In *Materialien zu Hegels "Phänomenologie des Geistes."* Edited by Hans Friedrich Fulda and Dieter Henrich. Frankfurt: Suhrkamp, 1973. 83–105.

Force and the Understanding

Baur, Michael. "Hegel and the Overcoming of the Understanding." *Owl of Minerva* 22 (1991), 141–58.

Bossart, W. H. "Hegel on the Inverted World." *Philosophical Forum* 13 (1982), 326–41.

De Nys, Martin J. "Force and Understanding: The Unity of the Object of Consciousness." In *Method and Speculation in Hegel's Phenomenology.* Edited by Merold Westphal. Atlantic Highlands: Humanities Press, 1982. 57–70.

Domenico, Nicola de. "Die 'Verkehrte Welt.' Ein erneuter Versuch, eine reflexive Paradoxie der *Phänomenologie des Geistes* Hegels zu interpretieren." In *Philosophie als Verteidigung des Ganzen der Vernunft.* Edited by Domenico Losurdo and Hans Jörg Sandkühler. Cologne: Paul-Rugenstein, 1988.

Dooren, Win van. "Der Begriff der Materie in Hegels *Phänomenologie des Geistes.*" *Hegel-Jahrbuch* (1976), 84–89.

Fink, Eugen. "Die verkehrte Welt." In *Weltaspekte der Philosophie: Rudolph Berlinger zum 26. Oktober 1972.* Edited by Werner Beierwaltes and Wiebke Schrader. Amsterdam: Editions Rodopi N.V., 1972. 41–52.

Flay, Joseph. "Hegel's 'Inverted World.' " *Review of Metaphysics* 13 (1970), 662–78.

Gadamer, Hans-Georg. "Hegel's 'Inverted World.' " In his *Hegel's Dialectic: Five Hermeneutical Essays.* Translated by P. Christopher Smith. New Haven: Yale University Press, 1976. 35–53.

Goldstein, Leon J. "Force and the Inverted World in Dialectical Retrospection." *International Studies in Philosophy* 20 (1988), 13–28.

Greene, Murray. "Hegel's Notion of Inversion." *International Journal of the Philosophy of Religion* 1 (1970), 161–75.

Hartnack, Justus. "Hegel's Inverted World." In *Méthexis: Études néoplatoniciennes présentées au Professeur Évanghélos.* Athens: C.I.E.P.A., 1992. 235–42.

Horn, Joachim C. "Hegel's 'Wahrheit des Sinnlichen' oder die 'zweite übersinnliche Welt.' " *Kant-Studien* 54 (1963), 252–58.

Narski, Igor S. "Die verkehrte Welt, List des Verstandes und List der Vernunft bei Hegel." *Annalen der Internationalen Gesellschaft für Dialektische Philosophie* 1 (1983), 136–40.

Smith, Henry B. *The Transition from Bewußtsein to Selbstbewußtsein.* Philadephia: University of Pennsylvania Press, 1947.

Verene, Donald Phillip. "The Topsy-turvy World." In his *Hegel's Recollection: A Study of Images in the "Phenomenology of Spirit."* Albany: SUNY Press, 1985. 39–58.

Walter, Eric. "Force and Its Other: An Interpretation." *Iyyun* 19 (1968), 260–61.

Zimmerman, Robert. "Hegel's 'Inverted World' Revisited." *Philosophical Forum* 13 (1982), 342–70.

Zviglyanich, V. A. "The Inverted World in the *Phenomenology of Spirit* and Its Significance for the History of Cognition." *Hegel-Jahrbuch* (1991), 205–9.

Self-Consciousness

"Self-Consciousness" in General

Gadamer, Hans-Georg. "Hegel's Dialectic of Self-Consciousness." In his *Hegel's Dialectic: Five Hermeneutical Essays.* Translated by P. Christopher Smith. New Haven: Yale University Press, 1976. 54–74.

Kline, George L. "The Dialectic of Action and Passion in Hegel's *Phenomenology of Spirit.*" *Review of Metaphysics* 23 (1970), 679–89.

Kozo, Kunio. "Zur Chronologie von Hegels Nürnberger Fassungen des Selbstbewußtseinkapitels." *Hegel-Studien* 21 (1986), 27–64.

Marx, Werner. *Das Selbstbewußtsein in Hegels "Phänomenologie des Geistes."* Frankfurt: Klosterman, 1986.

McCumber, John. "A Mind-Body Problem in Hegel's *Phenomenology of Spirit.*" *International Studies in Philosophy* 12 (1980), 41–52.

Onyewoenyi, I. C. "Self-Consciousness in the Philosophy of Hegel." *Thought and Practice* 2 (1975), 125–34.

Pöggeler, Otto. "Hegels Phänomenologie des Selbstbewußtseins." In his *Hegels Idee einer Phänomenologie des Geistes.* Freiburg: Karl Alber, 1973. 231–98.

Rauch, Leo. "Desire, an Elemental Passion in Hegel's *Phenomenology.*" *Analecta Husserliana* 28 (1990), 193–207.

Soll, Ivan. "Philosophy, Truth, and Human Activity." In his *An Introduction to Hegel's Metaphysics.* Chicago: University of Chicago Press, 1969. 3–46.

The Truth of Self-Certainty

Berenson, Frances. "Hegel on Others and the Self." *Philosophy* 57 (1982), 77–90.

Hanzig, Evelyn. "'Hemmung der Begierde'—Zur Dialektik des Selbstbewußtseins: Die Nahtstelle zwischen Hegel und Freud." *Hegel-Jahrbuch* (1984–85), 309–18.

Harris, H. S. "Les influences platoniciennes sur la théorie de la vie et du désir dans la *Phénoménologie de l'esprit* de Hegel." *Revue de Philosophie Ancienne* 3 (1985), 59–94.

Hyppolite, Jean. "Situation de l'homme dans la phénoménologie hégélienne." In his *Figures de la pensée philosophique: Écrits (1931–68).* Vol. 1. Paris: Presses Universitaires de France, 1971. 104–21. Originally in *Les Temps Modernes* 2 (1947), 1276–89.

Marcuse, Herbert. "Leben als Seinsbegriff in der *Phänomenologie des Geistes.*" In his *Hegels Ontologie und die Grundlegung einer Theorie der Geschichtlichkeit.* Frankfurt: Klostermann, 1968. 257–62.

Neuhouser, Frederick. "Deducing Desire and Recognition in the *Phenomenology of Spirit.*" *Journal of the History of Philosophy* 24 (1986), 243–62.

Rauch, Leo. "Desire, an Elemental Passion in Hegel's *Phenomenology.*" *Analecta Husserliana* 28 (1990), 193–207.

Römpp, Georg. "Ein Selbstbewußtsein für ein Selbstbewußtsein: Bemerkungen zum Kapital 'Die Wahrheit der Gewißheit seiner selbst' in Hegels *Phänomenologie des Geistes.*" *Hegel-Studien* 23 (1988), 71–94.

Lordship and Bondage

Adelman, Howard. "Of Human Bondage: Labor, Bondage, and Freedom in the *Phenomenology.*" In *Hegel's Social and Political Thought.* Edited by Donald Phillip Verene. Atlantic Highlands: Humanities Press, 1980. 119–35.

Becker, Werner. "Hegels Dialektik von Herr und Knecht." In his *Selbstbewußtsein und Spekulation: Zur Kritik der Transzendentalphilosophie.* Freiburg: Rombach, 1972.

———. *Idealistische und materialistische Dialektik: Das Verhältnis von Herrschaft und Knechtschaft bei Hegel und Marx.* Stuttgart: Kohlhammer, 1970.

Bernstein, J. M. "From Self-Consciousness to Community: Act and Recognition in the Master-Slave Relationship." In *The State and Civil Society: Studies in Hegel's Political Philosophy.* Edited by Z. Pelczynski. Cambridge: Cambridge University Press, 1984. 14–39.

Butler, Judith P. *Subjects of Desire: Hegelian Reflections in Twentieth-Century France.* New York: Columbia University Press, 1987.

Duquette, Daniel. "The Political Significance of Hegel's Concept of Recognition in the *Phenomenology.*" *Bulletin of the Hegel Society of Great Britain* 29 (1994), 38–54.

Fetscher, Iring. "Randglossen zu 'Herrschaft und Knechtschaft' in Hegels *Phänomenologie des Geistes.*" In *Wirklichkeit und Reflexion: Walter Schulz zum 60. Geburtstag.* Edited by Helmut Fahrenbach. Pfullingen: Neske, 1973. 137–44.

Gloy, Karen. "Bemerkungen zum Kapitel 'Herrschaft und Knechtschaft' in Hegels *Phänomenologie des Geistes.*" *Zeitschrift für Philosophische Forschung* 39 (1985), 187–213.

Gumppenberg, Rudolf. "Bewußtsein und Arbeit: Zu G. W. F. Hegels *Phänomenologie des Geistes.*" *Zeitschrift für Philosophische Forschung* 26 (1972), 372–88.

Hanzig, Evelyn. " 'Hemmung der Begierde'—Zur Dialektik des Selbstbewußtseins: Die Nahtstelle zwischen Hegel und Freud." *Hegel-Jahrbuch* (1984–85), 309–18.

Harris, H. S. "The Concept of Recognition in Hegel's Jena Manuscripts." In *Hegel in Jena.* Edited by Dieter Henrich and Klaus Düsing. *Hegel-Studien,* Beiheft 20. Bonn: Bouvier, 1980. 229–48.

Holz, Hans Heinz. *Herr und Knecht bei Leibniz und Hegel.* Neuwied: Luchterhand, 1968.

Janke, Wolfgang. "Herrschaft und Knechtschaft und der absolute Herr." *Philosophische Perspektiven* 4 (1972), 211–31.

Jarczyk, Gwendoline, and Pierre-Jean Labarrière. *Les premiers combats de la reconnaissance: Maîtrise et servitude dans la "Phénoménologie de l'esprit" de Hegel.* Paris: Aubier, 1987.

Jurist, Eliot. "Hegel's Concept of Recognition." *Owl of Minerva* 19 (1987), 5–22.

———. "Recognition and Self-Knowledge." *Hegel-Studien* 21 (1986), 143–50.

Kelly, George A. "Notes on Hegel's Lordship and Bondage." *Review of Metaphysics* 19 (1965), 780–802. Also in *Hegel: A Collection of Critical Essays.* Edited by Alasdair MacIntyre. Notre Dame: University of Notre Dame Press, 1976. In German as "Bemerkungen zu Hegels 'Herrschaft und Knechtschaft.' " In *Materialien zu Hegels "Phänomenologie des Geistes."* Edited by Hans-Friedrich Fulda and Dieter Henrich. Frankfurt: Suhrkamp, 1973. 189–216.

Kojève, Alexandre. *Introduction à la lecture de Hegel.* Paris: Gallimard, 1947. *An*

Introduction to the Reading of Hegel. Edited by Allan Bloom, translated by J. H. Nichols. Ithaca: Cornell University Press, 1969.

Lim, Sok-Zin. *Der Begriff der Arbeit bei Hegel: Versuch einer Interpretation der "Phänomenologie des Geistes."* Bonn: Bouvier, 1966.

Mayer, Hans. "Herrschaft und Knechtschaft: Hegels Deutung, ihre literarischen Ursprünge und Folgen." *Jahrbuch der Deutschen Schillergesellschaft* 15 (1971), 251–79.

Neuhouser, Frederick. "Deducing Desire and Recognition in the *Phenomenology of Spirit.*" *Journal of the History of Philosophy* 24 (1986), 243–62.

Ottmann, Henning. "Herr und Knecht bei Hegel: Bemerkungen zu einer misverstandenen Dialektik." *Zeitschrift für Philosophische Forschung* 35 (1981), 365–84.

Preuss, Peter. "Selfhood and the Battle: The Second Beginning of the *Phenomenology.*" In *Method and Speculation in Hegel's Phenomenology.* Edited by Merold Westphal. Atlantic Highlands: Humanities Press, 1982.

Rosen, Stanley. "Self-Consciousness and Self-Knowledge in Plato and Hegel." *Hegel-Studien* 9 (1974), 109–29.

Siep, Ludwig. "Der Kampf um Anerkennung zu Hegels Auseinandersetzung mit Hobbes in den Jenaer Schriften." *Hegel-Studien* 9 (1974), 155–207.

———. "Zur Dialektik der Anerkennung bei Hegel." *Hegel-Jahrbuch* (1975), 366–73.

Smith, Steven B. "Hegel on Slavery and Domination," *Review of Metaphysics* 46 (1992), 199–204.

Sonnenschmidt, Reinhard. "Ist Hegels Philosophie eine Philosophie des Todes? Eine kritische Bemerkung zur Dialektik von Herr und Knecht." *Hegel-Jahrbuch* (1991), 199–204.

Verene, Donald Phillip. "Masterhood and Servitude." In his *Hegel's Recollection: A Study of Images in the "Phenomenology of Spirit."* Albany: SUNY Press, 1985. 59–69.

Freedom of Self-Consciousness

Bednár, Jiri. "Die transzendentale Bedeutung des Hegelschen Begriffs 'Das unglückliche Bewußtsein' im Zusammenhang mit Hegels Religionskritik in der *Phänomenologie des Geistes.*" *Filozoficky Casopis* 14 (1966), 464–82.

Burbidge, John W. " 'Unhappy Consciousness' in Hegel—An Analysis of Medieval Catholicism?" *Mosaic* 11 (1978), 67–80.

Escohotado, Antonio. *La conciencia infeliz: Ensayo sobre la filosofía de la religión de Hegel.* Madrid: Ed. Revista de Occidente, 1972.

Gouhier, Alain. "Detresse materielle et conscience malheureuse." *Hegel-Jahrbuch* (1986), 211–22.

Greene, Murray. "Hegel's 'Unhappy Consciousness' and Nietzsche's 'Slave Morality.' " In *Hegel and the Philosophy of Religion.* Edited by Darrel E. Christensen. The Hague: Nijhoff, 1970. 125–41.

Jarczyk, Gwendoline, and Pierre-Jean Labarrière. *Le malheur de la conscience ou l'accès à la raison. Liberté de l'autoconscience: Stoïcisme, scepticisme et la conscience malheureuse. Texte et commentaire.* Paris: Aubier, 1989.

Jarvis, Simon. "The 'Unhappy Consciousness' and Conscious Unhappiness: On Adorno's Critique of Hegel and the Idea of an Hegelian Critique of Adorno." *Bulletin of the Hegel Society of Great Britain* 29 (1994), 71–88.

Le Dantec, Michel. "La Conscience malheureuse dans la société civile." In *Hegels "Philosophie des Rechts": Die Theorie der Rechtsformen und ihrer Logik.* Edited by Dieter Henrich and Rolf-Peter Horstmann. Stuttgart: Ernst Klett, 1982. 139–50.

Lessing, Arthur. "Hegel and Existentialism: On Unhappiness." *Personalist* 49 (1968), 61–77.

Marcel, Gabriel. "Le malheur de la conscience dans la philosophie de Hegel." *Europe* (1930), 149–52.

Mayer, Hans. "Hegel und das Problem des unglücklichen Bewußtseins." In his *Literatur der Übergangszeit.* Berlin: Volk und Welt, 1949. 7–16.

Stewart, Jon. "Die Rolle des unglücklichen Bewußtseins in Hegels *Phänomenologie des Geistes.*" *Deutsche Zeitschrift für Philosophie* 39 (1991), 12–21.

Ulrich, Ferdinand. "Die Onto-Theo-Logik des 'unglücklichen Bewußtseins.'" In his "Begriff und Glaube: Über Hegels Denkweg ins 'absolute Wissen.'" *Freiburger Zeitschrift für Philosophie und Theologie* 17 (1970), 344–99.

Verene, Donald Phillip. "The Unhappy Consciousness." In his *Hegel's Recollection: A Study of Images in the "Phenomenology of Spirit."* Albany: SUNY Press, 1985. 70–79.

Wahl, Jean. *Le Malheur de la conscience dans la philosophie de Hegel.* Paris: Presses Universitaires de France, 1951.

Reason

"Reason" in General

Kähler, Klaus, and Werner Marx. *Die Vernunft in Hegels "Phänomenologie des Geistes."* Frankfurt: Klostermann, 1992.

Kimmerle, Gerd. *Sein und Selbst: Untersuchung zur kategorialen Einheit von Vernunft und Geist in Hegels "Phänomenologie des Geistes."* Bonn: Bouvier, 1978.

Observing Reason

Bonsiepen, Wolfgang. "Zu Hegels Auseinandersetzung mit Schellings Natur-philosophie in der *Phänomenologie des Geistes.*" In *Schelling: Seine Bedeutung für eine Philosophie der Natur und der Geschichte.* Edited by Ludwig Hasler. Stuttgart: Frommann-Holzboog, 1981. 167–72.

Lamb, David. "Observation of Organic Nature (A)." In his *Hegel—from Foundation to System.* The Hague: Nijhoff, 1980. 111–36.

————. "Observation of Organic Nature (B)." In his *Hegel—from Foundation to System*. The Hague: Nijhoff, 1980. 137–64.

MacIntyre, Alasdair. "Hegel on Faces and Skulls." In *Hegel: A Collection of Critical Essays*. Edited by Alasdair MacIntyre. Notre Dame: University of Notre Dame Press, 1976. 219–36.

Sonnemann, Ulrich. "Hegel und Freud: Die Kritik der *Phänomenologie* am Begriff der psychologischen Notwendigkeit und ihre anthropologischen Konsequenzen." *Psyche* 24 (1970), 208–18.

Verene, Donald Phillip. "Phrenology." In his *Hegel's Recollection: A Study of Images in the "Phenomenology of Spirit."* Albany: SUNY Press, 1985. 80–91.

The Actualization of Rational Self-Consciousness through Its Own Activity

Andolfi, Ferruccio. "Die Gestalten des Individualismus in der *Phänomenologie des Geistes*." *Hegel-Jahrbuch* (1991), 211–25.

Gauvin, Joseph. "Plaisir et nécessité." *Archives de Philosophie* 28 (1965), 483–509. Also in *Hegel-Tage Royaumont 1964: Beiträge zur Deutung der "Phänomenologie des Geistes."* Edited by Hans-Georg Gadamer. *Hegel-Studien*, Beiheft 3. Bonn: Bouvier, 1966. 155–80.

Verstraeten, Pierre. "L'homme du plaisir chez Hegel et l'homme du désir chez Lacan." *Revue de l'Université de Bruxelles* 3–4 (1976), 351–94.

Individuality Which Takes Itself to Be Real In and For Itself

Hoy, David. "Hegel's Critique of Kantian Morality." *History of Philosophy Quarterly* 6 (1989), 207–32.

Kaan, André. "L'honnêteté et l'imposture dans la société civile (à propos du chapitre V. C. de la *Phénoménologie*: le règne animal de l'esprit)." *Hegel-Jahrbuch* (1971), 45–49.

Shapiro, Gary. "Notes on the Animal Kingdom of the Spirit." *Clio* 8 (1979), 323–38.

Verene, Donald Phillip. "Hegel's Spiritual Zoo and the Modern Condition." *Owl of Minerva* 25 (1994), 235–40.

————. "Two Forms of Defective Selfhood: The Spiritual Animal Kingdom and the Beautiful Soul." In his *Hegel's Recollection: A Study of Images in the "Phenomenology of Spirit."* Albany: SUNY Press, 1985. 92–103.

Spirit

"Spirit" in General

Litt, Theodor. "Hegels Begriff des 'Geistes' und das Problem der Tradition." *Studium Generale* 4 (1951), 311–21.

Solomon, Robert. "Hegel's Concept of *Geist.*" In *Hegel: A Collection of Critical Essays.* Edited by Alasdair MacIntyre. Notre Dame: University of Notre Dame Press, 1976. 125–49.

The True Spirit. The Ethical Order

Donougho, Martin. "The Woman in White: On the Reception of Hegel's Antigone." *Owl of Minerva* 21 (1989–90), 65–89.

Furth, Peter. "Antigone oder zur tragischen Vorgeschichte der bürgerlichen Gesellschaft." *Hegel-Jahrbuch* (1984–85), 15–30.

Gerald, Thomas J. "Hegels Familienbegriff in der *Phänomenologie des Geistes.*" *Hegel-Jahrbuch* (1984–85), 229–34.

Gossens, Wilfried. "Ethical Life and Family in the *Phenomenology of Spirit.*" In *Hegel on Ethical Life, Religion, and Philosophy: 1793–1807.* Edited by A. Wylleman. Leuven: Kluwer Academic Publishers, 1989. 163–94.

Hyppolite, Jean. "L'état du droit (La condition juridique). Introduction à un commentaire." In *Hegel-Tage Royaumont 1964: Beiträge zur Deutung der "Phänomenologie des Geistes.*" Edited by Hans-Georg Gadamer. *Hegel-Studien,* Beiheft 3. Bonn: Bouvier, 1966. 181–185.

Mackay, L. A. "Antigone, Coriolanus, and Hegel." *Transactions and Proceedings of the American Philological Association* 93 (1962), 166–74.

Mills, Patricia Jagentowicz. "Hegel's Antigone." *Owl of Minerva* 17 (1986), 131–52.

Piertercil, Raymond. "Antigone and Hegel." *International Philosophical Quarterly* 18 (1978), 289–310.

Willett, Cynthia. "Hegel, Antigone and the Possibility of Ecstatic Dialogue." *Philosophy and Literature* 14 (1990), 268–83.

Self-Alienated Spirit. Culture

The World of Self-Alienated Spirit

Boey, Conrad. *L'aliénation dans la "Phénoménologie de l'esprit" de G. W. F. Hegel.* Paris: Desclée de Brouwer, 1970.

———. "L'alienation hégélienne. Un chaînon de l'experience de la conscience et de la *Phénoménologie de l'esprit.*" *Archives de Philosophie* 35 (1972), 87–110.

———. *L'esprit devenu étranger à soi-même: Une Monographie consacrée à la figur du même nom dans la "Phénoménologie de l'esprit" de G. W. F. Hegel.* Paris: Desclée de Brouwer, 1968.

Hulbert, James. "Diderot in the Text of Hegel: A Question of Intertextuality." *Studies in Romanticism* 22 (1983), 267–91.

Jauss, Hans Robert. "*Le Neveu de Rameau*: Dialogue et Dialectique," *Revue de Métaphysique et de Morale* 89 (1984), 145–81.

Lauener, Henri. "Die Sprache der Zerrissenheit als Dasein des sich entfremdeten Geistes bei Hegel." *Studia philosophica* 24 (1964), 162–75.

Mougin, Henri. "Hegel et *Le Neveu de Rameau.*" *Europe* 24 (1946), 1–11.
Price, David W. "Hegel's Intertextual Dialectic: Diderot's *Le Neveu de Rameau* in the *Phenomenology of Spirit.*" *Clio* 20 (1991), 223–33.
Sobotka, Milan. "Das Kapitel über den sich entfremdeten Geist in der Hegelschen *Phänomenologie des Geistes* und Ludwig Feuerbach." *Wissenschaftliche Zeitschrift der Friedrich-Schiller-Universität Jena* 29 (1980), 387–93.
Stiehler, Gottfried. " '*Rameaus Neffe*' und die *Phänomenologie des Geistes* von Hegel." *Wissenschaftliche Zeitschrift der Humboldt-Universität zu Berlin* 13 (1964), 163–67.

The Enlightenment

Badie, M. F. "La doctrine et la vérité de l'Aufklärung dans la *Phénoménologie de l'esprit.*" *Tijdschrift voor de Studie van de Verlichting* 3 (1975), 125–39.
Besse, Guy. "L'utilité-concept fondamental des 'Lumières.' " *Hegel-Jahrbuch* (1968–69), 355–71.
Gauvin, Joseph. "La critique du salut chrétien par l'Aufklärung selon la *Phénoménologie* de Hegel." *Recherches de Science religieuse* 68 (1980), 391–417.
Hinchman, Lewis P. *Hegel's Critique of the Enlightenment.* Gainesville: University of Florida Press, 1984.
Ulrich, Ferdinand. "Begriff und Glaube: Über Hegels Denkweg ins 'absolute Wissen.' " *Freiburger Zeitschrift für Philosophie und Theologie* 17 (1970), 344–99.

Absolute Freedom and Terror

Hyppolite, Jean. "La signification de la Révolution française dans la *Phénoménologie* de Hegel." In his *Études sur Marx et Hegel.* Paris: Librairie Marcel Rivière et Cie, 1955. 45–81.
Granier, Jean. "Hegel et la Révolution française." *Revue de Métaphysique et de Morale* 85 (1980), 1–26.
Grlic, Danko. "Revolution und Terror (Zum Kapitel 'Die absolute Freiheit und der Schrecken' aus Hegels *Phänomenologie des Geistes*)." *Praxis* 7 (1971), 49–61.
Nusser, Karlheinz. "Die französische Revolution und Hegels *Phänomenologie des Geistes.*" *Philosophisches Jahrbuch der Görres-Gesellschaft* 77 (1970), 276–96.
Ver Eecke, Wilfred. "Hegel's Dialectic Analysis of the French Revolution." *Hegel-Jahrbuch* (1975), 561–67.
Wildt, Andreas. "Hegels Kritik des Jakobinismus" In *Stuttgarter Hegel-Tage 1970.* Edited by Hans-Georg Gadamer. *Hegel-Studien,* Beiheft 11. Bonn: Bouvier, 1974. 417–27.

Spirit That Is Certain of Itself. Morality

Bernstein, Jay. "Conscience and Transgression: The Persistence of Misrecognition." *Bulletin of the Hegel Society of Great Britain* 29 (1994), 55–70.

Calvez, J. Y. "L'âge d'or: Essai sur le destin de la 'belle âme' chez Novalis et Hegel." *Études Germaniques* 9 (1954), 112–27.

Dahlstrom, D. O. "Die schöne Seele bei Schiller und Hegel." *Hegel-Jahrbuch* (1991), 147–56.

Friedman, R. Z. "Hypocrisy and the Highest Good: Hegel on Kant's Transition from Morality to Religion." *Journal of the History of Philosophy* 24 (1986), 503–22.

Gram, Moltke S. "Moral and Literary Ideals in Hegel's Critique of 'The Moral View of the World.' " *Clio* 7 (1978), 375–402.

Hirsch, Emanuel. "Die Beisetzung der Romantiker in Hegels *Phänomenologie*: Ein Kommentar zu dem Abschnitte über die Moralität." *Deutsche Vierteljahress-chrift für Literaturwissenschaft* 2 (1924), 510–32. Also in *Materialien zu Hegels "Phänomenologie des Geistes."* Edited by Hans Friedrich Fulda and Dieter Henrich. Frankfurt: Suhrkamp, 1973. 245–75.

Jamros, Daniel P. "The Appearing God in Hegel's *Phenomenology of Spirit*." *Clio* 19 (1990), 353–65.

Kaan, André. "Le mal et son pardon." In *Hegel-Tage Royaumont 1964: Beiträge zur Deutung der "Phänomenologie des Geistes."* Edited by Hans-Georg Gadamer. *Hegel-Studien*, Beiheft 3. Bonn: Bouvier, 1966. 187–94.

Labarrière, Pierre-Jean. "Belle âme, mal et pardon." *Concordia* 1 (1982), 11–15.

Robinson, Jonathan. *Duty and Hypocrisy in Hegel's "Phenomenology of Mind": An Essay in the Real and the Ideal.* Toronto: University of Toronto Press, 1977.

Sax, Benjamin C. "Active Individuality and the Language of Confession: The Figure of the Beautiful Soul in the *Lehrjahre* and the *Phenomenology*." *Journal of the History of Philosophy* 21 (1983), 437–66.

Sedgwick, Sally S. "Hegel's Critique of the Subjective Idealism of Kant's Ethics." *Journal of the History of Philosophy* 26 (1988), 89–105.

Shklar, Judith. "The *Phenomenology*: Beyond Morality." *Western Political Quarterly* 27 (1974), 597–623.

Verene, Donald Phillip. "Two Forms of Defective Selfhood: The Spiritual Animal Kingdom and the Beautiful Soul." In his *Hegel's Recollection: A Study of Images in the "Phenomenology of Spirit."* Albany: SUNY Press, 1985. 92–103.

Well, Karlheinz. *Die schöne Seele und ihre sittliche Wirklichkeit.* Frankfurt: Peter Lang, 1986.

Westphal, Kenneth R. "Hegel's Critique of Kant's Moral World View." *Philosophical Topics* 19 (1991), 133–76.

Wilden, Anthony. "The Belle Âme: Freud, Lacan, and Hegel." In *The Language of the Self: The Function of Language in Psychoanalysis.* Baltimore: Johns Hopkins Press, 1968. 284–308.

Religion

"Religion" in General

Dooren, Willem van. "Die Bedeutung der Religion in der *Phänomenologie des Geistes*." In *Hegel-Tage Urbino 1965*. Edited by Hans-Georg Gadamer. *Hegel-Studien*, Beiheft 4. Bonn: Bouvier, 1969, 93–101

Flay, Joseph C. "Religion and the Absolute Standpoint." *Thought* 56 (1981), 316–27.

Heintel, Peter. "Die Religion als Gestalt des absoluten Geistes." *Wiener Jahrbuch für Philosophie* 3 (1970), 162–202.

Jamros, Daniel P. *The Human Shape of God: Religion in Hegel's "Phenomenology of Spirit."* New York: Paragon House, 1994.

Lauer, Quentin. "Hegel on the Identity of Content in Religion and Philosophy." In *Hegel and the Philosophy of Religion.* Edited by Darrel E. Christensen. The Hague: Nijhoff, 1970. 261–78.

Luther, O. Kem, and Jeff L. Hoover. "Hegel's Phenomenology of Religion." *Journal of Religion* 61 (1981), 229–41.

Ulrich, Ferdinand. "Begriff und Glaube: Über Hegels Denkweg ins 'absolute Wissen.' " *Freiburger Zeitschrift für Philosophie und Theologie* 17 (1970), 344–99.

Natural Religion

De Nys, Martin J. "The Appearance and Appropriation of Religious Consciousness in Hegel's *Phenomenology.*" *Modern Schoolman* 62 (1985), 165–84.

Dubarle, Dominique. "De la foi au savoir selon la *Phénoménologie de l'esprit.*" *Revue des Sciences Philosophiques et Théologiques* 59 (1975), 3–36, 243–77, 399–425.

Leuze, Reinhard. *Die außerchristlichen Religionen bei Hegel.* Göttingen: Vandenhoeck and Rupprecht, 1975.

Vieillard-Baron, Jean-Louis. "La 'religion de la nature': Étude de quelques pagés de la *Phénoménologie de l'esprit* de Hegel," *Revue de Métaphysique et de Morale,* (76), 1971, 323–343.

Religion of Art

De Nys, Martin J. "The Appearance and Appropriation of Religious Consciousness in Hegel's *Phenomenology.*" *Modern Schoolman* 62 (1985), 165–84.

Dubarle, Dominique. "De la foi au savoir selon la *Phénoménologie de l'esprit.*" *Revue des Sciences Philosophiques et Théologiques,* 59 (1975), 3–36, 243–77, 399–425.

Leuze, Reinhard. *Die außerchristlichen Religionen bei Hegel.* Göttingen: Vandenhoeck and Rupprecht, 1975.

Yon, Ephrem-Dominique. "Esthétique de la contemplation et esthétique de la transgression: À propos de passage de la Religion au Saviour Absolu dans la *Phénoménologie de l'esprit* de Hegel." *Revue philosophique de Louvain* 74 (1976), 549–71.

Revealed Religion

De Nys, Martin J. "Mediation and Negativity in Hegel's Phenomenology of Christian Consciousness." *Journal of Religion* 66 (1986), 46–67.

Devos, Rob. "The Significance of Manifest Religion in the *Phenomenology.*" In *Hegel on Ethical Life, Religion, and Philosophy: 1793–1807.* Edited by A. Wylleman. Leuven: Kluwer Academic Publishers, 1989. 195–229.

Fruchon, Pierre. "Sur la conception hégélienne de la 'religion révelée' selon M. Theunissen." *Archives de Philosophie* 48 (1985), 613–41; 49 (1986), 619–42.

Garaudy, Roger. *Dieu est mort: Étude sur Hegel.* Paris: Presses Universitaires de France, 1962.

Link, Christian. *Hegels Wort "Gott selbst ist tot."* Zürich: Theologischer Verlag, 1974.

Schöndorf, Harald. "Anderswerden und Versöhnung Gottes in Hegels *Phänomenologie des Geistes*: Ein Kommentar zum zweiten Teil von VII. C. 'Die offenbare Religion.' " *Theologie und Philosophie* 57 (1982), 550–67.

Sölle, Dorothee. *Stellvertretung: Ein Kapitel Theologie nach dem Tode Gottes.* Stuttgart: Kreuz-Verlag, 1965.

Vieillard-Baron, Jean-Louis. "L'idee de religion révélée chez Hegel et Schelling." *Hegel-Studien* 24 (1989), 97–105.

Welker, Michael. *Das Verfahren von Hegels "Phänomenologie des Geistes" und die Funktion des Abschnitts: "Die offenbare Religion."* Heidelberg: Ruprecht-Karls-Universität, 1978.

Absolute Knowing

Coreth, Emerich, "Das absolute Wissen bei Hegel." *Zeitschrift für Katholische Theologie* 105 (1983), 389–405.

———. "Zu Hegels Absolutem Wissen." *Aquinas* 24 (1981), 213–44.

Cunningham, G. W. "The Significance of the Hegelian Conception of Absolute Knowledge." *Philosophical Review* 17 (1908), 619–42.

De Vos, Lu de. "Absolute Knowing in the *Phenomenology.*" In *Hegel on Ethical Life, Religion, and Philosophy: 1793–1807.* Edited by A. Wylleman. Leuven: Kluwer Academic Publishers, 1989. 231–70.

Esposito, Joseph L. "Hegel, Absolute Knowledge, and the End of History." *Clio* 12 (1983), 355–65.

Gretic, Goran. *Das Problem des absoluten Wissens in Hegels "Phänomenologie des Geistes."* Zagreb: Universitäts-Verlag Liber, 1975.

Grimmlinger, Friederich. "Zum Begriff des absoluten Wissens in Hegels *Phänomenologie.*" *Geschichte und System: Festschrift für Erich Heintel zum 60. Geburtstag.* Edited by Hans-Dieter Klein und Erhard Oeser. Munich: Oldenbourg, 1972. 279–300.

Horn, J. C. "Absolutes Wesen/Absolutes Wissen," *Kant-Studien* 66 (1975), 169–80.

Labarriére, Pierre-Jean. "Le savior absolu de l'esprit." In *The Meaning of Absolute Spirit.* Edited by Theodore Geraets. Ottawa: Éditions de l'Université d'Ottawa, 1982. 499–507.

Lemaigre, Bernard. "Le saviour absolu comme réalisation de soi dans la philosophie de Hegel." *Études Freudiennes* 1–2 (1969), 249–83.

Ludwig, Walter D. "Hegel's Conception of Absolute Knowing." *Owl of Minerva* 21 (1989), 5–19.

Miller, Arnold V. "Absolute Knowing and the Destiny of the Individual." *Owl of Minerva* 15 (1983), 45–50.

Miller, Mitchell. "The Attainment of the Absolute of Hegel's *Phenomenology.*" *Graduate Faculty Philosophy Journal* 7 (1978), 195–219.

Pätzold, Detlev. "Das absolute Wissen als Theorie des Gesamtzusammenhangs." *Annalen der Internationalen Gesellschaft für Dialektische Philosophie* 1 (1983), 33–37.

Ulrich, Ferdinand. "Begriff und Glaube: Über Hegels Denkweg ins 'absolute Wissen.'" *Freiburger Zeitschrift für Philosophie und Theologie* 17 (1970), 344–99.

Index

a priori knowledge, 15, 49, 62, 464f.
Absolute, 2, 17, 26, 32, 33, 50, 340, 343,
    345, 346, 387, 465
absolute idealism, 464–66 passim
absolute knowing, 21, 23, 25, 31, 32ff., 43,
    44, 47, 267, 278, 289, 291, 453, 454,
    455–58 passim
Absolute Notion, 459, 462, 463
Absolute Spirit, 21, 383, 386 (defined),
    440, 442, 443, 452, 455, 456, 462
Aeschylus, 426. *See also* tragedy
"Also," 68–78 passim, 83f., 131, 206, 207,
    209, 211, 259, 389
Antigone, 290, 294, 299–309 passim, 315,
    319, 385, 431
aperception, 20
appetite, 107
Aristophanes, 426. *See also* comedy
Aristotle, 49, 96, 196, 215, 402
art, 408–36 passim
aufheben, 39f.

Battle of Jena, 6f.
Bauer, Bruno, 8
beautiful soul, 295, 374–83 passim, 458
being, 54ff., 64, 72, 108f., 114, 119, 163,
    174, 184, 227f., 229, 269f., 299, 301,
    358f., 368, 393, 394, 456, 457
Bosanquet, Bernard, 12
Bradley, Francis Herbert, 12
Brokmeyer, Henry Conrad, 11
Brown, John, 191

Caird, Edward, 12
categorical imperative, 358
categories of the understanding, 15ff.,
    37, 49, 207f.
certainty, 109f., 170, 234, 348, 376, 378

comedy, 426, 433–35
common sense, 33–38 passim, 40, 44, 45,
    46, 47, 53, 55
Concept. *See* Notion
Congress of Vienna, 4, 8
conscience, 374–83 passim, 458
Critical Journal of Philosophy, 6
Croce, Benedetto, 9
culture, 319ff.

Descartes, René, 5, 15, 27f., 128, 222, 347
desire, 105, 107ff., 114ff., 132, 139, 148,
    151, 158f., 242, 244–48 passim, 302f.,
    321
determinate negation, 41ff.
Dewey, John, 11
dialectic, 39ff.
Diderot, Denis, 290, 317, 326
Dilthey, Wilhelm, 12, 47
divine law, 300–9 passim
dualism, 33, 34, 37, 38, 45, 47, 50, 53, 76,
    101, 102, 111, 116, 119, 149, 154ff.,
    176, 179, 197, 213, 258, 259, 266,
    267, 272, 402, 425f., 433, 446, 447f.,
    450, 452, 464

Egypt, 401–7 passim, 408f., 411
Engels, Friedrich, 349
English Reform Bill, 4
Enlightenment, 4, 249, 290, 316, 326,
    327, 331–49 passim, 357, 385, 457
epic, 426, 428–30 passim, 432
Epictetus, 143, 144, 148
ethical life, 235, 236 (defined), 237, 278,
    286, 299ff.
existentialism, 10

faith, 327–31 passim, 333–49 passim, 351